CHAPPAQUIDDICK

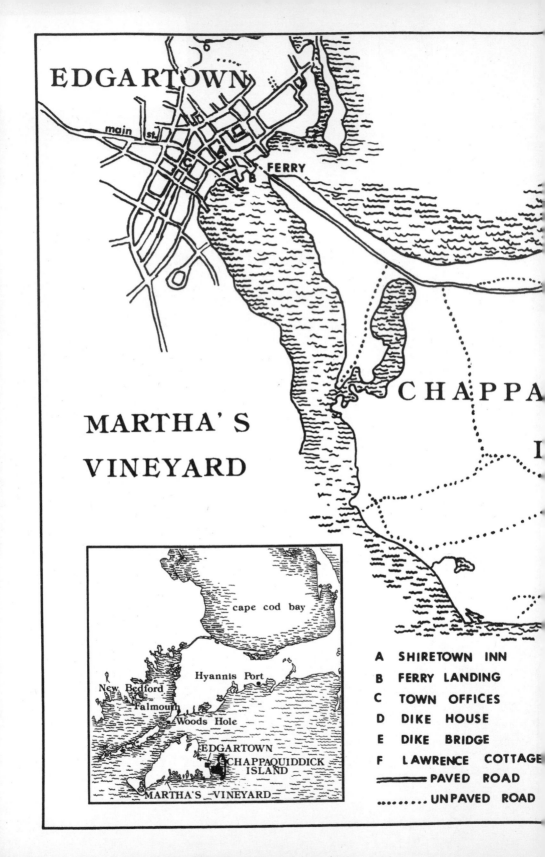

EDGARTOWN

main st.

FERRY

MARTHA'S
VINEYARD

CHAPPA

I

cape cod bay

Hyannis Port

New Bedford
Falmouth

Woods Hole

EDGARTOWN
CHAPPAQUIDDICK
ISLAND

MARTHA'S VINEYARD

A   SHIRETOWN INN
B   FERRY LANDING
C   TOWN OFFICES
D   DIKE HOUSE
E   DIKE BRIDGE
F   LAWRENCE COTTAGE
━━━━━━ PAVED ROAD
········· UNPAVED ROAD

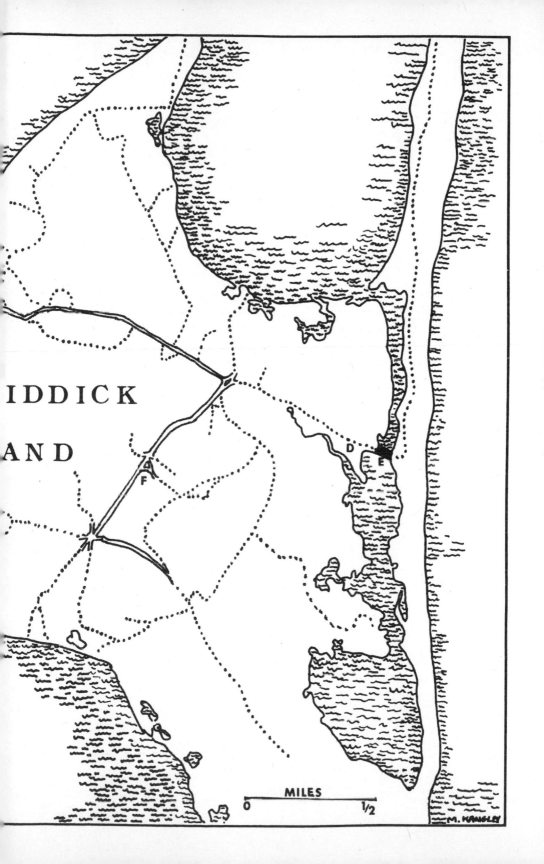

IDDICK

AND

D

E

F

MILES

0   1/2

M. KANGLEY

CHAPPAQUIDDICK

POWER, PRIVILEGE, AND THE TED KENNEDY COVER-UP

LEO DAMORE

Foreword by Howie Carr, author of *Kennedy Babylon*

REGNERY
PUBLISHING
A Division of Salem Media Group

Originally published in hardcover under the title *Senatorial Privilege*

Cataloging-in-Publication data on file with the Library of Congress

ISBN 978-1-62157-818-5
eISBN 978-1-62157-819-2

Published in the United States by
Regnery History, an imprint of
Regnery Publishing
A Division of Salem Media Group
300 New Jersey Ave NW
Washington, DC 20001
www.RegneryHistory.com

Manufactured in the United States of America

10 9 8 7 6 5 4 3 2 1

Books are available in quantity for promotional or premium use. For information on discounts and terms, please visit our website: www. Regnery.com.

Contents

Chronology

JUNE 5, 1968

Senator Robert Kennedy is assassinated in Los Angeles.

JULY 25–27

First party for "The Boiler Room" is held in Hyannis Port and Nantucket.

JULY 18–19, 1969

Senator Edward Kennedy's car plunges off Dike Bridge on Chappaquiddick Island. A passenger, Mary Jo Kopechne, is killed.

JULY 19

At approximately 9:45 a.m., Senator Kennedy gives a statement to Edgartown Police
Chief Dominick James Arena saying he had, at 11:15 p.m. the previous evening, taken a wrong turn en route to the ferry landing on

Chappaquiddick and gone off Dike Bridge. He had escaped the accident car and returned to his hotel room. He had contacted police when he "fully realized" what had happened almost ten hours later.

JULY 22
Mary Jo Kopechne is buried in Plymouth, Pennsylvania.

JULY 25
Senator Kennedy pleads guilty to leaving the scene of an accident and is given a two month suspended sentence and a year probation by Edgartown District Court Judge James A. Boyle.

JULY 25, 1969
At 7 p.m., Senator Kennedy describes the accident in a nationally-televised speech. He characterizes his conduct in not going to police sooner a "indefensible" and asks the voters of Massachusetts to advise him about whether to resign from the Senate.

JULY 31
Senator Kennedy returns to Washington to resume his Senate duties.

JULY 32
District Attorney Edmund S. Dinis requests an inquest into the death of Mary Jo Kopechne.

AUGUST 8
Judge Boyle sets an inquest for September 3, 1969.

AUGUST 27
At a pre-inquest hearing, Judge Boyle allows the press to cover the inquest, but no lawyers will be allowed to cross-examine witnesses.

SEPTEMBER 2

Senator Kennedy's lawyers ask for a temporary inquest injunction from the Massachusetts Supreme Judicial Court.

SEPTEMBER 18

In a Petition for Exhumation and Autopsy of Mary Jo Kopechne's body, district attorney Dinis claims blood was seen in her mouth and nose.

SEPTEMBER 24

Mr. and Mrs. Joseph Kopechne file a petition to bar the autopsy.

OCTOBER 20–21

Judge Bernard C. Brominski of Wilkes-Barre, Pennsylvania, presides at a hearing on the exhumation and autopsy petition.

OCTOBER 30

The Massachusetts Supreme Judicial Court orders the press and the public barred from the Kopechne inquest and orders inquest documents impounded until after all possibility of prosecution against Senator Kennedy is ended.

DECEMBER 10

Judge Brominski denies the exhumation and autopsy petition.

DECEMBER 11

Judge Boyle sets January 5, 1970, for the Kopechne inquest.

JANUARY 5–8, 1970

Senator Kennedy and 26 other witnesses testify at a secret inquest at Edgartown.

FEBRUARY 18
Judge Boyle files his report and the transcript of inquest testimony with Edgartown Superior Court clerk. The documents are brought to Boston Superior Courthouse for safekeeping.

MARCH 10
Dinis examines Boyle's report.

MARCH 17
Leslie H. Leland, Edgartown grand jury foreman, requests a special session to be reconvened in order to investigate the death of Mary Jo Kopechne.

MARCH 26
Chief Justice Joseph G. Tauro of the Superior Court calls a special session of the court to convene April 6 in Edgartown for the grand jury to hear evidence in the Chappaquiddick case.

APRIL 6–7
The grand jury calls four witnesses and returns no indictments. District Attorney Dinis says, "The case is closed," and inquest documents can now be made public.

APRIL 29
Inquest documents are released to the public.

MAY 14
The results of a secret registry of motor vehicles hearing finds Senator Kennedy to have been speeding and to be "at serious fault" in the accident.

NOVEMBER 4

Senator Kennedy is re-elected to the Senate.

NOVEMBER 27

Kennedy takes a driver's test in Plymouth, Massachusetts, and his license is reinstated.

Cast of Characters

EDWARD M. KENNEDY

Senator from Massachusetts.

DOMINICK JAMES ARENA

Police Chief, Edgartown, Massachusetts.

WALTER STEELE

Special Prosecutor for the County of Dukes County, Martha's Vineyard.

EDMUND S. DINIS

District Attorney for the Southern District.

JAMES H. SMITH

Assistant District Attorney and former Kennedy political campaign advance man and campaign coordinator.

ARMAND FERNANDES
Assistant District Attorney.

GEORGE KILLEN
State Police Detective Lieutenant, in charge of the Cape Cod office of the district attorney.

BERNIE FLYNN
State Police Detective Lieutenant, assigned to the Cape Cod office of the district attorney.

DR. DONALD R. MILLS
Associate Medical Examiner, Edgartown.

EUGENE FRIEH
Undertaker, Vineyard Haven, Martha's Vineyard.

JOHN FARRAR
Scuba diver and head of the Search and Rescue division of Edgartown Volunteer Fire Department.

CHRISTOPHER "HUCK" LOOK
Deputy sheriff and part-time "special" police officer.

RUSSELL PEACHEY
Manager-owner, Shiretown Inn, Edgartown.

STEPHEN SMITH
Brother-in-law of Ted Kennedy, frequent campaign finance manager, and Kennedy family business manager.

HERBERT J. MILLER

Washington attorney, former head of the Criminal Division, U.S. Department of Justice under Attorney General Robert Kennedy.

EDWARD HANIFY

Attorney, Chief Counsel for Senator Kennedy at the Kopechne inquest.

ROBERT CLARK, JR.

Attorney for Senator Kennedy, former District Court Judge.

RICHARD MCCARRON

Attorney for Senator Kennedy, Edgartown.

DAN DALEY

Attorney retained to represent eight witnesses who attended the party at Chappaquiddick.

PAUL REDMOND

Attorney, associate of Dan Daley.

JOSEPH DONEGAN

Court stenographer.

ANDREW TUNEY

Former Massachusetts state police detective-lieutenant employed as a private investigator for criminal lawyer, F. Lee Bailey.

F. LEE BAILEY

Criminal lawyer.

JAMES A. BOYLE
District Court Judge, Edgartown, Massachusetts.

BERNARD C. BROMINSKI
Presiding Judge of the Court of Common Pleas, Wilkes Barre, Pennsylvania.

JOSEPH AND GWEN KOPECHNE
Parents of Mary Jo Kopechne.

JOSEPH FLANAGAN
Attorney for the Kopechnes.

DUN GIFFORD
Aide to Senator Kennedy.

RICHARD DRAYNE
Press secretary to Senator Kennedy.

ROSS RICHARDS
Yachtsman, Hyannis Port.

STANLEY MOORE
Automobile dealer and Edgartown Regatta participant.

DAVID BURKE
Administrative Assistant to Senator Kennedy.

AT THE PARTY:

JOSEPH A. GARGAN
Lawyer, Ted Kennedy's cousin, and co-host of the party at Chappaquiddick.

PAUL MARKHAM
Lawyer and former U.S. Attorney for Massachusetts.

RAY LAROSA
Former fireman and Kennedy campaign worker.

CHARLES TRETTER
Lawyer, head of the Boston Redevelopment Commission, and a Kennedy campaign aide.

JOHN CRIMMINS
Senator Kennedy's part-time chauffeur.

THE BOILER ROOM GIRLS
Mary Jo Kopechne
Rosemary "Cricket" Keough
Esther Newberg
Susan Tannenbaum
Nance Lyons
Mary Ellen Lyons

To James Harold Smith
Class of 1947
B. M. C. Durfee High School
Fall River, MA

Foreword
by Howie Carr

If anyone ever truly deserved a Profiles in Courage Award, it was the late Leo Damore, the author of this book.

Of course, the awards are handed out by the Kennedy family, and they are all about, not courage, but Political Correctness. But no one can dispute the fact that Damore put himself and his career on the line to write this book, and that one way or another, he paid the ultimate price—as a suicide, in 1995, at the age of 65.

Senatorial Privilege: The Chappaquiddick Cover-Up was a *New York Times* best seller in 1988. It sold more than a million copies. Damore's volume established a little-known publishing house, Regnery, as a major force in the book trade. Its success also disproved what New York publishers had long believed, or perhaps just hoped, that there was no real market out there for books that spoke, really spoke, truth to liberal power.

If you are just now discovering *Senatorial Privilege,* you may not be aware of the controversy that surrounded its initial publication. Damore seemed a most unlikely person to blow the lid off the Chappaquiddick cover up. Born in Ontario, he was a reporter for the *Cape Cod Times*. His first book, in 1967, had been a standard post-JFK assassination hagiography, *The Cape Cod Years of John Fitzgerald Kennedy*.

In the final scene of *Cape Cod Years*, JFK returns to Boston for the final time, in October 1963, for a major black-tie fundraiser with the Democrat governors of New England. As Damore told the story, after the dinner a Hyannis housepainter named Fred Caouette approached the president and was "brusquely challenged" by a Secret Service agent.

Then JFK spots his humble Cape neighbor and yells to the agent, "Let the little guy through!" Shaking Cauouette's hand, the president says, "Freddy, it's awfully nice to see you," and finally tells him, "I'll see you next year."

That's the way all Kennedy books were written back then, even by Leo Damore. Little did Damore or anyone else know that earlier that evening, the tuxedoed president had summoned Mimi Alford, the intern he had deflowered in the White House a year earlier at the age of 19, to his suite at the Sheraton Plaza, where he ordered her to fellate his younger brother Teddy.

"You've got to be kidding, Mr. President," she recalled herself replying in her 2012 memoir.

Damore got a $150,000 advance from Random House, and he spent years digging up the truth. His most important source would be Joe Gargan, Teddy's first cousin who rented the cottage that evening. Like Michael Skakel, the convicted murderer in the next generation, Gargan was a kinsman, but not really a Kennedy. And like Skakel, in his fury against his mistreatment by the family, Gargan would eventually spill the beans.

The most explosive charge in *Senatorial Privilege* came from Gargan. After the accident, and the repeated rescue attempts of Mary Jo by Kennedy, Gargan and former US attorney Paul Markham, Teddy floated an alternative story:

"Why couldn't Mary Jo have been driving the car? Why couldn't she have left me off, and driven to the ferry herself and made a wrong turn?"

To which Gargan eventually responded: "You told me you were driving."

When Damore handed in his manuscript to Random House, all hell broke loose. This was the home, after all, of William Faulkner, Andre Malraux and Robert Penn Warren, not to mention Babar the Elephant. Imagine the reaction of the Random House editors as they read Damore's account of the court hearing in Pennsylvania on the exhumation of Kopechne's body, as the state medical examiner of Maryland blurted out a very inconvenient truth:

"It was apparent to me from the record that she lived for a certain time underwater... So she breathed, that girl. She *breathed!*"

You just couldn't write things like that about the Kennedys back then. Seldom was heard a discouraging word about America's First Family. Even the biggest names in journalism were muzzled, like James "Scotty" Reston, the columnist for the *New York Times* who owned a little paper on Martha's Vineyard. Reston was there at the police station in Edgartown that Saturday morning as Teddy shakily wrote out the accident report. Damore quoted Scotty in his manuscript:

"I'd love to tell the story but they won't let me."

If it came down to a fight with the Kennedys, Random House couldn't win. In 1967, Jackie Kennedy had tried to stop publication of another, much more innocuous book, *The Death of a President.*

Jackie famously told the author, "Anybody who is against me will look like a rat unless I run off with Eddie Fisher."

In retrospect, Damore was lucky to have found any publisher willing to stand up to the wrath of the Kennedys. When it was finally published by Regnery, *Senatorial Privilege* was ignored by the critics, but Damore's expose was so thorough and so damning that even with no publicity, it still skyrocketed to the top of the best-seller lists.

But then, Chappaquiddick was a scandal for the ages, even by Kennedy standards.

Mary Jo Kopechne, for instance—everything about her screamed Kennedy girlfriend. She wasn't wearing underwear when she died, and she was drunk—her blood-alcohol level was .09. Her first boss in Washington was Sen. George Smathers of Florida, JFK's best friend in Congress, who used to travel with the future president to Havana in those pre-Castro days, where they were treated to the finest prostitutes in Cuba, compliments of gangsters Meyer Lansky and Santo Trafficante Jr.

In Washington, Kopechne's landlord was Bobby Baker, the longtime bagman for, among others, Lyndon Johnson. Baker also ran a private DC "club" which offered the services of high-priced hookers, among them Ellen Rometsch, a suspected East German spy who was being investigated by a Senate committee for her relationship with JFK when she was suddenly deported in 1963.

The Kennedys may not have been able to stop publication of *Senatorial Privilege*, but revenge, as they say, is a dish best served cold. And after those first few big royalty checks, nothing was ever the same for Damore. As his wife divorced him, he fell into a deep depression and began threatening suicide. At the same time, Damore also started research on a new book about Mary Pinchot Meyer, one of JFK's last blue-blooded girlfriends.

Meyer was the drop-dead gorgeous sister-in-law of Ben Bradlee, later of the *Washington Post*. Bradlee was so close to JFK that in 1962 he was given the assignment of using his magazine, *Newsweek*, to spike the scandalous true story of Kennedy's first marriage, to a twice-divorced Protestant socialite in Palm Beach in 1947.

Meyer was another fascinating subject—during her affair with JFK, she got into drugs, and had begun visiting LSD guru Dr. Timothy Leary just before the assassination. Less than a year after Dallas, she was mysteriously shot to death while jogging on a canal path in Georgetown.

An obviously innocent young black man was arrested and charged, and then acquitted. The evening of her murder, Meyer's brother-in-law Bradlee went to her house to retrieve her secret diary about the affair with JFK. Inside, in the dark, Bradlee discovered that another intruder had gotten there first—James Jesus Angleton, the legendary CIA spook, who had his own sneaky eyes-only reasons for wanting the diary of the late president's paramour.

In short, Leo Damore had emerged from one Kennedy rabbit hole only to tumble into another, perhaps even deeper one. One of Meyer's biographers quoted Damore as telling him:

"What do you think it would do to the beatification of Kennedy if this woman said, 'It wasn't Camelot, it was Caligula's court.'"

I met Damore in 1994, on the 25th anniversary of Chappaquiddick. I was doing my radio show from the cottage on Chappaquiddick, and I booked some of the surviving principals. Only Damore asked for money—$100. Every time I spoke to him, he seemed nervous, agitated. The day after the show he telephoned again, begging me to send him the money ASAP, which I did.

Fifteen months later, Damore was depressed and broke, about to be evicted from his rented house in Essex CT. As a visiting nurse and a constable (who was there to serve the eviction notice) looked on in horror, Damore pulled out a gun and shot himself in the head.

Ted Kennedy died of brain cancer in 2009, at the age of 77. In his later years, it was considered bad form to even mention Chappaquiddick in polite company. Teddy himself seemed oblivious to the scandal—he named his last dog Splash.

The Kennedys' official fanzine has always been the *Boston Globe*. Every sixth year, when he was running for reelection, the *Globe* would run stories about how Teddy was "turning his life around," and how in an amazing feat of self-discipline, he had totally sworn off alcohol until his birthday—Feb. 22. On the day after Chappaquiddick, the *Globe* ran a front-page headline saying "Senator Wandered in Daze for Hours."

In 2003 the *Globe* perfectly summed up the mainstream media's revisionist take on Chappaquiddick:

"If she had lived, Mary Jo Kopechne would be 62 years old. Through his tireless work as a legislator, Edward Kennedy would have brought comfort to her in her old age."

In 2015, the Edward M. Kennedy Institute for the Senate opened in Dorchester. One of its exhibits is entitled "the Senate Immersion Module." Immersion—you can't make this stuff up.

Near the end of his life, in 2009, Teddy wrote a sorrowful letter to Pope Benedict XVI:

"I have always tried to be a faithful Catholic, Your Holiness, though I have fallen short through human failings... I know that I have been an imperfect human being but with the help of my faith, I have tried to right my path."

Then he added, in a somewhat incongruous attempt at penance, "I have worked to welcome the immigrant."

Somehow I don't think Teddy was referring to Leo Damore.

Few of the principals ever talked about what happened. The prosecutor, Walter Steele, was quickly appointed to a state judgeship—another nationwide search, as we say in Massachusetts. As a judge, his most famous case involved allowing a convicted child predator to leave the state without restrictions, after which the offender moved to Montana and then murdered and cannibalized a 7-year old boy.

When Steele reached the mandatory retirement age of 70 in 1996, the local New Bedford paper ran a story about him without a single mention of Chappaquiddick. But Judge Steele did obliquely mention the difficulty of explaining to victims and their survivors how sometimes an obviously guilty party gets off scot-free:

"It's awful hard to explain to them that you think you're doing justice."

Do you think the Kopechnes would have understood what Judge Steele was getting at?

As for Gargan, Damore paid him $15,000 for "legal and editing work" on *Senatorial Privilege*. Gargan eventually ended up with a hack job in Boston as chairman of a state board that essentially returned licenses to convicted drunk drivers.

Ironically, despite his intimate knowledge of what happened at Chappaquiddick, Gargan became the leading proponent on the board for allowing convicted drunkards back on the road. When Republicans regained control of state government in 1991, Gargan was summarily fired.

Gargan died in Virginia at age 87 in December 2017. By then he was such a forgotten figure that when his paid death notice appeared in the *Globe*, no Boston reporters even noticed it for three weeks.

According to the paid obituary, "Joe was dedicated to helping those who suffer from alcohol addiction."

The boiler-room girls you will soon be reading about have maintained *omerta*—silence—for almost half a century. But as Damore notes in Chapter 54, on the fifth anniversary of Mary Jo's death in 1974, Rosemary "Cricket" Keough did issue the following terse statement:

"My friend Mary Jo just happened to be in the wrong car at the wrong time with the wrong people."

In a strange way, Damore's life turned out like Mary Jo's—*Senatorial Privilege*, now retitled as *Chappaquiddick: Power, Privilege, and the Ted Kennedy Cover-Up* is an unforgettable book, muckraking in the best sense of the word. But for Damore personally, it was the wrong book at the wrong time about the wrong people, and it cost him his life.

But at least we still have his book—and the truth.

Introduction

CHAPPAQUIDDICK HAS BEEN CALLED "THE MOST BRILLIANT cover-up ever achieved in a nation where investigative procedures are well-developed and where the principles of equal justice prevail, at least during some of those moments where people are watching." The fascination for the most famous traffic fatality in the history of American politics remains strong today. The mysteries of the case continue to haunt Senator Edward Kennedy's career. For many, Chappaquiddick stands as the single obstacle in his path to the Presidency.

Those mysteries haunt not only the Senator, but investigative authorities. Charges of ineptitude and lack of diligence abounded, as did insinuations that the machinery of justice crumbled beneath the power and the prestige of the Kennedy family. To his dying day, George Killen, former State Police Detective-Lieutenant, and chief of a never-revealed investigation, was rankled by Chappaquiddick. Failure to bring that case to a satisfactory resolution was, he lamented, "the biggest mistake" of a long and distinguished police career. Two months before his death in

1979, Killen decried the injustice of Chappaquiddick; Senator Kennedy, he said, "killed that girl the same as if he put a gun to her head and pulled the trigger."

It is to George Killen that I owe the original inspiration and encouragement to undertake a reinvestigation of Chappaquiddick. To Killen's associate, State Police Detective-Lieutenant Bernie Flynn, I owe a special debt for revelations about the critical part he played in the case.

This book would not have been possible without the wise counsel of Joseph Gargan, Jr., and the generosity of former Assistant District Attorney Jimmy Smith. Reluctant to revive memories of a painful episode that resulted in the ruin of his own political career, former District Attorney Edmund Dinis nevertheless disclosed to me his conviction, "There's no question in my mind that the grand jury would have brought an indictment against Ted Kennedy for manslaughter, if I had given them the case." Former Assistant District Attorney Armand Fernandes was generous of his time and information about the part he played in the preparation of the inquest case. Peter Gay, Lance Garth and State Police Detective-Lieutenant Gordon Clarkson also provided helpful information.

District Attorney Philip Rollins and his staff made possible complete access to the official files of the case at Barnstable courthouse. Police Chief Dominick Arena, now of Lincoln, Massachusetts, was of enormous assistance in sharing his recollections and documents about his key role in the case, as were Carmen Salvador, George Searle, and former Deputy Sheriff Christopher Look.

I owe special thanks to attorneys Richard McCarron and Paul Redmond, to Edward Harrington, Frank Keating, F. Lee Bailey and, in particular, Andrew M. Tuney, for their insights into the case, and to Charles Zimmerman and Ed McGrath for expertise and technical assistance.

Introduction xxxiii

I am indebted to Court Stenographer Joseph Donegan for revealing the part he played in the inquest. Cleo O'Donnell was an invaluable source of information about his brother, Kenneth. Stanley Moore and Marilyn Richards Gilbert both provided important information.

Former Registrar of Motor Vehicles Richard McLaughlin and Registry Inspector Herbert Burr, and in particular, Registry Attorney Paula Golden, were very helpful in providing hitherto unavailable official records dealing with the Chappaquiddick accident under Registrar Allen Mackey's policy of open files. Richard Gill, Marianne O'Brien, James Igoe, William Camara, Andrew Martin, Frank Trabucco and Ronald Andrews helped to secure important records. Maurice G. Lauzon and Marguerite Habicht of the *New Bedford Standard-Times* provided generous assistance, as did Harvey Ewing, Ralph Gordon, Francis Broadhurst, Don Moore, Gerald R. Kelly, Margaret Kangley and columnist Jack Anderson.

I am grateful also to Dr. John McHugh and Lieutenant James Sharkey of the Massachusetts State Police Chemistry Lab; Dr. Henry Lee, Dr. Sidney Callis, Barry Crawford, Sally Elberry, John Ryan; and John O'Connor of the New England Telephone Company. Bobbi Galiani and Cynthia Field were unfailingly helpful; David Surette, Ralph Mairano and Brian Jermainne assisted in the preparation of the manuscript. Sally Merry and William Woods provided important support.

My wife, Dr. June King Davison, made it possible for me to undertake this work.

Those others who requested their contributions be made in confidence will recognize the help they gave me in a case in which the cause of justice was frustrated.

The problem of securing public officials against unwarranted legal harassment was anticipated by the Founding Fathers, who shielded members of Congress against arrest during their attendance at sessions of their respective houses in all cases, except treason, felony and breach of the peace. The Supreme Court clarified in 1907 that senatorial privilege did not, however, preclude criminal prosecution altogether.

At Chappaquiddick, it did.

Old Saybrook, Connecticut
March 3, 1986

For thou hast lost thy princely privilege
With vile participation.

—HENRY IV, PART I ACT III, SC. II

Chapter 1

THE FERRY AT EDGARTOWN, ON MARTHA'S VINEYARD, WAS NOT scheduled to begin operation until 7:30 A.M. on Saturday, July 19, 1969. Nevertheless, ferryman Richard Hewitt beckoned a blue Ford waiting at the dock at 7 A.M. on board the *On Time,* a raft-like vessel that crossed the 150-yard channel to the island of Chappaquiddick in under four minutes.

The Ford proceeded on Chappaquiddick Road to a sweeping, hairpin curve, leaving the asphalt for the dirt ruts of Dike Road. A bumpy half-mile away was a wooden structure perched on pilings spanning a tidal pool called Poucha Pond. After negotiating the narrow bridge, the Ford discharged Robert Samuel, a high school science teacher, and 15-year-old Joseph Cappavella. Burdened with fishing gear, they continued on foot along a sand track between ranks of dunes to East Beach. After an hour of fruitless casting into the surf along that deserted stretch of shoreline, the two returned to the car.

Samuel was contemplating fishing off the bridge into the pond when his attention was drawn to the glint of metal reflecting off a dark shape in the water ten feet away, on the south side of the bridge.

Looking closer through the ripples of tidewater, he discovered the shadowy outline of an automobile turned onto its roof, front end angled toward the bridge. Samuel made out the wavery numbers of a license plate on the car's inverted bumper.

Samuel and Cappavella headed at once for a cottage 400 feet from the pond. "Dyke House," read the printing on a mailbox beside the weathered shingles of the former hunting camp owned by Chappaquiddick resident Antone Bettencourt and leased for the summer to Mr. and Mrs. Pierre Malm of Lebanon, Pennsylvania. A self-possessed woman of middle age, Mrs. Malm was preparing breakfast when she responded to Samuel's knock at her back door and received his report that a car was overturned in the pond. Then, Samuel and Cappavella returned to drop fishing lines off the bridge, oblivious to the car submerged on the other side.

Mrs. Malm telephoned the Island Communications Center maintained by the Dukes County sheriff's office at Martha's Vineyard airport.

At 8:20 A.M. a call from the Center was logged at the two-room police station located on the first floor of Edgartown's white clapboard town hall.

Policewoman Carmen Salvador relayed the information that an automobile was under water at Dike Bridge on Chappaquiddick to Police Chief Dominick James Arena. She said, "Do you want to send somebody over there?"

"No," Arena said. "I'll go."

Arena left the station with the cruiser's blue dome-light flashing. A sultry, clouding-up morning presaged poor weather for the second day of the Edgartown Yacht Club's annual regatta. For 13 years a

Massachusetts state trooper assigned traffic duty and security at Boston's Logan International Airport, Arena was later attached to the Attorney General's criminal division, handling evidence of government corruption unearthed by the Massachusetts Crime Commission. "Because of my personality, and because I could handle people, I was running the jury room as far as witnesses were concerned to keep them happy and keep the lawyers happy," Arena said.

A newspaper story about a town meeting voting to raise the salary of its police chief to $10,000 in hopes of filling the vacant position prompted Arena to apply for the job even before he knew where that town was. The town, which he found on a map, would turn out to be Edgartown, a picturesque former whaling port described as "tidy, shipshape and sparkling clean." In May 1967, Trooper Arena became Chief Arena, taking on a job which, in many ways, cast him as a virtual legate of the Chamber of Commerce: Policing the occasional excesses of seasonal pleasure-seekers upon whom Edgartown's tourist economy depended.

Pulling up to the ferry landing at the foot of Daggett Street, Arena asked Dick Hewitt, "You hear anything about an accident at the Dike Bridge?"

"Not until now," Hewitt said.

Chappaquiddick looked no more than two swimming-pool lengths away, the channel as close-quartered as everything else was in Edgartown, including the two-car ferry that chugged Arena across. Apart from the modest swank of the beach club's cabanas, the island was a backwater of modest cottages midst groves of scrub pine and pin oak. In twenty years, the bridge at the end of Dike Road never had been the locale of an automobile accident.

Arena parked the cruiser beside the bulkhead. He asked the young men fishing off the bridge, "Is there a car over there?"

"On the other side," Samuel replied.

From the slope of the humpbacked bridge, Arena saw an automobile submerged but for rear tires beginning to show above the waterline. Gouges in a curbing of caplogs traced the path the automobile had taken before plunging into the pond. Arena judged the markings on the bridge's dusty planks, "Weren't really what you could call skid marks. They were more like scuff marks that probably were brought about by tires going sideways, sliding more than skidding across something."

Arena observed a woman approach the pond. Mrs. Malm was taking a look at the accident herself. She'd heard a car pass the house "going faster than usual" around midnight the previous evening, but nothing else.

Arena was amazed she had not heard the car hit the water. He asked if her husband had a bathing suit he could borrow. He followed her into "Dyke House" to change into plaid boxer trunks that, to his surprise, for he was 6'4" tall and weighed 230 pounds, fit him perfectly.

Arena walked to the pond and waded in until the banking dropped off. He swam towards the car, encountering a turbulence of current. He dived underwater. He caught only a blurred glimpse of the automobile before he was dragged away by the inexorable force of an outgoing tide he estimated was running to a depth of six feet, because he could touch bottom.

Arena had a presentiment of dread: Whoever had driven off the bridge might not have escaped from the crushed and upended position in which the vehicle had landed and could still be trapped inside. Any survivor would have reported the accident by now; and there had been no report on the answering machine that recorded calls after the police station closed, or on the log Arena checked when he arrived at the station that morning.

Arena radioed the Communications Center from the cruiser. He told the on-duty dispatcher to have the police station send an officer, and the fire department's scuba diver to the scene.

Arena asked the two small boys standing near the bridge if they knew where there was a face mask he could use.

One of the boys said, "I think there's one in the boat." He ran to a flat-bottomed punt beached on shore and tossed a mask to Arena.

Arena dived into the pond again. The current repeatedly sent him out of control. He let himself be swept to the bridge pilings where he caught his breath; then swam back to the car. Hoisting himself onto the undercarriage, he found seating space beside the gas tank, there to await the arrival of help.

Arena had cut the inside of his big toe on some metal edge of the car, but he was too distracted to care whether the wound was bleeding. Word of the accident was bringing spectators to the pond's edge despite a light rain that had started to fall. After catching five bluefish, Samuel and Cappavella were packing up their gear, preparing to leave. Arena's activities in Poucha Pond had scared away the fish.

At 8:45 A.M., Arena recognized the blinking red bulb atop Edgartown Fire Chief Antone Silva's station wagon bumping down the Dike Road, followed by Antone Bettencourt's blue Jeepster. With Silva was volunteer fireman Laurence Mercier, the proprietor of an Edgartown grocery store, and police officer Robert Bruguiere. A "special" hired for the summer, Bruguiere was a teacher of business subjects at Natick High School. Arena told him, "See if you can get a registry listing for this license," and called out plate number L78 207 from the submerged car's inverted front bumper.

Bruguiere radioed the Communications Center to check the *Polk Directory* of Massachusetts registrations to find out who owned the car in the pond. Then, he drove the police cruiser to the beach side of the bridge.

Arena watched John Farrar adjust an oxygen tank across his back. Captain of the search and rescue division of Edgartown's volunteer fire department, Farrar had received a call at 8:25 A.M. to proceed at once to Dike Bridge on Chappaquiddick. Farrar left the Turf 'n' Tackle shop he managed in Edgartown for the fire station, where diving gear was maintained in immediate readiness. He was joined by Antone Bettencourt, a sprightly 70-year-old retired ferrymaster who drove him to the dock. Fire Chief Silva was waiting on the Chappaquiddick landing to help transfer rescue equipment to his cruiser. Farrar changed into a full diving suit en route to the accident scene, arriving there at 8:45 A.M.

Arena's attention was diverted by Bruguiere calling out information he'd received over the cruiser's radio. License plate L78 207 had been issued to Edward M. Kennedy, Room 2400, JFK Building, Government Center, Boston.

My God, another tragedy, Arena thought. His concern for the accident tuned to a higher frequency of alarm. But he had no time to ponder the stunning news that it was Ted Kennedy's car he was sitting on. Farrar was swimming toward him holding a safety line. He gave Arena one end of the rope, put an oxygen tube in his mouth and dove underwater.

When his mask cleared, Farrar saw in the wash of watery light he likened to the *sfumato* effect of a Rembrandt painting, an Oldsmobile sedan balanced on the brow of its windshield, tipped forward from the weight of the engine so that its rear end was tilted toward the surface. The car was facing the opposite direction it had been travelling before plunging off the bridge. Only speed could account for such aerial maneuvers, Farrar said later. "The car must have been going at a pretty good clip to land almost in the middle of the channel."

Farrar peered through the driver's side open window. It took 20 seconds for his eyes to grow accustomed to the gloom inside the car. The front seat was empty.

Farrar made his way to the back of the car, fighting a current he estimated was running four knots, hard to swim against for any length of time. Through the top right-hand corner of the rear window Farrar saw two motionless feet clad in sandals. So long as there was a possibility the occupant might be alive and breathing, he had to hurry and expand the air in the automobile and bring a resuscitator, if necessary.

Farrar moved quickly to the right side of the car. The rear passenger window had been blown out, shards of glass formed a ragged edge along the frame. Farrar thrust himself through the portal inside the car to his waist. Looking up, he found the body of a young woman. Her head was cocked back, her face pressed into the footwell. Both hands gripped the front edge of the back seat to hold herself in conformity with its upholstered contours. It was not a position assumed by a person knocked unconscious by the impact of a crash, Farrar said. "If she had been dead or unconscious, she would have been prone, sinking to the bottom or floating on top. She definitely was holding herself in a position to avail herself of the last remaining air that had to be trapped in the car."

Farrar took hold of the right thigh. As soon as he touched the body, he knew the woman was dead; the flesh under his grasp was hard as wood. "Instead of life-saving, I was evidence-gathering," Farrar realized. "Because I was the only person who would be able to observe this situation, it behooved me to think about what I saw underwater to be able to report it."

Farrar rotated the body inside the car, a maneuver complicated by the victim's hunched posture and outstretched arms made inflexible by *rigor mortis*. The body was "about one-quarter positively buoyant," Farrar observed. "There was still a little air left in her."

Farrar drew the body through the window head first. A gold chain clasped about the waist came undone and slipped off. He struggled to maintain his position beside the car against the current. Concerned he might lose the body when he swam to the surface, Farrar bound the safety line about the woman's neck. He tugged on the rope to signal he was coming up. Clasping the body over his head, Farrar pushed off. He broke the surface as Arena was gathering in the last feet of slack line. Farrar noted with satisfaction that the police chief's assistance was not required to bring the body up. The difficult recovery had taken him ten minutes.

The current took Farrar downstream toward the bridge. Holding the body in a cross-chest carry, he swam to the rear of Kennedy's car. For the first time in the several years he had known Arena as "a very placid individual, very calm and collected," Farrar observed him to be "excited and emotionally wrought-up." Arena had a quaver in his voice when he said, "My God, it's a body. Do you recognize her? Is it one of the Kennedy clan?"

"I haven't had a chance to see if I recognize her or not," Farrar said. He turned the body over in the water.

Arena examined the face for a Kennedy family likeness. Farrar observed "a great look of relief" on Arena's face before he said, "Thank God, no. I don't recognize her. It isn't one of the clan."

Farrar undid the safety line. The victim's blonde hair was tangled in the half-hitch knots he'd tied. Farrar helped draw the body out of the water onto Arena's lap. Holding the corpse in his arms, Arena scrutinized the pale, lightly-freckled face, rigid in death. The mouth was open, teeth gritted in a death grimace. Pale eyes stared through partially-closed lids. She wore a long-sleeve white blouse, and navy blue slacks. There was a friendship ring on her left hand; two gold bracelets dangled from a wrist. "She appeared normal in the sense that there were no injuries that I could see," Arena said, later. "If she hadn't been wringing wet, it was as if she was about to go to work, or to a party, because everything was in place. Everything was buttoned right up."

Fireman Laurence Mercier called from the bulkhead, "Do you want the boat?" before pushing it out into the pond on a rope. Arena and Farrar placed the body across slat seats. The boat was drawn to shore. Passed hand-over-hand to the bridge, the body was placed on a stretcher in the back of the police cruiser.

Arena ordered Bruguiere to summon the medical examiner and undertaker, and have a tow truck sent to the scene. As required in all fatal automobile accidents, the Registry of Motor Vehicles had to be notified, too. Arena said, "And see if you can find out where Ted Kennedy is and get him down here."

Arena asked Tony Bettencourt to drive to the landing to wait for the medical examiner to come off the ferry.

Farrar dove underwater to retrieve the chain belt that had detached from the body. He checked the rest of the car. On the interior roof near the front passenger seat he found a workman's lunch pail lacquered with a *decoupage* of flowers, and fashioned into a handbag. When Arena opened it, water gushed forth a spillage of cosmetics and articles of grooming. A wallet contained a Virginia driver's license and a pass for the United States Senate, identifying Rosemary Keough of Washington, D.C. There were two keys for room #56 at the Katama Shores Motor Inn of Edgartown.

Arena radioed the Communications Center to confirm that Keough was registered at the motel. Minutes later, he received confirmation she was one of six young women who had occupied three rooms there since Thursday. None of the beds had been slept in the previous night.

Arena told Farrar to check downstream, "It's possible there were other people in the car. They might be in the pond someplace." He was walking off the bridge when the Depot Corner garage tow-truck pulled up with Jon Ahlbum at the wheel. The truck had emblazoned on its side panel: "You Wreck Em—We Fetch Em."

Arena didn't want Ahlbum to remove the car from Poucha Pond until registry inspectors arrived, he said. "They don't like it when an accident scene is disturbed before they can do their investigation." Concerned about the hazard presented by a growing crowd of spectators at the pond's edge, Arena changed his mind. The registry's office in Oak Bluffs was closed on Saturday. "I don't think we can get a hold of the registry today. You better get the car out as soon as you can and hold it at the garage." Arena added, "That's Ted Kennedy's car down there in the water."

"Gee, I just saw him at the ferry landing on the Chappy side," Ahlbum said.

"Oh, God. I better get a hold of him," Arena said.

Arena was walking down Dike Road when a Pontiac station wagon pulled up.

"Jim, can I help you?" Christopher "Huck" Look said. Look was a deputy sheriff and "special duty" police officer. A call to his cottage on Chappaquiddick suggested Look might be needed at the accident scene.

"You probably can help keep traffic away from the bridge," Arena said. "There's a car overturned in the pond. We're trying to find out if there's anyone else in it."

"I saw a car last night," Look said. "I hope to God that isn't the same one."

Arena was too preoccupied to continue the conversation and walked off.

Look got out of his car and watched the chief head for "Dyke House." Arena was going to call the police station to send somebody down to the ferry to locate Ted Kennedy.

Chapter 2

ARRIVING AT THE LANDING ON THIS ERRAND AT 9:30 A.M., ANTONE Bettencourt addressed Dick Hewitt on the docked *On Time*. "Do you know about the accident? It's Ted Kennedy's car and there's a dead girl in it."

Hewitt nodded in the direction of a weathered ferryhouse at the landing. "Well, he's standing right over there with two men."

Bettencourt confronted Ted Kennedy. "Senator, do you know there's a girl found dead in your car?" he said. "Do you need a ride down to the bridge?"

"No," Kennedy said. "I'm going on over to town."

Bettencourt watched the *On Time* leave the landing for the crossing to Edgartown. Minutes later the ferry was back. Hewitt made several round-trips during the next fifteen minutes. He observed Ted Kennedy and two other men "milling around" the ferryhouse. Hewitt wondered if the Senator knew about the accident. The same idea had occurred to Steve Ewing, the ferry's 16-year-old deckhand. "We realized by this time the Senator's car was involved in the accident," he said. "We thought he was waiting there for news."

Kennedy had boarded the ferry shortly after Ewing reported for work at 9 A.M. The Senator greeted the boy with a cheerful "Hi!" when Ewing collected three 15-cent fares. After the boat ride to Chappaquiddick the three men had gathered at the ferryhouse, which was furnished with benches and a public telephone.

Hewitt and Ewing walked off the docked ferry. At their approach, Kennedy edged toward a row of parked cars. He was within hearing distance when Hewitt called out, "Senator, are you aware of the accident?"

A tall man wearing glasses answered, "Yes, we just heard about it."

Hewitt and Ewing returned to the ferry. Kennedy and the tall man wearing glasses followed. "This time," Ewing noted, "Kennedy looked worried."

Steve Ewing's father was standing at the Edgartown dock. Vineyard bureau chief for the *New Bedford Standard-Times,* Harvey Ewing had heard about an accident at Chappaquiddick involving a member of Ted Kennedy's regatta party and had gone to the landing to cover the story.

It was 9:50 A.M. when he spotted Ted Kennedy on board the *On Time* bound for Edgartown. Ewing made ready to take a photograph, but before the ferry docked, Kennedy jumped off and was striding up Daggett Street at such a brisk pace, he walked out of focus. "That's why the picture isn't very good," Ewing apologized later. "Because I didn't get him full face coming at me off the ferry; I got him sideways."

Ewing wasn't sure why he had taken the picture. "I figured if someone in his party had been in an accident, it was a normal reaction for him to be over there checking things out, that he'd be concerned," he said. Kennedy looked "in fine shape," smartly turned out in light blue pants, white polo shirt and canvas deck shoes.

Ewing went to a pay phone at the dock to call Bob Hyde, his summer assistant. Ewing wanted Hyde at the accident scene while he maintained telephone contact with his paper in New Bedford. Ewing told him, "All I know is a car went into the drink and whoever was in it is involved with the Kennedy party. They think there's more than one person in the car."

Ewing was joined at the landing by Colbert Smith, assistant editor of the *Vineyard Gazette*. Boarding the ferry was undertaker Eugene Frieh, with the Buick station wagon he used as a hearse; his assistant, David Guay; and associate medical examiner, Dr. Donald Mills.

Mills had been alerted by his receptionist, Mrs. Thomas Teller, "Don't be surprised if you get a call to go to Chappy. I hear there's been a fatal of some kind over there."

Mills received the call because it was Medical Examiner Dr. Robert Nevin's day off. He left his office and drove to the ferry landing. Frieh invited him into the hearse for the journey to Chappaquiddick.

Mills observed a dozen bystanders on Dike Bridge. Wearing a bathing suit and a wet T-shirt, police chief Arena was entering "Dyke House." Arena used Mrs. Malm's phone to call the police station. He told Carmen Salvador to send someone down to the ferry to find Ted Kennedy.

"He's right here, Chief," Salvador said. "And he wants to talk to you."

"I'm afraid, Senator, I have some bad news," Arena said. "There's been another tragedy. Your car was in an accident over here. And the young lady is dead."

"I know," Kennedy said.

"Can you tell me, was there anybody else in the car?"

"Yes," Kennedy said.

"Are they in the water?"

"No," Kennedy said. "Can I talk to you? Could I see you?"

"Do you want to come over here?" Arena said. "Or do you want me to go over there?"

"I prefer for you to come over here," Kennedy said.

Not bothering to change clothes, Arena rushed out of "Dyke House" to find a ride to Edgartown. He asked "Huck" Look for a lift to the ferry. Look didn't have his car there. Look approached Dr. Edward Self, standing near the bulkhead. A prominent New York surgeon and president of the Chappaquiddick Association of island residents, Self agreed to chauffeur Arena to the landing.

Arena was getting into Self's Land Rover when Bruguiere reported "Huck" Look had seen the accident car—or one just like it—"up at the corner" around 12:45 A.M. the previous evening.

Arena didn't give much notice to the report. Look was a year-rounder with a variety of part-time vocations, including off-season heating oil dealer. Arena would have plenty of time to question Look later. Right now, Arena was more concerned about his forthcoming interview with Senator Ted Kennedy at the police station.

Police officer Roy Meekins was waiting at the Edgartown landing, as he had been instructed when Bruguiere radioed to have a cruiser meet Arena there. Then Bruguiere greeted Dr. Mills. He explained that a young woman had been recovered from the overturned car in the pond.

Mills wanted the body brought to the front of the cruiser so as not to expose it to spectators standing on the bridge. The stretcher was placed near the cruiser's front grill. Mills uncovered a blanket to find "a well-developed, well-nourished, very attractive young woman" in complete *rigor mortis*. Her arms were stretched outward from her shoulders as if to ward off an assault; hands were frozen in a "semi-claw. " There was a fine white froth about the nose and mouth flecked with a barely visible cobweb of blood that went directly to a capillary area on the left nostril.

It was, in Dr. Mills' opinion, "the characteristic foam that goes with a drowning case."

Mills ran his fingers through the wet hair for evidence of skull fracture, then the throat and neck. He unbuttoned the blouse to expose a lacy blue brassiere. He placed a stethoscope over the heart. There was no sound. He felt the rib cage; then tapped the chest, repeating the procedure with varying degrees of pressure. Each time, water welled up from inside the lungs, creating a splashing sound. The lightest pressure produced water from the mouth and nose.

Mills did not remove the brassiere to examine the breasts for injury. He slid the slacks over her hips "exposing her enough to make an adequate examination," he explained. "I couldn't have removed her clothes without cutting them off because of *rigor mortis*."

Frieh closely followed Mills' examination. As a mortician, "I more or less kept my eyes open," he said. Water seeped from the nose and mouth when the body was turned onto its left side, Frieh observed, "That probably came from her stomach."

"No, I'm pressing her chest," Mills said. "That's water from her lungs."

Mills passed his hands over the back and abdomen. He found no evidence of trauma of any kind. He diagnosed "an obvious and clear" case of drowning. "After all," he said, later, "the girl was found in a submerged automobile."

Mills overheard several bystanders speculating that the accident victim was a secretary employed by the Kennedy family. Mills ordered Frieh to remove the body to his funeral home, but to hold off embalming. In view of "certain non-medical factors and personalities" he had heard only as a rumor, Mills wanted to consult the District Attorney's office about a possible autopsy, he said. "If there's any Kennedy mixup in this, it's more than I want to handle alone."

Mills rode back to Edgartown in Frieh's hearse. Although he viewed the death of "this lovely young person" as a "shame," he was more concerned, at that moment, about the patient in labor he had sent to Martha's Vineyard hospital in Oak Bluffs, seven miles away.

The hospital's emergency room had monitored transmissions to and from the Communications Center concerning a fatal accident on Chappaquiddick involving Senator Ted Kennedy's automobile. The information was reported by on-duty nurse Barbara Ferry to her husband, at 9:30 A.M.

Richard Ferry, an employee of the Woods Hole, Martha's Vineyard, Nantucket Steamship Authority that provided boat service to the islands, called the Authority's chairman, Jimmy Smith, in Falmouth on Cape Cod. "There's been an accident," he said. "It's Ted Kennedy's car and somebody's dead. We don't know who it is yet. I thought you'd like to know."

Ferry promised to call back when he had more information.

Stocky, somewhat brash and outspoken but a well-liked lawyer, Smith had used his influence to secure hard-to-get reservations for Ted Kennedy's Oldsmobile to be transported to Martha's Vineyard on Wednesday. Return passage was booked for Sunday morning at 9:50 A.M. out of Oak Bluffs. An assistant district attorney within whose jurisdiction the accident had occurred, Smith had taken Ferry's call in a library furnished with the photographic memorabilia of his work as advance man and coordinator for various Kennedy campaigns. Captivated by John F. Kennedy "as the one politician in Massachusetts who didn't have his hand out," Smith had enlisted early, as one of an army of young, idealistic lawyers who were to become the foot soldiers in a Kennedy march to the White House.

In 1960, Smith advanced campaign appearances in North Dakota, Montana and Wyoming, states in the Northern Plains, under the charge of Ted Kennedy. When Ted himself became a candidate for the U.S.

Senate in 1962, Smith was floor monitor at the Democratic state convention that gave the first-time office seeker the party's endorsement. After that election, Ted Kennedy inscribed a Philipe Halsman portrait of himself: "To James Smith, who helped us fight the good fight." Smith had gone on to work Kennedy campaigns in 1964 and 1968.

"Cape Codders have wondered for some time if one of their number actually might be close to the Kennedy apparatus," the weekly *Cape Cod News* reported, "Jimmy Smith appears to be mighty close."

Smith called Kenneth O'Donnell. The former White House appointments secretary and political strategist lived in Jamaica Plain, a suburb of Boston. O'Donnell had little reaction to the news of the accident. He asked Smith to keep him "informed."

Smith called O'Donnell's brother, Warren, in Worcester. An advance man for both Kennedy and Johnson presidential campaigns, he had played football at Harvard with Ted Kennedy. More volatile than his brother, Warren wanted to "do something," he said. "How can we find out what's happening?"

Smith knew Chief Arena as a "very friendly, congenial guy with a lot of sophistication," and had rejoiced when he'd been chosen Edgartown chief of police. "I thought he would be good for Edgartown because they're so provincial over there."

Smith wasn't concerned about Arena "calling a shot a shot," whatever the case turned out to be. But he wasn't going to use his position in the district attorney's office to find out what was going on in Edgartown.

Chapter 3

ARENA STRODE INTO TOWN HALL AT 10 O'CLOCK WITH NO INKLING of what was ahead of him. He wasn't surprised to find Harvey Ewing and Colbert Smith waiting to see him, given the lightning speed with which Edgartown's gossip network had broadcast the news that Senator Kennedy was at the police station.

Arena asked the two local reporters to wait outside.

Ewing raised an eyebrow. Arena had never denied him access to the police station before.

Arena greeted Carmen Salvador at the station's front desk. A sweet-faced woman of an unexcitable temperament, she had been relaying messages to and from the Communications Center about the accident at Chappaquiddick when Ted Kennedy appeared at her desk.

"How are you?" Kennedy said. "Can I use your phone."

"You can use the Chief's," Salvador said. She let Kennedy into an adjoining office.

Kennedy looked "really nervous," Salvador reported. "He seemed to think I knew all about what had happened, but I didn't. I thought someone had taken his car for a joy ride."

A tall man had followed Kennedy into the station. He, too, had asked to use the telephone. Salvador watched him misdial the phone on her desk, make two calls that made no sense to her, then join Ted Kennedy in Arena's office and close the door.

Kennedy was using the phone when Arena entered his office and said, "Hello, Senator. I'm Jim Arena."

Kennedy hung up, came around the desk to shake Arena's out-stretched hand and said, "Hello, Jim."

From his state trooper days at Suffolk County Courthouse in Boston, Arena recognized the other man in the office as former U.S. Attorney Paul Markham. He said, "I'm sorry about the accident."

"Yes, I know," Kennedy said. "I was the driver."

"Nothing in my prior career as a police officer," Arena recalled later, "had prepared me for standing in a wet bathing suit and shaking hands with a United States Senator—and a Kennedy—who tells me he is the driver of a car from which I have just removed the body of a beautiful young girl. I was stunned."

Arena was struck by the incongruity of the situation. "Our roles could have been reversed. The Senator was in clean, dry clothes—poised, confident and in control, using my office and telephone. I'm standing in a puddle of water in a state of confusion thinking I had only minutes before broken the news of a personal tragedy he's now telling me quite calmly he knows all about." Arena had assumed the accident victim had driven the car off Dike Bridge herself. He said, "Do you happen to know where Rosemary Keough is from so we can notify her next of kin?"

"It isn't 'Cricket' Keough; it's Mary Jo Kopechne," Kennedy said. "I've already notified her parents."

Arena asked how to spell the last name.

Kennedy only knew how to pronounce it.

"We can find out how to spell it later," Markham suggested.

"What would you like for me to do?" Kennedy said. "We must do what is right or we'll both be criticized for it."

The Senator's demeanor "certainly worked a calming effect on me," Arena said later. "I automatically fell back on years of police training and began to process the matter as though it was a routine traffic case." As far as Arena could see, it was a motor vehicle accident, he said. "The first thing we have to do is to have a statement from you about what happened."

"Would it be all right if I wrote it out?" Kennedy said, requesting time "undisturbed" to prepare the statement.

Arena led the way to an unoccupied town office down the corridor from the police station, "so the Senator could have some privacy."

Kennedy asked Arena to return to Chappaquiddick to see that his car "got out and cleared OK."

Arena was glad for the reprieve. The admission that Senator Kennedy had been the driver of the fatal accident car thoroughly rattled him. On the way to the ferry, Arena collected his thoughts around self-reminders of the proper police procedures to follow, when he returned to the station to receive Kennedy's statement, in this suddenly-extraordinary automobile accident.

Dr. Mills was also taking pains in dealing with a case in which so famous a name was rumored to be involved. As medical examiner, Mills could call for an autopsy to be made on the accident victim, or one could be ordered by the district attorney. A modest man of cautious disposition, Mills hesitated to exercise his own authority. Instead, he called the state police barracks at Oak Bluffs, following a directive that all communications with the district attorney's office be routed through the state police.

Mills told officer Richard DeRoche to contact the district attorney's office in New Bedford. "Tell them I have the case of a girl who was trapped in a submerged vehicle for a matter of hours and has obviously drowned; that I am fully satisfied with my diagnosis of drowning by immersion; that I don't know who she is, but she is reputed to be an employee of the Kennedy family. And if it is the judgment of the district attorney or his assistant that an autopsy is indicated, then I am asking for one."

Mills wasn't making the request for medical reasons. "We almost never do autopsies in drowning cases on the island. I was requesting the consideration of an autopsy because of the connection with a prominent person—that was particularly important in my mind. I felt it was too big an issue for me to handle single-handedly. I felt the evidence of drowning was conclusive, but I'm no detective."

Chapter 4

REGISTRY OF MOTOR VEHICLES INSPECTOR GEORGE "RED"
Kennedy, and his assistant Robert Molla were waiting for Arena at the
ferry landing. Kennedy was fishing when he received a radio call that
Edgartown police were looking for him. A fourteen-year veteran of the
registry, Kennedy was reputed to be "a good investigator" by his
colleagues. Arena thought he was "a nice guy, but not too bright."

The automobile had been righted in Poucha Pond when Arena
returned to Dike Bridge; but the current was still too swift for the car to
be pulled from the water.

John Farrar had observed large air bubbles rise to the surface when
the automobile turned over. He was continuing to dive, looking for more
bodies. Arena told him, "You can call off your search; I have the driver.
We know who the girl is. There was nobody else in the car."

Arena joined registry inspectors taking measurements of the accident
scene. Dike Road was 15 feet wide at the bridge and the bridge was built
at a 27 degree angle to the road. The car had landed 51 feet from the

start of the bridge and catapulted 23 feet, 7 inches forward, and 5 feet outward from the exit gouges on the rub rail.

Inspector Kennedy noted: "According to the skid marks, the wheel of the right side of the car skidded some 18 feet before it went over the rub rail. The wheel on the left side showed skid marks of 33 feet, 2 inches to the point where the car left the bridge and flipped into the water."

Arena's inspection revealed, "No skid marks on the bridge or dirt road prior to reaching the bridge that I could see."

When tide approached dead low, the car was dragged from the pond. As the rear end license plate emerged, "Huck" Look, watching the salvage operation from the bridge, walked over to officer Bruguiere to say, "That is the same car I saw last night."

Bruguiere reported what Look told him to Arena.

"Do you know who was driving that car last night?" Arena said.

Look hadn't the slightest idea, "Only what I told Bob. It appeared to be a man and a woman, and maybe somebody else in the back seat."

"Well, it was Senator Ted Kennedy," Arena said.

One of the few registered Democrats in Edgartown, Look was horrified. "Holy Jesus!" he said. Then, in mock recantation, "I didn't see a thing!"

To Registry Inspector Kennedy, Look confirmed having seen "a vehicle with similar description to vehicle in the accident" whose occupants "looked like two persons, 1 male and 1 female, with male operating vehicle."

Farrar waded to the car, rear wheels resting upon the banking, front end partially submerged. The windshield, though shattered, was still held intact by safety film. Extensive damage had been done to the passenger-side doors and the car's top. The upper right edge of the roof had broken the impact of meeting the water; momentum had carried the car over onto its roof, Farrar said. "For that reason I believe initially a large amount of air was trapped inside." That one window was open and two others broken would not prevent an air bubble from forming.

Farrar opened the driver's side door and checked the dashboard. The key was in the ignition; the light switch was in the "on" position; the gear wand was in "drive." The car was full of broken glass. A hairbrush and a sodden *Boston Globe* for Friday, July 18, were on the floor of the back seat. When the trunk was opened, Farrar observed it to be "remarkably dry."

Arena's inspection of the car only added to his growing puzzlement about the accident. "I was far from being an expert, but I did have certain training beyond that of the average lay person in the matter of accidents. The driver of the car would have to have taken a really hard blow to the head—the windshield on the driver's side was badly smashed in." Arena found it difficult to reconcile Ted Kennedy's appearance at the police station with that of the driver of a car in such an accident.

Before the car was hitched to Jon Ahlbum's wrecker, Arena took from the glove compartment a leatherette folder containing the automobile's registration, several maps and "personal effects," and a lease for the rental of a cottage on Chappaquiddick to Joseph Gargan for ten days beginning July 10.

A New Hampshire news photographer and some-time *Newsweek* correspondent vacationing on Chappaquiddick, Jack Hubbard, had been alerted to the accident at Dike Bridge in time to shoot on-the-scene photographs of the car being dragged from Poucha Pond. Believing then it was strictly a local matter of no particular significance, Hubbard offered his roll of exposed film to Bob Hyde of the *Standard-Times*. An English teacher at Martha's Vineyard regional high school, Hyde had ridden a bicycle to Dike Bridge to cover the story.

Hubbard wasn't the only reporter on holiday in Edgartown. The crowd in front of town hall had grown considerably in the hour Arena was gone, and there were a number of journalists, indistinguishable from tourists and townspeople, who had stopped to find out what was going on.

Arena was dismayed to find James Reston, political columnist and executive editor of the *New York Times,* waiting to see him in the corridor. "I'd only just found out about the accident," Arena said later. "And right off the bat I've got one of the most powerful newspapers in the country camped on my doorstep."

Arena asked Reston to wait outside with other reporters.

A long-time summer resident of Edgartown, Reston had purchased the *Vineyard Gazette* in 1967. To Harvey Ewing, Reston appeared to be enjoying the role of police-beat reporter sniffing out a breaking story. "Reston was reverting to the style of an aggressive newshawk. He was a lot more excited than I thought he should be about the accident; but he was obviously putting things together faster than the rest of us were at this point." Reston had slipped a note through Carmen Salvador asking Ted Kennedy to see him, and stationed a reporter at the back door of town hall to prevent the Senator from eluding the press. To Ewing he said, "We want to see if we can catch him before he gets away."

Arena recognized Jack Crimmins standing in the corridor. Crimmins had chauffeured Ted Kennedy when Arena was assigned to Logan Airport in Boston as a state trooper.

When Arena walked into the town accountant's office, Paul Markham was seated at a desk and Ted Kennedy was pacing.

The statement was "nearly finished," Markham said.

Arena took the opportunity "to take a real close look" at Ted Kennedy. "I found it hard to believe the Senator had been in a major automobile accident. His face bore no traces of any marks. He never sat down or appeared in any kind of physical discomfort. If he had been injured, in shock, or confused, nothing of it lingered in our meeting, to my observation. But the Senator made it a point to tell me three times, without my asking, that he was the driver of the accident car. It was as though he wanted to make sure I got it right." Arena could think of no reason why Ted Kennedy would admit to that if it were not true.

Arena was summoned to the police station to take a call from Robert Carroll, chairman of Edgartown's Board of Selectmen. A real estate developer and entrepreneur chronically embroiled in controversies with local planning boards, Carroll was a fervent Kennedy supporter. He said, "I understand somebody went off a bridge in Teddy Kennedy's car."

"Yeah," Arena said. "And the worst of it is, Ted was driving."

"Oh, Jesus!" Carroll said. "If there's anything I can do to help, let me know."

Markham came into Arena's office with the accident report. Since Arena wasn't sure he could read Markham s writing, he said. "Do you mind if I have this typed?"

Markham thought that was a good idea.

Arena intended to have Carmen Salvador transcribe the two pages, but she was busy answering the station's two telephones. Arena sat at his desk to type the statement himself. He had no difficulty deciphering the spiky scrawl, complete with cross-outs and write-overs with which Markham had transcribed the Senator's dictation. But what Arena read astounded him. No wonder Ted Kennedy was showing no ill effects from the accident. According to his verbatim report, the accident had occurred more than ten hours ago:

> On July 18, 1969, at approximately 11:15 P.M. in Chappaquiddick, Martha's Vineyard, Massachusetts, I was driving my car on Main Street on my way to get the ferry back to Edgartown. I was unfamiliar with the road and turned right onto Dike Road, instead of bearing hard left on Main Street. After proceeding for approximately one-half mile on Dike Road I descended a hill and came upon a narrow bridge. The car went off the side of the bridge. There was one passenger with me, one Miss Mary ————————————————,

a former secretary of my brother Sen. Robert Kennedy. The car turned over and sank into the water and landed with the roof resting on the bottom.

I attempted to open the door and the window of the car but have no recollection of how I got out of the car. I came to the surface and then repeatedly dove down to the car in an attempt to see if the passenger was still in the car. I was unsuccessful in the attempt. I was exhausted and in a state of shock.

I recall walking back to where my friends were eating. There was a car parked in front of the cottage and I climbed into the back seat. I then asked for someone to bring me back to Edgartown. I remember walking around for a period and then going back to my hotel room. When I fully realized what had happened this morning, I immediately contacted the police.

Arena left his office with the typed statement. Walter Steele was standing in the corridor. Skinny, balding, owlish in appearance behind thick glasses, Steele had not yet logged two months as a special prosecutor. Steele's curiosity had been aroused by the crowd gathered outside town hall. Amazed to see the usually-impeccable police chief barefoot, wearing a damp T-shirt and swim trunks, Steele wanted to know, "What the hell is going on?"

Arena nodded toward the door of the town accountant's office. "Ted Kennedy's in there," he said, suggesting Steele stick around. "I might need you later."

Arena gave Ted Kennedy a copy of the statement. He retained a carbon to check over for typing mistakes.

Kennedy read the statement in silence. "OK," he said. Then, "We are trying to get a hold of Burke Marshall."

Markham described Marshall as "a Kennedy family lawyer."

The Senator wanted the statement looked over by his attorney before it became "part of the record," he said. "Could you please hold it until I talk to Burke Marshall?"

Arena had some questions he wanted to ask, principally about the long delay in reporting the accident.

Markham assured him, "The Senator will answer questions after he has consulted his attorney."

That Kennedy asked to talk to a lawyer seemed "a reasonable request" to Arena. "I figured Kennedy would be eager to clear the matter up." Arena agreed to hold the statement and forego further questions, a decision he would come to regret as "something of a low point in my particular case."

Arena asked to see Ted Kennedy's driver's license.

The Senator didn't have it with him, he said. "I can't find my wallet."

Arena wanted to know if the license had been "properly renewed."

Kennedy was "sure" it had been.

Massachusetts law required every driver to have a license "upon his person" or in some easily accessible place for presentation after an accident. Police could arrest without warrant and keep in custody for 24 hours any person operating a motor vehicle who did not have a license in his possession. The Senator's inability to produce a license was in clear violation of the law.

Arena gave no thought to pressing the charge. "A lot of guys forget their license when they change pants," he said. As a state trooper, Arena told drivers without licenses to report to the nearest police station. If they failed to show up or couldn't produce a valid license, he then issued a citation.

In Kennedy's case, Arena was bending enforcement to a breaking point. Possession of a license was required only when "actually engaged in operating a motor vehicle," Arena said. "There's nothing in the law that requires a driver to have his license on him when he walks into a police station to report an accident."

The lack of a license, combined with the delay in reporting the accident, unexplained by the statement it had taken Senator Kennedy more than an hour to compose, were unwished-for complications in an accident Arena had thought he could handle as "a routine traffic case." He was anxious to discharge the statutory requirement to report the fatality to the district attorney's office.

But Arena was reluctant to contact Edmund Dinis in New Bedford. Instead, he called State Police Detective Lieutenant George Killen, chief investigator for the district attorney's office on Cape Cod.

Killen didn't have much to say when Arena reported Senator Ted Kennedy had been the driver in a fatal automobile accident. He did offer the "assistance" of the district attorney's office, if Arena wanted it. Arena didn't. The Senator had given him a statement. Arena and a registry inspector were conducting an investigation.

Steele caught a glimpse of Ted Kennedy when Arena left the town accountant's office. He was gratified the Senator waved, apparently remembering their days together at the Suffolk County District Attorney's office. Fresh from law school, Kennedy had been paid $1.00 a year as an assistant district attorney. The caseload for assistants was backbreaking, but Kennedy had handled no more than a dozen prosecutions in his year of employment. He had argued one case in court. Kennedy spent most of his time giving speeches all over Massachusetts, preparing to run for office.

After 14 years as an assistant district attorney, Steele resigned only two months before to devote himself to private practice and the newly created position of special prosecutor for Dukes County District Court.

Steele spotted District Court Clerk Tommy Teller entering the town hall. Teller had learned about the accident from his brother-in-law,

"Huck" Look. Teller said, "Jesus, Walter! Ted Kennedy's in big trouble. I heard he was driving a car that was in a bad accident."

Steele walked into the police station to have Arena corroborate Teller's story and recognized Paul Markham seated on a bench across from Carmen Salvador's desk. Steele said to him, "How are *you?*"

Clearly, Markham wasn't very well. Red-eyed, his face drawn with exhaustion, Markham looked like he'd had a rough night. He stood up and abruptly announced, "I'm going over to the Shiretown Inn."

Steele volunteered to go with him.

There was about Markham s craggy good looks an air of such anguish that Steele's curiosity about the accident was momentarily subdued. Highly regarded in Boston legal circles, Markham had resigned as U.S. Attorney for Massachusetts in April and was rumored to be in line for a judgeship.

Markham was silent the two blocks to the Shiretown Inn, a shabby-genteel establishment of two nondescript houses connected by a brick courtyard. An outside stairway led to a second-floor porch and a meager room with scant furnishings. Markham collected various articles to stuff into a canvas bag. By the time he had returned to town hall, Steele had pieced together from Markham's muttered half-sentence responses to his tentative questions an incredible story: Ted Kennedy had driven a car off Dike Bridge. He had escaped the accident uninjured, but a young woman accompanying him had drowned. The accident had gone unreported for more than nine hours.

Steele was astonished "Jesus Christ, Paul!"

"I know," Markham said.

Steele suggested, "There might be a problem." Arena was a decent man, a fair-minded chief of police. But the district attorney with jurisdiction over the case was Edmund Dinis, an ambitious politician with a demonstrated penchant for publicity, Steele said. "He can be a pretty intractable guy."

Senator Kennedy was sequestered in Arena's office with Registry Inspectors George Kennedy and Robert Molla. After formally introducing himself, Inspector Kennedy read from a Miranda card of rights: "You have the right to remain silent. Anything you say can and will be used against you in a court of law. You have the right to talk to a lawyer and have him represent you while you are being questioned. If you cannot afford to hire a lawyer, one will be appointed to represent you before any questioning, if you want one."

The Senator listened glumly to the recitation usually given prior to an interrogation. He said he understood his rights.

Inspector Kennedy asked for the Senator's driver's license and registration.

The Senator thought the registration was in the accident car. He didn't have his license with him, he said. "Sometimes I leave it in my car in Washington, because I own two cars. I will place a call for you immediately and see if I didn't leave it there."

Kennedy called his Senate office in Washington. He asked his administrative aide, David Burke, to see if the license had been left in the other car, and to provide the complete name, address and date of birth for Mary Jo Kopechne required for the registry's report of the accident.

Inspector Kennedy read over the Senator's statement. He said, "I would like to know about something."

"I have nothing more to say!" the Senator said, brusquely. "I have no comment."

Markham assured Inspector Kennedy, "The Senator will make a further statement after he has contacted his lawyer."

Inspector Kennedy did not insist on asking questions about the accident in order to make a report. The Senator had let him know in no uncertain terms he had no intention of saying more. The cool manner the Senator had maintained throughout the three hours he had spent at the police station was beginning to unravel. The Senator was anxious to leave the premises. Markham was calling air charter services seeking to book a flight to Hyannis.

Arena called Robert Carroll, a licensed pilot who owned a Piper Commanche. "Can you fly the Senator to Hyannis?" Arena asked. "One of the motor vehicle guys is going to use his own car to drive him to the airport."

Carroll agreed to leave his office at once.

Senator Kennedy was fretful about reporters Carmen Salvador told him were waiting outside the police station to see him. Arena was sympathetic to Kennedy's dilemma. He wasn't looking forward to meeting the press himself, but for the Senator, Arena provided an escape route that would allow him to evade reporters. Clearing the corridor of "unauthorized personnel," Arena led Kennedy and Markham to a utility room in the rear of the building. A door provided access to a parking lot.

Bob Hyde of the *Standard-Times* was standing vigil outside the door when Kennedy dashed for Registry Inspector Robert Molla's unmarked Plymouth. He tried to get a statement, but Kennedy wouldn't say anything. The Senator appeared "very shook," Hyde observed. "He looked like the wrath of God."

En route to the airport Kennedy muttered, "Oh my God, what has happened? What has happened?"

He repeated the phrase during an uneventful ten-minute flight to Hyannis airport.

Carroll taxied the plane to a parking area without waiting for directives from lineboy John Celentano. The passenger-side door opened and Ted Kennedy climbed out, drenched in perspiration. Kennedy walked, then jogged to a car parked near the runway's tarmac. Celentano thought he looked "in a semi-state of shock."

Chapter 5

ARENA TOLD REPORTERS ALLOWED INTO THE CORRIDOR HE could not release a statement about the accident from Senator Kennedy until he received permission.

Furious that police had collaborated with the Senator to avoid confronting reporters, James Reston demanded the statement be released at once, with an accompanying story.

Arena politely declined to do so. He was bothered the victim's last name had been left blank in the Senator's report. The handbag he had brought back to the police station from the accident scene inspired the only investigative initiative Arena would find time to demonstrate in the escalating, pressurized atmosphere at town hall. It hadn't seemed "out of line" for the handbag to be found in the accident car, since Rosemary Keough was identified as a Senate employee. "That kind of lulled me into thinking she was just one of Kennedy's crew," Arena said. "That maybe here's a bunch of girls from Washington, and if Mary Jo was in the regatta group staying at the motel, then this other girl has got to know her."

Arena called the Katama Shores Motor Inn and asked to speak to Rosemary Keough. "Basically, I wanted to find out how to spell Mary Jo's last name, not what the handbag was doing in the car."

Keough sounded wary and suspicious after Arena identified himself as chief of police. He overheard a muffled consultation going on at the other end of the line before Keough came back on to spell out Mary Jo Kopechne's name. Keough was sending someone to the police station to pick up her handbag, she said.

Arena turned it over to a man "who looked reputable," an hour later. He didn't question him. "Maybe I gave it away too easy, but I figured he knew what bag to ask for. And there was nothing compromising in it."

It didn't occur to Arena until later that from the tremulous quaver in her voice, Rosemary Keough had known about the death of Mary Jo Kopechne. "She seemed very down in the dumps, like she knew what had happened. I'm thinking: 'She's way out at Katama, and I'm down here. How the hell does she know about the accident?'" But it was too late for Keough to be questioned. When Arena called the motel again, she had checked out.

Arena didn't get to question Jack Crimmins either. He wasn't sure what Ted Kennedy's driver was doing hanging around the police station after the Senator left. "I thought maybe he's with Ted and just waited around to see me, that maybe he was there to put the arm on me. To say: 'Hey, go easy on the boss.' Or did he want to tell me something."

When Arena went out to the corridor looking for him, Crimmins was gone. Arena's only source of information about the accident was Senator Kennedy's report. And that statement "didn't add up at all," in Walter Steele's opinion. The "wrong turn" was particularly contradictory. Kennedy was familiar enough with the geography of Chappaquiddick to know to bear left instead of turning right on Dike Road—properly identified in his report—if he were going to the ferry.

Yet he'd made the turn anyway. The Senator's approximation of the distance from the Main Street intersection to Dike Bridge was right on the money. Questionable too, was the "shock and exhaustion" Kennedy said he'd suffered after the accident. The Senator had not sought medical attention after the accident nor did he appear to be injured at the police station—factors which combined to suggest that the Senator may have tried to avoid responsibility by delaying his report. As it was, Kennedy hadn't done so until after the accident was discovered and a body been recovered from his car. Unless there were mitigating circumstances to account for the ten-hour delay, Arena had no choice but to seek a complaint against Ted Kennedy for leaving the scene of an accident, Steele said. "That's all you can do. The statement is in clear violation of the statute."

That Arena had been asked to hold the statement until it had been "cleared" by Burke Marshall, Steele thought, was utterly foolhardy.

"You can't release this to the press! It's a goddamn confession for Christ sake." Any lawyer advising Ted Kennedy was likely to be calling up any minute to say not to release anything, Steele said. "They can't want this made public."

Steele wanted to know if the district attorney's office had been notified about the fatal accident.

Arena said he'd called George Killen.

"The statute says you have to notify the district attorney," Steele said. "Let's not take any chances with that son of a bitch."

Reluctantly, Arena called Edmund Dinis in New Bedford. He recited only that portion of Kennedy's statement in which the Senator had admitted to driving the car.

Dinis didn't take it very well. "We're in this case right now!" he shouted. "He's all done; he's *gone!*"

"Jesus!" Arena said when Dinis hung up. "I don't know what's going on. It sounds to me like he's coming into the case."

Dinis had authority to take over any investigation within his district merely by announcing his intention to do so.

Before Arena could absorb the implications of the conversation with Dinis, the telephone rang again. George Killen said, "This is just a motor vehicles case. You must have had a hundred of these damned things when you were with the state police. You don't need our help." Killen once again offered the "assistance" of the district attorney's office, but he made it clear, "It's *your* case."

What was even clearer was that Dinis had talked to his chief investigator on Cape Cod and Killen had cooled the district attorney's ardor about taking over. Arena said, "Killen was right in some respects to think this was a state trooper kind of thing, knowing my experience as a highway cop. It wasn't the classic kind of case you called the district attorney's office about. My reaction was, with somebody like Ted Kennedy mixed up in it, if I didn't let Dinis know about the accident, he'd go apeshit."

In 1967, Dinis had proclaimed, "On Cape Cod I depend heavily on Lieutenant George Killen. He is one of the most outstanding police officers in the country today. He speaks for me. I trust him with my life."

As senior officer responsible for the investigation and prosecution of all criminal matters on Cape Cod and the islands of Martha's Vineyard and Nantucket, Killen had achieved near-legendary status. Tall, dapper, with great dignity of bearing, Killen's monumental reserve enhanced a strict adherence to the highest standards of rectitude in the investigation and preparation of cases for prosecution in Barnstable Superior Court. Killen deployed a small investigative staff with the skills of a field general. Lately, his office had been swamped with cases. "It seemed every time the telephone rang it was somebody else telling me: 'I got a body.'"

Killen was winding down the investigation of the most sensational murder case in Cape Cod history. Under arrest for killing four young women whose mutilated bodies were found buried in Truro woods was

Antone Costa of Province town. Killen gave the major credit for breaking the complex case to Lieutenant Bernie Flynn, a veteran detective
assigned to his office in 1967.

A former New Bedford police officer who had placed first on the
state police examination, Flynn was given the choice of assignment to
the district attorney's office in New Bedford or Barnstable courthouse.
Flynn jumped at the chance to work on Cape Cod.

Killen tracked Flynn to the Falmouth Country Club, and had him
paged off the greens.

"There's been an accident," Killen announced portentously.

"An accident?" Flynn said. "For Christ sakes, we don't investigate
accidents."

"We'll investigate this one," Killen said. "It's Ted Kennedy. You
better get over to Edgartown and see what the hell is going on."

Killen also contacted the state police barracks in Oak Bluffs about
an autopsy request made by Associate Medical Examiner Donald Mills.

Mills was attending a patient when officer Robert Lucas called with
a message from Killen: If Mills was satisfied with his diagnosis and there
was no evidence of foul play, no autopsy was necessary. Should Mills
care to discuss the matter further, he could reach Killen at home.

Mills was "perfectly satisfied with Lieutenant Killen's decision," he
said when he instructed Eugene Frieh to go ahead with embalming. Killen had suggested a blood specimen be taken for identification and
analysis.

Then, Mills put the accident at Chappaquiddick out of his mind. "I
couldn't give it any more thought at the time," he said. Mills had a baby
to deliver at Oak Bluffs hospital.

Frieh was surprised no autopsy had been ordered in the case. "I
figured there should have been one for three reasons: the type of accident
it was; the important people involved; and the fact that insurance companies would be hounding officials over double indemnity claims."

Frieh and his assistant undressed the body in a basement preparation room. A blood sample was drawn from the left armpit. As was customary in drowning cases, a body block was affixed under the diaphragm. From abdominal compression, Frieh observed "a very slight bit of moisture and a slight bit of froth of a pinkish hue." He estimated it to be less than a tea-cup. "I did raise an eyebrow in the sense that I was expecting much more moisture."

Frieh examined the scalp when he shampooed salt water and sea weed from the victim's hair. Because the car had gone over a bridge, Frieh wondered if there might be some injury Dr. Mills had overlooked during his brief on-scene examination. Frieh discovered no bruises or marks on the body, except for a slight abrasion on the left-hand knuckle.

After washing the body with a solution of germicidal soap and spray-rinsing it, Frieh cleaned all body orifices with an astringent. But, he put off embalming because he still expected Dr. Mills to change his mind about wanting an autopsy.

Frieh held everything in abeyance, awaiting identification of the body and specific instructions from the deceased's family when he received a call from the Kielty Funeral Home of Plymouth, Pennsylvania. John Kielty had been authorized by Mrs. Joseph Kopechne to take charge of funeral arrangements. Frieh was told to prepare the remains and forward the body to Pennsylvania as quickly as possible.

Kielty provided the vital statistics Frieh needed to make out a death certificate. The accident victim was Mary Jo Kopechne of 2921 Olive Avenue, N.W. Washington, D.C., born in Wilkes-Barre, PA, on July 26, 1940. She was formerly employed as a secretary to the late Senator Robert Kennedy. The information had been supplied by the victim's mother. She described her daughter as 5'4", 110 pounds, Roman Catholic and "being maiden."

Frieh used a trocar—a large, hollow needle—attached to a vacuum motor to penetrate the abdominal wall, pelvic area and heart spaces to remove excess body fluids that might be detrimental to good embalming. Sixteen ounces of formalin were inserted into the trunk; then an additional 16 ounces on aspiration. Frieh's assistant did the embalming under his supervision. Frieh carefully recorded all procedures "to keep ourselves refreshed in case we had to be questioned," he said, later. "We knew we had a hot cookie on our hands."

Chapter 6

AT 2:15 P.M., ARENA LOGGED ANOTHER CALL FROM GEORGE Killen. Concerned about an autopsy request from Dr. Mills, Killen wanted Arena's opinion because he'd been at the accident scene when the body was recovered.

"That's up to the medical examiner, it's not my say-so," Arena said. He saw no reason to question the finding of death by drowning. "To the best of my observation, nothing else was wrong."

Killen was satisfied to leave the case in Arena's hands. He said, "You've got a tiger by the tail, Jim. But I'm sure you can handle it."

Arena was still waiting for permission to release Senator Kennedy's statement to an increasingly impatient corps of reporters standing outside the police station when *CBS News* correspondent Ben Silver and a television crew invaded his office. An aggressive, take-over reporter, Silver brushed aside Arena's protests in his determination to interview the police chief.

Francis Broadhurst noticed more reporters were packing into the hot and airless corridor, when he arrived at town hall. Cape Cod stringer for the *Boston Herald Traveler,* Broadhurst received word around 9 o'clock that one of Ted Kennedy's secretaries had been killed on Martha's Vineyard. He took the *Island Queen* out of Falmouth for Oak Bluffs and hailed taxi-operator, Christopher Look, Sr., on the dock.

"You here on the Kennedy thing?" Look said en route to Edgartown. Look suggested Broadhurst talk to his son. "He knows a lot about it."

Look pulled up to a curb on Main Street when he spotted his son on the sidewalk. After introducing him to Broadhurst, he said, "Now, tell him what you told me about the accident over at Chappy."

Recognizing Broadhurst as a reporter, "Huck" Look backed away. He said, "I'm not saying a goddamned word!"

Look joined a group of locals near the courthouse that included Edgartown attorney Dick McCarron. Look appeared so solemn during the discussion about an accident at Dike Bridge, McCarron asked him, "What do you know about all this, 'Huck'?"

"More than I want to know," Look said. But he wouldn't say anything else.

"You ought to go down and talk to young Farrar," Look, Sr., suggested when Broadhurst got out of his taxi. The first reporter to talk to the diver who had recovered the body from Poucha Pond, Broadhurst was impressed by the good-looking, muscular man, just returned to the Turf 'n' Tackle from Chappaquiddick. Farrar had been diving since he was 15 and was a real enthusiast, technically knowledgeable and articulate to the point of compulsion about his specialty. Farrar was eager to discuss the recovery of the body he'd found in eight feet of water in the back seat of Senator Kennedy's Oldsmobile.

"She was in, what I call, a very conscious position," Farrar said. "Her head was at the floorboards where the last bit of air would have been. It seems likely she was holding herself into a pocket of air to breathe." There had been no air in the car when Farrar reached the body. "If an air bubble had been there earlier, her moving about would have dispersed it. But, she could have been alive a good while after the car went off the bridge." How long, Farrar couldn't say. He'd read about persons trapped in submerged automobiles who had survived up to five hours by breathing a pocket of air. If he'd been called soon after the accident, Farrar thought, "There was a good chance the girl could have been saved."

At town hall, Broadhurst was told by Bob D'Orio, a *Herald Traveler* reporter flown from Boston with press photographer Jimmy O'Callahan, a big story was about to come out of Arena's closed-door police station: Ted Kennedy was rumored to be the driver of a car in which a young secretary had been killed.

A woman in the corridor Broadhurst didn't know said to him, "This won't see the light of day. This will all be covered up."

But word of the accident was beginning to seep out. The *Cape Cod Standard-Times* was delivering to subscribers a front-page bulletin supplied by its parent paper in New Bedford from a story Harvey Ewing had filed to beat a one o'clock deadline:

> BULLETIN
> Edgartown. The body of a young woman believed to be a secretary for Senator Edward M. Kennedy was recovered from the waters of Chappaquiddick Island following an auto accident.
> It was not immediately determined if the woman was alone in the car. Some members of the Kennedy family are on the island for the annual Edgartown Regatta.

Another report of the accident was spreading the news farther away. At 2:45 P.M., an "urgent" message addressed to The Director was put on the FBI teletype in Boston:

On this date, Dominick J. Arena, Chief of Police Edgartown, Martha's Vineyard, Mass., advised body of female found in overturned car in water.

Tentatively identified as above was secretary to former Senator Robert F. Kennedy. Chief Arena confidentially states that driver of automobile was Senator Edward M. Kennedy who was uninjured. Stated fact Senator Kennedy was driver is not being revealed to anyone.

Chapter 7

BERNIE FLYNN WAS AMAZED AT THE SCENE OF CONFUSION AT
Edgartown police station when he greeted a harried Arena. Arena wasn't
surprised to see a representative of the district attorney's office inasmuch
as he had talked to Killen. And, Bernie Flynn observed, "He was probably relieved. Like, if anything too heavy comes up, the D. A.'s office is
there to take the weight off his shoulders. That's the usual reaction a
local police chief has that's on to something big. He's thinking: 'This is
where I can get off the hook.' Until that happens, he's going to handle
it."

Flynn read over Ted Kennedy's report of the accident. "Personally,
I thought it was bullshit," he said, later. Flynn kept his disbelief to himself. "As far as I'm concerned it's an automobile accident; I'm not
involved. I'm there so Dinis can say: 'Somebody from my office is on the
case.' Only we aren't on the case. Nobody said, 'Let's go and investigate
this thing. Why don't we take over?' So I'm standing in the background;
I don't want to get in the way of Arena's game plan. I backed off and let
him run it."

Flynn was careful to avoid displaying his presence too conspicuously to local reporters who might recognize him. He went to the small district attorney's office maintained at Edgartown's courthouse. Flynn had "no emergency" to report to Killen. In his judgment, the case wouldn't amount to anything. Flynn doubted Ted Kennedy would even be brought to court on a charge of leaving the scene, "Because he'd covered himself in the report saying he was exhausted, and in a state of shock. The law was vague on how long you had to report an accident. And Kennedy did, finally, report the thing."

In Flynn's opinion, "Arena was in way over his head. My impression was he wanted to help Ted Kennedy but he didn't know how to go about it. He didn't know what the hell to do with the case. He was trying to get out of doing anything."

George Killen wasn't anxious to do anything about the case either, or so it appeared when Walter Steele called him. Steele had reviewed the medical examiner statutes, he said. "Maybe we should think about doing an autopsy. You know what they say: 'When in doubt, do an autopsy.'" The diagnosis of drowning had been assumed because the body of Mary Jo Kopechne was found in a submerged automobile. That method of drowning was "sensitive" to misinterpretation.

Killen wasn't enthusiastic about the idea. Dr. Mills was satisfied there was no evidence of foul play in the death. Steele abruptly ended the conversation, telling Arena, "OK, we've covered all bases. The D.A.'s been notified; an autopsy has been suggested. It's our case to do with what we think best."

Steele was unhappy at the direction the case was taking. "Kennedy isn't being very nice to us, leaving a statement then taking off," he said. "It's a terrible position he's put us in. We've got a motor vehicle death here, and he's left us holding the bag. He's almost forcing us to charge him with leaving the scene."

Arena was mystified why he had not yet received permission to release the statement. The press had grown clamorous in the corridor. Arena didn't blame them. The accident begged more answers than the Senator's report supplied. Arena had a number of questions he wanted to ask Ted Kennedy himself, and regretted now he hadn't. "If everything had been clicking, I would have interrogated him more thoroughly," Arena said later. "But unfortunately, at the time, there was so much confusion. And I was laboring under the idea that it wasn't going to end when he left the police station. I told myself, 'We'll be following up on this thing. Everything'll ultimately come out. We'll clear everything up!'"

When Arena went out to the corridor to soothe the impatience of reporters, James Reston was the most insistent that the Kennedy statement be released. The accident was a matter of public record to which the press was entitled to have information. Reston suggested Arena was being "uncooperative."

Arena went back to his office to consult Steele. "They want the statement," he said. "It's been more than three hours. Nobody's called me. I'm going to release it."

Steele cautioned Arena to hold off. The statement contained an admission of guilt that could be prejudicial to Kennedy's case. If Arena released it, the Senator would have a constitutional defense. "He can say he can't get a fair trial because of the publicity you created by giving his statement to the press."

Arena thought it over. He didn't think an automobile accident was likely to have constitutional issues attached. The Senator had known reporters were outside town hall waiting to talk to him when he sneaked out the back way. Kennedy expected the statement to be made public.

Arena went into the corridor. He signalled for the attention of reporters. He said, "Senator Kennedy has given me the following statement."

Arena was asked to read the statement a second time so reporters could take it all down. He was in the midst of a third recitation when he was called into the police station. Paul Markham was on the phone.

Markham said, "Chief, we haven't been able to get a hold of Burke Marshall. Could I ask you to hold up the statement a little bit longer?"

"I'm sorry," Arena said. "I've already released it."

"Oh, Jesus!" Markham said.

"Well, I had to. It's been too long a period of time. What did you expect me to do with people beating on my door?" Arena held on to his equanimity. The medical examiner had diagnosed death by accidental drowning, Arena said. "I'm treating it strictly as a motor vehicles investigation, that's all."

Markham hung up before Arena could ask when Senator Kennedy expected to get back to him to answer more questions as he had promised to do.

Arena had little beyond the statement to give reporters. The Senator had been "cooperative" considering the strain he was under, Arena said. "He must have been in a state of shock after the accident."

Arena's own efforts to dive against the strong tidal current in Poucha Pond had exhausted him, he said. "And I think I'm a pretty good swimmer."

Steele sidled up to the police chief. "Don't do any more talking," he said.

On his way home, where he maintained the bureau's office, Harvey Ewing recollected his observations of Senator Kennedy at the Edgartown dock: "I'd watched him closely and his movements were completely normal. My impression was, he looked in good shape. At that point I didn't know he had been the driver of the car or had done all the things he said he did in the statement—it was a complete mystery to me, the more I thought about it. The biggest mystery was: What the hell had he been doing for ten hours until he reported the accident?"

To add to the puzzle, Ewing's son reported he'd taken Ted Kennedy over and back on the *On Time* and asked him if he knew about the accident an hour before the Senator reported it. Obviously, Ted Kennedy had not, as he had said, "immediately contacted the police."

Not that such incidents were unheard-of during Regatta weekends. A unique sailing event, the Regatta was also something of a trial for Edgartowners. An invasion of sailors multiplied opportunities for the kind of high-spirited mischief that was as much a part of the event as the races themselves. Ewing knew from experience, "You could count on at least a dozen people getting into trouble during most Regatta weekends. Minor stuff, like drunk and disorderly, assaults, and sleeping on the beach."

The accident at Chappaquiddick went beyond the standard rowdiness of Race Week, however. Ewing's paper was sending a reporter from New Bedford to work with him on a major story for Sunday's edition.

Ewing set about gathering details on the accident. "Basically, it was Ted Kennedy had driven a car off a bridge and some woman is dead. The larger implications of the accident hadn't registered yet." Ewing had no idea whether Kennedy could be cited for negligent operation or driving to endanger. "That," he thought to himself, "was left up in the air." Arena had said nothing about filing charges.

Ewing was also serving a number of small radio stations as correspondent. "They wanted anything I could give them, a voice on the scene." He used the same copy for an hour or so, "Then, if I heard something new I thought was important, I'd add it and delete something else." Ewing was picking up tidbits from out-of-town reporters who had turned his dining room into an improvised press headquarters, sharing what little information there was about the story. One of the first to arrive at Ewing's house was Cornelius Hurley of the Boston bureau of the Associated Press. Hurley had enjoyed privileged access to the Kennedys for years. He was able to reach a source at the compound in

Hyannis Port who asked not to be identified. Hurley was told Senator Kennedy "was still in a state of shock and unable to hold a press conference to discuss the accident."

Chapter 8

IN FALMOUTH, JIMMY SMITH HAD WAITED ANXIOUSLY FOR further reports from Dick Ferry about the accident at Chappaquiddick. A second call confirmed a fatality was involved, but the identities of neither the victim nor the driver of the car were known.

Around three o'clock, Ferry called to say that Ted Kennedy had been identified as the driver of the accident car. Ferry didn't know what charges, if any, were to be lodged against the Senator by Edgartown police.

Smith was stunned. He had spent most of his boyhood in Martha's Vineyard when his father worked for the phone company. He knew the island mentality well. "All my relatives over there hated the Kennedys. It was the old prejudice against Irish Catholics." Smith feared the consequences of a Kennedy accident occurring "in enemy territory."

Smith called Kenneth O'Donnell.

O'Donnell knew only what Smith had told him about the incident, he said. "I haven't been called."

The first thing anybody advising Ted Kennedy should find out was who the registry inspector handling the case was. Smith said, "It's a fatal, so you've got to have a registry guy there making out a report in addition to the Edgartown police. That's the key guy right there on any reckless driving charge."

Smith didn't know any registry people on Martha's Vineyard, but he did know Joe Greelish, who ran the Hyannis office. It was no secret registry problems could be "fixed" on Cape Cod, Smith said. "Before Frank Keating came to town Falmouth lawyers couldn't tie their own shoelaces on traffic cases. If you had a license problem you gave Hank Jonah two hundred dollars and that usually took care of it." Jonah ran a bookie operation out of the Leeside Cafe in Woods Hole. Jonah and Greelish were very close friends.

Greelish was a savvy operator, politically well-connected. In September 1966, he had sought Smith's assistance in securing a post-mastership at South Yarmouth on Cape Cod for his son. Smith recommended "a Democrat and a very deserving young man" to Ted Kennedy's office. Greelish had been badgering Smith about the appointment ever since.

O'Donnell told Smith to "keep in touch." If Smith couldn't reach him, O'Donnell suggested he contact his aide, Paul Kirk, Jr. Recently hired as counsel to a Senate sub-committee on administrative practices and procedures chaired by Ted Kennedy, Kirk was a natural pipeline for any information Smith might be able to provide from his strategic vantage point inside the district attorney's office.

Smith didn't call Edmund Dinis immediately. He thought about it for a while. He enjoyed good personal relations with the volatile and unpredictable district attorney. "He always acted like a teacher and a benefactor to me," Smith said. "He treated me like his kid brother." Despite his reputation, Dinis ran a four-county district with an able staff of assistants he left pretty much alone on cases. "That's why Dinis was re-elected three times," Smith said. "He ran a good shop."

When Smith finally did call, Dinis cut off his breathless recitation of the "known facts" about the Kennedy accident. "I know all about it. I've already been called."

But this demonstration of loyalty from the acknowledged "Kennedy man" on his staff put Dinis in teasing good humor. "We've got your buddy this time!" Dinis crowed. "We're going to get an indictment off a first degree. We're going to throw the book at him!"

Dinis let Smith dangle for a minute, then told him he was only kidding. "It's just a motor vehicles accident," he said. Dinis was content to leave the matter in the hands of Edgartown police, Smith reported to Paul Kirk.

Smith was confident the information would get passed along the Kennedy political network and eventually find its way to the compound at Hyannis Port.

But the Kennedy network had already been alerted to the crisis by the Senator himself. David Burke received the first call at Falls Church, Virginia, around 9:30 A.M. Kennedy was calling from a public phone at the ferry landing on Chappaquiddick to say he'd been in an automobile accident the previous evening. Despite the urging of his cousin Joe Gargan and Paul Markham, the accident had yet to be reported to the police. While he was fearful his car would soon be discovered in a tidal pond beside a bridge, Kennedy was still reluctant to go to the police.

The most admired of Kennedy's staff, Burke was a Harvard graduate and the son of a Brookline, Massachusetts, policeman. Burke's low, intensely urgent voice had battered down the last obstacle of Kennedy's resistance, making him understand there was no alternative but to report the accident as Gargan and Markham wanted him to. "You've got to listen to those two guys and report this thing. Go and do it right now!"

Kennedy asked Burke to locate Burke Marshall, "stand by" at his senate office, and expect a deluge of inquiries about the accident.

Burke called the office to let press secretary Dick Drayne know, "The Boss went off a bridge on Martha's Vineyard and one of Bobby's secretaries got killed."

Drayne was in the middle of a magazine interview.

"Anything wrong?" the interviewer asked.

"No, nothing really," a shaken Drayne replied, reflexively voicing the first in a series of evasions and half-truths he would be required to deliver about the accident in the next several days.

When Senator Kennedy called the office, Drayne could tell, "He was very upset, very depressed. But he could still come up with answers." Some of the answers were the stuff of which a major scandal could be made: The accident had occurred on a dirt road, late at night, following a party for a group of young women, and gone unreported for ten hours.

The Senator wanted no information about the accident given to the press. Drayne sat there all through the morning "waiting for the roof to fall in." By the time reporters descended on his office, "The story was on the wires about a former Kennedy secretary getting drowned," he said. "I knew what they didn't, that *he* was driving the car. And I could only give them what was already public."

Drayne was joined by Burke in the office to attempt to wrest some control over the exploding situation. The Senator had called several times from Edgartown's police station where he was writing a report of the accident. Kennedy wanted the telephone number of the accident victim's parents so they could be notified of her death. Burke came up with a number for Joseph and Gwen Kopechne in Berkeley Heights, New Jersey.

The Senator called Mrs. Kopechne around 10 o'clock. He asked to speak to her husband.

Gwen Kopechne sensed "a sorrow or sadness in the way his voice came over the telephone."

Kennedy reported, "Mary Jo was in an accident."

"Was it in a car?" Mrs. Kopechne asked.

"It was an automobile accident," Kennedy said. "Mary Jo was returning to take a ferry back to the mainland when the accident occurred."

Mrs. Kopechne asked if her daughter had been killed.

Kennedy hesitated, then said, "Yes."

The Senator gave her no details, Mrs. Kopechne said, later. "He just told me what happened and I broke down. I remember screaming: I'm alone here.' From then on, I don't remember anything. I must have let out some awful noises. A neighbor was outside hanging clothes. I must have let her in because I had the doors locked. She tried to get me to tell her what happened."

Burke Marshall was in Waltham, Massachusetts, that morning, preparing archives for a proposed John Fitzgerald Kennedy memorial library, when he got the call for help from Kennedy's staff in Washington. A self-effacing man of incorruptible character and strong moral convictions, Marshall had been selected by Robert Kennedy to head the civil rights division of the Justice Department in 1961. Marshall had defused an explosive racial confrontation in Birmingham, Alabama, by negotiating an agreement to provide a measure of desegregation, following a campaign led by Martin Luther King to end discrimination in department stores and lunch counters. Of him, Robert Kennedy said, "Burke Marshall has the world's best judgment on anything."

Marshall agreed "to help wherever I can," leaving at once for the two-hour drive to the Cape.

Marshall was already at the compound when Kennedy arrived from Edgartown "so upset...the question really was where to begin." Marshall found him "obviously disoriented but he appeared coherent." Kennedy said he hadn't reported the accident for some ten hours because he was convinced Mary Jo Kopechne had somehow gotten out of the car and survived the accident. "I don't think he shook that idea for a while," Marshall said. After he was with the Senator for a time,

Marshall came to the conclusion he'd suffered a "blockage," he said. "A lot of his mind wasn't accepting yet what was happening to him."

Marshall read over a copy of the Senator's accident report Markham brought back from Edgartown. An anti-trust lawyer, vice president and general counsel for IBM, Marshall was entirely ignorant of Massachusetts criminal codes and motor vehicle statutes. He needed time to consult lawyers experienced in those matters.

Marshall had Markham call Edgartown police chief Arena to postpone release of the accident report. The statement had been made public, Markham learned; but Arena appeared loath to press charges.

Marshall instructed the Senator not to answer any questions publicly or privately about the accident. "The reason I thought he shouldn't make a statement to the press was that I didn't know enough about his legal situation," he said. In addition, Marshall was concerned that Kennedy could break down at a press conference, he said. He "truly did not know whether he might have a medical problem."

Marshall advised Kennedy to see a doctor.

The Kennedy family physician on Cape Cod, Dr. Robert Watt, was summoned to Hyannis Port. The Senator told him he'd been in an automobile accident on Martha's Vineyard. There was a lapse in his memory from hitting Dike Bridge and struggling to get out of the submerged car. At the last moment, he'd grabbed the side of an open window and pulled himself out. He remembered diving repeatedly to get a passenger out of the car, without success, going for help, and returning to the accident scene. Again, efforts to rescue the passenger failed. Kennedy was driven to the ferry slip and swam to Edgartown. Returning to his hotel room, he had slept fitfully until 7:00 A.M. the next morning.

Watt's examination disclosed a half-inch scrape above the right ear, a bruise with spongy swelling at the top of the Senator's head, and a muscle spasm in an area about the nape of the neck. He diagnosed: concussion, contusions and abrasion of the scalp and acute cervical strain.

His determination of concussion was predicated "upon objective evidence of injury and the history of the temporary loss of consciousness and retrograde amnesia. Impairment of judgment and confused behavior are symptoms consistent with an injury of the character sustained by the patient."

Watt prescribed a sedative to relieve the headache, neck pain and generalized soreness Senator Kennedy complained of. Later, criticized that sedation was contraindicated in cases of concussion, Watt said he'd been misquoted, "But I wouldn't say he didn't get a sedative." Subsequently, Watt revealed he'd prescribed an oral muscle relaxant, hcat and bed rest and qualified his diagnosis. Kennedy had sustained "a mild concussion, was bruised and shaken up." He'd received a "blow on the head, but he was all right."

Chapter 9

OTHER MEDICAL AUTHORITIES FOUND WATT'S CONCUSSION
diagnosis far-fetched—"highly-unlikely," as one put it in a *Boston Globe*
interview. In that same interview, Watt admitted that part of his
diagnosis about Kennedy's post-accident memory loss had been based
"simply on what Kennedy told him." Another medical source familiar
with the case told the *Globe* Dr. Watt's conclusion about Kennedy's
behavior after the accident was open to question because, "It seems to
be stretching the facts to fit the diagnosis."

Retrograde amnesia, impairment of judgment and confused behavior were symptoms identical in all respects to yet another "malady":
intoxication by alcohol.

Nor did Watt's examination confirm the type of severe physiological
"shock" which would have caused Senator Kennedy to delay reporting
the accident for more than nine hours.

With Senator Kennedy undergoing medical examination, the compound at Hyannis Port was mobilizing for action. After her son called
from the Edgartown police station to tell her that he was all right after

an automobile accident, Rose Kennedy was advised to cancel a scheduled appearance at the annual St. Francis Xavier Church bazaar. Mrs. Kennedy notified daughter Jean and son-in-law Stephen Smith, vacationing in Spain; Patricia Kennedy Lawford in California; and Eunice Kennedy Shriver in Paris, where her husband was then serving as United States Ambassador to France.

Having presided at a Special Olympics at the University of Connecticut that morning, Bobby's widow, Ethel Kennedy, returned to Hyannis Port around two o'clock. She telephoned former Secretary of Defense Robert McNamara—a key figure in Jack Kennedy's administration—telling him, "Come up here, Bob. There's nobody here but women."

Barnstable Chief of Police Albert Hinckley was advised to supplement security personnel beyond standard traffic control needs in anticipation of a significant increase in activity at Hyannis Port. Not long afterwards, barricades went up, closing off Scudder Avenue to through traffic.

The former summer White House of John E Kennedy was made ready as a command post. From Truro on Cape Cod came writer Richard Goodwin. Goodwin, who was also a lawyer, had been tapped to help out by David Burke should a further statement about the accident need to be written.

Burke also alerted Dun Gifford at his family's summer house, "Heather Hill" on nearby Nantucket Island. A legislative aide in Kennedy's office, Gifford arranged immediately to island-hop to Martha's Vineyard, his chartered plane dipping over Dike Bridge on Chappaquiddick to see the Senator's car submerged in Poucha Pond.

Landing at Edgartown airport around 11 o'clock, Gifford first called Senator Kennedy, who was still at the police station to corroborate the instructions Burke had given him, then took a taxi to Martha's Vineyard funeral home in Vineyard Haven.

Gifford walked into mortician Eugene Frieh's office, introduced himself as an aide on Senator Kennedy's staff, and announced he was available "to help in any way that makes sense," in making the funeral arrangements.

Frieh was annoyed at the intrusion, telling Gifford, "You have no authority as far as I'm concerned. I'm taking all my orders from the Kielty Funeral Home."

Frieh wouldn't allow Gifford into his basement preparation room to identify the body. When Gifford asked to use the phone, Frieh accommodatingly left his office. Gifford called Burke in Washington for further instructions. He was told to do whatever he could to expedite the paperwork required to get Mary Jo Kopechne's body off the island as quickly as possible. Gifford learned that the other young women who had attended a party at Chappaquiddick preceding the accident were being hustled off Martha's Vineyard on a three o'clock ferry for Woods Hole.

On Frieh's desk was a copy of the Record of Death, certifying that Mary Jo Kopechne had died of "asphyxiation by immersion (overturned submerged automobile)." Gifford asked Frieh what that meant.

"Drowning," Frieh said. "Dr. Mills made the finding."

But Frieh was beginning to doubt the validity of the medical examiner's diagnosis. The lack of water evacuated from the body was "unusual" in a drowning case. Frieh wondered if the accident victim might not have suffocated to death. When he suggested Dr. Mills change his finding, the medical examiner told him he "didn't want to cause any problem." Nor would Mills make an independent decision about ordering an autopsy.

When Frieh proposed his assistant "run down and catch Dr. Mills in his office to have him sign a death certificate," Gifford asked if he could go along. Frieh had no authority to stop him.

Dr. Mills had begun office hours at 2:15, but had scarcely been able to treat a waiting-room full of patients; instead he had repeatedly been called to the telephone to answer questions about the accident at Chappaquiddick.

The first call was from Medical Examiner Dr. Robert Nevin.

"The reporters are here, Don," Nevin said. "Tell me what to tell them."

By 3:30 P.M., inquiries were pouring in from all over the country. Mills' wife said, "I'm going down to see the police chief and find out what on earth is going on." Returning to the office a short time later, she passed her husband a note: Senator Edward Kennedy was the driver of the car.

Mills was glad he had reported the case as fully as possible to the district attorney's office and had asked about an autopsy. Mills now called the police station. "What should I do, Chief?" Mills asked. He was getting a lot of pressure from reporters about ordering an autopsy in the case.

Arena was under pressure himself. "If the district attorney wants it, or it's up to you, OK. But if you don't think it's necessary, don't do it." Arena thought to himself that Mills was "looking for support or something."

Mills mistook Dun Gifford for a reporter when he showed up at his office with a death certificate. Gifford wanted to know if an autopsy had to be performed before the body of Mary Jo Kopechne could be released for burial.

The district attorney's office had left the decision to him, Mills said. And he was satisfied that the cause of death was accidental drowning.

By the time Gifford returned to the funeral home, Frieh had arranged for the Hathaway Air Funeral Arrangement Service of Fall River to transport the body to Wilkes-Barre the next morning. Frieh could have shipped the body out that night but held off "I still felt," he said, later, "that Dr. Mills might change his mind and order an autopsy—or, someone in higher authority might direct the autopsy to be done."

Before the body could legally be shipped out of state, a burial certificate and transit papers had to be filled out. Gifford went to town hall,
introduced himself to Arena and explained, "I've come up here to help
things along."

Arena knew of nothing standing in the way of releasing the body,
he said. "The required forms aren't my forms, anyway." He did not
question Gifford as a representative of Senator Kennedy about the accident, explaining later: "I wouldn't go out on a limb by talking about it
with him."

Arena had heard no word from Burke Marshall or anybody else
about the accident, a silence that intensified the pressure he was under
as the afternoon wore on from reporters at the station demanding more
information. Doubts were gathering about the Senator's accident report
like moths around a summer porch light. Arena told the reporters he
still had made no determination of any charges he intended to file,
because "I was still expecting to hear from these [Kennedy's] guys."

Between sessions with the press, Arena was conferring with Walter
Steele and Tommy Teller, clerk of the district court. "We were just honestly trying to figure out: 'What have we got here? What the hell are we
going to hit him with?'" Arena denied he was sweeping the case under
a rug. "There was no effort by anyone to say: 'Let's get Ted Kennedy,'
or, 'Let's take care of him.'"

A manslaughter charge was mandatory in Massachusetts in cases
where a driver left the scene of a fatal accident, if negligence was proved.
Arena said, "We talked about manslaughter. We even looked up the
wording in the statutes. You had to have wanton, reckless and wilful
conduct"—the legal equivalent of intentional conduct involving a high
degree of likelihood that substantial harm would result to another.
However, the mere happening of an accident where the circumstances
immediately preceding it were left to conjecture was not sufficient to
prove negligence on the part of the driver. For those reasons, Arena did

not think he had cause to make such a serious charge. He had found no evidence of negligence from his examination of the accident scene.

Walter Steele could have told him driving a car off a bridge was a *prima facie* case of negligence—but Steele was as timorous about making the complaint as was Arena. On the other hand, Steele was convinced, "There was absolutely no evidence for a manslaughter charge."

Perhaps influenced by the recollection that there had not been to that point anything resembling a serious investigation to gather evidence, Steele would say, later: "I really should have known better. If I had to do it over again, I would have held out for a probable cause hearing for manslaughter and an autopsy." Steele was sure no judge would have found probable cause, "But it would have wiped out a lot of doubts."

Arena, too, would eventually conclude that he had made a mistake. "A state trooper friend of mine in the traffic bureau said to me, 'You really could have gotten Kennedy on involuntary manslaughter: The taking of another's life by an act not performed.' That's probably true."

But Arena blanched at the idea of making so serious an accusation against Ted Kennedy. Even a "driving to endanger" conviction required proof that the operator of a vehicle was so grossly negligent as to be liable for injuries sustained by a passenger. With no evidence of negligence, nor witnesses to testify to recklessness, inattention, speed or drunk driving, Arena did not believe he could make that lesser charge stick, either.

That left "leaving the scene," less-objectionable nomenclature in Massachusetts for a "hit-and-run accident." The offense seemed clear enough from Kennedy's admission that he had delayed nearly ten hours before reporting the accident. But Arena hesitated to pursue even that misdemeanor charge because of a recent case he had lost in district court. "The defense lawyer argued that the statute didn't say within what particular time period you had to report an accident, and that his client had completed his legal obligation by reporting it when he did," Arena said. "So there was that little technicality."

But such legal hair-splitting wouldn't wash in an accident in which a person had been killed, and there was a gap often hours between the accident and the time it had been reported—particularly with so many reporters looking over Arena's shoulder. Reluctant as Arena was to press any charge at all, this one, Steele told him, was inescapable. "I don't see what else you can do except ask for the complaint."

Arena's solicitous treatment of Ted Kennedy, and his failure to interrogate the Senator, left him with a single piece of evidence, but one which was indispensable to the case: the Senator's own statement. There was no presumption under Massachusetts law that the owner of an automobile involved in an accident was the driver. No statute commanded a passenger to report an accident. Had Kennedy denied knowledge of the event, or had he said that Mary Jo Kopechne was driving the car, Arena would have had to accept the story since there were no witnesses to the accident.

Arena started drawing up a traffic violation complaint charging Edward M. Kennedy with a violation of Chapter 90, Section 24: Any operator of a vehicle who, "without stopping and making known his name, residence and the registration number of his motor vehicle, goes away after knowingly colliding with, or otherwise causing injury to any person, shall be punished by imprisonment for not less than two months or more than two years."

To complete the citation, Arena needed to know Ted Kennedy's driver's license number and expiration date. Since the Senator had been unable to produce a license at the police station, Arena called the Registry office in Oak Bluffs. He was told, "We don't have the license information yet. We'll get back to you."

Inspector George Kennedy was being deliberately evasive. At 4:10 P.M., David Burke had telephoned him to report that he couldn't find

Senator Kennedy's license in his Washington car. Inspector Kennedy called Registry headquarters in Boston to request a license check for "D.O.B. 2/22/32 Edward M. Kennedy."

On duty in the radio room to provide license and registration information to police calling in from around the state was Registry Inspector Joseph Mellino. Mellino went into the Registry's file room where license cards were kept in alphabetical order. ("It's the application for renewal that's in the files," Mellino explained later. "Not the license itself.")

Mellino found a white duplicate card, issued October 17, 1968, for a lost license valid until February 22, 1969. Mellino did not realize that the expired license in his hand belonged to a United States Senator. "I'd always thought of him as Senator Ted Kennedy, not Edward Kennedy. So I didn't make the connection until the next day, when I read about the accident and realized which Kennedy it was."

Mellino was instructed to pull the license renewal from the file and put it together with the car's registration in an envelope on Registrar Richard McLaughlin's desk. It was, he reflected, an unusual request.

Disturbed to learn that the Senator had been driving on an expired license at the time of his accident, Inspector Kennedy was less complacent about the infraction than Arena was about the Senator's lack of a driver's license at the police station. The Senator was running up a skein of motor vehicle violations, and while both offenses were misdemeanors, they were evidence of "some negligence."

The inspector called Joe Greelish in Hyannis. Regional head of Motor Vehicles for southeastern Massachusetts, Greelish wielded authority over all district supervisors. An abrasive, stony-faced authoritarian, Greelish ordered Kennedy to give no information about the expired license to anyone—including Edgartown Police Chief Arena. To conceal important information from investigating authorities was highly irregular. Nevertheless, Kennedy agreed to stall Arena about license information, and hope the police chief didn't run a check at Registry headquarters himself.

Greelish next tracked Registrar McLaughlin to his summer house in Harwich on Cape Cod. McLaughlin told him to handle the Kennedy accident as a routine vehicular fatality. "We get 800 to 1,000 of these damn cases every year," McLaughlin told him. "This is just another one. Don't do anything different because of who he is."

McLaughlin changed his mind, however, when Greelish told him Senator Kennedy's license had expired. He ordered Greelish to take over the case personally, "So it doesn't get screwed up."

Chapter 10

EFFORTS TO CONCEAL OR "MISPLACE" INFORMATION ABOUT THE accident were building a momentum of reaction. Much of the pressure was being applied to Dr. Mills. Having relinquished the hour he customarily spent playing the organ at St. Andrew's Episcopal Church as a respite from the tensions of his practice so as to stay close to his office telephone, Mills was being challenged by reporters about the lack of an autopsy in the case. By 5 o'clock, Mills was "pushed to the point of irrationality and blackout as I tried my best to answer a barrage of questions. It got into such a chaotic state," he called George Killen to plead for help. "I'm being swamped with calls from newspapers all over the country," Mills complained. "What do I tell these people?"

"Tell them the girl died of accidental drowning and don't say anything else!" Killen snapped. "If they persist, slam down the receiver."

Killen was being hounded about the accident himself. One call came from his friend Frank Keating. A former assistant district attorney,

Keating had worked with Killen at Barnstable courthouse. He wanted to verify reports of an accident involving Ted Kennedy.

"Yes, it's true," Killen said warily.

"And the girl was killed?" Keating said.

"She drowned," Killen said. Dr. Mills had called three times about the case. "I told him, 'If you want an autopsy let me know and we'll get a pathologist.' I left that strictly up to him. I asked if he was satisfied with the cause of death and he said he was."

"What a lucky son of a bitch Eddie Dinis is. He's got a United States Senator in the palm of his hand," Keating said. "He's got Teddy Kennedy for manslaughter."

Killen sputtered in protest, "Where's the manslaughter? Where's the evidence of negligence?"

"If Ted Kennedy was driving that car when it went off the bridge, there's no question of negligence about that, is there, George?"

Killen knew better than to argue criminal law with Keating. "We aren't in it at all; Arena's handling the thing himself. It's a local motor vehicles accident," Killen said. "What do *you* know about this case?"

"I don't know anything," Keating said.

"Well, nobody does, at this point," Killen said.

Eugene Frieh was not surprised to hear from Killen. He was expecting the district attorney's office to order a "hold for autopsy" on the body of Mary Jo Kopechne. Instead, Killen wanted to know the scheduled departure time of the remains off the island, and verification that a blood sample had been taken.

State police had left a message at the funeral home that the sample would be picked up. After Killen's call, Frieh suggested David Guay drop the sample off at the barracks in Oak Bluffs. Guay turned it over to state trooper Richard Lucas at 7 o'clock. When he got back to the funeral home, Guay took a call from Dun Gifford, asking if there was anything more he could do to help with arrangements.

Guay told him, "No, everything's fine."

Gifford had spent a busy day on the island. He had seen the young women off on the ferry at Vineyard Haven with the assurance that he would escort the body of Mary Jo Kopechne to Pennsylvania the next morning. Before he flew back to Nantucket, Gifford reported the progress of his efforts to David Burke at Hyannis Port.

Leaving Dick Drayne to deal as best he could with Washington reporters flooding Kennedy's senate office with inquiries about the accident, Burke flew to Boston late in the afternoon. A reporter on board recognized the gaunt, pock-marked Burke and took the seat beside him. Reports of Senator Kennedy's accident on news wires were contradictory and incomplete, the reporter said. "Don't you think you should make some kind of full disclosure soon?"

Burke was offended by the idea. "I don't think we're going to do that," he said. "The Senator is not in very good shape. I'm going to go up there and maybe sit under a tree with him. And then we'll have to see."

But keeping a lid on the story was impossible. Before leaving Washington, Burke dispatched William vanden Heuvel to Berkeley Heights to hand-hold the grieving parents.

A former Justice Department lawyer, vanden Heuvel had traveled with Robert Kennedy during his presidential campaign. He arrived at the modest first-floor apartment in a two-family house too late to prevent the Kopechnes from talking to reporters.

A well-spoken, good-looking insurance salesman, Joe Kopechne disclosed his wife had lapsed into shock after Senator Kennedy telephoned the news of their daughter's death. Ethel Kennedy had called. "She talked about faith, how it could help. She said, 'We will be at the funeral.'" No one at the Kennedy compound had volunteered any information about the accident. "Nothing was explained," Kopechne said to *Boston Globe* reporter Ken Botwright. "We still don't have any real details of what happened."

Kopechne didn't know what to make of a wire service story containing Kennedy's report of the accident Botwright read to him over the telephone. "We didn't even know she was with Kennedy—that kind of upset us. There we were, the last to know." The Senator had neglected to say he was the driver of the accident car when he called to report Mary Jo had been killed. Kopechne found Kennedy's evasiveness and lack of candor baffling. He had known about his daughter's trip to Martha's Vineyard with several other young women.

"We assume the girls went to the island to see the Regatta with the Senator, but we're not certain. Mary Jo loved sailing. She went sailing at the Kennedy place on Cape Cod. Ted invited her up with some other girls right after Senator Robert Kennedy was killed."

Mary Jo was almost one of the Kennedy family. She was pretty well wrapped up with the Kennedys, Kopechne said. "Politics was her life. She didn't seem to have any time for anything much outside of politics. She wasn't engaged or anything like that."

"It was a good career, working with the politicians. It was what she wanted to do," Gwen Kopechne said. "She would have been 29 years old next Saturday."

Mary Jo Kopechne had graduated in 1962 with a degree in business administration from Caldwell College for Women, in New Jersey. After a year teaching at the Mission of St. Jude in Montgomery, Alabama, she joined the staff of Florida Senator George Smathers, then went to work in Robert Kennedy's office when he was elected to the Senate in 1964. In December she was hired by Matt Reese Associates, an organization that set up campaign headquarters for politicians. Reese confirmed, "She left on Thursday and said she wouldn't be back until Tuesday morning. She wanted to spend the long weekend on Cape Cod with friends she had made while on Bobby's staff."

Mary Jo had never worked for Ted Kennedy, Mrs. Kopechne said. "He just entertained them up there at Hyannis Port. After Robert

Kennedy was killed, Ted Kennedy seemed to try to hang on to his brother's staff."

Mrs. Kopechne had spoken to her daughter on Tuesday, July 15, about the Regatta weekend on Martha's Vineyard. "We were talking on the telephone. I said, 'Honey, be careful of the water.' She said to me, 'Mother, you know me. I only like to sunbathe.'"

Mary Jo Kopechne had shared a house in Georgetown with three young women, among them Nance Lyons, an aide in Senator Kennedy's office. Her housemates were reluctant to talk about her. So were members of the Senator's staff who referred all inquiries to Dick Drayne.

That the Kopechnes had tipped off the press about a weekend party on Martha's Vineyard was bringing reportial furies down on Drayne's head. This was powder-keg information, bound to hurt the Senator if it wasn't defused fast. Drayne tried to lift the lid on the party just enough to remove some of the stigma beginning to attach to it. Mary Jo Kopechne was one of eight young women invited for a reunion of former campaign workers to a party in honor of David Hackett, Drayne explained. An aide in Robert Kennedy's presidential campaign, Hackett was in charge of the "Boiler Room" where trusted workers compiled intelligence reports on how delegates to the national Democratic convention intended to vote. "Ted came by to thank the girls for their work with Bobby. Then, this one girl had to leave. They were trying to catch a ferry when the accident happened."

Party guests had included the crew of the Senator's sailboat entered in the regatta: Paul Markham, former U.S. Attorney; Kennedy's cousin Joseph Gargan; and Jack Crimmins. Drayne described Crimmins as "a friend and long-time political aide" to Senator Kennedy. The presence of the Senator's chauffeur at the party begged more questions than Drayne had answers for. The most obvious one was: Why had Ted Kennedy driven himself to the ferry when his chauffeur was at the party?

Drayne suggested the Senator's wife had planned to fly to Edgartown on Sunday and sail back to the mainland with her husband. The truth was otherwise: Joan Kennedy had not been invited to the Regatta weekend.

That Senator Kennedy made no mention of the party at Chappaquiddick during the three hours he'd spent at the police station "really bothered" Arena. "That's one thing I objected to, that I had to hear about it from reporters. When I found out there'd been a party and everybody had left the island, I really got put on the spot."

Arena defended his ignorance as best he could. "I know nothing of any party. It's only a rumor," he told reporters. "Nobody has proven to me anyone connected with Kennedy was there, only that Joseph Gargan rented the house."

Virtually a prisoner in his own police station, Arena had had nothing to eat since breakfast. "I just kept answering telephones and giving interviews." His sister called from Michigan to say, "Gee, I just saw you on the news." More reporters were packing the station to be briefed on the progress of Arena's investigation. There hadn't been any progress. Arena had been too busy dealing with the press to do any investigating.

Arena passed out copies of Kennedy's accident report but could give reporters little else. He was waiting to receive more information about the accident from the Senator or his lawyers. He said, later, "I was still living in a dream world, thinking I'd hear from them."

Impressed by the distances some reporters had travelled to cover the story, Arena said, ingenuously, "Boy, this is really a big one, isn't it."

Unlike reporters who had clamored for the Senator's statement, satisfied with anything Arena gave them, newly arrived newsmen assigned a big story were more demanding. Arena was sitting on his citation, hoping he wouldn't have to use it. But hours of relentless inquisition by the press had wrought a change in his perception of the case. "Reporters helped me realize a lot of things about the accident I hadn't had a chance to think about. If the press hadn't been there all the time, things might have been different." Arena was suggesting a "likely possibility" a formal complaint against Ted Kennedy would be filed in connection with leaving the scene and failure to report the accident within a reasonable time. Arena emphasized, "This is the only aspect of the case on which I intend to press charges."

If reporters helped Arena to perceive the case in a different light, their demand for answers to the accident's mysteries was forcing him to make precipitous judgments based on nothing more substantial than two brief visits to Dike Bridge. Kennedy's wrong turn had led him to "a very narrow bridge that could easily be mistaken for something else when looked at with automobile headlights," Arena explained. The approach to Dike Bridge was unmarked by warning signs. Lack of "tire marks" on the bridge indicated to Arena that Senator Kennedy never attempted to brake the car, but drove straight over the side of the bridge in the belief he was still on the road, although the bridge angled to the left. The investigation conducted at the scene revealed, "No criminal negligence was involved in the accident," Arena said. "There's nothing to indicate excessive speed or reckless driving."

Arena's sense of public relations did not fail him. Senator Kennedy had been "as cooperative as he possibly could be," he said, a declaration that hardly matched the Senator's refusal to answer a single question about the accident.

Arena couldn't conceive of anything Kennedy gained by delaying the report of the accident, he said. "But once again, I don't know what went through his mind. He very well could have been in a state of shock after the accident." Arena wanted to talk to the Senator about the accident that was still under investigation only so far as failing to report it was concerned. Some details were lacking, but those involved Kennedy's actions after the accident, Arena said. "At this time, I find the accident is strictly accidental."

A weary Arena left the police station at midnight. He walked to the house on Cook Street that he had spent a year renovating before marrying a widow with three children, and put his telephone off the hook. He had left the house that morning the obscure police chief of a small tourist town. Fifteen hours later he was making the front page of every newspaper in the country, involved in "the most dismaying case" of his police career.

Chapter 11

IF ARENA HAD CALLED IT A DAY WITH REGARD TO THE ACCIDENT at Chappaquiddick, lights blazed into the night at an enclave of houses known as the Kennedy compound in Hyannis Port. To the command post on Irving Avenue came a procession of advisors, friends and hangers-on to mourn in the wake of what already was being referred to in early reports of the accident as "the latest Kennedy tragedy." Among those arriving was Edward Hanify of the distinguished Boston law firm of Ropes and Gray. Like Burke Marshall, Hanify was a dignified man of impeccable legal credentials and brilliance—to some, further evidence of legal overkill to defend an automobile accident case.

To the command post around 9 o'clock came Joseph Gargan, mentioned in early dispatches about the accident as the "owner" of a cottage in which a party at Chappaquiddick had taken place.

Personable, athletically trim, with a lively wit and pleasant good looks, Gargan enjoyed "total personal confidence" with Ted Kennedy as his "cousin and boyhood chum,"—the standard reference accorded Gargan in rare press reports about him. The least-known member of the Kennedy clan, whatever information available about Gargan had been filtered through the Kennedy publicity apparatus. The impression created was that he was the orphan child of Rose Kennedy's sister to whom charity had been extended. "Gargan is used by Kennedy largely as a companion for carrying out miscellaneous chores, making reservations, ordering food, emptying glasses and drawing baths," *Time* said. "His parents died when he was very young and Rose and Joe Kennedy saw to his education."

While his Aunt Rose and Uncle Joe had always been "very lovely" to him, Gargan said, "The kind of things you read about me just don't happen to be so."

His mother died when he was six. Gargan and two sisters had gone to live with his Uncle Bill and Aunt Ann in Lowell, a small industrial city north of Boston where the Gargans were bricklayers, building inspectors—strong, devout Catholic stock.

Joey Gargan had been invited to Hyannis Port for two weeks during the summer of 1940. An overweight, good natured 8-year-old Teddy Kennedy was delighted with his new playmate. Muscular and athletic, Joey Gargan could take care of himself. And, it turned out, Teddy, too. Used to doing chores, Gargan was handy with tools, something alien to his cousin who couldn't change a tire on a bicycle or use a screwdriver. So resourceful was his cousin, Teddy came to rely on him, confident that whatever the problem, "Joey'll fix it."

Gargan was asked back to Hyannis Port the following year. "The intention was I stay for one month, but I stayed the whole summer. The reason being, it did work out well. I could do things for Ted and his parents could stop worrying about him; they knew he was in good hands. I was two years older, so he was protected in a way." So long as Gargan kept himself and Teddy out of trouble, "I knew my vacation would extend to Labor Day. So it balanced off: I took care of Teddy; and I also took care of my summer vacation."

But Joey Gargan was no urban waif to whom a Fresh-Air Fund summer had been charitably bestowed by a rich and powerful uncle. "*My* father was the big shot to me in those days, not Joe Kennedy," Gargan proudly recalled.

And, truly, Joseph Gargan, Sr., was someone to be proud of. Orphaned at two, and raised by an aunt, he was regarded at 16 as the best featherweight prospect in the East and offered a contract to turn pro. The "schoolboy sensation" of Lowell High School recruited by Notre Dame in 1912, Gargan played first-string backfield on a team with Knute Rockne. Cited as "athlete, actor, politician and debater," by Notre Dame's *Scholastic* magazine, "His handsome face may yet grace the Faculty Room, for if the University ever establishes a chair of Good Fellowship, Gargan will certainly be its first occupant."

Gargan served in France during World War I as a first lieutenant of the 7th regiment, U.S. Marines, and was decorated for bravery under fire. Wounded while commanding a company at Belleau Wood, he had refused anything but first aid. Wounded again at Soissons, Gargan had returned to the front when the Armistice was signed. Discharged as a captain, he was the most decorated marine of World War I.

Gargan performed postwar army intelligence work in the Far East; played polo on a team in the Philippines with General George Patton and was an intimate of air power pioneer Billy Mitchell, providing important testimony at his famous trial. He had established a successful practice of law, married the beautiful younger sister of Rose Kennedy and regaled his nephews with tales of the gridiron at Notre Dame, barnstorming tours during college vacations giving "boxing exhibitions" to earn tuition, and hand-to-hand combat in the trenches. It was a mixture of battlefield courage, athletic prowess, and derring-do that was the stuff of Kennedy family lore. By contrast, Joseph P. Kennedy had neither distinguished himself on the playing field, nor served his country in the armed forces. "My father looked down on Joe Kennedy. He regarded him as a slacker in World War I," Gargan said. Kennedy had made "a ton of money" running the Fore River shipyards during the war and making his first important contact with then-assistant Secretary of the Navy Franklin D. Roosevelt, and spent years "chasing the dollar" in such enterprises as Wall Street speculation, motion pictures and the sale of imported liquors. "It was *my* father who took Teddy and me to sit on the Notre Dame bench when Elmer Layden was coach, at a time every kid in America knew he was one of the Four Horsemen," Gargan said. "Joe Kennedy had to go to *my* father to get tickets to the Army-Notre Dame game."

Named assistant to undersecretary of war Robert Patterson in 1941, Gargan was the leading lobbyist on Capitol Hill for the War Department. After serving as U.S. Ambassador to Great Britain on the eve of war, Joseph P. Kennedy sat out the war in disgrace, branded as an appeaser and isolationist as a result of his pessimistic view that, "Democracy is finished in England." Gargan said, "It was the death of Joe, Jr., during the war and Jack's heroism in the Pacific that brought Joe Kennedy to some sense of being an honorable man, which he was not in the eyes of many patriotic Americans because he had opposed the war."

Hired as lobbyist by Juan Tripp to secure lucrative air routes for Pan American Airways after the war, Gargan died of a heart attack in 1946. Orphaned at 16, Joey's education at Georgetown Prep had been paid by his father's estate. There was no question where he was going to college, Gargan said. "To me, Harvard was a crap school. In those days, you were kind of a fairy if you went to Harvard."

If Harvard lacked the manly image of Notre Dame, it was plugged into the circuits of power Joseph Kennedy had in mind for his sons. "I think that went back to Joe Kennedy's own beginnings. He himself had gone to Harvard the same way he went to New York and Wall Street, to make his mark, because he recognized, right or wrong, that he couldn't make it as an Irish-Catholic in Boston at that time," Gargan said. "So a parochial education was not the thing he wanted for his sons because he connected it with his own experience; whereas I grew up with a father who was terribly dedicated to the Blessed Mother, as most Notre Dame people were in the old days." When Ted Kennedy was expelled for Harvard cheating, however, it was briefly considered sending him to Notre Dame. But Ted had, "within 24 hours," gone into the army instead.

Gargan graduated from Notre Dame law school, married a pretty Indiana girl employed in the university's graduate school and passed the bar. He served a political apprenticeship in the 1952 campaign in which Jack Kennedy defeated Senator Henry Cabot Lodge. His career as an able trial lawyer in damage cases was subservient to the political ambitions of the Kennedy family. Gargan's status as "advance man" for Ted Kennedy, arranging the minutiae of campaign travels, was a perpetuation of their boyhood friendship, Gargan performing those tasks beyond Ted's ability or willingness to do so for himself. With no ambition of his own, and no press secretary giving out image pieces about him, Gargan was consigned by those who did not understand the close bonds of friendship and dependency that existed between the two men to the status of "bag carrier" and "factotum." Nor was Gargan taken seriously by the hard-driving professionals jockeying for positions of influence about the Kennedy brothers.

But none of this diminished the effortless intimacy he enjoyed with Teddy Kennedy. Family ties, and those Penrod-and-Jasper,

Booth Tarkington summers at Hyannis Port had cemented strong and permanent bonds. Gargan was granted automatic ranking as an "insider." What might seem to others a cheerful diffidence was merely a sense of easiness about himself. The boyishness that lingered well into his 30s disguised the tough Lowell kid who had broken horses at ten. A better athlete than the ponderous and heavy-footed Ted Kennedy, it was Gargan who caught the "long bombs" Kennedy quarterbacks liked to throw in the famed touch football games at the compound. And, it was generally conceded, Gargan was a better sailor, too.

There was a streak of tenderness and nurture in Gargan, the kind of dependable strength demonstrated by his sister Ann, in her devotion as companion to Joseph Kennedy during the last difficult, invalided years of his life. As one Gargan intimate remarked, "There's a lot of his father in Joe, a lot of character. He doesn't pound his chest or anything like that, but when the chips are down, he's there."

———

That character would be tested now more than ever before. Gargan would remain as steadfast under fire as had his father before him on the field of battle. And he would suffer in silence wounds inflicted on him by the accident that killed Mary Jo Kopechne.

As co-host of the party at Chappaquiddick, Gargan was about to achieve an unwanted prominence in a drama threatening to shatter the Camelot mystique of the Kennedy clan. That role had its roots in the frenetic and tragic Robert Kennedy campaign for the presidency in 1968.

As campaign chairman, Gargan's name appeared on all campaign literature. He brought to that campaign not only his considerable experience as advance man, but an ingratiating temperament and warmth rare in the hard-driving competitiveness of a campaign forged from often competing factions and loyalties bound together in uneasy alliance to secure the presidential nomination for Robert Kennedy. On one side, there was Bobby's fiercely devoted staff, suspicious of outsiders. On the other was Jack's Old Guard from White House days, ostentatiously displaying PT-boat tie clasps. Yet a third group was made up of Ted Kennedy men on loan to the campaign (who wore tie clasps in the shape of the state of Massachusetts, which had been used in his 1962 campaign). One aide recalled, "There were a lot of elbows out when we first started, but there was so much to do we had to work together."

Gargan shared an office with David Hackett, boss of the "Boiler Room" girls. It all came to an abrupt and shocking end on June 5, 1968, with Robert Kennedy's assassination. After the funeral, Gargan arranged for the charter of the 60-foot sloop, *Mira,* which he and Ted Kennedy sailed to Hyannis Port from Mystic, Connecticut. Gargan was virtually Ted Kennedy's only companion on aimless sails around Cape Cod in the wake of a death that left him floundering and adrift with grief. "It's inaccurate to say he was drunk most of the time," one confidante revealed. "It's also inaccurate to say he wasn't drunk at all."

If alcohol helped Ted Kennedy obliterate the memory of his brother's murder, it also eased the fear about his own safety. "I know I'm going to get my ass shot off...and I don't want to."

Suffering under the weight of a political legacy suddenly thrust upon him, Teddy fled to Spain, then cruised the Mediterranean aboard the Aristotle Onassis yacht *Christina.*

Gargan stayed behind to help close down campaign offices. "After Bob died there was a great deal of sadness cleaning out his headquarters. The girls who worked so hard were devastated, like all of us were." One of the most grief-stricken had been Mary Jo

Kopechne. "She was very hurt by Bobby's assassination, deeply wounded."

It was Gargan who conceived the idea, later that summer, of giving the young women a respite from their heart-breaking work, to invite the "Boiler Room" to Hyannis Port for a sail on the *Mira*. Dun Gifford thought it was a great idea, Gargan said. "So, we combined to give these girls a break in this sad ordeal, with a three-day trip to Dun's house in Nantucket."

Gargan invited 9 girls. Twelve came. Joan Kennedy invited the group to a cocktail party, "Then we all went to my house for a backyard cookout," Gargan said. The party swam out to the *Mira* anchored in Hyannis Port harbor before the boat sailed the next morning with campaign advance men Gargan asked along to serve as crew. A memorable day of sailing and swimming followed; then, a party at "Thirty Acres" restaurant on the island, the girls so young-looking they had to bring IDs to get served drinks.

The party sailed back to Hyannis Port the next day. Dun Gifford's two sons took turns at the helm. The "Boiler Room" girls stayed one more night, playing charades in Gargan's living room, he said. "We all had a great time."

An album of photographs memorializing the weekend presented "To Our Pal Joey, with Love and Thanks," was signed by "Cricket" Keough, "Esta"—for Esther Newberg, whose hard "er" was more than a Boston accent could handle; "Little Susie" Tannenbaum, Mary Ellen and Nance Lyons, and others who made the trip.

Beneath a photograph of Betty and Joe Gargan posed in front of their house in Hyannis Port, Mary Jo Kopechne wrote, "Who else could put up with all of the Boiler Room antics and come up smiling. Thank you, Betty for everything."

A photograph of the young women grouped around Gargan and Gifford on the *Mira* had captured the bittersweet ambivalence of the weekend. It was captioned:

BOILER ROOM 1968

... and they never even cried.

Chapter 12

HIS BROTHER'S ASSASSINATION CATAPULTED TED KENNEDY TO the front ranks of presidential contention. His first public appearance after the funeral provoked speculation he would seek the nomination. "Like my three brothers before me, I pick up a fallen standard," he said. "Sustained by the memory of our priceless years together, I shall try to carry forward that special commitment to justice, to excellence, to courage that distinguished their lives."

Gargan denied Ted was a candidate. "Yes, he picked up the standard, but you can pick up the standard without picking up the Presidency. The standard is the causes, the work, the poor, the blacks. He's got other things on his mind than being President."

Kennedy sent his brother-in-law, Stephen Smith, to the Democratic Convention in Chicago to canvass support. The nomination was there for the taking, if Ted Kennedy wanted it. Kennedy didn't. Dun Gifford explained, "He recognized that he had always been pushed forward too soon and knew that he just wasn't prepared to be the leader of the family in any respect." It had never been anticipated that Teddy would assume the mantle as exemplar of the Kennedys, one observer said. "He'd always been the spoiled kid brother to whom everything was handed and from whom nobody expected much." Ted often felt inadequate to his inheritance, Gargan said. "They were constantly measuring Ted against his brothers. And they were a tough act to follow."

Put in charge of advancing Ted's personal security, a responsibility frightening in light of the fear a third Kennedy could fall victim to an assassin's bullet, Gargan had witnessed first-hand Ted Kennedy's presidential stock soar. Election as the youngest majority whip in the history of the Senate only enhanced "already lustrous Presidential prospects," and "the luxurious presumption that the Presidency would one day come to him almost by inheritance." By the time Kennedy turned 37, he was "the most glamorous public figure in the U.S.," leading all polls for the nomination in 1972. Despite disavowals that he was seeking the office, one observer noted, "He wouldn't be a Kennedy if his goal were not the White House."

Submerging grief and self-pity in frantic activity, Kennedy's schedule was "like running the Boston Marathon." On a typical day, Kennedy climbed into a leased car and set out from McLean, Virginia, at breakneck speed for the Capitol, ten miles away, a "fearsome driver" already frightening the young, capable and "happy-to-be-anonymous" staff disinclined to reveal anything about a possible bid for the Presidency in 1972.

As Kennedy's stature rose in the Senate, in part as a leading anti-Nixon administration critic against the Vietnam war, his spirits revived, as well. He had become "tougher, more decisive, less ebullient" since his brother Robert's death. But "a general discouragement with Ted's off-hour antics" was being privately expressed within the Kennedy circle. Kennedy had been drinking more heavily since his brother's death, *Time* reported. "He has been a different and deeply-troubled man—but he is far from being a drunkard." Those close to Kennedy saw signs of a recklessness out of key with his expanding presidential prospects. Accepting an assignment from *Life* to cover Ted Kennedy after his brother's assassination, writer Brock Brower concluded that the insecurities, fatalism and fast-living showed Ted Kennedy was seeking to escape an inevitable candidacy for President. "The bad thing is the pressure everybody's putting on him that's making him come up with some pretty hairy avoidances."

A member of the press entourage that accompanied the Senator to Alaska in April 1969, Brower observed, "No one on board the return flight to Washington, D.C., was in any too great shape, but we were at least doing our drunken best to quell further display by the Senator himself." Kennedy started drinking on the plane, pelted aides and reporters with pillows and exhorted passengers in a chant for "Es-ki-mo Power." "A big, boiling broth of an Irish boy, all his anxiety clearly showing," Kennedy talked incoherently about Bobby's assassination, predicting: "They're going to shoot my ass off the way they shot Bobby . . . "

Seated beside Brower on the plane, John Lindsay of *Newsweek* saw "another all too-familiar pattern emerging." Kennedy was slipping out of control toward some unavoidable crackup. "Some thought his drinking had got beyond the strains it was supposed to relieve," Brower said. As reporters, "We were going to have to say something about this distressful side of Ted Kennedy."

But Lindsay made no mention of the incident in his coverage of the trip, filing notes of the incident in a confidential interoffice memorandum. In fact, for a year after his brother's assassination, Ted Kennedy got favored treatment from the press. More often than not abrupt, bland or evasive with reporters, Kennedy was enjoying a period of journalistic grace, protected by a mantle of sympathetic coverage.

Gargan accompanied Kennedy to Memphis to commemorate the first anniversary of the death of Martin Luther King, Jr. Kennedy's appearance provoked a tumultuous demonstration. He was introduced as, "The President of the poor people, and the next President of the United States."

After speaking before the Atlanta Bar Association convention, Kennedy confronted "this 1972 talk," and in a rare moment of reflection voiced his own doubts about his candidacy for the Presidency to reporter Joe Mohbat of the Associated Press.

"The thing about being a Kennedy is that you come to know there's a time for Kennedys. And it's hard to know when that time is, or if it will ever come again," he said. "I mean, is the country going to be receptive? And if it is, is it really the best thing for me to do? How much of a contribution could I make? So even if the time is right, why should I? I'm just not sure running around the country talking on the tough issues and waving the Kennedy flag…stirring people up—is that helpful? Bobby did it, I know. Spoke right on up on what bothered him, raised all that excitement … "

Kennedy was unresolved about seeking the Presidential nomination in 1972. "Maybe over the summer…some sailing…the family. I think perhaps by fall, I'll be settled, have some idea." He didn't believe in making long-range plans. "We can never know what is just up ahead that might change everything."

Gargan was looking forward to a tranquil summer after months of gut-wrenching anxiety advancing Ted Kennedy's stepped-up personal appearances. He had accepted a position as vice-president of the Merchant's Bank in Hyannis which fit in with a resumed law practice, and was preparing to relocate his family to Cape Cod.

No Kennedy boats had raced in the Edgartown Regatta in 1968 out of deference for a period of mourning for Robert Kennedy. But both the *Resolute* and the *Victura* were entered in the 1969 races—"an ideal situation," Gargan thought, for the "Boiler Room" to repeat the great success of the 1968 weekend.

When Gargan broached the idea to Ted Kennedy who hadn't participated in the previous year's festivities, he said: "Gee, that would be a lot of fun. Let's do it."

In May, Gargan went to Edgartown seeking a cottage at South Beach as headquarters for the weekend. Everything on the water was rented. Gargan rejected other accommodations, "Because we liked to stay over Saturday night, have a leisurely sail back, enjoy a picnic and a swim, and get into Hyannis Port on Sunday afternoon. All the places I looked at in Edgartown you had to be out by Saturday night."

A cottage on Chappaquiddick was "way out in the sticks, but it's a good place to get the rest you need if you're racing," rental agent Steve Gentle said. "And it's not too far from the beach."

More important to Gargan, "We could stay through Sunday. That's the main reason I rented the place." Gargan intended to take possession on July 12. When her mother became ill, Gargan's wife left for South Bend, Indiana. The cottage remained empty until Wednesday, July 16, when Jack Crimmins drove a 1967 Oldsmobile Delta 88 off the ferry at Vineyard Haven. A 63-year-old bachelor, Crimmins described himself as "part-time weekend and evening chauffeur when Ted Kennedy was in Massachusetts." It was a job he had performed for the past nine years.

Crimmins spent an uncomfortable night alone at the Chappaquiddick cottage, unable to sleep because an animal of some kind scratched at the front screen door, trying to get in. "Jack was fit to be tied about that, and terribly upset at me for having rented that particular cottage," Gargan related. "He didn't like having to sleep out in the boondocks with strange animals he wasn't used to. There weren't any raccoons or skunks scratching at the door in South Boston where he lived."

Gargan sailed the *Victura* to Edgartown on Thursday with Howie Hall, a youngster from Hyannis Port, and Paul Markham as crew. He and Markham checked into the Shire town Inn. Gargan had secured rooms there for Ray LaRosa, a civil defense adviser and ex-fireman; and Charles Tretter, a young Boston attorney and Kennedy campaign aide. Adjacent accommodations had been reserved by Jack Driscoll, a Boston attorney and former state treasurer, for members of the crew of the *Bettawin* owned by Ross Richards, long-time racing rival of Teddy Kennedy.

On Thursday evening, Gargan had a vodka-tonic with Stan Moore in a bar close by the Edgartown dock. A good-looking, care-free bachelor, Moore was a successful automobile dealer on Cape Cod. His Wianno Senior sailboat *Uncle Benny* was entered in the Regatta. Gargan asked Moore to a "cookout" the following evening at Chappaquiddick. Moore recalled, "The invitation was sort of hush-hush."

Gargan complained of an upset stomach and "feeling woozie" and switched to drinking Coca-Cola before leaving for Vineyard Haven to pick up some of the "Boiler Room girls" who had arrived on the ferry and didn't have a car. The young women were taken to rooms at the Katama Shores Motor Inn Crimmins had reserved for the weekend, then to inspect the cottage at Chappaquiddick.

On Friday, the young women shopped the fashionable boutiques of Edgartown before they went swimming at East Beach on Chappaquiddick. Senator Kennedy was picked up at Martha's Vineyard airport by Crimmins around 1 o'clock. He crossed over on the ferry to Chappaquiddick, changed into swim trunks at the cottage and was driven down Dike Road and across a narrow bridge to join the others on the beach. After a swim, Kennedy returned to the cottage, changed clothes and was ferried back to Edgartown for a race scheduled to begin at 2:30 P.M., but delayed until the winds picked up. The young women watched the race from the charter boat, *Bonnie Lisa*.

For Gargan, "It was a lousy, uneventful sailing day; it was awful hot. Howie and I worked very hard." The *Victura* finished ninth to Ross Richards' *Bettawin*.

Stan Moore sent his Boston Whaler to take Ted Kennedy off the *Victura* for a victory party on board the *Bettawin*, tied up at the dock. Richards had run out of beer. Instead, "highballs" were being served. Moore and Ted Kennedy had three drinks each. Moore remembered that specifically because they both were drinking rum and coke.

Gargan stayed behind to put up the sails and batten down. Great care was taken with the *Victura*, Gargan said. "Ted Kennedy never allowed anyone else to sail the boat. The hatch had a lock on it, so other people couldn't get in there and fool around."

By the time Gargan joined the party, the Senator was ready to leave for the Shiretown Inn, checking in around six o'clock. Gargan ordered six bottles of Heineken beer from the inn's pub for a gathering on the porch outside the room he was sharing with the Senator. (Markham had checked out; he was spending the night at the Chappaquiddick cottage.)

Crimmins chauffeured Kennedy to the ferry, crossing to Chappaquiddick shortly after 7 o'clock. No one was at the cottage when they got there. Kennedy soaked in a hot tub; Crimmins made him another rum and coke. Then Gargan showed up with Markham and Tretter in a rented Valiant. Tretter took the Oldsmobile to Edgartown to buy ice, charcoal, soft drinks and cigarettes for the party. Markham made himself a vodka-tonic and chatted with Kennedy about politics.

Picked up at their motel by Ray LaRosa, the girls were dropped off at the Edgartown dock. LaRosa parked his Mercury at the Shiretown Inn, then joined the others for the ferry ride across. Gargan had gone to the landing in the Valiant at 7:30 to meet the party guests. He had been waiting almost an hour, the first in a series of aggravations he would suffer that evening.

Gargan was disappointed at the turnout. "I thought more girls would be there. It was supposed to be a repeat performance of last summer's weekend." Dun Gifford was invited. Jack Driscoll had been asked; so had David Hackett. Ed Martin from the Senator's Boston office was expected back from Cape Canaveral after the Apollo moon shot, but had gone on instead to NASA headquarters in Houston. Gargan had also mentioned the party to Billy Cleary, future Harvard hockey coach, and Jimmy Smith of Falmouth. "Local people from around Cape Cod who had worked campaigns were supposed to be there, too." The party had ended up even: six men and six women crowded into a small living room whose counter dividing the kitchen was stocked with liquor Crimmins had purchased "for a price" in South Boston.

Gargan had no idea what anybody was drinking. Still suffering from an upset stomach, Gargan himself was sticking to Coca-Cola, he said. "I was interested in the food. That was my deal. I was doing all the preparations."

As co-host, however, Gargan was displeased with the party. "A lot of things were a source of irritation. I wasn't feeling well; and it was still very hot. The charcoal grill refused to start. We couldn't get the thing going at all." Gargan had provided a cassette player for the party, but everyone complained about the music selection. Tretter volunteered to go to Edgartown to borrow a radio. Rosemary Keough went with him. Then, Gargan discovered he could cook only three steaks at a time, "So we didn't start eating until 9:45."

Tretter and Keough returned after 10 o'clock with a radio. A few couples danced. "Everyone sang old Irish songs," Susan Tannenbaum recalled. Most of the evening was devoted to conversation ranging in subject from Dr. Benjamin Spock to politics; from jet noise complaints on Long Island to the Senator's poor performance in the Regatta.

Esther Newberg teased the Senator "about coming in ninth," she said. "He laughed and took it as a joke, blaming one of his crewmen."

Despite the noise level, the evening never got off the ground—at least as far as Gargan was concerned. While the young women seemed in high spirits, "The party was not that exciting. Some people were bored to death with it," Gargan observed. Paul Markham had injured his leg and was drinking heavily. "I would have been drinking, too, if I had had his pain." Crimmins was scowling and increasingly irascible. "Jack had become his usual arrogant self, as only he can get after 5 or 6 scotches," Gargan said. By eleven o'clock, "We started getting the heave. Jack was coming to me in the kitchen saying, 'Get all these douchebags out of here. I want to get some sleep. The last ferry leaves at 12 o'clock. I want everybody out."

Crimmins had not spared Senator Kennedy his distemper, either, but that was standard procedure. Kennedy and his chauffeur customarily engaged in ritual dialogues at parties the Senator provoked by complaining, "Jesus, Jack, you're stiff! How am I going to get home?"

Crimmins would invariably answer, "Take a fucking cab!"

"They talked that way to each other all the time. It sounded hostile, but it really wasn't," Gargan said. "And here you have another party, and Ted is kidding Crimmins again, because Jack's had quite a few. And Jack is saying, 'Get these broads out of here. I want to go to sleep. I don't give a shit how you get home, Kennedy. I'm not driving you.' And the Senator's saying, 'Ok, Jack. That's what we're doing. We're going. We're leaving right now.

Within 15 minutes of this conversation, Gargan had "a vague memory" of Senator Kennedy leaving the party. "I was in the kitchen area. I wasn't paying too much attention, except I clearly observed him go out the front door of the living room with Mary Jo."

Gargan didn't ask where the Senator was going, "I didn't question him. When he decides to go, he goes. He left when he felt like it."

Kennedy didn't announce he was leaving or say good night to anyone. Neither did Mary Jo.

Gargan thought it could have been as late as 11:50 P.M. when the Senator left the party, but he wasn't wearing a watch. "Maybe time went by faster than I realized, since I was cleaning up after cooking the meal, but he clearly left before 12 o'clock. I made a mental note—no particular reason—that he was going to make the ferry. When he left, the assumption was he was going to the landing, but I don't know where he went." During the course of the party, guests were coming in and out of the cottage, Gargan said. "It was very hot. Some people were going on walks. It's possible the Senator went for a walk before getting into the car, or did all kinds of things. I know he still had time to get the ferry—if he was going to the ferry."

Gargan had spoken to the ferryman about keeping the *On Time* running until one o'clock, "But I hadn't driven over to say, 'We're still having a good time, do you mind waiting?' Whether I didn't have time, or I forgot, somehow it got screwed around. I had in mind that if you were going to get the ferry, you had to get there by 12 o'clock. My idea was, the girls had better hurry if they were going to make the ferry, but they don't leave. The 'Main Event,' so to speak has left, but people are still talking. How it drifted past 12 o'clock was just the immobile situation people get into talking and letting the time go by."

Gargan observed, "Some people at the party had had quite a few, no question. Frankly, everybody's a little bombed, except for Ray LaRosa." A circumspect 41, LaRosa didn't drink. Although it was after twelve, Crimmins wasn't letting up. "Jack wanted everybody out. He's agitated because the girls are still hanging around. He kept saying, 'Joey, get the douchebags out of here; get 'em to hell out.'"

Gargan wondered if the girls weren't leaving because of Mary Jo. "They might have thought she hadn't left the party permanently and were waiting for her to come back from wherever it was she'd gone with Ted Kennedy."

Chapter 13

GARGAN WAS IN THE KITCHEN WHEN LAROSA TOLD HIM, "THE Senator is outside. He wants to see you."

LaRosa indicated that the Valiant was parked close to a split-rail fence.

Gargan was getting in the car when the Senator said, from the back seat, "You better get Paul, too."

Gargan asked LaRosa to call Markham outside.

Markham came out. He got in the car. He put his arm on the back of the front seat. He said, "What do you want?"

"There's been a terrible accident," Kennedy said. "The car's gone off the bridge down by the beach, and Mary Jo is in it."

Gargan recalled, "He didn't bark out any orders or anything. He made it clear he was driving the car; and Mary Jo was with him. He didn't say how the accident happened. All he said was, 'There's been an accident.' That's all I needed to know. The only thing that hit my mind was: 'Go to the bridge as quickly as possible.'"

Gargan gunned the Valiant down Chappaquiddick Road to the intersection. He made a sharp turn onto Dike Road. He was proceeding slowly over the bridge when the Senator said, "The car is there, on the right."

Markham said, "Holy God!"

Gargan expected to see "an automobile that had been driven into the water with the top sticking out." He saw something entirely different: The car was completely underwater upside-down in the middle of the pond. He said, "As soon as I saw that I got sort of butterflies in my stomach. I realized if Mary Jo was in that car, there was no hope. I said to myself, 'Oh, shit, this is over! This is done. She's *gone.*'"

Considerable time had elapsed since the accident, Gargan calculated. "My timing was based on the fact that the Senator had left the cottage, then come back. I knew from the distance he travelled that at least half an hour to 45 minutes had to have elapsed from the time of the accident to the time we got back to the bridge." The situation was hopeless as far as Gargan was concerned. "There had been one solution to the problem. If a rescue attempt could have been made within the first few minutes after the accident, then, maybe, you've got a shot."

Gargan turned the Valiant around at the beach-side of the bridge so headlights shone over the water. Their beams impaled a small house on Dike Road not far from the edge of the pond.

Markham got out of the car. He was preparing to dive into the water when Gargan called him back. Gargan was standing beside the Valiant's front fender, taking off his clothes. He told Markham to do the same, "Because if we are going to get in that car, we could get caught on the door handle or something else."

Gargan stood naked on the bridge. It was a warm night. There was no breeze from the beach. Markham went into the water first. Gargan followed. "All I was interested in was saving the girl; I wasn't thinking about anything else. I felt there was only one thing to do and that was get into that car as quickly as possible. Because if we didn't, there was just no chance in the world of saving Mary Jo."

Gargan swam out to the car. The water was cold, but not uncomfortable. The current was tremendous. He grasped a rod on the car's undercarriage and was able to hold on and still keep his head above water.

Gargan began to slide his feet down the side of the car. "I was trying to feel where there was a window or a door handle, sliding down and sliding down, then letting go and trying to get underwater."

Gargan couldn't do it. The force of the current dragged him away, so that he was 25 to 30 yards beyond the car before he got back under control.

Gargan stationed Markham at the rear of the car to intercept him as he went by, he said. "Paul had all he could do to hold onto the car against the current that was flowing through the channel. He'd been drinking, how much I don't know; but he was capable of going into the water and, on the occasions when I came up for air, he was functioning perfectly well."

Gargan continued sliding his feet down the side of the car, trying to duck underwater. After several more attempts, he realized, "That wasn't going to work."

Gargan swam to the front of the car. Working himself down the side, he found an opening he presumed to be a window and passed his body through, "groping around to see if I could touch anything," he said, later. "You had to operate by feel only. The current forced your eyes closed." The car was full of water, the current was running right through it. "There was no air inside the car," Gargan said. "There couldn't be. It was completely submerged."

Gargan started losing breath. He tried to get out and couldn't. He got stuck inside, "Because in turning to feel around, I'd gotten jammed in. Instead of turning again calmly, I kind of pushed myself out fiercely."

He felt something sharp rake his arms and chest as he passed out of the car. He came to the top of the water gasping for air, and was flung backward by the current. Markham missed him as he went by. Gargan ended 25 yards from the car. Markham swam up and grabbed him.

Ted Kennedy had observed the rescue attempts from the bridge, calling out, "Can you see her? Is she in there?" Now, in the wash of the Valiant's headlights, Gargan saw the Senator stretched out on the bridge on his back. Hands clasped behind his head, knees drawn up, the Senator was looking into the sky, rocking back and forth, repeating, "Oh, my God. What am I going to do?"

Gargan recovered his breath and swam back to the car. He conceived the idea of trying to open one of the car's doors. He dove straight down. Holding onto the side of the car, he located a door handle and yanked. The door wouldn't budge. Puzzled, because he could move the lock button up and down, Gargan put his knee against the body of the car and pulled. The door wouldn't move. Gargan couldn't understand why he was having such a hard time getting into the car. Being buoyant, and tossed around by the current made it difficult for him to gain leverage.

Gargan surfaced and sputtered for breath.

Markham swam alongside him.

"I can't do it," Gargan gasped. "I just can't get into the car." Gargan couldn't fight the current, as swift as any he had ever experienced, he said later. "The water was bad; it was rough. I almost drowned."

Gargan and Markham climbed out of the water and got on the bridge. Ted Kennedy was standing in front of the Valiant. His hair was matted and very curly, his trousers clinging wetly to his legs. He asked if there was any way Gargan could think of to get inside the car.

Gargan said there wasn't.

"I just can't believe this happened," Kennedy said.

"Well, what the hell happened?" Gargan said.

He was driving down Dike Road, Kennedy said. "Before I knew it, I was on the bridge." The car had gone over the side. Water had risen up to his chest. "I thought for sure I was going to drown; I thought that was it. And I just gave up. And the next thing I know, I'd come to the top of the water." He had tried going back into the car to get Mary Jo out, but he couldn't do it. The only thing he could think of, was to go back to the cottage to get help, he said. "I don't believe this could happen to me. I don't understand it. I don't know how it could happen."

"Well, it *has* happened," Markham said.

"What am I going to do?" Kennedy said. "What can I do?"

"There's nothing you can do," Markham said.

Gargan got dressed by the side of the car. "I had one thing in mind at the time, and that was to report the accident. I didn't say that when I was dressing, but I was thinking what happened had to be reported immediately. Not in terms of calling the fire department or making another rescue attempt—there was nothing to rescue. The thing was over."

Kennedy said, "OK, take me to Edgartown."

Gargan got into the car "not thinking of anything, and the car moved forward." He saw no lights on any of the houses on Dike Road. "They may have been lit, but I didn't notice."

Gargan drove slowly to the intersection. "There was a discussion— 'What do we do now?'—that was done in a sort of half-trance, like sleep-walking. We were all stunned; we were all horrified. We were discussing the situation, trying to decide what to do; trying to get the story together prior to reporting the accident. The accident is over. We're reporting the situation now. How that was to be done."

Gargan's intended destination was the ferry landing, "Because that was the location of safety; that's where we could get help to report this thing."

In the back seat, Kennedy kept repeating, "Do you believe it, Joe? Do you believe it happened?"

"We have got to report this accident immediately," Gargan said. He suggested the Senator call his administrative aide, David Burke, then go to the police. "I thought he should let the family know what had happened and, because of all these circumstances, let David Burke take care of the details. The family was in various places. We couldn't call all these people at once."

Gargan s first consideration was for Rose Kennedy, he said. "She was constantly on my mind. I didn't want Mrs. Kennedy to hear about the accident on the radio or TV; or have somebody call her up in the middle of the night to say, 'I understand your son has been lost in an accident.' She'd heard on the radio that Jack was shot. She heard about Bobby the same way. I wanted to make sure she was told Ted had been in an accident, that he was perfectly all right, and that she had nothing to fear."

Markham was interjecting only an occasional, "You're right, Joe," into the discussion. He was in no position of authority with Ted Kennedy. He did not enjoy the level of intimacy with him Gargan did. "Paul was really in pain. He wasn't being as forceful as I was about reporting the accident."

The Senator was silent about his intentions, but it appeared he did not want to report the accident at this time. Kennedy was having alternative ideas about the situation: Why couldn't Mary Jo have been driving the car? Why couldn't she have let him off, and driven to the ferry herself and made a wrong turn?

Kennedy asked to be brought back to the cottage to establish the story. After a while he could leave. Kennedy suggested that when he was back at the Shiretown Inn, Gargan could "discover" the accident and report to police that Mary Jo had been alone in the car. How this was going to be worked out insofar as "details" were concerned, the Senator didn't say.

Gargan rejected the idea out of hand. Mary Jo was the only other person who could possibly have been driving the accident car, but neither the Senator nor Paul Markham knew her very well, Gargan said, later. "Nobody had any idea if she could drive a car, or even owned a license."

And besides, Gargan reminded Kennedy, "You told me *you* were driving."

Gargan doubted he could persuade the girls at the party to allow Mary Jo to take the blame for the accident, or that he could concoct a story to persuade them of the veracity of the Senator's alternative version of the accident. The rescue efforts he and Paul Markham had performed had entirely changed the situation, making any revision of the accident out of the question, Gargan explained. "We weren't being quiet. There was shouting back and forth. The bridge is a very public place. There was no way of knowing how many people in the area saw or heard us, how many witnesses were going to come forward to say, 'Oh, I saw Ted Kennedy at the bridge with two other guys, and the lights of the car ... '" The Senator could be placed at the scene of the accident.

Making a false report to the police required a web of lies involving a disparate group of people. In addition, Gargan would be risking his integrity and reputation as a lawyer. Should he be found out, he said, "I could lose my ticket"—his license to practice law.

To drive home the importance of reporting the accident, Gargan invoked the name of Burke Marshall. "Because Bobby had said in my presence he was the most capable lawyer he knew. I was advising the Senator of this because he had a very serious problem and it was important to get who, in Bob's opinion, was the best lawyer. That's what I thought Ted needed at the time."

Of no less significance, Gargan was calling upon the memory of Robert Kennedy as a reminder of the responsibility the Senator bore as exemplar of those ideals. Gargan said, "When we were both boys, Bob spent so much time with Teddy, working on his sailing; but more than that, to tell him, 'Be disciplined. Be courageous. Meet every challenge with what ability you have. Be prepared for whatever opportunities may come your way.

What Burke Marshall would advise, Gargan was certain, was for the Senator to do exactly what he was insisting be done. "There was constant pressure on my part, saying it over and over. That he had to report the accident at once."

The discussion was at a stalemate when Gargan pulled up to the ferry landing looking across to the Edgartown lighthouse. Boats bobbed in the harbor's waters, but nothing stirred. The channel was smooth as glass. The ferry was moored on the opposite shore, but the dock looked deserted.

Gargan had used the public telephone at the landing's ferry house that weekend, but there was no thought to using it now. He said, "I was expecting to go to the police station with the Senator to report the accident—once we got the story together." The discussion about what had to be done continued in the car. Gargan's sequence was to call David Burke and Burke Marshall, then report the accident to the police. "This conversation went around and around: 'You've got to call these two people. And you've got to report this thing immediately!'"

The Senator appeared unmoved by Gargan's arguments, his silence an eloquent argument against reporting the accident. The famous Kennedy temper was stirring. Gargan had a short fuse himself. There was an edginess now to his reiteration. "I was in complete charge of the situation. I was pushing that sort of thing, saying it over and over: That he had to report the accident."

The Senator's toleration of Gargan's "nagging" was wearing thin. Finally, he'd had enough. He said, sharply, "All right, all right, Joey! I'm tired of listening to you. I'll take care of it. You go back. Don't upset the girls. Don't get them involved."

Kennedy bolted from the car, took three steps and dove into the water.

Gargan and Markham leaped from the car after him in astonishment. Gargan was more than astonished; he was furious. As Kennedy started swimming away, Gargan said, "I hope he drowns, the son of a bitch!" The Senator's departure was unexpected. "That hadn't been discussed in advance; the Senator merely left. Our conversation was cut short," Gargan said. The point was: nothing had been decided.

Gargan watched the Senator swim beyond the half-way mark in the channel. He wasn't concerned about Kennedy's ability to make it across. The Senator's final statement before diving in the water had been "reasonably clear," Gargan said. "He was going to report the accident, and I was going to take care of the girls." Gargan did exactly what the statement suggested, "I got in the car and started driving back to the cottage."

En route, Gargan had second thoughts. "I wasn't satisfied the thing for the Senator to do was to venture alone to Edgartown. I didn't think it was good he was attempting to do what he was doing by himself."

To Markham, Gargan said, "I think one of us should be with him. We better go back to the ferry slip and I'll swim across." Markham couldn't do it, Gargan realized, "His leg was in such bad shape, he never would have made it."

There was no sign of Ted Kennedy in the water when Gargan returned to the landing. He assumed the Senator had made it safely to the other side. Gargan "seriously considered" swimming to Edgartown, "To make sure the Senator was going to do what he clearly had said he was going to do." The reason he didn't was, "The Senator said he was going to take care of it. Since our discussion had been about reporting the accident, I presumed that's what he was going to do—take care of it. Whatever 'take care of' meant."

Gargan was the only person on Chappaquiddick who knew the Boiler Room girls well, he said. "I felt I should go back to the party, because I was the best one not to alarm them and to keep them calm at this time."

Gargan drove back to the cottage. He did not encounter another car, nor had he seen any vehicle or pedestrian on Dike Road, or in the two round trips to the landing. Chappaquiddick was a vacuum of stifling emptiness, Gargan said. "The night was hot. There was no air. There was that deadness."

It was "after 2:30 A.M." when Gargan returned to the party. The cottage was dark. An outside light had been left on.

Crimmins came out of a bedroom, lit a cigarette and commenced to grumble about being disturbed.

Gargan told him, "Jack, it's late. Let's get some sleep. The ferry's stopped running. We'll go over in the morning."

Gargan observed other guests "lying around in various degrees of a comatose state, trying to sleep."

Markham collapsed on the living room's studio couch, occupied by Susan Tannenbaum and Esther Newberg. "They were not in a very good mood at this point," Markham said, later. When Markham "kind of slumped back," Newberg told him, "Watch out! You're laying on my legs."

"I'm sorry," Markham said. "I'm exhausted. You aren't going to believe what happened."

Markham's slurred diction, his alcohol breath, did not encourage further conversation. Newberg got up and went into a bedroom occupied by the Lyons sisters, finding sleeping space on the floor.

Gargan was in the room talking to the girls.

Mary Ellen Lyons asked him where he'd been.

Gargan said, "Oh, don't even ask! We've been looking for boats."

Lyons recalled, "They said they had been down at the ferry landing swimming around; that the Senator dove in the water because there was no ferry available for him and he wanted to get back to the other side. Because of his back, they said, they sort of instinctively dove in after him."

And where was Mary Jo? one of the girls asked Gargan. Lyons said, "He told me she was at the Katama Shores, that she had taken the car on the last ferry."

Rosemary Keough had also asked Gargan where the Senator and Mary Jo were, she testified later, "He said not to worry about it, that Mary Jo and the Senator had probably taken the ferry."

Hard-pressed to explain his absence from the party and his dishevelled appearance, Gargan had to keep the young women at the cottage. Should they return to their motel, they would know Mary Jo was missing and could raise the alarm. And that couldn't be done until the Senator reported the accident.

Gargan was trying to keep conversation about the accident to a minimum. "I did not want to discuss what had happened. My attitude was one of being very negative, explaining nothing. The Senator had indicated what he was going to do by his statement before he went into the water. My job was to do exactly what I was doing, which was to stay with the party and wait."

Gargan lay down on the floor next to the screen door in the living room "to be the first to know if anybody came to the cottage." He had no idea of what to expect, but he was sure the Senator was going to report the accident. "I'm dealing with a guy I have some confidence in," he said, later. "If he dives in the water and says, 'I'll take care of it,' I may not know exactly what that means, but he's always acted responsibly. He's always been able to go forward with what he said he'd do in the past. So that's the thing to expect; that he's going to work it out. He's going to do what he's supposed to do—whatever that is."

Gargan's expectations were based, "on the confidence I ascribed to him in the past. Because...I saw him right after Jack's assassination; I saw him after Bobby was killed. He was a man under control—terribly shocked from the loss of his brothers, but still able to function. I knew a confident, tough, disciplined guy who handled a crisis very well. That's the guy who took three steps, and dove into the water."

After an hour passed, Gargan wasn't so sure. He wondered if the Senator had managed to report the accident without involving the party at the cottage, but he couldn't imagine how that would be possible. It occurred to him the Senator might consult attorney Jack Driscoll at the Shiretown Inn about reporting the accident, he said. "In fact, I was hopeful that he would."

Gargan was aware of the stirrings of would-be sleepers in the living room behind him. Preoccupied by the death of Mary Jo, and the Senator's dilemma, he was increasingly apprehensive, unable to sleep.

Several hours remained until dawn. Gargan took comfort from the thought that, in daylight, he would be able to figure out what the hell was going on.

Markham, too, was suffering a turmoil of doubts about Ted Kennedy's intentions. When the Senator dove in the water, neither he nor Gargan was sure what was going to happen, Markham said later. "We hoped Ted was going to report the accident, but we didn't know for sure what he was going to do. We hadn't gotten a real commitment from him, so we were foggy on that point."

———

In pain, unable to sleep, Markham walked out into the sultry darkness. He came back inside to sit in a rocking chair in front of the fireplace. He went outside again, stretching out on the back seat of the Valiant to try to get some sleep. It was dawn when Markham came back into the cottage.

Gargan was awake, too. "There were a lot of people up at this time, around 5 or 5:30," Gargan observed. "Nobody slept very well."

Gargan was anxious to get to Edgartown as quickly as possible. The first ferry went over at 7:30 A.M. He took Markham and Charles Tretter with him when he left the cottage. Rosemary Keough and Susan Tannenbaum wanted to go along, too. Gargan regarded them as "excess baggage," he said. "I didn't want to talk to them, have them along or anything. I wanted to get away from them." But he couldn't refuse.

Gargan left the Valiant at the landing and took the *On Time* to Edgartown. As he hurried up Dagget Street to the Shiretown Inn, Gargan made a determination "based on instinct" that the accident hadn't been reported.

Gargan and Markham parted company with the others at the bottom of a stairway leading to a second-floor porch. Gargan said, "We'll see you."

Rosemary Keough recalled looking up and seeing Senator Kennedy standing on the porch outside his room.

Chapter 14

ROSS RICHARDS WAS WALKING ON NORTH WATER STREET AROUND 7:15 A.M. when he met Stan Moore. Moore had rented a room at the Harborside Hotel in which a number of friends were staying. During some horseplay, one of the guests was thrown through a railing of a terrace, landing at the feet of a security guard. Moore and the others had been evicted from the premises—but not before having to pay damages, Moore related. "Nobody had any money. We had to take up a collection before they'd let us leave." Moore had been wandering around Edgartown since 5 A.M.

Richards and Moore encountered Ted Kennedy in the alley that separated the Shiretown Inn from the Colonial Inn next door. Kennedy joined them to walk back to the second floor porch. The Senator was coming from the inn's small lobby where he had asked the desk clerk, Mrs. Frances Stewart, to reserve the *Boston Globe* and the *New York Times*. He said, "By the way, could I borrow a dime? I seem to have left my wallet upstairs."

Mrs. Stewart produced a coin from the desk's cash drawer. Senator Kennedy was freshly shaven, dressed in "yachting clothes." He appeared "normal in every way" when he walked thirty feet to an outside porch and the inn's only public telephone.

Kennedy called Helga Wagner, a former German airline stewardess with whom he had established a romantic liaison.

Kennedy told her nothing about the accident, Mrs. Wagner said, later. "He just said something very serious had happened and I need to have Stephen Smith's number in Spain. He knew I had it because I was on my way to Europe to join Stephen Smith and his wife, Jean."

Kennedy returned to the desk to give back the dime he'd borrowed. Flustered to be in the presence of a prominent person, Mrs. Stewart impulsively introduced herself. She was surprised how weak the Senator's handshake was. Kennedy's skin felt "cold and clammy" to the touch.

Ross Richards went into his room to awaken his wife. He said, "Ted's outside. He wants to see you. Why don't you get up?"

A beautiful, slender blonde, Marilyn Richards complained, "Ross, it isn't eight o'clock yet!" When she joined the group on the porch, she observed Ted Kennedy was "all dressed up." A quarter-hour of innocuous conversation followed, she recalled. "Mostly, it was Stan Moore telling us about getting thrown out of the Harborside. We were all chatting on the porch when Joey Gargan arrived."

Mrs. Richards was surprised at Gargan's appearance. "Joey looked awful. His clothes were all wrinkled, and his hair was sticking out."

Even more startling was the uncharacteristically loud and coarse manner with which Gargan announced his presence, demanding to speak to Ted Kennedy at once.

Gargan was "very definite about wanting to see him. My directness, my aggressiveness, the sense of urgency I had may have startled him. I more or less ordered him into the room. It was: I'd like to see you right now! Get in there!'"

In his haste to get to the Shiretown, Gargan had worked up a sweat. "I was soaking wet, because it was a hot, muggy morning and I was very agitated and eager to find out what the hell was going on." After a sleepless night of mounting anxiety, Gargan's temperature had soared even higher when he'd looked up from the bottom of the stairs to see Ted Kennedy posturing on the porch, chatting unconcernedly with the others, pretending there was nothing wrong. From that tableau, it was clear to Gargan the Senator hadn't reported the accident.

It was obvious to Markham too, "That nothing had been done; there was no commotion."

Markham went to Kennedy's room. The door was locked. The Senator had left the key inside.

Gargan went to the lobby to fetch another key.

Ross Richards asked the Senator to join him for breakfast. Kennedy said he couldn't right now, but he "might" join him later.

Gargan returned with a key. Kennedy and Markham followed him into the room and closed the door.

"What happened?" Markham said.

Kennedy reclined on one of the room's twin beds. He said, "I didn't report it."

Markham recalled, "When we got over there and found out he hadn't reported the accident, we almost shit. We couldn't *believe* he hadn't reported it."

"What the fuck is going on?" Gargan exploded. "You were supposed to report the fucking accident."

Kennedy had swum the channel. He had slipped into the Shiretown Inn unseen, changed clothes and established his presence by asking an employee patrolling the premises the time. He had gone to bed and awakened around 7 o'clock. He had betrayed no sign of having been involved in an automobile accident to a number of witnesses. It wasn't too late for the scenario he had proposed to be put into effect. It wouldn't be difficult to convince people he hadn't known about the accident until the next morning.

The Senator had expected the incident to have been "taken care of when Gargan and Markham showed up the next morning, that Gargan would have reported the accident and told the police Mary Jo Kopechne had been driving the accident car. The Senator had counted on Gargan to realize, after an hour or so had passed and nobody showed up at the cottage, that he had no choice but to report the accident. It was, after all, the kind of clean-up detail Gargan customarily performed as advance man, a dependency that went back to the "Joey'll fix it" days of their boyhood. So long as there was a chance Gargan would reconsider his objections to the plan, the Senator had not reported the accident himself.

Gargan was mortified by his sense of the Senator's motive for swimming the channel: to force him to follow a course he had made clear in the car he wanted followed, irrespective of Gargan s objections. That the accident had not been reported was bad enough. For the Senator to have misrepresented his intentions by subterfuge, saying he was going to report the accident and then not doing so, and start putting an alibi into play only compounded the tragedy, Gargan said. "This thing is worse now than it was before. We've got to do something. We're reporting the accident right now!"

Kennedy said, "I'm going to say that Mary Jo was driving."

"There's no way you can say that!" Gargan said. "You can be placed at the scene."

Into the room burst Charlie Tretter.

Furious at the interruption, Gargan told him, "Hey, you! Get out of here!"

Tretter had looked through the room's window and thought the Senator had motioned him inside. "I thought that in his eyes and in his face there was something wrong," he said, later. "I thought he was angry or disturbed; but I didn't know whether it was at me for interfering with the conversation or what."

When Tretter left, Gargan said, "Jesus! We've got to report this thing. Let's go."

Kennedy was reluctant to do so, Markham observed. "He was still stuck on the idea of having Mary Jo driving the car."

The Senator wanted to know where there was a telephone he could use. The telephone at the inn was in an inconvenient place. Other telephones in Edgartown were equally public, Gargan knew from years of Regatta weekends. There would be two, three people lined up to use them. Time was of the essence, in Gargan's view. "I was very anxious for the Senator to get to a phone and do the things I thought he should do; then, report the accident." Gargan suggested the telephone at the ferryhouse on the Chappaquiddick landing.

Returning to the Shiretown Inn from a coffee shop where they had just breakfasted, Marilyn and Ross Richards passed Gargan, Markham and the Senator on their way to the ferry. "They were obviously in a big rush; and looked very preoccupied," Marilyn Richards observed. "They passed us without a greeting."

The Senator appeared untroubled on the short ride to Chappaquiddick. He went into the ferryhouse to call Dave Burke, "To alert him to take care of all the details that had to be taken care of," Gargan said. "Because now, obviously, the story was going to go out."

Gargan didn't hear the conversation. That the Senator was still reluctant to report the accident was clear to Markham from what he overheard.

Markham observed a tow truck's flashing lights bound for Chappaquiddick on board the *On Time*. He went inside the ferryhouse to bring the vehicle to Ted's attention, an indication the accident car had been discovered at Dike Bridge.

Gargan had spotted the truck too. Now it was essential to report the accident, he said. "You've got to do what I've been saying right along. Get your ass over there and report it as fast as you can."

Gargan suggested Markham accompany the Senator to the police station. Under normal circumstances, Gargan would have done it, but he was determined not to be a party to any false report. So long as there was a thread of hope that "somebody else" could be driving the accident car, the Senator would cling to that hope. Gargan didn't want to be placed in the position—if the Senator started to lie—of having to contradict him, or be forced to go along with whatever story he was going to tell police.

Gargan got into the Valiant parked at the landing to drive to the cottage. On the way he encountered LaRosa, Crimmins, the Lyons sisters and Esther Newberg walking on Chappaquiddick Road, heading for the landing.

———

Gargan stopped the car and told them to get in.

Looking at Gargan's face, Nance Lyons "knew that something was wrong." She said, "What's happened?"

"There's been an accident," Gargan said, but he wouldn't say anything else until he had returned to the cottage and the others were seated in the living room. "The Senator has been in an automobile accident," he said. "And we can't find Mary Jo."

Gargan refused to answer any questions. "I didn't know what had happened, so what I'm telling these people is limited."

Gargan ordered Crimmins and LaRosa, "Get all the stuff together: every bottle, every potato chip. I want this place cleaned up immediately. "He would return to pick them up later.

Nance Lyons found Mary Jo's handbag under a chair in the living room, she said. "Her pocketbook happened to be next to mine and I took it when I was collecting my own things."

Gargan was repeatedly questioned about the accident on the way to the landing: Where was the accident? What had been done about it? Had the Coast Guard been called?

Gargan had "no details," he said.

"Can't you do something?" Nance Lyons said. "Isn't there some way we can have somebody else as driver of the car?"

"That would be impossible," Gargan said.

"I don't know why *you* couldn't be driving the car," Lyons said. "Can't somebody else take the blame? There's no way we can do that?"

"Of course not," Gargan said. "That's absolutely out of the question."

It dawned on Gargan: "Goddamn it, Joe, you were smart not to tell anybody about the accident last night. Because you would have gotten everybody involved. They would have been making plans to have somebody else drive the car, and God knows what else. The damn thing would have been a total disaster."

Nance Lyons persisted, "Why can't we have somebody else driving the car?"

"We can't, that's all!" Gargan said bluntly, putting an end to the discussion. "The Senator was driving."

Gargan left the girls at the Edgartown dock to take a cab to their motel. He told them "to stay calm." He would call later with details.

Gargan went to the police station to find out what was going on. The Senator and Paul Markham were working on an accident report. Gargan didn't get a chance to talk to them. From the crowd gathered outside town hall he realized, "This thing was going to be highly investigated." Gargan had some understanding the accident car had been found, "But nobody specifically told me: 'We found Mary Jo in the car.'"

At the Shiretown Inn, Gargan suggested Tretter take LaRosa's Mercury to return Rosemary Keough and Susan Tannenbaum to the Katama Shores motel.

When the Lyons sisters and Esther Newberg arrived at the motel, they'd gone into Mary Jo Kopechne's room, expecting to find her there. Gargan had used the word "tragedy" to describe the accident. He hadn't said Mary Jo was dead, only that she was missing, Newberg said. "We girls kept hoping Mary Jo had somehow gotten out of the car, too; that maybe she was alive and wandering around dazed."

Tretter showed up with Keough and Tannenbaum. He said, "One of the girls already there came out of a room and said, 'There's been an accident. Something's happened to Mary Jo!"

Rosemary Keough was told, "The Senator drove off a bridge, and we don't know where Mary Jo is," she recalled later. "We said, 'How could it have happened? Does anybody know anything?' And nobody did."

Tretter returned to the Shiretown Inn. Gargan told him about the accident. Tretter was shaking his head, muttering, "Oh, God!" over and over. He said to Gargan, "I think you ought to go out and talk to the girls. They're upset. They don't know what to do."

———

Gargan intended to do that anyway. "I wanted to get them off the island as soon as possible. How I was going to do that, I wasn't sure."

Gargan called the Katama Shores and talked to Nance Lyons. She asked him if the accident car had been recovered. Gargan said it had. "I asked if Mary Jo had been in the car and he said, 'Yes,'" Lyons said, later. Gargan was coming to the motel to explain.

Gargan showed up around 11 o'clock. The Senator's car had gone off Dike Bridge, he told the girls. The Senator had dived repeatedly to rescue Mary Jo. Apparently, she was dead. "I want you to know," he said, "that every single effort possible was made to save her."

Gargan didn't mention his own rescue efforts, Tretter recalled. "He said the Senator had called him and Markham out of the cottage to tell what had happened and asked to be driven to the Edgartown ferry. The Senator was distraught. Neither one of them had talked to him. He was just saying, 'Get me to Edgartown. Get me to Edgartown.'" Tretter observed "a tremendous emotional breakdown of the girls around me so that for five or ten minutes, there was nothing but crying."

The girls' reaction was not pleasant, Gargan said, "They were highly critical. Some of them were very angry" they had not been told about the accident when he returned to the cottage.

Gargan was even more evasive than he had been at the cottage, "Because now I had the additional problem I didn't have the night before. The Senator is at the police station making his report of what happened in the accident. I don't want to say anything to these girls that would compromise whatever statement he was making. Plus, I had very little knowledge about the accident itself, except for Paul and I doing the diving. How much or any of that the Senator is going to tell the police I don't know. The only thing relevant to the report was how the accident had taken place, how fast the Senator was driving, where he was coming from and where he was going when he got to the bridge," Gargan said. "And I had no knowledge of any of that."

Having defended automobile accident cases for insurance companies for many years, Gargan was certain Kennedy would be sued. "First, I was thinking of this as a civil case. And, in addition to that, manslaughter definitely had to be considered, since Mary Jo had died in an accident. Because it's automatic in Massachusetts when a person is killed in an accident for the prosecutor to bring an action for criminal manslaughter. You've got to have a hearing."

"Now that I saw the magnitude of the situation, I was even less willing to give the girls any information. My client, so to speak—although he was sort of a semi-client—is now at the police station giving his report. I don't want anything I said at that time to change whatever factual situation he was presenting. I was in no position as a lawyer who had advised the Senator to report the accident to discuss this case with anybody, since it had now become a case."

Gargan told the girls, "I think what you should do is get off the island as soon as possible. Nobody knows at the moment that any of you are here, so go home and just keep quiet. Don't talk to anybody until we see what develops—that's the best advice I can give you right now." Gargan was trying to be kind, "I was thinking of them, basically, getting away from this whole thing."

Deputized to "take care of the girls," Tretter spent "a very uncomfortable hour or so" before he was told to remove them from the Katama Shores Motel. Gargan gave the order. He said, "Put them in the car, and take them to the ferry. Get them out of here!"

Gargan returned to the police station. Markham showed him the Senator's statement. Gargan "sort of perused it. I didn't read it at that time." He was satisfied the Senator had admitted being the driver of the accident car. He didn't have to know anything else.

Gargan checked out of the Shire town Inn. He returned to Chappaquiddick to pack up the debris left from the party and pick up LaRosa and Crimmins. He called Steve Gentle to say the cottage was now vacant.

Gargan turned up at Edgartown dock to pay Captain Manuel DeFratus $50 cash for the charter of the boat on Saturday, then rushed off without explaining why the young women would not be observing the races.

The fleet of Regatta boats was becalmed in the harbor. Gargan sought out John Linehan of the Hyannis Port Yacht Club to ask if the committee boat could tow the *Victura* back. "Will you do us that favor after the races today. We're all screwed up."

The Wianno class event was cancelled at three o'clock. "That was a bad summer," Gargan recalled. "The winds were not good all that summer."

Gargan spoke briefly with Jack Driscoll at the Shiretown Inn. Driscoll was concerned about rumors he'd heard about an accident involving Ted Kennedy.

The Senator had not, as Gargan hoped, consulted Driscoll about reporting the accident when he returned to the Shiretown Inn. Gargan couldn't tell Driscoll much, except to confirm an accident had occurred, the Senator was driving, but had not been injured.

When Driscoll asked why the accident had not been reported for ten hours, Gargan said, cryptically, "He didn't take my advice."

Marilyn Richards thought the whispers between Driscoll and her husband had started around 1 o'clock. "We weren't asked to the party at Chappaquiddick, but Jack was and he told us about it. When Ross told me around 3 o'clock what had happened, I was absolutely floored. I wondered what on earth Ted Kennedy had been up to wanting to chat at that hour of the morning—and he hadn't said one word about the accident. I thought it was all very strange."

Gargan telephoned his wife in South Bend, Indiana. He charged the call to the Senator's credit card used for advance and scheduling expenses. Others in Kennedy's office carried the card, including Dun Gifford.

Betty Gargan had heard about the accident on the radio. She was saddened and distressed by the news. The party at Chappaquiddick was typical of the kind of campaign get-together she had happily participated in the year before, Gargan observed. "It wasn't a scandalous party, but in the light of unfolding events, it was starting to look like one."

But given the record of previous Kennedy Regatta parties, Gargan had grounds for concern his sentimental reunion for the "boiler room" could be misinterpreted. Parties held in 1966 and 1967 had been riotous affairs. The 1967 party had left a rental cottage at Katama beach in shambles. Ted Kennedy's date had reportedly "begun an affair with him during the weekend" that had continued for over two years. Gargan hadn't had much to do with that weekend's festivities, attorney Jack Driscoll having made the rental arrangements.

Ray LaRosa's wife was "upset" when she was told about the accident. LaRosa hadn't known a party was planned when he accepted an invitation to come to Edgartown for the Regatta.

LaRosa helped load the party's leavings into his Mercury. Then Gargan returned the Valiant to a Hertz agency in Edgartown.

LaRosa drove to Vineyard Haven to get a ferry to Woods Hole. Gargan called the Senator's house in Hyannis Port from the dock. "We're on our way," he said. "We're leaving the island right now."

Gargan had accomplished his clean-up detail with his customary dispatch and efficiency. He had left no evidence behind that a party had taken place at the cottage on Chappaquiddick. And all the guests who had attended had escaped the island before Edgartown police even knew they were there.

On the ferry to Woods Hole, Jack Crimmins was "doubly furious" at Gargan for having rented a cottage on Chappaquiddick given the incident that had occurred there. Gargan conceded Crimmins had a point.

"The whole problem about reporting the accident was that damn little island," Gargan said later. "If the accident had taken place in Edgartown it would never have shaped up as it did. There would have been communication. We would have all been together. That little spit of water the ferry goes back and forth on is what screwed up the whole situation. The channel was like an obstacle. If it had been a bridge instead of a landing, we could have driven across and been in the center of Edgartown in a matter of 30 seconds, gotten out of the car and walked over to the police station. Only there wasn't any walking over—unless the Senator was Jesus Christ and could walk on water."

Gargan regretted having rented a cottage on Chappaquiddick. Had he gotten to Edgartown earlier and taken a place on South Beach the way he wanted, "The whole thing would never have happened."

Gargan unloaded the Mercury at his house in Hyannis Port. Then he walked over to the command post on the compound. The councils already in progress there were no more than hand-wringing sessions of commiseration. "There were people involved who did not understand the laws of Massachusetts regarding insurance coverage and other things, people who thought that because of this accident, there was going to be millions and millions of dollars of lawsuits," Gargan said. "Although others were excited about that, I was not. There wasn't much likelihood of anything in the way of heavy damages coming out of the accident, because it would be impossible to prove 'pain and suffering' on account of the way the accident happened."

Gargan wanted no part in the discussion of the accident, or why it hadn't been reported for ten hours. He'd come to rescue Paul Markham from the post mortems and take him back to his house as an overnight guest. Friends since they had played football together at Georgetown Prep, and former associates in the U.S. Attorney's office, Gargan and Markham "talked about the accident and what Ted had said about it in his statement."

Markham had written out a description of the accident from the Senator's dictation. He had corrected errors in grammar, but played no part in the deception the Senator had practiced in failing to mention the party at Chappaquiddick and his claim to have been "in shock" after the accident.

Gargan couldn't make that judgment in the drive to the ferry, he said. "Maybe I should have realized the Senator was in more serious trouble than I thought, so I missed the boat and so did Paul." Gargan had no idea what happened after the Senator took three steps and started swimming. "Up to that point," Gargan said, "I'm still dealing with a guy I've known for 30 years who's always done what he said he was going to do."

The Senator had told Markham nothing at the police station regarding his rate of speed, or the quantity of alcohol he'd consumed at the party. Gargan couldn't tell how much the Senator had to drink, he said. "He didn't appear to be under the influence, but I don't know whether he was or not."

The "wrong turn" was particularly puzzling. When he saw the Senator leave the cottage, "The assumption was he was going to the ferry. Where he went, what he did, if he stopped somewhere or did something else, I don't know," Gargan said. "He could have changed his mind about getting the ferry; all kinds of things could have happened after he went out the door of the cottage. It's entirely possible he went down that road deliberately to take a swim."

But Gargan didn't believe the Senator was taking Mary Jo to the beach to make love to her. He said, "They both had comfortable hotel rooms to go to, so it didn't make sense for him to go down there for that purpose."

The Senator had not mentioned the rescue attempted by Gargan and Markham at the bridge in his police report. Kennedy told Markham, "Look, I don't want you people put in the middle of this thing. I'm not going to involve you. As far as you know, you didn't know anything about the accident."

With Markham at the police station, and Gargan putting in two appearances there, Arena would have had two witnesses available to corroborate the Senator's accident report. By not "involving" them, the Senator was guaranteeing Markham and Gargan wouldn't be questioned. Was

Kennedy protecting himself from revealing that two lawyers had known about the accident hours before he'd gone to the police, and that those lawyers had repeatedly urged him to report the accident—advice Kennedy refused to follow?

While the Senator had not said so specifically, the impression Arena was bound to get was that Markham was acting as his attorney at the police station, a presence that might have inhibited his interrogation. As it was, Arena was a police officer of unusual good will, accommodating to the point of indulgence in his treatment of the Senator, Markham said. The police chief appeared to have accepted the Senator's accident report at face value. When Markham last spoke to him, Arena had given no indication he intended to press charges against the Senator and was handling the accident "as a routine motor vehicles case."

Chapter 15

SHORTLY AFTER INSPECTOR HERBERT BURR CAME ON DUTY IN the radio room at Registry headquarters on Sunday morning, he received a call to see if he could find a license for Edward M. Kennedy. When Burr found no record in the files, he went to the Tab Room. Here, licenses were key-punched on IBM cards attached to perforated renewal forms. Upon separation, the license was mailed to operators; the renewal card placed on circulating metal trays before being put in the Registry's files. The procedure took from two to six weeks. "When I looked in the trays, there were all yellow renewal cards there," Burr said, later. Among them was a license in the name of Edward M. Kennedy, valid until February 22, 1971. Burr had, on other occasions, found licenses that had been in the Tab Room for some time and hadn't been put in the files, but not for five months. Burr couldn't explain the anomaly in the report on the license check he made to Carl Catalano, chief of special investigations.

Having received confirmation of a valid license, inspector George "Red" Kennedy went to Edgartown police station, accompanied by

Joseph Greelish. Greelish delivered the license number and expiration date to Arena.

Arena completed his citation. He was sending the "offender's copy" by registered mail to Ted Kennedy at Hyannis Port. In doing so, Arena wasn't following standard police procedure; such "tickets" were ordinarily delivered in person.

That he was seeking to prosecute the Senator for leaving the scene of the accident after causing personal injury marked the end of his investigation, Arena told a dozen reporters at the police station. From his examination of the accident scene, Arena was "firmly convinced" there was no criminal negligence involved. "But in the matter of the time period after the accident, there is in my eyes a violation concerning going from the scene, leaving the scene." That the delay lasted ten hours was not important, Arena said. "If he sat in his house for 5 minutes without reporting the accident, he was in violation of the law."

Reporters wanted to know if Arena had looked into the possibility the accident was related to drinking at a party prior to Ted Kennedy driving off Dike Bridge. Having been deceived about the party, Arena had not asked that question of the Senator, he said. "There was no other physical evidence at the scene that there might have been drinking. I'm not pursuing that line at all. I'm still standing on the fact that there was no negligence involved. I really believe the accident is strictly accidental."

Arena had no plans to question those who had attended the party. The only witnesses to Kennedy's conduct on the night of the accident had been Kennedy's friends. In Arena's judgment, none could be expected to contradict his account or say anything to worsen his situation—so he saw no point in questioning them.

"I'm firmly convinced the Senator told me the correct story. He impresses me as a Senator, and as a man who would tell the truth," Arena said. "I think the Senator was more than cooperative with me because he released a statement more openly than most citizens might. Most citizens would want to talk with their attorney first." Arena conceded he'd given Kennedy a chance to speak in private with former U.S. Attorney Paul Markham who accompanied him to the police station.

Arena was surprised neither Ted Kennedy, nor his representatives had called him to provide more details about the accident. "I wouldn't say I was left out in the cold," he said. "But I did expect some additional information."

So did reporters. Arena was not likely to be the one to provide it. Reporters liked Arena because he was pleasant and accessible. But the consensus was that Arena seemed incapable of hanging a rap on Ted Kennedy more serious than a misdemeanor traffic violation. Nor was he galvanized into action by the mysterious aspects gathering around the accident to do much investigating, appearing more concerned with explaining away any possible wrong-doing on the Senator's part.

Arena thought the case so wrapped up he'd even disposed of the original police report. "It wasn't in Kennedy's handwriting, so I copied it and threw it away."

Weeks later, Carmen Salvador admitted she'd fished the document from a wastebasket to keep as a souvenir. Arena demanded the statement returned. "I felt it would be good for my files, because I figured I'm the one guy that's going to get questioned about this thing for the rest of my life." But even after it had been returned, the document proved elusive. "The truth is, one page of the damn thing did disappear again," Arena said. "I don't know where the hell it went."

Arena had to be reminded by reporter Ed Crosetti of *The Boston Record-American,* "Chief, you better talk to 'Huck' Look." Arena had neglected to question the deputy sheriff in the confusion of events on Saturday. Look's comments at Dike Bridge hadn't seemed critical. Whether the accident occurred at 11:15 P.M. as Kennedy said in his report, or after Look saw the car, didn't make much difference insofar as a leaving-the-scene charge was concerned. Arena said, "The question of time only became an issue after the press picked up inconsistencies in Kennedy's report."

A husky man with the high color of the outdoors, and a plainspoken, country-boy manner, Look was reluctant to retell his story officially for the record in view of the Senator's published account of the accident. Look regretted having blurted out information before he realized its significance.

Look had seen a dark car between 12:40 A.M. and 12:45 A.M., Saturday morning approaching the bend on Chappaquiddick Road at the center of the intersection of Dike Road. Arena noted, "He is positive there was a man driving and that there was someone next to him. He thinks there may have been someone else in the back seat but he's not sure." The car appeared "unsure or lost." Look stopped, and started to walk toward the car, but the driver had sped off down Dike Road.

Look's story sounded OK to Arena. "The thing that bothered me about it was, 'Huck' was so adamant about his time. I did believe he saw this particular thing, but I was between a stone and a hard place because I couldn't disprove Kennedy's time."

Look was more closely interrogated by George Killen and Bernie Flynn when the two detectives arrived in Edgartown around noon. Arena hadn't asked for their help. The chief had left the station, telling reporters, "It's my day off. I'm going home to my family."

"This was more a spectator thing," Flynn explained. "George didn't want us involved, but he wanted to know what was going on. Because if Dinis stepped in, our office would get the case."

Flynn and Killen made a formidable pair, at opposite ends of the police spectrum. Taciturn and rigidly principled, Killen was in austere contrast to the good-looking blond with a fiery temper, as likely to crash through a door as to knock. A tough street cop, Flynn was "like a dog in heat" when he sank his teeth into an investigation.

    Killen had taken an instant dislike to the younger man when Flynn
joined his office in January 1967, regarding him as "an angle-player and
a wise guy." Flynn had few scruples when it came to beating criminals
at their own game. Cape Cod was tame stuff after violent, gritty New
Bedford, upon whose mean streets Flynn had worked his way up from
patrolman to captain of the uniformed branch. Flynn had cut a considerable law enforcement swath through the economically depressed
former mill city, riddled with municipal corruption. Before moving over
to the state police and leaving town, Flynn sent a former mayor to jail
for taking payoffs, and made a host of enemies, not the least of whom
was a prominent physician with whose wife Flynn had carried on a
scandalous love affair. The doctors political connections reached into
the office of Governor John Volpe. Dismissal from the state police or
banishment to some remote corner of Massachusetts was in the offing
for Flynn, Killen confided to Frank Keating. "George told me the colonel of the state police was going to call Bernie in," Keating said. "And
they were going to move him out, because of this affair."

    Unlike Killen, Keating admired Flynn's quick intelligence and dash-
ing style as a police officer, and so it was Keating who warned him of
trouble brewing. Flynn used political connections of his own to head off
a hearing and retain his plum assignment on Cape Cod. Outstanding
detective work on several difficult cases over those two years had earned
Flynn Killen's admiration; then ultimately, his trust.

    Killen knew "Huck" Look as a reliable and responsible court officer
from cases he'd prosecuted in Edgartown. Look agreed to accompany
the police officers to Chappaquiddick to reenact his encounter with the
"Kennedy car."

    Look had worked as a special police officer at the Edgartown Yacht
Club Regatta dance from 8 o'clock to 12:30 on Friday night. Brought
to Chappaquiddick in the yacht club's launch, Look got into his car
parked at the landing and headed home. He had seen the headlights of

a car coming toward him near the curve at the intersection. "Knowing the road, I slowed down, because there's a sharp corner that people usually will cut too close," Look said. "I wanted to make sure I didn't get sides wiped." Look came almost to a complete stop. A black sedan passed in front of his headlights. "There was a man driving, a woman in the front seat, and either another person or some clothing, a sweater, or a pocketbook in the back seat—what appeared to be a shadow of some kind." The car went off the pavement into the private, dirt Cemetery Road.

By this time Look had proceeded around the corner a little bit, he said. "I observed in my rear view mirror that the car was parked. And it looked like they are going to back up. I thought they wanted information, that they were lost or something."

Look got out of his car and walked toward the other vehicle. He was 25 to 30 feet away when the car started backing up toward him, tail lights showing all over the deputy sheriff uniform he was wearing. Look believed the driver must have seen him, as the lights glanced off the badge and whistle on his shirt. He started to call out an offer of help, but the car took off down Dike Road in a cloud of dust. He observed a Massachusetts registration letter "L", he said. "And I did sort of a photostatic thing in my mind that it had sevens in it, at the beginning and the end."

Look returned to his car. A short distance from the intersection he saw two women and a man doing a snake dance down the middle of the road, "like a conga line." He stopped to ask if they needed a lift. The tall girl of the trio said, "Shove off, buddy. We're not pick-ups." The man in the group apologized. "Thank you, no," he said. "We're just going over there to our house."

Look mentioned the "lost car" to his wife when he got home at one o'clock. "I figured it was a man and his wife arguing about what direction to go—that's the first thing that came into my mind," he said. "So many visitors come to Edgartown in the summer, you kind of get used to people getting lost."

Look wondered where the car was headed at that time of night. There weren't many places to go on Chappaquiddick once the ferry stopped running.

Given without hesitation, guile, or calculation, Look's story was in clear contradiction of Senator Kennedy's report about the time the accident had occurred, and the wrong turn he said he'd made at the intersection.

If it was Kennedy's car—and every indication was that it was—to make a "wrong turn," a driver would have to ignore: (1) A directional arrow of luminized glass pointing to the left; (2) The banking of the pavement to accommodate the sharp curve; (3) The white line down the center of the road. To accomplish such a maneuver, a driver would also need to slow to a stop to make an abrupt 90 degree turn onto the unmistakable jarring ruts of Dike Road, a buckboard ride Flynn and Killen endured on their way to take a look at Dike Bridge, no more than a frail platform standing over Poucha Pond.

"Dyke House" was so close to the bridge, "There's no way you could go down that road and not see that house," Flynn observed. "It stuck out like a sore thumb." Diagonally across the road from "Dyke House," yet another residence was clearly visible from the road. Flynn counted two more houses Senator Kennedy had passed when he'd returned to the cottage after plunging into the pond. It took Flynn and Killen 23 minutes to walk the 1.2 miles from the bridge to the cottage, a nondescript house of weathered cedar shingles only 150 yards from the Chappaquiddick Volunteer Fire Station. A red bulb burned over the unlocked door of the cement-block fire station; a switch inside tripped a roof-mounted siren. Had the alarm been sounded, "I would have been there in three minutes. And my volunteers and half the people on the island would have shown up within 15 minutes," Fire Captain Foster Silva said.

Silva challenged Flynn and Killen when they came up the flag-stone path from a split-rail fence to the property he was guarding from curious reporters and tourists. Watchman for various summer residents and the Trustees of Reservations that maintained a wildlife refuge on the eastern shore of Chappaquiddick, Silva had let himself in with a caretaker's key provided by the cottage owner, Sydney Lawrence of Scarsdale, New York. Learning of the accident Lawrence immediately went to Edgartown and inspected the place on Saturday night. He found it swept clean of any evidence a party had been held there. Lawrence told Silva, "They were real cute about that. I only found 8 empty Coke bottles. Even the trash barrels had been emptied."

Silva lived less than 100 yards from the cottage. He had no trouble remembering the party held there on Friday night. He had watched television until 10 P.M., when his dogs started barking. "I went outside with my wife to quiet the dogs and saw two, three cars at the Lawrence house," he said. "There was a lot of singing and laughing coming from the house. I would say it was just a normal cocktail party. They were damned loud, though."

Silva went to bed around midnight but couldn't sleep with all the noise the dogs were making because of the party next door. Silva thought the revelers were inconsiderate in not lowering their voices after 11 P.M. "By one o'clock I was pretty well damn fed-up with the whole thing. It was a damn farce at that hour of the morning. If they had kept it up any longer I would have called the police."

Silva's son-in-law also described the party as "one of those loud, noisy brawls" put on by summer people. "There was yelling, music and general sounds of hell-raising." The talk and laughter continued until 1:30 A.M., then quieted down. Silva's wife, Dodie, said, "You could still hear people talking, but the noise level was not so bad. It was still going on when I went to bed at 2:30 A.M."

Silva hadn't known Senator Kennedy was at the party until the next morning when the accident car was hoisted from Poucha Pond. His wife recognized the automobile immediately. She'd noticed the car go by the house several times that afternoon, driven by "a middle-aged man with grey hair," she said. "I saw the same man driving the car after nine o'clock in the evening. He was heading towards the ferry."

Flynn was surprised at the modesty of a premises hired for "a Kennedy party." The living room-kitchen was panelled in knotty pine. There was a dining table and four chairs, a floor lamp, and a studio couch wrapped in flowered cretonne. A 9 x 12 Sears & Roebuck carpet filled the living room's entire floor space. A waist-high counter divided the living room from a galley kitchen. Flynn found four packages of frozen crabmeat, butter, milk, and three bags of ice cubes in the refrigerator. A bathroom separated two bedrooms identically furnished with a varnished chest of drawers, a bottle lamp and mirror. A blanket was rolled at the foot of each twin bed, each so neatly-made Flynn wondered that they'd been slept in.

Silva pointed out a backyard building. "That's Mrs. Lawrence's studio; she paints there."

The studio was locked.

Flynn and Killen took a place in the line of automobiles waiting to board the *On Time*. The ferry was packed with visitors returning from Edgartown's newest tourist attraction. The traffic broke all previous records by more than one hundred cars, owner-operator Jared Grant revealed.

Grant had taken Senator Kennedy and a man he didn't know to Chappaquiddick around 6:30 P.M., Friday night. He had operated the ferry until 12:45 A.M., when he made his last run to Chappaquiddick. Grant puttered around the boat for another half hour. "The reason I stayed was, it was too hot to sleep." He had observed "a lot of people in the area on the Edgartown side." Several youths were fishing off the dock; boats were running back and forth in the harbor, he said. "It was a beautiful night, very calm. The water was like glass."

Grant closed down at 1:20 A.M. He didn't recall taking Senator Kennedy to Edgartown. "I was dead certain I didn't bring him back until I got to reading the papers. He might have been on, I don't know."

The ferry could be summoned at any hour. "We come out for any legitimate reason," Grant said. "It doesn't have to be a case of an accident or injury."

Ferryman, Dick Hewitt said, "If someone wanted ferry service after midnight, they would call Jared's or my house. The numbers are posted on a sign on either side of the ferry." There was a public telephone inside the ferryhouse at Chappaquiddick. A bell was attached to the side of the building. "What people do is drive up to the ramp and leave their lights on; and we come across to get them. If you walk down, you ring the bell."

Hewitt was highly critical of Senator Kennedy's report of the accident. He said, "You tell me, is Kennedy finished? Or are they going to paper this over with $20 bills?"

By the time he debarked from the *On Time*, Flynn had put together a scenario for the accident.

"I figure, we got a drunk driver, Ted Kennedy. He's with this girl, and he has it in his mind to go down to the beach and make love to her. He's probably driving too fast and he misses the curve and goes into Cemetery Road. He's backing out when he sees this guy in uniform coming toward him. That's panic for the average driver who's been drinking; but here's a United States Senator about to get tagged for driving under. He doesn't want to get caught with a girl in his car, on a deserted road late at night, and driving drunk on top of it. In his mind, the most important thing is to get away from the situation. He doesn't wait around. He takes off down the road. He's probably looking in the rear-view mirror to see if this cop is following him. He doesn't even see the fucking bridge and bingo! He goes off. He gets out of the car; she doesn't. The poor son of a bitch doesn't know what to do. He's thinking: I want to get back to my house, to my friends'—which is a common reaction. There are houses on Dike Road he could have gone to report the accident, but he doesn't want to. Because it's the same situation he was trying to get away from at the corner—which turned out to be minor compared to what happened later. Now there's been an accident; and the girl's probably dead. All the more reason not to go banging on somebody's door in the middle of the night and admit what he was doing. He doesn't want to reveal himself."

The crowning irony was, "Teddy Kennedy was running from nothing," Flynn said. "Huck" Look couldn't have made an arrest even if he wanted to; he didn't have the authority. You're only a special police officer at the place you're assigned. Kennedy doesn't know that. All he knows is some guy in uniform is coming after him. And the funny part about it was, 'Huck' is only trying to help him find his direction."

Chapter 16

KILLEN DIDN'T MENTION FLYNN'S THEORY WHEN HE REPORTED to Edmund Dinis what his informal investigation of the accident had revealed. Killen had talked to the district attorney that morning. Dinis was questioning Dr. Mills' diagnosis of death by accidental drowning, and wondered about an autopsy. Mills was satisfied with the cause of death, Killen said. The issue was moot anyway. The accident victim had left Martha's Vineyard at 9:30 A.M.

But Killen hadn't bothered to check with undertaker Eugene Frieh. As it was, the body of Mary Jo Kopechne was in a garage section of the Edgartown airport. Dun Gifford was waiting to serve as escort. So far, neither a plane nor permission to take off had materialized. Gifford was concerned the delay was due to a "Hold for Autopsy" placed on the body by authorities.

Frieh assured him there was no such order. Poor visibility made it impossible for a single engine aircraft to make the flight. Frieh had given permission for a twin-engine plane to be used instead. Then, an oil failure necessitated finding another aircraft. The plane did not leave Edgartown until 12:30 P.M. on Sunday afternoon.

Gifford had never met the Kopechnes. "I just wanted to help them in any way," he said. David Burke was announced "in charge" of funeral arrangements, but when Gifford arrived in Wilkes-Barre, he learned, "Mr. Kopechne had already spoken to Mr. Kielty and made the arrangements." The Senator paid for flying the body to Pennsylvania, but the Kopechnes refused "repeated offers" by the Kennedy family to pay for the funeral. The money they had put aside for their daughter's wedding, Joseph Kopechne said, "We are using instead for her funeral." The Kopechnes had moved when Mary Jo was a year old, but decided to have her buried in Plymouth, "Because this is where her roots are."

The medical examiner's report that Mary Jo had drowned had been accepted "without qualification." Her death was "an unavoidable accident." Senator Kennedy telephoned on Sunday afternoon, Kopechne revealed, "He said he wished he had died in the accident instead of Mary Jo."

Senator Kennedy also called Dr. Robert Watt to say he was feeling better and did not require him to make a house call. The Senator would remain under his care for a period of time, Watt said. "We are playing it by ear."

Kennedy was reported despondent, in seclusion, refusing to be drawn out about the accident during meetings with his staff and advisers with regard to the complaint Arena was seeking in the case.

In Gargan's view, "There was no prosecutable charge against Ted Kennedy for leaving the scene. All the law said you had to do is make known you've had an accident causing more than $200 damage or that has injured somebody. It doesn't say report it to the police, the fire department, or anyone else.[1*] All it says is you are to report it." The Senator had not left the scene without reporting the accident, "Because he made known to me and Paul Markham that he was the driver of an automobile

1   * As of this writing in 1988, Massachusetts still has not plugged this loophole in its motor vehicle laws.

that, as far as he knew, had seriously injured a girl who was in the vehicle with him, and brought us to the scene to make a serious rescue effort," Gargan said. In addition to having reported the accident to two persons, "We happened to be two lawyers, so that was frosting on the cake, that was so much the better to report to, because we were officers of the court. And that forfeited the state's case." It would be very difficult to prove leaving the scene under those circumstances, Gargan said. "Whether he should have taken quicker action to rescue the girl, or all of those other factors, that's a different question."

Gargan had known cases of death resulting from automobile accidents which had been prosecuted for manslaughter. "That was quite common. There was nothing exceptional about it. That didn't mean a lot of times the person wasn't acquitted. But you had to go through a trial." Gargan had defended hundreds of automobile cases, some involving serious injury and sometimes death. "Once a school teacher killed a child in the street, no drinking involved or anything like that, a perfectly nice man with five children who is being torn apart because he is on trial for manslaughter."

Despite his wide experience with accident cases, Gargan didn't think he was the best lawyer to advise Ted Kennedy, "Because I was involved and therefore not objective." Gargan suggested the Senator get a lawyer knowledgeable about such matters. As respected for his legal ability as Edward Hanify was, he was no lawyer for this kind of case either. The best available lawyer in Gargan's opinion was Dave Kelly, of his former law firm, Badger, Parrish, Sullivan and Frederick, whose principal business was defending insurance companies. Kelly was a tough trial lawyer. "He could care less who Ted Kennedy was," Gargan said. "He'd keep his eye on the facts, irrespective of the press or the people on Ted's staff giving him totally unwarranted advice and only confusing things."

Gargan considered this an automobile accident case that should be handled like one, he said, later. "Unfortunately, a good friend of mine got killed—which made it much more serious an accident, but the only thing that made it different from an ordinary accident was that Ted Kennedy was involved. Granted, he was a United States Senator and also a Kennedy. But the facts of the case, the incident itself, was just an automobile accident. I never lost sight of that fact, as I think some others did."

Though Gargan gave what he thought was the best advice, "Ted didn't have to take that advice, and neither did anybody else," he said. "As a matter of fact they didn't take my advice in several respects." He wasn't being allowed very close to the situation, or to some conferees at the compound. Gargan was a pariah, as responsible for the incident as Senator Kennedy.

"I don't know about blaming me for the accident and not reporting it," Gargan said. "But some staff members, would-be friends and others did try to indicate blame for me having the party, the location of it and other arrangements that led up to this disaster—that I had put the Senator in the middle of this situation, which I resented a great deal. They were saying: 'If it weren't for that damn Joey Gargan, who wanted to have his party for the 'Boiler Room,' this never would have happened.' And they knew that wasn't so. We'd been going to Edgartown Regattas and having parties for years and years; this was nothing new. Except that girls from Bobby's campaign were being entertained by me and the Senator. It wasn't just my party, sort of to placate Joey. It was something everybody wanted to do. The Senator had fully participated in these plans."

If Gargan could eventually blame himself for anything, it was when he returned to the landing with Paul Markham the second time and didn't swim across. He said, "If I had dove into the water and followed the Senator to Edgartown, things would have turned out differently. I didn't do that. The judgment I made at that time was a mistake."

Among the advisers at the compound, Gargan found a measure of sympathy from Burke Marshall. He said, "You've got no reason to hang your head, Joe."

Gargan wasn't sure if Marshall had been told about his rescue effort at Dike Bridge. It was apparent, however, Marshall had not been apprised of the scenario the Senator had proposed—the one underlying the long delay in reporting the accident. Groping for a rationale to explain the lapse of ten hours, Marshall said, "That night, in that situation, I think Ted Kennedy might very well have functioned so that the people with him, particularly if they weren't strong-minded people, would think he knew exactly what he was doing."

That was a dead giveaway. The Senator wasn't levelling with his own advisers and was sticking with his police report, attributing his failure to notify authorities to shock. Had Marshall been told the truth, Gargan suspected he wouldn't have wanted anything to do with the case.

There was no question Dave Burke knew about the Senator's reluctance to report the accident up to the time he'd spoken with him from the Chappaquiddick ferryhouse. It was Burke who at that late hour persuaded Ted Kennedy to go to the Edgartown police.

Burke encountered Gargan coming off the private beach at the compound where he'd gone swimming. Burke suggested Gargan photograph the deep scratches on his chest and upper arms as "evidence" of the rescue effort he'd made at Dike Bridge.

Gargan dismissed the idea out of hand. "As far as I was concerned, I was just a witness to a certain aspect of the accident," he said. "My injuries had no bearing on the case at all."

Edward Hanify set Gargan straight on exactly what bearing he would have on the matter. Because he was representing Ted Kennedy, Hanify couldn't talk to him about the case, suggesting Gargan discuss the accident with a lawyer. Hanify told Paul Markham the same thing. "You people are going to be highly criticized," he said. "I think you ought to protect yourselves."

Since they had risked their lives to get Mary Jo out of the car, Gargan wasn't sure what it was they could be criticized for, he said.

"Hanify recognized that as lawyers, Paul and I might feel we could represent our own interests. He thought we should get some objective, outside advice."

Gargan failed to recognize the difficult position he and Markham were in until Hanify told him Ted Kennedy considered he'd had a lawyer-client relationship with them. Whatever advice they had given him after the accident, the Senator didn't want disclosed to anyone. Kennedy was invoking privileged communication to prevent Gargan and Markham from revealing what had happened on Chappaquiddick after the accident.

Gargan supposed a quasi-case could be made that he had advised the Senator as a lawyer to report the accident. There was no question Gargan had done that, in the car, at the landing, and at the Shiretown Inn the next morning. According to the code of ethics drawn up by the American Bar Association and adopted by most state boards, attorneys could not "counsel or assist" clients to take an action the lawyer knows to be illegal or fraudulent. And "assist" is exactly what Gargan would have done had he gone along with Kennedy's plan.

By failing to report the accident, the Senator had made of Gargan and Markham unwitting accomplices in his effort to conceal it from police for more than nine hours, involving them in a net of intrigue so as to avoid his own responsibility for the death of Mary Jo Kopechne. Now he was invoking lawyer-client privilege to prevent them from telling anybody what they knew.

Paul Markham was offended by the suggestion he'd acted as the Senator's attorney. He had hardly participated in the discussion in the car and at the ferry landing at all, merely seconding Gargan's reiterated insistence the accident be reported immediately. Markham confided to his law partner, Edward Harrington, "Ted wasn't looking for legal advice from anybody at the time." The Senator had ordered them not to do anything, "Not even tell the people back at the cottage the accident had happened." What had "really blown" Markham's mind the next morning was that Ted Kennedy hadn't reported the accident—and was still insisting on not reporting it.

Markham's advice had not been sought at the police station. The Senator had participated in lengthy telephone conferences with his staff in Washington while composing his statement.

Gargan recognized the convention of advisers at the compound was single-minded. "They were only concerned about protecting the Senator. They didn't care about protecting Paul Markham, Joe Gargan, the girls or other fellows at the party, or anybody else. They let us fend for ourselves."

Gargan had made up his mind years before, if he ever got into any trouble of a personal nature, "I would go to Joe Donahue. I'd known him since I was a child; he was a great friend of my father's. I had a high degree of respect for his ability. There weren't many kinds of cases he hadn't tried. At that time, not feeling that I would need a lawyer at all, I thought I would chat with him about the accident."

The famous "Jiggs" Donahue of Lowell was a legend in the Massachusetts bar, a widely admired criminal lawyer. Donahue agreed to meet Gargan the next day, Monday. Despite Hanify's warning, Gargan feared no liability for the part he'd played in the accident. "In fact, I was rather proud of myself for what I had done under those particular circumstances. Neither the press nor anyone else had gotten the information as yet that Paul and I had made a serious rescue effort, had done the diving in the water, and all those things. So I was feeling that, whatever happened, I would be exonerated of any blame."

The scale of the disaster was brought home to Gargan when he made his way out of the compound, past a swarm of reporters at the police rope-off on Scudder Avenue. Gargan recognized Sylvia Wright of *Life* magazine, and Joe Mohbat of the Associated Press, reporters who had been on trips Gargan had advanced that spring for Senator Kennedy.

But other members of the press paid him no attention. "I'd pass them by and they never asked a question. I was never approached for a statement," Gargan said. "Simply because I don't think they knew who I was."

But reporters were concentrating their expectations on the release of a statement of further clarification about the accident from Senator Kennedy. The compound was filling up with advisers; but nothing was coming out.

A telegram sent by Senate majority leader Mike Mansfield to Ted Kennedy, delivered to the compound on Sunday afternoon, was immediately leaked to reporters.

> DEEPLY SHOCKED AND DISTURBED OVER TRAGEDY WHICH OCCURRED OVER WEEKEND. WHAT HAPPENED TO YOU COULD HAVE HAPPENED TO ANY ONE OF US. YOU HAVE OUR FULL CONFIDENCE AND IF IN ANY WAY I CAN BE OF ASSISTANCE PLEASE LET ME KNOW.

Mansfield didn't think the accident had damaged Kennedy's political career at all. "After all, Senators are human beings, too. It's just one of those things that could happen. I'm sure the police chief is aware of all the facts, and I don't think it will affect the Senator in any way." Kennedy's efforts to dive in search of Mary Jo Kopechne supported his report he was dazed after the accident, Mansfield said. "He's been going around with a back brace for several years since he was almost killed in an airplane accident. It would have been directly against his doctor's orders to dive into the water. This could have contributed to his exhaustion and shock. It's quite understandable that Senator Kennedy could have been stunned and might not have known what he was doing for several hours after the accident."

Mansfield hadn't talked to Senator Kennedy, only his staff. Obviously, Mansfield had been prevailed upon to issue a sweeping and unqualified public endorsement of the Senator's version of the accident. Others in Washington were not so indulgent. Concern was being privately expressed the accident could damage Kennedy's career if he didn't disclose more information than his report to police.

Aides in the Senator's office declined to answer questions about the Senator's movements after the accident. Dick Drayne had "no details" about the incident, he said. Drayne refused to provide a guest list of "at least 20 people" who had attended the party.

Ethel Kennedy released a statement from Hyannis Port. "Mary Jo was a sweet, wonderful girl. She worked for Bobby for years and she was in the boiler room, the phone room used for delegate counts during the campaign. Only the great ones worked there and she was just terrific," she said. "She often came out to the house and she was the one who stayed up all night typing Bobby's speech on Vietnam. She was a wonderful person."

The statement provoked ripples of derision from information-starved reporters at the barricade. Ethel had not acknowledged an accident had occurred, mentioned that Mary Jo had been killed or that her brother-in-law was driving the accident car.

The statement was "patronizing as hell" in one reporter's opinion. "Typing was the operative word to signify Mary Jo had been devoted in service to the Kennedys. All that was required to account for her death, apparently, was a posthumous pat on the head. The situation didn't lend itself to smug tributes to former employees." In the opinion of this female reporter, "No amount of public relations was going to get around the fact that Mary Jo Kopechne had died in Ted Kennedy's car and he had taken ten hours to tell police about it." The Kennedys had had their share of troubles, but tragedy was not their exclusive province. "And this tragedy more properly belonged to the Kopechne family." Ted Kennedy had survived the accident; Mary Jo Kopechne hadn't.

More significantly, such patronizing effusions reflected an evasiveness to confront the issue of the accident head-on, and the confusion of purpose inside the compound. The Kennedy apparatus, so skilled at manipulating the media, was losing its sure and practiced grip on the press which had played so large a part in their political ascendency. With a legion of friendly reporters only too happy to tell "Ted's side" of the incident if provided the information to do so, the silence within the compound was all the more baffling. A list of questions about the accident sent by the *New York Times* through an intermediary inside the compound received no response. Security police were used to relay word to reporters that Senator Kennedy had "nothing further to say" about the death of Mary Jo Kopechne. Speculation about the accident multiplied as a result of the blackout, prompting reportorial mutterings of discontent.

First newspaper accounts of the accident had been nearly uniformly sympathetic. the *Boston Globe* published ten stories about the accident, pushing the Apollo moonshot to the bottom of page one. ("Our coverage was justified," managing editor Ian Menzies said. "The Kennedys are one of the most important families in history.")

The *Globe* described the Senator as "the only surviving brother in a family pursued by tragedy." The same mournful tone echoed in a *New York Times* reference to the "doom-haunted Kennedy family." Curiously, the *Times* failed to acknowledge the major contributions made to its coverage by James Reston. (Returning a rental car to a garage in Falmouth, Reston was asked by owner Alvan Nickerson, "What's going on over in Edgartown?" Reston replied, "I'd love to tell the story, but they won't let me." Other Timesmen had since arrived to cover the accident.)

The *Times* published the "lousy picture" of Ted Kennedy taken by Harvey Ewing. Unsatisfactory as it was to Ewing, the photograph captured the Senator in mid-stride, looking fit and trim, graphic evidence that, at approximately 9:45 A.M., Saturday morning, he had been neither in a state of exhaustion nor shock, nor appeared to have suffered any significant injury as a result of the accident.

As a humid, overcast Sunday afternoon rolled around, reporters at the barricade had nothing to do but monitor the occasional automobile allowed past the roadblock. When it started raining, most reporters abandoned their posts. A hard core were huddled under umbrellas when a boy ran across Scudder Avenue, calling out, "They've just landed on the moon."

But the accident at Chappaquiddick was casting a shadow over an event that was to have been "one of great personal pride for Senator Kennedy," the *Globe* reported. "Instead, he was being forced by tragedy and controversy to remain cloistered in Hyannis Port, reported by aides under a doctor's care."

It was John F. Kennedy who had launched the program to put an American on the moon before the decade ended. In anticipation of the triumph that would attach to the Kennedy legacy when the Apollo mission fulfilled that dream, television networks had prepared advanced interviews with Ted Kennedy. Only ABC intended to show the program as scheduled. "It's strictly on the subject of the moon landing," a spokesman said. "It has nothing to do with the incident at Martha's Vineyard."

Senator Kennedy spent the better part of Sunday with members of his staff, preparing a formal statement to the press about the accident. But at the last minute a decision was made to withhold comment.

By the time Dun Gifford got back to Cape Cod from Pennsylvania and saw Ted Kennedy, "He was in a state of mind I'd never quite seen him in before—down but determined. He wanted to make a statement, go to court and get the whole goddamned thing settled right then."

Chapter 17

JIMMY SMITH SPENT SUNDAY WATCHING THE MOON LANDING ON television, reading newspaper accounts of the "Kennedy accident," and reflecting on his invitation to the now-famous "cookout" at Chappaquiddick.

On Wednesday, July 16, Joe Gargan had come to Falmouth. Smith had taken him around to meet local builders and developers with a view to Gargan's new position as vice-president of the Merchant's Bank in Hyannis. During lunch at the Coonamessett Inn, Gargan mentioned he was sailing the *Victura* to Edgartown the following day. A cookout was planned for the girls who had worked Robert Kennedy's boiler room, he said. "If you're in Edgartown for the Regatta, drop in and see us."

"The invitation was given in the spirit of having something to eat after the races, with the same old crowd that had something in common," Smith recalled. "A lot of people who held Bobby in high regard suffered a personal crisis when he was killed. There was an awful sense of loss. So these gatherings were a chance for people who'd had a similar experience to get together, like a reunion of guys that had been in battle."

Smith declined the invitation. Saturday, July 19, was his wedding anniversary. He was taking his wife out to dinner. Besides, Smith knew only one of the Boiler Room girls. Her name was Mary Jo Kopechne. Now, reading about the "Kennedy secretary" killed in the accident, the remembrance of the girl added to his sense of pain.

As a campaign coordinator for Allegheny county in western Pennsylvania in 1968, Smith had maintained daily telephone contact with Robert Kennedy for President headquarters in Washington, where a half-dozen young women compiled delegate intelligence in black loose-leaf notebooks of the states. Mary Jo Kopechne had been "in charge" of Pennsylvania. Smith had talked to her almost every day. To refer to her as a secretary, however, was to misrepresent the work of the Boiler Room. The importance of that work was, in fact, the subject of a memorandum Smith had received from Paul Kirk, aide to Kenneth O'Donnell in the campaign:

> **MEMORANDUM FROM:** Paul Kirk
>
> **REF:** Delegate reports to Ken O'Donnell from Illinois, Michigan, New Jersey, Ohio, Pennsylvania and Connecticut.
>
> As we well know, the above states have been described in the press as "the crucial battleground" for the August Convention. Although fully aware that there is varying leadership control of the delegations in each of the above states, we are nevertheless attempting to compile information on each of the delegates or potential delegates to be elected or chosen. To help us initially in this effort we would like to get, as soon as possible, the following kinds of information on each of the delegates on the attached list with whom you may be familiar:
>
> Phone numbers
>
> Age
>
> Occupation

Marital status

At large, district delegate (what district) or alternate

Full vote or fraction vote

Public official (what office)

Candidate (if so, for what office and against whom)

Whether a delegate in 1964 or 1960

Present voting tendency

Feelings about RFK

What or who will most influence his vote

What advice or suggestions you can submit to the candidate or to us to assist you in influencing his vote

What progress has been made by you or your people in your respective states on each delegate

Any other comments

This list of names and any pertinent information can be updated to us by daily memo, or at your convenience, but we do ask that we hear from you or your representatives by Friday of each week (c/o Kennedy for President Headquarters, 6th floor, 2000 L St., Washington, DC).

Some of the principals in the Washington Headquarters may have further helpful information on the delegates in your state which we will communicate to you as soon as possible so that you may follow it up. Kindly let us know where you can be reached by phone if you change your location.

All of the above information should be submitted to us or to the girls in the boiler room who are maintaining the delegate files. They in turn will keep us informed.

No mere file clerk of intelligence on delegates, Mary Jo had directed Smith's attention to potential volunteers to assist him on his field work. In Smith's opinion Mary Jo and the others brought to their work a precision and shrewd judgement that marked them as "politically savvy, not mere secretaries."

Mary Jo recommended "a Vietnam veteran and freelance writer who knows two delegates who could be picked off," and the president of a small company in Erie, Pennsylvania, who had worked for JFK in 1960. She said, "I checked and this is true. He was a delegate-at-large and Democratic Committee chairman. Worth looking into."

In addition, the Boiler Room was the conduit for "policy statements" composed by media-control managers of the campaign to be planted in newspapers. On April 26, 1968, Smith had been advised, "As major a figure as possible in each state should say whatever best suits him regarding Kennedy vs. Humphrey, with the following suggestions:

1. Humphrey had time after Johnson's withdrawal to enter primaries in California and South Dakota like Kennedy and McCarthy but waited until filing deadlines passed to avoid submitting his candidacy and his Administration's record in Vietnam to the people.

2. Now, a gangup to stop Kennedy is under way—combining Southern Governors from Maddox to Connally with George Meany (whose organizers are totally blanketing the country high-pressuring political and labor leaders to support Humphrey), and enlisting both the special interest lobbies from Wall Street to oil and the major Republican newspapers. But the people are with Kennedy and they are fed up with this kind of power politics and propaganda.

3. By supporting the candidate of the status quo which Nixon is attacking, by picking him in the back room instead of the primaries, and by trying to label Kennedy "ruthless," because he is tough-minded and determined,

or "too young" because he has energy and drive, this unholy alliance is playing right into Nixon's hands. The people want leadership, not labels; and they want Kennedy, not Humphrey."

"I called this in to all my coordinators," Mary Jo told Smith. "It is suggested that they use whichever one they felt best for their state, or not use any at all."

Increasingly, newspaper accounts of the party at Chappaquiddick probed deeper into the accident. The assumption that drinking had taken place at the party, combined with the ten-hour delay in the report of the accident, made Smith anxious to gauge Edmund Dinis' thinking. Smith was particularly concerned about a rule in the district attorney's office dealing with motor vehicle fatalities.

Because "drinking has a capacity to impair driving, and has become the cause of 75% of fatal crashes," Dinis had directed police chiefs in his district to charge with manslaughter "all defendants accused of operating under the influence of liquor when such operation resulted in the death of another person." District court judges were to bind over to Superior Court all matters accompanying such complaints if "probable cause" was found. No complaint of driving under the influence was to be dismissed by a prosecutor or police officer, except by a judge. Assistants in the district attorney's office had reduced the policy to a formula called 3D: Drunk Driving + Death = DA. Dinis prosecuted such cases.

When Smith called New Bedford on Sunday afternoon, he reached Dinis' mother with whom the bachelor district attorney lived. Mrs. Dinis was praying for Rose Kennedy, she said. "That poor woman; my heart goes out to her. She's been through so much." However, Mrs. Dinis found the silence from the Kennedy compound about the accident puzzling. "Why don't they just come out and tell the truth?"

To Smith, Mrs. Dinis confided the results of a blood-alcohol test telephoned to her son by state police chemists in Boston. The results showed Mary Jo Kopechne had been "drunk" at the time of her death.

The report escalated Smith's concern about the Senator's possible liability in the case. He said, later, "It was common knowledge that Teddy Kennedy had suffered a bad depression over what had happened to Bobby; everybody was worried about his mental health." It was also common knowledge that Ted Kennedy was drinking more than it was wise for him to do on public occasions.

Smith had worked himself into such a state of anxiety by the time Dinis called him back, he launched a furious defense of Ted Kennedy's delay in reporting the accident even before the district attorney could say anything. "Don't forget the guy got hit on the head. He's got a bad back, so he was in some pain. If he laid low for a while and said, 'My God, *again*!'—meaning another disaster, put yourself in his place." Everyone in the United States had been affected by the deaths of John and Robert Kennedy, Smith said. "How would it be if they were both your brothers? And having your father upstairs not right. I just think the guy's been through so much."

"I feel sorry for him," Dinis said. He dismissed newspaper accounts beginning to question gaps in the Senator's report of the accident. "What's all this business about a conflicting statement? That's nothing! Never mind the press. Never mind being President. Let's save him."

Dinis outlined what would happen in the case: A complaint by Edgartown police would be issued on leaving the scene, and a trial scheduled at Kennedy's convenience. The registry inspector handling the case would file a report. More than likely the registry would lift Ted's license for six months. Dinis said, "It's a local matter anyway, a motor vehicles case."

Dinis didn't sound entirely convinced of that himself. He had more on his mind than expressing sympathy to a Kennedy partisan on his staff.

"You get a hold of Ted Kennedy," Dinis said. "You tell him I'm not going to prosecute him. I want to stay out of it."

Dinis had a message he wished Smith to deliver, "From me through you to Ted, and nobody else!" he said. "I won't touch this case unless Ted wants me to."

Chapter 18

SMITH HAD A LIST OF TELEPHONE NUMBERS FOR THE COMPOUND.
He dialed Ted Kennedy's house in Hyannis Port. He said, "It's Jimmy Smith of Falmouth, a personal friend. I'm also assistant district attorney. I have something important to tell the Senator."

Smith was told Ted Kennedy was "not available."

"I impress upon you the importance of this call," Smith said. "It's urgent that I talk to Senator Kennedy."

"He's not available," a male voice insisted, identifying himself as "a member of the staff."

Smith's temper flashed, "Do you have a *name*?"

The telephone was abruptly clicked off.

Smith was outraged. "It was a real bangdown. I thought, 'To hell with *them*!' I never kissed a politician's ass in my life."

Smith thought it over. "In my heart, I wanted to help Ted Kennedy. And if Eddie Dinis thought enough of me to ask that I deliver an important message, I wanted to make sure I did."

Smith then called Kenneth O'Donnell telling him of his conversation with Dinis. Dinis was "understanding and concerned," his whole reaction to the accident was sympathetic, not hostile. Dinis was not out to hurt Ted Kennedy; but as district attorney he had an official duty to perform. He wanted the Senator to know no "dirty politics" was going to be involved—because of the doubts there might be about him on account of his reputation for being a capricious wild man. If the fear of prosecution could be relieved in the minds of people at the compound giving the Senator advice, it could change how the situation was being handled. Smith said, "Dinis just wants Teddy Kennedy to know he has nothing to fear from him, that's all."

"Tell him," O'Donnell said cryptically.

"I just got off the phone. They won't let me talk to him," Smith said. "I can't get through to the guy."

"Stay here," O'Donnell ordered. "I'll get back to you."

But Smith didn't hear from O'Donnell. Instead, he got a call from Ben Smith, John Kennedy's former Harvard roommate. Named to fill the Senate seat vacated by Kennedy's election as President, Smith had relinquished the office in favor of Ted Kennedy s candidacy. ("Ben's for the family," Ted said at the time.)

Long active in Kennedy campaigns, Ben Smith said, "Let's do all we can to help Teddy, never mind Kenneth's attitude. He's waiting to be called. He's not volunteering."

Jimmy Smith didn't have to be told O'Donnell had been too proud to call the compound and asked Ben Smith to do it. And Ben Smith hadn't been able to get through either.

Dinis wanted his message delivered personally, didn't he? Ben Smith suggested, "Why don't you go over there?"

"How can I drive to Hyannis Port?" Smith protested. "The eyes of the world are trained on the place. I'm assistant district attorney. How would that look?"

Ben Smith said, "You could park up by the golf club and walk over that way ... "

"Jesus, Ben! Can you just see me climbing the wall with ten guys taking my picture?"

Ben Smith agreed that wasn't such a good idea.

Neither Kenneth O'Donnell nor Ben Smith were going to clear the barriers keeping outsiders at bay, Smith realized. The people he had contacted were a different faction, "The nuts-and-bolts campaign guys—the workers. Never mind the glamor stuff, like the star volunteers" assembling at Hyannis Port offering advice, Smith said. "It was like the jealousy of the court, like the guys that protect the potentate. Nobody else was going to get a chance to help. You couldn't get through."

Smith had one more "High Irish" connection to the Kennedy political apparatus left. A former marine captain who'd won the Silver Star, John Nolan had given Smith his "marching orders" when he ran the scheduling for Jack Kennedy in 1960. Nolan held the same position for Robert Kennedy's presidential campaign.

Nolan was out sailing when Smith called him in Maryland. Smith made no mention of the Dinis message when Nolan called him back. "John was such a straight arrow, I was in awe of him. I would never want to put myself in a position where I was conveying any impropriety to him," Smith said. "I wasn't talking about a 'fix' or anything like that. It was a situation where I wanted to be true to my job, and help Teddy Kennedy, too."

Smith had to talk to them over at the compound. How could he get through to these people? He knew Edgartown like the back of his hand; he knew all the people involved, he said. "I'm in a position where I can help with this thing."

Nolan was reluctant to jump in. He thought Ken O'Donnell could handle it.

"Kenneth's not in it," Smith said. "They're ignoring him. I don't think they know what they're doing over there—that's why I called you. Somebody better talk to them. Somebody's got to alert them that it's way off-track." The moon landing was taking a lot of attention away from the accident, "But that isn't going to save him."

Smith had despaired of penetrating the compound when he received a call from Burke Marshall. Smith recognized, "They had some kind of a brain trust going on over there and they needed local information. Who were they going to call? They called me."

Marshall asked Smith to recommend a lawyer in Edgartown to represent Ted Kennedy.

Smith ran down the list of attorneys on Martha's Vineyard. He recommended Dick McCarron. Smith had gone to law school with him. While it was always a good idea to have a local lawyer defend a case on his home ground, Smith said, "Why go to trial?" The Senator was only going to be charged with leaving the scene after causing personal injury—"That's no big deal. The insurance should cover any civil liability." There were many options available. "Why don't you plead him?" Smith said. "Why don't you plead *nolo*?"

"How do you plead *nolo*?" Marshall said.

Smith was astonished. "Maybe it was just a quick thing on his part, but that's what he said, 'How do you plead *nolo*?'" (*Nolo contendere*, "I am unwilling to contend," or "no contest" was a common plea in Massachusetts courtrooms.) The advantage of the plea in a motor vehicles case was, "You might not lose your license if there isn't a guilty finding," Smith said. Clearly, Marshall had no idea how to defend the case. Smith outlined the applicable motor vehicles statutes. Arena had blown any driving to endanger or involuntary manslaughter charges by saying there was no evidence of negligence in the accident. "You can't very well contradict the police officer in charge of the case."

Smith had tried to call Ted Kennedy personally, but hadn't been able to get through with a message from District Attorney Edmund Dinis, he said.

Marshall cut him off. They would be "in touch" as soon as they reached a lawyer. They weren't going to deal directly with the district attorney's office.

Smith was stung. This message was coming through loud and clear: "They didn't trust Dinis—not Teddy Kennedy, but the people around him." Advisors at the compound were only adding layers between themselves and the situation—a serious miscalculation, in Smith's opinion. "The case was being handled by people who knew nothing about Massachusetts law or the local personalities involved. You didn't go over everybody's head on a thing like this. You had to deal with the case on the level it was on. Dinis had a job to do. He was the guy you dealt with. You don't ignore him."

The line-up of big names reported at the compound giving advice, made it look like a gang-up of special privilege. "Inviting all those people to advise on a motor vehicle accident case made it look like Teddy Kennedy was in more serious trouble than he was," Smith said, later. The conferences at the compound were distorting the whole weight of the case. This was nothing that needed to be "handled." Just a straightforward explanation of the accident was all that was needed.

Smith didn't know which attorney would be chosen to represent Ted Kennedy in Edgartown. He hoped his recommendation to retain Dick McCarron would be followed. McCarron was a solid bread-and-butter lawyer, knowledgeable in the local way of doing things. Maybe he'd be able to talk some sense into the counsellors at the compound.

The summons did come in a call to McCarron from Ed Hanify around 8 o'clock on Sunday night. McCarron knew Hanify by reputation. If the Supreme Court ever wanted to hear an important issue of law, McCarron said, "Ed Hanify is the kind of lawyer they would pick to argue it." For Hanify to be in charge of defending Ted Kennedy in an automobile accident case was high-powered legal artillery.

Slight and soft-spoken, McCarron referred to himself as "a Boston-Irish lawyer." He had moved to Edgartown in 1966. He agreed to represent Ted Kennedy on the charge of leaving the scene of an accident.

McCarron went to work immediately drawing up a petition for a hearing on the complaint application Arena was going to file the next morning in district court. A standard maneuver to discover what evidence police had about the accident, the petition gained time to prepare a case should the Senator seek to defend the charge. Without a hearing, Kennedy could be arraigned within a few days.

McCarron called Arena to let him know he was representing Ted Kennedy. McCarron knew and liked the police chief. They saw each other socially, he said. "Our kids played together."

Arena was delighted a local lawyer had been retained. "At least now, I've got somebody I can talk to," he said. Reporters were driving him nuts about the party at Chappaquiddick which had preceded the accident. "I'm under terrific pressure from these press guys to do something about the party. That's all everybody's on my back about, that goddamned party," Arena complained. "Jesus, Dick! I ought to be able to get statements from some of these people. I ought to be able to talk to somebody who was there."

McCarron wasn't sure what he could do, having just taken the case. But he would try to see if he could line up somebody for Arena to talk to.

Arena made the same request of George Killen. "I asked him if he could do me a favor and send somebody over to the compound to get statements from some of these people." Arena wanted Killen to report, "Any facts he might be able to pick up from Cape Cod people who had attended the party."

Arena was in a bind. "Here I was, chief of a 5-man department, all guys who grew up on the island. They were supplemented by Rent-a-Cops you pinned a badge on and told to go out and be a policeman for the summer. I'm not belittling them; but I didn't have any sophisticated people. What am I going to do? Send one of my guys over to Hyannis Port? The poor soul would get stuck at the gate. He wouldn't know where to go."

Arena was soliciting Killen's help as a fellow former state police officer. "When you were a member of the alumni—as we liked to think of it—you could call on these people to do things for you."

Arena wasn't sure what Killen was going to do, he said. "My impression was, George was going to look into it."

Arena settled back to watch a momentous television event: Neil Armstrong and Edwin Aldrin, Jr., open the hatch of their depressurized landing vehicle, climb down nine rungs of a ladder to set foot on the moon and pronounce, "One small step for man. One giant leap for Mankind."

Watching the epochal event with Arena was writer Brock Brower. The *Life* article on Ted Kennedy which he had recently finished writing had been bumped by the Apollo mission. Brower had then flown back to Martha's Vineyard to recast his piece in the light of the accident at Chappaquiddick, the result of pressures to run for President in 1972 which had "helped push him to folly" at Dike Bridge.

But Arena's attention wasn't fixed on the moon walk. He was preoccupied by Senator Kennedy's failure to report the accident for some ten hours. He told Brower, "Why didn't he call me? That's what I still can't understand. I mean, I couldn't have fixed it for him or anything like that, but it would have been so much better. For him. This way…I just don't understand. Why didn't he call?"

Chapter 19

ARENA GOT TO THE POLICE STATION EARLY MONDAY MORNING TO write his accident report.[1*] In it, he wrote that a car had been operated "at an unknown rate of speed," and been "unable to stop upon entering Dike bridge." The accident had occurred "between twelve midnight and 1 A.M.," he said. ("I was"—Arena would confide later—"leaning more in 'Huck' Look's direction as to the time, than I was Senator Kennedy's.")

Inspector George Kennedy, by contrast, put the time of the accident at "about 11:20 P.M." in a report he filed with the Registry of Motor Vehicles on Monday morning. Preliminary investigation revealed, "Operator lost control of car and was at fault in the accident."

The report was immediately suppressed by Registry officials. "No decision" could be made about releasing it to the public, a spokesman said, because Registrar Richard McLaughlin was at "summer camp" with the Air National Guard.

---

1   * See Appendix 1.

The Registry also received the Findings of the Medical Examiner regarding an accident which had occurred "at midnight." But Dr. Mills couldn't document his conclusion that Mary Jo Kopechne's death had occurred "six hours or more" from the time of his examination. He hadn't taken the body's temperature nor attended to other routine procedures recommended by the *Handbook for Medical Examiners,* such as the removal of ocular fluid to test potassium content in order for a reasonable time of death estimate to be made. Without an autopsy, it was not possible to do more than guess the time Mary Jo died, Mills said. "I'm no pathologist."

Hounded by reporters for the results of a state police lab test of Mary Jo Kopechne's blood alcohol content, Mills complained to District Attorney Edmund Dinis on Monday morning, that as a physician, he was used to keeping a patient's affairs secret. Mills found it repugnant to release the figure.

"Keep it to yourself for a while and let's see what happens," Dinis said, suggesting Mills stay in close touch on the case. What Mills had found was "a very moderate, very slight level of alcohol" in Mary Jo Kopechne's blood, "The kind of thing anyone would have with a couple of drinks before dinner and maybe a highball afterwards." Mills refused to reveal the test figure.

Pressed by reporters about the lack of an autopsy, Mills said he had not done one because, "It was an open-and-shut thing, a clear case of death by drowning. There were no bruises, no marks, no kinds of injuries. No nothing."

In 15 years as associate medical examiner, Mills had handled six cases of accidental drowning. In none of them, he said, had an autopsy been performed.

Arena left for the regular session of Edgartown district court at 10 A.M. A crowd of photographers, reporters and interested spectators followed him to the police station where he obtained a complaint application then back to the courthouse. It was a scene "worthy of Cecil B. DeMille," the *Vineyard Gazette* observed, mocking the occasion as "The Great Event."

Under television lights, Arena presented court clerk Tommy Teller with papers seeking authorization to issue a complaint against Senator Kennedy. Arena was advised the Senator's request for a hearing had been filed by Dick McCarron at 8:30 A.M.

Teller scheduled the hearing for Monday, July 28, at which time he would hear evidence to determine whether police had "probable cause" to prosecute Kennedy on the charge. The hearing was no different from the four or five misdemeanor cases he conducted every week. Teller had two choices: Deny Arena's application, or issue the complaint and set a trial date.

Arena emerged from the courthouse to confront two dozen reporters for an impromptu press conference on the courthouse steps. That he was seeking to prosecute Senator Kennedy had brought him considerable criticism, Arena said. "Some people feel I've gone too far. Others think I haven't gone far enough. The emotions surrounding this case have resulted in a personal situation where I'm damned if I do and damned if I don't.'"

Arena had received many telephone calls and telegrams urging him not to yield to "political pressures" to drop charges in the case, he said. "There has not been one single iota of pressure from the Kennedy family or anyone else. With any man of stature, in a case like this, the pressure is on the police department. But to me, this is a case of leaving the scene of an accident, period. I'm treating it like any other police case."

Arena was focusing his prosecution on the time-lag in reporting the accident. "I may very well be tampering with my own case, but the Senator's whereabouts will be his defense. He's going to have to prove where he was between 1 A.M. and 10 A.M." Arena wanted to look more closely at the circumstances surrounding a party Senator Kennedy and

Mary Jo Kopechne had attended prior to the accident. "There's been a lost of hearsay and a lot of talk. As a result, I have requested the assistance of Lieutenant George Killen of the district attorney's office to talk to Joseph Gargan who rented the house at which the party was held, in order to ascertain if the Senator was there." Arena wanted Killen to find out whether and how much the Senator had been drinking. Arena emphasized, he had "no evidence" the Senator had been intoxicated at the time of the accident. Many questions remained unanswered. Who had driven Kennedy from the party the second time? How had the Senator returned to Edgartown after the ferry made its last run? And did his friends at the party know about the accident and Mary Jo Kopechne's death before they were reported to the police?

Arena disclosed a witness had seen a car similar to the one Senator Kennedy was driving near the accident scene at 12:45 A.M. and that the car "looked lost." Arena declined to identify the witness, but he was no match for reporters covering the same ground with the breadth of investigative resourcefulness his small department could not equal. Almost immediately, accounts identified Deputy Sheriff Look as having seen a car whose driver appeared "confused" at an intersection on Chappaquiddick.

But Look's story was being challenged by Arthur Egan of *The Manchester Union-Leader.* The conservative New Hampshire newspaper, unsympathetic to the Kennedy family, called on Monday morning, July 21, 1969, for Senator Kennedy to resign because of an accident in which "a married man was driving a young secretary around the countryside at midnight." In that front-page editorial, Publisher William Loeb demanded to know: "Had you been drinking and was that the reason why you drove off the road into the pond?" How much of a "daze" could Kennedy have been in, to be able to find his way back to the cottage, but not think about calling police "to see if the girl's life could still be saved," Loeb charged. "Senator, do you really think you are really fit to sit in the United States senate? Don't you think you ought to resign immediately?"

County Prosecutor Walter Steele had been puzzled by the discrepancy of the two accounts. At first, he believed Look's story to be accurate. Steele now "accepted" Kennedy's accident time. Investigation had "completely discredited anything Look has said," Steele told reporters Monday afternoon. In his opinion, Look was just "seeking a little publicity on a big story."

(Angered by Steele's remarks, Look replied, "I know what I saw. I saw that car and saw that 'L' and two digits. My memory's too short to lie.")

Arena's request to the district attorney's office for assistance was to make plain that the investigation of the case had been pursued as far as possible by local authorities, Steele said. Although Arena said his investigation was over, it was, in fact, just beginning. The chief would say later: "Once Kennedy applied for a hearing, I thought: 'We better get our fannies going and talk to people.' There hadn't been much investigating up to that point."

Arena's announcement that the district attorney's office had entered the "Kennedy accident case" brought reporters to Edmund Dinis' second floor law offices and the two-room district attorney's suite at Bristol County superior courthouse in New Bedford, 30 air miles across Buzzard's Bay from Edgartown (or two-and-a-half hours distant by car and ferry).

Unprepared for the assault, Dinis was, nevertheless, assured and poised meeting the press. Remarkably handsome, there was about him the florid and Latin good looks of an opera singer, with temperament and sonorous baritone to match.

Arena's request was the first time Edgartown police had asked his office for help in an investigation, Dinis explained. "Tremendous pressure has built up—not from the Kennedy family but from public opinion. Chief Arena felt he could handle this but then, because of these pressures and the extreme interest both locally and nationally, he asked that we enter to help him." Dinis described Arena as "an extremely capable police officer."

Dinis used the occasion to defend himself from criticism beginning to surface about his lack of activity in the case. "Some members of the press get irritable because they believe all I have to do is wave a magic wand and everyone concerned with this incident will talk. But those close to it are extremely reluctant to talk," Dinis said, a veiled reference to the impenetrable silence surrounding the Kennedy compound. The investigation would take some time, "But I assure you, it will be thorough and will produce all facts surrounding this unfortunate incident."

So clear and unequivocal an assurance that the district attorney's office had entered the case had hardly a chance to draw reaction before Dinis retracted it. He denied his office had decided what, if any, action to take in the Kennedy accident. "Until we have more information from law enforcement officers," Dinis said, "We can make no decision."

Killen hit the ceiling when Dinis reported Arena's courthouse remarks. Arena had asked him as a personal favor to talk to Gargan, and maybe some other people on Cape Cod who might have attended the party at Chappaquiddick. Killen hadn't committed the district attorney's office to an investigation. He had no intention of talking to anybody. "It's not our case; we don't have to get involved," Killen told Dinis. If all Arena was prepared to go after was a misdemeanor traffic charge, "He doesn't need our help. All he's got is an automobile accident without conviction. Let him get a complaint from the district court." Bernie Flynn was unhappy with Killen's tactics. "George was telling Arena, 'Yeah, yeah … ' but he wasn't going to do anything. That's why I felt uncomfortable. Because we'd been over there, but we're not really investigating. It's like window-dressing to protect the office." Killen was leaving Arena to flounder ineffectually on an investigation that was beyond his capacity to deal with. "I think he had something to do with public relations during the crime commission, like a publicity man for the state police, giving out stories," Flynn said. "I liked the guy, but he's no detective." Flynn also observed a certain ambivalence on the part of the police chief about surrendering the case to the D.A.'s office. "Positively not! He liked it. He was enjoying all the attention."

But Killen was keeping his foot on the brake regarding involvement of the district attorney's office, Flynn noticed. "George was on the phone with Dinis three, four times a day. It was strictly hands-off."

Dinis was also on the phone to Jimmy Smith.

"Did you deliver the message?" Dinis asked.

Smith said he hadn't.

"Okay," Dinis said.

Smith confided to Killen the message Dinis had wanted delivered to Ted Kennedy as an indication Dinis was sincere in not wanting anything to do with the case.

Kennedy's political career depended on more facts about the accident coming out, Killen said. The compound was swarming with advisers and speechwriters. Something was bound to break soon. Ted Kennedy would issue a statement to clear up all the questions about the accident, Killen said. "Let *him* explain it; and let us stay the hell out of the case."

That was exactly what Smith thought should be done, and the sooner the better, he told Paul Kirk. The silence from the compound was confounding. The longer it went on, the more sinister the situation looked. It was a serious mistake to stall for time, Smith said. "What are they doing over there? What's holding them up?"

Kirk didn't know what was going on. Kenneth O'Donnell had yet to be called.

Smith thought Ted Kennedy should hold a press conference and open himself up to questions—*that* was the Kennedy style of confrontation politics, not hiding behind a wall of advisers.

"What did they think he could do? Leave a statement and just walk away?" Smith said. "They've got to move on this thing before it snow-balls."

Dinis was waiting for some kind of signal to come through about his hands-off position on the case. Dinis was loath to do anything for now, but that could change. The press was building up a huge beef against the district attorney's office for inaction. If something didn't come out of the compound soon, the press was going to blow the lid off the case. Then Dinis would have to do something. Smith knew one thing about the district attorney: "If he's attacked, Eddie always reacts."

Smith had been waiting for immediate clarification of one critical point he expected Ted Kennedy would be anxious to clear up about the accident: What he was doing on Dike Road, travelling in the opposite direction from the ferry landing.

No aspect of Kennedy's police report was under more fire than his purported "wrong turn." Even Kennedy loyalists searching for innocent, understandable reasons Kennedy might have made the detour, conceded, "It could not have been a mistake. Nobody in condition to drive a car could confuse a dirt road with a macadam one." Because he had not explained this diversion, "The worst possible construction is being put on his lack of frankness here, which was inevitable."

Smith's main concern was, "Everybody's thinking, 'Why is he going down that way for?' And there was a logical explanation. All he had to say was, 'I *intended* to be on a dirt road. Because it was going to bring me to the ferry.'" That's all Smith wanted to get across to Joe Gargan when he called him. There was a second route to the ferry landing on Chappaquiddick that the Senator could use to explain his "wrong turn."

Smith had grown up in Edgartown. He was familiar with Chappa-quiddick. "Don't forget the geographical location of that cottage. Cars drive up facing the front of the house; the parking is perpendicular to the road. If you come out in the pitch black and you aren't familiar with the area and pull away from the cottage and take a left on the hard road, then a right on a dirt road, you'll go down to the bridge," Smith told Gargan. "But if you back out and take a right from the cottage, go down to the end of the macadam, then take a right on a dirt road—that dirt road brings you to the ferry landing. That would explain why Teddy Kennedy made a right turn off a paved road. It's the same configuration, only he turned wrong at the cottage. He went out, backed up and instead of going right and right, he went left and right. It's a simple mistake to make."

Gargan listened politely to Smith's advisory. He could give no assurances he'd be able to deliver the information, or the "Dinis message" Smith asked to be passed along to the councils at the compound.

The "wrong turn" was also bothering the 15 to 20 advisers already assembled at the compound. The Senator was sticking to his police statement that he had been heading for the ferry at the time of the accident.

Others at the compound were equally uncomfortable with other portions of the Senator's story, his reluctance to disclose more details about the accident or release information to an increasingly restless press. "Advisers saw what the dangers were in remaining silent and grasped what needed to be done," biographer Burton Hersh reported later. "But nobody was prepared to act without permission from Kennedy and risk his own reputation on the success of the consequences."

Kennedy put off any decision at all. "I didn't want to set up any kind of discussion with the funeral coming up, the grief of the family," he said.

Dr. Watt observed the Senator's condition was unchanged when he examined him on Monday afternoon. Kennedy continued to have pain and stiffness in his neck aggravated by activity and turning his head.

Watt recommended x-rays be taken. Kennedy was driven to Cape Cod hospital by his father's nurse, John Ryan. He underwent a standard four-position series and exposure of the first to seventh vertebrae of the cervical spine. Radiologist W. E. Benjamin found no evidence of fracture or depression. "The marked straightening of the spine in the lateral projection" indicated a rather marked muscle spasm.

Watt had Kennedy fitted with an orthopedic collar and contacted Dr. Milton Brougham, chief of neurosurgery at Cape Cod hospital for a consultation.

Kennedy complained of a stiff neck, lower back pain and a generalized headache, but was alert, oriented, his speech and vision normal when Brougham examined him.

In describing the accident to the doctor, Kennedy remembered driving down a road, and had "some recollection" of the car striking a beam along the side of the bridge. But he remembered nothing of any impact against water or the car turning over, a gap in his memory "of indeterminable length but presumably brief," Brougham noted. "His next recollection is of being in the front seat of his car which was filling with water. He somehow escaped from the car, but does not know how he did this. He states further that he can recall making repeated efforts to get back to the car by diving. Subsequent events are recalled in a somewhat fragmentary fashion, with an impaired recall of their exact time relationships."

Brougham diagnosed cervical concussion, contusion and abrasion of the scalp and acute cervical strain. He recommended an electroencephalogram.

Kennedy was in a tense and waking state during the test, which revealed "no abnormalities" to Dr. Robert Feldman of the Boston Neurological Laboratory. That finding appeared to call into question the symptoms of memory loss, impairment of judgment and confused behavior which Dr. Watt had reported. Any neurological symptoms or alternations of awareness, levels of consciousness or memory would show up on an EEG, according to medical authorities consulted by the *Boston Globe*. "It is safe to be dubious about the contention that there was a protracted period when Kennedy was alternately lucid and then terribly confused…because this behavior would almost certainly show up if the EEG had been properly administered and interpreted."

———

Dr. Watt recommended the Senator not attend Mary Jo Kopechne's funeral scheduled for the next day. Kennedy "hoped to go," barring any medical reason, Press Secretary Dick Drayne announced in Washington. "He's still under a doctor's care, and the doctor's opinion would have to be considered."

The Senator intended to give no further explanation of the accident, Drayne said. "As of this moment there are no specific plans for either a statement or a news conference."

Gargan recalled "a lot of different discussions and arrangements about the funeral." There was no question Gargan was going. He left Hyannis Port on Monday afternoon for Boston and a preflight meeting with his lawyer, Joe Donahue, at Logan Airport.

Gargan related the events of the accident at Chappaquiddick to Donahue, he said. "I told him the whole story, absolutely everything," including Ted's resistance to reporting the accident and his failure to do so in the expectation Gargan would come around to the scheme he'd proposed to avoid involvement.

Donahue wasn't impressed with the seriousness of the case. "He kind of brushed it off as not as exciteable as some people were making it out to be," Gargan said. "His reaction was that I had very little liability to be concerned about." Donahue said he would be available any time Gargan wanted to discuss the case. In his eighties and in semi-retirement, Donahue suggested Gargan rely on his son, Joe, Jr., a lawyer in the family law firm who had accompanied his father to the meeting. He told Gargan, "Dad is getting older now; and this isn't something he should get involved with."

But recapitulating the events of the accident had renewed the outrage Gargan had suffered at the Chappaquiddick landing when the Senator bolted from the car with a promise to report the accident. To Gargan, Teddy's attempt to conceal the accident, his child-like dread of facing the consequences of Mary Jo Kopechne's death, had betrayed an astonishing weakness of character.

On the other hand, Gargan had done nothing to be ashamed of. He'd gotten into the water, as treacherous as that effort had been and as hopeless as he knew the situation to be. He hadn't sat on his ass on the bridge feeling sorry for himself and refused to take responsibility for what he'd done. And he did not attempt to conceal the accident from authorities, then invoke lawyer-client privilege to prevent anybody from finding out.

The renewal of a Lowell connection revived in Gargan a renascent pride of place and family. "*Gargans* don't shit in their own bed," he said. "And that guy drove a car off a bridge and put everybody in the soup."

Chapter 20

THE JOURNEY TO WILKES-BARRE WAS A SAD OCCASION FOR Gargan, who was particularly anxious to pay his respects to Mary Jo's parents. Gargan introduced himself to the couple, "and I described what had happened. And I indicated in some way that I had done everything possible to save Mary Jo, saying that I was sorry I couldn't do more. But in the sadness of the moment, I don't think they understood much of what I said, that I had been at Chappaquiddick, or that I was the person at whose house Mary Jo had visited the year before. I understood that, of course. I'd lost a lot of my own family myself. They were terribly shocked by this whole thing; and I don't think they knew who I was."

Gargan exchanged greetings with the Boiler Room girls. "I didn't have a discussion with them about the accident or anything else." Gargan was present "strictly as a mourner." He was not advancing the funeral in anticipation of the Senator's arrival. That responsibility had fallen to Dun Gifford.

Gifford had returned to Wilkes-Barre on Monday afternoon. Reporters spotted him and several Boiler Room girls having a drink in the bar of the Holiday Inn. At their approach, the group got up and walked into a coffee shop. It was difficult to remain silent about the accident beyond the cloister of Hyannis Port and, at the same time, maintain requisite good relations with the press.

Gifford passed word to reporters that a doctor recommended against the Senator coming to the funeral. Asked if that meant Kennedy wasn't planning to attend, Gifford backed off. Trying to convey "how desperately anxious" the Senator was to pay his respects, Gifford quoted a Kennedy family friend who said, "He'd come if he were unconscious."

To his assignment to prepare the Kopechnes for Kennedy's appearance at the funeral and protect them as well as he could from reporters, Gifford brought a subtlety of purpose and consideration which won praise from Joseph Kopechne. "Dun Gifford was very kind and generous, he helped us a lot. He let us answer our phone. He never made any suggestions one way or another as to how we should handle ourselves. You have to respect somebody like that, because he was a Kennedy man ... "

But Gifford could render only moral support. He had nothing to tell the Kopechnes about the accident which had killed their daughter. Messages of condolence were pouring into the Kielty funeral home from all over the country. Kopechne revealed, "The first one we got was a newspaper clipping of Senator Kennedy. The sender had drawn a noose around his neck and written: 'This is what should happen to him.' These letters, they're all directed at Kennedy, but they're hurting us."

Senator Kennedy had telephoned again on Monday afternoon. "I still couldn't understand him. I could see he was trying to tell us about the accident, but he was still so broken up he couldn't talk." Kopechne didn't think the Senator would attend the funeral, "Because he was in such bad condition, mentally."

But the Senator had other plans. Senator Kennedy departed from Barnstable county airport before 7 A.M. on Tuesday morning on the private DC-3 owned by the Great Lakes Carbon Corporation, an enterprise of Ethel Kennedy's family. He wore a dark blue suit. A black tie was loosely knotted about a dress shirt opened to accommodate a cervical collar. On board was his wife, Joan, Congressmen John Tunney of California and John Culver of Iowa; Administrative Aide David Burke; and Massachusetts Democratic Committee Chairman David Harrison.

Harrison announced to a corps of reporters waiting at Scranton/Wilkes-Barre airport that Senator Kennedy expected to issue a statement "within the next few days" to explain what he had done during more than nine hours following the automobile accident in which Mary Jo Kopechne was killed.

The Kennedy party was driven in two cars to Plymouth, a town of 10,000 in the center of Pennsylvania's coal-mining region. Kennedy was met at the rectory of St. Vincent's Roman Catholic Church by Monsignor William Burchill and his curate. A parish secretary observed the Senator to be "uncomfortable" because of the neck brace he was wearing. "It was very difficult for him to even talk and walk," she said. "He looks like he's had a bad time."

The Senator's appearance had turned a somber, ceremonial occasion into a political celebration. An excited, curious crowd was spilling out into the street outside the elaborate, red brick church by the time the Kopechnes arrived in a car that stopped behind the funeral home's hearse. "They wanted to see the Kennedys. I understood that," Joseph Kopechne commented. "Nothing that big has happened around here since 34 settlers were killed by Indians. And that was before the Revolutionary War."

The TV crews, and the burst of flashbulbs, frightened Gwen Kopechne. "I'd seen so many people and their sadness on television," she said, later. "I didn't want to see myself that way." A small, dark-haired woman, Mrs. Kopechne was wearing sunglasses and a black linen dress. She was near collapse when Dun Gifford assisted her from the car.

The Kopechnes met Senator Kennedy in the rectory's shade-drawn front parlor. The priests withdrew after introductions were made. The conversation was "private," Gifford said. The accident was not discussed.

"Kennedy was talking and I still couldn't understand a word he said, he was so emotional," Joseph Kopechne said. "I think he really sacrificed a lot coming to the funeral, the way he was feeling."

The funeral party entered a side door of the church leading to the sacristy. Kennedy's appearance provoked an excited murmur of recognition from more than 500 spectators filling the church, most of them women.

Mrs. Kopechne wept inconsolably during a low requiem mass celebrated in an oppressive heat that permeated the large, ornately decorated church. Gargan stood at the back, apart from the fourth row pew the Kennedy party occupied. The Senator was a mask of anguish when he walked past the bronze casket to receive communion. The Kopechnes followed the casket out of the front door of the church. The Senator was delayed by women reaching out to touch him. He nodded to well-wishers, but said nothing. He left by a door near the altar.

Shouts of: "There he is!" greeted Kennedy's appearance at the front of the church. Photographers held cameras over their heads to take pictures. Above the tumult, the voice of Mayor Walter Burns could be heard, shouting: "Okay, you spectators, move back! Move back!"

Kennedy was visibly distressed by the implacable curiosity of the crowd. His wife attempted to smile at those pushing and jostling for a closer look at the famous couple. Kennedy said to her, "Let's get to the car."

Police locked arms to hold back the throng as Kennedy was guided to a white sedan. It took 10 minutes for a 25-car cortege to form. State police had to clear a lane on the winding, mountain road leading to the parish cemetery in Larksville, made impassable by cars parked on both sides to catch a glimpse of the Kennedy party as it went by. Spectators gathered on lawns and front porches along the route, some with cameras. A spattering of applause occasionally punctuated the procession, as if it were a parade.

The Kopechnes sat on folding chairs beneath a canopy at the graveside. Kennedy stood in the rear, staring distractedly at the surrounding green mountains scarred by slag heaps. The funeral over, he attended a post-funeral buffet.

"We had a great time at lunch," Kopechne recalled. "It was like one big family. I embarrassed him, I think. I called my nephew over. And I said to Kennedy, 'Here's a good Democrat.' The Senator took it beautifully. He laughed. He said to me, 'You're really something.'"

When Kopechne spoke to Ethel Kennedy, "I thought I was talking to my sister. That's the way she makes you feel. She's like that nice lady next door. She was interested in what was being done about safety in the mines. She asked all about the area."

Gwen Kopechne was "working automatically to greet people. I don't remember that I talked to anybody. I was under medication that let me forget all the things I didn't want to remember. I wasn't ever to the funeral. I don't remember any of it."

"She was in an absolute daze," Kopechne confirmed.

No additional information about the death of their daughter had been disclosed to the Kopechnes by Senator Kennedy or the Boiler Room girls. The young women had burst into tears at the funeral home on first viewing Mary Jo reposed in an open coffin and dressed in a blue peignoir. Her hands clasped a crystal rosary. A bouquet of yellow roses sent by Senator and Mrs. Kennedy stood on a pedestal, separate from other floral tributes.

The young women did not discuss the accident among themselves in view of a gathering furor of speculation about the party at

Chappaquiddick, Esther Newberg said. "We all talked at Wilkes-Barre, at Mary Jo's funeral. We said, 'Let people think whatever they want. Let our friend be buried.'"

Newberg had engaged in a brief conversation with Senator Kennedy. "He asked me how I was; I asked him how he was. He was concerned about my parents and their reaction. I was concerned about his wife."

Though out in force, the press kept a respectful distance from the Senator, at this, his first public appearance since the accident. The Senator was further insulated from reporters by a coterie of friends and aides. The funeral provided an opportunity to leak information about the accident without the formality of an official statement or attribution. This enabled Kennedy's handlers to stir a little sympathy for the Senator into the stew of controversy beginning to boil over regarding the silence maintained about the accident for four days.

Aides confided "first indications" of what had happened when Kennedy returned "dripping wet" from the accident to collapse in the back seat of a car parked in front of the cottage "where his friends had been holding a party." Kennedy was able to give them an account of the accident. He could remember thinking: "I'm drowning. This is incredible!" He had no idea how he had escaped from the submerged car. Aides refused to explain why neither the Senator nor his friends reported the accident for more than nine hours. Said to be "drawn and despondent" since his return to Hyannis Port, the Senator conferred with a half dozen friends and political advisers late Saturday night and early Sunday. Some had counselled him to remain silent about the accident. Kennedy favored a carefully worded explanation, but decided "not to make any statement in the foreseeable future about the accident, and might never make one."

Chapter 21

THE MATTER OF A STATEMENT WAS MORE AGGRESSIVELY pursued when the Senator landed at Hyannis airport around 2:15 P.M. Kennedy looked pained to be greeted by a cluster of reporters clamoring for "comment."

Kennedy turned away from the first confrontation with reporters since the accident. "This is the day of the funeral," he said. "This isn't the appropriate time. But I will make a full statement at the appropriate time."

He then walked determinedly away from trailing reporters. The most aggressive in pursuit was Liz Trotta of NBC News. "There has been some question as to what effect this will have on your political career," she said.

Kennedy whirled about in anger to confront his inquisitor. "I've just come from the funeral of a very lovely young lady. And this is not the appropriate time for such questions!" he said, indignantly. "I am not going to have any other comment to make."

Kennedy got into the front seat of a white car bearing Massachusetts license plates USS-1, his wife at the wheel, and was driven away.

Almost at once, "sources close to Kennedy" denied the Senator had any immediate plans for a statement. His remarks at the airport had been intended only to pacify the press.

Kennedy's return to Hyannis Port was preceded by the arrival of his brother-in-law, Stephen Smith. Manager of the Kennedy family fortune, and dispenser of campaign moneys, Smith was "the mysterious *eminence grise* who had always been associated with Kennedy invincibility." A backroom specialist with "the capacity to move into almost any situation with an abbreviated quick deadliness," Smith was dismayed by the scene he found in Hyannis Port. "Half the press of the world was standing outside in the street. Those guys acted like it was the 5 P.M. express. Christ! There were telephones all over the goddamn place. If this had been anybody but Edward Kennedy, we wouldn't have gotten the attention."

Smith found conditions inside the compound no better. The ongoing councils were fragmented, without focus, the Senator so self-absorbed as to be a non-participant. There were mutterings of discontent among the Senator's staff about the interference of outsiders, most of them former equerries of his brothers Jack and Bobby.

Smith took charge of what was proving to be the "prickliest crisis" in the history of the Kennedy family. Burke Marshall had put off his departure to attend a terminally ill father until Smith could take over. The elevated lawyerly arts that Marshall practiced were inapplicable on so low a rung of the legal ladder as an auto accident.

Smith conferred with Edward Hanify about the Senator's liability in the accident. "Our prime concern was whether or not the guy survived the thing; whether he rode out the still-possible charge of manslaughter," he said later.

To assist Richard McCarron to defend the traffic complaint, and whatever other charges might result from the accident, Hanify suggested former District Court Judge Robert Clark of Brockton. The preeminent motor vehicles specialist in Massachusetts, Clark had a summer house on Cape Cod.

Although the compound was already well-populated with advisers, Smith called in reinforcements of his own, principally Ted Sorenson, the rhetorician of the New Frontier. Former Defense Secretary Robert McNamara was on his way from a rented house on Martha's Vineyard, his arrival at the compound to inspire the most widely quoted jibe of the episode: "Well, Bob, you handled the Bay of Pigs and Vietnam. Now let's see what you can do with this one."

Gargan recognized who was in charge when he got back to Hyannis Port. "Steve's attitude was kind of organizing everything that was trying to help Ted, and whatever was going to happen. I never did talk to him about the accident. Directly, he did not get involved with me as to the factual details: 'What the Senator did. What I did.' He left that pretty much up to the lawyers."

If Ted Kennedy was going to tell anyone about his behavior at the landing at Chappaquiddick, and his delay in reporting the accident, that person would be Stephen Smith. Smith would have to know the whole truth to make sure Ted Kennedy was protected.

Gargan was following Hanify's orders not to disclose anything about the post-accident advice he had given Ted Kennedy. But he didn't require the muzzle of lawyer-client privilege to keep quiet. Bonds of friendship, family ties, and his real concern for the legal bind Kennedy was in were sufficient to guarantee silence. Gargan had no intention of betraying Kennedy's craven behavior at the landing to anyone. Concern that Gargan had become the focus of a new investigation undertaken by the district attorney's office grew when it was learned that Detective

Lieutenant George Killen had been asked specifically by Police Chief Arena to question Gargan about the party at Chappaquiddick.

As it happened, their concern was groundless. "I never heard from Killen or Arena," Gargan disclosed. "They never came near me."

Chapter 22

WHILE THE COMPOUND WAS HOLDING THE PRESS AT ARM'S length, Arena decided to hold twice-daily news briefings, beginning on Tuesday. It was the only way the chief could hope to get on with his investigation and also meet the rising demands of the press, Walter Steele said. "Unless we closed the police station."

By now, Chappaquiddick had burgeoned from a routine automobile case into a scandal tantalized into prominence by the inexplicable gaps in the Senator's delayed report, the baffling silence from the Kennedy compound, and an inept and barely launched police investigation.

Edgartown was suffering an invasion of reporters, photographers, major TV commentators and camera crews, the likes of which it had never seen before, local newsman Harvey Ewing observed. "Everyone was flying in media people. The number of press swelled to an incredible 450 within a couple of days—they beat the tourist mob any day. The place got to be a zoo very quickly."

The *Vineyard Gazette* added that the Kennedy accident was turning into "a story about getting the story." Never on the island had a single incident been the inspiration of so many individual investigations. "The digging for facts that began on Saturday has continued unabated since. The world, it seems, wants to know more than the fact that there was a tragic accident."

Pressure was applied mostly on Arena. "I left Boston to get away from all this commotion," he said before his first briefing. "Look at what I've got now. There are 50 million policemen saying: 'Thank God, it's not me investigating this case.'"

At 10 A.M., on Tuesday, July 22, Arena faced reporters for the first of a series of formal—and controversial—briefings, in a plain room in the Federated Church parish house normally used for church suppers and Sunday school, hastily improvised for the purpose. The room was furnished with mismatched wooden desk chairs, a locked upright piano and a framed mezzotint of Jesus Christ in the Garden at Gethsemane.

Arena presided behind a folding table. Walter Steele sat beside him to provide legal advice. If Arena was the genial host for the proceedings, full of smiles and boundless good will, Steele was physically miscast for the role of heavy. Frail and temperamental, he fairly vibrated with nerves. Intended to unravel the mysteries surrounding the death of Mary Jo Kopechne, the briefings only further clouded them, the *Boston Globe* observed. "The confusion indicated the pressure under which both Arena and Steele were working."

Steele started off the first session by contradicting Arena's Sunday statement that his investigation had ended with an application for a complaint against Senator Kennedy. Police were still working on the case. "One of the objects of the investigation is to determine if any additional charges will be placed against the Senator, and to determine whether drinking or heavy drinking" had occurred at the party Kennedy had attended prior to the accident. The Senator could face charges of driving to endanger, and driving under the influence of alcohol, "These have all been considered and have not been ruled out," Steele said. "But there is no material evidence now that the car was operated in such a manner."

Pressed to amplify such provocative suggestions, Steele declined to say specifically that an investigation was being made into drinking. "The investigation is continuing to determine whether other complaints should be sought, and the consumption of alcohol will be investigated." Since more than nine hours had elapsed from the time of the accident until it was reported, it was unlikely evidence could be mustered to sustain a charge of drunk driving. "I don't have, and probably will not have, any charges of a criminal sense," Steele said, promptly eliminating the charges he had just indicated were being considered.

Steele's reference to "other complaints," caught Arena unprepared. "That hadn't been discussed before the briefing," he said later. The most important requirement to prove drunk driving was a witness. "We need someone who saw him operating in that manner." Although Arena had not seen Senator Kennedy until nine full hours after the accident, nevertheless he told reporters he had no evidence to indicate Senator Kennedy had been intoxicated at the time of the accident. When Kennedy reported to the police station, Arena went on, "He walked steadily, he was clear of breath. I had no reason then to think he was drinking." Kennedy had undergone no sobriety tests on Saturday morning, Arena said. "It would have been a violation of his constitutional rights even to ask him to take the breathalizer test." Kennedy's crime began the moment he'd walked away from the scene. "It was strictly an accident up to that point."

To reporters at that first briefing, Arena insisted: "There's no proof of Senator Kennedy's faulty operation of the vehicle. I've got to repeat again, and say emphatically, there is no negligence involved in this accident."

"Aw, c'mon, Chief," a reporter called out. Ted Kennedy drove a car off a bridge. That was evidence of negligence, wasn't it?

"What do you mean, 'Aw, c'mon?'" Arena shot back. "What's the matter with you guys?"

Steele stepped in. Police had measured the distance of the car from the bridge and were satisfied the Senator had not been speeding at the time of the accident. Having received the evidence of the investigation, Steele was in agreement with Arena, he said. "There is not, and probably will not be, any evidence there was negligence in the operation of the automobile."

Arena's investigation was over. He would now limit himself, he said, to gathering evidence only in support of the misdemeanor charge, to make sure he had a strong enough case to secure a complaint against Senator Kennedy at next Monday's hearing. The hearing would be closed to the press. A transcript was not going to be made available to reporters, but they would be briefed on the proceedings. Steele told the reporters he felt it was "unfortunate" Arena had disclosed that Deputy Sheriff Christopher Look was scheduled to be called as a witness at the hearing. Look's testimony applied only to the "time element" of the accident, not as an indication of erratic driving by the operator of the car he'd seen at the intersection.

Steele prevented Arena from revealing whether his investigation had disclosed the Senator's whereabouts between the time of the accident and his report. "We have certain evidence on file in this case which we will prosecute in the next few days as to that problem," Steele said. "I'm asking the chief not to comment on it. It's for Kennedy to show the judge where he was."

Steele refused to comment on Kennedy's whereabouts himself. "I think it's unfair to this defendant, or any defendant, to comment." But in response to a later question, Steele absent-mindedly gave the game away. He said, "We have no evidence as to his whereabouts."

Asked if he thought Ted Kennedy had been "in shock" during the hours between the accident and the time it was reported, Arena replied, "Yes, but for how long?" Being in a state of shock was a legal excuse against the charge of leaving the scene, "But we felt, in our case, that we had evidence of some part of that morning when we believed that the state of shock was not present. That is why we went forward with the charge we did."

To determine how Kennedy had spent those hours, Arena had directed State Police Detective Lieutenant George Killen to interview the "12 or 14 people at the party"—none of whom had been questioned by police, "to establish the sequence of events before and after the accident." Arena had tried to question Ted Kennedy at the police station, "But the Senator said he wanted to talk to his lawyer first. I expected to hear from him, but I haven't heard from him yet."

Arena hadn't thought it necessary to advise Ted Kennedy of his constitutional rights before taking his statement, he said. "I just didn't think of giving him a Miranda warning—a Senator." If Kennedy's attorneys attacked the statement on that ground, "It might be thrown out."

Once again, in the presence of the reporters, Steele cautioned Arena to say no more about the matter. Failure to give the Miranda warning might be a factor in his case, Steele said. But he declined to reveal if he'd have a case to prosecute should the statement be ruled inadmissible.

Reporters at the briefing found absurd the suggestion that a U.S. Senator, in the company of a former U. S. Attorney, could deny knowing his constitutional rights and plead Miranda. [In the Miranda case, the Supreme Court held that, while police were obligated to advise suspects of their rights, "volunteered statements" were not bound by the Fifth Amendment protection against self-incrimination and were admissible in a trial. There was no requirement that a police officer stop any person from confessing to a crime.] As it was, Arena had not asked Ted Kennedy a single question about the accident.

Such inept waffling and trepidation provoked a tumultuous response from reporters. One blunt questioner asked whether Arena had been "influenced to mishandle the case."

Showing the strain of increasingly hostile questions, Arena resorted to pleading, "I've tried to cooperate with you fellows. And they're going to make a fool out of me in court, because I tried to cooperate."

But Arena recovered his good humor almost as soon as he lost it. He said, "About the only thing this case has done for me is help me to lose some weight."

Arena had lost fifteen pounds since Saturday.

————

Still smarting from the going-over he'd received at the two-hour briefing, Arena said at the police station afterward, "What bothers me is that people think I'm not doing my job. But I'm a conscientious Christian. I'll give Senator Kennedy the same shake that I would give to John Smith."

Arena was also being bombarded with letters and telegrams charging "preferential treatment" for Ted Kennedy, he said. "People can say what they want to, but we're in America where there is justice for all. Which includes U.S. Senators."

Walter Steele was less tolerant about the contemptuous treatment he had suffered at the hands of reporters at the briefing. Steele was particularly outraged about the unavailability of the partygoers for questioning by police—a sore point reporters repeatedly brought up at the briefing. Arena had granted Senator Kennedy every consideration at the police station. While the Senator was composing his accident report, the partygoers were being whisked off the island, Steele complained. "We played it straight and honest and they left us holding the bag. They were gone before we knew what had happened."

If Kennedy "sources" could plant misleading information in the press, so could Steele. Trying his hand at the technique for the first time, Steele leaked word that he expected to have statements by that weekend from the five men and five women who had attended the cookout with Senator Kennedy before the accident. The leak was attributed to "Dukes County officials close to the investigation," and said: "The state was prepared to take legal steps to compel the cooperation of the Senator's friends, if statements were not made voluntarily."

But like his tough-guy posturing at the briefing, Steele's threat had no legal force behind it. Arena confirmed, later, "There was no way we could make those witnesses talk, if they didn't want to."

But Arena's repeated pleas to Dick McCarron about the availability of partygoers for questioning had paid off. McCarron told him, "We can get Jack Crimmins for you to talk to." Arrangements were being made for a meeting with the Senator's chauffeur.

McCarron had petitioned Ed Hanify on the police chief's behalf, "To get Arena off the hook on this thing. He's got nobody to investigate the case but school-teacher specials." To McCarron's knowledge the only investigation of the accident had been conducted by the Registry of Motor Vehicles, "And they weren't that much help."

McCarron got Hanify s permission for an official guest list to be made available to the police chief, provided to him by Angelique Voutselas, Senator Kennedy's personal secretary. Four days after the accident, Arena would finally know who had attended the now-famous party at Chappaquiddick.

Chapter 23

KENNEDY'S FLIGHT FROM REPORTERS AT HYANNIS AIRPORT AND
the four days of silence about the accident had depleted press forebear-
ance. Coverage was turning sour. Editorial demands for more information escalated in volume and intensity. *Newsweek*'s cover story hit hard
at Kennedy's stubborn silence. "When the Senator's closest associates
are known to have been powerfully concerned over his indulgent drinking habits, his daredevil driving and his ever-ready eye for a pretty face,"
the accident cried out for more explanation than the Senator's "baf-
flingly-obscure" police report had provided.

Based in part on the memorandum filed by John Lindsay about an
episode of public drunkenness on a plane returning from Alaska in April,
the revelation shook the Senator's office with seismic force. It was a
signal that the Senators period of journalistic indulgence might be over.

Calling *Newsweek*'s charges "untrue," Press Secretary Dick Drayne
sought a spokesman outside his office to refute them. The best he could
do was Congressman Edward Boland of Springfield, Massachusetts. A
close political ally and protégé of Jack Kennedy campaign lieutenant

Lawrence O'Brien, Boland denied Ted Kennedy was a hard drinker, had never seen him drunk in their travels together and dismissed the girl-watching reference. But he couldn't supply the antidote to the poison of speculation about the goings-on at the party at Chappaquiddick. Only a guest could do that.

For purposes of defusing that dynamite, Kennedy's office delegated Esther Newberg as spokesman for the Boiler Room girls, none of whom had talked to reporters. "The word has actually gone out that they are not to talk to anybody," a former member of Robert Kennedy's campaign said.

An attractive, self-possessed young woman who held an administrative position with the Urban Institute in Washington, Newberg had gone to work for Robert Kennedy in 1967, joining the Boiler Room soon after he announced his candidacy for president. Newberg objected to the term 'Boiler Room girls' employed to describe the group, she said. "I am a professional; Mary Jo was a professional. We should be referred to as such."

Returning to her apartment in Arlington, Virginia, after the funeral on Tuesday evening, Newberg granted a series of interviews over the next four days. She refused to discuss anything about the accident that might be "prejudicial" to the hearing Senator Kennedy faced on Monday, "Because there will be a trial, as I'm sure you understand."

In contrast to the "noisy brawl" neighbor Foster Silva nearly called police about at 1:30 A.M., Newberg described the party as a quiet barbecue. "It was a steak party, that's the kind of party it was. There was not a lot of drinking at that party, at most one or two drinks apiece." Coals had been lighted in the front yard, "But everyone moved inside the cottage to eat, because there are these little bugs on the island." Guests had reminisced about Robert Kennedy's presidential campaign, discussed the Regatta race, "And there was talk about the weather and other things that friends talk about when they get together. It was a fun party," Newberg said.

"No one was sitting around watching the clock," or keeping particular track of who was there or who wasn't at any given time. No one had specifically missed Senator Kennedy and Mary Jo Kopechne, or noticed what time they left the party, Newberg said. "At some point, I guess we wondered where Mary Jo was and decided she had been lucky enough to make the ferry. We just assumed the Senator was exhausted and had gone back to his hotel in Edgartown. No one expected him to stay. No one was worried or concerned. I suppose if there had been a telephone in the cottage we would have called to check, but there wasn't."

Newberg was not aware that the Senator had returned to the cottage after the accident or that "someone outside asked for someone inside." Joe Gargan and Paul Markham had left the party "some time between 10:30 P.M. and 1 A.M.," but Newberg didn't know how long they were gone, what they'd been doing, or that anything was wrong. Having missed the last ferry to Edgartown, she and the others spent the night at the cottage, going to sleep around 12:30 A.M. Newberg said she had to guess at the time. Her "Mickey Mouse" watch, a topic of joking conversation at the party, wasn't working properly.

Newberg learned about the accident the next morning when she and the Lyons sisters were walking to the ferry landing, she said. "On the way, we met Joe Gargan driving back toward the cottage. He stopped and told us something terrible had happened. He told us about the accident. He said Senator Kennedy was all right, but that Mary Jo had not been found."

Gargan had telephoned her motel to say Mary Jo's body had been discovered in the accident car. She had drowned, although Senator Kennedy had tried to save her. The young women had left the island "rather quickly," Newberg said. "What else would you do?"

Mary Jo had known Ted Kennedy slightly before his brother's presidential campaign but had gotten to know him better at headquarters,

Newberg said. "Ted Kennedy's office was five doors down from the boiler room. Often he would come in along with other people like Ted Sorensen to get information."

The gathering at Chappaquiddick was the fourth Boiler Room reunion since Robert Kennedy's assassination. The first party had been given "by Mrs. Edward Kennedy at Cape Cod," the previous summer. The Senator had attended a second party in Washington in January, but failed to show up at a third party two weeks ago.

Newberg denied she had compared notes with others at the party to produce a consistent story of the accident, she said. "Nobody's trying to hide anything."

Two things were important to her: "First, Mary Jo is dead and there isn't anything we can do about it. Second, I know inside that Senator Kennedy tried to save her."

Susan Tannenbaum corroborated Newberg's version of the cookout as a decorous affair. "There was some vodka at the party, but drinking was very minimal, she said. She hadn't thought it unusual for Ted Kennedy and Mary Jo to leave the party together. The Senator often had conversations with the girls who had worked in his brother's Boiler Room. Tannenbaum assumed the Senator was driving to the ferry so Mary Jo could return to her motel. She described Mary Jo as "a serious, quiet girl. She wasn't a flippant-type person."

Tannenbaum reported for work as appointments secretary to New York Congressman Allard Lowenstein on Wednesday morning but she didn't stay very long. Looking tired and tense, she left before noon, refusing to talk to reporters.

Lowenstein's office issued a statement on her behalf: "During the weekend, I lost a dear friend, Mary Jo Kopechne. My sympathies go out to her bereaved family and to Senator Edward Kennedy and his family. I have nothing further to say."

But Tannenbaum would later complain about the intense interest in the press about the case. "You can't begin to understand what it's been like. I place a tremendous value on the right of privacy, but suddenly I'm infamous. The real meaning of what you are and what you value remains intact inside yourself; but there you are splashed all over the papers."

Tannenbaum was especially incensed about speculation of improper conduct having occurred at the party at Chappaquiddick. She said, "How would you feel if a reporter called your mother at 8 A.M. and asked whether she approved of her daughter's conduct in spending the night with a group of married men?"

Chapter 24

BUT EFFORTS TO DESTIGMATIZE THE PARTY HAD COME TOO LATE.
Speculation and rumor had erupted into such a contagion of suspicion
that even Arena was not immune. A message he found on his desk at the
police station on Tuesday night to call Judge Clark from Brockton
aroused suspicions where ordinarily there would have been none.

"I thought, 'Hey, what's this? Is somebody going to say to me: Chief,
would you mind going easy on the Kennedy accident case?'"

Judge Clark turned out to be attorney Robert G. Clark, Jr., informing Arena that he and his son had been retained to represent Ted Kennedy in association with Dick McCarron. Clark asked for a meeting with
Arena the next day, Wednesday.

Arena was wary of the idea. He didn't know what Clark wanted.
Would it be all right if Walter Steele attended the meeting, too? When
Clark agreed to meet with the prosecutor, Arena suggested Steele's camp
at Ocean Heights, several miles outside of Edgartown. Nothing clandestine was intended, Arena said. "We just wanted to be able to hold the
meeting without press coverage."

Clark arrived at Dick McCarron's law offices in a bungalow at the end of a lane off Edgartown's Main Street on Wednesday morning. A tall man, Clark had the compelling presence of a repertory actor. No ivory-tower lawyer like Burke Marshall, he was a former Brockton shoe-factory worker, with a strong record in hit-and-run and drunk-driving cases. A tough, hard-nosed advocate of exceptional competence in "dirty cases," a colleague observed, "Clark had always been a police-court kind of lawyer with occasional splashes of heavy guys with big dough that people told, 'Clark's the guy you should get. He's the best.' And he was a good lawyer in all other respects, a very common-sense guy."

Clark brought a portfolio of photographs of the accident scene, including aerial views taken by *Boston Herald Traveler* photographer Jimmy O'Callahan, and delivered to his law office courtesy of editor-publisher Harold Clancy. Invaluable as the photographs were as an aid to comprehending the facts of the accident and preparing a defense, Clark nevertheless wanted to take a look at Dike Bridge.

Clark was conspicuously well-dressed in a three-piece suit and car-rying a briefcase that virtually proclaimed his profession to the omnipres-ent reporters tracking McCarron's every move as Senator Kennedy's local attorney of record. McCarron loaned him a yellow slicker before driving to the landing to board the *On Time*.

After inspecting the bridge and retracing the route to and from the Lawrence cottage, Clark and McCarron left for a conference at the com-mand post at the Kennedy compound.

Hyannis Port was under siege. Wealthy residents were furious at the inconvenience of the roadblock at Scudder Avenue and the notoriety the Kennedy family had again inflicted upon their exclusive enclave. A mecca for tourists, the former summer White House of John Kennedy was a privately owned residence of modest white clapboards behind a high, stockade fence. To McCarron, the place was redolent of memories of John Kennedy greeting well-wishers at a rose-strewn fence during the

1960 summer of his presidential candidacy. The stockade had been added for security after his election to the White House.

McCarron found a sense of embattlement inside, aides bustling about opening doors and running errands. He was impressed by the number and distinction of those brought together to defend a motor vehicles complaint in the district court.

In command of the conference of lawyers in a formal dining room was Stephen Smith. A second conference was taking place upstairs attended by Robert McNamara, Ted Sorensen, Milton Gwirtzman, a Washington attorney who had written speeches for Ted Kennedy, and members of the Senator's staff. Sorensen was moving from the upstairs conference to the dining room gathering material, it was apparent, for a statement of some kind.

Edward Hanify made it clear, "If I have anything to say about it, he'll never make that speech."

The parallel meetings measured the schism that had developed between Kennedy's attorneys and his "political people," McCarron observed. "The lawyers wanted no statement made before Senator Kennedy went to trial. His advisers wanted to break silence for the sake of public relations and the Senator's career." The situation was at a stalemate. McCarron was surprised it was happening at all. Hanify wasn't the kind of lawyer who tolerated interference in the defense of a case.

McCarron provided a factual, comprehensive description of the case of leaving the scene. Arena had sufficient evidence to get a complaint from Monday's hearing. The notion that Senator Kennedy had discharged his legal obligation to report the accident by telling Joe Gargan and Paul Markham about it, "Didn't cover it at all," McCarron said. "The statute says you had to make known your name, address and the license plate number of your car. Presumably, someone has to be there when the police arrive at the scene, at least that was my interpretation."

A plea of *nolo contendere* wasn't in the cards either. Judge Boyle expected defendants to plead guilty or not guilty in his court. A *nolo* plea said, "Let's suggest everything you say is true. What are you going to do about it?" By accepting the plea, Boyle would be dismissing the case as unimportant. *Nolo* couldn't be applied to an accident where a fatality had occurred. McCarron said, "That's why it wasn't considered."

A guilty plea would dispose of the case quickly, but the statute provided a sentence of two months to two years. McCarron pointed out, "The law at that time had a mandatory 20 days in jail in all cases of leaving the scene after causing personal injury." Where a death had occurred in the accident, Boyle might feel obliged to impose the maximum two-year sentence.

Boyle had the reputation of being a "defendant's judge" in traffic cases. He had decried the injustice of arresting motor vehicle offenders after hearing a case in which a driver had been jailed for speeding. Boyle delivered a blistering lecture to island police for their "callousness. " He was critical of the double punishment drivers suffered in traffic cases, contending that the courts should decide loss of license and registration—not the Registry of Motor Vehicles, which did so without hearing all the facts.

McCarron recommended pleading guilty and asking for the case to be continued without a finding for six months. In that procedure, a judge heard the evidence, but said, in effect: "I'm not going to find you guilty or not guilty. If you behave yourself, I'll dismiss the case. If not, I'll sentence you."

McCarron gathered from the conference that Ted Kennedy had provided his attorneys with no additional information about the accident or the delay in reporting it. The Senator was a client *in absentia,* a non-participant in the conference of lawyers, leaving to others, in particular Stephen Smith as his surrogate, the task of deciding his next move.

Kennedy's remoteness alienated several of his advisers who thought he "wasn't levelling" about the accident and was "acting the hurt, small boy and not the reasonable adult man" in the crisis. Kennedy was reported to be "so rattled and unsure of himself, he had on reflex, turned over responsibility of decision-making to men, aides of his brothers, allowed them to grill him skeptically, openly dubious, as if he were an unreliable schoolboy."

Kennedy himself would later recall the week after the accident, "As a time of great and searching speculation over the incidents surrounding the whole tragedy, many cross streams, people coming up and saying, 'You ought to go to press conferences,' my own feelings about the circumstances. I don't know how you'd describe the period other than...enormously difficult and complex."

———

Another onlooker—former Jack Kennedy confidant Richard Goodwin—saw it differently.

Kennedy was "obviously panicky still, obviously really shaken up," Goodwin recalled. "And yet nobody else was really willing to make the kind of serious decisions a situation of this sort required." Goodwin composed an expanded version of the accident covering as many of the inconsistencies in Kennedy's report as possible to be attached to the Operator's Report of the Accident the Senator was required to file with the Registry of Motor Vehicles within five days of the accident. The idea was to make more information available to the press without holding a press conference or issuing a formal statement.

Hanify and Clark balked at the idea. Fearful of the impact should additional charges be brought, they wanted no additional disclosures made about the accident. Goodwin's version was scrapped in favor of an Operator's Report identical to the statement Kennedy had left in

Arena's office—but with significant deletions. Gone was the reference to a passenger, Kennedy's rescue attempts, and the "shock" he had suffered after the accident. Gone was his request to be "taken back" to Edgartown, and, with the realization of what had happened, having "immediately contacted police." But the report did contain one new piece of information: Kennedy estimated his rate of speed prior to the accident at approximately 20 miles per hour.

Chapter 25

AT SIX O'CLOCK WHEN WINE AND CHEESE WERE SERVED TO THE
lawyers at the strategy conference, McCarron decided he'd contributed
all he could to the discussion and asked to be driven to Woods Hole,
where he caught a ferry to Martha's Vineyard. McCarron wasn't going
to take part in the meeting Clark had scheduled with Arena and Walter
Steele for that same Wednesday night.

Apprehensive at that prospect, Arena was equally concerned about
Steele's growing agitation over the case. Still chafing over the beating
he'd taken from reporters during Wednesday's two press briefings, Steele
complained, "The nerve of these horses' asses, letting us handle the
whole goddamned press while they pull up the drawbridge and don't say
a goddamned word! In all my years in the district attorney's office, I
never had such crummy treatment. And from people that are supposed
to have some class."

By day two of the briefings—five days after Mary Jo Kopechne had
gone to her watery death—Steele had given up any pretense about a
continuing investigation. "There is not a scintilla of evidence," he told

reporters, "to point to any other charges. We are proceeding only on the charge of leaving the scene." And, he added, that investigation was closed, "Except for finishing touches."

Arena was as anxious as was Steele to put a stop to the notion of "other charges." "To quell all the inferences and rumors, let us not forget that this is a driving case from start to finish," he said at the briefing. "My investigation as an experienced police officer shows that this was a true accident, caused by natural conditions." No criminal negligence on Senator Kennedy's part was involved.

Under reporter probing, Arena acknowledged that the lack of blood or breath tests had inevitably aroused speculation that the Senator might have been drunk at the time of the accident. But, he added, "There is not one iota of evidence that operating under the influence of liquor was involved. We don't and probably will not have a case of negligent driving in the criminal sense. I don't see how that can change. We're satisfied that the accident is an accident. What happened after the accident is the reason for the complaint."

Arena told the reporters he was seeking telephone company records to determine whether Senator Kennedy had called anyone on Friday night or Saturday morning from the Lawrence cottage. But newsmen who had dug deeper than Arena, knew the remark only betrayed the poverty of information unearthed by his investigation. Had Arena inspected the cottage, he would have known there was no telephone there, only a jack for an extension to the telephone in a locked studio in the back yard.

Defensive as Arena was, Steele went even further to protect himself from accusations of ineptness and timidity in prosecuting the case. Police had talked to some of the partygoers, he said. But Steele refused to reveal their names or any details of the conversations. Failure to report an accidental death to the proper authorities within a reasonable time was a misdemeanor punishable by a $100 fine. Yet Steele wasn't contemplating bringing charges against any of the Senator's friends reputed to have been given an account of the accident when Kennedy returned to the cottage.

Surprised by Steele's fabrication, Arena tried to smooth it over. Lieutenant Killen, he said, was interviewing "persons who had attended the party."

Arena was promptly disputed by *New York Post* reporter Leonard Katz. Killen had denied he had been assigned the case.

Arena admitted that he hadn't heard from Killen since his original request for help. In fact, he didn't know what Killen was doing.

"Well, I've talked to him," Katz said. "And he's not doing anything. It's not his case."

Reported to be as "elusive" as Senator Kennedy, Killen went public on Wednesday afternoon. "It is not true that I have been assigned to this case. I have no intention of interviewing any witnesses. This investigation is being conducted by Chief Arena. All I know is, for all intents and purposes, the investigation is over." In view of Arena's statement to the press that there was no evidence of driving to endanger, and the finding of the medical examiner that the death was accidental, Killen said, "I see no need of any investigation being made by the state police bureau."

Privately, Killen scoffed at the notion, attributed to "Dukes County officials close to the investigation," that those who had attended the party at Chappaquiddick could be "compelled" to give statements about the accident. "This isn't Argentina," Killen said.

Killen had to "decline officially" to assist Arena in questioning witnesses, D.A. Dinis explained in New Bedford. A misunderstanding had occurred with regard to Killen's involvement in the investigation: That Arena had sought Killen's assistance directly should not be construed as action taken on the part of the district attorney's office. Unless specifically requested to do so by the police chief, "This office will not step into the Senator Kennedy accident case," Dinis said. He might take action after Monday's hearing, "At which time I am sure there will be more clarification of the issue. More facts will be presented."

Fairly driven once again from the press briefing, Arena only then began playing catch-up with reporters with a belated investigation. He brought "Huck" Look to Chappaquiddick to assist him in drawing a map of the intersection where Look said he saw a car he believed to be the Kennedy car. Skeptical that the automobile that passed "Dyke House" about midnight had been involved in the accident, Arena nevertheless secured a statement from Mrs. Malm, resident of the cottage nearest the bridge. Her daughter had been reading under an open window in a bedroom, facing the bridge, she said. Sometime "between 11:15 P.M. and 11:45 P.M." on Saturday night, her daughter heard a car "going fairly fast" on Dike Road, but nothing else. "Nobody ever heard a car hit the water," Arena said later. "It seems amazing if they were still up they couldn't hear anything."

Mrs. Malm had left a 25-watt light bulb burning all night at the back door of the house. The light was visible from Dike Bridge. A light had also been left on in one of the children's bedrooms in a house across Dike Road occupied by the Reverend and Mrs. David Smith. Both were mystified Senator Kennedy had not sought their help after the accident, because of the house's proximity to Poucha Pond.

Back at the station, Arena received the report of an interrogation of Russell Peachey conducted by police officer George Searle. Co-owner and manager of the Shiretown Inn, Peachey had refused to talk to reporters about Senator Kennedy's accommodation at his establishment during the weekend of the accident. The Senator had checked in around six o'clock, but Peachey hadn't seen him again Friday night or Saturday, he said. "But I believe Mrs. Stewart did. She was the desk clerk that morning."

Arena was intrigued to learn Mrs. Stewart had talked to an apparently normal Senator Kennedy several hours before he had reported the accident. But Arena wasn't sure when Kennedy had appeared at the police station, variously reported to be 8:00 A.M. to 9:30 A.M. Saturday morning. Arena requested the negative of the photograph Harvey Ewing had taken of Ted Kennedy coming off the ferry "around 9:45 A.M." as evidence. He said to Ewing, "You are probably nearer the time than I am. You may be a witness."

The investigation was uncovering nothing but additional mysteries about the accident. No piece of the puzzle fit at all. One thing was clear: Senator Kennedy had not told the whole truth about the accident in his report.

With his belated investigation going nowhere, Arena was to suffer another setback. A reporter called the police station to ask, "Did you know the Registry has determined Ted Kennedy was at fault in the accident? They've just suspended his license because of negligence."

Arena was stunned. " 'Red' Kennedy was supposed to be co-operating on this thing," Arena said later. "And I had to hear about Ted's license being suspended from a reporter."

Arena called the Registry's office in Oak Bluffs. As required by law in all cases of fatal motor accidents where there were no witnesses, the Senator's license had been suspended until a statutory hearing could be held. If the hearing resulted in a finding of "serious fault," the suspension would be changed to a revocation which, by law, remained in effect for at least six months. The hearing couldn't be scheduled until Registrar McLaughlin received a full report from inspectors investigating the accident. Meanwhile, a standard-form notice that his license was suspended for an "indefinite period" was sent to Edward M. Kennedy on Wednesday, July 23. He was ordered to surrender his license at once. "You must not again operate a motor vehicle until your license has been reinstated."

The Registry's action was "a matter of interpretation," Arena told reporters at Wednesday afternoon's briefing. "I didn't recommend it, but I'm not opposed to it. It's just some more stuff to add to my woes." Walter Steele explained that the preliminary finding by the Registry should not be construed as "fault in the criminal sense." That Kennedy's license had been suspended, Steele added, would have no bearing on efforts to convict him of leaving the scene.

Arena had the feeling "people were pulling the rug out from under me left and right. And there wasn't one son of a bitch who was cooperating. Even Walter Steele made me feel like I was alone in this thing. At the morning press briefing somebody asked him, 'Have you ruled out operating under the influence?' And Walter said, 'No.' And that really shook me up. I said to him afterward, 'Walter, dammit! We don't have anything to hook him on for operating under.' All these different things were putting me on the spot." Arena felt isolated even from other law enforcement agencies, he said. "I got the feeling they were all avoiding me."

Arena was surprised when Bill Carpenter sauntered into the police station. FBI resident agent on Cape Cod, Carpenter was "a nice, easygoing guy," Arena said. "Bill loved the Vineyard." Despite his casual dress and relaxed manner, it was clear that Carpenter was working. Arena thought he'd been "directed by Hoover, by way of somebody else, to snoop around."

Walter Steele denied reports the FBI had expressed interest in the case. He was wrong—again.

At 5:35 P.M., on Wednesday, July 25, Kitty Henley, senior secretary to the assistant to the director of the FBI, took down in shorthand a report telephoned by special agent James Handley of Boston:

> The car that was driven by Kennedy was found in the water
> near the beginning of the bridge. Skid marks were very short,
> indicating he was traveling at no great speed. The case of

leaving the scene without reporting the accident will be based partly on his going by two houses near the scene to allegedly get back to his cottage instead of stopping at the nearest house and summoning the authorities.

The Registry of Motor Vehicles is consistent with the local police investigation in that there is no evidence of speed that could be called negligence. Chief Dominick J. Arena is of the opinion, and this is only an opinion, that Kennedy was not in shock for any 9 or 10 hours and he desires to get the answers from Kennedy. The Chief does not know how he could have been in shock that length of time.

You have seen in the papers that the Chief failed to advise Kennedy of his rights when Kennedy furnished the statement—partly because Markham, former U.S. Attorney, and Gargan, who is a cousin of Kennedy were present, and because the Chief said he did not think of it at the time since Kennedy voluntarily appeared at the station. The Chief said that now they have a witness who can show the Kennedy car was seen at 12:40 A.M. at the intersection near the bridge, which offsets the fact that Kennedy said he left the party with the victim at 11:15 P.M.

The police have as yet no witnesses as to seeing Kennedy driving the car at any reckless speed prior to the accident or being under the influence. The Chief suspects that Teddy Kennedy came from Chappaquiddick Island to Edgartown early in the morning and not shortly after the accident as he said in his statement, but the Chief has no real good evidence to prove this. The Chief suspects that the possibility exists that Kennedy may have been too loaded to report the matter immediately after the accident, but he has no evidence at all to support this. The common consensus on the island, the

Registry and the police, is that a complaint will be issued for Kennedy having left the scene of the accident. The police department is being deluged with letters from all over the world, 90% of which are against Kennedy and urging them to be thorough in this investigation so Kennedy can be convicted of the worst.

"Life" magazine, according to the Chief, is coming out with a statement pointing out that Kennedy has been living recklessly of late, probably since Bobby's death, as a protest against running for the Presidency. In other words, he is being pushed to run for the presidency whereas Teddy does not feel at this time he wants to run for it."

Arena suffered total humiliation at Wednesday's afternoon press briefing, having to confirm that he had never made a direct request to the district attorney's office for assistance in the Kennedy accident. Killen had seen no need to become involved in the case because the Senator was only going to be prosecuted for a traffic misdemeanor. "This is the case—and the *only* case I have."

For the first time since the accident, Arena complained about it. "This is my baby—not a very nice baby, but *my* baby" he said. Showing the strain of five days of publicity and pressure, Arena revealed he was "taking tranquilizers because of this thing."

Chapter 26

WALTER STEELE WAS SUFFICIENTLY CALMED DOWN BY THE TIME
Judge Clark and his son arrived in Edgartown for their Wednesday night
meeting. Clark came prepared to do business. Arena had filed a complaint application charging Senator Kennedy with leaving the scene of
an accident after causing personal injury. Clark wanted him to know,
"There are technical defenses to this charge."

However, Clark had to be guided "by other considerations that
transcend the usual criminal case," he said. He proposed Senator Kennedy admit to sufficient facts for a finding of guilty. The procedure
precluded a *plea* of guilty and said, in effect, "I don't want evidence of
my wrong-doing presented as a case against me." The procedure required
the consent of the prosecutor and the presiding judge.

The idea was so obviously a whitewash even Steele, timorous as he
was about prosecuting anything more serious than a misdemeanor in a
fatal accident, objected. "The judge won't go for it," he said. "And neither
do I."

"There are defenses to this charge," Clark reiterated, implying a not guilty plea could be in the offing.

Steele wasn't fooled. "We've got enough to hook him in court," he said.

For the sake of argument, Clark said, "If we pleaded guilty, what would you recommend to the judge?"

Steele would recommend a suspended sentence for any first offender on a leaving the scene complaint, he said. "A suspended sentence would be fair to everybody."

Clark wanted "an assurance" Judge Boyle would go along.

You could never be sure about anything with Boyle, Steele said. "You'll get a fair shake before this guy. He won't be influenced by the press, by Kennedy or anybody else. He goes strictly by the book."

Clark couldn't commit his client to anything so tentative. He wasn't a free agent; another attorney was in charge of the case. Clark had to clear everything first. Stephen Smith and Ted Sorensen had the most to say about the Senator's defense, he said. "They're calling the shots." Clark had to return to Hyannis Port before anything in the way of a plea could be decided.

That a suspended sentence could be forthcoming because Senator Kennedy was a first offender wasn't as comforting a resolution of the case to Clark as it was to Arena and Steele, because he knew what they did not: Kennedy had never been involved in a hit-and-run accident before, but there was a record of serious traffic violations. Their nature formed a pattern of deliberate and repeated negligent operation. Particularly bothersome to Clark was a June, 1958 conviction for "reckless driving."

On March 14, 1958, Deputy Sheriff Thomas Whitten had been on routine highway patrol outside Charlottesville, Virginia, when an Oldsmobile convertible ran a red light, sped off, then cut its tail lights to elude pursuit. A license check revealed the car belonged to Edward M.

Kennedy, a 26-year-old law student attending the University of Virginia. Kennedy had in March 1957 been fined $15 for speeding.

Whitten was on patrol at the same intersection a week later, he testified, "And here comes the same car. And to my surprise, he did exactly the same thing he did before. He raced through the same red light, cut his lights when he got to the corner and made the right turn."

Whitten gave chase. He found the car in a driveway, apparently unoccupied. Looking inside, he discovered the driver stretched out on the front seat, hiding. Whitten issued a ticket for "reckless driving; racing with an officer to avoid arrest; operating a motor vehicle without an operator's license (Mass. registration.)"

At his trial in Albermarle county court, Kennedy testified that his tail lights had a short circuit—a condition a garage mechanic confirmed finding a few days after Kennedy's arrest. Convicted of all charges, Kennedy paid a $35 fine. It had taken three months for his case to be heard, his attorneys able to win postponement after postponement. Court officials never filed the mandatory notice of the case in the public docket. Kennedy's name had not appeared on any arrest blotter. A local reporter spotted the case after discovering 5 warrants in Kennedy's name in a court cash drawer.

Three weeks after his trial, Kennedy was speeding again, and still operating without a valid license. In December 1959, Kennedy was stopped again for running a red light and fined $10 and costs. In Whitten's view, "That boy had a heavy foot and a mental block against the color red. He was a careless, reckless driver who didn't seem to have any regard for speed limits or traffic ordinances."

The offenses in Virginia had occurred on Ted Kennedy's Massachusetts driver's license. But neither the Registry of Motor Vehicles in Boston nor the office of probation in Cambridge had any record of the out-of-state convictions when Clark checked with that agency. Though "clean" on the record, there was always the chance the press might rediscover the ten-year-old history of Kennedy's reckless driving and jeopardize his first offender status in Edgartown court, should a plea of guilty be made.

The technical defenses Clark threatened Arena and Steele with were: The vagueness of the statute as it pertained to reporting a one-car accident; the constitutional issue of self-incrimination through the statement Kennedy left with Edgartown police; and, a medical defense of "shock."

But the body of documentation gathered from the Senator's various examinations and treatment had undercut the medical argument. Instead, that body of evidence indicated Kennedy had not been seriously injured in the accident, but had suffered a slight concussion, a bump on the head, a scratch behind the ear, and a stiff neck. No medical evidence supported a diagnosis of shock. Nor did Kennedy's behavior at the Shiretown Inn the next morning reflect the condition. According to Arena, the Senator had looked "depressed, but physically OK," at the police station.

A not guilty plea required a trial open to the press and public, cross-examination of the Senator and the presentation of evidence against him. All those who had attended the party could be subpoenaed and made to testify. Deputy Sheriff Christopher Look was scheduled to be a witness to enter into evidence the controversial question of the time the accident had taken place. Look's observations that the driver appeared "lost" and "confused" could provoke inferences of impairment, such as drunk-driving, although neither Steele nor Arena had drawn that conclusion from Look's information.

Look's story "disturbed" other lawyers, McCarron said. "They were upset about it. The time difference was baffling to everybody." McCarron talked to Look himself and believed he had seen the car an hour and a half after Ted Kennedy said the accident happened. But McCarron wasn't concerned about the discrepancy. "I didn't think it would take that much for Senator Kennedy to conform his story on the question of time with 'Huck' Look's."

Despite the peril he could be placed in by his traffic record, Senator Kennedy might be wiser to take his chances with a guilty plea to leaving the scene rather than expose himself to more serious charges of driving to endanger and, possibly, manslaughter, as a result of more information coming out of a trial to defend a misdemeanor.

As to manslaughter, the rule in Massachusetts was clear: "Any person who wantonly or in a reckless or grossly negligent manner did that which resulted in the death of a human being was guilty of manslaughter, although he did not contemplate such a result." Negligence in exposing another to injury by doing an act, supplied all the intention the law required to make a defendant responsible for the consequences.

A further manslaughter charge possibility had developed from John Farrar, the Edgartown fire department scuba diver. In a number of interviews, Farrar repeatedly expressed the opinion that Mary Jo Kopechne might have lived for some time underwater by breathing a bubble of trapped air, and that she could have been saved if rescue personnel had been promptly called to the scene of the accident.

As a result of the famous Coconut Grove night club fire in Boston in 1942, the Massachusetts Supreme Judicial Court had broadened "wanton and reckless conduct" to consist of "an intentional failure to take such care in disregard of the probable harmful consequences." In upholding the guilty verdict of manslaughter brought against Barnett Welansky, owner of the nightclub, for failing to keep his establishment safe for patrons, the Court had ruled failure to do an act was as culpable as driving an automobile or accidentally discharging a firearm. "Grave danger to others must have been apparent, and the defendant must have chosen to run the risk rather than alter his conduct, so as to avoid the act or omission which caused the harm." Even a defendant "so stupid or heedless" not to have recognized the danger, could not escape the imputation of "wanton or reckless conduct in his dangerous actor omission."

If Senator Kennedy's failure to secure rescue assistance had contributed to the death of Mary Jo Kopechne, his omission to act was negligent. He was liable for prosecution under the *Welansky* decision. That was, in fact, the major legal prop under which District Attorney Edmund Dinis had successfully prosecuted for involuntary manslaughter in 1967 a Christian Scientist for failing to provide medical treatment for a child who had died of pneumonia.

Senator Kennedy confronted a legal dilemma: A not guilty plea required a trial, which could uncover damaging evidence against him. A guilty plea avoided a public inquisition and further revelations of wrong-doing, but made him liable to a possible jail term and provided an admission on the record that was one element required to prove manslaughter, should that charge be subsequently brought against him under *Welansky*.

If the hardest decision was what plea to make, Kennedy also faced the increasingly urgent need for a statement of explanation about the accident.

Kennedy's dependence upon speechwriters was legendary. In the preparation of a speech, most politicians briefed their writers before a draft was written. But Kennedy's writers completed a draft, then entered into discussion, during the course of which he was "unusually receptive to other people's suggestions." Kennedy had assigned others to compose the famous eulogy delivered at his brother Robert's funeral. One of the speechwriters, "Felt pretty funny about it. Because, how could we know what he felt about his brother? He just said write something on the theme of love. I thought maybe that was one speech he shouldn't have asked us to write."

But composing any explanation of the Senator's accident at Chappaquiddick required a legal and verbal dexterity to explain away the ten hours it had taken for authorities to be notified. That task was assigned to Ted Sorensen, the literary light of the Kennedy White House.

Honored four days before the accident by the University of Nebraska as "a graduate having influenced national affairs and life more than any other living Nebraskan," Sorensen arrived at the compound, "full of brooding reproach for what Ted's mischief was going to do to the legacy."

Sorensen could hardly conceal his distaste for the whole affair. When Senator Kennedy called upon him to give legal counsel, "I responded to the call," Sorensen said, but he thought Kennedy's action at the time of pressure was indefensible. "The presence of a girl in his car and liquor at the party fanned the flames of ugly suspicion and wild speculation about his motivations for not going to the police immediately." Sorensen found it difficult, "To suspend my own moral judgments in working on a matter of that kind. And I therefore was insistent that whatever he said to the public, it did not contain misstatements of facts."

Sorenson consulted Gargan, "about certain things he was not aware of, that he wanted to make certain about." Gargan confirmed the rescue efforts he and Paul Markham had undertaken at Dike Bridge, his urging that the accident be reported, and Ted Kennedy's "impulsive dive" into the Edgartown ferry channel. Gargan said nothing about the alternative plan for reporting the accident Kennedy had proposed or Kennedy's suggestion that it was Mary Jo Kopechne who drove the accident car.

As the crisis passed into a fifth day of silence, editorial and political heat intensified. A leading Democrat, critical of Kennedy's behavior since the accident, suggested, "He can't let this thing deteriorate. I can't help but think he's been badly hurt. He may be able to come back if he's got some answers."

Reported under sedation, "still suffering from the traumatic shock of not rescuing Mary Jo Kopechne—a girl he hardly knew—from the car," Kennedy had made no decision to delegate a spokesman with authority to make statements or answer questions. It was unlikely the Senator would reveal more information about the accident before his court appearance, an aide said. Any comment might have a "prejudicial effect" on the hearing scheduled for Monday.

But the change in editorial winds brought increasingly strident demands for complete disclosure of the accident. Kennedy's report to Edgartown police was woefully inadequate. "Worse, there are good reasons to doubt that it is even accurate," the *Washington Post* charged. If, the *Post* said, Kennedy remained silent, he could expect not only honest doubts to remain about his post-accident behavior, "But also the bitter whispering campaign that has already begun. The talk will go on amplified about the initial timidity of the police and how the Kennedys managed that; about the drinking and the calls to lawyers and the various damaging versions of what actually transpired that night." Saying nothing would do Kennedy grave harm, "Which is why he would be better advised to get the politics out of it and clear up the record of this tragic affair."

"To end speculation and rumor that was vilifying the Senator's reputation and undermining public confidence in our law enforcement system," the *Boston Record-American* suggested it was "appropriate and essential in the interests of justice that an inquest be held into the death of Mary Jo Kopechne."

Chapter 27

THE GROWING CLAMOR FOR MORE INFORMATION FOUND ECHO when, for the first time, Dukes County Medical Examiner Robert Nevin made a public statement that the circumstances attending the death of Mary Jo Kopechne warranted an autopsy. "We don't know if the girl died of a heart attack, a stroke, or from drowning," he said. Nevin said he would have asked the State Police to send a pathologist to Edgartown. "I wouldn't have let that autopsy go. I would have gone to Washington, if I had to. It wasn't too late when Dr. Mills learned the entire story around 2:30 A.M. The corpse had been embalmed, the presence of formalin couldn't change the picture."

Mills had performed his function of medical examiner by satisfying himself there was no evidence of foul play in the death, Nevin said. "But the point is that there are so many nasty questions, it would have been a kindness to Senator Kennedy to have an autopsy—so that all the nasty questions could be answered."

An autopsy could still be possible, Nevin said. "The order could come from the district attorney."

Dinis passed the buck. He would have preferred an autopsy be performed, he said. But it was up to Dr. Mills whether to order one or not. District attorneys rarely became involved in automobile accident cases, Dinis said. "In my 11 years as a district attorney, we've never investigated a motor vehicles accident."

Arena had reported the accident to him, "And then for some reason bypassed me and contacted State Police Lieutenant Killen." Walter Steele hadn't invited Dinis to participate either. "For some reason they are not desirous to get me into the case at all and I can't understand why." With newspaper reports indicating other charges could be brought in the case, "It would seem to me the more manpower the better," Dinis said. "It is an extraordinary investigation and unusual. They are in the position where, if the case begins to crumble, people will start talking."

By his attack on Edgartown authorities, Dinis was hoping to deflect criticism about his office remaining aloof from the case. Dinis had shown no eagerness to become involved. In fact, Dinis protested that he wouldn't step into the Kennedy accident case unless specifically asked to do so by Edgartown authorities.

That Dinis had known about Senator Kennedy's involvement in the accident by noon on Saturday and not called for an autopsy was defended by Assistant District Attorney Armand Fernandes. "You're saying that since Dinis was factually aware at noon, that he was legally aware for purpose of intervening. I say no, no, no. You're saying he was supposed to change his opinion right away in Senator Kennedy's case, whereas with Joe Blow he wouldn't."

Dinis' office announced the district attorney "would not be available for any further comment on this matter."

That it was not customary for the district attorney's office to become involved in motor vehicle accidents came as news to Jimmy Smith. In

February, Smith had tried a hit-and-run accident on a direct indictment for involuntary manslaughter. "I got hung with it because the guy involved was a New Bedford fireman and a former high school star athlete," Smith said. "No other assistant wanted the case. It was kicking around the office waiting to be tried for months."

The lack of information about the Kennedy accident was "deeply troubling," Dinis said, when he called Smith to complain of the inept handling of the situation by the Senator and his advisers. "Where's all this Kennedy expertise? Where are all the pros? Can you imagine them just letting this thing ride?"

Smith could only agree. With nothing coming out of the compound, Dinis' position was growing untenable. Smith wasn't concerned about the district attorney's office entering the case, "So much as the political time-bomb of no action on this thing. The beauty of the Kennedy's earlier was that they acted, they didn't react. But this was a *non*-action. All they had to do was come up with some answers. The longer it waited, and they couldn't, the worse it got."

The whole reaction of the parties was creating the suspense and mystery about the accident, whether it was intentional or not, Smith told Warren O'Donnell.

O'Donnell was grim, "Because of what was going on at Hyannis Port," Smith said, later. "Because Kenneth was being frozen out. They were giving out his name as being there as an advisor to make it look like all the old Kennedy hands were rallying around, hoping that meant to people that Teddy couldn't be guilty of anything serious—but that wasn't working at all."

O'Donnell thought Ted Kennedy was "screwing up" by delaying a public explanation of the accident. He had had direct experience with an earlier and notorious occasion when Ted had gotten himself in trouble. O'Donnell had arranged for his Harvard roommate, Bill Frate, to take a Spanish examination in Kennedy's stead. When Frate got caught, he and Ted Kennedy had been expelled for cheating. Warren called his brother.

In the midst of preparing John Kennedy's campaign against Henry Cabot Lodge, Kenneth O'Donnell told Ted Kennedy to pack his bags, but not to leave the dormitory until he received further instructions.

When the telephone rang, Warren recognized the voice demanding to speak to Ted as former ambassador Joseph P. Kennedy.

"You're in the army. Report to Fort Dix at eight o'clock tomorrow morning!" the Ambassador announced, then hung up. O'Donnell swore it was "the real story" of the famous cheating episode.

Ted Kennedy had denied there was anything unusual about his interrupted education at Harvard. The Korean war was on and he thought it was "a good time to get my service over." Kennedy had served as an infantryman assigned to military police honor guard at SHAPE headquarters in Paris. A curtain of secrecy had enveloped the incident until 1962 when *Boston Globe* reporter Robert Healy discovered the story. Kenneth O'Donnell had participated in White House conferences seeking to persuade Healy not to release the information as a news story. A compromise had allowed Ted Kennedy to confess the incident, with a statement of contrition. The public had been forgiving of the "schoolboy prank," and the incident was defused as an issue in the election.

That wasn't going to be possible with the accident at Chappaquiddick, Warren O'Donnell said. Jack wasn't in the White House, and Bobby was dead. Whatever happened at Chappaquiddick was bound to come out. Attempts to "manage" the crisis were so blatant, nobody was going to believe anything but a complete disclosure.

Smith was worried the pressure on the district attorney's office was starting to tell. Reluctant as Dinis was to do anything, Smith said, "He can't duck the case forever."

On Thursday morning—now six days after the accident—Dinis called Dr. Donald Mills to ask, "I don't think an autopsy was necessary, do you?"

Surprised to hear Dinis mention autopsy for the first time, Mills said, "I really agree. I'm sticking to my guns on that."

Mills wanted the district attorney's office to issue an official statement about the accident. That way, he would be spared having to reiterate the known facts of the case to reporters who were continuing to pester him about the lack of an autopsy, and Mary Jo Kopechne's blood alcohol test figure.

Dinis was staying out of the case, he said. "I don't want another Lee Harvey Oswald affair. If I get involved, it's going to stir up a big Roman holiday in Edgartown. We don't want that; so we'll let Arena handle it."

Under pressure from reporters, Mills released the blood-alcohol test figure of .09%. He characterized it as "a very modest, very slight" level of alcohol in Mary Jo Kopechne's blood, an interpretation that immediately was challenged by other medical authorities.

The test had been conducted by Dr. John McHugh, director of the state police chemistry lab in Boston. McHugh said, "In this particular case, the figure means a person weighing 110 pounds or thereabouts has an alcohol intake of about 3.75 to 5 ounces of 80 to 90 proof liquor—that's up to five drinks within one hour prior to death, more if you measure over a longer period, since alcohol diminishes in the bloodstream with the passage of time."

The standard of interpreting blood alcohol in terms of human behavior demonstrated a figure of .09% was at a level which adversely affected driving. All European countries and Canada established .08% as the point which a person should not operate an automobile.

Massachusetts provided .15% as legal intoxication, but legislation was pending to conform Massachusetts to the federal standard of .10%

According to existing statutory guidelines, a test result of .05% was presumption of sobriety. With percentages of more than .05%, but less than .15%, "There shall be no presumption," McHugh said. Mary Jo Kopechne may not have been legally intoxicated by Massachusetts standards, but she was closer to drunk than sober when she died.

Plagued by the return of reporters to his office and the eruption of another medical controversy about his role in the accident, Dr. Mills announced a press conference for Friday morning.

Chief Arena cancelled the Thursday-morning press briefing. The Federated Church parish hall was booked for the annual "Whale of a Sale" bazaar.

Arena was now suffering a different species of pressure than he had from reporters. Massachusetts Attorney General Robert Quinn had called to say, "Chief, you're talking too much." Quinn suggested Arena cancel all further press briefings.

Identified as an "aide" to George Killen, Bernie Flynn announced from Barnstable courthouse, "Pretrial publicity has gotten to the stage that it's unconstitutional." Killen "sincerely hoped" Arena was keeping in mind some of the recent Supreme Court decisions, particularly those bearing on pretrial publicity.

"The two press conferences a day were driving Killen crazy," Flynn said. "It got so bad, I told Arena myself: 'For Christ sakes, take it easy!' He'd say: 'Oh, all right, I'll knock it off.' Then, an hour later he'd be going at it again. You couldn't control the guy as far as the press was concerned." Arena was in such thrall to reporters, "If they stuck a potato in front of him he'd talk into it like it was a microphone."

Killen was appalled at the escalation of the publicity in the case since Arena's briefings. "Every time you turned on the television there's his mug making exculpatory statements about there not being any negligence in the accident—giving his whole goddamned case away." Arena should not be revealing details of his investigation like a detective reporting his progress to a superior officer, Killen said. There was no prosecutable case left except for leaving the scene. And if Arena didn't mind his public statements, he could very well lose that one, too.

Killen asked his friend, Al Hinckley, chief of Barnstable Police, to call Arena about talking to reporters about his prosecution of Ted Kennedy. Hinckley did, telling Arena, "Better not blow your case."

"I don't think I was told to shut up," Arena said. "There were some calls from law enforcement people informing me I was endangering my case, but those calls were made in good will. They were friendly calls."

Arena sent offIcer Robert Bruguiere to tell reporters gathered at the parish house for the afternoons briefing, "There will be no further press conferences on the advisement of special prosecutor Walter Steele."

Reporters regretted the end of the briefings, given the sobriquet, "The Walter and Dominick Show" by a *Chicago Today* reporter, and referred to less fondly by others as "Ted Mack's Original Amateur Hour."

Arena and Steele "might understandably have been awed" at having to deal with a U.S. Senator and a potential presidential candidate and hesitated to question Ted Kennedy aggressively, "But it is beyond belief entirely why answers—complete and satisfactory ones—to the obvious questions in this case have not been forthcoming voluntarily from those who participated in the events," The *Nation* complained. "Many questions which should have been asked as a matter of course in circumstances such as these have not even been asked."

No purpose had been served by the press briefings except to afford Arena and Steele the opportunity to defend their maladroit handling of the case. Arena had tried to make up for his lack of investigation, "By talking a lot," one observer noted. "The more he talked, the more he invited ridicule from reporters for knowing so little."

Yet, Arena had won over the press by an unflagging good humor. He'd initialed scores of personal checks so reporters could get them cashed—no small accomplishment in tourist-wary Edgartown; refereed the repeated squabbles for territorial space between rival television correspondents Ben Silver and Liz Trotta, and never refused a reasonable request for information, such as he was able to provide.

Selectman Robert Carroll chose the occasion of the cancelled news briefings to declare his complete satisfaction with Arena's handling of the Kennedy accident. "He is not only the best chief this town has ever had, but one of the best in the country," Carroll said. "Unlike the district attorney, our chief is not looking for headlines to further his own career,"—a gratuitous swipe at Dinis, given the district attorney's obvious reluctance to involve himself in the case.

But Carroll's encomiums had fallen short of the mark. Arena had been duped about the party by Senator Kennedy, then had failed to press Kennedy on his promise to provide more information about the accident. He'd been deprived of important license information by the Registry and straight-armed by Killen; then been persuaded by Walter Steele into filing the least charge possible in a fatal automobile accident. Arena himself had come up with no evidence except that provided by the Senator's report, and "Huck" Look's volunteered testimony which contradicted it with regard to the time the accident had occurred and the reason for the Senator's "wrong turn" on Dike Road. Nor had Arena corroborated either version.

As Ted Kennedy's leading supporter in Edgartown, Carroll was only confirming what reporters knew already: The great job Arena had done absolving Ted Kennedy of any blame for the death of Mary Jo Kopechne.

Chapter 28

BUT ARENA WAS, FINALLY, GOING TO QUESTION JACK CRIMMINS, one of the guests at the Chappaquiddick party. Accompanied by Walter Steele and Tommy Teller, Arena drove to the Registry office at Oak Bluffs to meet Registry Inspector "Red" Kennedy. There, they boarded Kennedy's cabin cruiser for the ten-mile journey across Vineyard Sound to Falmouth and their rendezvous with Jack Crimmins.

Crimmins met the delegation at the door of his room at the Catamaran Motel. A tall man with coarse skin, he was the fastidiously dressed bachelor who "liked to hang around cops" Arena had known from his state trooper days at Suffolk County courthouse. Crimmins was then employed as "a legal aide and investigator" in the district attorney's office. Arena wasn't sure what Crimmins did.

"Jack was one of those typical, hail-fellow-well-met Irish guys who probably wouldn't have to work a day in his life on a strenuous job because of these 'little things' that kept coming up." Arena figured Crimmins to be the beneficiary of a "no-heavy-lifting" patronage sinecure favored by Massachusetts politicians.

Arena regretted not having spoken to Kennedy's chauffeur on Saturday morning, he said. "I thought, 'Gee, that would have been a great feather in my own cap, because right from the beginning I might have had an idea what the hell had gone on the night before.'"

Crimmins had come to the police station to talk to Arena, but spotted a *Newsweek* reporter in the corridor he didn't like, and left.

Crimmins was now suspiciously eager to cooperate. Five days of dealing with reporters had rubbed some skepticism off on Arena. He wondered if Crimmins didn't have another purpose in mind, he said. "Here's a guy who's going to say we've got the interview with him, so we don't have to bother anyone else who was at the party."

Arena asked Crimmins, "What can you tell us about the night of the accident?"

"Do you mind if I write it?" Crimmins said.

A statement was "better than an interrogation," in Arena's opinion, "So we all stood around like Joe Bananas gabbing, while Jack wrote out his statement in longhand:"

> My name is John B. Crimmins. I live at 164 Marine Boad, South Boston. On July 18, 1969, I was on Chappaquiddick at a cottage rented by Joseph Gargan where a cookout was held for girls who had worked for Robert Kennedy in his presidential campaign.
>
> There were twelve people present: myself, Senator Kennedy, Paul Markham, Charles Tretter, Joe Gargan, Ray LaRosa, the deceased, Susan Tannenbaum, Rosemary Keough, Esther Newberg, Mary Ellen and Nancy Lyons.
>
> It was a friendly party. The group was reminiscing and discussing politics. There was liquor available for those who wanted it. We all ate between 9:30 P.M. and 10:30 P.M. as the steaks came off the grill. Joe Gargan prepared and served

frozen hors d'oeuvres until the steaks were ready. At about 11:15 P.M. Senator Kennedy asked me for the keys to the car so he could get back to Edgartown. I talked briefly with him at this time. He was perfectly normal at that time. There was nothing unusual about his appearance or behavior.

Immediately thereafter the car pulled away from the front of the house. Some time later I went to bed in the cottage. I first learned of the accident the following morning.

Arena didn't ask Crimmins why he hadn't driven the Senator to the ferry; how much Kennedy had to drink at the party; what time the Senator had returned to the cottage after the accident; and why Crimmins hadn't been told about it until the next morning.

Arena's new reticence about making public statements about the case prevented him from revealing he had, at last, questioned one of the partygoers—one of the most embarrassing holes in his threadbare investigation. To have released the statement would have been asking for trouble. The Crimmins interview was a transparent effort to allay suspicion that the party had been a riotous affair. Even Arena recognized the effort to absolve the Senator of any blame, he said. "The statement certainly seemed to be one that would cover everything. Here's somebody who was at the party saying: 'It was a nice time. Everybody was sociable.' In other words, he's corroborating Ted Kennedy."

Arena had copies of the Crimmins statement delivered to Dick McCarron's office. McCarron had just received a telephone call from Clark, asking him to draft a statement waiving the Senator's right to a hearing to contest Arena's complaint application.

McCarron read the two paragraphs over the telephone to Stephen Smith at the compound. Smith turned him over to Ted Sorensen. Sorensen made two minor changes in the text. Then the statement was held pending further developments.

The decision to withdraw objections to the complaint had been worked out at a major conference at the compound, giving rise to rumors that the long-awaited statement about the accident was forthcoming.

The conferences were the target of such scathing press criticism that it was plain the Senator's decision could wait no longer. The *New York Times* reacted sharply to the picture of Senator Kennedy locking himself up in his Hyannis Port compound for a solid week with high-powered advisers. This, the newpaper said, "Reinforces the suspicions aroused by his failure to report the accident until after he had conferred or tried to confer with a battery of lawyers that his priority interest from the moment of the accident was to avoid assumption of responsibility for the tragic situation."

To the *Chicago Daily News* Kennedy's "almost Pavlovian response" to the accident had been a flight to the seemingly safe world of advisers and public relations experts. Their presence alone had changed the whole scale of the event.

The compound planning sessions were like a parody of the Cuban missile crisis, *Life* said, "All the surviving New Frontiersmen scheming to extract their man from the scandal of an accident." All they had to account for was, "The classic rich kid's stunt—running away from an accident that dad can fix with the judge."

———

Even Clark was unhappy with the resolution. Reputations such as his were not made by pleading clients guilty—the "solution" proposed by Hanify, seconded by Stephen Smith and agreed to by the Senator as a way of throwing a bone to prosecuting authorities and not dragging the case out. "It's what lawyers traditionally do," Dick McCarron agreed, "Plead to a lesser charge in hopes of avoiding a more serious one."

Clark arranged to go to Edgartown on a chartered plane to work out the details of Kennedy's court appearance with Arena and Steele.

Arena wasn't prepared for another meeting. "We didn't get much advance notice. I didn't know what to expect, if it was going to be a pitch or what."

Arena agreed to meet Clark in a vacant office at Martha's Vineyard airport. "It was at this meeting," he said, "they threw the bomb at us."

Senator Kennedy was going to waive the hearing and face arraignment on the charge of leaving the scene. Clark said, "How would you feel about pleading guilty and asking for probation?"

Copping a plea was fine with Steele. But he thought the idea of a United States Senator on probation was absurd.

Clark proposed "a plea and a suspended sentence." McCarron would make a statement on mitigation and hope Judge Boyle would go for it. Clark wanted to move quickly. There were security problems to be considered. The Senator's staff feared that a crank might be lurking about Edgartown, so inflamed by the controversy over the accident as to do injury to the Senator. Extraordinary measures would have to be taken to protect Ted Kennedy. Clark proposed going to court, "First thing in the morning. We'll waive our rights to a hearing, make our plea and get the hell out before anybody knows what's happening."

The idea made sense to Arena, provided he could arrange police protection that fast. Before Clark flew back to Hyannis, another pre-arraignment meeting was agreed upon, to coordinate the Senator's court appearance.

Arena was calling in reinforcements from other island police forces when Walter Steele burst into the police station. He said, "Jesus! We forgot to tell the Judge!"

Steele called court clerk Tommy Teller. No cases were docketed for the next morning. Boyle wasn't scheduled to hold court. The Judge was off-island, visiting relatives in New Bedford, not due to return until evening.

Boyle refused to discuss the matter over the phone when Teller called him. He didn't sound much taken with the idea of arraigning Senator Kennedy the next morning. Boyle said, "Why should we put the case down for any date they ask for?"

"That's when we all pushed the panic button," Arena recalled. "When Tommy said we better not do anything without Boyle's approval, because he'll get upset."

Arena and Steele went to Dick McCarron's house. McCarron scrambled some eggs, but nobody was hungry. McCarron left for the airport to meet Judge Clark; Steele and Arena went to Ocean Heights. Arena had a cold drink before Clark arrived with two copies of the Operator's Report of the accident and confirmation that arrangements for the next day's court appearance had been made at the Kennedy end.

Steele gave Clark the bad news: "We don't know if Judge Boyle will be sitting tomorrow." Steele was leaving for a meeting with Boyle in Vineyard Haven. He instructed the others to stay clear of the uncurtained windows and to keep quiet should anyone come to the door. If reporters learned the Senator's lawyers were meeting secretly with the chief of police and county prosecutor, it would be on the news wires in an hour that a deal was being cooked up.

Clark asked Arena what he would do if Senator Kennedy pleaded guilty.

Arena would give, "The normal summary of the facts of the case like I usually do."

"Would you mind putting it together now?" Clark asked.

Arena went into another room. He used Steele's typewriter to bang out a statement. "I was very pleased my initial preparation was acceptable to all," he said, later. "That was word-for-word the testimony I gave the next morning in court."

Arena waited for Steele to return as twilight fell. "A lot of time went by. We were all wondering what the hell was happening."

A voice boomed from outdoors calling Walter Steele. Arena observed a large man of unmistakable albino complexion placing planks across the back porch steps from a panel truck backed into the driveway.

Arena told Clark and McCarron to hide in a bedroom. He opened the door and greeted Bill McClure.

"I've brought Walter's refrigerator," McClure said.

"Go right ahead," Arena said. He thought it was pretty funny that in the middle of a secret meeting some guy shows up to deliver a refrigerator. "I'm trying to be so coy, making small talk. And this guy's probably wondering, 'Where did all these cars come from? Who do they belong to?'"

Steele returned around nine o'clock with good news. Boyle would hear the case first thing in the morning. Although it would undermine security arrangements, it was decided to hold a press conference to announce the Senator's arraignment. There was no way Ted Kennedy could be sneaked in and out of Edgartown district court to make his plea.

Arena sent his officers to hotels and popular drinking spots in Edgartown rounding up as many reporters as possible.

McCarron planned to deliver the statement he'd written but developed last minute stage fright. Judge Clark did it, instead. He said, "I've got a brief announcement to make. I cannot elaborate on it. This is it. I can say no more."

Senator Kennedy was waiving his objection to the issuance of a complaint against him. He would "accept service" on the charge of leaving the scene tomorrow morning in district court.

Kennedy's decision to face arraignment came as "a complete surprise," Arena told reporters. "I have no idea what they based their decision on. As of this moment, there is nothing to indicate this is more than a motor vehicles case." If Kennedy pleaded guilty, Arena was prepared to present his case. "If a not guilty plea is entered, we'll ask for a continuance." Arena didn't think Steele was prepared to prosecute.

Steele promptly, and predictably, contradicted him. "I'm ready to go to court I tell you. I have the witnesses ready."

Steele was asked about a report of the accident filed with the Registry of Motor Vehicles in which Senator Kennedy was purported to have been driving so carefully, he could not have been negligent when the car went over Dike Bridge.

Steele confirmed a report had been filed, but refused to show it.

Reminded such documents were routinely made available to the press, Steele said, "That's right, they are; but this one isn't. So sue me!"

When the reporter wanted to know if Steele had served as an assistant district attorney for Suffolk County with Ted Kennedy in 1961, and what their "relationship" was, Steele exploded. "That's true! And if you're going to ask questions like that, you can leave. In fact, I'll have you shown out." Steele ordered two Edgartown police officers, "Take him out."

The prosecutor had cooled down by the time reporters submitted their names and affiliations in the hope of being assigned to a 35-member press pool allowed inside the courtroom to cover the arraignment. Harvey Ewing and Colbert Smith would be admitted without question, Steele said. "Because they represent the local press."

Steele sat up until 3 A.M. selecting the press pool and preparing his appearance in court for the next morning.

After the press conference, Clark called court reporter Joe Donegan in Brockton, Massachusetts. District courts did not provide verbatim transcription of proceedings. Donegan understood why Clark wanted Ted Kennedy's arraignment taken the next morning.

"If a lawyer had a serious case in the district court he'd always get a stenographer to have a permanent record," Donegan said. "What they want that for is to study the Commonwealth's case to prepare their defense for a Superior Court trial, if there is one. Usually, the defense doesn't put on a case in the district court; they just let the Commonwealth put their case on, then rest. Especially, if they know there's a strong case against their client."

Donegan agreed to be in Edgartown the next morning.

At his office, Richard McCarron received a telephone call from Joe Gargan to go to Oak Bluffs to await the arrival of attorney John Driscoll. Gargan had suggested Driscoll be sent to Edgartown, "Not as a legal advisor, but to coordinate the Senator's appearance the next morning, the arrival of the other lawyers, and the going to court." Gargan usually did this kind of advance work, but he was out of favor insofar as Kennedy's staff was concerned. In addition, nobody wanted Gargan, the co-host of the party at Chappaquiddick and a key witness who had thus far avoided interrogation by police on conspicuous view the morning Ted Kennedy made his plea.

Because it was late when this was decided, Gargan suggested Driscoll go over on the Kennedy yacht, *Marlin*. The boat was on call at all times for any kind of trip, Gargan said, "So it wasn't difficult to make arrangements."

Gargan accompanied Driscoll on the voyage across Vineyard Sound. He did not talk about the accident with him. "I never discussed the accident with Jack Driscoll," he said. "Or anyone else for that matter."

McCarron recalled the *Marlin* coming out of the darkness "like some mystery ship." Driscoll was dropped off at the dock. He wanted to check the route Kennedy was to travel to the courthouse the next morning, but it was too foggy. McCarron put him up for the night in an apartment in a building he owned on Edgartown's Main Street. Driscoll roused McCarron very early the next morning in order to review security arrangements made in advance of Kennedy's court appearance.

Edgartown was shrouded in grey mist and uncomfortably warm when Arena walked to town hall at 8 A.M. Police in foul weather gear were directing traffic on Main Street. Arena had brought in reinforcements from other police departments to provide what security he could. But the number of newsmen gathering in front of the courthouse, and the tiers of television cameras ranked across the street made him uneasy. It was impossible to provide absolute protection for Ted Kennedy without closing off Main Street altogether.

Senator Kennedy, his wife and Stephen Smith boarded the *Marlin* at Hyannis Port for the hour-long crossing through fog and heavy seas to Martha's Vineyard. McCarron met his client for the first time when the *Marlin* docked at Oak Bluffs. Kennedy looked grim and tense. He wore a blue suit and a dark tie, but had left his cervical collar at home. A detachment of state police escorted him to Edgartown.

Dike Bridge. Arena is seated on the submerged accident car in the location it landed following the accident. Rub rail on the right side of the bridge describes the path the car took before plunging into Poucha Pond. *Inquest Exhibit #10—Courtesy Philip A. Rollins, District Attorney.*

Scuba diver John Farrar about to enter the partially removed car on a banking after the body of Mary Jo Kopechne had been removed from the back seat. *Inquest Exhibit #25—Courtesy Philip A. Rollins, District Attorney.*

Edgartown Police Chief Dominick Arena, seated on the submerged accident car awaiting the arrival of help at the accident scene, is unaware that Mary Jo Kopechne is in the back seat of the car. *Inquest Exhibit #23— Courtesy Philip A. Rollins, District Attorney.*

The ferry channel separating Edgartown on the left with the island of Chappaquiddick on the right. Ferry is pulling away from the landing. *Inquest Exhibit #19—Massachusetts State Police Bureau of Photography. Courtesy Philip A. Rollins, District Attorney.*

The accident car is dragged by a wrecker out of Poucha Pond. When Farrar opened the trunk of the car he found it to be "remarkably dry." *Inquest Exhibit #6—Courtesy Philip A. Rollins, District Attorney.*

Accident car removed from Poucha Pond is examined by Registry Inspector George "Red" Kennedy. *Inquest Exhibit #24—Courtesy Philip A. Rollins, District Attorney.*

The view of Dike Road from the bridge. *Inquest Exhibit #8—Massachusetts State Police Bureau of Photography. Courtesy Philip A. Rollins, District Attorney.*

Dike Road, Chappaquiddick, heading toward the bridge. *Inquest Exhibit #21—Massachusetts State Police Bureau of Photography. Courtesy Philip A. Rollins, District Attorney.*

Chappaquiddick Road intersection. On the right is Dike Road, ahead is Cemetery Road. *Massachusetts State Police Bureau of Photography. Courtesy Philip A. Rollins, District Attorney.*

Chappaquiddick Island. In the foreground is the curve of Chappaquiddick Road leading to the ferry landing. On the right is Dike Road leading to Dike Bridge (far right). *Inquest Exhibit #5—Massachusetts State Police Bureau of Photography. Courtesy Philip A. Rollins, District Attorney.*

Sketch of Mary Jo Kopechne's position in accident car prepared under the direction of John Farrar. *Inquest Exhibit #14—Courtesy Philip A. Rollins, District Attorney.*

The Lawrence Cottage, where the party was held. *Inquest Exhibit #20— Massachusetts State Police Bureau of Photography. Courtesy Philip A. Rollins, District Attorney.*

Chapter 29

WHEN KENNEDY ENTERED THE COURTHOUSE, ARENA PRESENTED him with a "forthwith summons," making his appearance in court official. The Senator was taken to the probation office to fill out an identity card required of all defendants. Then, he met privately in a second-floor grand jury room with Clark and McCarron.

Clark had received no assurance Judge Boyle would go along with a suspended sentence. "I never had a case like it," Clark said, later. "I didn't know a single thing about that judge and I didn't know what he was going to do. He could have sent my client to jail."

McCarron was concerned about the mandatory 20-day jail term in all cases of leaving the scene of an accident where personal injury had occurred. Boyle was a stickler for strict construction of statutory commandments when it came to sentencing.

Kennedy tried to put McCarron at ease, telling him, "Don't worry about it. He's already made up his mind." Boyle wasn't likely to make a precipitous decision from the bench.

McCarron entered the courtroom first, followed by Ted Kennedy. All eyes observed the Senator walk slowly to a captain's chair in the row of seats behind the defendant's table. Kennedy clasped his hands together, rested his chin on his fingers and stared at the floor.

Seated at a table reserved for local press in the courtroom, Harvey Ewing contrasted the fast-stepping Ted Kennedy he'd photographed on Saturday morning with the "beaten man" in the courtroom. Kennedy looked whipped, Ewing said. "He looked like: 'There's one Senator that should have gone down with the car.'"

The Methodist church bell next door tolled the hour, although the electric clock in the courtroom read 8:58 A.M. Kennedy flinched when a bailiff banged a gavel for quiet and intoned, "The District Court of the County of Dukes County is now in session. God save the Commonwealth of Massachusetts."

Judge James Boyle entered the courtroom. A tall man with a thinning ridge of red hair, mustache and ruddy complexion, Boyle settled himself behind a raised oak desk.

Court clerk Tommy Teller called the first case on the docket, *Commonwealth* v. *Edward M. Kennedy.*

"This complaint charges that Edward M. Kennedy of Boston, Mass., on the 19th day of July, 1969, at Edgartown, did operate a certain motor vehicle upon a public way in said Edgartown and did go away after knowingly causing injury to Mary Jo Kopechne without stopping and making known his name, residence and the number of his motor vehicle."

Teller addressed Kennedy directly, "How do you plead? Guilty or not guilty?"

After one week of studied silence closeted with advisers at Hyannis Port, this was the climactic moment of truth reporters had been waiting for: Whether Kennedy would admit guilt or seek to defend himself from the charge.

Kennedy hesitated. He looked at his attorneys. His lips moved, but no sound came. "Guilty," he said, in a choked near-whisper, hardly audible. He swallowed hard, then repeated in a louder, but shaking voice, "Guilty."

As was his custom, Boyle wanted to hear a summary of the evidence.

Arena was sworn. He received permission to read a precis of the case from personal notes written on a single sheet of yellow paper.

Kennedy slumped in his chair, his eyes shut. Not once did he raise his head while Arena testified.

Arena dropped his summary in mid-recital. He spent several seconds crouched on the floor of the witness stand retrieving the document. More than one reporter in the courtroom thought the incident symbolized Arena's handling of the case.

McCarron had, "No questions of the officer."

Boyle had a question. Peering over his glasses, he said in a harsh voice, "I would be most interested in determining from the defendant or the Commonwealth if there was a deliberate effort to conceal the identity of the defendant."

The question encapsulated all speculation "that Ted Kennedy had tried to avoid being implicated in Mary Jo Kopechne's death by delaying his report" of the accident.

Arena looked confused.

"Identity of the defendant?" he asked. "Not to *my* knowledge, your Honor."

Steele stepped in. "Thank you, Chief," he said, getting Arena off the witness stand in a hurry.

Boyle had addressed his question to the defendant *or* the Commonwealth. Senator Kennedy had chosen not to respond to the question everybody in the courtroom knew only he could answer. Arena and Steele would have no idea what the Senator had done after the accident.

Boyle turned his attention to the *defender's* table. Clark and McCarron stiffened. If Boyle asked Ted Kennedy the question directly, he would be required to answer or plead the Fifth Amendment to avoid self-incrimination.

Boyle let the question go. He said, "I should be glad to hear you gentlemen on disposition."

It was an incredible gaffe. If Boyle wanted to find out what Kennedy had done in the hours after the accident, this was the time to do so.

Unsettled by the close call, McCarron said, shakily, "The attorneys legal defenses that could be presented in this case … "

Boyle cut him off. "I don't think that is a proper statement to make," he said, sharply. "On a plea of guilty that's a confession! I don't think you should argue there are legal defenses." Boyle was concerned now with the question of mitigating circumstances. He didn't want any public relations posturing in his court.

Senator Kennedy was adamant in his wish to plead guilty, McCarron said. "It is his direction that his plea be entered and to leave the disposition to this court." In the view of the defendant's attorneys, confinement of the defendant, "Would not be the proper course. I believe his character is well-known to the world," McCarron said. "We would, therefore, ask that any sentence that the court may impose be suspended."

Steele proposed incarceration in the Barnstable House of Correction for a period of two months. Having in mind the character of the defendant, his age and reputation prior to the accident, Steele said, "The ends of justice would best be served were he given a suspended sentence."

Boyle asked chief probation officer, Helen Tyra, "There is no record?"

Under a Charlottesville, Virginia dateline, the Associated Press had circulated a story appearing in that morning's newspapers listing Ted Kennedy s record of previous traffic offenses.

Apparently, Tyra hadn't read the papers. "*None,* your Honor," she said.

Boyle paused. The courtroom held its collective breath. Clark called it, "The longest minute of my life, waiting for the judge to announce his decision."

"Considering the unblemished record of the defendant," Boyle said, "and insofar as the Commonwealth represents this is not a case where he was really trying to conceal his identity … "

Steele interjected a firm, "No, sir!"

Where it was Boyle's understanding that Kennedy, "has already been, and will continue to be punished far beyond anything this court can impose, the ends of justice would be satisfied by the imposition of the minimum jail sentence and suspension of that sentence—assuming the defendant accepts the suspension."

McCarron wasted no time in saying, "The defendant will accept the suspension, your Honor."

Kennedy stood up.

Teller said, "Edward M. Kennedy, on the complaint the court has found you guilty and has sentenced you to serve two months in the House of Correction at Barnstable. Sentence is suspended."

Boyle adjourned the court.

The proceeding had taken seven minutes.

Kennedy, his wife and Stephen Smith were led by two state troopers down a back staircase to the front of the courthouse. Kennedy paused on the top step to confront a corps of reporters shouting questions in a light drizzle.

Kennedy ignored the questions. He said, "I have made my plea and I have requested time on the networks tonight to speak to the people of Massachusetts and the nation … " His last words were lost as the crowd surged forward, nearly knocking him to the ground. State troopers shouldered through the crowd to allow the Senator to reach a car parked at the curbside, sparing him any further contact with reporters. The car sped off to Martha's Vineyard airport. A chartered airplane was waiting for the return flight to Hyannis Port.

Chapter 30

ANTICIPATING THE OUTRAGE OF REPORTERS EXPECTING "MORE facts coming out of the hearing," but having received no more than Arena's truncated version of the case, Steele, Teller and Arena were engaged in a struggle inside the courthouse.

Teller urged the police chief, "You go out and tell them it's all over."

"Nobody else would go out, that's how I ended up in front of the television cameras again," Arena recalled. He told reporters "We have prosecuted on the facts we have, and there are no additional facts warranting further investigation. I'm satisfied I did my job and the case is closed."

Arena thought the sentence had been fair. Any defendant with a clean record was entitled to a suspended sentence. He felt the most relief since Clark had mentioned a possible guilty plea, he said. "I thought of letting out a big yell: 'Hey, everybody, let's all go out to South Beach and go swimming or something.' I honestly thought the whole thing would be over. That his speech would be the end of it."

Arena returned to the police station, talked with reporters and just tried to relax. CBS correspondent Ben Silver proposed coming to Arena's house to film the police chief watching the Senator's broadcast. Arena did not think that was a very good idea. Silver returned to the station an hour later, Arena related. "He said he'd called New York and been told he really had to do it. It was at this time that I gently but firmly reminded him that I was the chief of police. And that if he or any of his people came on my property, I would arrest them for trespassing."

Walter Steele thought justice had been done, telling reporters when he left the courthouse, "This case is closed."

The haste with which the case had been disposed of, the appearance of a show trial, combined with a guilty plea that precluded cross-examination and the taking of evidence, smacked of a deal worked out in advance of Kennedy's court appearance. Steele allowed that he had held "the customary discussions" with defense attorneys, who informed him their client was considering a guilty plea. He said, "I let them know what my recommendation to the court for sentencing would be, if such a plea were entered."

Steele refused to speculate about the questions that remained unanswered about the accident. Presumably, Senator Kennedy would address those mysteries in his speech. "People think once you present a case to trial you know everything," Steele said, later. "You never do. There will always be doubts."

Senator Kennedy had been urged to defend the charge against him, McCarron revealed. "It was his decision and his decision alone to plead guilty." Had the jail sentence not been suspended, the Senator would have appealed to the Superior Court for a trial by jury.

The adjudication of the case was "justified and perfectly proper," McCarron said. "You had to enter a sentence, but you could suspend." The mandatory 20-day jail term he'd feared could be dispensed with— a view other legal authorities were beginning to challenge. Suspension of a mandatory sentence was not legal, George Killen's close friend, Falmouth attorney Frank Keating said. "The statute called for no less than 20 days in all cases. That meant if you gave any sentence at all, it's got to be a minimum 20 days in jail. You can't give two months, then suspend." The only way Boyle could have gotten around that was to give Senator Kennedy straight probation, with no sentence at all.

McCarron remained at the courthouse to deal with probation papers. Helen Tyra intended to treat Senator Kennedy like all her other probationers, she said. "I see no reason, and neither did he, why the Senator would be any different."

Kennedy's reporting dates were "a private matter, and just like everyone else, reached on an individual basis." The Senator had to report by letter, phone or in person. Tyra refused to disclose how often she would require Kennedy to do so during his year's probation. Ordinarily, convicted persons were forbidden from leaving the court's jurisdiction, she said. "But Senator Kennedy will be free to travel at will."

Pestered by reporters for a copy of the transcript he had taken of the brief proceedings, court stenographer Joe Donegan started to cooperate, then thought better about it. As an employee of Senator Kennedy's lawyers, he wondered if he should provide reporters with access to the document. Donegan asked McCarron if it was all right.

McCarron wasn't taking any chances. He called the compound in Hyannis Port and received permission from Stephen Smith. Donegan figured that wrapped up his involvement in the Kennedy accident case. But he was to play a much more significant role as part of a daring effort to prevent any more information about the accident coming out than was available from the brief transcript of Kennedy's trial he had transcribed or the speech the Senator was scheduled to make that evening.

———

Gwen Kopechne was "looking forward" to Senator Kennedy's broadcast, she said. "I'm waiting for him to discuss his part publicly. There are a few things that happened that haven't been cleared up to the public yet." Mrs. Kopechne would take further action if Senator Kennedy did not clarify these points. "I know there are a lot of sick people in the world, and maybe we should expect a little vicious mail. If we can't clear up all the little snide remarks and everything, I would have an autopsy performed—if that's the only way I can clear my daughter." Her only interest in the case was the light in which Mary Jo's "character and background" was being shown.

The furor over the fact that an autopsy was not done was totally unfounded, Dr. Mills told a press conference one hour before Senator Kennedy's court appearance. Mills had consulted the district attorney's office, "Although this call is not required of me, I made it because the case involved personalities of national importance and it was altogether more than I wanted to carry without further advice." Lieutenant George Killen had sent word that if Mills was satisfied as to the cause of death, "Which I was, then he was satisfied to close the matter with my original finding." He said, "My feelings have not changed in this respect. Neither Lieutenant Killen nor I had the slightest inkling of Senator Kennedy's involvement in the case at the time. The decision not to autopsy was based on the facts at hand and was, in effect, a joint decision between Lieutenant Killen and myself. On a strictly objective basis, we have no reason to regret this decision." Had the district attorney considered an autopsy after embalming advisable, Dinis would have ordered it, Mills said. "Certainly he knew of the Kennedy connection as soon as I did."

Mills had been asked numerous times if an autopsy would have been ordered had he known Senator Kennedy was the driver of the accident car. "I believe," he said, "the district attorney's office would agree with me that the answer would be 'yes,' in view of the Senator's prominence as a national figure and the need to protect his public image against speculation." Had Mills known the extent of the Senator's involvement, "I would have told the district attorney's office an autopsy was needed— not for medical reasons, mind you; but just to have avoided all this awful hue and cry about nothing and to make sure the Senator's name was cleared."

In view of the clear-cut evidence of drowning, "and the knowledge we had at the time, an autopsy was not indicated and, if done today, would add absolutely nothing we do not already know." The public concept that an autopsy was the total and final answer to all circumstances surrounding a death was a myth, Mills said. "I would urge the press to drop this angle once and for all."

If Mills hoped the issue had been laid to rest, it wouldn't stay buried. An hour after his press conference, "Reporters had a story that Mrs. Kopechne was willing to have her daughter's body disinterred, if that would clear her reputation," Mills said. "It was implied that I would have to initiate such a step, which I was perfectly willing to do."

Mills called the district attorney's office in New Bedford to plead with assistant Armand Fernandes, "To send somebody down to help me."

Fernandes "didn't know the law on the subject," he said.

It was clear to Mills, "that he fervently wished me to take full responsibility for the 'no autopsy.'"

The case disposed of in the district court, a most curious ritual occurred at the Registry of Motor Vehicles office in Hyannis. Judge Clark personally turned over Senator Kennedy's license to Registrar Richard McLaughlin. Where the license came from was neither explained nor questioned. The Senator had not been able to produce a license at the police station, and David Burke had not found one in Kennedy's Washington car.

The license was mailed to Registry headquarters. That a license renewal had been found in the Tab Room aroused Inspector Joseph Mellino's suspicions. "When I learned it was Senator Kennedy's license I'd done the check on, I was surprised." Mellino hadn't looked in the Tab Room, "Because I had a file card in my hand; I had no reason to look anywhere else. I didn't figure there was any other card because, after five months, I wouldn't be looking for one. Anything I might find in the Tab Room couldn't be there more than 2 or 3 weeks," he said. "I don't think it would have been in there at all. It seems funny as hell."

Mellino had been alone in the radio room when he'd checked Kennedy's license. He hadn't seen anyone in the building, "But a while later, I heard talk going around that McLaughlin was there on Saturday night," he said. It wouldn't take much for someone to keypunch a new license, to spare the Senator the embarrassment of not having one.

McLaughlin denied the Senator's license had expired, then dismissed the issue as not relevant to an accident. "The expiration of a license of a person who's had one for a long time is not an indication of his ability to operate a motor vehicle."

That the license had expired—and that fact been concealed by the Registry—was confirmed when Hank Jonah telephoned assistant district attorney Jimmy Smith. Jonah's friend Joe Greelish wanted Smith to know the "problem" with the Senator's license, "had been taken care of."

Gargan didn't know the Senator was driving on an expired license at the time of the accident, but he wasn't surprised to learn later this had been the case. "Jack Kennedy often drove with an expired license; and so did Bobby. That doesn't make it any better, of course. Ted probably just forgot to have his license renewed," Gargan said.

Gargan had no idea why the Senator should want to conceal the fact, or that Registrar McLaughlin should later claim, "Senator Kennedy's license never expired." McLaughlin claimed Registry records showed Kennedy had applied for renewal on February 6, 1969. "In fact, he made it right here in this building. We have girls downstairs who handle things like that, just like any Registry office." Forgetful of the Senators two charges of driving without a license in Virginia, McLaughlin added, "He was always prompt in renewing his license."

Kennedy had been in Massachusetts on February 6. He had followed an early morning appearance in Quincy with trips to Taunton, Fall River and New Bedford. Kennedy's Boston office had advanced the three-day barnstorming tour. Gargan said, "We never went near the Registry."

Back and forth to the compound during the week of councils, Gargan on occasion said only a brief "hello" to Ted Kennedy. He was pointedly excluded from the strategy sessions. The Senator did not feel like talking about the accident. Gargan was an embarrassment and a potential threat. To those who didn't know the real story he was a puzzle wrapped in conspiratorial silence—but silence the Senator had demanded. Gargan wouldn't talk about the reason the accident hadn't been reported for ten hours. Because of his friendship and regard for Gargan, Paul Markham wasn't going to blow the whistle on Ted Kennedy either. Markham told reporters "I see no prospect of talking about it. Not today, not tomorrow and not the next day. I see no necessity of talking about it ever!"

Markham and Gargan were given the opportunity to examine the speech of explanation Senator Kennedy was going to deliver on television. Gargan hadn't actually seen Ted Sorensen writing it, "But I was of the opinion he prepared most of it." There was nothing wrong with the speech as far as Gargan and Markham were personally concerned. "However, we felt that the tone of the speech, the way it was written, wasn't going to be helpful to the Senator and we didn't think he should make it," Gargan said. "My main objection to the broadcast was it was totally against my training of keeping your mouth shut, don't give your case away."

Because the speech referred to his client, Joseph Donahue, Jr., read over the draft. Donahue found it acceptable with regard to Gargan's legal position, but otherwise was appalled. He urged Gargan to go personally to Ted Kennedy to dissuade him from delivering the speech. Donahue said, "Can't you get to him? Can't you tell him how damaging this is?"

"We indicated our feelings, but others had theirs," Gargan said. "It seemed to me they'd already made up their mind to go ahead with this explanation. We weren't being asked for advice at this time." While the speech presented an accurate portrayal of the rescue effort Gargan and Markham made at Dike Bridge—the only part of the incident in which they had played a direct part—the rest of it was a fake, Gargan said, later. "It was made up, all of it, including thoughts and emotions."

Chapter 31

BECAUSE THE SENATOR'S ADDRESS WAS REGARDED AS A NEWS story, all three television networks donated 15 minutes of prime time to the broadcast. Boston's WHDH-TV was selected to originate the program, an arrangement made with Harold Clancy, general manager of the station and publisher of the affiliated *Boston Herald Traveler*. Clancy was spotted on board the *Marlin* in the zoom lens of a photographer standing at the periphery of the compound, one of a crew of reporters who jeered at the huge remote truck emblazoned with Channel 5's logo that was waved through the checkpoint on Scudder Avenue.

Among reporters who had stood a week's vigil waiting the release of a statement regarding the accident was *Herald Traveler* stringer, Francis Broadhurst. Learning WHDH had been chosen to provide the "feed" for the broadcast, Broadhurst proposed he masquerade as a member of the television crew to observe first-hand the speech and write a background story. Broadhurst was outraged when Clancy vetoed the idea. "I was pretty disillusioned that the Kennedys could exercise so much control over the press," he said. No reporter was to be allowed inside the house. The Senator wasn't going to answer any questions after his speech.

Following the remote truck in a small van was audio technician Don Moore. Assigned a crew to provide live coverage of the Miss Massachusetts beauty pageant in Attleboro, Moore had been chosen as part of a crew of five and told, "You're going to Hyannis Port."

Facilities for the broadcast were to be set up at the Senator's house. Moore drove to the causeway at Squaw Island, got out of the van and measured the distance between two entrance pillars. The remote truck couldn't get through. The location of the speech was moved to the home of Ambassador Joseph P. Kennedy.

The remote truck was proceeding down Marchand Lane, used by the Kennedy family and other residents, when a highly agitated man ran out of an adjacent house, demanding the caravan stop. He told director Bob Kincaid, "You see those overhanging branches of that tree on my property? If one leaf falls, I'm suing Channel 5 for damages!"

To assuage the irate neighbor, Kincaid stationed two crew members on top of the remote truck to divert branches from its path. Despite such precautions, Moore observed one leaf disengage. Kincaid was able to distract the tree-owner's attention as the leaf fell earthward. When it was within reach, Moore grabbed it and stuck it in his pocket.

While some facilities existed from previous television coverage originating from the compound, it was a race against time to install a hookup of television lines to deliver picture and sound beamed from Cape Cod via Providence, Rhode Island, to New York, where networks would distribute the program nationwide at 7:30 P.M., when the Senator was scheduled to deliver his speech.

At 7:20 P.M., the crew got a picture. Five minutes later the audio came in. Moore was asked by CBS for a microphone test.

CBS was in the midst of broadcasting the *Nightly News* with Walter Cronkite. The program featured an interview with Dr. Donald Mills conducted by correspondent Ben Silver, during which the medical examiner revealed the decision not to perform an autopsy on Mary Jo Kopechne had been "jointly made" with the district attorney's office.

At the interview's conclusion, Mills received a telephone call from Edmund Dinis. He said, "Mills, you let me down by not ordering an autopsy."

"He started to scream over the telephone about what a liar I was, how incompetent I was, and worse," Mills recalled. "When he launched into a personal attack, my wife picked up the extension phone and screamed right back at him. I will not give you exactly what he said, but he was unpleasant, quite impolite and he hung up the receiver in my face."

A light layer of pancake makeup was applied to the Senator's face to dull a surface reflection of lights. Kennedy asked his mother to join Stephen Smith and his sisters, Jean and Patricia, in a room off the library to watch the speech on television. Joan Kennedy was more persistent in her attentions until she was ordered from the room by a short-tempered and tense Senator Kennedy as time for the broadcast drew close.

Kennedy took a place behind a desk. The desk and chair had been built up, using books as support blocks, so that the cameras were at eye-level, to give a more natural angle when Kennedy delivered his speech.

Kincaid was directing operations from the remote truck outside. Two cameramen were on the floor with Moore. At 7:30 P.M., Channel 5 newscaster Jack Hynes announced Senator Kennedy's talk was being produced by WHDH-TV Boston.

On cue from Moore, Kennedy began reading from a manuscript gripped tightly in his hand:

My fellow citizens:

I have requested this opportunity to talk to you, the people of Massachusetts, about the tragedy which happened last Friday evening.

This morning I entered a plea of guilty to the charge of leaving the scene of an accident. Prior to my appearance in court it would have been improper for me to comment on these matters, but tonight I am free to tell you what happened and to say what it means to me.

On the weekend of July 18th, I was on Martha's Vineyard Island participating with my nephew, Joe Kennedy, as for 30 years my family has participated in the annual Edgartown Sailing Regatta. Only reasons of health prevented my wife from accompanying me.

On Chappaquiddick Island off Martha's Vineyard, I attended on Friday evening, July 18th, a cookout I had encouraged and helped sponsor for a devoted group of Kennedy campaign secretaries. When I left the party around 11:15 P.M. I was accompanied by one of these girls, Miss Mary Jo Kopechne. Mary Jo was one of the most devoted members of the staff of Senator Robert Kennedy. She worked for him for four years and was broken up over his death. For this reason and because she was such a gentle, kind and idealistic person, all of us tried to help her feel that she still had a home with the Kennedy family.

There is no truth whatever to the widely circulated suspicions of immoral conduct that have been leveled at my behavior and hers regarding that evening. There has never been a private relationship between us of any kind. I know of nothing in Mary Jo's conduct on that or any other occasion—and the same is true of the other girls at that party—that would lend any substance to such ugly speculation about their character. Nor was I driving under the influence of liquor.

Little over a mile away the car that I was driving on an unlit road went off a narrow bridge which had no guard rails and was built on a left angle to the road. The car overturned into a deep pond and immediately filled with water. I remember thinking as the cold water rushed in around my head, that I was for certain drowning; then water entered my lungs and I actually felt a sensation of drowning; but somehow I struggled to the surface alive. I made immediate and repeated efforts to save Mary Jo by diving into the strong and murky current, but succeeded only in increasing my state of utter exhaustion and alarm.

My conduct and conversation during the next several hours, to the extent that I can remember them, made no sense to me at all. Although my doctors inform me that I suffered a cerebral concussion as well as shock, I do not seek to escape responsibility for my actions by placing the blame either on the physical and emotional trauma brought on by the accident, or on anyone else. I regard as indefensible the fact that I did not report the accident to the police immediately. Instead of looking directly for a telephone after lying exhausted on the grass for an undetermined time, I walked back to the cottage where the party was being held, requested the help of two friends, Joe Gargan and Paul Markham, and directed them to return immediately to the scene with me (it then being sometime after midnight) in order to undertake a new effort to dive down and locate Miss Kopechne. Their strenuous efforts, undertaken at some risk to their own lives, also proved futile.

All kinds of scrambled thoughts—all of them confused, some of them irrational, many of which I cannot recall, and some of which I would not have seriously entertained under normal circumstances—went through my mind during this period. They were reflected in the various inexplicable, inconsistent and inconclusive things I said and did—including such questions as whether the girl might still be alive somewhere out of that immediate area, whether some awful curse actually did hang over all the Kennedys, whether there was some justifiable reason for me to doubt what had happened and to delay my report and whether somehow the awful weight of this incredible incident might in some way pass from my shoulders. I was overcome, I am frank to say, by a jumble of emotions—grief, fear, doubt, exhaustion, panic, confusion and shock.

Instructing Gargan and Markham not to alarm Mary Jo's friends that night, I had them take me to the ferry crossing. The ferry having shut down for the night, I suddenly jumped into the water and impulsively swam across, nearly drowning once again in the effort, returning to my hotel around 2 A.M. and collapsed in my room. I remember going out at one point and saying something to the room clerk. In the morning with my mind somewhat more lucid, I made an effort to call a family legal adviser, Burke Marshall, from a public telephone on the Chappaquiddick side of the ferry, and then belatedly reported the accident to the Martha's Vineyard police.

Today, as mentioned, I felt morally obligated to plead guilty to the charge of leaving the scene of an accident. No words on my part can possibly express the terrible pain and suffering I feel over this tragic accident. This last week has been an agonizing one for me, and for the members of my family; and the grief we feel over the loss of a wonderful friend will remain with us the rest of our lives.

Kennedy put aside the prepared text. He folded his hands, looked directly into the camera and appeared to continue the speech extemporaneously. However, large cue cards, picking up the text of the speech were held up out of camera range by Joe Gargan:

> These events and the publicity and innuendo and whispers which have surrounded them, and my admission of guilt this morning, raises the question in my mind of whether my standing among the people of my state has been so impaired that I should resign my seat in the United States Senate. If at any time the citizens of Massachusetts should lack confidence in their Senator's character or his ability, with or without justification, he could not, in my opinion, adequately perform his duties, and should not continue in office.
>
> The people of this state—the state which sent John Quincy Adams, Daniel Webster, Charles Sumner, Henry Cabot Lodge, and John F. Kennedy to the United States Senate—are entitled to representation in that body by men who inspire their utmost confidence. For this reason I would understand full well why some might think it right for me to resign.
>
> This would be a difficult decision to make. It has been seven years since my first election to the Senate. You and I share many memories. Some of them have been glorious, some have been very sad. The opportunity to work with you and serve our state has been much of what has made my life worthwhile.

And so I ask you tonight, the people of Massachusetts, to think this through with me. In facing this decision, I seek your advice and opinion. In making it, I seek your prayers. For this is a decision that I will have finally to make on my own.

It has been written:

"A man does what he must—in spite of personal consequences, in spite of obstacles and dangers and pressures—and that is the basis of all human morality. And whatever may be the sacrifices he faces if he follows his conscience—the loss of his friends, his fortune, his contentment, even the esteem of his fellow men—each man must decide for himself the course he will follow. The stories of past courage cannot supply courage itself. For this each many must look into his own soul."

I pray that I can have the courage to make the right decision. Whatever is decided, whatever the future holds for me, I hope I shall be able to put this most recent tragedy behind me and make some future contribution to our state and mankind whether it be in public or private life. Thank you and good night.

Kennedy got up from the desk and went into the adjoining room to watch a commentary on his performance delivered by Howard K. Smith of ABC News.

The speech hit hard at the one specter Kennedy's attorneys feared most: a charge of manslaughter. It did so through his outright denial of drunk driving, and a reaffirmation of his efforts to save Mary Jo Kopechne, fortified by the revelation of the rescue attempted by Joe Gargan and Paul Markham. While no prosecutable offense, Kennedy denied any sexual misconduct, the shadow issue that had represented so serious a threat to his political career as to have preoccupied the counselors at Hyannis Port in the composition of his speech. Richard Goodwin said, "They were trying to say something and still avoid the connotation of immorality—the old Irish Catholic fear of ever suggesting that you were screwing anybody outside of marriage."

The rest of the speech was a painful, bedraggled account constructed around the pitfalls of his statement to Edgartown police. A week of conferences had failed to fill in the gap of ten hours the accident had gone unreported. Despite a disclaimer, Kennedy was clinging to the "shock and exhaustion" of his police report as the only handhold to defend his delay in reporting the accident. Yet, by pleading guilty to leaving the scene of the accident, in the eyes of the law he had forfeited that medical defense. Furthermore, no doctor had ever given him or anyone else a "shock" diagnosis. The injuries Kennedy sustained in the accident had not been manifested in the extraordinary catalogue of symptoms his speech inventoried.

Kennedy's escape from Gargan's nagging at the landing had been transformed into an effort to swim to Edgartown so strenuous as to have incapacitated his ability to report the accident. It was a piece of legalistic logic that covered all bases, but failed to explain why Mary Jo Kopechne should have been left immersed for more than ten hours while the Senator grappled with "scrambled thoughts." Nor did it explain why the simple task of informing police had been beyond his ability to perform. In wondering "whether somehow the awful weight of this incredible incident might in some way pass from my shoulders," Kennedy came close to expressing the hope that "somebody else" take blame for the accident—the aborted scenario he'd proposed that left a number of loose ends to account for, such as his alibi-seeking encounter with a room clerk at the Shiretown Inn.

Unable to explain Kennedy's failure to report the accident, advisers had re-focused the incident as a political problem through a contrived and irrelevant issue of whether he should resign his Senate seat. To ensure against that threat, Kennedy had asked for a vote of confidence under the guise of advice.

The speech ended with a passage cribbed verbatim from his brother Jack's *Profiles in Courage*, an effort to elevate the episode into a heroic mold more suitable to the Kennedy hagiography. But, as *Time* later observed, "There was nothing heroic about fencing with half-truths, falsehoods, omissions, rumors and insinuations of cowardice," and above all, Kennedy wanted it both ways: "He asked to shoulder the blame for what happened, at the same time he was obviously begging to be excused." Kennedy was accepting responsibility for the death of Mary Jo Kopechne, he said. What he wasn't willing to accept were the consequences.

Amidst the fabrication, one poignant truth surfaced in the speech. Because of his close friendship with the Kennedys, Joe Gargan knew the reality behind the "health reasons" preventing Joan Kennedy from attending the regatta and party: "She was having a very tentative pregnancy and was trying to stay as quiet as possible in order to keep the baby. She wasn't expected to go to Edgartown this particular sailing weekend."

Minutes after the speech, telephone calls began to pour into Senator Kennedy's Boston office. "We got 100 calls in half an hour. We would have had more, but people couldn't get through," Press Secretary Richard Drayne reported. Response to the speech "was overwhelmingly favorable from both men and women, and from in-state and out-of-state, but you can't really tell until the telegrams come in." No formula or organized poll had been established whereby Massachusetts voters could register their opinion, Drayne said. "We're going to be no more specific than that." There was only one candidate in this election. And his staff was going to count the votes.

But the Kennedy political apparatus was not relying upon the spontaneous eruption of public opinion alone to persuade the Senator to remain in office. Mobilized at the barricades was a lineup of "reactions" to the speech.

An indefatigable defender since the accident, Senator Mike Mansfield thought Kennedy's speech had answered all his critics. He said, "Senator Kennedy has made his case to the people and they are now in a better position to make their judgment on him. He has my full confidence and support. Senator Kennedy has been beset by tragedy and trouble and has become a marked man because of this. He has been the target of slander and innuendo."

Another fellow Democrat, Congressman Edward Boland of Massachusetts hoped "ugly rumors" had been put to rest. "Knowing Senator Kennedy as well as I do, and also having known Mary Jo Kopechne, I am convinced there was no kind of improper relationship between them." Boland was sending a telegram encouraging Kennedy to remain in office. The Senator's service to Massachusetts and the nation was "too significant, too outstanding to have it concluded." Boland was confident, "Senator Kennedy has the strength of character to weather this latest tragedy."

Kennedy's position in the Senate had not been damaged by the accident, in the opinion of the Democratic Congressman (and later House Speaker) Thomas "Tip" O'Neill. "I say that Senator Kennedy can still be an effective leader. We need him badly."

O'Neill grew angry, however, when asked to compare the broadcast with the "Checkers speech" of Richard Nixon in 1952. "I have seen a growing disgust in Washington with the press of America, with the way you have handled this," O'Neill said. "I don't think the Nixon incident should be dragged into this by you people."

But that comparison was inevitable and ubiquitous. A post-speech television commentary by John Chancellor that drew the parallel prompted more than 800 calls of protest. An NBC spokesman defending the analogy revealed reaction to the speech to have been, "Unanimously anti-Kennedy."

One hour after the speech, Gwen Kopechne stepped onto the porch of a neighbor to read haltingly from a hand-written text: "I am satisfied with the Senator's statement and do hope he decides to stay on in the Senate." Mrs. Kopechne explained, later, "I was satisfied that he came forward and said *anything*. Before that I was going out of my mind. Questions? There are lots of questions. That's what I go on from day to day, the unanswered questions."

In the week the Senator had been in seclusion with advisers, he had maintained as calculated a silence with the Kopechnes as he had with the press, without the pretext of jeopardizing his legal position. No word had been disclosed to them about the death of their daughter, Mrs. Kopechne said. "The only people who told us anything were the reporters. Nobody else told us what was going on. They seemed to forget about Mary Jo, as though she didn't count."

Unlike his wife, Joseph Kopechne was not satisfied with the speech. "Why didn't he speak out on that relationship between the Kennedy family and their workers that included all the other girls?" Kennedy had explained the accident, "not enough, but he explained it."

In light of the broadcast, however, the Kopechnes no longer felt an autopsy of their daughter was "necessary."

Jimmy Smith had watched the speech with growing dismay. All signs of deception were apparent in Kennedy's effort to cover up fear and distress, making a perfect performance difficult. "Whatever guilt was there, came out," Smith said. "You'd have thought they had taken a tape and slowed it down. It was so depressed it was sickening. I wanted him to finish. It was 'My God, hurry up and *stop!*'"

Nevertheless, when the *Cape Cod Standard-Times* sought the reaction to the speech of "an assistant district attorney and ardent worker in election campaigns for the Kennedy family," Smith sang a different tune, "I think he was sincere. It was certainly satisfactory to me," he told the newspaper.

The speech came as a profound embarrassment to George Killen. "It was just foolish political talk. You'd have thought he was running for reelection from the gist of it. He didn't explain a goddamned thing about the accident. If that's all he was going to say, he'd have been better off saying nothing at all."

Killen shared his dissatisfaction with Bernie Flynn. "All this time Killen's telling Dinis: 'Stay out of it; let them handle it. Kennedy's going to give out all the details. We don't have to get involved,'" Flynn said. "He's trying to keep Dinis away from the thing, because Dinis would only fuck it up. And the speech just pulled the rug out from under George's arguments."

Flynn was convinced Senator Kennedy had lied in his police report. "Watching that speech, I'm saying to myself: 'Jesus, this goddamned guy is lying *again*!' He should never have gone on the air, he came off so badly. The speech was an insult to your intelligence. Whoever came up with that speech ought to be shot."

Armand Fernandes confirmed the devastating effect of the Senator's television appearance on the district attorney's office. He said, "About 20 seconds after the speech, I knew Eddie would have to do something."

Chapter 32

IN EDGARTOWN, RUSSELL PEACHEY IDENTIFIED HIMSELF AS THE
room clerk Kennedy had referred to in his television address. Peachey
was patrolling the Shire town Inn, "because Regatta weekends can be
wild. We like to make sure the parties don't disturb other guests."

Peachey had observed Senator Kennedy standing in the shadows at
the bottom of a stairway leading to a second floor where his party was
being accommodated.

Peachey said, "May I help you in any way?"

The Senator had been disturbed by noises coming from a party next
door, he said. "I've looked for my watch and seem to have misplaced it.
What time is it?"

Peachey looked through a window to a clock in his office. It was
exactly 2:25 A.M. Because the Senator appeared somewhat distressed,
Peachey asked him, "Is there anything else I can do to help you?"

Kennedy replied, "Thank you, no," and returned to his room.

Peachey called the Colonial Inn to ask the management to quiet the party. He continued patrolling his premises until 4 A.M. He had not seen the Senator or any members of his group again that night.

Peachey had not revealed the conversation before because he'd been uncertain it was Senator Kennedy he'd spoken to, he said. "The courtyard was lit by floodlights, but there were shadows. I couldn't see very clearly. I wasn't absolutely sure it was the Senator." The man Peachey had spoken to was tall and had a Boston accent that sounded like Ted Kennedy, "Although at that time I thought it might have been Gargan's voice. I wasn't sure it was Kennedy then, but after hearing him say on television he saw a hotel employee, I'm certain now I was the person he saw. I was the only person he could have been referring to. I was the only one around at that time."

Peachey believed the Senator's explanation of the accident. "He could have swum the channel. It's impossible to measure a man's strength under such conditions," he said. "I hope he stays in the Senate. He's too fine and talented a man for this state or country to lose in high office."

On Saturday morning, Peachey posted a notice on the Shiretown Inn's bulletin board "fully endorsing" Senator Kennedy and encouraging him to remain in office.

While confirming one aspect of the Senator's speech, Peachey's endorsement also added a new dimension of mystery about it. Kennedy had specifically identified a room clerk in the darkness while in a turmoil of emotional trauma. In full command of his faculties, Peachey had to deliberate a week, so uncertain was he of the Senator's identity. Kennedy couldn't have it both ways: be in shock sufficient to prevent him from reporting the accident, but appear only distressed to have his sleep disturbed, and establish his whereabouts by asking the right time—a detail left over from the aborted scenario he'd proposed to Gargan at the Chappaquiddick landing. In addition, Kennedy had made no reference to his automobile accident, foregoing another opportunity to inform authorities.

Arena was mystified by Peachey's story. "I thought, 'Where the hell did he get *that* from?' I figured he's giving Ted Kennedy an alibi." By doing so, Peachey was contradicting his police interrogation in which he denied seeing the Senator after he'd checked in on Friday night. "I probably should have gone back to him on that, but I never did," Arena said. "Once we got through the trial, I figured, It's over, unless somebody comes up with something new!'"

Kennedy's speech left Arena totally confused, "Because I thought I was going to hear the complete explanation, and that didn't happen. I had his initial statement—now here was a variation."

The variations were considerable. In his police report, Kennedy designated his destination as the ferry landing. In his speech, he failed to mention that, or his controversial "wrong turn" on Dike Road, and "unfamiliarity" with the area. The police report had omitted mention of the party and the rescue efforts of Gargan and Markham, but revealed Kennedy had been "brought back" to Edgartown. In his speech, Kennedy said he swam the channel—one factor that, in particular intrigued Arena. "Why the hell didn't somebody see Kennedy when he went back to Edgartown, even if he went over in a skiff or something? Nobody ever came forward to say they saw him coming out of the water or off the banking up to the Shire town Inn, as busy as that place was." For the Senator to have walked from the landing to the Shiretown Inn unseen on a Regatta night suggested a deliberate avoidance of witnesses.

Despite his private reservations, Arena told reporters on Saturday morning, "It was a moving and eloquent speech. The Senator bared his soul to the country and you have to admire a man for that." Had Ted Kennedy made the television speech at the police station when he reported the accident, "It wouldn't have changed a thing. The only charge still would be for leaving the scene. We feel there is no need to go into the matter any further."

But Arena was in a minority with regard to the broadcast "not changing a thing." Edgartown was in the grip of a media frenzy. Television cameras grinding up and down Main Street recorded residents' "reaction" to the speech. The most hotly debated issue was Kennedy's ability to swim the channel.

"I'm not saying it's impossible to make the swim, but I don't believe it," ferryman Richard Hewitt said. If Ted Kennedy were a normally healthy man and well-rested, "There's no question in my mind he wouldn't have even attempted to swim this channel. His speech was a lot of baloney."

Hewitt had supported Ted Kennedy in past elections, he said. "But I wouldn't vote for him for dogcatcher now. How could he leave that girl in the water for nine hours?"

Senator Kennedy's credibility was put to a public test when John Farrar—scuba diver and captain of the search and rescue division of Edgartown's volunteer fire department—dove into the ferry channel from the Chappaquiddick side, swimming the distance in five minutes. Farrar found the crossing "tiring," he said. "A man of Kennedy's swimming ability could probably do it, but I think it was quite a feat based on his physical condition."

But Farrar was critical of the Senator's speech. "He didn't answer any questions, he brought on more," Farrar said. Assuming Kennedy was in shock, why hadn't Markham and Gargan contacted police if they were concerned enough about the girl to risk diving into Poucha Pond in the middle of the night?

If the fire department had been called at the time of the accident, "There was a great possibility we could have saved Mary Jo's life," Farrar said. "There would have been an airlock in the car—there always is in such submersions—that would have kept her alive." Farrar had equipment to administer air to a trapped person directly or to augment an air pocket inside a submerged automobile. "If we had been called, I could have reached the scene in 45 minutes. I say 45 minutes because it was dark." It had taken Farrar 30 minutes from the time he got the call until he recovered the body from the accident car, he said. "That was in daylight. The lack of light might have caused a delay of 15 minutes."

Arena disapproved of the carnival-like spectacle at the town wharf: A 40-year-old man followed Farrar into the water fully clothed: then six young men made the swim *ensemble*. But there wasn't much he could do about it except maintain order.

Arena had grown impatient with Farrar's pronouncements about the accident. "John had all this stuff down pat about the air bubble and how long Mary Jo could have lived. The thing that bothered me about it was, John didn't know when he went down into that car what he would find. I'm thinking: 'Was he really doing all this investigating when he was underwater for about ten minutes?' I didn't think so."

But Arena had to reconsider his opinion in light of a clipping from the *Boston Herald Traveler,* dated three days before the Kennedy accident and mailed to the police station. A New Hampshire woman had spent five hours in a submerged automobile. Amazed to find the driver unconscious, but alive, police rushed the victim to a hospital where she was given respiration and treated for immersion. Doctors said only an air bubble trapped inside the car had saved her life.

Arena also received accounts of an accident in Salem, Oregon, in which the passenger in a car that crashed through a chain on a ferry crossing the Willamette River had drowned. Having escaped from the car to swim to shore, the driver was charged with negligent homicide. Arena's correspondent suggested, "This is near what happened in your town. I think you filed the wrong complaint, don't you?"

Carmen Salvador acknowledged, "Chief Arena is getting a lot of letters. They're about evenly divided. Those who like the Senator will stick with him." As for Ted Kennedy's swimming ability, "When the kids around here can swim that channel they know they have it made. It's the thing to do."

Arena himself believed Kennedy. "Despite his bad back, Senator Kennedy looks healthy to me. I think he could do it."

Arena told reporters, "about a dog we used to see every day downtown that was soaking wet and bothering people. Finally, one of my officers grabbed it and looked at his collar. The dog belonged to somebody on Chappaquiddick. Apparently, every day the dog would jump in the water and swim to Edgartown, have his fun, then swim back at night. And we chuckled about that at the police station. We figured: If the dog could do it, Ted Kennedy could do it."

Arena was not so amused about the rescue attempt made by Gargan and Markham and disclosed for the first time in the Senator's speech, "This revelation stunned police who clearly feel that this information should have been given them at the outset and cannot see why it was not." Though both Markham and Gargan were at the police station neither had given any indication they had a connection with the accident. Arena thought charges could be brought against a person who had known about the accident and hadn't reported it, but "research" showed Gargan and Markham to have only "a moral, not a legal obligation" to report the accident. Neither was liable for prosecution because of their knowledge of the accident for an undisclosed number of hours, Arena said. "There's no violation on their part of any statute."

While under no legal obligation to do so, "Gargan and Markham could reasonably have been expected to report the accident," *Time* pointed out later. "A prompt call to the police would have saved the Senator from some of the innuendo that followed—if indeed, he was innocent of drunkenness." The suspicion was bound to linger, "That the only reason the two men did not call police is that they were afraid that Kennedy was in no shape to undergo breath or other tests for alcohol.

Thus, they might have chosen to risk the lesser charge of leaving the scene of an accident over the graver charges that might have arisen from drunken driving." The harshest deduction *Newsweek* made about their behavior was, "That their efforts were devoted almost exclusively in trying to get Teddy Kennedy off the hook."

Indeed, the role of Markham and Gargan touched off the strongest reaction to the speech, a wave of editorial revulsion and reproach. By acknowledging belatedly their rescue efforts at Dike Bridge, Kennedy had passed the onus of not reporting the accident onto Gargan and Markham. If Kennedy was in shock, he could not be wholly blamed for failing to report the accident. How defensible was the inaction of two men, "In full possession of the facts, not in any state of shock, trained in the law and politically astute?"

Gargan's "was irritated and angry" about the furor. But, he said, "At the same time I understood the press didn't know the real situation; they didn't know what had gone on. So the criticism was rightly taken from their point of view. But from my point of view, I did exactly what I thought I should have done, and what I would do again." All Gargan was interested in when he dove into Poucha Pond was saving Mary Jo, he said. "I wasn't thinking about the Senator's political career at the time. And the press had no understanding of that."

Gargan may have been the worst person to return to Dike Bridge with Ted Kennedy, he said, "because we had grown up together; we did that kind of thing, go into the water and try to save people. This was an automatic reaction. When an incident takes place on the water, you don't call the Coast Guard. You better do something damn quick, or it may be too late. The thing to do was get into the nearest speedboat or dive in—and that's what we did. A person not having that experience might have looked at the car and said, 'Oh, Christ! There's nothing I can do.' If it had been some guy who came upon the scene all hysterical and ran for the nearest telephone to call the fire department—that isn't helping

Mary Jo. That wouldn't have saved her. You're doing that because you don't have the guts to take your clothes off and get into that dark, cold water and try to make a rescue in a car you may be stuck in. But you're doing everything the press loves."

In the speech Ted Kennedy did not claim that he intended to report the accident as soon as he swam the channel. Gargan observed, "The Senator never did actually say in so many words that when he jumped into the water he told Paul and me that he was going to report the accident. He wasn't in shock at that point. What happened to him after that, I don't know. So as far as press criticism goes, it may be well taken. Except to Paul and me, when somebody says, 'I'll take care of it,' we presumed that's what he was going to do. It wasn't our position to report the accident. We had a guy right up to the moment he went into the water capable of reporting his own accident. But he did not live up to what he said he was going to do."

Legally, Gargan was on solid ground. "Nothing under the law would criticize what Paul Markham and I did. If I drove by that bridge and saw the accident take place and just continued on my way and did nothing about it, there's no law that would put me under any obligation to report the accident," Gargan said. "Everybody is saying, 'Those two guys are sons of bitches,' and this and that. Granted, we may be. But there's no liability under the law in being a son of a bitch."

———

It would have been unethical for Gargan and Markham to do anything about notifying police about the accident. As lawyers to Senator Kennedy, they would have breached the canons of ethics had they reported the accident without his permission, Philip Sisk, president of the Massachusetts Bar Association said. "There's no evidence they knew any time after the accident what the Senator wanted them to do." The question was: When did Kennedy realize he should have reported the accident?

Sisk was more concerned about the press briefings Edgartown officials held during their investigation, he said. "If a man is a United States Senator, that doesn't mean he is stripped of his rights, and they definitely were trampled on."

Sisk was impressed with the Senator's speech. "I think he assumed a lot more responsibility than he had to." It was his personal opinion, not as president of the bar, "that Senator Kennedy could never have been found guilty of leaving the scene."

District Attorney Edmund Dinis agreed the press briefings had been unwise. With such an explosion of publicity, "No one could get a fair trial until it's over." He hadn't gotten involved, "Because I didn't want to become part of this carnival atmosphere where the news media take over and conduct their own investigation. They do it every time." Reporters used "psychological gimmicks" to get public officials to talk, Dinis complained. "You're always on the defensive, you're wide open. I tell myself again and again: 'No comment. No comment.' You begin talking and God help you."

Dinis would have ordered an autopsy in the case had he been aware of all the circumstances surrounding the accident, he said. "When the medical examiner made his examination of Mary Jo Kopechne, it wasn't known that Senator Kennedy was the driver of the car."

Dinis' remarks angered Walter Steele. "It's awfully easy to be a Monday morning quarterback. Apparently he is speaking from the living room because it was too hot for him in the kitchen." If Steele were to seek advice "during the turbulent time that we had with the press, Dinis would be the last person from whom I would seek advice."

Steele discounted Dinis' autopsy talk. Not only had the district attorney known Senator Kennedy was the driver of the accident car, it was his office which had suggested an autopsy not be performed, Steele said. "Dinis was notified last Saturday in my presence by chief Arena of the death of the girl soon after the tragedy happened. Dinis said, 'You handle it. It's just an automobile accident case. If you want help, I'll come down.'"

Later, when the news was released that Senator Kennedy was driving the accident car, there was no move on the part of the district attorney's office to request an autopsy. Mary Jo Kopechne's body had remained in Edgartown until Sunday, Steele said. "Dinis had at least 24 hours to make a decision on whether or not to enter the case and hold the body for autopsy and chose to do neither."

In Steele's opinion, "An autopsy in this matter would only result in the unnecessary surgical mutilation of the body of a blameless girl. It would add nothing to the fact pattern of the Commonwealth's case."

That the Commonwealth's case was "complete" without autopsy or further investigation, however, was arguable, Arena conceded. "A lot of local people took the burn when Kennedy went on TV. They got aroused thinking he was putting them on."

The most vociferous of these made public his displeasure. On the scene when the accident car was removed from Poucha Pond, Dr. Edward Self had driven Arena to the landing for his meeting at the police station with Senator Kennedy on Saturday morning. Senator Kennedy's explanation of the accident contained "discrepancies and hiatuses" which demanded answers, Self said. Had the Senator made a wrong turn on Dike Road, "His headlights would have revealed water and the bridge in adequate time for him to stop the car. For him to drive off the bridge implied that judgment and reaction time were impaired," raising such serious doubts that Self could not accept "the highly-polished, indeed politically masterful TV statement of July 25 without retorting: 'Just whom do you think you're kidding?'"

If Edgartown was suffering a miasma of doubt over the Kennedy broadcast, the Senator was faring much better on the mainland. "It seems like we've handled 95,000 calls since Kennedy went on television," Western Union's traffic chief in Boston said. "Most of the people sending telegrams are for him."

An estimated 10,000 telegrams delivered to the Hyannis Port compound on Saturday morning were running 100 to 1 in favor of the Senator remaining in office, Dick Drayne said. "Obviously moved" by the outpouring of support, Kennedy was reserving decision on whether to return to the Senate. No announcement was planned over the weekend.

While the speech was generating a flood of messages of support in Massachusetts, editorial response to the speech nationally was harsh. Nothing Senator Kennedy said had explained his conduct convincingly to the *Baltimore Sun*. Kennedy remained "a man who failed badly in long hours—not just a moment of crisis." The Senator had given no real explanation why Miss Kopechne should have been abandoned in the car all night, or why the accident was so long in being reported to police "when others had known about it," the *Hartford Courant* charged. So long as Kennedy had not seen fit to explain the night's events, "Further investigation might be necessary."

Reference to "the health of my wife" brought inquiries about a possible pregnancy to Kennedy's office. When Press Secretary Dick Drayne called the compound, Kennedy told him, "Just say she's pregnant. She's expecting a baby in February." Concerned the information might be construed as a bid of sympathy, Drayne delayed releasing it. Desperate for something to give reporters against a deluge of negative reaction to the speech, Drayne announced on Saturday that Joan Kennedy was expecting a fourth child.

That couldn't help matters very much, but it was the best Drayne could do. Proscribed from commenting about the accident, he had nothing to say in the face of a torrent of critical complaints about the speech. The Senator was unwilling to answer any questions about the accident. To all inquiries, Drayne made a standard reply, "The Senator made that clear in the statement. And if it wasn't clear, I'm not going to elaborate."

On the defensive, anxious to salvage something from "the ugly and destructive gossip that was being spread about the accident," Rose Kennedy disclosed in an interview at the compound, "Teddy has been so magnificent under a tremendous strain which people don't know about. He has been overly conscientious about his father and about me and about Ethel, in addition to his own obligations. He has been so faithful in caring about us all, it has really been unfair—the burden."

Mrs. Kennedy was writing to the Kopechnes, she said, telling them that having experienced the death of one of her own daughters at the same age, she understood their suffering; "and how badly I felt that my son was in any way involved in their loss; and that my sympathy and prayers were with them."

Through her maternal testimonial, Mrs. Kennedy echoed the chords of a familiar family mythology. "I've always brought my children up with the idea that you have ordeals and triumphs," she said. "Some people call them the agonies and the ecstasies, the ups and downs." Putting the accident in detached perspective, Mrs. Kennedy explained, "God does not send us a cross any heavier than we can bear. How you cope is the important thing—not the events themselves. I'm sure Ted can rise above all this."

Chapter 33

THE SENATOR'S FIRST PUBLIC APPEARANCE SINCE HIS broadcast was also calculated to subdue the negative response to his speech. That the press had been tipped off in advance was evident by a company of photographers awaiting the arrival of a Chevrolet convertible driven by Joan Kennedy that pulled into the parking lot of St. Francis Xavier church in Hyannis on Sunday morning.

Kennedy got out of the car to absolute silence. Then, a scattering of applause began to build. A voice called out, "We're with you, Ted!"

Kennedy walked with his head bowed into the church. He sat staring at an altar dedicated to the memory of his brother, Joseph, Jr., while Monsignor William Thompson read from the Epistle of St. Paul: "No test has been sent you that doesn't come to all men." The Mass concluded with "America the Beautiful." The anthem had been sung in the church on previous occasions, Msgr. Thompson explained. "Today, we used it in tribute to Senator Kennedy."

The Senator's exit provoked another outburst from an unruly crowd that ignored the pleas of four police officers to maintain order. An usher escorting the Senator to his car shouted, "This is church ground! Let's not make a carnival out of it."

Another demonstration greeted Kennedy's return to Hyannis Port. Circling about the post office, seventeen college-age "Youth for Truth," carried hand-lettered signs: CAN YOU BUY JUSTICE? and SWIM, DON'T RUN IN '72. The group was "disgusted, dismayed and shocked" by the Senator's speech, "because it appealed strictly to the emotions."

The demonstrators were pelted with eggs by neighborhood youths who shouted obscenities and let the air out of the tires of one or two cars that had brought the group to Hyannis Port.

Kennedy spent the afternoon on board the *Marlin*. The yacht was anchored for a picnic; then Kennedy returned to the compound for a meeting of advisers and staff to evaluate the depth of a disaster in the making. National press monitors in the Senator's office reported nearly-uniform editorial condemnation for his "emotion-charged" address which had raised more questions than it answered "for a gross failure of responsibility." By delaying reporting the accident, Kennedy "had possibly sacrificed whatever slight chance there might have been of saving Mary Jo Kopechne in the hope of somehow keeping his name out of it."

In David Halberstam's opinion, "The speech was of such cheapness and bathos as to be a rejection of everything the Kennedys had stood for in candor and style." With all witnesses silenced, it was not clear why the moral issue should have been raised to voters "who have no way of questioning the cast of characters," James Reston said in the *New York Times*. To ask for a referendum on the basis of unknown facts was ridiculous. The only way Kennedy could get from the voters the kind of endorsement he sought was to resign and seek re-election on a platform of vindication, the *Providence Journal* suggested. "Anything short of a formal submission of the issue to the electorate was an exercise in emotional bathos." For Kennedy to have resigned would have been "an act of wisdom, clear perception and high courage that would have been a healing service to himself, to his family, and to so many people who want so badly to believe him."

Spokesmen put as good a public face on the collapsing situation as possible. Ignoring the editorial furor, Eric Cochner of the Senator's staff said response to the speech in Washington was "tremendous." "We've had calls from all over the country urging him not to resign." Cochner had no idea what Senator Kennedy was going to do. "If he has made a final decision, he hasn't communicated it to us."

———

Registrar Richard McLaughlin chose Sunday evening to announce Kennedy's license, suspended because of a preliminary finding of fault in the accident, was being revoked for an indefinite period, as required by his conviction for leaving the scene of the accident. Kennedy had to appear at a statutory hearing scheduled for Wednesday, August 6, at the Registry's Hyannis office, but his attorneys would be permitted to answer questions put to him, McLaughlin said. "We are interested in his functions at the wheel, what happened immediately before the accident. We're trying to establish the level of performance." The hearing could find "serious fault" or "no serious fault," but nothing in between.

The results of an investigation into the accident conducted in cooperation with Edgartown police "to avoid friction" was not being released, McLaughlin explained. "All such reports are held in confidence to avoid giving any party the advantage in a court case that might stem from a fatal accident."

McLaughlin denied "favored treatment" had been granted to Senator Kennedy. Described as "a politician whose arm-twisting tactics [resulted] in getting his own way around the State House" in his six years as registrar, McLaughlin had been named to the post in 1964 for a term to expire on December 12, 1967. His appointment had been extended two years by special legislation passed over the veto of Republican Governor John Volpe. Cited as "the finest registrar the state has ever had," McLaughlin won praise for his mission to rid the state of drunk drivers—the number one problem of highway safety in Massachusetts. In recommending legislation to reduce from .15% to .10% alcohol blood levels at which drivers were considered too drunk to operate an automobile, McLaughlin had charged courts were too lenient. Drunk drivers accounted for 600 traffic deaths a year, yet less than one percent were ever found guilty and punished. Mandatory jail sentences were needed if the law was to be enforced, McLaughlin said. "We must make the consequences of drunken driving in terms of punishment so severe that that alone will discourage persons from getting behind the wheel when they drink."

McLaughin's private opinion of the Kennedy accident was rather more severe than his official stance. Leaving the scene of an accident and delaying a report for more than nine hours, for all practical purposes foreclosed a drunk driving charge. "It effectively deprives officers of evidence of chemical testing and direct observation of the operator," he said. "So if you wanted to avoid a drunk driving charge after an accident—that's how you do it."

———

Twelve sacks of mail delivered to Kennedy's Boston office on Monday morning were running "heavily in favor of the Senator," according to an aide. Other reports had responses varying from "generally favorable" to reaction split evenly "with both sides strongly opinionated."

Drayne had nothing to say against the tide of editorial incredulity about the speech. Instead, he relied on "counts" of telegrams and mail bags "overwhelmingly supporting the Senator," and expressions of political coquetry about whether the Senator would resign. Drayne didn't know how long Kennedy would take to make up his mind, he said. "He has no immediate plans."

Drayne refused to identify the "second car" mentioned in Kennedy's speech, raising the possibility deputy sheriff "Huck" Look had seen the Senator and two friends en route to the accident scene at 12:45 A.M., and not the accident car itself. But Gargan had rented a white Valiant for the weekend that neither matched the license plate configuration nor the appearance of the "black sedan" Look had encountered at the intersection. Look dismissed the notion he could have confused the two cars, he said. "I know black from white."

That Look could have seen another car unrelated to the Kennedy party was not in the cards either. No one had come forward to say he'd been driving on Chappaquiddick at that hour of the morning, a prospect an aide in Kennedy's office conceded was "probably unlikely."

Gargan found Look's story puzzling, "Because at the time Look said he saw the Senator, I'm convinced under all the circumstances that Paul and I had to be swimming in the water. How that incredible coincidence could have taken place with what Look says about the number plate and the color and style of the car, I don't know." Gargan wasn't as upset about the story as the Senator's lawyers were. "I simply thought Look was wrong."

The witnesses Gargan had feared, at the time, might appear to say they'd seen the Senator at Dike Bridge and contradict the alternative scenario Kennedy had proposed at the ferry landing had not materialized. The only witness to have surfaced had participated in a singular encounter with the Senator before the accident had taken place.

Suffering under the glare of press vituperation as an "accomplice" in failing to report the accident, Gargan was keeping as low a profile as he could. The Senator's speech was generating considerable support, he said, "But it was also highly criticized and raised a lot of anguish and anger that, had it not been given, would not have happened." Much of the "anguish" was reserved for Gargan and Markham, singled out for the "angriest questions" about the speech and labelled "more guilty of wrong-doing than Kennedy." The notoriety had dispensed with Gargan's previous anonymity. Gargan was being pursued by the press.

A pretty, diminutive woman, Betty Gargan was furious to find Ben Silver of CBS at her door, looking for her husband. Excusing herself, she took down a motto from above her kitchen stove, telling Silver, "Take this and read it. And get off my porch and leave this yard. I don't want to see you again!" (The motto said, "Great Spirit: Grant that I may not criticize my neighbor until I have walked a mile in his moccasins.")

Gargan thought it was "awfully funny" his wife had chased CBS News off their property. Outraged at the vilification levelled at her husband, Betty Gargan was even more incensed by the treatment accorded the young women who had attended the party at Chappaquiddick. "She wanted to go on a talk show and give everybody a blast, because the press had been so unfair to the girls about this whole thing," Gargan said. "To say what nice girls they were."

Gargan could only concur. "The truth was, these were girls of high reputation who I liked very much. They had been very loyal to Bobby. The purpose of the reunion was to talk about the campaign the year before—that was strictly the limits of that particular party." Gargan was tired of reading about "six men and six girls" at the party, he said. "Other people who had worked campaigns were supposed to be there and didn't show up. So it could have been 10 fellows and 8 girls, or vice versa. It was as willy-nilly as that."

Gargan bore the withering characterizations of him by the press in silence. He was in no position to clarify the issue, Gargan said. "I wouldn't have tried to clear myself under circumstances where I wasn't at liberty to discuss things I was privy to as a witness, information that was nobody's business. It had nothing to do with Ted Kennedy. It may have been easier if the person involved in the accident owned the fish

market in Hyannis—but that wouldn't change the fact that your obligation is the same."

———

A telegram delivered to the compound on Monday afternoon was
immediately made public:

THE DEMOCRATIC CONGRESSIONAL DELEGATION
FROM MASS. STRONGLY URGES YOU TO RETAIN
YOUR SEAT IN THE U.S. SENATE.
WE PLEDGE TO YOU OUR CONTINUED FRIEND-
SHIP, SUPPORT AND CO-OPERATION. AS MEMBERS
OF THE CONGRESS, WE ARE AWARE OF WHAT
GREAT CONTRIBUTIONS YOU HAVE MADE TO THE
COMMONWEALTH AND TO THE NATION. YOU
HAVE EXERCISED YOUR ROLE OF LEADERSHIP IN
THE SENATE WITH GENUINE BRILLIANCE AND
DEDICATION. WE URGE YOU TO CONTINUE IN
THAT ROLE.

That message was signed by John McCormack and all six Democratic congressmen. To some reporters, it was pure "partisan politics."

Other political pressures were encountering resistance. A nonparti-
san bill in the form of a resolution urging Senator Kennedy to remain in
office was introduced to the Massachusetts House by speaker David
Bartley. He would not force the issue, "If there was less than unanimous
support," Bartley said. "If a vote would prove an embarrassment to
anyone, I wouldn't have it take place." The resolution died in committee.

The Fall River city council voted 5 to 3 against a similar resolution.
In nearby New Bedford, those seeking to register their support for Ted

Kennedy could sign a petition posted in the lobby of city hall by Democratic Mayor Edward Harrington. A New Bedford radio station promptly demanded that a second petition be made available for those who wanted Senator Kennedy to resign. Station WBSM said in its editorial that such a petition was needed because of the "inescapable conclusion that the overriding consideration that motivated Edward M. Kennedy during those tragic hours was the effect the event would have on his public image and his career. What was at risk here was the Kennedy image. Balanced against it was the life of a girl."

Edmund Dinis had "no comment" when asked if his office was looking into the Kennedy accident case. With uncharacteristic understatement, Dinis added, "It's a tough spot for me."

Chapter 34

HAVING FAILED TO RESOLVE THE SUSPICION AND DOUBT
attached to the accident, the lid Kennedy's advisers hoped to place on
the episode was threatening to be lifted by demands—most of them
directed upon the district attorney's office—for a new investigation. The
most dangerous of these was coming from Edgartown grand jury foreman Leslie Leland. A young Vineyard Haven pharmacist, earnest and
conscientious about "fulfilling our civic responsibilities," Leland
requested a conference with Dinis and Attorney General Robert Quinn.
Leland wasn't as interested in calling the grand jury into session to look
into the death of Mary Jo Kopechne, "as I was with our legal rights as
jurors," he said. "I wanted to clarify in my own mind if it could be done,
because the press was putting so much pressure on me to call for an
investigation."

Leland learned that the grand jury had "no legal right" to call for
an investigation at this time. In Quinn's opinion, "It's up to the attorney
general, the district attorney or a judge," Leland reported. "He didn't
say which judge; that's the way he put it: a judge."

Leland wouldn't comment on what Dinis told him, "Because of possible political repercussions," he said. But Dinis had made it clear he had no intention of bringing the case before a grand jury.

But Quinn's "advice" was faulty; and Dinis knew it. The grand jury had the right to investigate any matter it wanted to. All Leland had to do was file a written request with the chief justice of the Superior Court, asking for the grand jury to be reconvened in special session to conduct an investigation into the death of Mary Jo Kopechne. Leland had to make the request through the district attorney's office, but Dinis could not prevent him from doing so.

A grand jury investigation required Dinis to present evidence of a specific crime against a specific defendant. Should the grand jury indict Ted Kennedy, Dinis would be stuck with prosecuting the case. To head off the grand jury, and retain control over the case—if it should come to that—Dinis was exploring his options "at one of the many meetings we had about this matter," on Monday morning, July 28, Armand Fernandes recalled. "Eddie thought he should have gone in at the beginning, but George Killen countered with, 'Let's handle this like we handle all other accidents. Let's leave it to the local police.' And George had prevailed, until the speech."

Had those attending the party at Chappaquiddick talked to police instead of sneaking off Martha's Vineyard, no further investigation would have been necessary, Fernandes said. "The effort to conceal the party, and what had gone on before and after the accident was what brought about all the suspicion in the case." A judicial inquest had been talked about in the newspapers, "But nobody knew how to go about getting one."

Dinis assigned Lance Garth to research the statutes on inquests. A former New Bedford police officer attending law school, Garth was employed in the district attorney's office as indictments clerk.

Dinis also discussed his dilemma with famed criminal attorney F. Lee Bailey, a friend.

"We talked about this entire situation which was unfolding at the time," Bailey recalled. "At first, Ed kind of dropped the thing. It was an automobile accident and he was trying to stay out of it—and the press didn't like that very much. Ed was kind of complaining that he was trying to do the right thing, but he had a Hobson's Choice." Dinis would be criticized no matter what he did.

An inquest was the only procedure short of a grand jury or a trial in which testimony under oath could be obtained, Lance Garth reported on Tuesday morning. Used when questions arose about the circumstances of a death, an inquest was conducted by a judge with the power to subpeona witnesses, hear testimony under oath and consider investigative reports. The judge made a finding of facts as to how the person met his death and reported to the Superior Court whether criminal proceedings were warranted. The judge's determination could be accidental death, criminal negligence, conspiracy to hide facts, or the report could draw no conclusions at all.

If the judge found fault, such as negligence, and the person charged in the report with the commission of a crime was at large, "The magistrate shall issue process for his arrest." If the judge found murder, manslaughter or assault had been committed, he could bind over for appearance in court on a criminal case such witnesses as he considered necessary or as the district attorney designated. But the district attorney was not bound by anything the judge found. The inquest report could be used as a basis for bringing a case before the grand jury or be ignored—and that suited Dinis just fine. The procedure allowed the case to be reopened, but for Dinis to maintain a "hands-off" position, and let the judicial process pursue an investigation.

George Killen demanded to know what "crime" Dinis was seeking to prove by asking for an inquest.

Dinis wasn't looking to hang a rap on Ted Kennedy. He was considering an inquest in order to gain access to witnesses who had attended the party. If people had submitted sworn statements at the time of the accident, the purpose of a new investigation would be questionable. Dinis was considering entering the case, "Because the press is on my back to do something."

"To hell with the press!" Killen said. "Look what they did to Arena! And all he was trying to do was cooperate." Whatever questions remained about the accident—and Killen agreed there were plenty of them—it wasn't a case of any kind. Unsatisfactory as the explanation of the accident was, it was likely to be all Ted Kennedy and his friends were prepared to say about it. Kennedy was going to resume his Senate seat. The controversy was bound to die down. Why revive it?

Killen couldn't stay on at the meeting. He was escorting a possible accomplice in the Costa murders to Boston to undergo lie detector tests. The Costa case and the death of Mary Jo Kopechne were vying for attention not only in Killen's office, but on the front pages of Massachusetts newspapers, two sensational investigations running concurrently. Costa was scheduled to go to trial in September. Killen had 169 other cases to prepare for the special criminal sitting of Superior Court. He wasn't interested in reopening an investigation into the Kennedy accident. Killen said, "We don't prosecute all the cases we know about."

That Killen was downgrading the Kennedy case and counselling Dinis to stay out of it was "good advice," in the opinion of Frank Keating, Killen's friend and himself an ex-assistant district attorney. "George had so much pride, he was far more interested in making sure Dinis didn't look like a goddamned fool and therefore humiliate the office George had such a big part of. I don't think in his wildest Boy Scout dreams George ever thought Ted Kennedy was going to give out enough evidence of willful, wanton and reckless conduct to amount to a manslaughter case." The clamor in the press for a new investigation had been brought about by the mismanagement of the case by Kennedy's advisers. "There was Ted Kennedy, surrounded by sycophants, people who wanted to please him. Had one person controlled his attention it should have been Bob Clark. He was the motor vehicles expert. He'd tried a million of these cases; he knew them backwards and forwards. It was probably the only case Clark wouldn't have his way with a client because he's dealing with a Kennedy. And with those Washington people, and Ted Kennedy being no lawyer himself, the ball just got fumbled." Keating thought the speech so ill-advised, "I couldn't watch it. I was just so ashamed of that whole approach."

Killen was politically neutral about wanting to keep the district attorney's office away from the Kennedy accident; but Dinis was a different breed altogether, "a pure political animal," Keating said. "I could just see Eddie Dinis *trembling* with the possibilities of the thing."

Killen was not the only one in the district attorney's office opposed to a new investigation of the Kennedy accident. Assistant District Attorney Joseph Harrington, brother of New Bedford's mayor, threatened to resign. He said, "I won't have anything to do with it. I'll leave."

Dinis did not consult First Assistant Peter Gay who ran the office administratively and issued all cases. "Eddie knew better than to ask me because he knew I'd say not to do it," Gay said. Gentlemanly, soft-spoken, an experienced trial lawyer with a successful private practice in Taunton, Gay was a former "campaign secretary" for John Kennedy. As a delegate to the state Democratic convention in 1962, he'd been offered a judgeship and other inducements to change his vote to Edward McCormack. Gay had taken an active part in swinging Bristol County to support Ted Kennedy's endorsement.

Jimmy Smith was not aware of the meetings in New Bedford. When he heard about them, "My personal reaction was, I wanted to stay the hell away from it. All the assistants agreed—Joe Harrington, Roddy

Sullivan, Ernie Rottenberg—no way did we want anything to do with an inquest. We said, 'We're out of it. Let those guys go at it.' Dinis only trusted Armand [Fernandes] anyway. It was the Portuguese connection."

Modest, hard-working, content to remain in the shadow of the flamboyant Dinis, Fernandes was the only assistant in the district attorney's office without political ambitions, he said. "I only wanted to be a lawyer."

If Dinis was finding his decision to enter the case difficult, indecisiveness was epidemic at the Kennedy compound, the machinery of public relations faltering in the face of overwhelming editorial hostility. The "election returns" were winning emotional public support, but Kennedy's "too contrived, too blatantly emotional" speech had done him "more harm than good with political professionals and the press." Kennedy had left so many questions unanswered about the accident, "No fair assessment could be made about his resignation." It had been as indefensible for him not to have offered a full explanation for the accident as it was not to have reported it in the first place. With so many questions still hanging over him, it was questionable how effective Kennedy would be in the Senate.

A decision to field a creditable candidate to challenge Kennedy's seat in 1970 had been made before the accident. Republican State Chairman Josiah Spaulding didn't know whether his party's chances of defeating Ted Kennedy had been enhanced by the accident at Chappaquiddick. "It could hurt his image, but I wouldn't want to beat him on this basis," Spaulding said. "Senator Kennedy's situation is not a partisan matter. One can only feel great personal sympathy for him. But there are a great many questions involved, some of which may never be answered. Eventually, he is going to have to make speeches and demonstrate his ability to lead."

Spaulding's analysis wasn't taken very seriously. Political observers doubted Kennedy could be defeated in Massachusetts no matter what he did, "Because he was a Kennedy and could get away with anything, even the death of a young woman under mysterious circumstances." The real damage to his career was as a national leader.

Kennedy's post-accident behavior had permanently knocked him out of presidential contention, in the opinion of liberal Democratic Congressman Emmanuel Celler of Brooklyn. "I think the nation itself has come to realize he is not a shining white knight." There were so many gaps in Senator Kennedy's "cunning" TV speech, "that it causes us to lose considerable confidence in Teddy Kennedy."

As a result of the accident, pressures pushing Senator Kennedy toward a presidential candidacy had subsided, Mike Mansfield confirmed. "I never thought he'd run in 1972 unless he bowed to the pressures that built up. Now, I feel more certain than ever that he won't run."

Before Chappaquiddick, Kennedy could have had the nomination "for the asking," Senator Edmund Muskie said. "The controversy may have brought about an unfortunate shift in his fortunes." Muskie, a Maine Democrat with his own presidential ambitions, would not operate on the assumption that Ted Kennedy's troubles—"And I suppose he has troubles—would be of any political advantage to me. I wish him well in every way." It was premature to write off the Senator's future. "I would never count a Kennedy out of anything," Muskie said. The continuing tragedy and phenomenon of the Kennedy family "did not lend itself to common measurement."

With neither Kennedy nor his friends planning to say anything more about the accident "In the face of demands by almost every major newspaper for clarification," the press that had played so large a part in the success of the Kennedy dynasty was now "more solidly and righteously anti-EMK than perhaps any other element in the political community," columnists Evans and Novak observed. So long as Kennedy remained silent about the accident's unanswered questions, "He risked a hostile press. As a result, most politicians read EMK out of the 1972 presidential race. He may be out of the presidential picture for good. His entire political career hangs in the balance."

The collapse of Ted Kennedy's presidential chances, however, was suggesting a possible escape route out of the dilemma of Chappaquiddick. A poll published by the *Boston Globe* on Tuesday, July 28, revealed 78% of Massachusetts voters wanted Ted Kennedy to retain his Senate seat. Although 56% believed he'd left a number of questions about the accident unanswered, an NBC-sponsored survey revealed the next day that 81% of his constituents wanted Kennedy to remain in office. As presidential preference, however, Kennedy's position had dropped from a pre-accident high of 72% to 55%. Advisers at the compound concluded from that result that a first step toward his political rehabilitation would be to take himself out of presidential contention in 1972, a fact that appeared already a *fait accompli*. Withdrawal from the presidential race, combined with an expression of interest in remaining in the Senate, should—in their view—end the harassment in the press about a new investigation into the accident.

"No decision" had been made on Tuesday, when the Senator cruised Nantucket Sound aboard the *Marlin,* then went fishing from the breakwater in Hyannis Port. But Kennedy could not afford to dawdle in the expectation of a tide of public support rising up against the implacable criticism in the press. Editorials and cartoons were getting worse. Kennedy was not an unfortunate man confessing panic and poor judgment in his speech, "But a personage engaged in an elaborately devious piece of stagecraft." The surge of public support was falling off. Western Union officials confirmed earlier estimates of messages sent to the Senator to be well below the 100,000 mark previously announced. The Senator was reading many of the messages, "To help him decide about resignation," Dick Drayne said. "Whether he will say 'yes' or 'no,' isn't known."

But Kennedy's appeal to constituents had reduced the credibility of his resignation talk. The longer the decision hovered, the less likely it was anyone would believe he ever considered resigning. A "source close to the decision" later claimed the suspense about the Senator's intentions had been a Kennedy-created sham. "There was never any essential doubt about resignation. It was just a matter of timing the statement" to announce his return to the Senate.

The editorial furor, the letters and telegrams, had played no part in the matter. Kennedy had determined from the start, "I've just got to gut this thing through."

Chapter 35

OF THE FIRST 400 LETTERS OPENED AT THE SENATOR'S BOSTON
office on Wednesday morning "only three or four" were anti-Kennedy,
aide Jim King revealed. Because the Senator had expressed the wish to
see everything that came into the office, the mail was being forwarded
to Hyannis Port. The Senator was "heartened and encouraged" by such
messages of support, but King didn't know how long he would take to
decide whether to resign.

Dick Drayne, too, persisted in the claim that resignation was possible, he said. "I have no reason to believe the Senator has made any
decision, or if he has, communicated it to anyone." Kennedy ended his
self-imposed exile, boarding a plane at Barnstable County airport in
Hyannis at one o'clock to fly to the funeral of Burke Marshall's father
in Plainfield, New Jersey. It was then that his Boston office distributed
mimeographed copies of a statement to reporters:

Senator Edward M. Kennedy is returning to Washington to resume his duties as United States Senator and assistant majority leader.

He is grateful to the people of Massachusetts for their expressions of confidence and expects to submit his record to them as a candidate for re-election in 1970. If re-elected he will serve out his entire six year term.

Dick Drayne refused to say if the Senator was foregoing a run for the presidency in 1972. "I don't interpret the Senator's statements," he said. "It seems unambiguous to me." Kennedy did not plan to hold a press conference or to submit to questions about the accident. His speedy response to an appeal to Massachusetts voters suggested to the *New York Times*, "A carefully-worked out plan to reestablish his political position in the eyes of the voters of his state" based upon "a partially irrelevant and totally unsatisfactory *ex parte* account" of the accident. "There are so many gaping holes in the story which he has so assiduously avoided filling, there is such an unmistakable atmosphere of calculated evaluation for maximum—or, as the case may be, minimum—public effect, that we cannot consider the matter to have been satisfactorily resolved in any sense."

Joseph Kopechne approved of Kennedy's decision to return to the Senate, but considered his week of silence about the accident ill-advised. "I think he was getting poor advice, I really do." Kopechne had yet to come to grips with his daughter's death. He said, "I still can't believe it's happened, even now. It's like watching a TV program and turning if off and it's all over."

Gwen Kopechne continued to think of her daughter "in the present, not in the past. We still expect her to come home, to walk through that door. We haven't had time to think and form any opinion of what is going on around us. When it really hits us, it will be too late."

Mrs. Kopechne did not hold Senator Kennedy "personally responsible" for her daughter's death and harbored "no hard feelings" toward
him, she said. "Mr. Kopechne and I can form no hate for anyone. There's
always something good in a person, no matter what his faults. Nothing
can help us with our daughter now. No one can bring her back or console
us. This could have happened to any one of those girls; it just so happened it was Mary Jo. It was an unfortunate accident. We want to believe
this!"

Senator Kennedy's return to the Senate had left Edgartown "with
the physical and figurative debris of its notoriety," the *Vineyard Gazette*
observed. Portions of Dike Bridge had been broken away for souvenirs;
tourists continued to pose for snapshots at the split rail fence in front of
the Lawrence cottage; and reporters returned for "second look" stories.
"All of them are bothered and intrigued that the known facts of the case
do not add up to a complete picture of the accident."

Kennedy's intention not to say anything more about the incident
brought new and heavy pressures on the district attorney's office. For
the past three weeks Dinis had been "deeply troubled," he said. "Miss
Kopechne was dead. Senator Kennedy said he was involved. I had a
choice of conducting an investigation myself or letting the local authorities do it." Dinis had no doubt the proper course was to leave the matter in the hands of the local police and medical examiner, "But as the
days went by and no new information came to light, I began to distrust
my own motives. I began to ask myself if my admiration of the Kennedys, and my sympathy for Senator Kennedy's personal situation were
preventing me from carrying out my duty as district attorney. Had my
decision to take no action been based on a misguided deference to the
Senator's high station? Clearly, I had to call my own courage into
account."

On Wednesday night Dinis decided he could stay out of the case no
longer. "A human being was dead. I was not satisfied that all pertinent

facts had been told," he said. "And it was my duty as a representative of the people of my district to demand an inquest."

———

Senator Kennedy looked tanned, rested and apparently recovered from whatever injuries he had suffered in his accident when he stepped into a crush of tourists and reporters awaiting his arrival at the Capitol on Thursday morning.

Reporters wanted to know if the statement released the previous day meant he'd eliminated himself as a candidate for president in 1972.

"That's right, I intend to fill out my full term if re-elected," Kennedy said and brushed aside other questions to hurry up the Capitol steps. Kennedy waited in an anteroom of the Senate until Majority Leader Mike Mansfield showed up; then, he entered the chamber.

Mansfield said, "Come in here, Ted. Right back where you belong." Taking Kennedy's arm, Mansfield escorted him to the front-row whip's desk, a ritual of reentry as obvious to those crowded into the gallery as was the Senator's subdued and ill-at-ease manner. Throughout the morning session, members of both parties approached his desk to shake hands, pat his shoulder and murmur words of welcome.

Kennedy reaffirmed his decision not to run for president in 1972 on his way to lunch. "The statement that I made was precise in saying to the people of Massachusetts—who have been so responsive—that I would serve my full term." Kennedy intended to say no more about the accident, he said. "I tried to the very best of my ability in the reports that have been made to give the facts of the accident. I wouldn't have any further comment."

So dark a cloud of doubt and mystery hovering over the incident, and the appearance of "a calculated suppression of many details," was a powerful argument for Senator Kennedy to abandon his intention not to say anything more about the episode, in the view of the *Washington Post*. "Because it is crucial for the Senator to dispel the impression given by his silence that there is something he is trying to hide." Kennedy's silence was "compelling evidence in support of the ugly suggestion that there was, and still is a careful, cold-blooded conspiracy to cover something up—a suspicion that, as things stand, is easily arrived at."

Jimmy Smith regretted the price of the presidency appeared to have been paid as a result of the serious mismanagement of the crisis by a clique of advisers at the compound.

Smith was glad, "You're back at work and the ordeal is over." He wrote Kennedy on Thursday, July 31, to express, "How I feel and where I stand, and that you know you can count on me now and any time in the future." Smith had talked to Joe Gargan, "And asked him to relay messages to you during the past two weeks. I hope they helped."

Disappointed that his mediation efforts between the district attorney's office and the compound had not been able to avert a disaster, Smith wanted Kennedy to know, "Ed Dinis proved to be a true friend. I'll explain when I see you."

But Smith's assurances were hollow. He didn't know what Dinis was doing. On the day of Smith's soothing letter, Dinis was asking Joseph Tauro, chief justice of the Superior Court to assign a judge, "To conduct an inquest into the death of Mary Jo Kopechne who supposedly died by external means on or about July 18, 1969." Later that afternoon, the district attorney's office released the text of the Dinis letter, without comment.

Word of the reopening of an investigation into the accident at Chappaquiddick struck Kennedy's office like a thunderbolt, only hours after the Senator had resumed his seat.

Dick Drayne learned of the Dinis letter when the Boston bureau of the Associated Press telephoned for "reaction." Summoned from the

Senate floor, Kennedy was reported to have "blown his top" at the revival of a crisis thought to have been disarmed.

Chapter 36

THE SENATOR WOULD HAVE "NO COMMENT" ON THE DINIS LETTER, Drayne announced, before a call from Kennedy's office went out to Judge Tauro in Boston.

Tauro was outraged the letter had been made public before he received it. "It is very bad judgment at the least on District Attorney Dinis' part to disclose information of this sort without first notifying the court." Tauro refused comment until he received the letter, which arrived by special delivery the next morning. Tauro dismissed the request out of hand. No provision of law permitted the Superior Court to conduct inquests, he said. "All relevant statutes clearly indicate that the district court has exclusive jurisdiction over such proceedings." Tauro scorned Dinis for "the confusion and misconceptions you have created in the minds of many regarding the judicial process. I do believe it is incumbent upon you to state the reason for your unusual and unprecedented action."

Dinis took Tauro's rebuke in stride. He had no quarrel with the Chief Justice and was following his advice. The law on inquests was "ambiguous about jurisdiction." While unprecedented, his request to the Superior

Court had been attempted anyway, "To express my preference of courts to conduct the inquiry. District court judges are appointed for life to serve in their community, Superior Court judges travel around—I like that better," Dinis said, with disarmingly cavalier disregard for proper procedure.

Dinis sent his request to Kenneth Nash, chief justice of the district court. While district attorneys might request them, "Inquests are practically obsolete," Nash said. An inquest did not have the power of indictment, "All it can do is recommend to a district attorney that grand jury action is advisable." A grand jury was used to ascertain the existence of a crime and the parties accused of doing it; an inquest was limited to the question of whether a crime had been committed. The difference was, "A judge is trained on determining legal causation, grand juries aren't."

Dinis may have hesitated to apply to Judge Nash following Dinis' highly publicized accusations that the Massachusetts district court system was "among the most corrupt systems in the world, because judges sit for life on one bench and exercise personal prejudices daily." Nash had "considered the source" in disdaining the charges as "hardly worth an answer." He said, "I'll challenge Mr. Dinis to name one corrupt judge in the system, but he can't."

Dinis should have filed his request with the presiding judge of the district court at Edgartown, Nash explained. Judge Boyle would "probably" disqualify himself from presiding at an inquest, having imposed a suspended sentence for leaving the scene and delivered himself of the extrajudicial opinion that Senator Kennedy had been "punished far beyond anything this court can impose."

Dinis had not followed the established procedure of consulting local officials who were familiar with the case before asking for an inquest, Walter Steele said. "We have had no discussion at all with Mr. Dinis since Senator Kennedy pleaded guilty." Steele was willing to sit down and "talk rationally" with the district attorney about evidence in the case, but he would oppose an inquest, "If I had any official standing to do that." Steele didn't think a new inquiry would produce any evidence of other crimes.

An inquest could resolve a number of unanswered questions about the accident that had aroused public curiosity, Arena said. He was surprised Dinis hadn't informed him of his request in advance or explained why he felt an inquest in the case was necessary, "After all, he is my district attorney."

Nettled by criticism that his handling of the case might have provoked demands for a new investigation, and still sensitive about his failure to have questioned persons who had attended the party with the exception of Jack Crimmins, Arena wanted it to be known that he had interviewed "a number of them" and so had Walter Steele. "Although the questioning did not develop any evidence to support new charges, it helped dispel some of the rumors about the case," Arena told the *New York Daily News*. Arena's questioning had turned up no evidence of excessive drinking at the party, nor information to support speculation that Senator Kennedy had conspired for a time to hide the fact he was driving the accident car. His interrogations had failed to clear up one mystery in the case: No one at the party to whom Arena talked could pinpoint the exact time Senator Kennedy and Mary Jo Kopechne had left the party.

An embarrassed Arena later confessed, "Maybe we were just trying to cover our asses or something, but that story is inaccurate. We only talked to Jack Crimmins. We never got to the other party people at all."

Arena's offer to help in the new investigation went unacknowledged. The district attorney had shown no interest in Edgartown police files, he said. "There's no rapport between the two offices."

———

As a first step in the investigation, Dinis ordered the accident car impounded as evidence. Bernie Flynn supervised the removal from the

Depot Corner garage to State Police barracks in Oak Bluffs. Shrouded in tarpaulin, the car had been stripped by souvenir-seekers of three ashtrays, the gas cap and pedal, pieces of shattered windshield and chrome trim. Flynn didn't think the car would provide much in the way of evidence and was dubious about a new investigation. "Dinis didn't want to go after the case at all; he was so scared of it, he wasn't answering his phone. He was forced by the press baying at his heels to do something. So, being a politician, he could see the handwriting on the wall," Flynn said. "Had he been smart, he would have kept 'hands-off,' like Killen told him to."

Killen was "fit to be tied and mad as hell" when he got word of the Dinis letter. In Killens view, Dinis was upset at criticism in the press, and had caved in to pressure. An inquest was as much to defend Dinis' own reputation as to investigate Senator Kennedy's accident.

Frank Keating thought there might be another reason the district attorney got involved. "One thing about Dinis, there was no hanky-panky with drunk driving cases. And that was strictly and solely because of publicity. If anything ever happened to a case that was going down the drain it was going to reflect on him—and Dinis wasn't about to give that up for drunks. He had that scathing attitude about anybody who drank because he never drank himself to any degree." The press had been pounding away with speculation that Ted Kennedy had been drinking at the time of the accident, needling Dinis into action.

Keating was curious to see if the matter ever went to trial. "It wasn't the kind of case Dinis would assign anybody; he'd handle it personally," he said. "I figured he'd fall flat on his face. He was hopeless trying cases. He never knew anything. Because he'd never take the time to prepare."

But Jimmy Smith commended the district attorney's conduct entirely. Dinis had been unfairly criticized for following the dictates of his office by staying out of the Kennedy accident. "Eddie turned sour when he was hammered and ridiculed by the press. He went into a rage, then he attacked, like he usually does," Smith said. Errors of judgment on the part of Ted Kennedy's advisers had been responsible for a reopened investigation. "Dinis was being kind, and they didn't take his kindness," Smith said. The arrogance of Kennedy's staff had prevented even so much as a telephone call to acknowledge what Dinis had tried to do.

Smith was grateful Dinis hadn't taken the case before a grand jury. "If he'd done that, they would have bagged it, and it would have been all over."

Dinis was amused when Smith told him he didn't want anything to do with the inquest. He said, "We didn't have any plans for *you* to be involved." With the inquest letter, "I was put in a back room," Smith said. "They were afraid I'd surface, so they had me tucked away."

George Killen wasn't concerned the press would discover the "Kennedy connection" in his office, so much as the focus of the case had moved to New Bedford, and he'd lost control. When Dinis announced a press conference "to state clearly the reason why I have called for a judicial inquest into the death of Mary Jo Kopechne," Killen was reminded of the debacle the previous March. Dinis had made such inflammatory remarks at a news conference to announce the arrest of murderer Antone Costa, that defense attorneys had won injunctive relief "following some of the most sordid pretrial publicity ever released to the press by investigative agencies." It was the first time an order for restraint had been brought by a district court. Killen urged Dinis not to discuss the Kennedy accident in public and fan the flames of controversy any higher than they were already.

Dinis called off the press conference as reporters were already gathering, so as to allow his letter to reach the district court for a ruling. In the statement he had prepared for the press conference—but which was never released—Dinis explained that his request for an inquest had not been based on the uncovering of new evidence, "but rather on the *lack* of information that would allow me to remain out of the case with a clear conscience," Dinis said. "The purpose of my action is to find the truth. Only a full disclosure of all the facts will allow us to lay this case, with all of its pain, finally to rest."

To deflect criticism that an inquest had, in any way, been "invited" because of the unavailability of witnesses, "three young women" who had attended the party at Chappaquiddick complained to the *New York Times* that they had yet to be approached by Massachusetts authorities to give statements about the accident. The Senator's office confirmed the two other young women and five men at the party hadn't been contacted by police either.

Senator Kennedy was cancelling a speech before the World of Youth Council in Liege, Belgium. "He doesn't feel now is the time to travel to Europe," Dick Drayne said. Kennedy wanted to be "available" in case his presence was required, "But he doesn't understand why Dinis is asking for an inquest."

Kennedy told reporters on the Senate floor, "It's still rather unclear as to the nature of it. I plan to cooperate in any way." But he was clearly dismayed by a reopened inquiry into his accident. It had been his understanding, "After I accepted the responsibility and appeared in a court of law, there wouldn't be any further kinds of legal action."

If Kennedy didn't understand why Dinis asked for an inquest, he was among the few in Washington who didn't. "The common sense and common conscience of the American people rejected the Senator's explanation of the accident," columnist James Reston wrote. An inquest, "Should be welcomed by the general public, and especially by Senator Kennedy himself," according to a WCBS radio editorial. Even the most partisan of Senator Kennedy's "supporters should be disturbed by the ugly suspicion that a conspiracy of official silence has surrounded the tragedy." Vital questions had been left unanswered, and material witnesses permitted to go unquestioned by police. Kennedy's televised explanation had been "at once self-pitying and unsatisfactory" in many respects. "There is about the whole incident an unpleasant aura of pro-tected privilege. Senator Kennedy and every other witness who will be called to testify must be prepared to give honest answers to the searching questions that remain to be asked."

The resumption of the crisis was very much on the minds of report-ers at Logan Airport in Boston who met Senator Kennedy on his way to Cape Cod for the weekend.

Asked if he thought the move to seek an inquest "smacked of an attempt to get publicity," Kennedy replied, "No, I wouldn't categorize that of Mr. Dinis. I think he has a responsibility. I respect him for fulfill-ing his responsibilities. I'm just hopeful we can get back to work and get back to the Senate."

The next day, however, "sources close to Kennedy" charged Dinis was trying "to turn tragedy into a political windfall."

But Dinis recognized, "Politically, this is not good for me. This is the home state of the Kennedys, and they are loved. How can anyone who is involved in prosecuting or investigating them come out with any advantage?"

Dinis' assessment was based upon years in pursuit of elected office as heir to a modest political dynasty founded by his father, Jacintho Diniz.

A native of the Azores, the elder Diniz had emigrated to Fall River, served in the U.S. Army in World War I, then taken up a career in pub-lic service. A tireless advocate of social legislation to benefit the poor immigrants who made up the majority of his supporters in the Eighth Bristol District, Diniz was the "stormy petrel" of the State House, "one of the most controversial personages ever to debate an issue on the floor of Beacon Hill," in which he had, one day, appeared wrapped in the Portuguese flag.

Edmundo—he later changed it to Edmund Dinis—Diniz had learned his father's trade in a household where politics was not only a preoccupation, "But a requirement for survival," Armand Fernandes said. "If his father lost an election, there wasn't food on the table."

Diniz died of a heart attack at a political rally in 1949, but not before his 24-year-old son had succeeded to his seat in the State House, a political *wunderkind* summoned from classes at Suffolk University law school to the legislature for roll-call votes.

A former city councilman and state senator, Dinis was, at 34, elected the youngest district attorney in Massachusetts. Reelected in 1962, he ran unopposed in 1966.

A delegate to the 1956 Democratic convention, Dinis had escorted John F. Kennedy to the rostrum to accept nomination as vice president, and "whole-heartedly" supported his election in 1960. Dinis displayed in his law office a pastel portrait of John Kennedy, alongside photographs of his other political heroes: James Michael Curley (former mayor of Boston, who served part of his term in a federal penitentiary); former President Franklin D. Roosevelt, and the late British Prime Minister Winston Churchill.

Ted Kennedy's Senate candidacy in 1962 had placed Dinis' standing in the Kennedy political network in jeopardy. Dinis resented the arm-twisting, "for-us-or-against-us" demand by Kennedy operatives for his support during a bitterly fought primary against Edward McCormack, nephew of House Speaker John McCormack. When Dinis had sought to fulfill his father's wish to be buried at Arlington National Cemetery, John McCormack had made the arrangements. Dinis felt he "owed" him. His support of Edward McCormack inevitably cost him in the powerful Kennedy camp. To this was added a growing reputation as an outspoken political maverick of unpredictable and mercurial temperament, chronically embroiled in public controversies.

Dinis attacked the probate court as "a little-known citadel of judicial patronage and favoritism operating in an atmosphere of intimidation."

The jury-selection system, he charged, was "absolutely discriminatory," and "a systematic denial of justice throughout Massachusetts."

Most aggravating of all had been Dinis' inability to extend his political horizons beyond the precincts of New Bedford. Seeking to unseat Republican Margaret Heckler in the U.S. House of Representatives in 1968, Dinis was criticized for misrepresenting his record. Then state Attorney General Elliot Richardson had warned the Kennedys not to support Dinis. Charging "widespread, notorious and systematic criminal offenses" occurring in Dinis' district, Richardson called a special grand jury to investigate police corruption in Bristol County. Dinis reacted by ascribing the probe to Richardson's record of motor vehicle violations, including several drunk driving convictions.

Ted Kennedy had campaigned on behalf of other Massachusetts Democratic House candidates facing tough competition, but he stayed away from New Bedford. Publicly, Dinis said nothing about the lack of Kennedy backing but blamed his crushing defeat on "insufficient funds," and two editorials in the *New Bedford Standard-Times*. According to the newspaper, Dinis had displayed more vigor outside the district attorney's office in developing his private law practice and extensive real estate interests. A newly acquired insurance agency had pursued business so aggressively, Dinis was censured for "unethical solicitation" by the State Department of Banking and Insurance, and was in possible conflict of interest. Since Dinis was entrusted with the prosecution of violators of motor vehicle statutes, "He can decide not to move against drivers who bring their insurance business to him."

Dinis scorned the newspaper as "John Birch-oriented" and regretted that "candidates must live with irresponsible editorial writers with their lies and innuendoes." Although he was "handsome, likeable, articulate, and on occasion straight-talking," Dinis had failed to attract the favorable notice of the leaders of the Massachusetts Democratic Party in Boston. Dinis, in turn, branded them as "a small clique of star-chamber coatholders." He said, "I think for the most part it's that I go my own way. I don't spend the time to cultivate them—and I couldn't care less."

A mural blow-up of a campaign photograph greeted reporters in the stairwell of Dinis' second floor law and insurance offices when they sought out the district attorney.

"I am controversial, and have been ever since I entered politics twenty years ago," Dinis conceded. "Sometimes I may have been wrong; but at least I have gone along doing what I thought was right." The primary duty of the district attorney's office was not to convict, he added, "But to see that justice is done."

This, then, was the man poised to plunge into a controversy without precedent in an already stormy career.

Chapter 37

GARGAN WASN'T SURPRISED DINIS HAD ASKED FOR A NEW investigation. "I wasn't confident at the time the Senator pleaded guilty in Edgartown that would be the end of the matter, particularly with all the publicity the case was getting."

The Senator's report of the accident had been composed in haste and ill-advised. A week of deliberations at the compound had produced a speech under the stress of an impatient and increasingly skeptical press.

But making unsworn statements to police and delivering a ghostwritten exegesis on television was one thing; repeating them at an inquest was another. To repudiate either statement was to admit having lied. To repeat lies for the sake of consistency under oath risked perjury. Senator Kennedy would have to tread carefully around his previous words, Gargan reflected, while at the same time making sure he maintained the same position. It had never been anticipated the Senator would be called upon to provide sworn testimony about the accident—a major consideration in his decision to plead guilty to leaving the scene.

Stephen Smith now took over the direct management of a crisis that no longer could be delegated to others, to deal with an inquest he scorned as, "An imprecise process devoted primarily to train accidents that hasn't been used in Massachusetts since I don't know, never."

"Steve Smith sort of came to dominate things after a while," a participant in the strategy sessions at Hyannis Port observed. "He decided at the compound that the girls shouldn't be left high and dry." Smith had expressed the view, "These kids came up here all alone, not a soul to look out for them. So we've got to watch out for their interests."

Smith later denied playing any part in retaining lawyers for the young women as a means of coordinating their testimony and to fend off reporters and investigators, "Because of what the girls might be asked about or get into." That idea had come from their mothers, "expressing some concern about what was going to happen to then-daughters," Senator Kennedy explained. "After an inquest was called for, there appeared to be some necessity to retain counsel. I felt they were innocent individuals who, as a result of my action, were being brought into court. I felt some responsibility to at least offer some compensation. Arrangements were made by which I paid their attorneys."

Judge Clark recommended that his friend Daniel Daley represent Ray LaRosa, Jack Crimmins and Charles Tretter, as well as the young women of the Boiler Room. (Reportedly, "One of the first actions the attorneys took was to instruct the women not to discuss the case with reporters or police.")

Clark was shutting off other avenues of information. He advised Registrar McLaughlin to cancel a scheduled hearing into the accident. Clark wanted no determination of "serious fault" made on the record that could prejudice the inquest by suggesting negligence to a presiding judge.

On September 11, Registry Inspector Joseph Greelish confirmed by telephone that the hearing was being postponed, "Until such time as the final outcome of proceedings now pending." Greelish was instructed to reschedule the hearing for Wednesday, May 6, 1970, at 10 A.M.—more than ten months after the accident.

McLaughlin had the Chappaquiddick file in a locked drawer in his office desk to prevent subordinates from leaking information to reporters. An interagency memorandum warned, "We have already made all the comment in this case that we legally can."

If the accident had provided anybody with "a political windfall," it was McLaughlin. His term of office was due to expire on December 17. He and other hold-over Democratic appointees were not expected to be renamed by Republican Governor Francis Sargent. By his assiduous accommodation on the case, McLaughlin was gathering up leverage to keep his job. The Kennedy political apparatus in Massachusetts would not want a Republican appointee dealing with the sensitive Chappaquiddick case.

In contrast to the week following the accident there was no rush of Jack Kennedy's New Frontiersmen to the compound. Most conspicuously absent was Ted Sorensen, principle author of the "now-regretted" television speech. Mention of a possible inquest had been sufficient to send Sorensen on television to moralize about Senator Kennedy's predicament and clarify his role in the affair. "As Senator Kennedy himself has declared, his conduct that night was inexplicable," Sorensen said. "He should have gone and gotten help that night now that he looks back on it. Of course, he should have."

Angered that Kennedy's staff was blaming the speech for the doubts about the case, which had prompted a new investigation, Sorensen was protecting himself in the event an inquest uncovered any deception he was not aware of in the speech. He said, "To the best of my knowledge there are no misstatements of facts."

The accident had "damaged, if not destroyed" Ted Kennedy's prospects for the Democratic presidential nomination, Sorensen said. "And

I don't think that that being so recent in the minds of the public, and that being so clear an indication of his action under pressure at this stage of his life that he should try for the presidency in 1972." Ted Kennedy was so young, he could run for president as late as 1988 when he was 56 years old, but no one could predict with certainty what his political future was. What happened at the inquest would tell whether Kennedy could ever run for president.

William vanden Heuvel, the former Bobby Kennedy aide dispatched to hand-hold the Kopechnes, criticized as "unprofessional" Sorensen's public remarks about the accident. Sorensen and vanden Heuvel were rumored to be rivals for the Democratic nomination to run for Robert Kennedy's former Senate seat from New York in 1970, a contest Sorensen was "actively considering." Drafting Kennedy's speech about the accident, however, had hurt his candidacy, Sorensen said. "There's no doubt it has diminished my chances, by how much we don't know yet."

The accident not only threatened Sorensen's embryonic political career but necessitated last-minute changes in the bound galleys of the *Kennedy Legacy,* a book in which author Sorensen intended to anoint himself as elder statesman of the New Frontier. Sorensen now deleted all references to Teddy Kennedy running for President in 1972 and re-cast the framework of his book "in light of these two remarkable brothers, John and Robert Kennedy." "The legacy of the two Kennedys," he wrote, did not depend "on their surviving brother being elected president for it to endure." Sorensen denied that the accident at Chappaquiddick "marked the end of the Kennedy era." In all, he virtually disinherited Ted Kennedy from his family's political heritage.

But Chappaquiddick tarnished the lustre of that legacy. Hostile critics perceived "disturbing similarities" in the handling of the accident with the Kennedy White House style: "The eagerness to put off hard decisions as long as possible, the absorption in secondary issues, the belief that rhetoric is enough and the heavy dependency on borrowed judgments of idea men and speechwriters."

Sorensen was not alone among New Frontiersmen distancing themselves from Teddy Kennedy because of Chappaquiddick. Frank Mankiewicz, former press secretary to Robert Kennedy, characterized the episode as, "A tragedy in the Shakespearean sense of a puzzlement of the will, of judgment suspended and flawed at a crucial moment." Even before the accident, Ted Kennedy was exhibiting "a moodiness and disorientation that worried friends," demonstrating to some observers "an emotional escapism and volatility that betrayed the absence of a central core of integrity."

But those "Elder Statesmen" defections pleased Ted Kennedy's "bushy-tailed staff," unhappy when "The Boss went outside for prestigious advice." In their view, part of the problem was due to an older generation of Kennedymen "whose print-out was at least ten years old." Sorensen's soaring Ciceronian phrases had acquired a fustian dust. This crisis called for a harder, more pragmatic approach.

The strain Kennedy was under was evident when he left Cape Cod early Sunday to greet President Nixon on his return from an eight-nation foreign policy tour at Andrews Air Force base in Washington. The President stopped to shake Kennedy's hand, and extend an invitation to the White House for a briefing of cabinet members and congressional leaders about his trip. Receiving him with "almost paternal sympathy," Nixon took Kennedy aside for a private, ten-minute talk in the Oval Room. Nixon had experienced "premature political burial" himself, and achieved a remarkable comeback six years later.

Nixon refused to say what he'd told Senator Kennedy or to comment on the accident at Chappaquiddick. "I don't know anything about it," he said. But, in anticipation of a possible Kennedy challenge in 1972, a surveillance of the Senator had been instigated and a private investigator was dispatched to Edgartown to gather intelligence about the accident.

The major threat to Nixon's re-election had disappeared in a cloud of scandal so tainting the Kennedy mystique, "It is doubtful that the Kennedy name for some time to come, will have its former appeal."

With the passage of weeks, a high degree of skepticism about the Senator's explanation of the accident and his behavior afterward had produced a sharp drop in Kennedy's popularity, a national Lou Harris poll reported. "Much of the doubt is focused upon whether or not Kennedy was drunk at the time of the accident." Public perception of the event reflected upon Kennedy's aptitude for the White House, that he had "panicked in a crisis and showed that he could not be given high public trust, such as being President." Unless Kennedy answered all questions about the incident, he would raise ineradicable doubts about his fitness for the Presidency, "And the public will continue to question his ability to make important decisions under pressure."

If there was one aspect about the accident more mysterious than any other, it was that, despite the damage done to his reputation, "Kennedy refused to clear the air," writer Robert Sherill observed. "Painful as his slippage in popularity and the raw jokes were, Kennedy apparently preferred them to making a full disclosure."

While full disclosure was unlikely, Judge Clark warned the conferees at the compound the new investigation would be no amateur affair like Arena and Steele had conducted in Edgartown. Chief investigator in the district attorney's office was George Killen, an experienced detective. Clark knew from personal experience of Killen's abilities: He had locked horns with him in several cases he had defended on Cape Cod. Killen was an able investigator, meticulous in the preparation of cases for prosecution in the Barnstable court. In Killen's office was Bernie Flynn, a tough and resourceful police officer. Together they had cracked the Costa murders, second only to the Boston Strangler case in the annals of famous contemporary crimes in Massachusetts.

On Monday, August 4, George Killen and Bernie Flynn arrived in Edgartown to begin their official investigation into the death of Mary Jo Kopechne. "They wanted the names of my witnesses and copies of the reports and everything else," Arena recalled. "But George and Bernie did everything on their own."

Arena's investigation was "practically worthless" to Killen; the case "as cold as Mary Jo Kopechne, or colder." A lot of leads had dried up since Ted Kennedy's police report. Most of all, Killen regretted the decision to release the body without autopsy, Flynn said. "George was kicking his own ass about that. Every day he's saying, 'We should have done an autopsy.

Flynn was amused by the sign on display behind the front desk of the Shiretown Inn: "Please do not ask us to answer questions concerning the Kennedy accident. Thank you. The Management." Besieged since he came forward to corroborate a portion of the Senator's broadcast, Russell Peachey was having second thoughts about his encounter with Ted Kennedy. "He didn't look to me like a man who had come downstairs to complain about noise," Peachey said. "He was just standing there. He was fully dressed. I think he was wearing a jacket and slacks. Usually, a man who just wants to complain about noise doesn't get up and get fully dressed to do it. Especially at 2:25 in the morning."

Reservations for seven people of the "Kennedy party" had been made under the names of John Driscoll and Joe Gargan for the Regatta weekend. The room adjacent to Senator Kennedy's had been occupied by Ross Richards. Peachey described Richards as "a friend and sailing companion" of Ted Kennedy.

Chapter 38

KILLEN DISPATCHED DETECTIVE–LIEUTENANT JOHN DUNN TO Rumford, Rhode Island, to interrogate Richards—and later came to regret that he did. Dunn was a thorn in Killen's side. A former Boston motorcycle traffic cop employed by the fire marshall's office in Springfield after joining the state police, Dunn had invoked seniority to win assignment to Killen's office. Killen tried to block Dunn's assignment because he wanted Bernie Flynn and not an inexperienced investigator working for him, but a state police review board backed Dunn. Killen had to pull Dunn off the Costa murder case when, in his judgment, Dunn botched the initial investigation. Killen referred to him as "that dopey son of a bitch." Nevertheless, Dunn was in his office to stay. If anybody was going to have to go, it was going to be Flynn.

———

Vice president in charge of production for the Narragansett Wire Company, Ross Richards was a hard-driving, dynamic sportsman.

Richards had photographs of himself with Ted Kennedy on display in his living room, but his feelings about the Senator were ambivalent, Marilyn Richards said. "Ross wasn't a member of the inner circle around Ted because he wasn't a political person. We were strictly sailing friends. We got invited to the compound on occasion for social things, but we weren't close. Ross had grown up in Hyannis Port. He and Ted had sailed against each other for years. The Kennedys were fun and had a lot of glamor. We thought they belonged in Hollywood, not Washington."

Richards was wary of talking to police. He had heard no disturbance from the Senator's room on the night of the accident. His conversation with Ted Kennedy the next morning had been about the previous day's Regatta, he said. "I happened to win the race and he congratulated me on it; and we discussed that back and forth for maybe 10, 15 minutes." Stan Moore had also participated in the discussion. Richards had observed nothing out-of-the-ordinary about the Senator's speech or appearance. Kennedy hadn't mentioned the accident. "I remember the bell at 8 o'clock. We asked the Senator if he would like to have breakfast with us. He said he couldn't, but he might join us later."

Kennedy had looked startled when Paul Markham and Joe Gargan showed up "soaking wet." The three men went into the Senator's room. Richards heard an argument going on, "But as to what it was about, I don't know."

"Are you thinking what I'm thinking?" Dunn said. "That Kennedy was finding out about the accident for the first time?"

According to the report of the interrogation Dunn submitted to George Killen, Richards replied, "It sure looked that way."

But Richards didn't tell police any more than he had to, Stan Moore said, "Ross was making faces whenever the accident was mentioned. He knew something had gone on." Richards had refused to discuss how much Ted Kennedy had to drink at a victory party on his boat after the Regatta race. Neither would Moore. "We weren't going to be the ones to stick Ted Kennedy with a drunk driving charge, if that's what police were looking for," Moore said. When Killen came to his automobile agency to interrogate him, "The police asked me if the Senator seemed nervous when I saw him on Saturday. All I can say is, he looked all right to me." Kennedy had made some innocuous remarks, "Things like, 'What a beautiful day,' and 'Isn't this a lovely place.' He didn't mention Chappaquiddick at all."

Moore refused to talk about drinking. "I was asked that question many, many times, but I have no comment," Moore said, later. "I didn't think it was anybody's business. Ted had three rum and cokes in about twenty minutes; but he wasn't laced or anything."

Moore didn't tell Killen about his invitation to the cookout or his view of the gathering as *"that* kind of a party." As for the accident and its aftermath, "I just thought it was a case of, 'A stiff dick has no conscience.'"

Killen added Moore and Richards to a list of witnesses to be called at the inquest. He was interested to find out if they would refuse to discuss liquor consumption under oath and risk contempt of court to protect Ted Kennedy. But Killen was baffled by the reports of Senator Kennedy's conduct on the porch of the Shiretown Inn on the morning after the accident. So was Bernie Flynn. Using Dunns' report as a basis, Flynn revised the scenario of "probable events," he'd put together after visiting Chappaquiddick with "Huck" Look.

The new scenario went like this: After fleeing from his encounter with the deputy sheriff down Dike Road, Kennedy had decided not to chance getting arrested for drunk driving, Flynn suggested. "So he pulled over. He got out of the car, and tells the girl to go down to the end of the road and come back to pick him up when the coast is clear. When she didn't show up, he thought she was stuck in the sand on the beach or got lost. He figures, 'Well, I'll go back to the cottage.' He tells Gargan and Markham what happened and asks to be taken to the landing. When he gets there, the ferry's closed down. He thinks, 'What the hell, I'll go back to the other side.' He dives in and swims across. The people at the party hung around the cottage waiting for Mary Jo to come back with Kennedy's car. When they realize she's missing they go looking for her—that's why everybody spent the night out there. It wasn't until morning Gargan and Markham spotted the car in the pond. They dive in to see if Mary Jo's in it, but they can't see anything. So they get on the ferry soaking wet and run like hell to the Shiretown Inn to tell Ted what happened. That's the first time he heard about the accident."

Flynn based his theory, "On the fact that a man like Ted Kennedy—or any man, except for a hardened criminal—could go through the experience of driving off a bridge and not report the accident if he knew that a girl was still in the car. I just can't believe Kennedy went to sleep, got up the next morning and was standing on the deck, supposedly prepared to go yachting, talking to people about the weather like nothing was going to happen, if he knew the girl was dead. You'd stay in your damn hotel room. You'd be biting your fingernails trying to figure out: 'What am I going to do. What am I going to say?' You'd expect to be locked up any minute; and you'd be frightened."

As Flynn visualized the scene, "Kennedy's talking to these people when Gargan and Markham show up. I think he received the information like, 'Ted, the car's in the water.' And he gets this startled look. Then, the three of them go into his room to discuss it. When they come out, Kennedy is shaken. This reaffirms my suspicion that this is the first time he knows the girl didn't make it back to the cottage."

Kennedy's first impulse was to go to the scene of the accident to see for himself what had happened, "Not because of any telephone—that sounded like a story to me," Flynn said. "There were phones he could have used in Edgartown. There was no reason whatsoever for him to go to Chappaquiddick, if he knew about the accident. What's he going to do? Look at the body and say, 'Oh, my God, she *did* stay in the car. She didn't get out?'"

Flynn could only surmise why Kennedy had given an altogether different version of the accident in his police report, "Not unless somebody said to him, 'We can make you look like a hero. You dove in, you tried to save her. You expended all your energy...' He might have gone for that; that sounds pretty damn good. Everybody thought it was only a minor automobile accident. They didn't realize how it would mushroom. All they wanted to do was protect him from an embarrassing situation: being drunk in a car with a girl late at night, parked on the road to the cemetery," Flynn said. "Kennedy could have been there for an hour and a half getting laid—or gone someplace else after he left the cottage. That would account for the time difference with 'Huck' Look seeing the car. If anything happened, it didn't happen at the beach. It had already happened. Kennedy's finished, and now he's ready to run."

Once he made the police report, Kennedy was stuck with the story. Later, he had to compound the lie by elaborating on it in his television speech. Flynn said, "Ted Kennedy wasn't in the car when it went off the bridge in my opinion. He would never have gotten out alive."

Killen tested Flynn's theory on Frank Keating with variations of his own. When Kennedy drove to the intersection, he'd gone straight into Cemetery Road, "That was deliberate. Kennedy wasn't confused. He did that when he saw Look pass in his car. And I suppose he said to the girl, 'That cop recognized me. I'm getting out. You drive back to the cottage. I'll walk.'" Mary Jo had driven off. Instead of going straight, she'd taken the "wrong turn" on Dike Road, Killen said. "That's why the details about the accident are so sketchy. Kennedy doesn't *know* what happened."

If that was truth, Keating countered, "Why wasn't it less harmless to say that rather than putting himself in the car, diving repeatedly and all the rest of it? Don't you think there's a strong possibility Ted was loaded? How much could he remember in detail except for finding himself in the water?"

In Killen's version, Kennedy took the last ferry to Edgartown, returned to the Shiretown Inn and said to himself, "To hell with it. I never should have been out with her in the first place."

But Killen could not corroborate his theories. Gargan would have told him they didn't hold water. Police had no hope of questioning Gargan or anybody else who had attended the party, Flynn said. "Everybody was represented by counsel. Once somebody gets a lawyer, you can't go to them and say, I want to question you.' You have to go to the attorney." It was rare in Flynn's experience that a witness hired a lawyer. Rarer still, was the district attorney's office writing letters asking witnesses to talk to police.

Armand Fernandes confirmed, "The letters we sent to the people involved received uniform answers that under Miranda, they refused to talk to police."

Dinis had not received an answer to his request for an inquest when he called on Attorney General Robert Quinn in Boston. A delegate to the 1968 Democratic convention pledged to Eugene McCarthy, Dinis proposed at the first Massachusetts caucus a resolution committing the delegation's 82 votes to Ted Kennedy, should the convention go to a second ballot, as seemed likely. As the delegation's vice chairman, Quinn had gavelled Dinis out of order, a move interpreted as in accord with Ted Kennedy's instructions not to encourage a draft.

Dinis suggested Quinn take over the inquest, as the state's chief law enforcement officer. "Quinn nearly fell out of his chair," Dinis reported, later. "He said, 'No! No!' He was terrified."

Although Dinis had brought up the subject, Quinn had no intention of becoming involved in the Kennedy accident, Quinn told reporters. "I have no more information now than I had three weeks ago that would require me to enter the case." Quinn was leaving Dinis to his decision to hold an inquest, although his cooperation was extended to him, as it was to any district attorney in the Commonwealth. "I've done a lot of research in the matter, *legal* research," Quinn emphasized to subdue speculation that, as a political ally of Ted Kennedy he had discouraged an inquiry by the Edgartown grand jury and ordered police chief Arena "to keep your mouth shut," and discontinue his twice-a-day press briefings.

But Quinn had made it clear where his sentiments were after the Senator's speech. Urging Ted Kennedy to remain in office, he said, "Let us hope that in the deep resources of his human capabilities, he can again redouble his efforts in service to the people."

Dinis was in Quinn's office when Judge Boyle's reply to his request for an inquest arrived in New Bedford. The gist of the letter was read to Dinis over the telephone by Armand Fernandes.

Boyle wanted to know if Dinis was exercising his mandatory power to "require" an inquest to be held, and intended "to submit evidence that an unlawful act or negligence caused or contributed to the death of Mary Jo Kopechne," contrary to the report of the medical examiner.

Dinis regarded the response as "satisfactory," and predicted an inquest could begin within a week to ten days. "All I'm trying to do is conduct a general inquiry into a situation that should be looked into a little further," Dinis told reporters on the sidewalk in front of his law offices when he returned to New Bedford. "We want to learn as much as we can about the incident from the people who were in the area at the time, so as to determine exactly what the facts were. All persons present prior to the death of the girl, and anyone else who can assist the Commonwealth will be called to testify." Dinis had "made no determination about calling Senator Kennedy yet."

As part of the inquest, Dinis was seeking to have Mary Jo Kopechne's body exhumed, "In order to have a pathologist perform an examination and once and for all close that aspect of the case." His office was researching legal procedures required to secure a belated autopsy. A "public clamor" had prompted a new look into the case, Dinis told Blythe Evans, district attorney for Luzerne County in Wilkes-Barre, Pennsylvania. Dinis wanted to know "what practices and procedures" were required to have an exhumation performed in his county.

Like Dinis, Evans was, at 36, the youngest man to hold the office. A Republican, he had squeaked to a 150-vote "surprise victory" in a heavily Democratic district. Evans made sure his constituents knew about his lack of enthusiasm for the idea. Dinis had to prove in his own state that an autopsy was necessary, he said. "I regard this as a major hurdle for Dinis. After all, there has been a medical finding in this case that went unchallenged and was accepted until now. I definitely will not do anything of my own volition. If a court of appropriate jurisdiction in Massachusetts hands down an order, then we are ready to cooperate. Everything will be done by the book."

But Evans knew even less about Massachusetts law then Dinis did about Pennsylvania procedure. Pennsylvania's coroner system required permission from the court to perform autopsies. Massachusetts district attorneys had authority to secure an autopsy on their own authority. All Dinis had to do was ask that an autopsy be made under the relevant Massachusetts statutes, then wait for a Pennsylvania court to accede to section 1, article IV of the U.S. Constitution which requires states to give "Full Faith and Credit to the public Acts, Records, and judicial Proceedings of every other State." On the surface, it looked easy. Reality would prove otherwise.

Fernandes was preparing a petition asking Pennsylvania to honor the Massachusetts law granting the district attorney's authority to order autopsies. Evans insisted, "It's a court order we're looking for, not a petition." For Pennsylvania courts to grant exhumation, it should be shown there were "imperative reasons" to disturb the sanctity of the grave. The wishes of the deceased's family were always taken into account.

Autopsies could be performed against their opposition, "If there was a suspicion that a serious crime had been committed."

Dinis was "fairly confident" of getting an autopsy. He had been studying Pennsylvania law and concluded that not much weight was given to family objections. He hadn't talked to the Kopechnes about exhuming their daughter's body, he said. "I wouldn't do that; I wouldn't want to bother them. They have enough trouble."

Gwen Kopechne confirmed, "Mr. Dinis never bothered to consult us, we've never heard a word. We've been left out of this as if it didn't matter who we are." Mrs. Kopechne was under the impression an autopsy had already been performed. "We were told, 'Everything has been taken care of.' I'm pretty positive it was somebody from Mr. Dinis' office. I don't know why in two weeks they decide to hold an autopsy. Maybe I'm a foolish person, but I just can't see this at all. Not after we buried her."

Nor, since the funeral, had the Kopechnes heard from another key figure: Senator Kennedy. "We have had no collusion with the Kennedys at all, not even information. They didn't bother to tell us anything." She added, however, that Kennedy's aide Dun Gifford had paid a number of visits. "He'd make a trip all the way to our home to tell us there was going to be something in the newspapers—maybe by Jack Anderson or somebody else, that might hurt us," Mrs. Kopechne said. "We thought that was nice, because we were prepared for it."

What Gifford wanted the Kopechnes prepared for were two Anderson columns scheduled to appear in the *Washington Post* and other newspapers in which the syndicated columnist had pieced together "from Kennedy intimates who would have no reason to falsify the facts," what had happened on the night of the accident.

Senator Kennedy had done his share of drinking at the party, but "intimates" insisted he wasn't drunk. He'd invited Mary Jo for a midnight swim, deliberately turned onto Dike Road heading for East Beach and hit the bridge going 20 miles per hour, "Too fast for safety and shot off the side of the bridge without skidding," Anderson said. Kennedy escaped from the car and made repeated dives to rescue his passenger. "After it was too late to save Mary Jo, he felt it might still be possible to save his presidential dream," Anderson wrote. Exhausted and in panic, Kennedy had rested beside Poucha Pond. "In this state, he conceived a preposterous, absurd idea. He would ask his cousin, Joe Gargan, to take the rap for him. Gargan had always been there when the Kennedys needed him. Although a lawyer, he was more a handyman who ran the errands and attended to arrangements for the Kennedys."

Gargan agreed to say he had driven the car and returned to Dike Bridge to familiarize himself with the scene of "his" accident. "It is entirely possible that Markham and Gargan attempted to retrieve the girl's body," Anderson said. "Then Gargan and Markham rustled up a boat and delivered Kennedy to the other side. The idea was to remove the Senator from the site of the accident." Kennedy had slipped unnoticed into the Shiretown Inn and established an alibi by talking to a room clerk. When Gargan and Markham had arrived at the inn the next morning, they had assumed they were the only ones who knew about the accident. "They wanted another look at the scene in daylight. As they were crossing the channel, however, someone mentioned that a car had been found bottom up in Poucha Pond." A shaken Ted Kennedy had walked off to get hold of his emotions, telephoned Burke Marshall, then reported the accident to Edgartown police. Kennedy's hope to avoid blame had occurred during "a nightmare of emotional trauma," Anderson explained. "But in the end he abandoned the scheme and manfully owned up to what he had done."

"There were no rowboats as reported by Anderson," Gargan said, later. "I wish to hell there had been! Then we would have been with him after he dove in the water." Publicly, Gargan denied any truth in

Anderson's columns. "There's no basis in fact whatsoever for the report. It's entirely untrue."

But Gargan was bothered Anderson had cited "Kennedy intimates" as sources. Knowledgeable in the art of media control as practiced by the Kennedy political apparatus, he suspected misinformation about the accident probably *had* come from friends, anxious to explain away the Senator's misbehavior. The reports had trivialized Gargan s dangerous rescue effort; the "handyman" reference was especially galling, but revealing of certain staff sentiments about him. Gargan made a good living as an able trial lawyer. His work in Kennedy campaigns had been voluntary and unpaid.

The efforts to mislead the press about the incident were well-intentioned, Gargan recognized. "I don't think anybody was trying deliberately to hurt Paul and me by these stories; they were only interested in protecting the Senator."

The speculation that Gargan had agreed to take blame for the accident came to him from *Time* magazine, Anderson said, later. "Their files contained this same report. I can't say *Time* bought it, because they didn't use it."

Anderson was working hard on "one of the great political stories of all time," he said. He had Jack Olsen as leg man in Edgartown gathering information on the case. "Jack was representing me on the short side, and working on a book on the long range."

In defending his columns, Anderson conceded Kennedy "intimates" might have fed him misinformation to protect the Senator and throw the press off the track of the case, he said. "Those things are possible. We only know what our sources tell us. That's the best we can do."

Chapter 39

AS A RESULT OF ANDERSON'S REPORTS, HOWEVER, C. REMINGTON
Ballou of Providence, Rhode Island, contacted the *New Bedford Standard-Times,* "Because I thought someone should know what we had seen."

In Edgartown for the Regatta, Ballou's Concordia yawl, *Sumatra,* was moored in the harbor close by the ferry channel. A little before 2 A.M. on July 19, Ballou overheard a hushed conversation from "the forms of three persons" passing by in a boat that doused its lights and outboard motor. Then, a larger boat with a powerful engine left Edgartown, crossing the channel to a beach near the Chappaquiddick landing, and also shut off lights and motor, Ballou related. "At this point the small boat was drifting, pointed towards the beach and the larger boat. It seemed to be waiting, like somebody casing the area to see all was quiet." Five minutes later the small boat's motor started up again, lights were turned on, and it moved out of the harbor.

Dick Drayne denied the story. "If there was a boat, he wasn't on it. The Senator swam across." Pending the inquest, Senator Kennedy would have nothing more to say about the accident other than to characterize the Anderson columns as "categorically untrue." Kennedy had no idea why such allegations should be published, but he was disturbed by reports he had planned to lie about his involvement to protect his political future and had left the scene of the accident while there was still a chance Mary Jo Kopechne was alive in his car.

Kennedy conceded he may have made a mistake in not going beyond his television explanation, but cited "legal restraints" and the "current rumor-filled atmosphere" for not going into more detail now. Kennedy "might" talk more about the accident after all legal proceedings were concluded. He said, "I can live with myself. I feel the tragedy of the girl's death. That's on my mind. That's what I will always have to live with. But what I don't have to live with are the whispers and innuendoes and falsehoods. Because these have no basis in fact."

Kennedy described himself as "comfortable" back in the Senate. Some thought otherwise. "He is ill-at-ease and far from the commanding figure he had developed before the accident." Kennedy was "ashen-faced, tortured eyes looking out tentatively for signs of loyalty or defection." Slouched in his Whip's chair, distracted and preoccupied, Kennedy retained a gaunt, hangdog expression.

Kennedy's staff was maintaining "an almost manic gaiety" throughout the crisis, coping with a flood of hate mail. Sponsors of some events had withdrawn invitations for the Senator to appear. His unsatisfactory explanation for the accident had been responsible for a climate of "gloom and defeatism" inside the Democratic Party.

Kennedy acknowledged the hard-going he was having to Jimmy Smith. Thanking him for his "thoughtful messages and very kind letter," he said, "I just wanted you to know how much I appreciate your warm expressions of friendship and support. It's good friends like you that have made this difficult period a bit easier for me."

On Friday, August 8, Dinis flew to Edgartown in a chartered sea plane, landing at a beach on Chappaquiddick. Dinis boarded the *On Time* for Edgartown. He was met at the courthouse steps by reporters and Judge Boyle. Dinis was led to Boyle's second-floor chambers for a private conference.

For Dinis to have asked the Superior Court to preside at an inquest was a direct slap at Boyle's court, a contempt Dinis had never hidden. When Boyle had directed 15 straight "not guilty" verdicts, because island police didn't know how to present evidence in trials, Dinis cited an increase in crime on Martha's Vineyard to widespread contempt for law enforcement because island police failed to obtain convictions in court.

Boyle returned Dinis' hostile feelings in kind, regarding the district attorney as an ambitious opportunist whose entry into the Kennedy accident case was the latest in a series of "publicity stunts" to advance his political career.

But, Boyle had also been offended by the noble posturing of Senator Kennedy in his television speech. By speaking of his "moral obligation" to plead guilty to leaving the scene, Kennedy had suggested he could not have been found legally guilty of the charge. In addition, the Senator, in his speech, had dredged up the medical defense Dick McCarron tentatively broached at the arraignment which had angered Boyle in court.

But Boyle was even more mistrustful of Dinis' motives in calling for an inquest—which he made abundantly plain to Dinis at their meeting. For what purpose was the district attorney seeking a new inquiry?

Dinis wanted to put to rest "all the rumors and speculation about the accident," he said.

A district attorney who had evidence to proceed against a possible defendant conducted a private, not a public investigation, the results of which led him to drop the matter or seek an indictment, Boyle said. Most states had reciprocal agreements for witnesses to appear before a grand jury. Out-of-state witnesses were not bound to honor a summons to an inquest, Boyle pointed out. Dinis might have trouble getting witnesses to testify, if they didn't choose to appear voluntarily.

Dinis ruled out a grand jury. He wanted to avoid any "intimation of criminality" by his reopened investigation.

But Boyle wasn't buying the argument. Taking the case to a grand jury was tantamount to seeking a prosecution. By "requiring" an inquest to be held, Dinis was placing responsibility for an investigation—and any charges that might come out of the inquest—onto the court.

Furious to be lectured about his motives, Dinis had questions about Boyle's. By discouraging an inquest, Boyle was seeking to protect his jurisdiction from accusations—quite correct ones in Dinis' opinion, that Edgartown authorities had bungled the case so badly, the district attorney's office had been forced to take over. Arena's investigation had given a new dimension to ineptitude; Walter Steele had "rolled over and played dead," his plea bargaining so facile as to have been viewed by the press as a "fix." Kennedy's trial was a farce. For Boyle to suspend a 20-day mandatory jail sentence wasn't even legal. That Boyle wasn't disqualifying himself from presiding at the inquest was further proof, if Dinis needed any more, of a determination to protect his judicial turf from outsiders and keep the Kennedy accident "an Edgartown case."

Boyle appeared in judicial robes before an audience of reporters in the courtroom to announce an inquest into the death of Mary Jo Kopechne to be held on Wednesday, September 3. The statute permitted the exclusion of all "not required" to attend; but Boyle was exercising judicial discretion by allowing "legitimate and accredited members of the press, television, radio or other news media" in the courtroom—a decision Harvey Ewing regarded as consistent with Boyle's policy of "open courtroom," he said. "For weeks media people had been scrounging around Edgartown for any tidbit about the Kennedy accident they

could find and pretty much getting nowhere—but an *open* inquest!"
Now that was a story to whet journalistic appetites.

Dinis had more modest expectations for what an inquest could
accomplish. The scope of his inquiry was, "To make an effort to establish for the official record all the facts surrounding the death of Mary
Jo Kopechne." Dinis would call "as many witnesses as we know about—
everyone involved." With regard to Senator Kennedy, however, he had
"no intention of calling him at this time," a declaration guaranteed to
provoke doubts about how thorough the inquest would be if Dinis really
believed he could bypass the driver of the car and the only eyewitness
to the accident. To many reporters, such reticence suggested Dinis was
more interested "in going through the motions" than uncovering the
accident's unsolved mysteries.

Although Dinis wasn't calling Kennedy to the inquest, Arena was
arranging to provide police protection for the Senator anyway, he
explained. "That's what he said today; but if you know that guy you
know we have to arrange for every possibility."

Dinis widened a credibility gap when he visited the accident site to
pronounce Dike Bridge "a traffic hazard." He said, "It's understandable
that in the middle of the night an automobile could easily go off the
bridge if the person who approached it wasn't aware it was there, and
that it veered off sharply to the left. The angle is quite acute." Dinis was
letting Ted Kennedy off the hook before a single piece of evidence had
been heard at the inquest, in the view of some reporters. Having
demanded Dinis engage in further investigation, "Now that he was
doing it, the press got all over his back for picking on Ted Kennedy," F.
Lee Bailey observed.

Bailey's appearance at the accident site excited speculation Dinis had
asked his friend to look into the case. Bailey was considering a commission from the *Ladies Home Journal* to "write something" about Chappaquiddick.

After flying over Dike Bridge in a helicopter, Bailey hung a movie camera out of the window of an automobile driven by his private investigator, Andy Tuney, to photograph the route from the cottage to the bridge, "To try to reconstruct the probable circumstances of the accident." Bailey crossed over the bridge, peered thoughtfully into Poucha Pond and posed for photographs. He concluded the accident wasn't anything that he could write about, he said. "I didn't think a trial lawyer jumping in with speculation that would level the finger of suspicion at Senator Kennedy would be my cup of tea, and I'd rather not get involved." But Bailey, and in particular his investigator, would become "involved" beyond anything they could have imagined, setting in motion a scheme to prevent any information contrary to Ted Kennedy's two public accountings of the accident being revealed at the inquest.

———

While required to demonstrate "the impartiality of the law, and to quell the disturbing, not unreasonable impression" that public officials had not followed their usual course in dealing with the Kennedy case, Dinis' unusual choice of a public inquest without a formal charge or the legal restrictions of a trial could turn into "a punitive venture against Senator Kennedy, unless conducted with great care," the *Standard-Times* warned. Dinis was quick to point out the decision to permit the press in the courtroom was Judge Boyle's. "The statute is very clear about that," Dinis said. "It says the Court will decide."

Senator Kennedy left it to his press secretary to remind reporters of his earlier pledge "to cooperate in any way" with an inquest, a declaration as far from the truth as it was possible to be. The prospect of a public inquisition, of testimony put under a daily press microscope was intolerable and dangerous. But for Kennedy to decline to participate in an open inquiry was a dilemma for a public man; he couldn't refuse on

the basis of the presence of the press in the courtroom. Some other pretext for enjoining the inquest under the auspices Boyle had decided had
to be found.

Kennedy was more candid about the initiatives undertaken to secure
an exhumation and belated autopsy of Mary Jo Kopechne. He could
have been talking about himself when he said, "I hope there will be no
more grief for the girl's family."

In the interest of speed "and to avoid procedural delay," Dinis sent
his petition to secure an exhumation and belated autopsy of Mary Jo
Kopechne to the Common Pleas Court of Luzerne County by certified
mail. Rather than based upon 4th amendment grounds, Dinis had constructed an elaborate rationale to justify his late entry into the case. An
autopsy was required, "So the circumstances of death be clearly established and the doubt and suspicion surrounding the case be resolved,"
Dinis said. The Senator's report to Edgartown police had differed from
his television broadcast, both statements silent on many important
details immediately preceding and following the accident. Persons with
knowledge of the event had not called authorities and, within hours after
the report to police, had left Edgartown and since that time have been
unavailable for questioning.

If Dinis hesitated to impute criminal implications in seeking a new
inquiry, he did not hesitate to do so in his petition. The purpose of the
inquest was to determine whether there was any reason to believe, "That
the sudden death of Mary Jo Kopechne may have resulted from the act
or negligence of a person or persons other than the deceased."

After weeks of pussyfooting around the issue, Dinis was sounding
the alarm. His petition didn't need to mention any names. The finger of
accusation was being pointed at Ted Kennedy.

Dinis asked Dr. Robert Nevin to co-sign the petition, "Because I've
favored an autopsy all along," Nevin said. An autopsy would have been
"distinctly to the advantage of Senator Kennedy, by putting an end to a

lot of shabby rumors and thrown light on many obscure and debated facts."

In Nevin's opinion, "Dr. Mills committed an error in judgment in not excluding foul play before signing a death certificate." Nevin described him as "a sweet, gentle, kind person who hooks rugs and plays the organ. He won't take a stand unless pushed."

Mills was "proud" to hook rugs, he said. Nevin was "a strange man, twice-married, who doesn't make friends and has formed an opinion in this case without knowing the facts." Mills had talked with Dinis and his aides numerous times since the accident. "It was crystal clear to me that the district attorney wished to keep out of this case completely." Two weeks later, Dinis had dropped his "hands-off" policy and was seeking to exhume the body of Mary Jo Kopechne for autopsy, a procedure that would probably settle public clamor, "But that's all it would accomplish. I've always been led to believe an autopsy after embalming is a pretty futile affair."

An autopsy would have spared Mills being accused of having been "bought off by Kennedy money," a charge made in crank letters he'd been getting, mainly from California, he said. "If the district attorney's office had gotten into this thing the moment they heard the word 'Kennedy,' and if they had backed me up rather than leaving me out on a limb, much of my ordeal could have been avoided."

"That medical examiner can't pass the buck to me," Dinis charged back. "Dr. Mills has tried from the first day to shift responsibility for his actions to the district attorney's office. He had full authority himself to order an autopsy and he didn't."

Dinis turned up the heat under the stew of controversy bubbling over the lack of an autopsy in the case. "On Sunday after the accident I ordered Lieutenant George Killen to call the state pathologist, but the medical examiner had already released the body," Dinis said. Killen had been in touch with Eugene Frieh and been informed that arrangements had been made to fly the body off the island at 9:30 A.M. Mills found it "strange that this should come out at this time," because of a number of telephone conversations he'd had with Dinis, "In none of these did he ever mention an autopsy."

Killen refused to become embroiled in the controversy. "The answer to these and many other questions will come to light during the inquest," he said. "I don't believe in trial by newspaper." But Killen was appalled Dinis should fabricate a story to defend himself against the charge he had been derelict in failing to execute his statutory authority to order an autopsy. Dinis hadn't mentioned a pathologist on Sunday morning. Killen said, "If he'd asked for an autopsy, he'd have gotten one."

Despite a request that his court act "expeditiously," Judge Bernard Brominski was giving no special consideration to the Dinis petition, he said. "I've got 16 other things on my desk to do, and I'm not going to be stampeded by what happens in other states."

There was no danger of Brominski being stampeded into doing anything. Dinis had again been tripped up on legal procedure. A mailed petition was inadmissible in a Pennsylvania court. Dinis was obliged to present it in person.

"They are a lot more formal here than in Massachusetts," a chagrined Dinis sought to cover up his mistake when he arrived in Wilkes-Barre. Dinis wasn't satisfied with the finding made at the scene of the accident. Dr. Mills' diagnosis of drowning was nothing more than a calculated guess. "We did not overrule him. We *should* have, but we didn't. Dinis hadn't interfered in the case, "Because it was a motor vehicle accident, and we did not want to accentuate and add to the confusion and hysteria that prevailed."

Escorted into the courthouse through a basement door to avoid reporters, Dinis was introduced to Judge Brominski. A stolid, hulking former college football player, Brominski was a party-line Democrat of limited judicial gifts who "called 'em as he sees 'em" on the bench. Dinis took no encouragement at all from the bust of JFK on display in Brominski's chambers.

After Dinis agreed to bear expenses for any witnesses he intended bringing to Pennsylvania, his petition was granted a hearing. Brominski would weigh the public interest against "the sanctity of the deceased" in dealing with the case, by far the most interesting he'd handled in 11 years on the bench. "It's rather exciting to be contacted by the national networks and other representatives of the news media," he said. "Legally, I can't change my perspective. Obviously, I will give no special consideration to this decision than I would if it did not involve a United States Senator."

The publicity pleased Brominski because he came up for reelection in November, a fact clear enough to Dinis who observed posters advertising the judge's candidacy "all over the place, even in the elevators of the courthouse."

Scheduled for August 25, the hearing would allow enough time to prepare for the inquest. Dinis had made "no decision" about what witnesses he would call. "Developments" would determine whether Senator Kennedy would be asked to testify. Ordering an exhumation was always "a difficult decision," but thousands of autopsies were routinely ordered by medical examiners and district attorneys every day, Dinis said. It was his understanding Mrs. Kopechne had wanted an autopsy for her daughter, but changed her mind.

When she learned Dinis was flying to Wilkes-Barre to present his petition, Mrs. Kopechne telephoned attorney Joseph Flanagan. "She was adamant in resisting exhumation of her daughter," Flanagan reported. "She wants it blocked if at all possible."

Dinis had not given any good reason for wanting an autopsy, Mrs. Kopechne said, "We can't understand why he waited so long to do this; he is only hurting us. I don't want my little girl's body dug up—my tiny, lovely baby. She'd never seen a doctor in her life except for a little sinus drip a month ago."

Mrs. Kopechne had accepted Senator Kennedy's failure to report the accident for more than nine hours because he was "in shock." But she questioned how he could appear in fresh clothes at the Shiretown Inn to ask the time several hours after the accident; and a possible conflict which had developed with a deputy sheriff regarding the time the accident had taken place. "Reading all the different versions of what happened really gets you confused," she said. "I would love to sit down and listen to the whole story—all of it pieced together, everything good and bad about how it happened."

The young women who had attended the party hadn't revealed anything about the night her daughter was killed, she said. "I guess those girls just aren't going to talk. It would ease the heartache so much if they could give us some answers." Mrs. Kopechne had "heavy questions" about the circumstances leading up to her daughter's death and afterward. The main question she wanted answered was the role Joseph Gargan and Paul Markham had played in the incident. She said, "There's no sense denying it, I wonder what those men were doing. Why wasn't help called for my daughter? I can understand shock, but I don't see where they went into shock. It is this question that plagues me every day."

Mrs. Kopechne was banking on an inquest, "To clear up the questions I have about Mary Jo's death." If other witnesses failed to answer those questions, "I certainly would want Senator Kennedy to testify."

Gargan didn't blame Mrs. Kopechne for questioning what he and Paul Markham did, he said. "She didn't know what the real situation was." Hurtful and unwarranted as her remarks were, Gargan didn't seek "to set the record straight."

But Senator Kennedy couldn't tolerate criticism from a grieving parent in silence. Neither the Senator nor his press aide were "available to comment." Dun Gifford was dispatched to Berkeley Heights with reassurances that the incident had been "entirely innocent." The Senator had left the party to give Mary Jo a lift to the ferry so she could return to her motel room. The damage control Gifford had practiced was so skillful, Joseph Kopechne explained several days later his wife's remarks had been "misinterpreted." She'd been "upset" when she said she wanted Senator Kennedy to testify at the inquest. "What she meant was, we would be interested in hearing Senator Kennedy's testimony, if the district attorney feels it's necessary to call him. This is what we've believed all along."

But defending against outbreaks of speculation about the entirely legitimate questions being raised about the accident was beyond even the capacity of the Senator's skilled and tireless publicity apparatus to control. No sooner was one rumor stamped out, others sprang up in their place.

On Wednesday, August 13, the *Manchester Union-Leader* reported Senator Kennedy had charged 17 long distance telephone calls to his credit card during the hours he claimed to have been "in shock" after the accident. Five calls had been made "before midnight" from the Lawrence cottage—the first to the compound in Hyannis Port lasting 21 minutes; then, two calls to Ted Sorensen, and Burke Marshall. Twelve calls had been made from the Shiretown Inn. Investigative reporter Arthur Egan had received the information from lawyer-realtor James Gilmartin of the Bronx, New York. Gilmartin claimed to have learned of the record of calls from a telephone company employee in "accounting procedures."

New England Telephone Company officials refused to confirm or deny the story. Federal regulations forbid the disclosure of the existence or contents of telephone calls except by court order, thereby giving credence to a story that was entirely false, but would attach permanently to the official history of the case. The record of calls charged to Senator Kennedy's credit card on July 18–19 Egan claimed to have access to would have shown none to have been made during the hours after the accident, or before Kennedy called Helga Wagner at the Shiretown Inn,

Dick McCarron confirmed when he talked to telephone company attorney, Bob Daley.[1]* "I looked at some of their records," McCarron said, later. Kennedy used a credit card issued by the Park Agency, Inc. of New York for calls made at the Chappaquiddick landing and the police station, "To keep the Senate stuff separate from the personal stuff."

At least half a dozen people had access to the Senator's telephone credit card, Dick Drayne said, "But I doubt that any of them made any calls that night. I think the whole story is a fabrication."

Sorensen denied Kennedy had contacted him on the night of the accident. "If he'd called me, I would have advised him immediately to do what he later realized he should have done. Namely, go to the police promptly."

Sorensen complained that "some elements in the press" were being unfair by "printing lies and exaggerating rumors" about the case. As the chief perpetrator of a misleading and now-discredited television statement, Sorensen was in a position to know much of the misinformation about the case had been Kennedy-created. The handling of the accident revived criticism of the Kennedy administration's penchant for news management in the form of "repression and distortion, pressure and propaganda." Kenneth O'Donnell had repeatedly been mentioned in dispatches as having "advised" at the compound, despite his denials.

"We knew he wasn't there, so we didn't talk about it. We tried to stay away from discussing Chappaquiddick." Jimmy Smith recalled a meeting with O'Donnell at the Coonamessett Inn in Falmouth on August 15. "All Kenneth would say about Ted Kennedy was, 'He's got problems.' His attitude was, 'We know what should have been done. They got shit on their shoe, let *them* handle it'"—the first "Kennedy crisis" O'Donnell would play no part in after more than a decade as a leading member of the Irish Mafia, and a political chieftain once

---

1   * See Appendix 4.

described as "the closest adviser and friend President Kennedy had in the White House."

Like Sorensen, O'Donnell was seeking to use his service as a New Frontiersman as a springboard for an independent political career. O'Donnell could "best carry the torch of John Kennedy's philosophy in a state position in Massachusetts," he said, announcing his candidacy for governor at a 1966 "Friendship Dinner" in Boston.

The "non-political tribute to the man who had served the President" was attended by Ted and Robert Kennedy; but spokesmen emphasized neither was endorsing O'Donnell's quest for office. In fact, Ted Kennedy was using the results of his own polling to persuade Robert Kennedy to tell his closest friend and former Harvard football teammate to drop out of the race. Ted's polls indicated O'Donnell couldn't win the nomination. Strictly a backroom operator, O'Donnell was a stiff, tight-lipped man of few words, a tense and interior personality that wouldn't come across as a candidate. Publicly, Kennedy intended to remain "neutral" in the contest, a stance Jimmy Smith had urged him to abandon by assuming party leadership in Massachusetts. "Your brother is moving boldly in New York. He is popular because he is fighting and winning," Smith said. "I'm constantly asked, 'What's the matter with Ted?'" Smith suggested, "Now is the time to support Kenneth O'Donnell."

Ted Kennedy told him, "Why should I help Kenneth O'Donnell? What's he ever done that makes him so great?"

O'Donnell "went dry in the mouth" when Smith reported the conversation back, Smith said. "Kenneth had made major contributions to both Jack and Bobby—he gave them his life. And it was coming down to rotten, first-grade politics, the kind of thing the Kennedys had danced away from in Massachusetts for years." ("There wasn't a major decision that was made by President Kennedy during the period of 1961 to November 22, 1963 that Ken O'Donnell did not share in," O'Donnell's campaign literature quoted Robert Kennedy.) O'Donnell ran a strong second to Ted Kennedy's old nemesis from 1962, Edward McCormack in the primary. "Kenneth made a strong effort and will be a future contender," Smith predicted. But relations between Ted Kennedy and O'Donnell remained strained. They clashed again when O'Donnell urged Robert Kennedy to run for president on the issue of ending the Vietnam War. Dun Gifford said, "Teddy didn't believe you should use up what capital you had on a moral issue." As political coordinator of the states in that campaign, O'Donnell spoke with Robert Kennedy by phone minutes before he'd descended to the Ambassador Hotel ballroom in Los Angeles to accept victory in the California presidential primary. Devastated by the assassination, O'Donnell observed, "That's two out of two, now. That's a helluva average for the Red Sox, but it's not very good in this business." Rather than auction his political acumen to the highest bidder in Washington, O'Donnell returned to Massachusetts for a second try for governor in 1970. Smith was affronted to learn at the meeting to prepare for the campaign that Ted Kennedy intended to remain neutral again. O'Donnell could expect nothing by way of support.

But O'Donnell had no such expectations. With the shadow of Chappaquiddick dimming the political horizon, Ted Kennedy had his own backyard to cultivate. O'Donnell had a pretty good idea why his advice hadn't been sought about the accident. Unlike Gargan, Paul Markham was not bearing his withering characterization about the role he had played in the accident in silence.

Cleo O'Donnell, Kenneth's older brother recalled, "Paul was calling Kenny up to talk about the accident, not for Teddy but for himself. Being a former U.S. Attorney, the leading federal law enforcement officer in Massachusetts, it didn't look good for him not to know enough to report an accident. Paul wasn't comfortable with the situation he was in, but he was stuck with Teddy's story. Kenny knew what went on, because Paul told him."

Kenneth O'Donnell confided what he would have done in the circumstances Markham described. "Kenny would have knocked Teddy out cold at the landing when he didn't want to report the accident, then called the Coast Guard, the U.S. Marines—you name it—and had Teddy taken to a hospital 'with serious head injuries,'" Cleo said. "Maybe the girl could have been saved, maybe not. But Teddy would have been all right. The thing would have been reported. That's what the problem was, not the accident itself, but running away and leaving Joey Gargan and Paul Markham holding the bag like that, to save himself."

In Cleo's view, "Teddy Kennedy was the weak kitten in the litter," never able to measure up to his brothers. The accident at Chappaquiddick had been illustrative of a chronic immaturity, Cleo said. "One problem Teddy always had was keeping it in his pants—even when other people are around."

The Senator's television speech was nothing more than "a sob story," Cleo said. "Kenny was amazed Teddy's people had allowed him to make it. He blamed Ted Sorensen. There was no love lost between them; they never hit it off."

Nevertheless, Kenneth O'Donnell called the Boston bureau of the Associated Press to register support for Ted Kennedy. "I think he should stay on. I'd be very disappointed if he didn't," O'Donnell said. "I thought he showed tonight the kind of courage his brothers showed."

Jimmy Smith was shocked when he learned of the endorsement. "How do you think Teddy Kennedy felt when Kenneth said that about courage, knowing what he'd been saying about him? It was the perfect political backhand. Like saying, 'Now you owe me one. See, I'm not such a bad guy.'

Smith was convinced O'Donnell could have saved the situation had he been called to the compound the week after the accident. "Kenneth was a moral man. His presence alone would have set some of those guys advising back light years." But Smith had intuited another reason

O'Donnell hadn't been asked: "Kenneth was drinking a little bit, so they didn't want him around—the powers close to the throne. They thought they had the next president of the United States all to themselves. And what they did was, they left Teddy Kennedy as a guy who would never be president. Because if he couldn't handle a fucking automobile accident, how could he handle anything else?"

Chapter 40

THE HANDLING OF THE ACCIDENT HADN'T IMPRESSED PAUL
Redmond, retained with his law partner, Daniel Daley, to represent eight witnesses at the scheduled inquest. "I thought the meetings Ted Kennedy had at Hyannis Port with the so-called 'wonder boys' had been a disaster," Redmond said. "I remember Ted Sorensen being asked: 'What were you doing at the compound?' And him saying, 'Well, I was just there to make sure he didn't lie.' I thought that was the classic example of, 'Lord, deliver me from my friends.'"

Redmond hadn't thought much of the speech Sorensen had composed either, he said. "When I became involved in the case, I very carefully went back and reread it. The statement was aimed at the elements of manslaughter: sobriety and reckless driving. The rest of it was strictly P.R."

A classmate of Ted Kennedy's at Harvard, Redmond was a brilliant trial attorney. "I was representing three guys and five very young girls. When I got the case it was a circus. There was tremendous speculation, a lot of rumor and gross untruth was being printed in the newspapers.

These girls had been put through the wringer," Redmond said. "For all the vaunted Kennedy P.R. machine, I was amazed no one ever came forward to say loud and clear that these girls had worked for Robert Kennedy, not only had there been previous reunions, they had been at Ted's house when Joan was there as hostess—that was the proper background and setting for the party at Chappaquiddick. These weren't six high-priced, international jet-set hookers flown in from all over the world for Ted's carnal amusement at the party."

Redmond dismissed the idea of a "Kennedy brain-trust" plotting strategies, he said. "Everybody was talking about the defense of this case being framed and postured by all these high-powered lawyers at the compound, but there was never any of that. The fact was, this case was being handled by guys who had tried literally thousands of criminal cases. We were not only very experienced trial lawyers, we had lived in Massachusetts our whole lives, so we knew the names and numbers of all the players. We were not unaware that District Attorney Dinis liked to bask in the sunlight of publicity, that he was prone to making statements both in and out of the courtroom." What Dinis said outside the courtroom, Redmond had no control over. "But I was going to make goddamn sure when I went into that inquest that I knew exactly what was going to happen. I'm not walking in there blind."

The first thing a trial lawyer wanted to know, "Never mind the facts of the case, or the law," Redmond said, "was what are the rules of the game going to be? Nobody knows anything about inquests. The only two cases on the books were railroad accidents, dating to the late 1800s." Redmond was drafting a letter to Judge Boyle requesting a conference to find out what kind of proceeding he was going to run. Redmond wanted to know whether lawyers would be present to advise clients during their testimony, and be allowed to object to questions put to them and other witnesses. Redmond said, "If I get over there with no ground rules and some local gossip gets up on the witness stand and starts spouting off material she's convinced herself is true because her third cousin's aunt flew over Chappaquiddick at 10,000 feet, I want the right to cross-examine to protect my clients' reputations. That's the reason I'm asking for things like the right of confrontation, and the right to present evidence. Christ! I'm not going into a courtroom where I can't do anything but just sit there."

Redmond was scouting the legal terrain seeking to locate an appealable issue to sabotage the inquest and tempt Judge Boyle into a legal snare. Boyle wasn't bound by law to hold hearings or entertain argument prior to an inquest, a procedure known to any lawyer as a judicial investigation into a death that did not require a defense, since no one was accused of any crime. Nor was an inquest a "case" calling for the pretrial maneuvering of a criminal prosecution.

A copy of Redmond's letter delivered to the district attorney's office prompted Armand Fernandes to inquire if Redmond intended to produce his clients voluntarily at the inquest.

Redmond regarded the ground rules as "the first order of business," he said. He wouldn't say whether his clients would volunteer or not.

But Redmond was stalling and Fernandes knew it. He said, "There was some question about extraditing out-of-state people as witnesses to an inquest, if that could be done. The four Washington girls couldn't be subpoenaed except through a long, drawn-out legal process—that's why the inquest situation came up in the first place. The idea was, Kennedy's lawyers would cooperate. If that didn't work to get the witnesses to talk, we would have gone to a grand jury, something Kennedy's people greatly feared. So word just sort of went out about voluntarily appearing, responding to a summons—or facing a grand jury subpoena." By going with an inquest, Fernandes thought Dinis had "outfoxed" the opposition.

In lieu of subpoenas, the district attorney's office was sending registered letters with return receipts asking those who had attended the party at Chappaquiddick to appear at the inquest "without further notice from this office."

Fernandes recalled, "There was no overwhelming response."

If Redmond refused to disclose what his intentions were, one of his clients did it for him. A gamine-like young woman, and former aide to Robert Kennedy, Rosemary Keough evinced a sophistication about her "legal position" well beyond her twenty-three years. Although not required to answer a summons, if she was invited by Massachusetts authorities, "I will voluntarily agree to testify at any legal proceedings in regard to the case," she said. "I will answer all questions fully and cooperatively."

Keough denied guests at the cookout had left Martha's Vineyard to avoid interrogation about the accident. She would have been glad to answer questions if police had asked her any. None did. Neither Senator Kennedy, his aides nor anyone else had suggested directly or indirectly that she not discuss the party. "Those rumors are untrue and false and very unfair," she said. "Mary Jo's death was an accident, of that I am sure. There is nothing to hide or cover up. I can't understand all the mysterious aspects that are being thrown around about her death."

One "mysterious aspect" Keough was anxious to clear up, however, was why her handbag had been found in the accident car. One version of the accident circulating in the gossip stage had Mary Jo Kopechne leaving the party to fall asleep in the back seat of the Senator's car some time before he and Keough had driven off together. Both had escaped the submerged car unaware Mary Jo was drowning in the back seat, "A ridiculous untruth," Keough said. "I was not in the car at the time." She had forgotten her handbag in the car when she left the party to get a transistor radio, "That's all there is to it."

Keough disagreed with conventional political wisdom that the accident had destroyed Ted Kennedy's presidential candidacy for 1972 and

1976. She said, "I'll do everything I can to help the Senator obtain the nomination."

Displeased to have his client go public about testifying at the inquest scheduled in ten days, Redmond appreciated the reason for it, dismissing Keough's remarks as "just more Kennedy P.R."

If Dinis couldn't match the emendations of a relentless publicity machine seeking to exculpate Senator Kennedy of any blame in the accident and denigrate the value of a new inquiry, neither could he head off the maneuvers designed to stall the inquest. The legal obstacles Dinis had encountered getting his inquiry off the ground were only half the difficulty, Fernandes observed. "The investigation was being blocked at every turn by Kennedy's people. We were handicapped by the fact that the major witnesses wouldn't talk to police." Much of the investigation undertaken in the case was amounting to nothing. Police chased leads to Washington, Vermont, and Pennsylvania, "But these were often wild-goose chases."

Killen had discovered a package store in South Boston where Jack Crimmins purchased three half gallons of vodka, four fifths of scotch, two bottles of rum and two cases of beer for the party at Chappaquiddick.

Killen had submitted the clothing Mary Jo Kopechne had worn at the time of her death to the state police chemistry lab in Boston. Wipings of reddish-brown stains on the back and left sleeve of a white blouse indicated the presence of blood, the "positive benzidine" on the collar significant to lab director Dr. John McHugh only insofar as it was "consistent" with the medical examiner's finding of the cause of death, he said. "When you drown like that in a car, or an enclosed unit, some of the flow of bloody froth from the mouth will pass along the edge of clothing."

The "serrated" blue stains McHugh observed when he spread the blouse out flat indicated the garment had been tucked under slacks. "We

knew that's how she was dressed when she died because the hours under-
water had transferred the dye over from the elasticized waistband. " That
Mary Jo Kopechne wasn't wearing underpants at the time of her death,
McHugh didn't think was "uncommon."

Examination under ultra-violet light disclosed nothing of evidentiary
value on the other clothes. Tests for semen stains were negative, but
McHugh doubted, "you'd get a positive on the acid phosphatase test for
seminal fluid under those conditions, the clothing having soaked in salt
water for many hours."

McHugh's examination of the accident car at state police barracks
in Oak Bluffs wasn't productive of any evidence either. "The trouble was,
everyone had been in that car; they'd stripped everything off. Somebody
had taken the radio, somebody else had cut himself. There was fresh
blood on the backseat. Obviously, there wouldn't be blood after the car
was immersed."

That the windshield had "caved in like a wave of water hit it from
the front," indicated that car had not merely toppled off Dike Bridge,
but had been travelling at a considerable speed. McHugh said, "The
logical person to survive an accident like that was the driver. Because
of the steering wheel he can orient himself. If you're on the passenger
side and a gush of water comes in going this way and that in the pitch
black, you don't know where the hell you are. You grab something,
and you don't know if it's a door-handle or part of the dashboard.
And you don't have any time. You're very fortunate to survive that
situation. You must be able to push the door open or have a window
close by." As it was, the drivers-side window measured 16" x 28".
How a 200-pound, broad-chested man wearing a back brace pinned
upside down behind the steering wheel had escaped from that space
suggested the dexterity of a contortionist or—more likely—that the
door had sprung on impact, then been closed again by the fast current
in Poucha Pond.

The "most interesting aspect" of the accident to McHugh was that Senator Kennedy had admitted being the operator, "Because nobody saw him in the car—maybe he thought somebody did." In McHugh's experience, "The most common thing we get in many of these accidents is, we find a guy in a car overturned in a field and the first sober word, the first return to consciousness he says, 'It wasn't *me* driving.' And you think to yourself, 'Well, buddy, you've got to prove that.'"

McHugh made no attempt to lift fingerprints from the steering wheel to verify a police theory that Mary Jo Kopechne had been driving the car at the time of the accident. Identification specialist state police sergeant James Sharkey explained, "Steering wheels can be difficult to start with because the corrugations often don't 'take' a fingerprint. The amino acids in the secretions that preserve a latent don't work on that surface." The Kennedy accident had provided an insuperable challenge. "Anything submerged in water like that is basically washing away the print," Sharkey said.

Frustrating and inconclusive as his investigation was, Killen was receiving an unprecedented volume of mail addressed to him as "Chief Investigator" at Barnstable courthouse. Correspondents charged "a whitewash" and a "cover-up" was going on. Others offered "suggestions" to help solve the mysteries of the case. "There were a lot of phone calls," Killen said. "There always are on highly-publicized cases." Killen ignored most of them. One call, however, "sounded like the genuine article," a witness who reported seeing Senator Kennedy "around 2 A.M. "on Saturday morning in the back seat of a blue Ford LTD sedan on Cape Cod. The caller "knew where the car was going," but refused to say. He suggested Senator Kennedy could have flown off Martha's Vineyard without being seen. "Nobody's at the control tower at Edgartown airport late at night," the caller said. "You sit on the runway. You open your radio and ask: 'Is there anyone out there?' When there's no answer, you take off."

The man refused to give his name, "because I don't want any trouble. The Kennedys can trace this information directly to me." Killen kept him talking as long as he could, but couldn't break him. From what he'd been told, Killen deduced the caller might have seen the car en route to the Kennedy compound. Killen asked Barnstable police chief Albert Hinckley to question the roster of "specials" assigned driveway duty and other security posts at Hyannis Port on the night of the accident. Killen started checking air charter services on Martha's Vineyard to find out if any planes had left the island late Saturday night or early Sunday morning. Of three airports, two were private grass facilities—one of them operated by Steve Gentle, the real estate agent who rented the Chappaquiddick cottage to Joe Gargan.

Gentle denied knowledge of such a flight. Killen could find no others from his inquiries on the island. Nor were the landing records at Barnstable county airport in Hyannis any help. Records were kept from 6 A.M. to 10 P.M., when tower personnel left. It was, however, "possible" for a plane to land at the field after hours.

At Killen's request, Dinis personally assigned state police Detective–Lieutenant Gordon Clarkson to investigate airfields in the New Bedford area. Clarkson compared a list of names Dinis gave him against the flight logs of the Gingras Air Charter Service of Fairhaven which flew seaplanes to Marthas Vineyard. "Everyone came up a blank," Clarkson reported. After hours of hard police work, Killen was forced to conclude the telephone tipster had been a "phony."

Hardly involved in the investigation that was the major preoccupation of the district attorney's office in New Bedford, Clarkson observed, "The place was a madhouse. The mail was staggering. They'd deliver it in baskets and just dump it on top of desks." Several letters threatened Dinis for "persecuting" Ted Kennedy. One letter, postmarked Binghampton, New York, said, explicitly: "I'm on my way to New Bedford to kill you."

On Saturday, August 23, state police Corporal Robert Enos reported to Clarkson for duty as bodyguard to Edmund Dinis. Spokesmen for the Bourne Barracks denied knowing about any death threats made against the district attorney. Enos had been assigned as "added manpower" for the investigation of the Kennedy accident case, Fernandes said. "What his duty is, only the district attorney knows."

Fernandes was wary of saying anything about the case. Convinced telephones in the district attorney's office were tapped, he devised a code with office secretaries. He spoke only Portuguese when discussing the Kopechne inquest with Dinis. He said, "The office was under terrific pressure; all kinds of calls were coming in. Dinis was dealing with some pretty powerful people." Reporters hovered about the premises "like vultures, you couldn't move. Eddie was taking all kinds of flak from these guys and they still expected him to cooperate." Dinis was not "as wild and woolly" about the case as he was being portrayed. He wasn't encouraging the attention he was getting from the media at all. Most of the time, Dinis was ducking the press.

Assigned by the *New York Times Magazine* to write "about the political implications of the Kopechne inquest," freelance writer John P. Marquand, Jr., requested an interview "to avoid the hysterical rumors and bad reporting that surround the event and obscured the truth."

But Dinis had more immediate concerns than the importuning of reporters, threats on his life and a staff of assistants mutinous in their opposition to a reinvestigation of the accident at Chappaquiddick. For all intents and purposes, the inquiry was being conducted by Dinis and Fernandes, two part-time prosecutors bound by the limited experience of a small, economically depressed former mill city confronting a Kennedy political organization, a choir of lawyers, advisers, media controllers and a network of Kennedy cultists in the press. A motion to dismiss his petition for exhumation and autopsy had raised enough legal points to require a conference. Judge Brominski wanted to accommodate Dinis as much as possible, but he didn't feel "obliged" to hold a hearing on the petition before the inquest. Brominski postponed it to hear arguments on the motion instead.

According to Joseph Flanagan, Dinis had lost his statutory authority to order an autopsy the moment the body of Mary Jo Kopechne left his jurisdiction, he said. "Having failed to act, he is now powerless." Dinis had not set forth in his petition sufficient facts to warrant an exhumation, particulars as to the manner in which an autopsy would diminish the "doubts and suspicions" surrounding the case, or allege that any crime had been committed. Flanagan challenged Dinis, "To reveal grounds for suspecting the death of Mary Jo Kopechne had resulted from the negligence of Senator Kennedy or anyone else."

Dinis let Fernandes argue that an autopsy was a necessary aid for the inquest, the purpose of which was the detection of a crime. It was Dinis' duty to uncover all facts of the accident "whether or not criminal intent was suspected." That there was to be an inquest was alone sufficient reason for exhuming the body.

"Holding an inquest without an autopsy would be like hitting a home run and not touching first base," Fernandes said. "We are counting on the courts to give us the evidence we need for the inquest."

Brominski took the motion under advisement. His decision would take a minimum of 48 hours, and could take considerably longer. Dinis insisted that an "autopsy is part of the investigation. Without an autopsy this matter will never be closed. We don't have ample legal evidence of the cause of death," Dinis said. "There must be an inquest with all witnesses under oath to get a complete story on the record. We must have an autopsy, but if we can't get one, we will proceed without it." The action of a Pennsylvania court would in no way delay the inquest. Dinis saw no tactical advantage in seeking a postponement. But "events in the next 24 hours" could change the picture, a sly reference to a secret request he had already made to Judge Boyle to postpone the inquest.

Chapter 41

THE SECRET WAS OUT THE VERY NEXT DAY. BEFORE OPENING A hearing to discuss inquest ground rules, Judge Boyle publicly challenged Dinis to make his postponement request in open court and give his reasons for it. Embarrassed to have his words so promptly and publicly contradicted, Dinis withdrew the request. The Commonwealth, he said, was prepared to go forward on September 3.

Because Boyle wanted "no secrecy" regarding the inquest, he had Redmond's letter about ground rules read in open court. Whereupon Redmond sprung his trap, handing Boyle two requests for rulings and a motion drafted from the legal questions raised in his letter. Redmond observed with satisfaction, "Boyle was surprised as hell to get requests for ground rules."

The hearing had been prompted solely by Redmond's letter to "discuss matters appropriate to an inquest," Boyle said. He was not convinced motions were "entitled to be filed" before an inquest. Boyle declined to officially receive them.

Redmond was astounded, "And so were all the other lawyers," he said. "We were absolutely flabbergasted when Boyle said he wouldn't accept motions—which is unheard of. You can file all sorts of motions every day in court. A judge might deny them, but he has got to hear them. Boyle's attitude was: 'This is an inquest, you guys just show up.' The statute on inquests was supposed to say it all, that he had *carte blanche* to do anything he wanted."

Redmond was "just not going to accept" Boyle's ruling. If he knew what the ground rules for the inquest were going to be, "We can know how to properly advise our clients." Without ground rules, "It may be we will have to take other procedural remedies in order to assure our clients are entitled to due process under the United States Constitution.

"Confronted by a constitutional issue, Boyle was at sea, and admitted it. "You've had more time to research the law than I," he said. "You should have come here this morning prepared with your memorandum of law as to whether a motion request was proper to an inquest."

Clark had a memorandum of law all right, but it had nothing to do with motion requests at an inquest. Redmond had fired the first shot. Clark was bringing up the legal artillery, but was scant on ammunition: a month-old United States Supreme Court decision, "that went to the very heart of this issue," Clark said. It didn't, but it was the best Clark could do. While a Louisiana Labor Management Commission's investigation into violations in labor relations did not operate as evidence of guilt in subsequent criminal proceedings, their findings became a matter of public record and were to be reported to prosecuting authorities. The Court found the Commission had exercised a function similar to an official adjudication of criminal culpability and ruled that any person who had "a stake in an accusatory proceeding was entitled to have the rights and privileges which were constitutionally guaranteed him." The Massachusetts inquest statutes "clearly fell within the Court's decision," Clark said and were "archaic under present-day circumstances." Inquests were used to explore criminal violations by specific individuals and performed an accusatory function when it appeared some criminal violation existed. (Clark chose to ignore a 1960 Supreme Court ruling which had upheld a U.S. Civil Rights Commission's refusal to allow Louisiana voter registrars to confront and cross-examine witnesses. In a majority decision the Court ruled, "The investigative process could be completely disrupted if investigative hearings were transformed into trial-like proceedings.")

Boyle refused to budge. It was his understanding inquests were a judicial inquiry, not an adversary proceeding. "It's an investigation, not a prosecution of anyone," Boyle said. Since no person was accused of any crime, the constitutional rights of a defendant did not apply. Boyle knew of no precedent for conducting an inquest under the rules of a criminal trial.

Neither did Clark. Nevertheless, he demanded the inquest be conducted, "So that the rights of every witness were fully protected." Clark proposed ground rules on behalf of Senator Kennedy: That he be represented by counsel throughout the entire inquest, have the power to compel witnesses to attend the hearing and be allowed to examine and cross-examine them, and seek rulings with regard to the relevancy, competency and materiality of their testimony, and to present evidence.

Redmond went even farther. "The Lord alone knows down what road this inquest is going to lead and what questions are going to be asked," he said. Were witnesses to be prepared "in the nature of a slander or libel case, where someone's whole life is wide open?" Redmond wanted to know the manner in which his clients would be examined.

The scope of the inquest would be such as to enable Boyle to report to the Superior Court all material circumstances surrounding the death of Mary Jo Kopechne, and the name of any person or persons "whose unlawful act or negligence appeared to have contributed thereto," Boyle said. The statute conferred broad powers upon the presiding judge of an inquest who bore the responsibility for running the proceedings according to his best judgment and in an attempt to arrive at the truth. The district attorney did not function as prosecutor but as an aid to the Court in presenting testimony and examining witnesses. But Boyle did not intend to be limited to witnesses Dinis presented. He would call other witnesses he thought might have "the information that I need to make a completely impartial investigation and report." If witnesses didn't appear voluntarily, they would be summoned at the instigation of the district attorney, Boyle said. "Except that I will make the statement now: It is *essential* that Mr. Kennedy be present as a witness." Failing other means, Boyle would subpoena Senator Kennedy himself, "Unless you represent to me that he will be here voluntarily without subpoena."

Here was the fearsome demand Dinis had quailed at making. Boyle's blunt declaration provoked consternation at the defender's table. Clark hastened to say, "At your request Senator Kennedy will be present in this courtroom at any time you designate."

Surfacing finally as Kennedy's chief counsel, Edward Hanify was not so agreeable. If the inquest was not conducted in accordance with constitutional details, "Then we are not going to make any commitment either with respect to our participation or that of our client."

Redmond could make "no statement" about voluntarily producing his eight clients—including the "Boiler Room girls"—until he knew what the inquest ground rules were going to be.

Joseph Donahue proposed a legal "process" be served on his clients Joseph Gargan and Paul Markham, suggesting they would not otherwise appear at the inquest.

Confronted by unanimous defiance, Boyle could only sputter, "You heard that, Mr. Dinis. I don't want any 'ifs.'"

Clark thought it was imperative a proper hearing on the allowance of motions be held in open court, "Before an inquest or anything else."

Senator Kennedy should have "his say as to what should be allowed at an inquest."

Boyle saw the roadblock ahead and tried to go around it. He set a hearing on the motion and request for rulings for the next morning. Boyle wasn't accepting them officially, he said. "I'm doing what Clark wanted. He wanted argument."

Clark had a right to file a motion in this case, he said. "People file motions in court every day, and they have got to be accepted and docketed!"

If Clark could find a precedent establishing a court should entertain requests for rulings of law and motions prior to the taking of evidence in an inquest, "Give it to me by tomorrow morning at ten o'clock," Boyle snapped. "I want some law on this!"

However, neither Clark nor anyone else could provide so much as a citation from a case, or a quotation from a legal textbook when the hearing resumed the next day. Boyle ruled both requests for rulings "improper."

Redmond demanded "an exception."

It was Boyle's turn to be "astounded." He said, "To what Court do you make your exception?"

Redmond would have to determine that at a later date. He said, later, "What I was saying in veiled terms—but very clear to any lawyer, was: 'Judge, you're going to find out what court.' Boyle was saying, I'm the law. I'm Judge Roy Bean and you guys are going to do it my way.' And I'm thinking, 'No, you're not. The Constitution of the United States doesn't end at Woods Hole. We have other remedies!'"

Mention of "another court" was sufficient to intimidate Boyle. A district court judge of something less than Olympian legal stature, graduate of a defunct Southeastern Law School of Fall River, Massachusetts, Boyle had served as Superior Court clerk before his appointment to the bench in 1961. Seldom was his court threatened by such lofty appeals. Boyle was accustomed to hearing cases of no more weight than theft from the five-and-ten, or taking a bushel of oysters out of season. Precedent or not, Boyle reversed himself, accepted the filing of the motion on due process, and fell into the trap Redmond set for him. Hanify had come to the courtroom prepared to argue with a brief "about an inch thick," McCarron observed, "he must have stayed up all night to produce."

Senator Kennedy had legal standing "to raise the issue of due process rights as applied to an inquest, the subject of which was a fatal auto accident in which he had been the driver," Hanify said. The fact Boyle had singled out Senator Kennedy's presence at the inquest from all others as "essential" made him "a person who had a personal stake in the outcome of the inquest."

Boyle had made the statement, "Because it had not been made clear to me that Kennedy would attend the inquest, and for no other reason," he said. How could any judge not require the presence of the only eyewitness to the accident and perform his duty to give from the best evidence obtainable the cause and material circumstances of death?

Although it was not among the issues Redmond had raised in his letter, Hanify got around to the major objection to the inquest. The death of Mary Jo Kopechne had generated "more publicity than any other fatal accident in the history of the United States and, perhaps, the world," Hanify said. How could the Senator be denied the right to have counsel present, cross-examine witnesses, and have the right to present evidence when the inquest was a public accusatory proceeding in which the spotlight of the media of the world would be focused on him?

Hanify wanted to repudiate any suggestion that, by adopting this position, Senator Kennedy was "being less than cooperative with the agencies of justice or distrustful of the fairness of this tribunal," he said. "But he comes here as Edward M. Kennedy, not as a U.S. Senator from Massachusetts, as a private citizen properly stripped of all indicia of his public office with the same rights as the humblest man in the United States. And it is those rights we seek to protect with respect to the Senator's participation in the inquest."

Paul Markham and Joe Gargan were in "the same situation," attorney Joseph Donahue declared. They were entitled to their constitutional rights, too. The inquest was accusatory to any witnesses, "Because the end result of the inquest would be a report and perhaps some further criminal action," Redmond said. "The witnesses want to come in here and lay the truth before your Honor. We have nothing to hide. We don't want to stall. But we want the basic fundamental rights to which the United States Supreme Court has said a man in an inquest situation is entitled."

Boyle wasn't persuaded the due process clause had been read into the inquest procedure by the single case cited, "That's for the U.S. Supreme Court to say, not for me." Boyle denied the motion.

This time it was Hanify who wanted an exception to preserve his client's rights.

Boyle laid down the ground rules for the inquest: Witnesses would come into the courtroom singly and be represented by counsel during their appearance on the stand for the sole purpose of advice on their rights against self-incrimination, and privileged communication. Counsel for the witness left the courtroom when the witness left.

Boyle's insistence that Senator Kennedy appear at the inquest pleased Dinis. "I was actually relieved when Judge Boyle assumed the burden of that responsibility," he said. If he had to call Senator Kennedy himself "There would be some people who would have read implications into it. I think it best that Senator Kennedy be there."

But Dinis continued to be tremulous with regard to the Senator's participation. It was not his custom to put a possible defendant on the witness stand in a preliminary procedure. "There are constitutional grounds of self-incrimination to be considered," he said. From the other witnesses called to the inquest, Dinis intended "to trace the movements of Senator Kennedy and all the others at the party, before and after the accident and explore not only the immediate questions surrounding the accident," but the "larger discrepancies" in the Senator's two accounts of the accident. Dinis confidently predicted, "All questions raised by investigators, by the press—by gossip, even—will be satisfactorily answered."

Dinis refused to say whether the inquest could lead to criminal proceedings or a grand jury investigation.

Grand Jury Foreman Leslie Leland wanted to see what developed, he said. "If Dinis is thorough, fine. If he isn't, it's another matter entirely."

Leland had "a bunch of questions" he wanted to ask about the accident if he was allowed to participate in the inquest. Killen dismissed the notion of Leland second-guessing the district attorney's office. Leland was chafing at the bit. If they let him into the inquest as foreman of the grand jury, he could take the play away from Dinis and decide the case on his own. Leland had no part to play in the proceeding, Killen told him. "You'll get a full report on the inquest from Judge Boyle."

But Redmond's provocation had borne fruit. The due process issue had made possible an objection to halt the inquest. Any legal proceeding that "could damage a person" was susceptible to appeal. Political strategy had dictated not seeking a secret inquest until after the due process motion was denied, then using the constitutional issue as a smokescreen to object to the press being in the courtroom. Weakly grounded as it was on a single Supreme Court ruling, the motion was sufficient to provide the pretext to take the issue to a higher court. Had Boyle granted all due process rights, Senator Kennedy could not have moved to enjoin the inquest on grounds of pre-trial publicity alone, when he was receiving all the constitutional protection of a trial which was always public.

A three hour meeting of Kennedy attorneys in Richard McCarron's office stimulated rumors that his lawyers would seek to delay the inquest pending an appeal to resolve the constitutional issues. Walter Steele saw it differently: "My educated guess is the Senator wants to get it over with as soon as possible," he said.

Edward Hanify followed the meeting in Edgartown with an even lengthier one at his office at Ropes and Gray in Boston, in the preparation of a writ of *certiorari* to the Massachusetts Supreme Judicial Court. Judge Boyle's rejection of the argument that a U.S. Supreme Court decision had read the due process clause into the inquest procedure may have caused "substantial injury and manifest injustice" to Senator Kennedy, Hanify suggested in the petition. To allow the press to cover the inquest "sanctioned publicity so widespread as to taint with irremedial prejudice any subsequent judicial proceedings." Judge Boyle had acted in error by saying Kennedy had to appear as a witness at the inquest. While not specifically demanding the Senator not be made to give testimony, the appeal suggested for him to appear would violate his rights.

When Hanify called the compound to disclose the basis for the appeal, the Senator was on a camping trip to Nantucket with his two oldest children, nephew John F. Kennedy, Jr., and Joe Gargan. He rushed back to Hyannis when alerted that Joan Kennedy had suffered a miscarriage on Thursday, August 28, and was taken to Cape Cod Hospital.

There was "no known cause" for the miscarriage, the third his wife had suffered, Kennedy told reporters the next day. An aide denied the "strain" of Chappaquiddick was responsible.

Chapter 42

BUT REPORTS OF OTHER WOMEN IN HER HUSBAND'S LIFE, "HURT
my feelings. They went to the core of my self-esteem," Joan Kennedy
revealed later. "It wasn't my personality to make a lot of noise, or to yell
or scream or do anything. And so rather than get mad or ask questions
concerning the rumors about Ted and his girl friends, or really stand up
for myself at all, it was easier for me to just go and have a few drinks and
calm myself down, as if I weren't hurt or angry. I didn't know how to
deal with it. And, unfortunately, I found out that alcohol could sedate
me. So I didn't care as much. And things didn't hurt so much."

Having been told nothing about the accident, and kept out of the
councils at the compound, Mrs. Kennedy accompanied her husband to
Mary Jo Kopechne's funeral, a public display of loyalty. She played her
assigned role in the public relations drama stage-managed by the Senator's staff. "I believe," she said, "everything Ted said. It was a very
unfortunate, tragic accident. I think it was a miracle Ted managed to get
out of that car. It was a very brave thing for him to do, to keep diving

down to rescue Mary Jo. I think anyone under the circumstances would be in a confused state."

Mrs. Kennedy denied speculation that her husband had been headed for a beach on Chappaquiddick with Mary Jo Kopechne when the accident occurred. "No, I'm sure they weren't," she said. "Ted left the party early so he could get a good night's sleep and be ready for the next day's race."

There was "a reasonable explanation" why he was driving down a dirt road in the opposite direction from the ferry landing, Kennedy said. But to tell it now would only lead to "more rumors." Kennedy expressed amazement at the doubts expressed that he'd swum the ferry channel, and that anyone could think him "so stupid as to attend a sex orgy in his own state accompanied by a middle-aged chauffeur and girls from his own and late brother's staff."

———

Despite Kennedy's assurances that he intended to "cooperate in every way" with the inquest, on Saturday, August 30, Court Clerk Tommy Teller issued a summons for Senator Kennedy, as well as for twenty other witnesses, to appear at the inquest. Teller also distributed "tickets" of admission to 103 newspaper, magazine, radio and television reporters permitted to cover the inquest—amid reports that reporters unable to squeeze into the 150-seat courtroom were offering one thousand dollars for tickets.

But unbeknownst to Teller, or anyone else—and protestations of innocence and assurances of willingness to talk "later" notwithstanding—the high-powered Kennedy legal team was already putting the finishing touches on their maneuver to block the inquest. On Sunday evening, August 31—during the long Labor Day weekend, and only 72 hours before the inquest was to begin—an appeal petition was signed in

Kennedy's name by Robert G. Clark II, then held, awaiting Justice Paul Reardon's turn to sit on a special branch of the Massachusetts Supreme Judicial Court that heard unusual writs and petitions. A member of an advisory committee of the American Bar Association studying the effects of pre-trial publicity on criminal trials, Reardon was co-author of the controversial "Reardon Report," proposing compulsory restraints on the publication of information released by prosecutors, defense lawyers and police officers that could be prejudicial to defendants in criminal trials. In Reardon's view, extensive publicity jeopardized not only the investigation and prosecution of cases, "But the integrity of the judicial process and the status of our legal institutions. "Reardon condemned "the careless, impulsive and inexact character of much of the nation's court reporting," and called for more specialization for journalists assigned to cover court news.

Clearly, Edward M. Kennedy could not have hoped for a better judge to hear an appeal grounded on the issue of pre-trial publicity.

That the case had achieved world-wide notoriety was evident from the list of accredited media posted in the lobby of Edgartown's courthouse: Ten British newspapers as well as the British Broadcasting Company; Reuters, the French, Italian, and West German newsmagazines, *Le Figaro, Epoca,* and *Der Spiegel;* and reporters from Australia, Japan, Spain, the Scandinavian countries and every major American and Canadian newspaper. Extensive coverage was planned by the three major American television networks. Rival correspondents Liz Trotta and Ben Silver were assigned adjacent places in the courtroom behind a raised platform where the deputy sheriff presided, forcing them to stand up to see the witness box. Harvey Ewing said, "That was Tommy's revenge for all the commotion those two had caused covering this thing."

Each network was spending $15,000 a day to cover the inquest live. Huge trailer trucks lined up like behemoths in front of the Methodist Church whose basement was being transformed into a "communications center" for reporters. Television cameras would stand upon a 50-foot scaffolding to be erected on School Street. Tiers of bleachers were going up on the front lawn of St. Elizabeth's Roman Catholic church to provide vantage places for still photographers. The furious activity of telephone crews and the din of portable transformers enthralled a record number of tourists. To the *Vineyard Gazette,* "It did look as if the circus had come to town."

Teller received notice that attorneys Stephen Moulton and William Looney would represent Paul Markham at the inquest. Markham's own law firm was taking over his defense.

Resentful of the status of accomplice her husband had been assigned in the Senator's speech, Claire Markham dismissed as "ridiculous" innuendos about the party at Chappaquiddick. "They have these political get-togethers all the time," she said.

Markham was suffering under the glare of a pitiless media spotlight. A television news team spent a week trying to photograph him entering or leaving his law office in Boston. "I never saw them myself," Gargan said, "but I was told there were crowds of reporters hanging around Paul's office waiting to see him."

Edward Harrington observed, "Paul was definitely having a hard time. A lot of people were shunning him because of the terrific criticism in the press." Harrington had served under Markham on the Strike Force of the U.S. Attorney's office. To Harrington, Markham revealed "what really happened" after the accident. Gargan had risked serious injury by his rescue effort at Dike Bridge. Harrington reported, "Paul told me Joe was the force that kept insisting the accident be reported. Teddy Kennedy didn't want to do it. He wasn't in shock, he was evaluating the situation, looking for a way out from under the thing. Ted couldn't accept the fact he was driving the car. He couldn't deal with it."

Markham's law partner, Dave Mazzone, was concerned about the effect intense public interest in the inquest was having on the district attorney's office. He placed a call to an old political crony: Jimmy Smith. (Mazzone and Smith had worked Pennsylvania together as field operatives in Robert Kennedy's presidential campaign.) Mazzone told Smith he had several concerns beyond the publicity one: Did the fact that Markham and Gargan had tried to rescue Mary Jo provide sufficient mitigation against manslaughter under the *Welansky* decision? Might Judge Boyle consider the speed of 20 miles an hour Kennedy had claimed in his Operator's Report as "negligent operation" on so primitive a public way as Dike Road?

And, above all, what about the risk of perjury should "certain statements" Senator Kennedy had already made be repeated under oath at the inquest? Mazzone noted that Kennedy's staff was "pushing the idea" that Gargan and Markham had acted as Ted Kennedy's attorneys after the accident.

Smith dismissed the idea out of hand. Kennedy's staff were trying to use privileged communication "as a fire shield to make sure what happened after the accident was client-protected," he told Mazzone. By their silence, "Markham and Gargan were taking the big fall to protect Ted Kennedy."

Paul Redmond doubted the lawyer-client issue would even arise at the inquest. "People were walking around Boston whaling the bee-jesus out of Paul Markham and Joe Gargan for not reporting the accident— that was so unfair. Here were two guys, good lawyers and fine men, made to look like stooges or worse by the press." Gargan had told him he could not have reported an accident in which a driver faced a possible manslaughter charge, Redmond said. "It's no secret Joe was a dear friend. When I left the U.S. Attorney's office, Paul Markham took my spot."

A week before the inquest, Redmond bumped into Gargan in the elevator of the building in which both had law offices. The Boiler Room girls were "upstairs," Redmond said. "They haven't seen you in a long time. I think they'd like to say hello."

Gargan went straight to Redmond's office for "a nice reunion, a pleasant chat. Very friendly." There was no discussion about the inquest. Gargan did not want to become involved in the preparation of anybody else's testimony. As one of two persons at the party who wasn't "a bit bombed," Gargan's memory of the occasion was "clear as a bell." So it was Gargan's description of the party that, along with the Senator's two public versions of the accident, would provide the scenario for inquest testimony.

———

If Gargan testified to the Senator's attempt to cover up his involvement in the accident as the reason he had failed to report it until the next day, he could blow the entire lid off the case. But that prospect became moot when a writ of *certiorari* was filed on Tuesday, September 2, asking the Massachusetts Supreme Judicial Court to determine whether "errors of law" had been made in Judge Boyle's ruling on the conduct of the scheduled inquest *in re: Mary Jo Kopechne*.

Justice Paul Reardon scheduled a hearing for three o'clock. Notified an appeal had been filed, Dinis drove to Boston from New Bedford. He was seated in a gallery reserved for lawyers when Reardon entered the courtroom. Tall and gaunt, with an aristocratic bearing, Reardon looked the very model of his reputation as a Tory elitist with grave misgivings about the role of the press in the judicial process.

Hanify pandered directly to those prejudices in presenting the appeal. From the "massive descriptions" of the scheduled inquest Hanify had read, Senator Kennedy was being made the focal point "of a gathering crescendo of publicity increasing in intensity with each passing hour," with regard to an investigation into his conduct over and above the misdemeanor charge to which he had pleaded guilty.

Hanify questioned whether it was consistent with the requirements of due process for an inquest to be conducted in a manner generating "massive publicity." Such a procedure, he argued, could taint subsequent judicial proceedings should the presiding judge find an unlawful act had contributed to the death of Mary Jo Kopechne. Senator Kennedy's rights could be "irremediably prejudiced" if the inquest were permitted to go forward in the manner Boyle proposed. Hanify called for "preliminary relief in the form of a temporary restraining order" to allow the Court to consider the "grave constitutional questions" of law presented.

Having had only hours to prepare, Assistant Attorney General Joseph Hurley struck hard at the double weaknesses of the appeal. The inquest was a judicial investigation into the circumstances of a death; no one was named as defendant. For that reason, the constitutional requirements of due process in a trial did not apply. There stood between an inquest and any accusatory proceeding a report to the Superior Court and possible grand jury action. Hurley did not deny an inquest could ultimately be the link in a potential chain of subsequent criminal proceedings, "But at this point we don't know if this chain can or will ever come into existence. It's purely speculative that the rights of any parties concerned are going to be harmed."

The statute left to the discretion of the presiding judge whether the public was to be admitted to an inquest, Hurley said. Faced with the problem of limited seating, Boyle chose to open the proceedings to the public "through the medium of the press."

To nobody's surprise, Reardon ordered the case retained for the full bench to decide the "grave constitutional questions" presented by the appeal and enjoined Boyle from proceeding with the inquest. Reardon added that he was considering an order "to terminate statements of wide circulation" about the case made by counsel and law enforcement officers which "carried the seeds of prejudice," but was satisfied to advise those to whom his admonition was directed, "To mind their conduct." Reardon stopped short of a "grave constitutional" assault of his own—on freedom of the press, guaranteed by the first amendment to the Constitution. The restrictions Reardon had proposed in his Report had been rejected by Chief Justice Earl Warren as presenting "serious constitutional problems," placing direct curbs on the press by restricting the release of information by law enforcement agencies about investigations.

Kennedy's attorneys couldn't have hoped for more. Not only had Reardon put off the dreaded inquest, but he had clamped a judicial lid on talking about it. Stunned by the speed with which his inquiry had been blocked, Dinis didn't feel it was "appropriate" for him to make any comment on the ruling, "In view of the Judge's feelings toward the publicity that has emanated."

Walter Steele was glad to see the question of inquests reviewed by the Court. In light of the U.S. Supreme Court changes in the law over the past few years, especially concerning a person's civil rights, "Now is the correct time for Massachusetts to update its inquest laws," he said.

Arena was also relieved the inquest was postponed. "We'll have a much easier time with things like traffic and other problems if the inquest is held later in the year." Arena was worried about protecting Senator Kennedy during the high tourist season. "We've only got one Main Street and we couldn't close that off."

But disbelief among reporters gathered for a briefing about the inquest turned to outrage when they discovered that Kennedy had waited until the last minute to have Justice Reardon, a known "anti-press jurist," hear the appeal, instead of filing the appeal after the previous Thursday's hearing.

Chapter 43

SENATOR KENNEDY CONFRONTED THE STORM OF CRITICISM about the blocked inquest when he returned to Washington on Wednesday, at the end of a three-week summer recess. The first question posed at a news conference before the Senate session at which Kennedy presided was whether he'd agreed with his lawyers to delay the inquest on procedural grounds.

"I signed that prayer for relief and I think that answers the question," Kennedy said. It didn't answer anything of the kind, but Kennedy took refuge behind Justice Reardon's admonition that, "There already had been sufficient comment by the principals in the case. I'll abide by the Justice's declaration."

According to the Kennedy media machine, postponing the inquest had been "a particularly difficult decision." A public inquiry could only have helped his image with the voters. Some of his advisers urged a news conference as the only way to end "corrosive speculation." Stories leaked from his office portrayed him as a man locked in a struggle between lawyers—unanimous in urging him to fight an inquest—and political advisers—equally adamant that no matter how persuasive the legal case, fighting the inquest would appear to be an effort "to worm his way out" of facing up to full disclosure of the facts of the accident. "He did not want it thought that he was seeking to evade all the inevitable, painful questions," one aide said. Only at the last minute, had Kennedy given in to pressure from his attorneys.

———

But such cosmetic claims paled alongside the additional moves made to block the inquest. Nine partygoers filed petitions to the Court, add-ons to Kennedy's own appeal, claiming their constitutional rights to privacy would be invaded by an open inquest. Said Redmond: "The press would sit as a jury. My clients will be subjected to innuendo and outrageous gossip." He sought, he said, to protect them from being "verbally assassinated."

Paul Markham did not join that appeal because, "with everyone else represented, he felt it wasn't necessary," Gargan observed. Markham was now being represented by his own law firm. Gargan would just as soon have testified at an open hearing, he said. "The reason I went along with objecting was I had a great deal of affection and respect for these girls and the other fellows involved. For this thing to turn into a public circus would be unfortunate—not only for the Senator but for all the other people I had invited for what was supposed to be a fun weekend for old friends that turned into a disastrous, uncomfortable and unattractive situation for years to come."

The appeal wasn't likely to be heard until January. The Court had 56 cases to decide before it could get to the Kennedy case. Supreme Court Clerk John Powers doubted, "There'll be any shuffling."

Having stalled the inquest, however, Kennedy didn't want the matter dragged out any closer to the election year 1970 than was necessary.

Powers' doubts notwithstanding, the Kennedy appeal was placed ahead of all other cases scheduled for the Court's October sitting. "This is not unusual when the Court thinks there's some reason that warrants it," a back-pedalling Powers explained. "The Court may have felt that the sooner the matter is disposed of, the quicker justice will be done."

But giving top priority to the Senator's appeal reinforced suspicions that "The state's judicial machinery was being manipulated in the Senator's behalf." In addition, Attorney General Robert Quinn wasn't very anxious to "win" this case. Quinn was, in fact, seeking additional ways to conduct judicial proceedings in secret.

Quinn didn't mention the Kennedy case, but it was clear what he had in mind by proposing to approach the Massachusetts Supreme Judicial Court to see whether rules might be promulgated to deal with the problem of pre-trial publicity. Public statements by court officers widely played-up in the media raised "grave doubts in many quarters whether defendants were capable of receiving a fair trial." Quinn was soliciting the aid of leaders of the Massachusetts Bar Association, "to join with me in this effort by submitting suggestions and recommendations as to what rules can conceivably be established to restrict this potentially dangerous practice."

———

While a "victory" for Kennedy's attorneys, winning postponement of the inquest had been purchased at the price of increased hostility from the press and even riskier alternatives. If Senator Kennedy wanted to keep reporters out of the courtroom when he testified, it was editorially suggested, "Why not move the whole proceeding to a grand jury?" which would dispense with the issues of due process and pretrial publicity since those proceedings were always conducted in secret. Should the Supreme Court rule that an open inquest would endanger the Senator's rights, it would be up to Dinis to decide where he wanted to take his investigation. The volatile and unpredictable district attorney might be provoked by the furor over the appeal to let Kennedy sink or swim in the grand jury room, then say, "*I* didn't indict him—the grand jury did."

Grand jury foreman Leslie Leland had heard nothing from Dinis, but "had a feeling" a call from the district attorney was forthcoming. When it wasn't, Leland took matters into his own hands. On September 9, Leland wrote Chief Justice Tauro of the Superior Court for permission to reconvene the grand jury into special session to look into the death of Mary Jo Kopechne.

Leland was advised it would be "premature" for the grand jury to look into the case before an inquest was held. But word of Leland's letter to the court alarmed Kennedy's attorneys, concerned about Dinis' "state of mind" regarding the postponed inquest.

"They were all shitting their knickers about a possible grand jury action," Jimmy Smith said after Judge Clark called him on September 14. "What he called me for was to tell me, rather than me tell him, what Dinis could do and what they could do."

The press was hacking away at Dinis. "If he didn't pursue the case, it was a whitewash. If he did, he was looking to advance his own political career," Smith said. "And all this time, he's trying to be a decent human being. He's trying to help Teddy Kennedy. He wasn't going after Teddy Kennedy, he was going after those people who attacked his own reputation."

But if Dinis had image problems, his legal woes were even greater—and multiplying. Dr. Robert Nevin notified newsmen he was withdrawing his support from the petition for exhumation and autopsy of Mary Jo's body. The relative value of what might be gained from a postmortem had diminished with time. Nevin did not want to become involved in a "militant effort" to secure an autopsy now that the emphasis had shifted from the precise cause of death to yet another issue: "The credibility of witnesses—a legal rather than medical area."

Nevin's actions caught Dinis unawares. "I haven't been contacted," he said.

Another surprise was the ruling on the Kopechne motion to dismiss Dinis' petition for exhumation and autopsy. While the petition did not specify what crime had been committed, that it was brought by a district attorney prior to an inquest suggested the inquiry was of a criminal, not civil nature. Brominski declined to view a forthcoming inquest as "sufficient reason" to order an autopsy. Dinis had not set forth "sufficient facts" to warrant exhumation, or show how an autopsy would resolve the "doubts and suspicions" surrounding the death of Mary Jo Kopechne. That millions of people had read about the accident could not be substituted for "allegations of fact" in a judicial proceeding. If Dinis had more information, Brominski said, "Let's have it." He gave Dinis 20 days to file an amended petition providing more details about why he wanted an autopsy.

Dinis was going to have to "name names and spell out a specific crime that may be involved," Joseph Flanagan said. While the Kopechnes were satisfied with Brominski's ruling, Flanagan, speaking as their lawyer, said they could change their mind, "If it were clearly established there was some compelling reason for an autopsy."

Joseph Kopechne said he was willing to meet with Dinis. "We offered to go to Massachusetts. He was supposed to come and see us, and he didn't.... We tried to meet him in Wilkes-Barre at the lawyer's office and he would never come," Kopechne explained later. "He could have talked to us, even though we were in opposite corners.... We probably could have come to some agreement. We wanted to find out why it was important to have an autopsy. We were made to believe the autopsy was primarily to find out if my daughter was pregnant.... That didn't mean a thing one way or another. It did to Gwen, being a mother, naturally. But to me, that would be ridiculous. What was it going to prove?"

Gwen Kopechne had her own answer for that. Her daughter had completed a menstrual cycle three days before her death. "I know she wasn't pregnant, so I wouldn't consider that. They had to come up with something else."

Dinis was measuring his options against the Supreme Court decision, he said. "In a way the appeal lets me off the hook, the same with the autopsy. If the court says she drowned, that's it. There's no point to it."

Dinis continued to be critical about the handling of the case, telling Smith, "Don't these assholes around Teddy Kennedy know what I can do?" Dinis wanted Smith to make sure, "Teddy Kennedy knows some day what I'm doing."

But Smith recognized the legal difficulties the district attorney's office had suffered in the courts had been largely self-inflicted.

Dinis did, indeed, have something else, detonating a charge so provocative it catapulted the Chappaquiddick case out of the legal mire into which it had sunk and back onto the front pages. On Thursday, September 18, Dinis announced that an investigation had revealed the presence of a certain amount of blood in Mary Jo Kopechne's mouth and nose, "which may or may not be consistent with death by drowning," he said in his amended petition submitted to Brominski's court. "Washed-out reddish brown stains" on the back of both sleeves and collar of a blouse worn by Mary Jo Kopechne at the time of her death had indicated the presence of residual traces of blood. Dinis didn't reveal the source of his new evidence, except to say the information hadn't become available until after internment.

Arena didn't remember seeing blood on Mary Jo Kopechne "when she was in my arms, waiting to be put in the boat. She didn't look unusual at all."

John Farrar hadn't noticed bloodstains either, "But I wasn't looking for stains," he said. "I was too busy getting the body out of the water."

Mortician Eugene Frieh refused to comment, telling reporters, "You are putting me on that well-known spot and I'm not going to give you an answer." Frieh confided to Dick McCarron, however, that he never saw any blood in Mary Jo Kopechne's mouth, "Only a slight, pinkish frothy exudate from the nostrils."

Senator Kennedy dismissed the blood evidence with something less than conviction. "I would say those who tend to look for things in this case are going to be disappointed." Kennedy's office hastened to reveal that a pathologist had told the Senator's attorneys Mary Jo's body might have been scraped when pulled through a window of the car during recovery, and this "could have caused an oozing of blood."

Kopechne lawyer Joseph Flanagan suggested blood might have resulted from slivers of shattered glass puncturing the skin during the accident.

But Brominski could not dismiss this "new evidence" redolent of violence and possible criminal wrong-doing. Brominski scheduled a pre-autopsy hearing on September 29.

Killen was dismayed that Dinis had taken state police tests out of context and inflated the results into sensational disclosures of new evidence to secure a hearing for his petition. The petition was harmless make-work to demonstrate the district attorney's office was doing something about the case. Still, Killen could think of no reason why an autopsy should not be welcomed by both the Kopechnes and Senator Kennedy if only to put an end to speculation with regard to immoral conduct having occurred before the accident, and a rumor that Mary Jo Kopechne was pregnant at the time of her death. Killen saw no harm in the procedure at all. "I figured we'd get the autopsy and it would be: 'She wasn't pregnant; she drowned. Case closed. Everybody go home.'" Instead, four lawyers in Wilkes-Barre were fighting like hell to prevent the body being exhumed; and Judge Brominski was avoiding every opportunity to rule on the issue.

Knowing the lab tests had been "consistent with drowning" Bernie Flynn was even more disenchanted with the case. "The investigation was unlike anything we'd ever done before," he said. "There was something unusual about the whole thing. It seemed like everybody wanted to get the damn thing over with as fast as they could to appease the press. Nobody in the district attorney's office said, 'Come up with information.' We were never told what crime we were investigating. Usually, we know what somebody's being charged with so we go out and dig up the evidence to support the charge. The scene was one of panic for many weeks, panic in the D.A.'s office, panic in the Registry and in the press. I'm standing there observing it every day, and ideas are going through my head."

Flynn admired the Kennedy family. "When Jack and Bobby got killed the whole country mourned. Because of my feelings, naturally, after two assassinations, I started feeling sorry for Ted Kennedy during the course of this thing. Because I'm thinking: 'What the hell is going on?' Dinis is supposedly prosecuting him; the press is like a goddamn lynch mob. My theory was Kennedy wasn't in the car. But even if he was, it was an accident. He certainly didn't qualify for this hangman vigilante gang going after him."

Flynn related his theory about the accident to journalist Jack Olsen, also embarked upon writing a book about the case, during lunch at a restaurant near the courthouse in Edgartown. "Ted Kennedy didn't want to admit being drunk with a broad in a car late at night. When he saw 'Huck' Look he got scared. He thought a cop was coming after him." Flynn couldn't prove Ted Kennedy had gotten out of the car before the accident; and he didn't expect the Senator to recant his previous statements. True or not, Kennedy was stuck with the other story. Flynn didn't think Olsen was very impressed by his theory.

Andy Tuney reserved judgment about the Senator's guilt in the accident. Tuney was working on a stolen art case in which the thief had offered to sell the paintings back to the insurance company. Because the robbery had occurred on Cape Cod, Tuney was consulting George Killen at Barnstable courthouse. After the meeting, Flynn invited Tuney to have lunch at the Coonamessett Inn in Falmouth. Flynn had never met Tuney before, "But I knew of him by reputation." Tuney was a celebrity cop, head of the Boston Strangler bureau which had cracked the famous murder case. After nineteen years with the state police, Tuney resigned to become F. Lee Bailey's private investigator.

During lunch, Tuney said, "I hear you're working on the Chappaquiddick case. How're things going?"

Flynn was glad Tuney brought the subject up. "I was telling him about my feelings about Ted Kennedy, the poor bastard, he's getting a raw deal," Flynn recalled. "That goddamned TV speech made him look like a jerk. I know he's lying, whatever the reason. He got bad advice. I thought he's really going to get it put to him when he gets to that inquest and keeps lying; he's going to be gone!" Flynn told Tuney, "Jesus, I'd like to help the guy out. I think he's in a bind." The only way Flynn could think of to help Ted Kennedy was to let him know what certain people were going to testify to at the inquest.

"Bernie was very anxious to be put in contact with Ted Kennedy's office in Boston," Tuney said, later. "He figured I'd know how to make the call because I'd worked both sides of the street as a state cop and a private investigator." Tuney was no "Kennedy lover," he said. "I wouldn't have stepped out of the way to help Ted Kennedy." Before Tuney did anything, he sought the advice of F. Lee Bailey.

"Andy said he knew where there was some information which could be helpful to Ted Kennedy with respect to the inquest," Bailey said. "He was asking me, 'Should I volunteer to pass it along, or just stay out of it?'" Bailey spent no time thinking about it at all. "It wasn't even a conference. Andy mentioned it and I said, 'Sure, if it's helpful to Teddy Kennedy, see that he gets it.'"

Bailey didn't know the informer was a police officer engaged in investigating the case. He had no idea somebody in Edmund Dinis' office was involved. "But I rather think, because I knew Ed's attitude, that wouldn't have bothered me," Bailey said. "Because I think Ed Dinis would have given Teddy Kennedy or his lawyers anything he had to prepare him for the inquest."

Tuney called Kennedy's Boston office. He had "urgent and important information about Chappaquiddick." He didn't want to talk "to any aide, secretary or anybody else," he said. "I only want to talk to Ted Kennedy." Tuney was sure his call would be returned when he gave his name as F. Lee Bailey's private investigator, he said. "I'd been chief of the Boston Strangler bureau. My name had been in the papers all the time."

The next day Tuney received a call from Stephen Smith. He recognized him as Ted Kennedy's brother-in-law. Tuney said he wanted to talk to the Senator.

Smith said, "Well, you can't do that. He's not here."

Tuney wasn't prepared to give out the information to just anybody, he said, later. "It had to be somebody close, or I wouldn't have said a word." Tuney told Smith, "Well, it's some very important information a state police officer wants to relay to Ted." Tuney didn't know what the information was. "Bernie didn't tell me anything except he was willing to show Ted Kennedy the district attorney's file on the case before he went to court—that's what he intended doing, because he admired Ted and the Kennedy family so much."

Smith assured Tuney the information would go to Ted Kennedy and nobody else. Smith would "relay it direct," he said. "I'll see that the Senator gets the message."

Chapter 44

FLYNN WAS SURPRISED TO RECEIVE A CALL FROM TUNEY AT
Barnstable courthouse. "At the time I talked with Tuney, I didn't think
he was serious about putting me in contact with somebody in Ted's
office. I wasn't expecting anything to come out of the conversation. We
were having a couple of drinks. I figured it was just barroom talk."

If Flynn wanted to help Ted Kennedy, Tuney had two numbers for
Stephen Smith in New York:

(Home) (212) RE7-9946

(Office) (212) TN7-4900

Flynn copied the numbers in a black address book he was keeping
for people he wanted to have a file on when he transferred from New
Bedford to Cape Cod.

Stephen Smith was expecting Flynn to call, Tuney said. "It won't be
cold."

"Tuney saying that helped me out," Flynn said. "Because I wouldn't
have to explain who I was."

Flynn "gave it a lot of thought" before he called Stephen Smith, aware of the risk involved in what he was contemplating doing. "This went beyond all my character to do this. The first time I've been on a case and gone over to the opposition and tell them what's going on. It's something I'm not comfortable with."

Flynn discussed the idea of passing evidence of the investigation with his girl friend, Jacqueline Buzzee. She thought it was a good idea to help Ted Kennedy. There was the matter of Flynn's vulnerability to transfer from Cape Cod to some less desirable assignment with the state police. It couldn't do any harm to have Ted Kennedy obliged to him about an investigation that wasn't going anywhere anyway. Dinis wasn't serious about hanging a rap on Ted Kennedy. He was only going through the motions to get the press off his back.

Flynn called Stephen Smith's office in New York. When he gave his name to the secretary, "I was put right through, there was no hesitation. There wasn't anything like, 'Who is this?' If I had to explain who I was, I probably wouldn't have gone through with it," Flynn said. "But everything was set up. Stephen Smith wasn't surprised to hear from me. He knew who I was."

Flynn had been told to call this number, he said. He wanted to talk about Chappaquiddick.

Smith asked him to call him at home. When Flynn did that evening, "I told him my position, but I think he knew it. He wasn't saying too much on the phone. Maybe he was afraid it was a police trap or something. My gut feeling about his attitude was, he's wondering: 'Why is this guy offering to do this?' The initial phone call indicated he was going to get in touch with Teddy Kennedy."

Smith had to "check this out with the Senator," he said. He wanted Flynn to call him back "in a couple of days, within the week."

Years of backroom maneuvering as financial director of Kennedy campaigns had prepared Stephen Smith to be the perfect confidential agent for Ted Kennedy, following a tradition that, "The most delicate political assignments were always kept in the family."

The team of lawyers working on the inquest had been compartmentalized by their specialty. Edward Hanify had overall legal command of the case and had handled the constitutional issues of the appeal. Clark, as a motor vehicles specialist, was given the "dirty work" of dealing with the Registry in matters bearing directly on the accident. Retained to defend Ted Kennedy in Edgartown district court, Dick McCarron was now no more than resident agent for Kennedy's interests on Martha's Vineyard.

Others played a role: Ted Sorensen, Richard Goodwin and Milton Gwirtzman. Burke Marshall and William vanden Heuvel later claimed a lawyer-client relationship with Ted Kennedy on the case. To this squadron of lawyers was added another, one who played out his crucial role in history's shadows.

His name was Herbert J. Miller, Jr. A top-flight defense lawyer, "the pragmatic, pun-loving" Miller had built a solid reputation in Washington after Bobby Kennedy picked him to head the Criminal Division of the Justice Department from 1961 to 1965. In that role, he captained Bobby Kennedy's final offensive in his long campaign to put Teamster chieftain Jimmy Hoffa behind bars.

With Kennedy's future hanging in the balance, Stephen Smith tapped Miller for a vital but volatile assignment: to receive evidence from Flynn of the ongoing State Police investigation into the accident at Chappaquiddick. Kennedy's brain-trust realized that, as tempting an advantage as it was to have access to those files, it was also flirting with charges of judicial espionage or obstruction of justice. Smith concluded that it would take a man of Miller's shrewd mind and legal acumen to handle such an explosive assignment.

That Miller had joined the Kennedy juggernaut was to remain the best-kept secret of the cover-up. His connection with the case never has, until now, been revealed.

———

Stephen Smith was ready to do business when Flynn called him back. "I'll give you this name and make arrangements for you to meet this person in Washington," Smith said.

Flynn had a ready-made "cover" story. He was working on a "picayune case, a breaking and entering involving larcenies of motel television sets," Flynn said. He needed to consult with Joseph Lanzetta, a former civilian employee of the Massachusetts State Police then working in a Washington crime lab, "To see what Lanzetta could testify to if the case ever came to trial. I had to go to Washington anyway, and I had *carte blanche* as to when."

Smith instructed Flynn to call Miller, "When you hit Washington." Flynn recalled, "He said his name was Herbert or Henry, but everybody called him Jack." As soon as he arrived in Washington, two days later, Flynn dialed the number Smith had given him for Miller, Cassidy, Larroca and Lewin. He was put through at once to Jack Miller.

Flynn told him he was calling from the airport.

Miller said, "Stay there. I'll meet you in 20 minutes." He directed Flynn to a lobby lounge area at the airport. Miller would be, "Hatless, wearing a black cashmere topcoat and carrying a briefcase," he said.

Flynn described himself, "Blond hair, no hat. And I'm wearing a trench coat, light color."

Flynn was disappointed Miller was coming to him, "Because I'd made the trip all the way down there, I figured he's going to say: 'Grab

a cab and come over to the office. We can have lunch or something.'"
Miller plainly preferred the anonymity of an airport.

Flynn spotted Miller from his description as soon as he appeared,
"A good-looking guy, late 40s, a little shorter than me, nice stature. And
very self-confident."

Miller introduced himself. He said Stephen Smith had contacted
him.

Miller took a seat on a bench in the center of the lobby. Flynn was
immediately put on guard when Miller placed a briefcase on the floor
beside him. "I said to myself, 'He's going to start taping.' What the
hell, I'm no dummy," Flynn said. "There was no reason for him to be
carrying a briefcase. He never opened it. He didn't say, 'I want to take
down notes on a yellow pad or something'—which I was expecting.
That's when I knew he was nervous. I can't blame him. He doesn't
know who I am or what I'm going to do. It kind of made me uneasy
knowing it was being taped, but I had committed myself. Plus the fact,
Miller is going to be using the tape to tell Stephen Smith and Ted Kennedy what I said."

Flynn was at pains to explain, "I'm doing this because Ted Kennedy
was not in the car. That was my opinion, I could be entirely wrong. My
main purpose is, I don't want Ted Kennedy to get caught in a big lie that
could really make him go down the drain. The reason I'm there is not
to have Ted Kennedy go into the inquest and start lying again. Because
in my opinion he'd already lied in the police report and the TV speech,
and I liked the guy. I knew he had presidential aspirations."

Flynn's meeting with Miller was primarily to give him evidence.
Flynn had copies of all investigative reports, but brought none of these
to the meeting. "I kind of selected in my own mind what I thought was
important," Flynn said. "Everything was to be delivered verbally."

"Huck" Look was going to be the major problem at the inquest. His
testimony checked out. The man is honest," Flynn said. "He has no

reason to lie. So there's a time-gap there, like an hour and a half off what Kennedy said it was."

Flynn delivered, "The whole context of Look's testimony. What he's going to say at the inquest. The reason Look knows he saw the car at 12:45 A.M., he was a special police officer at a party at the Edgartown Yacht Club. He knows what time he quit work, naturally. He's on his way home and he sees a car backing out of the road to the cemetery."

Then Flynn went into what he surmised: "Teddy Kennedy was in the bag, no question in my mind about that. And the most important thing to him at this time is not getting locked up for driving under."

Flynn revealed, "The new witnesses we had, Ross Richards and Stan Moore. They were going to testify to what happened the next morning on the porch of the Shiretown Inn. They had a description of Ted Kennedy talking, that he wasn't upset," contradicting what he told police about being in a state of shock after the accident. Moore had refused to talk to police about drinking on Richards' boat after the regatta race, which suggested Kennedy had half a bag on before the party at Chappaquiddick, information of vital importance, given a possible manslaughter charge emanating from the inquest. In addition, the investigation had uncovered several witnesses who could testify to the noise-level of the party, and the fact that it had not been "a quiet barbecue" as reported in the press. The Registry of Motor Vehicles was "walking on tiptoes" around the case, Flynn said, because Ted Kennedy's license had expired, information that was common knowledge in the district attorney's office.

Miller didn't ask for anything specific, Flynn observed. "He's just following the trend of the information I'm giving out. He's sitting there listening, not writing anything down. He isn't saying too much. He didn't want his voice talking on the tape."

After Flynn's recital, Miller said, "Is that it? Do you have anything else?"

Flynn didn't. If anything important came up, he'd get in touch with Stephen Smith.

Miller thanked him, shook hands; then left the lobby. The meeting took between twenty minutes to a half an hour. Flynn took a cab and checked into a hotel in downtown Washington. He called Joseph Lanzetta at 4:30 P.M. Lanzetta met him after he got off work for a drink at the hotel's lounge. More hospitable than Miller, Lanzetta asked Flynn to his house in Virginia, to meet his wife and have dinner. After a few drinks at a local bar, Lanzetta drove Flynn back to Washington. He observed the passing landscape of the capitol "All lit up at night," Flynn said. "And I really enjoyed that."

Flynn flew back to Cape Cod the next morning. He made out an expense voucher, charging the Washington trip to the district attorney's office. "Stephen Smith didn't send me an airplane ticket or anything," Flynn said. "He didn't say, 'I'll pay your way down.'"

Flynn didn't report his meeting with Miller to Andy Tuney. "I never called down to the Cape to find out whatever the hell it was Bernie did, whether he ever got together with Ted Kennedy and went over the case with him," Tuney said. He never mentioned the subject of Chappaquiddick again to F. Lee Bailey.

Bailey had the impression Tuney "gave something to somebody," he said. "I presumed it had something to do with areas of the investigation. But I don't know what it was, where he got it from or who he gave it to. I assumed, Judge Clark."

Bailey said nothing about the incident to Dinis. "By the time this happened, Ed and I didn't have an occasion to chat about Chappaquiddick." Bailey wouldn't have hesitated to mention that somebody from his office had passed information to Ted Kennedy, he said. "I don't think Ed would have objected. He certainly didn't have anything against Ted Kennedy. If he'd wanted to prosecute him for something, he probably could have gotten a manslaughter indictment out of a grand jury, but I don't think he felt disposed that way at all." Nor was the appeal pending before the Massachusetts Supreme Judicial Court at issue. Any secrecy order would be to prevent publicity in the event of a criminal prosecution, in Bailey's opinion, "The Supreme Court wouldn't rule that information be kept secret from the target of the investigation, Ted Kennedy."

Chapter 45

WITH "HUCK" LOOK IDENTIFIED AS THE MOST DAMAGING WITNESS at the inquest, Edward Hanify retained private investigator J. E. Gautreau of Confidential Services, Ltd., of Arlington, Massachusetts, to conduct an investigation of Look and other witnesses scheduled to testify.

Look was "a little bit upset" when he found out, "Investigators for Kennedy were knocking on doors all over Edgartown asking old ladies if I get drunk or run around with women. Well, everybody knows that I don't. But even if I did, that wouldn't change what I saw."

Gautreau's investigation was discontinued at Richard McCarron's request, "Because it didn't work. The press got on to him too fast, and so did people in Edgartown." Look's reputation was exemplary, McCarron said. "My attitude was, 'Why are we investigating 'Huck' if he's telling the truth?'" The fact an investigation had been undertaken was McCarron's only question about Look's story, he said. "I didn't have any doubt 'Huck' saw what he said he saw."

McCarron sought to resolve the mystery of that confrontation himself. Securing a registry list of property owners assessed at Chappaquiddick as of January 1, 1969, he questioned only a few residents seeking to locate a "black sedan" with an "L7" Massachusetts registration before giving up. "It was the same problem the investigator had," McCarron said. "People just got on too fast to what I was doing."

McCarron was deeply involved in an investigation of another kind, having received permission from George Killen for tests to be performed on the accident car impounded at state police barracks at Oak Bluffs. McCarron had asked the tests not be divulged, but Daniel I. Murphy, captain of the state police bureau, didn't want his agency accused of "favoritism" by allowing experiments to be conducted in secret. Murphy released the information that an investigation into the "physical factors" of the accident was being undertaken by a 10-man team from the Arthur D. Little Company, a research consultant firm of Cambridge.

Senator Kennedy was concerned about statements made by John Farrar that Mary Jo Kopechne could have breathed in a pocket of air long enough to have been rescued if help had been sought out immediately after the accident. "Above all, Kennedy has told friends, he wants to prove that Mary Jo could not have survived in the submerged car even if he had immediately summoned help, instead of waiting nine hours to report the accident," a delay which had provoked speculation "that Senator Kennedy had tried to avoid being implicated in any report of Miss Kopechne's death." The idea that Kennedy had bolted from the scene and abandoned Mary Jo Kopechne to die a slow, terrifying death by asphyxiation was so damaging to his case as to have prompted experiments to determine how long she could have survived after the accident.

A mannequin of her approximate size and weight was used in a test during which the accident car was flipped over and jarred with the same impact with which it had struck the water in Poucha Pond. The

mannequin was thrown into the rear seat of the car with a force "sufficient to stun, and possibly disorient a human being."

Hoisted by a wrecker into a position to simulate that in which it was
discovered, the car was filled with water from a state police garden hose
to determine how quickly air had been displaced in the back seat. Two
days of tests concluded that Mary Jo Kopechne had remained conscious
for "one to four minutes." She could have been revived up to ten minutes
after losing consciousness.

John Farrar regarded the tests as "worse than useless," he said.
"How they can recreate the conditions, I don't know. Filling a car with
water is not the same as having it submerged. It seems certain they are
doing all this to try to discredit my evidence. But the big difference is, I
went down to where a girl was trapped in a submerged car—the consulting firm didn't." In Farrar's opinion, there was no way to duplicate the
circumstances of the accident short of sinking the automobile all over
again.

Farrar's pronouncements about an air bubble having sustained Mary
Jo Kopechne's life, and that she might have been saved if he'd been called
at the time of the accident had brought him some highly critical mail,
he said. "But I stand on my belief."

McCarron was not concerned about Farrar's testimony, he said.
"John was a little screwy on the subject of the accident." A "summer
kid" who'd moved to Edgartown in 1965, Farrar had held press conferences at the Turf 'n' Tackle to explain his theories about the accident.
No matter how expert his testimony was, Farrar had, by pontificating
at such length about the accident, literally talked himself out of any
credibility as a witness.

But Arena, too, was skeptical about the value of tests conducted to
replicate the accident. The accident car's wiring having been destroyed
by vandals, a battery was placed directly on headlights to indicate the
dimmer switch had been on high-beam at the time of the accident. Using

a 1969 Chevrolet with the same headlight configuration as the accident car, a test of "visual factors" was conducted to reproduce what the human eye would see approaching Dike Bridge at night. Motion pictures revealed the bridge was visible "less than 3 seconds, if approached at 20 miles per hour." Still photographs taken under the same conditions showed at a distance in excess of 100 feet, headlights struck the ground in front and to the left of the bridge then were deflected upward, "Almost as though one's headlights have been turned out"—an abrupt change in light intensity that could well distract a driver. As the car reached the bridge, headlights came down to illuminate the rub rail, and the realization that the road over the bridge angled to the left.

Arena clocked the test car at 20 miles per hour for an experiment during which brakes were applied the instant front wheels touched the bridge. Although the automobile stopped in 31 feet and did not plunge over the side, the test indicated that, even allowing reasonable reaction time, "Braking only will not prevent a car traveling at a speed of 20 miles an hour from going over the rail," a result that appeared to confirm Registry Inspector George Kennedy's report of his examination of skid marks on the bridge and "other conditions." Inspector Kennedy had calculated the car had been operated "at approximately 22 miles per hour" at the time of the accident, an assessment Arena discounted entirely. "Maybe an engineer could do it," he said. "But I seriously doubted 'Red' Kennedy would be able to tell much from the smudge marks I saw on the bridge."

As a state trooper, Arena knew skid marks were evaluated on the basis of tire depth and length of skid. Dike Road was dirt, sand and gravel. If Senator Kennedy had attempted to brake before the accident, no skid marks would show up on that surface. Markings on wood were difficult to measure and even harder to evaluate. In Arena's opinion, Senator Kennedy had not attempted to brake at all but had driven straight over the side of Dike Bridge. Without braking there could be no skid marks. And without skid marks, no way for "Red" Kennedy—or anybody else—to estimate rate of speed.

As part of the tests commissioned on behalf of Senator Kennedy a plan and elevation of Dike Road's approach to the bridge was prepared from direct survey and aerial photographs. A consulting engineer found existing conditions at Dike Bridge "well below the minimum standards set by commonly used engineering criteria." The absence of warning signs, guardrails, lights or reflectorized markers made the accident site particularly hazardous at night. Underwater photographs of the tide and current patterns in Poucha Pond and the location of the accident car were taken by a scuba diver.

Senator Kennedy's swim across the ferry channel was restaged by a person of his approximate weight and stature, preceded by "some alcoholic intake" to approximate conditions the night of the accident. Dukes County Sheriff John Palmiera refused McCarron's request to administer a breathalyzer test, since "no criminal aspect" was involved in the experiment. Palmiera said, "We use the breathalyzer when someone is arrested. It isn't a toy."

Such elaborate and contrived experiments scandalized Edgartowners with rumors of thousands of dollars spent on, "The best evidence money can buy." In contrast to the sums at the disposal of Kennedy's defense team, a special appropriation bill passed by the legislature allowed the County of Dukes County to borrow $15,000 to pay for the scheduled inquest. In pursuit of justice, Edgartown couldn't compete with the Kennedy fortune.

With costs of the defense mounting up, McCarron requested compensation to cover day-to-day expenses. A check for $5,000 was issued from Park Plaza, Inc., the Kennedy family corporation. When McCarron complained he hadn't received the money, an investigation revealed the check had been stolen from a tampered mail chute in the Pan Am building in New York, and cashed the same day at a bank nearby.

But more than money, scientific and legal expertise was being thrown at the problem of Chappaquiddick. A tireless propaganda machine was seeking to disperse the cloud of scandal hanging over Senator Kennedy, described as "hurt and shaken" by rumors attaching to the episode. Kennedy was disturbed, in particular, by "one widely-accepted line of speculation that there was never any question of catching the ferry and that, after the accident, he at least entertained the notion of concealing his role by reporting that Miss Kopechne had been alone in the car."

To repair the damage done to his career as a political leader "willing to speak out on important issues," Kennedy used the occasion of a testimonial dinner in Boston for the retiring president of the American Cancer Society to deliver a harsh condemnation of the Vietnam war as a conflict that was "eroding the health, the economy and the moral and spiritual strength" of the nation "as surely as any disease that attacked the body."

Response from a distinguished audience was "lukewarm at best," the speech described as "a palpable dud," and "a lackluster performance," that revealed Kennedy was still suffering under the shadow of unanswered questions about the death of Mary Jo Kopechne.

That the speech had not aroused marked enthusiasm was less surprising than, "Ted Kennedy had been audacious enough, less than two months after Chappaquiddick," to speak so indignantly about such virtues as moral strength, Sylvia Wright observed in *Life* magazine. Wright ascribed Kennedy's regained spirit to his job as Senate whip, "And acceptance of the fact that he must—and will—face further questioning about the accident." Forbidden by court order from making public statements about the case, Kennedy had come to realize, "There was much more he should have said immediately after the accident. The advice taken, the solutions worked out in those rainy days inside the Hyannis Port compound were not, he now feels—along with many friends and family advisers—the best advice and solutions." Thus, the forthcoming inquest was "less frightening to him than it is essential." Kennedy was eager to satisfy the widespread demand for information about the accident, Wright reported. "If necessary, he would probably be willing to be interviewed by newsmen on a TV panel."

Kennedy had tried to answer questions the Kopechnes had about their daughter's death, he said. "For the rest, it will all come out. The questions ...all the answers. And I think people will understand. But it will just have to wait."

For the Senator's office to generate favorable stories, seeking to exculpate him of any blame in the accident and dismiss the dangers of the forthcoming inquest didn't sit very well with Edward Hanify, reflecting a continuing struggle between the Senator's lawyers and his political advisers. (Hanify had opposed the Senator making the TV speech, Dick McCarron said. "Everyone agreed it had been a mistake.")

Efforts to rescue the Senator's political reputation were jeopardizing the defense of his case. The peril of possible criminal charges issuing from the inquest was serious enough not to risk further damage to his legal position by indulging in a public dialogue about the accident. McCarron received a call from Hanify during a dull interval in the case. "Nothing much was going on," McCarron said. "Hanify felt there was just too much interference with Ted's political people in the management of the case; that we couldn't function properly as attorneys under those circumstances." Their insistence on issuing public relations statements was making a legal defense of Senator Kennedy virtually impossible. Hanify intended to resign from the case unless he was given free rein, without interference from Kennedy's staff or advisers. He was soliciting the support of other lawyers employed in the Senator's defense to present a united front. McCarron agreed to join Hanify, Judge Clark and his son, to walk off the case.

Hanify's ultimatum had its effect. McCarron said, "He stayed on; we all did." Kennedy could not bear the spectacle of his legal team abandoning his defense prior to the argument of his appeal before the Massachusetts Supreme Judicial Court.

Senator Kennedy would make no political appearances while court action was pending, his office announced. The "self-imposed moratorium" would prevent the Senator from participating in a special election in the 6th congressional district in Massachusetts. Kennedy had given his "implied endorsement" to Democratic candidate Michael Harrington before the accident, but since that time had no connection with the campaign. Because the election was regarded as a possible trend-setter for 1970, Edmund Muskie and George McGovern had appeared for the candidate. Hubert Humphrey and other prominent Democrats were scheduled to campaign. Kennedy wasn't going to take part, a Harrington aide said. "The decision was made not to invite him, because it wouldn't help."

But denying Senator Kennedy a public platform from which to discuss the accident didn't stanch the tireless efforts of his staff to defend the legal blockade imposed upon the inquest. Friend and political ally, Senator Birch Bayh, among others, took up the cudgel. Ted Kennedy was "anxious" to tell all he knew about the accident, Bayh said. "The matter has to be cleared up completely. I think Ted wants to make available all the information."

Bayh had been involved in an accident himself which had left him so confused he had assumed for 24 hours that he was responsible for someone's death. Not until he called the home of the deceased to extend his sympathy had he learned that another driver was to blame. Bayh cited the incident "as a possible explanation" for Senator Kennedy's failure to report the accident for more than nine hours. It was "too early to tell" how badly Chappaquiddick had hurt Kennedy's political career, Bayh said. "Some polls say he's completely through. My judgment is that this is not completely true. He has a tremendous hold on young people. It amounts to almost worship. And young people are prone to forgive and forget."

Bayh's analysis was not borne out by a survey published by *The Boston Globe* on September 22, revealing that the greatest drop in approval for Senator Kennedy in Massachusetts had occurred in 18- to 20-year-olds. The slide was so precipitous that it fueled rumors of an impending resignation. Governor Francis Sargent went so far as to request a review of the procedure for naming Kennedy's replacement. Should the Court strike down his appeal and require Kennedy to testify at a public inquest he might resign before facing revelations of wrongdoing. That speculation appeared uppermost in Edward Hanify's mind when he rose to argue the appeal before the Massachusetts Supreme Judicial Court.

Hanify wanted the Court to determine whether the inquest statutes had become "outmoded" by recent U.S. Supreme Court decisions. Unless new ground rules were laid down, the procedure could be unconstitutional, Hanify said. The evil to be averted was the use of a judicial proceeding prior to a formal indictment, generating massive and gratuitous publicity which could prejudice Senator Kennedy's case, and deprive him of a fair trial in any subsequent criminal action. As evidence, Hanify brought a "compendium" of press clippings to the courtroom, and cited the Dr. Sam Sheppard murder case[1*] as an example "of publicity developing from a flood into a tidal wave."

---

1   * On July 4, 1954, 31-year-old Marilyn Sheppard, wife of Dr. Sam Sheppard, a wealthy osteopathic neurosurgeon, was beaten to death in her suburban Cleveland home. Sheppard was tried and convicted of second degree murder in one of the most highly publicized and sensational trials of modern times. In November 1961, a young lawyer, F. Lee Bailey, appealed the case, charging that the press had "deliberately and with malice" published articles implicating Sheppard. At the culmination of a series of appeals, on June 6, 1966, the U.S. Supreme Court overturned Sheppard's conviction, citing "the trial judge's failure to protect Sheppard sufficiently from the massive, pervasive, and prejudicial publicity that attended his prosecution." At a second trial six months later, Dr. Sheppard was found not guilty.

Hanify asked the Court to bar the press and public from the inquest, disqualify Judge Boyle from presiding and, should the inquest reflect any wrongdoing on Senator Kennedy's part, to suppress the report and transcript of testimony until the conclusion of any prosecution or trial.

Assistant Attorney General Joseph Hurley hit the publicity issue head-on. The prejudice complaint in *Sheppard*, he argued, had occurred after the accused was arrested and during the course of his trial. In reversing the conviction, the Supreme Court had not held reporters should be excluded from the courtroom, but that the trial judge should have controlled them better. The principle that justice could not survive behind walls of silence had long been reflected in the Anglo-American distrust of secret trials. A responsible press was "the hand maiden of effective judicial administration," especially in criminal cases, not only publishing information about trials, "but guarding against miscarriages of justice by subjecting police, prosecutors and the judicial process to public scrutiny." The courts had, traditionally, refused to place any limitation on freedom of the press even while "sometimes deploring its sensationalism." The news media was not concerned with Senator Kennedy's guilt or innocence with regard to the death of Mary Jo Kopechne, but his career as a U.S. Senator and his future in national politics, Hurley said. The inquest should be public for the same reason Kennedy had gone on television, "To end innuendo and gossip." The peak of publicity had been reached following the Senator's broadcast.

The rights of privacy of the other petitioners had been lost, Hurley went on, "By their action of attending a social event with Senator Kennedy, a person of great prominence." Their constitutional rights would be infringed only if publicity adversely influenced the outcome of a judicial proceeding to which they became parties. Publicity about an open inquest did not make the publicity prejudicial; a secret inquest would also generate publicity. "Because of the extreme interest in the case, you might close the doors, but you couldn't keep secret what was going on inside," Hurley said. Reporters would work diligently to discover what was going on and, as a result, inaccurate information about the proceedings would be published.

An inquest could clear a person of suspicion as well as indicate guilt, "and preserve the good name of Mary Jo Kopechne, even though she is not a party to the hearing," Hurley said. Nor was an inquest a first step on a stairway leading to criminal prosecution, but complete in and of itself, its purpose served when the presiding judge filed a report to the Superior Court. "There may be criminal proceedings," Hurley said. "But I know of none."

If Hurley and Hanify were unwilling to declare exactly what was feared in the holding of an inquest, Henry Monaghan did not hesitate to do so in a brief filed on behalf of the Civil Liberties Union of Massachusetts as *amicus curiae*. Unless criminal prosecution were commenced against Senator Kennedy or some other person, "It is doubtful there is any constitutionally-acceptable basis for holding an inquest." Under Boyle's ground rules, Kennedy could stand publicly accused of Mary Jo Kopechne's death. Having pleaded guilty to one offense arising out of the accident, Kennedy could be reported to be the person "whose unlawful act or negligence appeared to have contributed thereto," Monaghan said. "Accordingly, he faces the possibility of a manslaughter proceeding."

If the district attorney desired a public trial, then Senator Kennedy must be afforded the procedural safeguards which attended the criminal process, Monaghan argued. If the Commonwealth wasn't willing to grant those rights, it could proceed by way of a grand jury whose proceedings were always secret. While an indictment may be returned, "Senator Kennedy would be spared the intense glare of one-sided publicity," which could jeopardize his right to a fair trial.

Chapter 46

DINIS DID, IN FACT, GET HIS CHANCE TO GIVE THE CASE TO THE grand jury when it reconvened in Edgartown on October 14. As he had done so often before in this case, he went to the brink—and then shied away from taking the plunge. Juror Theresa Morse recalled that Dinis was "all fire and brimstone" when he addressed the jury. "He said he wanted our help, because he was going to 'get' Kennedy if it was the last act of his life; he wasn't going to buy his way out of this one. It didn't matter how much money he had, or how much power he had, the facts were going to be known."

The jury could help the most "by not getting in the way at all," Dinis said. The body of Mary Jo Kopechne was going to be exhumed, an autopsy performed, and an inquest held. Dinis was going to get to the truth of the matter and then, "If he needed us, he was going to call us back," Morse said. "The grand jury was all in a loving spirit of cooperation. And we cooperated with Mr. Dinis."

That the grand jury was recessed, instead of discharged, provoked speculation Dinis was leaving the door open to present the case to them should the Supreme Judicial Court rule his inquest request was invalid. A recess allowed time for the Court to decide Kennedy's appeal.

But Dinis was either playing fast and loose with the grand jury or rehearsing in public a private ambivalence about prosecuting Ted Kennedy. He would not seek a grand jury investigation, regardless of the Court's decision, he said a week later in Wilkes-Barre. "Such an action would place me in control of the investigation and I prefer a judge to retain that responsibility."

Dinis was about to have his day in court. A second Kopechne motion to dismiss the request for an autopsy had charged the amended petition had included no new evidence to indicate an autopsy would add anything to what was already known about Mary Jo Kopechnes death. Nor was an autopsy needed to solve a crime Dinis had reason to suspect had been committed.

"Our position is quite simple: No crime, no criminal conduct, no autopsy," Kopechne lawyer Joseph Flanagan said. "We are going to do everything we can to stop the district attorney from going on a fishing expedition. He can't seek his evidence in the grave without providing facts that the evidence is there."

Judge Brominski dismissed the motion. In his ruling, he said the "interests of the public" and the Kopechnes could best be served "by developing the facts at a hearing" that would allow the court to resolve the question of exhumation and autopsy without further delay. It was a decision so obvious, some legal observers wondered why it had taken Brominski three months to make it.

Before the hearing, Flanagan visited Edgartown to interview potential witnesses, examine the scene of the accident and ask Arena "only routine questions about my investigation."

Flanagan denied Senator Kennedy was involved in the fight against exhumation. "Ted Kennedy would very much like to have an autopsy performed," Kennedy spokesman William vanden Heuvel said. The

Senator was "in close touch" with the Kopechnes, aides in his office revealed. "His battle against a belated autopsy was less than for legal reasons—his advisers think it could only help him—than in sympathy with their opposition." Flanagan refused to say whether "the Kopechnes are paying for this trip or is someone else?"

The Kopechnes had turned down "a few offers" of help with the legal expenses of barring the autopsy. "This is our responsibility," Joseph Kopechne said. "We haven't stopped to think about the cost of it all. We'll worry about that when it's all over. The lawyers have been very good, letting us pay what we could afford. Even if we're overruled, it won't be the end of it. We'll go as high as we have to."

George Killen was also in Edgartown lining up witnesses for the hearing. His most delicate mission was to persuade Dr. Donald Mills to testify on behalf of the petition. Killen wasn't blaming anybody but himself for releasing the body of Mary Jo Kopechne without autopsy. He had no intention of corroborating Dinis' claim to have ordered an autopsy on the morning her body left Edgartown.

Kopechne lawyers had already expressed an interest in having him testify, Mills said. It was debatable which side Mills would benefit the most.

There was no question whose side John Farrar was on when Killen took his detailed statement. As captain of the search and rescue division of Edgartown's volunteer fire department, Farrar had made his own study of the accident. In Farrar's version, the car had been travelling 30 miles per hour and had hit the water at a 45-degree angle. Kennedy had been able to escape, "Because with the roll of the car, the driver's side window would have been the last one submerged," Farrar said. Mary Jo Kopechne had assumed "a conscious position" in the back seat. "She was rebreathing her own air. The oxygen content was lowering from 21% as she used it up and replaced it with carbon dioxide," Farrar said. "As the CO2 builds up, you breath heavier and heavier; the emotional trauma is extensive. Try putting a plastic bag over your head and breathing. You can feel the anxiety coming over you. Then try to imagine that bag being held over your head by a 300-pound wrestler, and think of having to struggle to get out of that situation knowing you might be breathing your last. It's a very, very scary situation. The anxiety that sets in is just unbelievable."

The length of time a pocket of air remained in a submerged automobile was a matter "no human being can swear to, but she could have lived for a good while after the car went off the bridge." Farrar estimated, "She was alive, easily an hour."

Farrar produced a sketch of the body's position in the accident car redrawn three times by an artist, "To become as close as possible to that which I observed," to aid in the presentation of his testimony at the exhumation hearing.

Impressed by the passionate advocacy with which Farrar expressed his theories, Killen thought, "He's going to make one helluva witness."

So did Assistant District Attorney Armand Fernandes who accompanied Killen to take Farrar's statement which, if allowed to become part of the record could be very damaging to Ted Kennedy.

Thanks to a special $15,000 appropriation voted by the Massachusetts legislature to fund the investigation, Dinis was able to assemble a panel of 14 witnesses and experts to appear with him in Wilkes-Barre.

It was 10 A.M. on October 20, 1969, when Judge Brominski opened the hearing in Luzerne County courthouse. While welcoming reporters to the packed courtroom, Brominski also admonished them to observe certain rules for this case. "You will be required to remain in your assigned places until such time as Court recesses or adjourns a session," he said. If reporters left the courtroom, they would not be readmitted until the following day. Any violation of his guidelines would result "in the revocation of your press pass."

But no reporter was likely to chance missing out on the first courtroom confrontation in the case—a virtual preview of the postponed inquest.

Armand Fernandes, who had prepared the hearings case, opened argument by reciting the Massachusetts law granting district attorneys authority to request autopsies on their own authority. As his first witness, Fernandes called Police Chief Dominick Arena to the stand to relate the events of Saturday, July 19, after he had been summoned to Dike Bridge on Chappaquiddick and returned to Edgartown police station to receive a statement about the accident from Senator Kennedy.

Representing the Kopechnes, Joseph Flanagan objected to the Senator's statement being placed into evidence as "hearsay."

Fernandes was not concerned "with establishing what the Senator said at this time was true—*that* may be hearsay." The report was being offered "as a statement made of the facts and circumstances," he said. "We're not concerned with the truth of it."

Brominski refused to allow it. To rule an official police document inadmissible in a judicial proceeding stirred reporters in the courtroom to murmurs of disbelief—no matter which legal hairs were being split.

Dinis himself examined the next witness, scuba diver John Farrar. Battered by news media accusations that he was "prejudiced, biased and anti-Kennedy," Farrar had retained attorney Herb Abrams for advice and assistance in the preparation of his testimony. Farrar had anticipated being asked for "a professional opinion" as to whether Mary Jo Kopechne could have been alive upon her removal from the submerged car if sufficient air had been trapped. It was a chance he would not get. Brominski dismissed as "immaterial and irrelevant" the statement Abrams made to introduce Farrar's testimony.

Dinis did not ask Farrar about airlocks, or Mary Jo Kopechne's longevity underwater, restricting him to a description of the automobile's position in Poucha Pond, the damage sustained to it in the accident, and the process whereby Farrar had recovered the body.

If Farrar's potentially damaging testimony could be elided, "Huck" Look's couldn't be. His very appearance on the witness stand—robust and ruddy, a plain-spoken rustic—was a rebuff to those who had questioned his credibility. Look's description of a car whose driver appeared "confused," and his recognition of the same automobile the next morning when it was dragged from Poucha Pond was devastating in its direct and simply stated sincerity. Under oath, Look placed the time of his encounter at "approximately 12:40 A.M. to 12:45 A.M., Saturday morning," a direct challenge to Senator Kennedy's version of the accident.

There wasn't much Flanagan could do but try to cast doubt on Look's ability to read a license plate in the dark. But Look easily disposed of that cavil. "There were lights on the car—back-up lights, tail-lights and number plate lights."

"Did it appear to you that the driver of the car was in a confused state?" Flanagan asked.

"Yes, sir," Look said.

"Yet, despite the fact that this driver appeared to be in a confused state, you did not follow the car or make any attempt to stop it that night, did you?"

"No, sir," Look said.

"Did the car move away from you slowly?" Flanagan continued.

"No sir," Look answered. "I would say, hurriedly." Before he could call out an offer of help, the car had driven off at "approximately 25 to 30 miles per hour," Look said. "There was a lot of dust. All I could see was just the lights going down the road."

Look's appearance on the witness stand brought Herbert "Jack" Miller to the courtroom to confirm Bernie Flynn's intelligence about him as the most dangerous witness expected to testify at the inquest with regard to the time of the accident and the reason for Kennedy's wrong turn to avoid confrontation with a police officer.

Informed by two reporters during a recess that Miller was attending his examination of Look, Fernandes recognized his name "as a Washington attorney of some ability, like you would know F. Lee Bailey, by his reputation," he said. "But there was no association with anybody, as far as I was concerned."

If Look represented the most danger to Kennedy's case at the inquest, Dr. Donald Mills was the biggest obstacle Dinis had to get over in order to secure an exhumation and autopsy.

Dinis left his examination to Fernandes.

Mills was sticking to his diagnosis. His examination of Mary Jo Kopechne had revealed, "She had the characteristic foam that goes with a drowning case. She had no evidence of injuries..."

Flanagan drove the point home forcefully under cross-examination.

"In your examination of the body, Doctor, did you find any signs of foul play?"

"I did not," Mills said.

"Did you have any reason to believe there was any criminal conduct that may have resulted in the girl's death?"

"I have no reason to believe any such thing!" Mills snapped.

But Dinis had a corps of experts waiting in the wings to dismember Mills' testimony and to call into question the soundness of his drowning conclusion.

Among them was Dr. Cyril Wecht, coroner of Allegheny County, Pennsylvania. External examination alone frequently failed to reveal if body organs had been lacerated, several kinds of poisonings, a fractured skull or a broken neck, Dr. Wecht testified. It was possible for a competent forensic pathologist to perform an autopsy on an embalmed body buried four months and still arrive at "quite substantial and valid opinions with more than a reasonable degree of medical certainty" that could verify, modify or even completely negate Dr. Mills' findings.

That Mary Jo Kopechne had been found inside an automobile suggested the possibility that a significant injury may have occurred prior to her death, Dr. Joseph Spellman, medical examiner for the city of Philadelphia, testified. He found "little significance" in the pink froth about the nose and mouth of the victim, a phenomenon which appeared in other forms of death such as heart failure and drug overdose.

"Would this include manual strangulation?" Fernandes asked.

Flanagan objected to the question. So did Brominski. He wanted Fernandes, "To stay away from that line of questioning."

The question came up, "Because we were trying to find out what other kinds of injuries could result in the things the medical examiner found in Mary Jo Kopechne's case," Fernandes said, later. Dr. George Katsas, who performed most autopsies on Cape Cod, had alerted the district attorney that strangulation was one of several things that could have brought about the same conditions. "That," Fernandes would say later, "was why the question was used."

A highly respected forensic pathologist, formerly attached to the department of legal medicine at Harvard Medical School, Katsas would have performed an autopsy on Mary Jo Kopechne had Dinis ordered one.

On the witness stand, Katsas testified that an experienced forensic pathologist could recognize and evaluate aspects of disease and injury in an embalmed and exhumed body. In Katsas' opinion, external examination alone "did not exclude the presence of internal injuries, fractures or ruptures of organs which may have contributed to the death or even have caused the death."

Preparing Katsas to appear at the hearing, Killen had some questions of his own not put to him on the witness stand. Prudish and puritanical, disliking "smutty talk," Killen had, nevertheless, considered Bernie Flynn's opinion that a sexual interlude could have accounted for the hour and a half between the time Ted Kennedy said he'd left the cottage and the time "Huck" Look saw the car at the intersection. Lab tests for semen had been "negative," but Mary Jo Kopechne had not been wearing underpants, Flynn pointed out. "So obviously you couldn't make a test on underpants. Any seepage would be on the slacks."

Katsas had performed the difficult post-mortems in the Costa murders. Microscopic examination of vaginal smears taken from two badly mutilated bodies buried for six weeks in a Truro woods had revealed the presence of male spermatozoa. Killen wanted to know if it was possible to detect evidence of sexual intercourse in an embalmed body buried for over three months.

Finding sperm was "remote" in exhumed bodies, Katsas told Killen, but no one could be absolutely certain without an autopsy, and serological tests of a vaginal swab for "semen markers"—a number of common chemicals found in male ejaculate, a biological fluid rich in certain proteins. Semen contained 400 times more of the enzyme acid phosphatase than any other body fluid. An "AP-positive swab" would indicate "maybe" on sexual intercourse.

If sperm were not detected, the serologist looked for "sperming"— a chemical contained in seminal states—and P-30, a protein found only in semen. Sperm and P-30 were the only "conclusive tests." But, Katsas added, chances of finding either were slight. In Killen's judgment, the odds were so long that there was no point in raising these issues while Katsas was on the stand.

Now on the offensive, Flanagan called Dr. Werner Spitz, deputy chief medical examiner for the State of Maryland, who testified that it was "good as impossible" for a pathologist to determine whether a person had drowned or asphyxiated. "You may exhume the girl and examine her and still not know whether she drowned," Spitz said. Drowning was one of the most difficult diagnoses to make in forensic pathology because it so frequently resembled other causes of death.

How then, Dinis wanted to know, could Spitz be "so medically certain" Mary Jo Kopechne had drowned?

"Because of the circumstances which are being related to me," Spitz said. "The question here is: 'Shall the deceased be exhumed?'"

"That is *not* the question!" Dinis snapped. "The question is whether or not you can eliminate any other cause of death other than drowning."

"She may have injuries which I cannot determine upon external examination of the body and…"

That was good enough for Dinis. "No further questions," he said, cutting Spitz off.

"I didn't finish the sentence!" Spitz protested.

Brominski allowed Spitz to continue, and may have wished he hadn't.

"She may have injuries," Spitz went on. "There is no question in my mind that at this point she also inhaled water. It is also apparent to me from the record that she lived for a certain time underwater. Otherwise, why should the froth have developed? You're talking about pink foam," Spitz added, warming up to his subject. "That foam is the combination of water and protein that is being shaken. And the shaking action is the breathing action. So she breathed, that girl. She *breathed*! She wasn't dead instantaneously. You're not going to find a cause of instantaneous death whether you exhume her or you don't."

Flanagan looked stricken. In his peroration, Spitz had medically corroborated John Farrar's long-held opinion—heretofore excluded from testimony—that Mary Jo Kopechne had lived for a time in the submerged car, an admission that, because it came from a "defense" witness, was especially damaging.

Flanagan got Spitz off the witness stand in a hurry, but the damage was done. Not only had Spitz legitimatized Farrar's theories, he had floated a pretty good reason to exhume and autopsy Mary Jo Kopechne himself.

"The issue Kennedy's lawyers feared the most was the *Welansky* decision as a basis for bringing a manslaughter charge," Fernandes said, later. "They were scared to death of that case, because an omission to act constitutes negligence under the law." If Senator Kennedy had abandoned a living, breathing passenger in his car and his failure to notify police and rescue personnel could be shown to have contributed to her death, he was guilty of manslaughter.

Flanagan moved swiftly to recoup. He called Spitz' boss, toxicologist Dr. Henry Freimuth. Chief medical examiner for the State of Maryland, Freimuth testified that the stains on the blouse Mary Jo Kopechne had worn at the time of her death were "typical" of those produced by the pinkish froth discharged from the nose and mouth of drowning victims. "In a drowning case there will be blood foam in the airway from the rupture of very fine, little vessels. You don't need much blood to give it a pinkish hue," Freimuth said. The foam could come out of the mouth, roll down the side of the face and stain the clothing of a drowning victim, stains "that gave positive benzidine reactions." In a few, incisive phrases, Freimuth had disposed of Dinis' blood evidence.

From having heard the testimony in the courtroom, Joseph Kopechne felt more than ever, "We do not want an autopsy. My wife and I are unalterably opposed to it. It would be just like another funeral for us. We feel that they had a chance at an autopsy, it wasn't performed, and we absolutely do not want it now. We see no value in it at all."

Brominski adjourned the session at 9:00 P.M. Dinis was "very near completion." Asked if he planned to call Senator Kennedy as a witness, Dinis said, "That's always a problem, but not as of tonight."

It certainly would be a problem. Having cancelled a speech in August to be available in case his presence were required at an inquest, Kennedy was now out of the country, attending a NATO meeting in Brussels. Inevitably, speculation arose that Kennedy's lawyers did not want him testifying in open court, particularly when Dinis intended to present evidence of "inconsistency" between the Senator's two public statements about the accident.

Dinis took the witness stand the next day to defend himself against charges of inaction in the case and his failure to have called for an autopsy earlier. There was no provision of law which put Dinis under an obligation to make an immediate investigation of any case in his jurisdiction, he said. It was customary for district attorneys to take charge of cases, "When the investigation by local authorities was either unsatisfactory or incomplete." Dinis would not have ordered an autopsy, "Unless I was informed of sufficient facts to give me a reason to." After that information had been made available to him, Dinis had "positively ordered" an autopsy, only to be told, "The body had already been flown off the island by the Kennedy people." As chief law enforcement officer for the Southern District, Dinis was "not satisfied" with the cause of Mary Jo Kopechne's death as determined by Dr. Mills.

Brominski ordered Dinis' comment stricken from the record. It made no difference whether Dinis was a district attorney, a judge or a defense counsel, he said. "You cannot come to a conclusion unsubstantiated by facts."

Dinis was undaunted. An autopsy, he said, was necessary to ascertain the legal cause of death and to resolve the contradictions between Senator Kennedy's two statements about the accident. Dinis had wanted the statements entered into evidence in lieu of the Senator's presence as a witness in the courtroom.

But with Kennedy's accident report excluded there was no point in offering Kennedy's television speech as Dinis proceeded to do. Without the police report, there would be no basis for finding "inconsistency."

Once again Flanagan objected. The speech was "a self-serving declaration," immaterial and irrelevant to the issue of the hearing. Inexplicably, Brominski said he would allow it—if an accurate reproduction could be found. Dinis had a transcription of the broadcast supplied by radio station WBZ in Boston.

So it was that, into the packed courtroom, came the voice of Teddy Kennedy, delivering a speech that sounded to many just as facile and manipulative as it had originally, and every bit as "indefensible" as Kennedy said his actions after the accident had been.

Brominski adjourned the hearing at 3:15 P.M. An hour later, he was handing out refreshments and dancing with supporters at a campaign rally. Brominski bristled at the suggestion he intended to delay his decision to exhume and autopsy Mary Jo Kopechne until after the election. "That's unfair! I have to wait until the court stenographer completes the transcript of the hearing before I can make a ruling."

Dinis told reporters as he left the courthouse that he was satisfied that the allegations in his amended petition had been proved. "I can't think of a single instance where we were disheartened. Everything we tried to achieve was achieved." Dinis had been "treated fairly," he said.

"We will abide by the decision. I don't think we'll go any further on appeal if we lose."

Chapter 47

ON OCTOBER 30, 1969, THE MASSACHUSETTS SUPREME JUDICIAL
Court granted Senator Kennedy's request that the press and public be
barred from the inquest. The Court ruled that, while the procedure was
not accusatory, if it were held in public, "The activities of the news media
may be such as to make it difficult, if not impossible, for a long time to
insure a defendant a fair trial in any criminal proceedings which may
follow."

———

The Kopechne inquest presented unusual problems by arousing great
public interest which, in turn, had stimulated efforts by the press to
provide coverage. The difficulty had not been lessened by Senator Kennedy's own resort to television, "which may itself have increased public
interest and demand for a more complete investigation and explanation
of those events," the Court said. Nevertheless, the risk of prejudice from
pre-trial publicity remained.

The Court was not making "a special rule for a particular case." No other inquest was likely to arouse such public interest, but similar risks of prejudice could occur to citizens less well-known or able to protect themselves. They, too, must be afforded the protection that was now being accorded Senator Kennedy. The Court's ruling would apply to all future inquests in Massachusetts.

But to amend an 82-year-old procedure to accommodate one of the champion self-promoters of modern times was, indeed, a special case. That the Court should cite "great public interest" as a reason to close the inquest was an irony not overlooked by editorialists. Rather than "a gathering crescendo of publicity," the press had only exposed a crescendo of bungling in the legal process by authorities too willing "to absolve the Senator of anything beyond leaving the scene of the accident," the *Wall Street Journal* charged. Now, a curtain of secrecy was being dropped over the inquest, "So the bumbling can continue safe from prying eyes."

Public confidence in the administration of justice in Massachusetts had once again been seriously impaired by the special consideration given to Senator Kennedy. "Sooner or later the full and complete story about what happened that night on Chappaquiddick will come out despite all attempts to keep it smothered," the *New Bedford Standard-Times* said. "For this case, involving as it does a man who was—and may be again— considered almost a shoo-in for the Presidency of the United States has too many unanswered questions. So far, despite all the planted stories about how Senator Kennedy wants to tell the people the full and complete story of Chappaquiddick, he has consistently turned away from all opportunities to do so."

Senator Kennedy hadn't read the decision released while he was en route from Washington, he told reporters at Boston's Logan Airport, but he was satisfied the Court had acted "judiciously." Kennedy hoped the inquest would get under way as soon as possible, "So I can get on with representing the people of Massachusetts." Asked if he would be a witness at the inquest, Kennedy said, "I'll conduct myself in whatever way the Court recommends."

But no court ruling could relieve Kennedy of the requirement to put the full story of what had happened before or after the accident on the record. He had only bargained over the circumstances under which he would answer questions, not whether the questions had to be answered. The Senator couldn't give the account now because he would violate the order of the Massachusetts Supreme Judicial Court for secrecy, his office disclosed. But once the inquest was over and Kennedy was free to talk, he intended to give a detailed public accounting of what he knew about the death of Mary Jo Kopechne. Kennedy's plan to do so was based on the assumption "that the inquest would not produce any criminal action against him."

Although Senator Kennedy got what he asked for, the Court struck down the constitutional pretext upon which his appeal was based: No witness at an inquest was entitled to the due process rights accorded persons on trial. The Court did grant Hanify's request that inquest documents be made public only after all probability of criminal prosecution had passed, indictments sought or returned by a grand jury or following the trial of any person named in the inquest report as responsible for the death of Mary Jo Kopechne. The Court, however, refused to disqualify Judge Boyle, and left all other procedural aspects of the inquest to his discretion.

Boyle was not upset by the decision. He wasn't the least inclined to create a new interpretation of the concept of the inquest whose roots went back to 1887. "I never thought a court of my low rank had for its function the making of law," he said at a two-hour meeting with Kennedy attorneys, Dinis and his staff to discuss the Court's new inquest guidelines.

Boyle declined to set a date for the inquest until Judge Brominski ruled on the Dinis petition for exhumation and autopsy. He suggested

"No comment" be made by participants in that closed conference. Edgartown police had guarded the doors of the courtroom which had been searched for concealed electronic recording devices—a procedure to be followed every day of the inquest to guarantee the secret nature of the proceedings as ordered by the Supreme Court be maintained.

Gwen Kopechne didn't care whether the inquest was closed or open. "I just wish they'd hurry up and get it over with. We were disappointed when it was postponed, although we knew there were good reasons for it. But we're totally opposed to an autopsy. The answers to the question are in Massachusetts—not here," she said. "I just wish Mr. Dinis would have his inquest and clear up this whole situation."

On Tuesday, November 18, 1969, at 11:04 A.M., Joseph P. Kennedy died in his sleep at the age of 81. A White Mass was celebrated at St. Francis Xavier church in Hyannis by Richard Cardinal Cushing. Senator Kennedy paid tribute to Ann Gargan's "loyalty, devotion and great love" as companion to his father, invalided by a stroke in 1961. In lieu of a eulogy, Kennedy read a passage from a privately printed volume of family reminiscences, the *Fruitful Bough,* written by Robert Kennedy whose 44th birthday the funeral also observed. Three days later, a memorial Mass at the church marked the sixth anniversary of John Kennedy's assassination.

Senator Kennedy objected to "certain unjustified statements" in *Newsweek*'s obituary of his father, complaining, "We who are in public life must learn to live with petty gossip and baseless slander." Senate colleagues were reported "astounded" by Kennedy's resilience, his determination to reassert strong leadership on major issues. Kennedy was "regaining confidence and spirit," recovering remarkably from the gloom of Chappaquiddick. "Great spells of depression had been commonplace then for what he had done to the family name and the memory of his slain brothers." Among friends, Kennedy was again able to laugh and enjoy himself. Those who knew Kennedy said, "He's snapping back."

The Senator acknowledged he was feeling better. Not having to read about the case in the newspapers every day helped. He was now awaiting the inquest, "eager to clear up all the remaining questions" about the accident, and stepping-up his schedule of public appearances on behalf of his campaign for re-election. Kennedy denied he would seek to surpass his record 1.2 million winning margin in 1964, he said, "But I think we'll win big."

Crimmins was back chauffeuring Kennedy in Boston; Gargan was once again advancing campaign stops. It was politics as usual, and a public display of confidence. With an informer installed in the district attorney's office, Kennedy was assured of a pipeline to whatever disclosures might come out of further police investigation. But the inquest cast shadows nonetheless over an election it was conceded Kennedy had too formidable a lead to lose.

But the Senator had every reason to be optimistic. He had altered a judicial procedure which had stood for 82 years, stilled as much talk about the case as it was possible for his media controllers to do, and blocked a police investigation while at the same time maintaining a public posture of "cooperating fully" with the inquiry. His attorneys had won every legal round in the courts. Another victory was imminent.

On Wednesday, December 1, Judge Brominski barred the exhumation of Mary Jo Kopechne. There was, he ruled "No evidence" to indicate "anything other than drowning had caused the death of Mary Jo Kopechne." Even if an autopsy revealed a broken neck, a fractured skull or the rupture of internal organs, "None of these would be incompatible with the manner which this accident occurred," Brominski said. Evidence of blood stains on Mary Jo Kopechne's clothes had been "wholly consistent with death by drowning."

To justify his ruling required that Brominski travel peculiar corridors of logic. That the accident may have occurred at 12:50 A.M. on July 19, rather than 11:15 P.M. on July 18 did not suggest a cause of death other than drowning. While an acknowledgement of "Huck" Look's testimony, Brominski dismissed the idea that even if Senator Kennedy had lied about the time of the accident and his reason for turning onto Dike Road, this was not sufficient to cast doubts on other reported aspects of the accident. To consider any other cause of death at this time, "would give loose rein to speculation unsupported by any medical facts of record," Brominski said. In fact, the lack of an autopsy guaranteed speculation and rumor would continue to flourish.

Brominski had taken the opposition of the Kopechnes into account in making his decision, he said. While their disapproval was no absolute bar to an autopsy, "In view of the facts presented, their objections are well taken." In so holding, Brominski challenged a ruling by the Pennsylvania Supreme Court in 1956 which said that the purpose of an inquest was to protect the public. Any doubts about a death favored holding an autopsy. If a coroner failed to do so, "It is the duty of the Court to have the body exhumed and an autopsy performed." Yet, by finding Mary Jo Kopechne could have died from no other cause than drowning, and that an autopsy was not necessary to establish a legal cause of death, Brominski had established his own judicial precedent.

The decision came as no surprise to Dinis. As a candidate in a heavily Democratic district, Brominski had played politics every step of the way, holding the petition hostage to his own re-election bid. He even waited until he won a new ten-year term on the bench before making his ruling.

To criminal attorney Melvin Belli, "The irony is, the public's impression that the JFK autopsy was unsatisfactory, and now Teddy Kennedy's female companion gets none," he said. "The Kennedy family is hiding the actions of those two days. They've gone around parading themselves as sponsors of the little people and yet let that little person in the back seat of a car go unexamined to the grave."

Brominski's ruling pleased Gwen Kopechne. "I can't tell you how wonderful I feel," she said. "Now, I know my daughter will not be disturbed and will be at rest. I could never have gone up to that cemetery again, if I knew she'd been disturbed." She and her husband had agreed, "If in any way we had felt we were obstructing justice by fighting exhumation of Mary Jo's body, we would have yielded in favor of an autopsy. But I know what drowning is; I've seen drowned persons before. When I saw my daughter, I could tell she had drowned."

But speculation of sexual misconduct attached to the accident was clearly on Mrs. Kopechne's mind, anxious as she was to preserve her daughter's reputation against reports challenging the characterization of Mary Jo as the most straight-laced of the Boiler Room crew. One such report said that at a party in Washington one month before Chappaquiddick, Mary Jo was "somewhat vocal and demonstrative, even sitting on the lap of a man who was someone else's date. She had a little too much to drink and was flirting and more girlish than usual."

Mrs. Kopechne said, "Mary Jo was a wonderful girl, so aware and full of life. Nobody had announced it—how could you? But there was an examination of my girl. And it showed she was a maiden lady."

Now the Kopechnes were "patiently waiting" for the start of the inquest. That Judge Boyle had refused to allow them or their attorneys to attend was upsetting, "Because we're the parents of this girl and it's as if we don't exist," Mrs. Kopechne said. "The whole thing has been a mystery." Joseph Kopechne added, "There's a lot of questions we want answered. You have to have a daughter to know how we feel. People are saying: 'Your kid was dead before she hit the water.' But I don't give a damn about the public. I just want to know what happened."

Senator Kennedy telephoned the Kopechnes to express his pleasure at Brominski's ruling, "because I realize how much it means to the Kopechne family. It increases their peace of mind and I'm grateful for that." It was now Kennedy's hope, "that the authorities in Massachusetts will move forward so the entire matter can be concluded as soon as possible."

Judge Boyle scheduled the inquest for Monday, January 5, 1970. "We wanted him to have the inquest before Christmas," a Kennedy aide disclosed, "But the Judge couldn't make the arrangements."

Boyle wasn't being intractable, "That's just the way he is," Jimmy Smith told Dave Mazzone and Stephen Moulton, when Paul Markham's law partners called to find out what kind of a guy Boyle was.

Smith had known Boyle since his boyhood, "I used to live across the street from him in Vineyard Haven. Boyle's outspoken as hell. You either like him or you don't." Boyle was a Republican and a Protestant, Smith explained to the lawyers. "He's not our kind of Irish."

Chapter 48

ON DECEMBER 18, PRIVATE INVESTIGATOR J. E. GAUTREAU FILED a final "confidential report" to Edward Hanify. His investigation had found nothing to compromise witnesses expected to testify at the inquest. But Gautreau had uncovered one piece of information with disquieting implications for Ted Kennedy's defense: An eyewitness who could possibly corroborate "Huck" Look having seen the accident car hours after the Senator said it had gone off Dike Bridge. Gautreau had tracked Nancy McDonald to Burlington, Vermont. A college student employed as a waitress at the Harborside Hotel during the summer, she and the assistant manager had walked to Edgartown Lighthouse beach around 12:30 A.M. on Saturday, July 19. They were seated on the dock when their attention was drawn to an automobile traveling at a high rate of speed on the road leading to the ferry slip on Chappaquiddick 350 yards across the harbor. From the glow of the headlights, the car appeared to be neither a foreign nor a compact, "But a large, American-style automobile." The car stopped at the landing and the headlights were turned off. To Miss McDonald and her companion, that seemed "rather odd," since the ferry had closed down for the night.

That account suggested that Senator Kennedy had been driving around the island after leaving the party and could have approached the landing before his confrontation with "Huck" Look—information a state police investigation had failed to uncover. In fact, the investigation had produced no additional evidence since Bernie Flynn's meeting with Jack Miller in Washington, Flynn reported to Stephen Smith in late December. "The reason I called was to let him know we had nothing that's going to be embarrassing to Ted Kennedy at the inquest. They aren't going to ask him anything he doesn't know already."

Smith wanted to be sure, "There's nothing else you can tell us about evidence at the inquest?"

Flynn had "negative information" which could be helpful, he said.

Smith asked Flynn to call him the next day at his office. When Flynn did so, Smith proposed a meeting at Logan Airport in Boston. Smith wasn't taking any chances. He wanted the "negative information." Flynn recalled, "He told me the flight number and the time he was going to arrive."

Flynn was waiting at the ramp when Smith appeared, "A nice, athletic-looking fellow wearing a grey topcoat with a velvet collar," Flynn said. "I was kind of impressed with the mod haircut he had."

Flynn was surprised Smith was accompanied by Washington lawyer Jack Miller. Smith hadn't mentioned he was bringing Miller to the meeting. Miller was carrying a briefcase. He came over, shook hands and introduced Stephen Smith. Smith suggested a drink in the airport's cocktail lounge. Flynn was concerned someone might recognize him in the place. He was assured whoever knew him, wouldn't know Smith or Miller.

Flynn ordered a scotch and water. Smith and Miller had drinks, too. Miller was more at ease than he was in Washington, Flynn observed.

"He put the briefcase on my left, almost in my lap. Looking down at it, I was almost going to tell him: 'Take that briefcase and put it over there.' The first time in Washington, I didn't care. The second time around, I figured, 'Why should I let him tape it again?'"

Seated across the table from Flynn, Stephen Smith said, "Is there anything more you can tell us?"

Flynn filled them in on what he'd learned in regard to points that would be covered at the inquest. "What I was trying to do was—if they had any fears about something coming out at the inquest Ted Kennedy couldn't handle, I could allay those fears. It's a nice feeling to know nothing is going to be thrown at you that's going to put you off your equilibrium," Flynn said. "I'm thinking of Ted Kennedy going into the inquest frightened, not knowing what's going to be dropped on him. My whole thought was: I knew Ted Kennedy lied on TV. I didn't want him to go into an inquest and get caught in another lie. This time when he tells his lie in the inquest, he can stick with the lie and they have to swallow it. He could walk into the inquest knowing there wasn't going to be any bombs dropped on him. We don't have anything that could contradict Ted Kennedy, except for "Huck" Look and the witnesses I had already discussed with Miller. I wanted them prepared for that. So I put their mind at ease that there weren't going to be any surprises. And they seemed to like that."

Flynn did most of the talking. "They're interjecting once in a while," he recalled later. "This information I have is not like the last time I talked to Jack Miller. This is what I call 'negative information'—the fact that we have nothing new. Everything is what I've already told you."

Stephen Smith came right back at him. "Are you sure there isn't anything else?" he said.

"No, that's it. That's why this information is so good," Flynn explained. "I'm trying to show him, 'This is worth your trip to Boston.' This information is as important as me telling you something new. The fact that there isn't going to be anything Ted Kennedy won't be aware of. He can stick with the old story, because he has nothing to fear."

Flynn had no idea what Eddie Dinis' strategy was going to be at the inquest, "Except I know we had nothing, absolutely nothing. That's what I wanted to convey to them. The whole thing with me was I don't want to see Ted Kennedy get caught in any more lies at the inquest. The meeting with Stephen Smith and Jack Miller is to alleviate the feeling: 'Am I going to get caught?' I wanted Ted Kennedy to walk into the inquest and walk out—and he's protected." Flynn realized, "That's the reason the meeting was important to them, otherwise they would have said, 'We don't want to talk to you. Don't bother us.' But they *wanted* to talk to me, which indicated that Ted Kennedy was covering something up he didn't want to come out at the inquest."

That Kennedy's license had expired wasn't going to be brought up at the inquest, Flynn said. "That was nothing." Telephone records had been subpoenaed. Flynn had served telephone company branch manager John O'Connor at the Coonamessett Inn, he related. "John was sitting at the bar with his wife having a cocktail. I told the waitress, 'Take this Christmas card and give it to that man over there.' She brought it over to his table. He opened it and looked around. He was a very startled man. He wasn't expecting it. He came over to my table, laughing. He said to me, 'You bastard!'"

Stephen Smith said, "Are you *sure* there isn't anything else?"

Flynn assured him again, there wasn't. If anything came up before the inquest, "I'll get in touch with you."

Smith wanted to know what Flynn expected in the way of payment for his services. "What can I do for you?" he said. "What did *you* want?"

"You tell Ted Kennedy that I'm frightened. If this ever gets out, I'm cooked." Flynn was liable to a possible charge of conspiracy to obstruct justice or dismissal from the state police. The very least he could expect would be demotion and a punitive assignment to some remote and undesirable part of Massachusetts, Flynn said. "If I'm ever transferred to the western part of the state, I want help from Ted to get back to Cape Cod where I belong. I don't want to get struck riding a camel in Pittsfield someplace."

"That's no problem," Smith said. All Flynn had to do was, "Make one telephone call."

Flynn was satisfied he would never need to be concerned again about losing his plum assignment. To have helped Ted Kennedy was the best kind of job insurance to have—except the premium had come high. In order to preserve his career as a police officer, Flynn had to betray it.

Even so, Flynn tried to cover his tracks. Miller had placed his briefcase at Flynn's feet under the table. "While I'm talking to them, I'm tapping on it with my foot," Flynn recalled. "I'm kicking the side of the briefcase, to interfere with the tape that was there."

Flynn had "maybe two drinks" during the half-hour meeting. Smith and Miller caught the next shuttle back to New York. Smith turned up several days later to join Ted and Joan Kennedy on a skiing holiday at Vail, Colorado. Assured that "no bombs" were going to be dropped at the inquest, Senator Kennedy expressed confidence criminal charges were not likely to be developed against him at the inquest. He said, "Do you think that if I knew there was anything else that could come out of this I would not have given up my Senate seat? I know what happened there, and I'm the *only* one who knows. There's nothing else that can be said about it."

Kennedy returned to Washington on New Year's Day to meet with Jack Miller. He spent Saturday, January 3, and part of Sunday in Boston rehearsing his testimony with his attorneys of record. Kennedy was not looking forward to the inquest, "Like he would to a party," an aide at the compound said. "It's painful for him, painful for the family. He wants to clear it up once and for all."

The most painful question Senator Kennedy would be required to answer was, why he had abandoned a helpless young woman in his car for ten hours. His answer would have a lot to do with whether that action could be used to bring charges against him. Judge Boyle could contend his failure to alert authorities and rescue personnel had constituted criminal negligence and accuse Ted Kennedy of wilful, wanton and reckless conduct by not reporting the accident.

The Bridge at Chappaquiddick by Jack Olsen was published on Friday, January 2. To ensure against leaks, access to a single copy of the manuscript was restricted to three employees of Little, Brown and Company, of Boston. Despite precautions, a clandestine approach to a production supervisor at the Vail-Ballou printing plant was made by "a Democratic political figure," seeking a bootleg copy of the book in advance of publication. A bribe offer was made. Editor-in-Chief Elliot Fremont-Smith assumed "that it was ultimately from a Kennedy source."

But Senator Kennedy had nothing to fear from the book, produced under the pressure of a narrow deadline. Olsen failed to resolve any of the mysteries attending the accident. He'd had "no luck" with the Senator or anyone close the Kennedy family. To fill in the gap, Olsen had expropriated Bernie Flynn's theory that Senator Kennedy had not driven the accident car off Dike Bridge. Aware of the "political implications" of being on a deserted road late at night with a young, unmarried woman, Kennedy had stopped the car, gotten out and told Mary Jo to circle back to pick him up from fear a police officer would ask him questions. Seated behind the wheel of a strange and powerful car, she had no time to adjust the seat in order to reach the gas and brake pedals comfortably. Barely able to see the road ahead, Mary Jo had driven in a straight line off Dike Bridge. Kennedy had given a different version of the accident because he had "a public image to consider," Olsen explained. "No intelligent politician would begin a police report by writing: 'My brothers and I have a certain reputation. It is not deserved, but we have it. When I realized that I was in a very compromising position and might be interrogated by a police officer, I jumped out of the car'—a statement that would have ended Kennedy's career." It would be simpler for Kennedy to "fudge a few minutes off the time and claim he and Mary Jo had been headed for the ferry, and taken a wrong turn on Dike Road."

Olsen couldn't explain why Senator Kennedy should flee a police officer if he wasn't doing anything wrong. Driving a car on Chappaquiddick with an unmarried woman at any hour was no offense warranting an "interrogation," unless Kennedy was afraid of being arrested for drunk driving—a portion of Flynn's theory Olsen had omitted from his book. A more serious defect in the theory was: Why, knowing a police officer had seen the car, did Kennedy think he could "fudge" an hour and a half off the time with a witness available to contradict him, as had proven to be the case with "Huck" Look?

Olsen "thought a lot" about the differential in the time Kennedy said he'd left the party and Look had seen the car, he said, later. "The obvious answer was that they were playing around in the weeds—this wasn't in the book. I didn't want to get sued for libel. It was enough to say Ted Kennedy was at a party with six unmarried women," and had left with Mary Jo Kopechne. "She's had a few drinks. She's very giddy and excited. She's with a Kennedy—a lifelong dream. He's probably been loving her up a little. Just to be in the car with him in the middle of the night on a deserted island—I couldn't say that in the book, but she must have been beside herself with excitement, a spinster girl. What was she, 28?"

Olsen was "in a very weird spot" when he wrote the book. "The publisher and I were certain we were going to get hauled in for contempt of court or something like that—so many things were played down."

Olsen's book puzzled Arena. If Kennedy wasn't in the car and not guilty of the transgressions everyone was accusing him of, "Why throw yourself to the wolves and say you were driving?" That Kennedy felt the other story was the thing he should stick with, "Well, he's certainly stuck with it now, because if he changes his story, who's going to believe him?" Every time Arena thought about the various theories proposed to explain the accident, "I say to myself, 'How come Kennedy knew enough to come to the station and tell me she went off the bridge if he wasn't in the car?'"

On Sunday evening January 4, Arena held an informal press briefing for about 400 reporters and photographers at the communications center again set up in the basement of the Methodist Church. Security at the inquest would be strict. Witnesses would enter and leave the front door of the courthouse between a double file of police. Reporters would be required to stand behind barricades. Any witness who wanted to talk to the press could do so at the communications center. Otherwise, "Police will protect all witnesses," Arena said.

Court Clerk Tommy Teller was also observing the secrecy imposed on the proceedings by the Supreme Court, refusing to disclose the names of witnesses subpoenaed to appear at the inquest.

Dinis also declined to identify those he'd called to testify when he arrived at the Katama Shores motel on Sunday night. His entourage included bodyguard Robert Enos and staff assistants Peter Gay, Joseph Harrington and Armand Fernandes.

A cadre of Kennedy aides had arrived in Edgartown before the weekend to prepare for the inquest. Jim King of the Senator's Boston office had sought accommodations for Kennedy witnesses and lawyers, and arranged for domestic help and catering services to provide meals.

Richard McCarron rented a house on School Street as headquarters for Edward Hanify and Robert Clark, and provided an apartment in a building he owned on Main Street for Dan Daley and Paul Redmond where the Boiler Room girls would be served a daily luncheon.

McCarron hired two locals as drivers for the young women, who arrived by chartered plane from Boston on Sunday afternoon. Miniskirted, more attractive and younger-looking than their press pictures, they ignored shouted greetings from reporters and pleas from photographers to pose, moving resolutely toward the rental automobiles that would take them to the Blueberry Hill Guest Inn at Chilmark, 15 miles from Edgartown.

It was in those same yellow Chevrolet sedans that the girls arrived at the Edgartown courthouse the next morning for the start of the inquest. Police cleared the sidewalk for the unsmiling young women to pass into the courthouse. Once inside, they were served with subpoenas. Their lawyer, Paul Redmond, had waited until the last hour to volunteer his clients to testify at the inquest.

Chapter 49

SENATOR KENNEDY STEPPED OFF A CHARTERED PLANE AT
Martha's Vineyard airport at 9:15 A.M. He was "looking forward to
responding to any and all of the questions" to be asked of him at the
inquest into the death, not quite six months before, of Mary Jo
Kopechne. Kennedy was hopeful the record would be completed, "And
I can get back to the business of devoting my energies to the Senate."

Driven to the house on School Street, Kennedy conferred briefly
inside, then stepped off a front porch for the 100-yard walk to the courthouse, accompanied by his wife and four state troopers. Arena had
received instructions not to provide a heavy police escort when the
Senator entered or left the courthouse. Kennedy didn't want to look "like
a criminal" on television.

Kennedy was solemn when approached by a crowd of reporters he
acknowledged with a tense smile and a wave. One reporter called out,
"Are you glad it's finally under way?"

"Yes, I am," Kennedy said, waiting on the courthouse steps while
his wife weaved through a throng of spectators on the sidewalk.

Ready to open the courthouse door was Bernie Flynn, an "historic moment" preserved in a photograph he clipped from the *New York Times*. Though others did not then know it, Flynn was opening the door for Ted Kennedy to play the inquest game with "a stacked deck," he said, later. At stake was, "The pride of the Kennedys, and perhaps, the Presidency of the United States."

When Joan Kennedy came out of the courthouse ten minutes later, Dick Drayne drew reporters' attention to the fact that, under Judge Boyle's rules, "She couldn't stay inside; but she really wanted to accompany Ted to the courthouse."

Mrs. Kennedy returned to the house on School Street to be greeted by Mary Frackleton and Jim King of the Senator's Boston office, and court stenographer Joe Donegan. Donegan would reside at the house with Clark and Hanify for the duration of the inquest. Also staying there was Herbert "Jack" Miller, Jr. Looming over the occupants of the house was the worry that the Senator's two previous statements about the accident might be contradicted by witnesses at the inquest.

Before those proceedings began, Kennedy came into the courtroom, empty except for Assistant District Attorney Peter Gay at the prosecutor's table. Gay greeted the Senator warmly, showed him where the witness stand was, and was moved by the occasion to observe, "It was kind of sad. A U.S. Senator to be put on trial like that."

———

Promptly at 9:00 A.M., Clerk of the Court Tommy Teller formally opened the inquest *re: Mary Jo Kopechne*. The inquest was not a prosecution of anyone, Judge Boyle told all lawyers and witnesses he'd summoned to the courtroom in order to explain the purpose of the inquest, the results it was intended to accomplish and the rules of procedure under which it would be held. The courthouse did not provide facilities for the sequestering of witnesses.

However, he made it clear, "Witnesses after testimony, are ordered not to discuss their testimony with anyone except his or her counsel."

Boyle recognized a difficulty in this regard with Redmond and Daley representing a substantial number of witnesses. "I don't want any attorney who heard what one witness said in the courtroom to reveal to another witness what the testifying witness said," Boyle said. He was specifically ordering attorneys, "Not to discuss the testimony of one client with another client."

Hanify wanted to be sure he understood Boyle's order, "As an implicit instruction to all counsel present that we are to respect the privacy of the proceedings, and are not to discuss with the press what goes on."

But if Hanify and the other lawyers knew perfectly well what Boyle had in mind, that would not prevent Boyle's instructions from being repeatedly and deliberately violated.

Boyle excused everyone from the courtroom except Dinis and his legal staff. In keeping with the secrecy order imposed by the Supreme Court, state police trooper Robert Enos and George Killen were asked to leave. Killen joined Bernie Flynn, assigned security duty in the corridor outside the courtroom, to summon witnesses. Before the inquest in September was postponed, Dinis had proposed Chief Arena and other Edgartown locals testify first, followed by those who had attended the party at Chappaquiddick—with the exception of Paul Markham, Joseph Gargan and Senator Kennedy. Dinis had wanted them questioned last, and in that order. Judge Boyle, however, had in mind a different arrangement. He would not "Keep a U.S. Senator waiting."

Dinis now proposed Robert Malloy, general accounting supervisor of the New England Telephone Company, to lead off the inquest. Boyle suggested Malloy not be called until some foundation was made to indicate his testimony was relevant.[1*]

---

1 * Malloy's attorney Charles Parrot came to the courtroom prepared to offer four lists of telephone calls charged to Kennedy credit card accounts in Boston, Washington and Virginia and those billed to Park Agency, Inc., of New York—none of which showed any calls made during the hours after the accident or before Kennedy called Helga Wagner after 8 a.m. at the Shiretown Inn.

Dinis called Senator Edward Kennedy as the inquest's first witness. Kennedy entered the courtroom accompanied by Hanify and Clark. He took the witness stand in the near-empty courtroom to put on the record what he had avoided direct questioning about for more than five months. Because Kennedy had waited so long, "Anything he says will be weighed against two earlier statements that were less than persuasive," the *New York Times* said. "There is a risk that even the most dignified and straightforward mea culpa could bring his public career to a humiliating end."

But there was nothing straightforward about what Kennedy put on the record. It was, instead a lattice-work of evasions and omission, of half-truths and obfuscation, patched together by a phalanx of lawyers and advisers.

Arriving at Edgartown on Friday, July 18, Kennedy was brought to Chappaquiddick and driven over Dike Bridge as a passenger in a 4-door Oldsmobile 88 operated by Jack Crimmins. After a swim at East Beach, Kennedy was returned to Edgartown for the Regatta race, then checked into the Shiretown Inn, "visited with friends," and returned to Chappaquiddick to soak his back in a hot tub until party guests arrived in a rented Valiant around 8:30 P.M.

Kennedy had initially tended bar, "Then, I think, most of the individuals made their drinks after that." He had "engaged in conversation and recollections" with guests "which were old friends of myself and our families." He left the party at "approximately 11:15 P.M.," Kennedy testified. "I was talking with Miss Kopechne perhaps for some minutes before that period of time. I noticed the time, desired to leave and return

---

In a nine-page memorandum for his own files, Parrot observed, "There was no discussion about records of calls by putting dimes and quarters in the box, collect calls, or charging calls to your home number." Parrot denied any telephone company records had been withheld.

Fernandes said, "Judge Boyle was only interested in a list of calls made from Marthas Vineyard on July 18–19 as relevant to the issue of whether the Senator had telephoned anyone after the accident." Compiled in chronological time-sequence, the record, "Doesn't at the moment tell me anything," Boyle said, when Malloy was on the witness stand. Dinis saw "no harm" in offering the list into evidence. (See Appendix 4.)

to the Shiretown Inn and indicated to her that I was leaving and returning to town. She indicated to me that she was desirous of leaving, if I
would be kind enough to drop her back at her hotel. I said, 'Well, I'm
leaving immediately,' spoke to Mr. Crimmins, requested the keys for the
car and left at that time." While his chauffeur drove him on practically
every occasion, "Mr. Crimmins, as well as some of the other fellows
attending the cookout were concluding their meal, enjoying the fellowship and it didn't appear to me necessary to require him to bring me
back to Edgartown," Kennedy said, slipping easily into euphemism to
provide the first obfuscation in his testimony. (Drunk, truculent,
demanding everyone leave, Crimmins could hardly be said to be "enjoying the fellowship."[2*])

Although the question wasn't asked, Kennedy denied "any personal
relationship whatsoever with Mary Jo Kopechne." He had never been
out with her when "we were not in a general assemblage of friends,
associates or members of our family." He left the party for the ferry
landing, travelled down "I believe it is Main Street," and taken a right
turn on Dike Road.

Kennedy disposed of "Huck" Look's anticipated testimony in short
order: At no time had he driven into Cemetery Road, backed the car up
or seen anyone between the cottage and Dike Road, he said. "I did not
stop the car at any time. I passed no other vehicle. I saw no other person."

Kennedy was driving "approximately twenty miles an hour," taking
"no particular notice" that Dike Road was unpaved, or that he was not
heading for the ferry landing. He had applied brakes, "A fraction of a

---

2 * Crimmins testified he didn't know why he hadn't driven the Senator to the ferry. The Senator had
called him out of the cottage to the front yard. "He told me that he was tired and that he wanted to go
home and go to sleep. He told me he was going to take Miss Kopechne back, that she wasn't feeling well;
she was bothered by the sun on the beach that day." Kennedy asked for the keys to the car. "It was his
automobile and I gave them to him. I didn't question him." Crimmins was sure Kennedy left at 11:15
p.m., "Because I looked at my watch."
The District Attorney's office had information that Crimmins didn't want to give Kennedy the keys to the car and
offered to drive him to the ferry landing, Armand Fernandes revealed after the inquest, "But like other investigations
we did, it was nothing conclusive."

second before I was on the bridge and about to go off," he said. "The next thing I recall is the movement of Mary Jo next to me, the struggling, perhaps hitting or kicking me. And I, at this time, opened my eyes and realized I was upside-down, that water was crashing in on me, that it was pitch black. And I was able to get a half gulp, I would say, of air before I became completely immersed in the water. I realized that Mary Jo and I had to get out of the car."

Kennedy tried to get the door open by "reaching what I thought was down, which was really up," and feeling alongside the door panel to see if the window was open. "And I can remember the last sensation of being completely out of air and inhaling what must have been a half a lung-full of water and assuming that I was going to drown. And the full realization that no one was going to be looking for us until the next morning, that I wasn't going to get out of that car alive; then, somehow, coming up to the last energy of just pushing, pressing, and coming up to the surface," he said. "I have no idea in the world how I got out of that car."

Judge Boyle asked Kennedy to describe what he had seen as he was driving along Dike Road, "From the point when you first saw the bridge."

"I would estimate that time to be fractions of a second from the time that I first saw the bridge and was on the bridge," Kennedy replied.

"Your attention was not diverted by anything else?" Boyle said.

"No, it wasn't," Kennedy said.

"I want to go into the question of alcoholic beverages," Boyle said.

Kennedy had "two rum and cokes at the party," he said.

Boyle wanted "to go back before that," he said. "I think you said you visited friends at the Shiretown?"

Kennedy had "a third of a beer at that time." But Boyle hadn't gone back far enough. Kennedy didn't mention the victory party on Ross Richards' boat after the Regatta race—at which he'd drank three rum and cokes.

After Boyle was assured that Kennedy had been made aware of his constitutional rights with regard to self-incrimination, he said, "Were you at any time that evening under the influence of alcohol?"

"Absolutely *not*," Kennedy said. He had been "absolutely sober" when he drove over the side of Dike Bridge, the scene of the accident Dinis was anxious to resume his questions about.

After Kennedy escaped from the submerged automobile, he was swept away "by the tide that was flowing at an extraordinary rate" in Poucha Pond. Wading up to his waist, he started back to the car, "gasping and belching and coughing," to commence diving in an attempt to rescue Mary Jo Kopechne. Prevented from doing so by the fast current, he'd returned again and again to try to gain entrance to the car, "Until at the very end, when I couldn't hold my breath any longer."

"You were fully aware at the time what was transpiring?" Dinis said, leading up to the question of "shock" after the accident.

Kennedy knew what was coming and tried to slide under the question. "Well, I was fully aware that I was doing everything that I possibly could to get the girl out of the car. And that my head was throbbing and my neck was aching and I was breathless and, at that time, hopelessly exhausted." Kennedy was careful not to say "in shock" as Dinis was inviting him to.

"But there was no *confusion* in your mind about the fact that there was a person in the car?" Dinis asked, a direct reference to Kennedy's television speech.

Kennedy ducked the question again. "I was doing the very best I could to get her out," he said. On the last of seven or eight attempts to get into the car, he realized, "I just couldn't hold my breath any longer. I didn't have the strength to come down even close to the window or the door. I knew that I just could not get under water any more." He had lost contact with the car, let himself float to shore, "And I sort of crawled and staggered up some place and was very exhausted and spent on the grass."

Kennedy rested on the banking for 15 to 20 minutes. After he regained his breath, "I started going down that road walking, trotting, jogging, stumbling as fast as I possibly could. It was extremely dark and I could make out no forms or shapes or figures. The only way that I could see the path of the road was looking down the silhouettes of the trees of the two sides." To his knowledge, "I never saw a cottage with a light on," he said, artfully—not to say no lights were lit. The walk back to the cottage had taken "approximately 15 minutes." A white Valiant was parked 15 to 20 feet outside the front door. "As I came up to the back of the vehicle, I saw Ray LaRosa and I said, 'Ray, get me Joe.'" Kennedy climbed into the back seat of the car. Gargan came out; then, Paul Markham. Kennedy told them, "There's been a terrible accident. Let's go," and returned to Dike Bridge. "I believe that I looked at the Valiant's clock and believe that it was 12:20 A.M.," Kennedy said, contriving to establish the time of the accident. (When it was discovered by the *Boston Globe* in 1974 that the Valiant rented for the regatta weekend had no clock, Kennedy admitted, "I made a mistake about a clock being in the Valiant that wasn't there." Caught in the lie, he sought to correct his answer retroactively. "I am also aware that Paul Markham had a watch on and that I did determine the time.")

Kennedy had not participated in the rescue efforts undertaken by Gargan and Markham, he said. "But I could see exactly what was happening and made some suggestions."

"You were fully aware of what was transpiring at that time?" Dinis reiterated, giving Kennedy another chance to lay claim to the "shock" of his police report and the "scrambled thoughts" of his television speech.

Kennedy wouldn't do it. He was "fully aware" that Gargan and Markham "were trying to get in that car and rescue that girl."

But Dinis was now leading up to another, inevitable subject: "Was there any effort made to call for assistance?"

There was no way around this question. It had to be answered. Kennedy said, "No, other than the assistance of Mr. Gargan and Mr. Markham."

"But they *failed* in their efforts to recover Miss Kopechne…" Dinis said.

At this critical point in the examination, Judge Boyle interrupted to ask Kennedy to leave the witness stand and the courtroom.

Boyle told Dinis that, in his view, the purpose of the inquest was to determine whether criminal conduct had contributed to the death of Mary Jo Kopechne, and not whether poor judgment or duplicity may have followed.

Armand Fernandes recalled "quite a tussle with Boyle about all questions stopping after the car hit the water and Mary Jo died. He wanted only testimony relating to whether the Senator or anyone else had acted criminally in her death—not what anybody did afterward." To Fernandes a defendant's behavior *after* a crime was material to any inquiry, especially in view of the omission to act liability under the *Welansky* decision for manslaughter.

Vigorously protesting the limitations Boyle was seeking to place on his examination of witnesses, Dinis threatened to walk out of the inquest unless he was allowed more latitude to ask questions. Faced with the disruption of the inquest and the possible collapse of the entire enterprise, Boyle reluctantly acceded. But he would continue to cut Dinis off in the middle of questions to admonish him, "I want to avoid as much as possible any trial technique." Boyle did not suggest what other method there was to elicit information from a witness. Both were in the dark about inquest procedures. Neither Dinis nor Boyle had ever participated in one before.

———

"Was there any particular reason why you did not call either the police or the fire department?" Dinis said when Kennedy resumed the witness stand twenty minutes later.

Kennedy tried to duck the question. "Well, I intended to call for assistance and report the accident to police within a few short moments after going back into the car."

"Did something transpire to prevent this?" Dinis said.

Now at the most critical point in his testimony, Kennedy's answer on the record would be scrutinized, pondered and tested for years to come. Kennedy didn't want to undergo interrogation. He said, "If the Court would permit me, I would like to be able to relate to the Court the immediate period following the time that Mr. Gargan, Markham and I got back in the car."

Neither Boyle nor Dinis had any objection.

"I believe it was about 45 minutes after Gargan and Markham dove and they likewise became exhausted and no further diving efforts appeared to be of any avail. And they so indicated to me and I agreed," Kennedy said. "So they came out of the water and came back into the car and said to me, at different times as we drove down the road towards the ferry, that it was necessary to report this accident.

"A lot of different thoughts came into my mind at that time about how I was going to really be able to call Mrs. Kopechne at some time in the middle of the night to tell her that her daughter was drowned, to be able to call my own mother and my own father, my wife," Kennedy said, evading the issue of notifying the police and rescue personnel. "Even though I knew that Mary Jo Kopechne was dead and believed firmly that she was in the back of that car, I willed that she remained alive. I was almost looking out the windows trying to see her walking down that road." Gargan and Markham understood this feeling, but said it was necessary all the same to report the accident. "And about this time we came to the ferry crossing and I got out of the car and we talked there just a few minutes," Kennedy continued. "I just wondered how all of this could possibly have happened. I also had sort of a thought and the wish and desire and the hope that suddenly this whole accident would disappear. I related this to Gargan and Markham and they reiterated that this had to be reported and I understood at the time ...that it had to be reported. And I had full intention of reporting it. And I mentioned to Gargan and Markham something like, 'You take care of the girls; I will take care of the accident!'—that is what I said and I dove into the water."

Kennedy had been prompted to give instructions "not to alarm Mary Jo's friends that night," and conceal the accident from the others at the party, "Because I felt strongly that if these girls were notified that an accident had taken place and Mary Jo had, in fact, drowned, that it would only be a matter of seconds before all of those girls, who were long and dear friends of Mary Jo's, would go to the scene of the accident and enter the water with, I felt, a good chance that some serious mishap might have occurred to any one of them."

With that admonition, Kennedy dove into the channel. As he started to swim into the tide, "I felt an extraordinary shove, the water almost pulling me down. And suddenly I realized that I was in a weakened condition, although as I had looked over that distance between the ferry slip and the other side, it seemed to me an inconsequential swim. But the water got colder, the tide began to draw me out. And for the second time that evening I knew I was going to drown," Kennedy said. "I remember being swept down toward the direction of the Edgartown Light and well out into the darkness. And I tried to swim at a slower pace, to be able to regain whatever kind of strength that was left in me. And some time after that, I think it was about the middle of the channel, the tide was much calmer, gentler." Reaching the other shore he pulled himself onto a beach. He said, "And all the nightmares and all the tragedy and all the loss of Mary Jo's death was right before me again."

Kennedy found his way to a parking lot adjacent to the Shiretown Inn "almost having no further strength to continue, and leaning against a tree for a length of time, trying to really gather some kind of idea as to what happened." He went to his room, took off his clothes and collapsed on the bed. He was conscious of a throbbing headache, pains in his neck and back strain, "But what I was even more conscious of was the tragedy and loss of a very devoted friend," Kennedy added. Hearing noises "around me, on top of me, almost in the room," Kennedy put on dry clothes and opened the door to his room. "I saw what I believed to be a tourist or someone standing under the light off the balcony and asked what time it was. He mentioned to me it was, I think, 2:30, and I went back into the room," he said, and betrayed the guile and calculation of his prepared testimony. In his television speech, Kennedy had specifically identified "a room clerk." Russell Peachey had corroborated the conversation the next day. Now, in the lawyer-reworked version, it was more prudent not to be so exact following his traumatic swim, as to appear to suggest a motive in seeking a witness to his presence far from the accident scene. Kennedy also neglected to say he had descended the stairs to provoke the encounter; or that the "tourist" had asked if he required "any further assistance."

Dinis did not ask why Kennedy had not availed himself of this opportunity to report the accident. By his rambling discourse, Kennedy had avoided explaining why authorities had not been notified of the accident or help sought to retrieve the body of Mary Jo Kopechne from his submerged car.

"I never really went to bed that night," Kennedy continued. "Even as that night went on and as I almost tossed and turned and walked around that room ...I had not given up hope all night long that, by some miracle, Mary Jo would have escaped from the car."

Kennedy had spoken to the desk clerk the next morning, then to Ross Richards and Stan Moore. (He had been able to conduct these conversations without betraying any sign of distress about the accident, Kennedy explained in 1974 to the *Boston Globe,* "Because I was still in the frame of mind of false hope, that perhaps with the dawning of a new day, all the nightmare events of the evening before would have been washed away." But all hope "absolutely disappeared," when Gargan and Markham arrived at the Shiretown Inn, Kennedy said. "From just the look on their faces I could tell that as hard as I had prayed for her survival, that Mary Jo was dead. Up to that time I really tried to will her existence and her life.")

"They asked had I reported the accident and why I hadn't reported the accident," Kennedy said on the witnesses stand. "I told them about my own thoughts and feelings as I swam across that channel ...that somehow when they arrived in the morning that they were going to say that Mary Jo was still alive. I told them how I somehow believed that when the sun came up and it was a new morning that what had happened the night before would not have happened and did not happen. And how I just couldn't gain the strength within me, the moral strength, to call Mrs. Kopechne at 2 o'clock in the morning and tell her that her daughter was dead."

But Kennedy conceded he did "make a private phone call to one of the dearest and oldest friends I have," Burke Marshall. "I didn't feel that I could use the public phone that was available outside the dining room at the Shiretown Inn," the same one he used to attempt to reach Stephen Smith, calling a "party that I felt would know the number."

Dinis didn't ask who "the party" was. Kennedy didn't volunteer he'd called Helga Wagner.[3*] He had returned to Chappaquiddick and called

3 * Five years later Kennedy was still avoiding disclosure of who he had called, telling the *Boston Globe* he tried to reach Stephen Smith, "And I was unable to."
"Who did you call?"
"I think it's in the testimony," Kennedy said.

Burke Marshall, "Because it was my thought that once I went to the police station, I would be involved in a myriad of details, and I wanted to talk to this friend before I undertook that responsibility." Kennedy then returned to Edgartown with the intention of reporting the accident.

"But you didn't go *directly* from your hotel room to the police. . ." Dinis began to challenge the logic of the testimony.

But Boyle interrupted to say, "Excuse me, Mr. Dinis. We are now at one o'clock. I think we will take the luncheon recess." It was the second time during Kennedy's testimony that Boyle had rescued him from dangerous questions.

———

Kennedy "didn't seem confident of what he was saying on the witness stand," Assistant District Attorney Peter Gay observed. In his experience as a trial lawyer, "You can pick out those witnesses that are positive and assured. And Senator Kennedy impressed me that he wasn't. Whether it was his position, his status in life, he was insecure about what he was trying to say."

Senator Kennedy returned to the house on School Street for a salad and sandwich lunch with his lawyers. Kennedy's state of mind had been insufficiently explained to account for his failure to report the accident and to seek further assistance to rescue Mary Jo Kopechne as mitigation for the omission-to-act liability for manslaughter under the *Welansky* decision. The subject of alcoholic beverages had been introduced, but not aggressively pursued. Kennedy

---

Asked again, "Who did you call?" Kennedy replied, "A number of . . . he was in Spain at the time and I tried to call someone to get the number."

"Do you remember who that was?"

"I would have to check on it, I think" Kennedy said.

Not until 1980 did Kennedy reveal he'd called "family friend" Helga Wagner. After repeated denials, Mrs. Wagner confirmed the Senator had called her on the morning after the accident. She said, "He was trying to find a number for Stephen Smith."

hadn't been asked about the victory party on board the *Bettawin,* a point that had to be covered since Ross Richards was scheduled to testify. A fuller statement emphasizing Kennedy's sobriety was needed to head off that element of manslaughter showing up as "probable cause" for negligence in Boyle's inquest report. Miller, acting on information from Bernie Flynn, assured Kennedy that Richards was not going to testify about drinking. From his examination, Dinis appeared to be verifying Flynn's intelligence that "no bombs" were going to be dropped at the inquest. Still, Kennedy had some rough moments left when he resumed the witness stand at 2 o'clock. Dinis quoted from Kennedy's accident report: "When I fully realized what had happened this morning, I immediately contacted the police." Dinis asked, "Now is that, in fact, what you did?"

Once again, Boyle moved to the rescue. "Mr. Kennedy already said this was a copy of the statement he made. Now, won't you let the record speak for itself?"

Faced with repeated sabotage of his examination, Dinis finally exploded. "Well, I don't think it's possible, your Honor, at this late date in my life, to begin to change whatever style I have and the method of cross-examination."

"There is no cross-examination in this inquest!" Boyle pounced. "We don't need constant repetition of testimony."

"I know we don't *need* it, but we have to have it occasionally," Dinis said, furious. "I appreciate it and I apologize to the Court."

Clearly, Dinis was not going to be allowed to pursue the inconsistencies between the police report and Kennedy's television speech. Boyle simply blocked testing of testimony through reiteration—a trial technique Boyle wanted no part of in the inquest. Frustrated, Dinis had, "No further questions."

Neither did Boyle. He wanted to know if Kennedy would be available, "In the event we needed you back for anything."

Kennedy would make himself available. But he couldn't resist reminding the Court he was, after all, a United States Senator. He said, "I would hope to be able to return to Washington some time this week."

But so inadequate had his examination been, even Kennedy was dissatisfied with it. The record would show he'd been let off the hook too easily. Before he was released, Kennedy asked to consult his attorneys, "On one point that I might like to address the bench on."

Whether Boyle wanted repetition of testimony or not, he was going to get it. Kennedy wanted another run at the key question of the inquest: "Why did you not seek further assistance after Mr. Markham and Mr. Gargan had exhausted their efforts in attempting to reach Mary Jo?"

Kennedy said, "It is because I was completely convinced at that time that no further help and assistance would do Mary Jo any more good. I realized that she must be drowned and still in the car. And it appeared the question in my mind at that time was, what should be done about the accident."

"Since the alcoholic intake is relevant," Kennedy wanted to clarify the other element of manslaughter to which he was the most vulnerable. "Although I haven't been asked it, I feel in all frankness and fairness and for a complete record that it should be included as part of the proceedings." During the course of the Regatta race, Kennedy had shared two beers with members of his crew. "One other occasion in which there was some modest intake of alcohol would be after the race at the slip in which Ross Richards' boat was moored," he said. "I shared a beer with Mr. John Driscoll, the sum and substance of that beer would be, I think, less than a quarter of one." That gratuitous falsehood could be dropped into the record thanks to Bernie Flynn's assurance neither Richards nor Stan Moore were prepared to testify to the three rum and cokes Kennedy had imbibed at the party.

"Anything more?" Boyle said.

Having delivered himself of testimony prepared by his attorneys to explain "the various inexplicable, inconsistent and inconclusive things I said and did" after the accident, Kennedy couldn't think of anything else to say.

He came out of the courthouse looking "immensely relieved," and for the first time since the accident, "He again was the breezy and smiling, supremely self-confident Ted Kennedy."

His three hours of testimony had "generally paralleled" his two previous statements about the accident, Kennedy told reporters shivering in the 26 degree cold outside. "I'm satisfied I responded in the most complete way possible to all the questions put to me by the Judge and the district attorney." Kennedy wanted his testimony released as soon as possible, perhaps within days of the conclusion of the inquest, he said. "I expect to be vindicated and vindicated fully when the transcript is made public and I am then allowed to answer questions."

Kennedy enjoyed an escort of reporters to the house on School Street, all shouting questions at once. One of them asked, "Who else testified, Senator?"

Kennedy replied, "Now, you don't expect me to give away any secrets do you?"

Chapter 50

A SUMMARY OF SENATOR KENNEDY'S TESTIMONY WAS DICTATED by Clark and Hanify to Joe Donegan, a recital by necessity foreshortened, "Because how much could they take down in longhand of what he said in the courtroom?" Donegan said, later. "It was no substitute for a transcript."

Donegan did not know why such a record was being made of inquest testimony in contravention of the Massachusetts Supreme Judicial Court's ruling on secrecy. But, surrounded by lawyers, Donegan wasn't concerned about the legality of his assignment. "The only testimony they were interested in getting was the people that were at the party. The average take was a couple of pages, if that much. It didn't take me very long. It was just an outline of their testimony, very meager, really."

But it was sufficient to provide a working script to keep succeeding witnesses on the track of the Senator's testimony and prevent anything contrary to it from getting into the inquest record Boyle wanted kept secret. The judge had gone so far to insure that, as to demand the stenographic notes of official court stenographers Sidney Lipman and Harold

McNeil be destroyed after daily transcription was accomplished. (When Lipman protested the transcript might not be "official" without his original notes, should he later be called upon to recheck what had been said in the courtroom, Boyle agreed to have the tapes impounded, rather than destroyed.)

But no matter how hard the Kennedy legal team tried to shape the outcome of the inquest, risks remained. Ray LaRosa came close to placing the credibility of the Senator's testimony in serious jeopardy. A former fireman employed by the Federal Office of Civil Defense, LaRosa testified that he had not seen Senator Kennedy leave the party with Mary Jo Kopechne. He wasn't sure what time "a voice which I recognized as Senator Kennedy's" had called out his name twice outside the cottage. After Gargan and Markham left the party, LaRosa had gone for a walk with Nance and Mary Ellen Lyons. A car coming from the direction of the ferry had stopped, "A man asked whether we needed help or something. And one of the girls made some kind of statement. I think she said, 'Shove off,' or something of that nature," LaRosa said.

Before that occurrence, however, another car had come along heading toward the ferry in the same direction LaRosa was walking, he said. "And I held my hands out to kind of protect the two girls. The car slowed down and didn't stop and just continued on its way."

That LaRosa had seen another car between the cottage and the intersection at the same time one was observed there by "Huck" Look was a revelation that could explode the Senator's testimony about the time the accident had taken place. (Distressed when he later realized the significance of the "other car," LaRosa said, "Hell, it could clear Kennedy once and for all if I told you it wasn't his Olds—but I really can't say.")

But the bomb LaRosa dropped on the inquest didn't detonate to any effect: Neither Dinis nor Boyle pursued the subject of the "other car." La Rosa's testimony inflicted only minimal damage on Kennedy's story.

"The lawyers coached us pretty good," he said, later. "We knew what to expect."

———

A young Boston attorney and Kennedy campaign aide, Charles Tretter, also grazed the Senator's testimony. Tretter told the inquest he had not seen the Senator and Mary Jo Kopechne leave the party, but became aware of their absence around 11:30 P.M. when he went for the first of two walks with Rosemary Keough. He said, "I had to go by where two cars were parked. There was only one car—the white Valiant."

During the walk it had been necessary for Tretter to step off the road for passing automobiles, one of which he thought was the Valiant. He'd returned to the cottage between 30 to 40 minutes later, "And there was no one there, no cars." Tretter assumed party guests had returned to Edgartown without him.

But Tretter had walked into a time trap. Had the accident occurred when Senator Kennedy said it did, and had he returned to the cottage at 12:15 A.M. to fetch Gargan and Markham, Kennedy would have encountered Tretter and Keough on their walk toward the intersection. Kennedy later acknowledged it was "unlikely" he could have missed anyone on so narrow a road. But the contradiction in Senator Kennedy's testimony wasn't pursued. Judge Boyle adjourned the first day of the inquest at 4 P.M. As he was to remind all witnesses, Boyle warned Tretter not to discuss his testimony with anyone except his lawyer, "And particularly with no other witnesses."

Tretter resumed the witness stand the next day. He hadn't known about the accident or that Senator Kennedy had called Joe Gargan and Paul Markham out of the cottage, until Saturday morning. Tretter said, "Mr. Gargan said the Senator was distraught, that neither one of them talked to him. He just kept saying, 'Get me to Edgartown. Get me to Edgartown.'"

It was clear from his testimony that Tretter hadn't been paying much attention to anything but Rosemary Keough that weekend.

When it was her turn to testify, Keough stumbled badly with regard to time, finding it difficult to keep in mind the hour and a half differential between the Senator's version of the accident and that of "Huck" Look. Keough thought it was 12:15 A.M. or 12:30 when she left the cottage for her first walk with Tretter. Returning to the cottage some 45 minutes later, she found the place empty, except for Jack Crimmins asleep in the bedroom. Keough had resumed her promenades with Tretter for another hour and a half. By the time she returned to the cottage again, people were settling down to sleep.

Keough had seen the Senator and Mary Jo leave the party "at 11:20 P.M.," having looked at Susan Tannenbaum's watch. But, despite her avowal in August to answer all questions "fully and cooperatively," she had little else to say. "As far as I'm concerned," she said, later, "there's only one person who really knows what happened from the beginning of the incident to the end and that's Edward Kennedy."

But Keough and Tretter were suffering a problem unique to Kennedy witnesses. Having gone to the Shiretown Inn to borrow a radio, danced together at the party, disappeared for two midnight walks lasting over two hours, and slept side-by-side on the living room floor, it was clear a flirtation had blossomed during the weekend. Tretter's wife was reported furious at the episode of dalliance, Paul Redmond said. "In preparing Tretter's testimony it was Dan Daley's idea to keep him walking—to save his marriage." Having to account for his own activities didn't leave Tretter much time to verify Kennedy's story or contribute significantly to the transcript Donegan was making of the inquest.

But the transcript was not only serving as an *aide memoire* for witnesses, but as a means of exerting control over them by lawyers, "whose main interest was Ted Kennedy," Esther Newberg recognized. Every witness knew what they said in the courtroom was going on the private record—sure to inhibit any spontaneous deviation from that script on the witness stand. The procedure was devised by Jack Miller, who reported on the progress of the inquest to Stephen Smith from one of five telephones installed at the house on School Street. So tightly was control being exercised, the Boiler Room girls excused from testifying at the second day's inquest session were not allowed to leave the courthouse unsupervised. Lawyer Paul Redmond asked Judge Boyle for permission to leave the courtroom, "Just to escort them by the press outside," he said. "They have to pass reporters with microphones."

As the second day of the inquest progressed, attention centered on Joe Gargan and Paul Markham, "the lawyer friends," as *Newsweek* observed, "who though not suffering from shock had joined Kennedy in his long post-accident silence." Their testimony was second only to Kennedy's in interest. In many ways, Gargan and Markham had more to clarify than Senator Kennedy, "Since they were presumably lucid when Kennedy returned to the cottage 'dazed' after his accident." Not only would they be asked about Kennedy's activities, but their own, particularly why neither had summoned help to the scene or reported the accident to police. As the only witnesses who could corroborate Kennedy's post-accident behavior, they could be expected to be the target of Dinis' most probing questions.

Gargan said he wasn't worried. "I was simply going to tell what I saw and what I did and what I heard."

Gargan did far better than that. Building on his image as "bag carrier" and "factotum" projected by the press, Gargan played it for all it was worth on the witness stand. He poured out a torrent of irrelevant details about the sailing weekend, even to describing his role as crew during the Regatta race, "having to hold onto the stay, forcing my back out in this position with the pole holding the spinnaker out."

Gargan even larded his testimony with details of culinary techniques he had employed at the cookout. Chatty as a neighbor exchanging recipes across a backyard fence, Gargan explained, "I took out of the refrigerator what you would call frozen hors d'oeuvres—some which have sausage and some which had cheese. I turned the oven to about 450 degrees—they take about 12 minutes to cook—and I put in some of these hors d'oeuvres at that time. After they were ready, I took them out and started to pass them around."

Dinis later confessed he had been disarmed and amused in spite of himself, and regaled his staff with Gargan s testimony. "Eddie was laughing," during a call to Jimmy Smith during the inquest. "He thought it was hysterical about the oven temperature and all the cooking instructions."

Between working at the kitchen stove and the grill outdoors, Gargan said he hadn't noticed which guests at the party were drinking, or how much. The Senator was holding "a tall glass with a dark fluid in it—I would say was Coca-Cola. Whether there was anything else in the glass besides Coca-Cola, I cannot honestly testify to," Gargan said. "But I would say, frankly, that the Senator does consume rum and coke and I would assume he was drinking rum and coke at that time." Kennedy left the party between 11:25 P.M. and 11:30 P.M. "I saw him go out the door of the cottage with Mary Jo Kopechne. Where he went from there, I don't know." Gargan assumed they were going to the ferry because of a conversation the Senator had joined in with Jack Crimmins prior to his leaving. "Mr. Crimmins was somewhat agitated by the fact that we weren't moving out," Gargan said. Crimmins had complained "that it was 11:15 and that we ought to think about leaving because the last ferry left at 12 o'clock." Gargan did not mention Crimmins urging him "to get these douchebags out of here," or his state of intoxication. ("I didn't think it was necessary to testify to that," he said, later. "The gist of the conversation was that Jack wanted everybody to go home.")

Gargan testified he next saw Senator Kennedy in the back seat of the Valiant when Kennedy announced, "The car has gone off the bridge down by the beach and Mary Jo is in it." Gargan drove, "just as fast as I could" to the accident scene. When attempts to rescue Mary Jo failed, "I didn't think there was anything more that could be done." The Senator had been "very emotional, extremely upset, very disturbed," Gargan said. "He told me he was going down the dirt road headed toward I don't know what. He suddenly saw the bridge in front of him and that was it, he went right off into the water."

Gargan couldn't testify to the dialogue word-for-word, "But I do recall that the thrust of the conversation—and I was the one who said it—was that we have got to make a report of the accident immediately." Before the Senator did so, however, Gargan suggested he call David Burke, "to let the family know he was all right," and Burke Marshall, "because Burke Marshall is the best lawyer I know." The Senator told him to go back to the party, "Don't upset the girls; don't get them involved," and dove into the water. Gargan watched him swim until he was "about three quarters of the way across," confident of his ability to make it to the other side. "The Senator can swim that 5 or 6 times both ways."

Gargan said he then drove to the cottage, turned the car around and returned to the landing. He decided, "The Senator was going to report the accident." Following the Senator's instructions, Gargan said nothing about the accident when he returned to the cottage "around 2:15 A.M."

Quick arithmetic would have revealed Gargan's timing didn't jibe with Senator Kennedy's. Had the rescue efforts taken "approximately 45 minutes" from the time Kennedy said he had returned to the cottage to seek help "around 12:15 A.M."—that would have placed him at the landing at one o'clock. Gargan had left more than an hour unaccounted for.

Given the difficulty of tracking such vague testimony, Dinis did not pick up on the time discrepancy, asking only about the time the Senator had left the cottage. Dinis did not ask Gargan if the Senator had been in shock after the accident, or what excuse Kennedy had offered the following morning when Gargan learned the accident had not been reported.

Gargan had seen the sheet of paper the Senator was working on his report at the police station, but hadn't read it or mentioned being at the accident scene to Chief Arena, he said. "I never spoke to the police, not about that or anything else."

Despite the widely published speculation that Gargan had agreed to take the blame for the accident, Dinis failed to ask if the Senator had proposed the alternative scenario Gargan had carefully edited out of his one hour of testimony. Gargan was prepared to say, "Yes, that was discussed—but not acted upon." Dinis had spared him the necessity. For all his outrageous garrulousness, Gargan walked off the witness stand in triumph, neither having betrayed Ted Kennedy nor having committed perjury.

If Paul Markham couldn't match Gargan s performance, he did comport himself well on the witness stand. Kennedy had "a rum and coke with me before other guests had arrived," but Markham did not know how much more the Senator had to drink at the party, nor did he "expressly recall" Kennedy leaving at any specific time. By Markham's best estimate, it was shortly after 12 o'clock that Kennedy returned to the cottage seeking help to rescue Mary Jo Kopechne at Dike Bridge. "We were singularly unsuccessful in trying to get into the car; the current was very, very strong," Markham said. "The girl was apparently gone. We had to get help and report the accident."

En route to the landing, Markham observed the Senator to be "very emotional. He was sobbing and almost on the verge of actually breaking down crying." Kennedy had said the next morning he hadn't reported the accident, "because, I don't know, it was just a nightmare. I wasn't even sure it happened."

As Fernandes understood Markham's testimony, "The reason that you or Mr. Gargan did not seek assistance or notify the police was that you assumed that Mr. Kennedy was going to do so when he arrived in Edgartown after the swim?"

"That is what he told us," Markham said, truthfully.

The two witnesses "who besides Kennedy, have the most explaining to do," had gotten cleanly away. Unlike Senator Kennedy, both had testified without knowing in advance what questions were to be asked.

Gargan was shocked when he later learned about the meetings Stephen Smith and Jack Miller had held with Bernie Flynn of the district attorney's office. "It was the kind of overkill that perhaps took place as a result of people trying to protect not only Ted Kennedy but the Kennedy image, the record and the reputation," Gargan said. "They were going through an enormous effort and extent to do that, and in their enthusiasm, I'm afraid some people over-reacted and did things that were unnecessary."

In Gargan's opinion, Ted Kennedy could have handled inquest questions. "He didn't need that kind of help," Gargan said. "Unfortunately, a lot of people aren't going to believe Paul Markham and I were not familiarized with that situation when we testified—but we were not."

Chapter 51

COLLECTING AS MANY SIGNATURES OF INQUEST PARTICIPANTS as he could, Assistant District Attorney Peter Gay asked Paul Markham to autograph his copy of the *Bridge at Chappaquiddick*. Markham wrote in it, "Don't believe everything you read." Because Markham's examination had been left to Armand Fernandes, rumors circulated through the press corps that Dinis had quit the inquest. Dinis showed up at the communications center with assurances, "I'm still on the case. I'm not leaving." He didn't know what all the commotion was about, "But I'm going to find out."

Dinis traced the rumor to Dick Drayne, the Senator's press secretary. Drayne had told reporters, "Dinis is folding up. He's leaving and not coming back." State Police Captain Charles Harrington, in charge of courthouse security, had told Drayne he "thought" the district attorney was leaving the island that afternoon.

Dinis was uncharacteristically subdued at the communications center. "I've led a very controversial life. I keep hoping that controversy will leave me, but it won't," he told reporters. "I just do the best I can." Far from being relentless in the pursuit of a criminal case against Ted Kennedy, Dinis said he "expected" to vote for him in November, "if he's renominated."

Taking his lead from Dinis, Armand Fernandes was not aggressive in his questioning of witnesses either. He did ask Markham about the victory party after the Regatta race, eliciting the laconic reply, "People were drinking several cans of beer."

But Fernandes failed to question the host about the party when Ross Richards took the witness stand. Instead, Fernandes confined his questioning of Richards to events the morning after the accident.

Richards had spent half an hour in Senator Kennedy's company on the deck of the Shiretown Inn talking about the previous day's race. He had observed no injuries, or anything out of the ordinary about Kennedy's speech, appearance or attitude. "There wasn't a word mentioned about Chappaquiddick," he said.

Markham and Gargan had appeared "ruffled" when they arrived. "I would say they looked damp; their hair hadn't been combed in some time," Richards said. "They might have been wet from the night's dew or fog or something." Richards denied telling a detective from the district attorney's office both men had been "soaking wet." He said, "I did not say that, I'm sure."

Fernandes wanted to refresh Richards' recollection by reading from Lieutenant John Dunn's report of his interrogation, but Boyle wouldn't allow it. Fernandes didn't question auto dealer Stan Moore, "Because he had nothing to add" to Richards' testimony. Moore expected to testify, "Because I'd been with Ted on Ross' boat, and at the Shiretown Inn the next morning." All inquest witnesses were being kept in a large room on the second floor of the courthouse adjacent to the courtroom. "When it was somebody's turn, a court officer came in and got them." Moore observed the Boiler Room girls, "Playing cards, shooting the breeze and laughing. They seemed lighthearted, a bit nervous maybe, but not real anxious about testifying."

Moore was pondering how he would get around telling the inquest about the "highballs" Ted Kennedy had enjoyed on Ross Richards' boat when he was excused.

Moore and Richards left the courthouse together, to share a chartered flight to Hyannis. Moore noticed he was being followed, presumably by members of the press, and ducked into his automobile agency to switch cars. Then he headed for Hyannis Port. Richards wanted to say "hello" to Ted Kennedy.

When Richards knocked on his door, Kennedy opened it himself and thanked him for testifying, Moore recalled. "We were on Ted's doorstep 2, 3 minutes at the most. It was a sunny day but very cold. Ross was very offended Ted didn't ask him in. He'd come all the way from Florida and hired an attorney. He'd spent time and money to make sure Ted didn't get bagged for drunk driving. And all the thanks he got was a fast brush-off."

Killen hit the ceiling when he learned Moore had been excused from testifying at the inquest. Killen wanted to find out if Moore would refuse, under oath, to discuss the drinking that went on Regatta day, as he repeatedly had done during police interrogation. The decision not to put Moore on the stand had been made by Dinis, Fernandes said, later. "Both Richards and Moore had refused to talk to police about drinking. It was obvious they were protecting Ted Kennedy. There was no reason to believe they wouldn't do the same thing on the witness stand. That's why Moore wasn't called."

As the second day of the inquest neared an end, the first of the Boiler Room girls was called to testify. Other witnesses could follow the script of the Senator's testimony without difficulty; Esther Newberg had to square hers with a number of interviews she'd granted the week after the accident. In those interviews, she had gone on record as saying, "No one specifically missed Senator Kennedy or Mary Jo Kopechne or noticed what time they left the party," she had described as "an informal group with no one keeping particular track of who was there and who wasn't at any given time."

But the time element had become crucial to shoring up Kennedy's version of the accident. Now under oath, five months after the accident, Newberg managed to remember that Kennedy had left the party at 11:30 P.M. "I have a rather large watch I wear all the time and I looked at it," she said on the witness stand. "I saw him walk out of the screen door. Miss Kopechne was directly behind him." Mary Jo had appeared completely sober, "If you can use me as an expert."

"If I tell you that Mary Jo's blood had a content of .09 per hundred percent of alcohol which, by expert testimony, would be somewhere between 5 or 6 drinks, would this change your testimony in any respect?" Boyle asked.

Mary Jo was not a drinker, Newberg said. "Five or six drinks would have been completely out of order with the way she lived."

"I am only telling you what a chemical analysis shows," Boyle said, ruffled by the stridency of the witness. "And the chemical analysis is practically irrefutable."

"Then, I'm the wrong person to be asked!" Newberg replied, sharply. "Because as far as I was concerned, she was completely sober."

"And you saw her the time she left?" Boyle said.

"*Exactly* the time she left," she shot back.

But Newberg didn't know where Mary Jo was going when she left the cottage. She overheard Gargan tell the Lyons sisters, "Something to the effect that the Senator swam across. Perhaps, in my own mind I then assumed that Mary Jo was back at the motel."

Boyle wasn't buying it. "How did you believe Miss Kopechne got back to the motel?"

"She had driven the black car back. They had left before midnight, so I knew they could make a ferry without any trouble."

"She had driven and he swam?" Boyle said, incredulously. "Nothing is said by her to you or anyone else as to where she is going; now you make an assumption that she is going back to the motel?"

Newberg assumed Mary Jo was going into the front yard. "Later I had the assumption that it was a long day watching that race, she was exhausted and the Senator was probably driving her back to the motel so that she could get some rest."

"Without her saying a single word to you or to anyone else at the party?" Boyle said, aroused from complacency on the bench to challenge, for the first time, a witness' testimony at the inquest.

"That is right," Newberg said.

"At that time you and the other girls are expecting to go back to your motel. Didn't somebody walk out and see two motor vehicles gone?" Boyle asked. "Suddenly you are left without transportation on an island and none of you girls said, 'What are we going to do? What is happening? This isn't the plan?' No questions of any kind are discussed among you?"

"There was some concern about whether we could make the ferry," Newberg said. "After one o'clock we realized we weren't going to go back that night. Something was said, 'We have to make the best of a bad situation and attempt to sleep.' We had no reason to be unduly alarmed. We knew that if we had to stay that night at the island nothing was going to happen."

"You could think of no reason why two men should leave and take the last transportation available without saying a single word to you, not even a by-your-leave," Boyle said, acidly. "That didn't excite you at all?"

"We all wondered where Mr. Gargan and Mr. Markham went," Newberg responded. "Nobody volunteered any information. Later, when Mr. Gargan said the Senator swam across, it was almost as if we didn't need to know. He didn't seem to want to talk in detail about what happened. By that time, we couldn't get off the island anyway. And we assumed that Mary Jo was back in that motel room."

The most argumentative of witnesses, Newberg had won the sympathy of Armand Fernandes. "She seemed like a nice girl put in a tough position," he said. "It was obvious Boyle had taken a dislike to her."

Dislike or not, Boyle had no intention of letting her off the hook. "Did you at any time have any interview or conversation with any reporters?"

Newberg braced herself for what was coming. "The last time was the week of the accident, the day after the funeral," she said. "I was in a state of extreme duress."

But Boyle wasn't referring to those interviews, but a report published in December.

"No, I'm sorry," Newberg said. "I can see what you are reading from. That looks like one of the trash sheets like the *National Enquirer*. I never talked to that reporter. I never talked to anyone after July."

Because neither Boyle nor Dinis had done a background on the witness—including reading the July interviews Newberg had given to the *New York Times* and other newspapers—Boyle could press her no further. (Confronted much later with the contradictions between her interviews and inquest testimony, Newberg said it was "unfair" to pinpoint conflicts, "Because, Christ, I can't remember what I told a Worcester [Mass.] reporter five years ago.")

———

Since the Boiler Room group was lodged together, Boyle specifically ordered Newberg, "Not to discuss any portion of your testimony with any of them."

Newberg didn't have to worry about disobeying Boyle's instructions; Paul Redmond did it for her. If Boyle was going to question his other clients as searchingly as he had Newberg, Redmond wanted them prepared—warnings about witnesses disclosing testimony be damned.

If Boyle wanted "discussion" among the young women at the party as to what was going on, Redmond was happy to supply it through the testimony of Mary Ellen and Nance Lyons. When Markham and Gargan had returned to the cottage around 2:30 to 2:45 A.M., they'd been asked: "Where have you been? What is going on? What is happening?"

"They stated that they had gone with the Senator to the ferry and the ferry wasn't there," Nance Lyons said. "They said they couldn't find a boat and the Senator dove in and swam across, that Miss Kopechne had taken the car to the Katama Shores."

"Didn't you say to them, 'Well, how come Mary Jo takes the car and the Senator swims?'" Boyle said. "Did you have some thoughts in your mind that this was most peculiar?"

"No, not really," Mary Ellen Lyons answered. "We weren't asking anything because there was no reason to," Mary Ellen said. "We were just saying, 'Where is everybody?' The only thing we could think of was that a car was stuck in the sand."

Mary Ellen had noticed Senator Kennedy and Mary Jo Kopechne were not at the cottage around 11:15 P.M. or 11:3 P.M., "Just after a while they weren't there."

Nance Lyons gave a similar account. She had seen the Senator and Mary Jo walk out the door of the cottage. Although she wasn't wearing a watch, "I would say it was 11 :oo P.M., 11:15 P.M." It hadn't registered they were leaving the party permanently, "Simply because people were moving in and out of the cottage all evening." An hour later, Ray LaRosa came in from outside, "And said in a rather loud voice—because people were talking, 'Mr. Gargan, Mr. Markham, Senator Kennedy would like to see you.'" She added that LaRosa told her during the walk she and

Mary Ellen had taken with him that the Senator had returned to the cottage.

———

Susan Tannenbaum followed the Lyons sisters to the stand. She'd seen Mary Jo—but not Senator Kennedy—leave the party. She'd looked at her watch at twenty-five minutes of twelve, "And Mary Jo had already left."

"Were you surprised," Boyle asked, "to find out that, without your knowledge, all the transportation had gone, so you couldn't get back to Edgartown?"

"Yes, I was surprised," Tannenbaum said.

"Was there not some discussion between you and your friends about it? No one said, 'Well, gee, this is unusual to leave us stranded here?'"

"Not that I remember," Tannenbaum said.

"You are not accustomed to being deserted in that fashion are you?" Boyle said with obvious irony. It was a question without an answer—but Boyle had made his point: A pattern of collusion in the testimony of the young women, all of it clearly aimed at corroborating the time Senator Kennedy claimed he had left the party.

Exasperated, Boyle dismissed the witness. He said, "You may leave the courtroom and go, I assume, right to your friends."

———

The prettiest of the Boiler Room girls, Tannenbaum was as unhappy about her testimony as Boyle was. Her participation in the inquest continued to rankle. A year later, she demanded of Joe Gargan, "Would you just do anything the Senator asked you to do?"

As Gargan read her question, Tannenbaum was insinuating "that I may have been either put in the position, or that I did whatever had to be done under the circumstances to protect Ted Kennedy. What she was asking was whether I would sacrifice my own reputation and career to protect Ted Kennedy."

Gargan gave her an honest answer. "If you mean the time of Chappaquiddick, no I would not," he said. "I didn't do it then, and I wouldn't do it now."

The transcript of Kennedy witnesses completed with the testimony of the Boiler Room girls, court stenographer Joe Donegan was free to enjoy the social aspects of his assignment, "having a few drinks at night after dinner," and a surprise birthday party for Judge Clark "that was a lot of fun."

"That's the only time I saw Jack Miller at the house on School Street," Paul Redmond recalled. "Jack was at the party. Clarkie was deeply touched, really moved. He was a super guy. An old-style barrister," and a great storyteller. "I used to say to him he should be in Hollywood," Donegan said. "Because he was more of an actor than anything else—that's how he tried his cases. He'd put on a long face and act everything out to the jury. It was very effective."

Clark's performance at the inquest had occurred off-stage. He had more to celebrate than his birthday. No Kennedy witness had departed from the "official" Kennedy line. Nor was the omnipresent press the wiser. Walking with Clark one afternoon, "Some of the newspaper people asked what connection I had with the case," Donegan recalled. "They were curious about everybody."

But no reporter ever came to the house on School Street. The population of reporters in Edgartown had dropped to half after Senator Kennedy's inquest appearance. For *New York Times* columnist James Reston, newsmen left in frustration over "a non-story, held behind closed doors, to repeat old tales which few people quite believe anyway. Seldom in the wonderful-goofy history of politics and the press have so many reporters and so much expensive gear been transferred at such cost to cover so little news as the current Kennedy inquiry."

Reston lived next door to the house on School Street. Like other newsmen, however, he never discovered the inquest was being managed by Jack Miller from a script crafted by Kennedy lawyers and transcribed by Joe Donegan.

Susan Tannenbaum's testimony made the crucial time factor unanimous: Every Boiler Room girl had seen Senator Kennedy and Mary Jo Kopechne leave the party between 11 o'clock and 11:30 P.M., a remarkable display of unanimity for those whose memories had lapsed about any other event at the party. But such multiple endorsements had been required to support the Senator's accident time and to overwhelm "Huck" Look's anticipated testimony by a sheer weight of numbers.

Chapter 52

TO CORROBORATE KENNEDY'S VERSION OF THE ACCIDENT,
witnesses had to know what they could not know: Where the Senator
had gone after leaving the party. Esther Newberg conceded, "The real
story is what went on in that car and what went on during the next eight
hours—and I have no knowledge of anything in that period."

Neither did anybody else. But one man believed he knew something
about the missing hours that no one else did.

———

Taking the witness stand on Wednesday, the third day of the inquest,
"Huck" Look repeated testimony he had given at the exhumation hearings at Wilkes-Barre: A "dark car" with an "L7" license plate had passed
in front of him at the intersection of Dike and Chappaquiddick Road in
the early morning hours of July 19.

Boyle wanted Look to be more specific than a "dark car."

The vehicle was, "Either black, deep blue or dark green," Look said.

"Then you are unable to positively identify this car you saw taken out of the water as the identical car you saw the previous night?" Boyle asked.

"No, I can't," Look answered.

Despite his challenge to Look's testimony, Boyle also took steps to corroborate it. The district attorney's office had not conducted an investigation through the Registry of Motor Vehicles to determine how many cars in Massachusetts had registration plates with "L7" configurations. "Maybe no other car happens to have that combination, or is a Volkswagen, I don't know," Boyle said. But he thought the information so important, "I will even postpone the inquest," in order that an investigation be made. But a recess was not necessary.

Fernandes told Boyle "I will get on it with Lieutenant Killen right away."

Killen assigned Bernie Flynn the task. "It was like 3:30 P.M., on Wednesday afternoon when I called the Registry," Flynn recalled. "I got some assistant in McLaughlin's office. I gave him the information I wanted," and a number at the state police barracks at Oak Bluffs where he could be reached.

The Registry was already on the defensive. Registrar McLaughlin had told Arthur Egan of the *Manchester Union-Leader* that Senator Kennedy's license showed no traces of salt water, raising serious questions about Kennedy's testimony.

Kennedy's office hadn't been discussing details of the case outside court, "And we aren't going to now," a spokesman said. "However, if the *Union-Leader* story is an attempt to allege that the Senator was not in the car when it went into the water, we would refer that newspaper to the Senator's comment on the Jack Olsen theory that Miss Kopechne was driving alone: 'Nonsense.'"

McLaughlin denied he'd spoken to Egan or anyone else at the *Union-Leader*. "It would be improper for me to talk to anyone on the subject until the case has been adjudicated." He couldn't speculate on whether the license had been in water or not.

McLaughlin changed his story when the full realization of the important information he'd supplied hit him later in the day. Egan charged and produced a letter from the New England telephone company verifying two person-to-person calls completed to McLaughlin's office on Tuesday, January 6.

McLaughlin continued to insist he hadn't received the calls, "And I don't believe anyone else did who would have access to the license," he said. The Associated Press declined to circulate the story because, "It's not news when a newspaper catches a prominent official in a barefaced lie."

The day after denying he'd talked to Egan, McLaughlin was reappointed Registrar. Republican Governor Francis Sargent was not doing so out of political considerations, he said. "How he votes is his own concern. How he functions as Registrar is mine. And on that basis I make the reappointment with satisfaction."

Not everyone agreed. The *New Bedford Standard-Times* scorned the appointment as a "payoff," and "an open acknowledgement of McLaughlin's influence in the Democratic-dominated legislature with which Governor Sargent must do business." McLaughlin's agency was so maladministered, "Police have first-hand experience with the frustration of trying to extract, when most needed, quick information on the ownership of motor vehicles from the registry's muddled files."

But Flynn had no trouble receiving the very next morning a list of "L7" license plate owners from Carl Catalano, chief of the Registry's special investigations. Only eight of the 50 plates had been issued to operators of Oldsmobile-type vehicles.

Flynn called automobile owners on the list and asked, "Was your car on Chappaquiddick on the night of July 18?" None had been.

Flynn turned the results of his investigation over to Killen. Though the results seemed to prove conclusively that the car "Huck" Look saw had to be the one Ted Kennedy was driving, Flynn learned later that the evidence was not used at the inquest. "I don't know what the reason was, whether it came in too late or what," Flynn said. Fernandes had a different explanation: Boyle had decided such an investigation would not be "conclusive," and so he wasn't interested in knowing the findings. But Boyle himself later revealed, "The attempt disclosed that it would not be feasible to do this since there would be no assurance that the end result would be helpful." While the elimination of all other cars within that registration group "would seriously affect the credibility of some of the witnesses," Boyle said, it wouldn't alter his findings.

Flynn's detective work was not the only Registry evidence kept out of the record of the inquest. Three Registry inspectors en route to the inquest on Thursday morning to testify about the license plate investigation were told, "They weren't needed."

Not that the Registry itself was entirely forthcoming in producing evidence, either, as was demonstrated when George "Red" Kennedy took the witness stand. Kennedy's report of the accident had been kept out of the hands of the district attorney's office until Fernandes formally requested a copy of it on December 15, two weeks before the start of the inquest. When Senator Kennedy had been unable to produce a driver's license at Edgartown police station, a check at Registry headquarters had revealed, "His license was valid until February, 1971," Inspector Kennedy said on the witness stand. "This was the same day. On the 19th."

With the report of two license checks in hand, Fernandes was surprised the witness was prepared to lie under oath. He gave Kennedy another chance. "Did they produce the license *immediately*?"

Realizing he'd been caught in the lie, Kennedy changed his testimony. The license was produced, he said, "At another date."

Inspector Kennedy's remaining testimony was equally questionable. Based upon the measurement of skid marks at the start of the bridge continuing in a straight line to the end and over, and his experience investigating more than 100 accidents, Kennedy was of the opinion the accident car was travelling "approximately 20 to 22 miles per hour," corroborating the Senator's estimated rate of speed in his Operator's Report. Skid marks on the gravel surface of Dike Road preceding the bridge, however, could not be measured "very well," Kennedy said.

Boyle broke in to cut off his line of questioning. "Now you are going into something that may not exist."

Fernandes protested, "He doesn't know." Because skid marks on Dike Road couldn't be measured didn't mean there weren't any. If Senator Kennedy had started braking before he hit the bridge, he could have been going much faster than 20 miles per hour when the accident occurred. To Fernandes it was an important point because it cast doubt on the inspector's report. The Registry's "official rate of speed" prior to the accident was based on partial and inconclusive evidence. There was a significant difference between not being able to measure skid marks on gravel and saying there weren't any.

"Let's ignore that," Boyle said. He wanted "no conjecture" on the record.

But conjecture did not prevent Boyle from allowing the Arthur D. Little study of the "Physical Factors" of the accident into evidence. Boyle refused to consider those portions of the study dealing with experiments conducted with regard to Mary Jo Kopechne's possible longevity under water. He was not concerned "with the problem of survival in an immersed automobile." Since there was no evidence that any air had remained in the car, "Testimony was not sought nor allowed concerning how long Mary Jo Kopechne might have lived had such a condition existed, as this could only be conjecture and purely speculative," Boyle said, later. Whether additional assistance would have been of any material help in rescuing her from the car had not been pursued either, "Because such failure, even when shown, does not constitute criminal conduct." This was an astonishing ruling in view of the omission-to-act liability Kennedy's attorneys had feared as a basis for a possible manslaughter charge. "Either Boyle didn't know the Supreme Court decision on the *Welansky* case," one colleague observed later, "or he didn't understand how it applied to the Kennedy accident."

John Farrar disputed Boyle's contention there was "no evidence" air had remained in the car after it was submerged. "Two of us in the fire department saw air emanating, but were not allowed to testify on that aspect."

Next on the stand, Farrar testified he had found "the victim's head cocked back, face pressed into the footwell, hand holding herself in a position such as she could avail herself of the last remaining air in the car."

Fernandes cut Farrar short. "You don't *know* what was done," he said. Farrar was to describe, "Exactly what you saw," and not speculate on whether professional rescue efforts, if promptly made at the time of the accident would have saved Mary Jo Kopechne's life, or to deliver himself of the opinion, "She suffocated in her own air void—she didn't drown."

Boyle suggested a description of the car's length and weight would be helpful in making his report. After receiving specifications from a local Oldsmobile dealer, Richard McCarron dictated an affidavit to Donegan at the house on School Street.

In concluding the inquest, Boyle had gone over the evidence to make sure he had not omitted anything that might be available, and "then find out there was something I didn't obtain."

But Boyle's self-congratulation was vainglorious. The inquest had been conducted in a haphazard manner, gaping contradictions in testimony allowed to go unchallenged during the incomplete questioning of witnesses, called in no particular order or sequence. No attempt had been made to confront one witness' testimony with another's with regard to continuity and consistency. Skeptical as Boyle was about the testimony of the Boiler Room girls, he had confined himself to making ironic remarks about it from the bench.

Other relevant witnesses had not been called to testify, including Sylvia Malm and her daughter—reading under an open window facing Dike Bridge "some time between 11:15 and 11:45 P.M." on the night of the accident. Dinis did not bother to call other Dike Road residents who left lights on in their houses to challenge the Senator's testimony there were "absolutely no lights in that area that I noticed."

Foster Silva was not called to testify about the "yelling, music and general sounds of hell-raising" at the Lawrence cottage that had continued to 1:30 A.M., a report at variance with the duration and character of the party as described by inquest witnesses. Dinis had kept Flynn's investigation of license plates off the record; and Stan Moore and three Registry inspectors off the witness stand, testimony that—had it been given—would have tended to discredit Kennedy's version of the accident.

Fernandes defended the inept character of the inquest. "You've got to remember this wasn't a trial. It was an informational process, hence no cross-examination," he said. "Boyle decided what got on the record and what didn't. Some purely hearsay evidence—like Kennedy's beer with Jack Driscoll—was allowed, other hearsay evidence was not. We were hidebound by that," Fernandes said. "Under Boyle's guidelines you couldn't really question testimony, it was merely received."

———

Dinis was satisfied, "We put on the record all the witnesses that were available," he told reporters outside the courthouse. "When we started we had nothing. Now, we have a helluva lot more."

Dinis declined to speculate on the possibility of criminal charges against Ted Kennedy coming out of the inquest. He could make no decision about prosecution before Boyle filed his inquest report. But it was unlikely the grand jury would take action in the case. Dinis said, "Traditionally, the grand jury does not function without the advice of the district attorney." Should Boyle's report find negligence on the part of Senator Kennedy had contributed to Mary Jo Kopechne's death, Dinis would have no choice but to seek an indictment for manslaughter if Boyle didn't make the complaint for him.

Word of the inquest's end was telephoned by Jack Miller to Stephen Smith, reported to be "in conference" with Senator Kennedy at the compound in Hyannis Port.

Kennedy left Cape Cod immediately. "I'm glad it's over," he told reporters at Washington National airport, a short distance from the lobby where Bernie Flynn had disclosed inquest evidence to Jack Miller. "I answered the questions to the best of my ability," Kennedy said. "I am hopeful now of getting back to the business of the Senate."

———

But the drama's denouement was yet to come. Judge Boyle asked to be relieved of court duties in order to devote himself to reviewing 763 pages of inquest testimony. On February 18, a tightly sealed cardboard box containing the inquest transcript and report was carried from Edgartown to the clerk of Suffolk County Superior Court for Criminal Business in Boston, to be locked in an office safe. The documents would be available to Dinis, Attorney General Robert Quinn and counsel for any person named in the report as having been responsible for the death of Mary Jo Kopechne. Lawyers for other witnesses would be allowed to check their client's testimony for accuracy and submit corrections. Any person seeking to examine the transcript and report had to set forth in writing the basis for his claim of access.

Edward Hanify's petition requesting review of Senator Kennedy's testimony was promptly granted. A week later, Hanify was allowed to examine the inquest report.

A step-by-step recapitulation of the known facts of the case based upon testimony that contained "inconsistencies and contradictions" too numerous for Boyle to attempt to enumerate, the report placed the time of the accident "between 11:30 P.M. on July 18 and 1:00 A.M., on July 19," straddling both Kennedy and Look schedules of the accident.

Under the statute, Boyle had to report the name of any person whose unlawful act or negligence appeared to have contributed to Mary Jo Kopechne's death. Based upon inquest evidence, Boyle inferred "that Kennedy and Kopechne did *not* intend to drive to the ferry slip and his turn onto Dike Road had been intentional."

Dike Bridge constituted a traffic hazard, particularly at night, and must be approached with extreme caution, Boyle said. "A speed of even twenty miles per hour as Kennedy testified to operating a car as large as his Oldsmobile would be at least negligent and possibly reckless. If Kennedy knew of the hazard that lay ahead of him on Dike Road his operation of the car constituted criminal conduct. Since Kennedy was driven over Dike Bridge twice on July 18, Boyle believed it was "probable" he knew of the hazard, "But for some reason not apparent from his testimony, he failed to exercise due care as he approached the bridge."

Boyle, therefore, found, "There is probable cause to believe that Edward M. Kennedy operated his motor vehicle negligently ... and that such operation appears to have contributed to the death of Mary Jo Kopechne."

Having found "probable cause" of negligent motor vehicle operation, Boyle failed to exercise the statutory requirement "to issue process for the arrest of the person charged in the report with the commission of a crime." By citing the law requiring him to issue a warrant if evidence indicated guilt—and not doing so—Boyle was admitting his action was unlawful.

But whether Boyle made the charge officially or not, the damage was done. Not only had he impugned fault to Kennedy's driving, but suggested he and others had lied at the inquest, consolidating all public doubts and suspicions about the case in one damning and devastating conclusion.

Kennedy's lawyers were stunned. "We, of course, read the report in advance," McCarron recalled. "If Boyle thought Senator Kennedy was guilty of a crime, we thought he should have bound the case over to the Superior Court."

But McCarron was glad Boyle hadn't. The judge had left a narrow loophole, perhaps large enough for Senator Kennedy to slip through.

In guiding himself with regard to the proof required of the commission of an unlawful act, Boyle had applied the standard of "probable guilt" in grand jury hearings to bring an indictment. Having fulfilled that portion of the statutory commandment pointing to Kennedy's criminal negligence, Boyle was virtually inviting Dinis to do something about it. Angered that the district attorney had "required" him to hold an inquest, instead of taking on responsibility for conducting an investigation himself, Boyle was bouncing the case back where he thought it belonged. If anyone was going to bring charges against Ted Kennedy, it was going to be Dinis.

On vacation in Portugal, Dinis told *Diario Popular* the Chappaquiddick case had not been shelved. "The judge is preparing his report," he
said. "When I get back the report will be presented to me and will be
studied in detail. Two things can happen: either the process is reopened
and a new investigation is carried out, or it is closed." Interviewed by a
television talk show host puzzled that a small city district attorney had
authority to prosecute so important a political personage as Senator
Edward Kennedy—something unheard of under the dictatorship of
Antonio de Oliveira Salazar—Dinis explained, "Our system is a rule of
law—not a rule of men."

Dinis was going to get the chance to prove his words when he was
ushered into Suffolk County courthouse and shown Boyle's report. "Son
of a bitch!" Dinis muttered, stormed out of the building and refused to
talk to reporters. In Dinis' view, if Boyle thought Senator Kennedy was
probably guilty of a crime, he had a "moral duty" to seek a complaint.

Boyle had gone as far as he could go, but fell short of an indictment,
Fernandes explained. "He could have, in his discretion, brought charges,
but he didn't. What he said, in effect, was 'Yes, there's some evidence of
negligence here, but not enough to bring a charge.'" How much negligence was required to become legally criminal "was a line very difficult
to draw," Fernandes said.

Clearly, Dinis was not prepared to draw that line. His experience in
investigating the case had been sobering. Prodded by the press to enter
the case, once he did so, he had been subjected to ridicule and accusations of seeking to advance his own career. In seeking answers to the
mysteries of the accident he had encountered a judicial stone wall, the
courts doing everything to favor Kennedy's cause. Fed up with being the
scapegoat of the inquiry, Dinis complained, "Others in appropriate
power avoided everything."

Dinis had run out of options. There was no alternative now except
to prosecute Ted Kennedy on the basis of the inquest evidence as Boyle

was challenging him to, or fail to bring charges and be accused of dereliction of duty and God knows what else when the inquest documents were published.

With Boyle's report a ticking time bomb ready to explode when it was made public, Dinis made no decision at all. But he was clearly unwilling to prosecute the case, Jimmy Smith recognized. "Dinis didn't want to go down as the guy who put the bullet in Teddy Kennedy. He wanted to save him."

Chapter 53

THAT INQUEST DOCUMENTS HAD NOT BEEN MADE PUBLIC immediately suggested to grand jury foreman Leslie Leland that the report had been "unfavorable" to Senator Kennedy. Leland conferred informally with members of the grand jury. Questions about Kennedy's explanation of the accident remained. Jurors suspected the Senator had devoted a considerable portion of his nine-hour delay to report the accident to grope for some way of escaping involvement. "Most of us felt Kennedy was morally responsible for the death of that girl," one juror said. "We talked about bringing in Kennedy and some of the girls present at the cookout."

On March 17, at his drugstore in Vineyard Haven, Leland composed a letter to Chief Justice Joseph Tauro of the Superior Court asking the grand jury be called out of recess to consider the Kennedy accident. The grand jury had "a duty and a responsibility to come up with answers that have been long overdue and try to close the case once and for all," Leland said. It was the feeling of most Edgartown residents that the death of Mary Jo Kopechne, "Should have been disposed of a long time ago.

Everyone feels that a great injustice has been done to the democratic process, that there's been a whitewash, a cover-up and that things have been swept under the rug. A great deal of time has passed since the girl died and it's time the public found out what happened." The main purpose of Leland's request was to examine the inquest transcript and report, he said. "We want to see what's there and what isn't there."

Leland followed proper procedure by directing his letter to the court through the district attorney's office. Reluctant to go forward himself, Dinis now faced the prospect of the grand jury taking the case away from him and deciding it for themselves. "Leland wanted to keep it an Edgartown case—that's the island mentality," Jimmy Smith said. "They wanted Teddy Kennedy on a spear and they weren't going to let anybody take him off. And this was on an island where they didn't have anybody smart enough in all five police departments to prosecute a case in the district court."

Dinis received an advisory opinion on March 24 from Justice Tauro that he could reconvene the grand jury into special session at any time. Leland was "very pleased" his request for authorization to conduct an investigation into the death of Mary Jo Kopechne had been granted. Dinis had been asked to seek the court's permission to reopen the case, but the district attorney would play only a minor role as "counsel" to the grand jury. Leland intended to conduct the investigation himself.

Leland "hoped" the inquest report would be made available. If it wasn't, the grand jury could subpoena all those who had attended the party at Chappaquiddick and commence their own investigation from scratch. "We want to finalize this matter once and for all as far as Dukes County is concerned," Leland said. "It's been my attitude since the accident that the public is entitled to know what happened—instead of this air of secrecy that has floated over the case."

That Dinis had not taken the initiative in seeking further prosecution had indicated to defense lawyer Dick McCarron that no further charges against Senator Kennedy were "justified." McCarron was disturbed by rumors that Leland had been getting advice on how to proceed with the case from one particularly aggressive television reporter. Other grand jurors were being interviewed by the press, "A violation of common law," McCarron complained to Dinis. "They could be getting evidence to use in their deliberations."

There wasn't anything McCarron could do to head off the new investigation but procure a grand jury list and commence a rundown on members. The grand jury was beyond the reach of hearings on ground rules or appeals to a higher court. Senator Kennedy faced the most serious liability from the accident since Dinis had asked for an inquest. What his attorneys feared was an indictment for manslaughter emanating from the grand jury when it assembled at 10 A.M., on April 6, at Edgartown courthouse, three months after the inquest.

But judicial good fortune continued to favor Ted Kennedy. Assigned by Chief Justice Tauro as custodian of impounded inquest documents was Judge Wilfred Paquet. A portly man with a stentorian voice and a reputation for indulging his disagreeable temper from the bench, Paquet was a curious choice. A former member of the Democratic state committee, rewarded with a judgeship for running the successful campaign of Governor Paul Dever, Paquet was, of all jurists assigned to hear aspects of the Chappaquiddick case, "The one person you could call a Kennedyphile," a colleague on the bench remarked. In addition, Paquet was a former client of Edward Hanify.[1]* Citing "judicial ethics," Tauro declined to say whether Paquet should have disqualified himself from presiding at the special session of Superior Court to receive any indictments the grand jury might hand down.

At the opening of the court session, a priest's invocation called upon grand jurors to be guided by "mercy, meekness and compassion" in their deliberations—qualities conspicuously lacking in Paquet's instructions.

---

1   * In 1961, Paquet sentenced two bookies to ten years in jail, then ordered their release because he considered his sentence, "too harsh." Hanify had represented Paquet before the Massachusetts Supreme Judicial Court which had upheld Paquet's "honor and integrity."

For over an hour, Paquet harangued the jurors against being "too zealous," stressing the need for "an unbiased investigation." "You must bear in mind that you will not be trying this case. Your function is to indict those people who you believe committed a crime. You decide an indictment strictly on the evidence that is submitted to you." Jurors could consider only what was called to their attention by the Court, the district attorney, or what individual members know "personally" about the case. More importantly, Paquet "didn't think it was legal" for the jurors to see inquest documents and refused to permit them to examine the transcript and report unless the Supreme Court revised its decision for the documents to remain impounded until no possibility of further legal action was contemplated—a construction of the new inquest guidelines set by the court on Kennedy's appeal that was "way off base" in Assistant District Attorney Peter Gay's opinion. "The reason to impound inquest records was to avoid pre-trial publicity. That wouldn't be reason to keep it from a grand jury because their deliberations are always secret. The Court impounded these things to keep them out of the hands of the public."

Even when he was arguing before the Massachusetts Supreme Judicial Court, Edward Hanify had considered the inquest procedure accusatory because "a report could lead to a grand jury proceeding and further criminal process." The Supreme Court had demanded a closed hearing to avoid "premature publicity about an investigation preceding an indictment being sought or returned against a potential defendant," indicating the legitimate expectation of grand jury access to inquest documents.

The grand jury could have appealed to the Supreme Court for the release of inquest documents to them—or started their own investigation. But, they were led to believe they couldn't subpoena Senator Kennedy or any witnesses who had testified at the inquest—a critical error in their interpretation of Paquet's instructions.

Dinis did nothing to disabuse them of that mistaken notion. Jurors could only summon witnesses who had "new information," he said.

One juror suggested, "Well, you were at the inquest. We can call you as witness to what was said."

Dinis had "no evidence" to present, he said. "We don't really believe he did it on purpose do we? We know that a murder wasn't committed. It was just an unfortunate accident."

"We definitely discussed involuntary manslaughter with the grand jury," Fernandes recalled. "We tried to explain what was required to make that charge." The lack of eyewitnesses to the accident made prosecution of any serious charges against Senator Kennedy difficult.

Dinis derided talk of a traffic complaint being brought against the Senator as "Mickey Mouse" stuff. "He just kept saying there wasn't much sense going into it," Leland said. "That we would get no significant charges out of it."

By law, Dinis was required to present evidence and avoid expressing an opinion as to whether an indictment should be handed down. But Dinis deliberately steered the grand jury away from the pursuit of charges against Senator Kennedy, suggesting there was nothing in the inquest record upon which to base an indictment. Despite having read the report himself, Dinis led jurors to believe Boyle had found no wrongdoing.

Leland went personally to the judge's chambers to plead again for a copy of the inquest documents. Paquet refused. With the transcript and report impounded, and forbidden to call key witnesses who had appeared at the inquest, the grand jury's investigation was narrowed to a focus of a handful of secondary witnesses and what they knew personally about the case.

As its first witness, the jury called Stephen Gentle, owner of the Katama Air Park. Gentle denied rumors a plane had left his airfield during the early hours of July 19. Mrs. Nina Trott, desk clerk at the Shiretown Inn, had so little to offer as evidence that she testified for only five minutes. Resuming the next morning, the jurors heard from Edgartown resident Benjamin Hall, who told them he had overheard an argument during the early hours of Saturday, July 19, between Russell Peachey and a person "who sounded intoxicated" but whom he couldn't identify. Having sent someone from his office to mingle with reporters to find out who the grand jury was calling to testify, McCarron learned, to his delight, these witnesses "didn't know anything about the case."

Though reluctant to stop there, the grand jury had no choice. "It was very discouraging," one juror said. "We had no cooperation, so we felt we might as well go home."

At 10:55 A.M., the grand jury filed into the courtroom. Leland announced he had "no presentments" to make. Paquet excused the jurors from further deliberations, reminding them of their pledge of secrecy. "I don't mean for a day, I mean forever."

"It was made quite clear and emphatic that I can't talk to anyone," a dejected Leland told reporters leaving the courthouse. Leland was returning to his drugstore, "Because it's necessary to make a living and support my family."

Dinis was hardly able to contain his relief "at the end of this particular investigation into the death of Mary Jo Kopechne," he said. "The case is closed."

———

Dinis intended to file appropriate certificates notifying the Superior Court no criminal prosecution of Senator Kennedy was contemplated, clearing the way for the release of inquest documents. The grand jury was "without purpose," Dinis said, later. "They were on a wild goose chase. I challenged them to come up with more evidence, more witnesses, but they couldn't produce anything." If Dinis was seeking to shift blame for the lack of prosecution in the case, he admitted later, "There's no question in my mind the grand jury would have indicted Ted Kennedy for involuntary manslaughter if I had given them the case."

That Dinis had chosen not to do so was an exercise of "prosecutorial privilege," Armand Fernandes said, later. "The investigative portion of the case had been more or less accomplished by the inquest, fulfilling the need to interrogate witnesses. Their testimony did not indicate a trial would lead to a successful prosecution. There was no point in pursuing an indictment when you know you don't have a winnable case—that isn't ethical. Actually, Dinis did the right thing, although he knew he would be criticized for it." To indict Ted Kennedy for manslaughter knowing you couldn't prove the case in court would definitely have been "publicity-seeking," Fernandes said. "And Dinis didn't stoop to doing that."

Paquet's refusal to allow access to the inquest documents had been crucial in keeping the case out of the grand jury's hands, Fernandes said. "If our office had appealed to the Court for an advisory opinion, I think it's fair to say the odds were 1,000 to 1 Paquet would have been over-ruled."

Gargan agreed the ruling had been "a questionable call." Paquet was a judge of the old school, he said. "He'll do you a favor and do it publicly—and be damned."

Paquet refused to discuss the case, telling reporters, "To hell with you! I don't have to talk to you."

McCarron flashed word to Angelique Voutselas, Senator Kennedy's secretary, in Washington of the termination of the grand jury proceedings. Senator Kennedy was "happy with the findings of the grand jury." (One juror bristled, "There *were* no findings. We weren't allowed to make any.")

The Senator was anxious for the inquest transcript to be released "to eliminate any suspicion in the case." But the report was bound to have a devastating effect on his career. There was, however, a trade-off worth the price: According to the Supreme Court's ruling, release of inquest documents would forever prevent Ted Kennedy from being prosecuted on any charges dealing with the death of Mary Jo Kopechne. Whether Judge Boyle had found him "probably guilty" of manslaughter and suggested he'd lied at the inquest didn't matter. Legally, Kennedy couldn't be touched.

But release of inquest documents was blocked by court stenographer Sidney Lipman on April 8. Claiming "valuable property rights," Lipman filed suit to prevent the distribution by the Superior Court of inquest documents for the $75 cost of their reproduction, as opposed to $820.20 at Lipman's professional rates.

Dinis knew of no other case in which an official stenographer had been denied the right to sell copies of a transcript. Lipman was relying on payment from the news media for his services. Dukes County could not afford to pay him for some time.

On April 23, Edward Hanify filed a petition on behalf of Senator Kennedy asking the Supreme Judicial Court to release the documents "to insure order and decorum in the public examination." No person had private property interests or the exclusive right to make copies of court documents, the Court ruled, only hours later, ordering the transcript and report made public.

On April 29, more than 50 reporters crowded into Suffolk County Superior court in Boston for the release of the bulky documents. What reporters read staggered them, detonating another explosion of controversy about the case. The effort to manage inquest testimony had backfired. That Senator Kennedy had not spoken the truth about the accident was, "The only finding a jurist of integrity could make," the *New Bedford Standard-Times* charged. That Judge Boyle had not ordered further legal process after finding Kennedy had contributed to Mary Jo Kopechne's death would lead many to conclude, "Where justice in Massachusetts is concerned, there is one door for John Doe and another for Senator Kennedy."

Grand jury foreman Leland was "trying to digest what I've heard" about the inquest documents. He still had not had a chance to read them. Dinis had sat through the grand jury session knowing what was in the transcript and report "without letting us know," he said. "Things might have been different," if the grand jury had seen the documents, "But we couldn't get our hands on it." There was still a possibility to reconvene the grand jury which remained impanelled until May 11, Leland said. "But I'll have to wait until I read the report."

"A bigger bunch of dumbbells you'd never hope to find—I most certainly include myself," grand juror Theresa Morse observed. "We were dupes and boobs, and let ourselves be manipulated. Nobody ever briefed us properly about what we could do. We were a powerful body made impotent by Mr. Dinis."

Arena was "a little bit surprised" by Boyle's report. In his opinion, "There were contributory factors to negligence. The bridge is a hazard." Arena hadn't had enough evidence to go forward for a negligence complaint. "I don't care what Boyle said. He has only to look for probable causes, but the district attorney has to determine whether a complaint will hold up in court. If Boyle is saying Kennedy did something wrong, I'd be interested to see what the indictment says. Because, if they could prove something else, it was all right by me."

Release of inquest documents marked Judge Boyle's last day on the Edgartown district court, leaving in the wake of his retirement a furor, not a resolution. Chappaquiddick had ended as it began: "In mystery, with many questions unanswered both by Senator Kennedy and by authorities," the *Standard-Times* said. A classic example of how the ends of justice can be frustrated, "the case may be closed in the eyes of the law, but it leaves Senator Kennedy under a cloud," the *Boston Record-American* said. "And though that may diminish in time, it will cast a shadow on his future."

———

In a statement issued from his office on the day inquest documents were made public, Senator Kennedy announced, "The facts of this incident are now fully public and eventual judgment and understanding rests where it belongs. For myself I plan no further statement on this tragic matter. Both our families have suffered enough from public utterances and speculations."

In Kennedy's personal view, "The inferences and ultimate findings for the Judge's report are not justified and I reject them."

Attorney general Robert Quinn confirmed, "No criminal action is likely against Senator Kennedy. The legal aspects are over," he said. "Politically, it remains to be seen."

Chapter 54

POLITICALLY IT WAS DISASTROUS, JUST WHEN KENNEDY
appeared to be re-emerging as a possible presidential candidate. According to opinion polls, public opinion nationwide turned decisively against the Senator after the publication of the inquest documents, with more people believing he had concealed what happened at Chappaquiddick. The heart of Kennedy's problems stemmed from a widespread belief "That his own testimony at the inquest was not accurate or truthful."

Strolling Boston's Public Garden with William Honan of the *New York Times* several days after release of the inquest transcript, Kennedy refused to respond to doubts being expressed about the credibility of his inquest testimony. "Every time I say something—for example, that I swam the channel—15 people turn up who said they were in a boat at about that time and they didn't see me swimming. So then I have to explain that," Kennedy said. "Everything just adds. There doesn't seem to be any way to end it."

Reminded he had wanted to reveal "the full story" of the accident but considered it unwise to do so because of the "rumor-filled atmosphere" and pending legal proceedings, Kennedy reneged on his promised press conference to respond to questions left unanswered by the inquest. "That was last summer, before the inquest," he said. "It's all in the transcript now. So I don't have anything more to say."

That the Kopechnes might file a civil damage suit on the basis of Boyle's finding of criminal negligence in the accident was "always a possibility," Kennedy said. But he had received no indication they were contemplating such action.

The inquest transcript was "the most difficult and disturbing reading we've ever done," Gwen Kopechne said. "We finally realized how unfortunate it was we hadn't been allowed to attend the inquest and hear the witnesses first-hand. Because we found in the testimony so many inconsistencies and contradictions. The questioning of witnesses was so incomplete and superficial—it was all left hanging. Nobody seemed to be following the case properly. The district attorney was falling apart, going from question to question; he'd get an answer but didn't follow through. There were so many questions I could have asked he never thought of asking." The testimony of the young women had been particularly unsatisfactory. "It all sounds alike; it's too pat. I think Judge Boyle might have thought it was rehearsed."

From reading the transcript, "I began to disbelieve in the legal process," Joseph Kopechne said. "To me, it was unbelievable."

George Killen could only agree, stung by accusations that those charged with official responsibility in investigating the case "fairly and impartially" had, instead, shown "a lack of vigor and diligence." For Dinis not to have sought an indictment from the grand jury was an embarrassment to his office. Too good a cop not to recognize a prosecutable case when he saw one, Killen knew court procedures backwards. There was enough evidence for "reasonable inferences" to be made from the facts, Killen said. "If Senator Kennedy was at the wheel of that car and he drove down Dike Road in a certain way, there's no question about his negligence."

Not only had Dinis kept evidence from the grand jury, but Killen "only got to read the case after we couldn't do anything about it." A "legal trick" had prevented prosecution after the inquest testimony was made public. Killen never suspected his investigation into the accident had been betrayed by Bernie Flynn.

Privately, Flynn blamed the collapse of the case on Edmund Dinis. "Boyle's report put the ball in his court, and Dinis dropped it like a hot potato." Flynn agreed, "The testimony at the inquest was all rehearsed. Everybody knew what they had to say to corroborate Ted Kennedy." That the Senator had accepted the assistance Flynn had rendered to protect himself from criminal charges issuing from the inquest, Flynn regarded as "characteristic of the man." "Ted Kennedy cheated at Harvard; and he cheated at the inquest."

Because the Senator's Oldsmobile was a total loss, "The insurance company had to pay on it," McCarron recalled. "So they owned the car legally." Edward Hanify purchased the automobile back from the insurance company to prevent it from falling into the hands of a promoter for display at a freak show as "The Chappaquiddick Death Car." McCarron towed the vehicle from the state police barracks to the dock at Oak Bluffs. Jimmy Smith arranged for transportation by ferry to Woods Hole. A wrecker brought the automobile to Plymouth to be gutted for parts, then crushed into scrap.

Jimmy Smith was also dealing with the residual consequences of the accident. Joe Greelish was pushing hard for the postmastership, making not-so-subtle references to the suppression of license information and other "favors" the Registry had performed in the Kennedy accident case, Smith said.

Smith had some bad news for Greelish: His son wasn't going to get the job.

Greelish had some bad news for Senator Kennedy a month later, following the long-postponed Registry hearing into the accident held in

Hyannis on May 18. On the basis of the facts of the case presented, "It would appear that Kennedy did not see the bridge in time and put on his brakes, losing steering ability and slid off the right side of the bridge. I believe there was operation too fast for existing conditions," Greelish reported.[1*] "I do not find that the accident occurred without serious fault."

On May 27, Registrar McLaughlin informed Senator Kennedy, "Upon investigation and after a hearing, I am unable to find that the fatal accident in which a motor vehicle operated by you was involved was without serious fault on your part." Kennedy's license was revoked for an additional six months. Any driver "aggrieved" by the hearing's decision could appeal. But Kennedy didn't bother. On June 11, Kennedy formally announced his candidacy for re-election.

Four days later, on June 15, Kennedy was driving—in violation of his license revocation—the thirty-five miles from Boston to Haverhill in less than an hour "despite fairly heavy traffic" accompanied by author Lester David and campaign aide Paul Kirk. "The Senator never drove a car when Jack Crimmins was available," Gargan said, but Crimmins was helping him advance a campaign appearance. "There was a problem at the cutoff on Route 93 getting where we wanted to go." Crimmins and Gargan were waiting by the side of the road when Kennedy drove up, got out of the car and climbed into Crimmins' automobile.

Kennedy was waiting for the start of a parade celebrating Haverhill's 100th anniversary as a city when a portable cannon was practice-fired close by. Doubled up, hands clutching his stomach, Kennedy fell against the car seat, his face drained of color. Moments later, he was smiling and jaunty, marching the four-mile parade route, waving at crowds lining the curbside.

"Good work, Senator!" a bystander shouted when Kennedy passed. Two girls kissed him during a pause in the parade's route. The Senator

---

1 * See Appendix 6.

received a centennial hat and was proclaimed: "Kennedy Our Next President."

The Senator disclaimed any intentions of seeking the nomination in 1972. He would remain in public life, "As long as I felt that I could be effective in the United States Senate on the issues."

Kennedy was running a "shoe leather" campaign for re-election, widely heralded as a preliminary to seeking the Democratic presidential nomination. "But Chappaquiddick changed all that," James Reston observed. "And the paradox of it is, that he is probably a more reliable man today than he was a year ago—sadder, wiser, more disciplined, but rejected for the Presidency in 1972 by his party and by himself."

A "different" Ted Kennedy stumped New Bedford in July: hair shaggy and greying, wearing a somber suit, more soft-spoken and reflective since the release of inquest documents. The *Standard-Times* was endorsing Kennedy's re-election, "even though the Chappaquiddick incident has left a sour taste in our mouth. To this day, Senator Kennedy has never fully answered all questions about his actions during the tragic episode."

Kennedy himself acknowledged the incident was an issue in the election. "The voters need reassurance. They need to see me to be convinced that I'm reliable and mature," he said. "You can't counter the Chappaquiddick thing directly. The answer has to be implicit in what you are, what you stand for and the way they see you."

———

One place Ted Kennedy wasn't going to be seen was the Edgartown Regatta. He wasn't entered in the 1970 races.

Dike Bridge remained a popular tourist attraction, access to which was facilitated by a new *On Time* with an expanded three-car capacity. In vain did island residents brandish a new bumper sticker: Chappy's Our Home—Leave Us Alone.

Arena was anticipating, "At least one TV man will be here to cover the anniversary of the accident."

The Kopechnes marked the occasion at their daughter's grave. A bouquet of red and white carnations was sent by Senator Kennedy. Rosemary Keough carried a basket of daisies to the cemetery. She said, "My friend Mary Jo just happened to be in the wrong car at the wrong time with the wrong people."

The Kopechnes received a check for $140,923.00 from the General Accident Group of Philadelphia which had carried $1 million accident policy on Senator Kennedy's car. Their lawyer, Joseph Flanagan, revealed the figure to end speculation about a settlement rumored to be as high as half a million dollars. The figure, proposed by a professional actuary of Mary Jo Kopechne's potential lifetime earnings, had been "accepted without protest" by Kennedy's insurance company, Flanagan said. Kennedy had "paid nothing out of his own pocket."

But both statements were false. The insurance company had refused to pay more than the $50,000 maximum allowed under Massachusetts law for accidental death the Kopechnes could recover if they were unable to prove their daughter had "consciously suffered" before she died.

Informed the Kopechnes planned to sue, Senator Kennedy agreed to pay the $90,923.00 difference. "Obviously, a financial settlement could never compensate the Kopechne family for the loss of their daughter or for the tragedy of the accident," Kennedy said. "But if there was to be one, I thought it should be fair."

Flanagan also negotiated the sale of Gwen Kopechne's story to *McCall's*, written, she said, "To put to rest the ugly rumors that have been torturing us."

Judge Boyle's conclusion that Senator Kennedy had lied when he said he and Mary Jo had been driving to the ferry, "leaves a bad taste in our mouths and we absolutely reject it and any implications that flow from it." Her daughter, she insisted, had not been involved in a romance over the Regatta weekend. "Among her boyfriends, there was not one named Senator Edward Kennedy."

Mrs. Kopechne was convinced the Senator had done all he could to save Mary Jo by diving down to the car. "We also believe that the Senator was in shock when he started back to the cottage after his unsuccessful rescue attempt. If his judgment hadn't been impaired, we're certain that he would have tried to get immediate help at one of the houses along the way."

Although the Senator was "obviously distraught," Joseph Gargan and Paul Markham had been in full possession of their senses. "Mr. Kopechne and I have been very disturbed by their actions. Why did they assume that Mary Jo was dead and then not seek help? Whoever knows when it's too late for rescue?" By not notifying authorities promptly, Gargan and Markham had invited all kinds of awful speculation. She said, "Many people will always think there was more to this tragedy than just an accident."

But compensating the Kopechnes for the death of their daughter was only part of the cost of Chappaquiddick. Kennedy paid $32,000 to Paul Redmond and Dan Daley for their representation of eight witnesses at the inquest. Other lawyers retained in the case submitted bills—"some of them were heavy hitters," one insider said. Stephen Smith was surprised to learn that Joseph Donahue was not charging for his services. Out of friendship and regard for Gargan, Donahue said, "There will be no fee."

Chappaquiddick also exacted a price in the election, over 100,000 blank votes reducing Kennedy's percentage of victory to 58%, far short of his record 1964 plurality.

But Kennedy was sufficiently buoyed by his victory to reassert claims of national leadership in a victory speech televised from his heavily guarded headquarters in Boston. "I look forward to being a voice for peace in the U.S. Senate, a voice of reconciliation that appeals to the best within people," Kennedy said. "I return to the Senate to give voice to the powerless groups that exist within our society."

On November 27, Kennedy went to Plymouth to undergo a full driver's license examination. He used a Cadillac to take—and pass—his driver's test, and received his license. For all practical purposes, the consequences of Chappaquiddick were over.

———

Edmund Dinis had been confident he would be re-elected to a fourth term as district attorney. His opponent was "too new in politics to have any guile or malice in his attacks." Dinis was wrong.

That "guileless" Philip Rollins won an "upset" victory, was "more a repudiation of Dinis," than a vote of endorsement for "an unknown aspirant for public office," the *New Bedford Standard-Times* opined, having editorially supported Rollins.

Dinis didn't think Senator Kennedy had played "a direct role" in his defeat. But pro-Kennedy voters had perceived his handling of the Chappaquiddick case to be "against" the Senator. Ethics prevented Dinis from discussing the case after it was closed, "But I would not hesitate to handle the matter in the same way if I had a chance to do it all over again."

Privately, Dinis was bitter to have saved Ted Kennedy's career by preventing a grand jury from charging him with manslaughter, at the expense of his own. He perceived a singular irony in the Senators reelection: "The girl died. And *I* got defeated."

Preparing to take office in November, district attorney Rollins ordered the transfer of all Chappaquiddick records from New Bedford to Barnstable courthouse. Indictments clerk Lance Garth removed several state police photographs of the accident car as a souvenir of the case. Fernandes claimed proprietary rights to documents he had worked on during the exhumation and autopsy hearings.

But the district attorney's office was not alone in suffering the displacement of records in the case. Edgartown police files vanished. The Registry of Motor Vehicles had "lost" Herb Burr's report on Senator Kennedy's license check, a "diligent and thorough search" failing to turn up the record.

George Killen set about retrieving all the documents he could. On December 26, 1970, he requested return of exhibits submitted as evidence at the inquest by the district attorney's office from Dukes County Superior Court clerk Sophie Campos. Three days later, Mrs. Campos inquired of Chief Justice of the Superior Court Walter McLaughlin what the procedure was to return the requested items.

What motives a young, unknown Republican district attorney might have in seeking to consolidate evidence in the Chappaquiddick case prompted a letter, dated October 5, 1971, from Edward Hanify. Citing "our usual Massachusetts procedure," Hanify asked that exhibits presented at the Kopechne inquest "be returned to the parties who introduced them or to whom they respectively belong."

The exhibits introduced by Kennedy attorneys at the inquest had been affidavits: a partial study of the "Physical Factors" of the accident; an engineer's report of his examination of Dike Bridge and environs; and the medical records of Kennedy's physicians to the injuries he had suffered from the accident. According to Lieutenant Killen, the "procedure" Hanify referred to applied to items of value, such as stolen property used as evidence in robbery and breaking and entering cases. "There was nothing of value presented at the inquest that I knew about."

The next day, Killen learned what Hanify was after. Joseph Flanagan telephoned the district attorney's office from Wilkes-Barre to inquire about, "The return to the parents of Mary Jo Kopechne of any exhibits introduced at the inquest" which belonged to her: the clothing she had worn on the night she was killed. Flanagan confirmed the conversation by letter and was expecting to hear from the district attorney's office on Monday, October 11.

"I couldn't figure out what the hell the Kopechnes wanted their daughter's clothes back for in the first place." Killen said, later. In the second, whether the clothes "belonged" to Mary Jo Kopechne was debatable. The deceased owned no property rights to exhibits presented by the district attorney's office in a judicial hearing. Standard operating procedure was for evidence to be kept a minimum of five years in storage bins in the basement of the courthouse, longer in cases under appeal or subject to reinvestigation.

To his amazement, Killen received an order dated October 31, 1971, from Superior Court Judge Walter McLaughlin, brother of Registrar Richard McLaughlin, for "all exhibits introduced at the inquest to be returned to whom they respectively belong, or by whom they were respectively presented or introduced," language virtually identical to Hanify's inquiry.

On November 3, Killen received all inquest exhibits, including Exhibit #5, consisting of:

1 white, long sleeve, button front, blouse or shirt

1 pair, color blue, slacks

1 bra, blue trim

1 pair of leather sandals

Two days later, Flanagan called the district attorney's office. Rather than *receiving* the clothes, the Kopechnes wanted them destroyed. Killen was loath to do it, but with a court order, he had no choice. The district attorney was agreeable to having the clothing destroyed, Killen told Flanagan, but he wanted a letter to verify the request.

Flanagan wrote to Killen on November 10, 1971, on behalf of Mr. and Mrs. Kopechne requesting "the specific articles of clothing be destroyed," and for Killen to let him know when the district attorney's office had complied with the request.

Killen made copies of all correspondence and memoranda for his personal files to protect himself should it later be revealed he had participated in the destruction of evidence in a highly controversial case. On Tuesday, November 16, 1971, Killen went to the basement of Barnstable courthouse accompanied by Bernie Flynn and a custodian. As Killen reported to Flanagan, "The clothing and sandals were sprayed with lighter fluid prior to being thrown into the fire to insure total burning."

Chapter 55

THE OTHER ELEMENTS OF CHAPPAQUIDDICK WERE NOT SO EASILY disposed of as the clothes Mary Jo Kopechne had worn the night she died. One immediate consequence of Chappaquiddick was Kennedy's defeat, in January 1971, as Senate majority whip. He admitted, "It hurt like hell to lose." What hurt even more was the collapse of his presidential prospects. But Ted Kennedy's preeminence as a potential Democratic candidate had been "primarily a biological phenomenon," conservative columnist William F. Buckley, Jr., wrote. "What he now faces is a long struggle. His assets are his name, his talents and his wealth; his liabilities are Chappaquiddick." If over the next ten or more years Kennedy was able to show by his achievements "a sobriety of purpose, a strategic manliness, and a sense of destiny and resolve," he could transcend the episode.

Efforts to rehabilitate his political career were already underway. In the view of his political handlers, his presidential stature would rise as the memory of the accident faded. Kennedy had "faced up to the humiliation of being called a coward and a liar after Chappaquiddick." The task now was to resurrect the mystique of a Kennedy dynasty. Said one advocate: "In the minds of millions of Americans, he has no choice. The White House is his legacy, his ultimate responsibility, even his debt to society." Kennedy tried not to think about being President, he said. "I don't discuss it with my family. We just don't talk about it. That business about promising my mother not to run, well that's just not true."

In November 1971, Kennedy toured five midwestern states. His first "avowedly political trip" since his re-election in Massachusetts was, inevitably, looked upon as "the commencement of the third Kennedy quest for the Presidency of the United States."

But even the most partisan of his supporters were uneasy in their assessment of Kennedy's temperament and character. Writing in the *New York Times* on April 10, 1972, historian James McGregor Burns observed: "In this context, Chappaquiddick is the issue that will not die." Nothing had been learned about the accident to challenge Kennedy's characterization of his behavior as anything but "indefensible." Still, Burns wrote, Chappaquiddick had forced Kennedy "to come to grips with himself, a self-confrontation which had brought iron into his soul." Burns insisted Kennedy had to be reckoned with as a potential presidential candidate in 1972. "A genuine draft would mean that his post-Chappaquiddick period of probation was over, that the politicians considered him electable. It would be hard to respond to such a gesture with a refusal."

To other observers, Kennedy was not far enough removed from the scandal to be a viable candidate. The notion of a draft rested upon the premise that enough voters had forgiven his misbehavior at Chappaquiddick. A pollster's test of voter attitudes published by *Harper's* magazine in July 1972, revealed the stigma not only persisted, "It may be getting worse." Seventy percent of those polled expressed the view Kennedy, "Didn't tell the whole truth about what happened at Chappaquiddick." Sixty percent said they "trusted Richard Nixon more than Edward M. Kennedy."

Nevertheless, political professionals were taking a hard look at Kennedy's chances. With a view to supporting a possible candidacy, Jack Conway, political lobbyist for the United Auto Workers, commissioned Joseph Walsh to make a study of the Chappaquiddick case. Walsh had left a position as public relations chief for the UAW in Detroit to form his own communications company. A tough, shrewd, former lobbyist for liberal causes, Walsh secured a copy of the inquest transcript, made numerous marginalia in questioning testimony and submitted a confidential memorandum to Conway on November 18, 1971.

Kennedy's biggest problem was, "He is thought of as an indecisive weakling, a scoundrel or worse as a result of the accident. People believe he panicked under pressure, that he was out with an unmarried young woman for immoral purposes, and that when he had to face the facts, lied about his conduct," Walsh said. "It is almost conventional wisdom that his explanation of what happened is not credible. While the facts strongly suggest something occurred altogether different from Kennedy's account, it is with this record as background he must run for President."

Yet Richard Nixon was proof that public memory was short. His farewell tirade after his defeat for governor of California should have finished him off, "but now he is President," Walsh said. "The same could be true in Kennedy's case." Walsh suggested Kennedy pull out of the 1972 race, campaign extensively for whoever turned out to be the nominee and duplicate Nixon's efforts in the 60's with hard, party-regular work. Then, given well-publicized efforts in the Senate, make the run in 1976 or 1980 from the first primary to the last. Any other course would be disastrous for Kennedy's political career and the Democratic ticket in 1972.

Kennedy conceded the potential for *The Education of Edward Kennedy* to rescue his reputation from the residual swamp of Chappaquiddick, telling biographer Burton Hersh, "My political fortunes are tied to your book."

In an exhaustive examination of Kennedy's career, Hersh dismissed Chappaquiddick as "wholly a fluke and inevitable, absurd and tragic, over-reported and misunderstood hours after it happened and now." To Hersh, Kennedy said, "I really think I did all I could have, given the situation, my condition. All anybody else could have done."

The handling of the case continued to rankle Jimmy Smith, complaining to Kennedy's senate aide Paul Kirk that the persistence of memory about Chappaquiddick was largely self-inflicted. Smith got a call-back from Kirk, telling him, "The Boss wants to see you."

Smith went to Washington, "Because I wanted to deliver the message in person. I thought Eddie Dinis had been improperly attacked by the press. He wasn't out to hurt Ted Kennedy. Dinis had tried to save him."

Kennedy said, "What's on your mind?"

Smith was bothered about what went on during Chappaquiddick, he said. "I don't think you're getting information. You're surrounding yourself. Guys who tried to help couldn't reach you. And it's a shame you didn't get the message, because a lot of the mess could have been avoided."

Kennedy "dodged the bullet," Smith observed. "He went right into the cover-up."

"Ask me anything you want. I've answered everything," Kennedy said. "There's nothing more I can say; it's been fully covered."

Kennedy was considering taking second place on a ticket headed by George McGovern, "If that was the only way to beat Nixon;" his advisers suggesting "the cleansing effect that a vigorous, progressive national campaign would have on the sour memory of Chappaquiddick." But if Kennedy were a candidate, he could expect Chappaquiddick to be brought up repeatedly. The Nixon White House had a file of information about the accident—"Nickel and dime stuff," Kennedy said. "They haven't come up with anything really new."

Kennedy was urged to claim jurisdiction for his sub-committee on administrative practices and procedures over a burglary at Democratic National Committee headquarters at the Watergate apartment and office complex. A Kennedy-chaired investigation of the break-in could make Watergate, "The biggest political television show since the McCarthy hearings," according to columnist Stewart Alsop.

Kennedy hesitated to become involved in a political scandal coming so close upon his own. Watergate burglar E. Howard Hunt had spent time investigating Chappaquiddick. Under the alias, "Albert Patterson," Hunt had written the clerk of the Edgartown Superior Court on December 3, 1971, to inquire about "the availability of several exhibits connected with the Kennedy-Kopechne inquest." Hunt was seeking "a good, clear copy" of scuba diver John Farrar's drawing of Mary Jo Kopechne under water; and the Operator's Report of the accident Kennedy had filed with the Registry of Motor Vehicles. Patterson was referred to the district attorney's office at Barnstable courthouse.

A three-month investigation undertaken in October 1972 by Kennedy's sub-committee behind closed doors disclosed findings sufficient to persuade the Democratic leadership to create a Senate select committee to hold hearings on Watergate. Nixon's men saw "the fine Kennedy hand" behind the inquiry, and discussed seeking FBI files to show improprieties had occurred during the Kennedy administration and in the obstruction of justice in the Chappaquiddick case.

Kennedy kept a discreet distance from the burgeoning scandal. Not until September 1973 did Kennedy rise in the Senate to declare that if

President Nixon defied a Supreme Court order to turn over tapes of Oval Office conferences with his staff, "A responsible Congress would be left with no recourse but to exercise its power of impeachment."

Until all the facts about Chappaquiddick were known, Kennedy was "the last person in the country to lecture us" on Watergate, Senator Barry Goldwater said. Even liberal political columnist Tom Wicker of the *New York Times* suggested that the question implicit in Kennedy's remarks was, "How the country would react to the man of Chappaquiddick leading an impeachment battle against the man of Watergate."

Unlike other politicians, Senator Kennedy did not believe the Watergate scandal had expanded the problem of Chappaquiddick. Polls were reporting Kennedy the first choice for the 1976 nomination by a majority of Democrats, including Joseph and Gwen Kopechne. They harbored "no bitterness" toward Senator Kennedy about the accident. "We have only pleasant feelings for him. We wish him well," Joseph Kopechne said. While some aspects of the Chappaquiddick investigation could have been handled better, "It's all over now. These shocking, terrible accidents do happen," Kopechne said. No purpose would be accomplished by raising the issue again.

———

Kennedy felt confident enough about the matter to return to Edgartown on January 19, 1973, to hold three days of meetings to hear local opinion about legislation he'd proposed to establish a national park of shorelands, including Chappaquiddick. Arena assigned a detail to protect the Senator, "Not on account of Chappaquiddick but because we thought they were going to hang him. The national park proposal was a very unpopular idea." Under the Kennedy plan, half of the island's land area would be removed from the control of local officials. Kennedy had observed the ineffectiveness of local zoning boards "in serving as a barrier to the almighty developer." Kennedy clashed with his friend and biggest supporter, Robert Carroll, co-chairman of the "Islands Action Committee" opposed to the bill.

———

With operatives spreading the word Ted Kennedy was "definitely running," for President in 1976, a climate of gloom was enveloping those in the Democratic Party who believed the stain of Chappaquiddick would defeat Kennedy in a general election.

Appearing on "Face The Nation" on March 14, 1974, Kennedy denied the incident would have any bearing on his political future. "There's a full response and the inquest has been made public," he said. "And I would expect that people are going to have to make a judgment out of it, and I'm prepared to go to the people, were I a candidate, and be judged."

Kennedy supporters were convinced "Watergate had obscured public memory of Chappaquiddick, and that the ghost of Miss Kopechne will not again be raised in a serious way." With Kennedy's candidacy all but declared, the fifth anniversary of Chappaquiddick brought a flood of retrospectives about the accident. The most devastating was a replication of the case as "a multilayered, complex mystery that remains as baffling today as it was five years ago," by Robert Sherrill, Washington correspondent for the *Nation*. Sherrill provided "a case study of how a famous politician—by delays, by obfuscation, by propaganda, by all kinds of tricks and wiles—can kill somebody under mysterious circumstances and still regularly receive more than 40% of the support in presidential preference polls."

On July 30, 1974, three articles of impeachment voted by the House Judiciary Committee charged President Nixon with having obstructed and impeded the administration of justice in order to cover up unlawful activities, withheld material evidence and information and caused false and misleading statements to be made to lawfully authorized investigative officers and judicial proceedings—charges critics had unofficially made about Chappaquiddick. Cries were again heard for the same kind of disclosures about the accident from Kennedy as were being demanded of Nixon about Watergate.

There was no chance of the Chappaquiddick case being reopened and given a Watergate-style going over, Massachusetts Attorney General Robert Quinn said. Kennedy's press secretary pointed out 125 to 200 of the nation's best reporters had looked into Chappaquiddick "and have found nothing beyond the record."

But a symbolic connection between the two scandals was forged after Nixon resigned, on August 8, and retained Herbert "Jack" Miller as his criminal attorney. Miller had played a key role in defending Ted Kennedy in the Chappaquiddick case. Now he was employed to perform the same task for the fallen president.

And that Miller did brilliantly. After conferring with Nixon at the compound in San Clemente, Miller met with special prosecutor Leon Jaworski. Should evidence of an investigation point to criminal conduct, an indictment would be sought against the former president on the likely charge of conspiracy to obstruct justice.

In a memorandum of law he submitted to Jaworski, Miller echoed Edward Hanify's brief on Senator Kennedy's appeal before the Massachusetts Supreme Judicial Court, arguing that "intense publicity" about Watergate made it "inconceivable that a jury free from actual bias" could be found. Nixon's constitutional rights of due process would be seriously threatened by prosecution. Like Hanify, Miller cited the Sheppard murder case as an example, "Where pretrial publicity had subverted a fair trial." Two days of intense negotiations produced an agreement for the turnover of White House tapes and other documents to the General Services Administration in exchange for a full presidential pardon.

Secure in the knowledge his own cover-up was of a more enduring nature, Kennedy scorned the "preferential judicial treatment" his former attorney had negotiated on Nixon's behalf. "Do we operate under a system of equal justice under the law, or is there one system of justice for the average citizen and another for the high and mighty?" Kennedy thundered in the Senate. But his moral posture had been made crooked by Chappaquiddick. Kennedy denied any relationship between the two episodes. "I think there may be some people who draw that kind of parallel but, of course, Chappaquiddick is an entirely different situation," he said. "Watergate was an attempt to corrupt the political processes and to violate basic constitutional rights and liberties of individuals in a premeditated and deliberate way. The other was a tragic accident."

Chapter 56

MARY JO KOPECHNE WAS NOT THE ONLY CASUALTY OF THAT
"tragic accident." To some, Chappaquiddick had a decisive impact on
the Nixon presidency, too. First, there was, in the Nixon White House,
euphoria at the prospect of not having to face Kennedy for re-election.
But that euphoria had hardened into an atmosphere of spite and ven-
detta, Dan Rather observed in the *Palace Guard*. "It may be said that
Chappaquiddick helped unleash the forces that in time would make a
wreckage of Richard Nixon's presidency."

It also made a wreckage of Kennedy's presidential hopes. His second
chance at the White House since Chappaquiddick was swamped in the
wake of Watergate. Citing "family responsibilities," Kennedy announced
on September 23, 1974, his "firm, final and unconditional" decision not
to seek the presidency in 1976. Kennedy denied Chappaquiddick was
what drove him from running. He said, "I can live with my testimony."

The trouble was, few others could. Had Kennedy sought the nomination, "His most obvious problem is Chappaquiddick and the still unexplained discrepancies between his story and what seems to be

indisputable facts," *McCall's* observed in November 1974. Chappaquid-dick would have neutralized Watergate as a Democratic attack weapon. The lingering doubts about the accident had threatened a bitter, nasty, mud-slinging campaign. Already battle lines were being drawn. Bumper stickers had appeared to proclaim: Nobody Drowned at Watergate.

In anticipation of a Kennedy candidacy in 1976, the *Boston Globe* had undertaken an ambitious reinvestigation of the accident over the summer of 1974. "We are not out to drive Ted Kennedy from office," editor Tom Winship explained. "We are trying to get more details on an important story affecting a public figure who will continue to be important."

Senator Kennedy granted a two-hour interview to a team of investigative reporters to discuss the accident for the first time since the inquest. He continued to insist his version of the accident was accurate. The widespread skepticism about his inquest testimony was "unwarranted and unjustified," he said. "I attempted during the course of the inquest to respond to these questions completely, candidly, honestly and to the best of my ability." His conduct had been "irrational and indefensible and inexcusable and inexplicable," he said. "I was, at that time, obsessed by grief at the loss of a life. It was strictly a state of mind." But Kennedy cleared up none of the contradictions involved in the accident or "the nearly 100 discrepancies in the testimony and statements by several key inquest witnesses. Preferential treatment by law enforcement and judicial officials had saved Kennedy from being charged with serious crimes, including manslaughter, the *Globe* concluded in its four-part series. Routine investigative and judicial procedures had been either altered or botched numerous times by apprehensive officials in overwhelming deference to Kennedy's power and prestige. "Justice was not served, hard questions were not asked of witnesses and complaints and indictments not pursued."

Kennedy protested the *Globe's* use of unnamed sources to give prominence to charges that were "ugly, untrue, and grossly unfair," he said. "It is regrettable in the atmosphere of doubt and suspicion which enshrouds us as a people that the truth cannot compete with the unnamed source, the groundless suggestion and speculation which is nurtured by articles of sensationalism."

The facts, as Kennedy related them, "Are harsh, complete and cold on their own and no alteration of them to satisfy new suspicions could relieve me from the remorse and regret of which they constantly remind me." Kennedy attributed renewed interest in the accident to "a post-Watergate mentality," rather than any questions about the accident. "The problem is, they haven't been answered the way the writers would like to have them answered," he said. "The real story has been told. They're not going to find other kinds of facts, because they just don't exist."

———

The unanswered questions about Chappaquiddick had left Gwen Kopechne angry and frustrated. "Sometimes I'd like to scream a lot, but I'm trying to hold it back," she said. "It would be nice if somebody would speak up." Senator Kennedy had called her about the *Globe* articles. "He was worried that I might read some of it and become upset."

The Kopechnes came to Edgartown in June 1975, to seek answers to the case for themselves. Crossing on the ferry to Chappaquiddick, Gwen Kopechne pointed out the public telephone in the ferryhouse at the landing. Joseph Kopechne said, "I was rather afraid what her reaction would be when we went up to Dike Bridge. In fact, she reminded me of what part of the bridge the car went over—I had clean forgotten."

Among those they tracked down was "Huck" Look. Resigned to having his story questioned, Look said, "It just becomes, as I told everybody, a thing of credibility. If you want to believe him, fine. If you want to believe me, I've got nothing to gain in any way, shape, or form." (Evidently, Edgartown believed Look. They'd elected him sheriff.)

Look would "never live long enough" to believe he hadn't seen Ted Kennedy's car going down Dike Road an hour and a half after the Senator said the car went off Dike Bridge. "He's so sure of what he saw that it makes me think better about what really might have happened," Joseph Kopechne said. "It looks to me like there's a lot of unanswered questions now that I look at it objectively. The Senator gave me the story. I believed it, it's possible," Mrs. Kopechne said. "But at the same time I didn't have any questions to ask him. I was only listening to anybody that was saying anything to me. Now, I think I would give a little argument. Now, I'd have something to say."

The Kopechnes hesitated before entering the Turf 'n' Tackle shop to talk to John Farrar. "After all the inconsistencies and evasions," Farrar was "more convinced than ever the truth had not come out." Mary Jo Kopechne could have been saved if rescue personnel and equipment had been immediately called to the accident scene, he said. "I know she suffocated when her oxygen ran out. She didn't drown."

"I felt that boy is experienced enough so that he can make those statements. He convinced me real good," Mrs. Kopechne told Gerald Kelley, a local freelance journalist. She added: "No matter how you look at it, it was an accident. What hurts me deep is to think that my daughter had to be left there all night. This is why we hold so bitter a feeling towards Markham and Gargan ...I think Kennedy made his statement when he was still confused. In the state he was in, I do believe he couldn't think clearly. I think he was taking all this bad advice, and it just continued for days. He got so deeply involved in it, he couldn't back out and tell the truth. How is he going to change his story and get out of it? Now, he's in worse trouble than he would have been if he had come out and given the story himself without anybody advising him."

Mrs. Kopechne wanted to talk to someone who had attended the party at Chappaquiddick. "I'd like to know what went on, what they were doing, what led up to Mary Jo leaving, and what happened afterward," she said. "I'm still waiting for something to happen. If you wait long enough you get what you're waiting for. That one day, I'll know everything I want to know. I don't want to hurt anybody. I think even the Senator has got enough problems."

The Kopechnes stayed at the Katama Shores motel where their daughter had been lodged during the regatta weekend. The bathroom wallpaper had fish floating through clouds of seaweed, Mrs. Kopechne said. Her daughter's death was with her "every time I entered that bathroom last night. It is with me every time I take a bath."

Chappaquiddick continued to hurt the Senator politically, but it did not affect his re-election to the Senate in 1976. A request for security personnel made through the State Police got Bernie Flynn assigned as Senator Kennedy's bodyguard for a campaign fund-raising party at Padanaram, a suburb of New Bedford. Told to mingle inconspicuously with guests, Flynn engaged Jack Crimmins in conversation and disclosed he'd been an investigator for the district attorney's office on the Chappaquiddick case. "I'm the guy that helped the Senator out," Flynn said. "I'm the one that told Stephen Smith about inquest evidence."

Flynn observed Crimmins in conversation with Senator Kennedy a short time later. "He was standing like ten feet away. I just happened to turn around at the right moment to catch Crimmins whispering in his ear. Kennedy was looking right at me with this startled look on his face, so I guess Crimmins told him who I was."

After the political affair, Kennedy invited Flynn to a private steak and lobster dinner in Plymouth hosted by Jack Campbell, a long-time supporter and owner of radio station WPLM. Campbell memorialized the occasion by taking photographs. Flynn wanted to have his picture taken with the Senator. Kennedy was happy to oblige his Chappaquiddick benefactor.

———

Kennedy won re-election, but the beneficiary of Watergate was Jimmy Carter. Outraged that a restoration should have been usurped by a political upstart from Georgia, Kennedy supporters revived rumors of a possible candidacy in 1980.

Returning to Edgartown again in 1978, the Kopechnes threatened to go on national television and "ruin Kennedy" if he tried to run for president. But by 1979, they had changed their mind. They still "didn't know the full story of the accident," but saw no reason to bring everything up again. Gwen Kopechne said, "Everyone makes mistakes. If he runs, we won't interfere."

Kennedy telephoned the Kopechnes to express regret for another avalanche of publicity as the tenth anniversary of Chappaquiddick approached. In fact, much of the publicity could have been avoided had Kennedy himself not granted numerous interviews, motivated by a desire to put the issue to rest before the campaign. Kennedy was now inviting reporters to ask him any questions they wanted about Chappaquiddick, "Because I will answer them, as I have answered them in the past."

The answers "seemed almost memorized," the *Washington Post* complained. An interview with the Senator about Chappaquiddick was "a distinctly unenlightening exercise, frequently punctuated by denials before the questions are complete. Sometimes Kennedy tries to fob off questions by alluding to what he said at the inquest. Occasionally he has to be reminded that he was never asked the question."

On the eve of the tenth anniversary of the accident, the Senator
called the long-promised press conference to answer questions about the
accident the inquest had left unanswered. "Many of the actions that I
was involved in on that night were irresponsible," Kennedy said. But he
did not believe Chappaquiddick posed the kind of tests he had met for
17 years in the Senate and would face as president. Kennedy had confronted issues of war and peace in public life since the accident, "And I
felt no hesitancy about involving myself in them, and taking stands on
many of them."

Kennedy hadn't been asked "a new question" about Chappaquiddick in ten years, he said. "There hasn't been a new fact that has questioned the position that I stated at the time of the tragedy and there
cannot be." No information would ever challenge his sworn testimony,
"Because it doesn't exist."

Chief Arena shared that view. In the ten years since the accident,
"No one has ever found anything to support more than what I initially
charged him with."

Still, one question continued to intrigue Arena: What had gone on
from the time of the accident and Kennedy's report the next morning?
"Expanding on it might lead to something that is beneficial to him, or
it might not," he said. Arena wasn't sure he could vote for Kennedy if
he ran for president. "I certainly couldn't wipe Chappaquiddick out of
my mind." If Kennedy was a candidate, an investigation should be
reopened and every facet of the accident reexamined, Arena said. "I still
think the whole case deserves scrutiny."

Senator Kennedy had "cooperated fully and completely" with all of
the law enforcement agencies involved, his press secretary replied, "What
does Chief Arena want to be done?"

But Arena's doubts about a presidential candidacy were shared by
others. "I don't think anybody can forget Chappaquiddick," Republican
Congresswoman Millicent Fenwick told *McCall's*. Asked if there was

any other issue besides Chappaquiddick that would defeat Senator Kennedy if he ran for president, Republican candidate Ronald Reagan replied, "Well, you mentioned one pretty good one."

Historian and former White House adviser Arthur Schlesinger, Jr., doubted Chappaquiddick would be a decisive factor in a presidential campaign. Ever since the accident Kennedy had been trying to redeem himself for those hours of panic. "He has become ever more serious, more senatorial, more devoted to the public good," Schlesinger said. "I think this ceaseless effort at self-redemption may be for Teddy Kennedy what polio was for FDR."

By June 1979, Kennedy was leading President Carter better than 2 to 1 in public opinion polls. Twice as many Democrats had "unfavorable" ratings for the President as for Ted Kennedy. All signs were pointing to Kennedy "positioning" himself for the run.

But Kennedy was adamant: He was not running, he said. "As I've said many times, I expect the President to be renominated. And I expect to support him."

Carter dismissed opinion polls as an accurate gauge of presidential popularity. "We've had some crises where it required a steady hand, a careful and deliberate decision to be made," he said. "I don't think I panicked in the crises,"—an observation regarded as a "coded reference" to the Senator's failure to report his accident for ten hours.

Kennedy did not expect Carter to bring up Chappaquiddick in the election, should he decide to seek the nomination, he said. "I think the President wants to talk about issues that are important to the country."

But the Senator got a foretaste of what he could expect as a presidential candidate at a political rally in Louisville, confronted by placards bearing Mary Jo Kopechne's name, and the effigy of a female corpse. In the face of continued questions about Chappaquiddick, Kennedy said, "People may not believe me or accept some of my answers, but the idea that the people who were there that night are holding back some secret is just all wrong." Repeated efforts by the *New York Times* to persuade Kennedy's friends to discuss the period after the accident were fruitless. "They refused, as they have for ten years to clarify the sequence of events on a night still cloaked in mystery."

Kennedy denied forbidding anyone to talk to the press. "Some have chosen to engage in interviews and conversation, others have not," he said. "I left that completely up to their discretion." However, Kennedy still had "a lawyer-client relationship with those who had given him legal advice after the accident." He did not want Joe Gargan or Paul Markham talking to reporters. On "Meet the Press," he continued to insist, "There is not going to be any new information that is going to challenge my testimony." If there was, "There would be absolutely no reason that I should consider remaining in public office, let alone run for the Presidency of the United States."

Chappaquiddick had not figured at all in Kennedy's decision to seek the nomination, Stephen Smith reported. "The only major negative as always, was the assassination fear. But the judgment of everyone in the end was that you can't let that rule your life forever." Kennedy had made known, "His family was ready—if he was."

Chapter 57

BUT KENNEDY WAS APPARENTLY NOT SO READY AS HE THOUGHT.
On September 29, 1979, Roger Mudd of CBS News arrived in Hyannis
Port to conduct an interview. Mudd tossed out a question he expected
the Senator to hit out of the ball park: "Do you think, Senator, that
anybody really will ever fully believe your explanation of Chappaquiddick?"

Kennedy struck out. He had found his behavior "beyond belief"
himself, he said. Aired as part of a one-hour documentary special, Mudd
devoted half the broadcast to the accident, asked Kennedy about other
women in his life and characterized his marriage as "existing only on
select occasions."

In an atmosphere of euphoria and great expectations, Kennedy
formally announced his candidacy on November 7 at Faneuil Hall. But
the promise of that candidacy, heralded since 1968, proved to be more
seductive than the candidacy itself. Kennedy's campaign disintegrated a
month later. Chappaquiddick was partly responsible for the dramatic
plunge in Kennedy's popularity in opinion polls. "Doubts about the

propriety of Kennedy's behavior at Chappaquiddick have risen significantly" in the six months since polls the previous spring showed most Americans "willing to forgive and forget" the incident.

Kennedy was having trouble attracting support from politically active women. Feminist Betty Friedan "still felt queasy" about Chappaquiddick, she said.

By the following January, Kennedy's advisers were preoccupied with the impact Chappaquiddick was having on the campaign. The issue had been seriously misjudged. Kennedy had allowed himself to be misled by pollsters, friends and advisers into believing Chappaquiddick had faded as a potential source of trouble. Campaign manager Stephen Smith called a press conference to refute a *Washington Star* report questioning Kennedy's claim to have "nearly drowned" swimming the channel after the accident. Hitherto undiscovered evidence relating to tides and topography placed a crucial element of his story in doubt. Aerial photographs taken on May 15, 1969, had revealed the Katama opening had sealed off, making Chappaquiddick not an island separate from Edgartown. A rising tide no longer flowed out of the harbor but in a reverse direction from that which Kennedy described in his inquest testimony.

To challenge the story, Smith brought two admiralty lawyers and an ocean engineer to the press conference, the same team of experts that accompanied Kennedy to a second conference the next day. Kennedy characterized the articles as "inaccurate, irresponsible and incomplete," and charged the newspaper had misrepresented what it had been told by tidal experts.

Edgartown Harbormaster Robert Morgan speculated, "The tide that night could not have been other than what Mr. Kennedy testified." Morgan had taken a sailboat under tow to a pier close to the ferry landing shortly before midnight on July 18, he said. "The tide was low and quite slack, not moving in either direction," a condition that meant within the next 30 minutes to an hour, the tide would be running strongly out of the harbor.

———

The integrity of the entire Edgartown community was being seriously questioned by a barrage of national press stories about the accident, the *Vineyard Gazette* complained. When the *New York Times* questioned editorially whether Senator Kennedy had used "his enormous influence to protect himself and his career by leading a coverup of misconduct," readers would be led to believe investigative and prosecution officials on Martha's Vineyard had been negligent, inept or "subjected to influence," the *Gazette* observed. "The clearly-documented facts are that the tragedy was investigated by honest, competent police officers before it became known Kennedy was the driver of the car, and no basis was found for a complaint of speeding or reckless driving." The conduct of the entire case by Judge Boyle was "legally precise and impartial. One will go far in legal annals to find an abler judicial exercise."

Denouncing an article in *Reader's Digest* as "a very serious misrepresentation" of the operation of the automobile before the accident, Stephen Smith pointed out Senator Kennedy's rate of speed had been "officially accepted" by a Registry of Motor Vehicles investigation.

An accident analyst hired by the *Digest* to recreate conditions by computer revealed Kennedy had been driving on the wrong side of Dike Road, going approximately 34 miles per hour at the time of the accident. Kennedy had slammed on the brakes when he saw the bridge, skidded 17 feet along the road, another 25 feet up the bridge, and jumped the rub rail. Despite his braking effort the car had been travelling between 20 to 22 miles an hour when it hurtled 35 feet over Poucha Pond. That the Registry of Motor Vehicles had refused to release to the *Digest* a copy of its report of the accident "without written notarized authorization from Senator

Kennedy himself," came as a surprise to Ronald Andrews, a private investigator specializing in laws pertaining to public records. He said, "I knew that according to Massachusetts law, anyone was able to gain access to the report." Andrews' request for a copy of the report was refused, because the document was protected "under The Fair Information Practices Act." (Registry counsel Rico Matera explained later, "The invasion of personal privacy in many instances outweighs the public's right to know, for the pertinent facts in this case have been spewed out to the public by the news media for many, many years. ") Andrews appealed to the supervisor of public records of the department of the Secretary of State. Registrar McLaughlin was informed that a fatal accident report was not exempt from disclosure exceptions and directed him to provide Andrews a copy of the report.

Most interested to discover that Senator Kennedy's license had been thought for a time to have expired, Andrews turned the report over to Ralph Gordon, a veteran court reporter for the Springfield newspapers bureau in Greenfield, Massachusetts.

Gordon started checking out the story. Registry Inspector John Mellino told him, "I never liked all this cover-up stuff going on." Mellino dismissed the idea a license renewal could be left in the Tab Room for five months. Inspector Herb Burr couldn't explain the delay either, he said. "I have nothing to say about that."

Gordon was surprised to receive a call from Registrar McLaughlin himself. "I understand you've been talking to some of my men about Chappaquiddick," he said. McLaughlin had the Chappaquiddick file in front of him, he said. The Registry was the only agency "that went straight down the line on the case." Kennedy's license had been revoked on July 20, 1969, and surrendered to him personally by his lawyer, Judge Robert Clark.

Asked to explain the five-month delay in Kennedy's renewal card being replaced in the Registry's files, McLaughlin grew impatient. "You're insinuating something that doesn't exist and ascribing it to the 11-year-old memory of an inexperienced man working in the radio room." When Gordon emphasized he was reading from Inspector George Kennedy's report, McLaughlin hung up. His office was "not accepting any calls from you," Gordon was told when he tried to reach the Registrar again.

Gordon wrote the story and sent it to Springfield. "Beyond that, I didn't hear a thing, until I realized they weren't going to print it," Gordon recalled. "I finally called to ask why. They didn't question the story. The response was: 'Well, we just thought there had been enough on Chappaquiddick.' They were supporting Kennedy and decided, as a political thing, not to use it."

But Kennedy's campaign was haunted by Chappaquiddick. Spectators in Chicago spit on the candidate and called him "killer" as he went down State Street in a parade. A retired doctor carried a sign: "Do You Want the Coward of Chappaquiddick for President?" outside a senior citizen center Kennedy visited. Kara Kennedy, the Senator's 19-year-old daughter was told, "Your father killed a young girl about your age." "Negative feelings toward Kennedy are growing each month," the *Washington Post* reported in March. Nearly half the Democrats nationwide had "unfavorable views" of him, reversing polls conducted in November. The issue of the campaign had devolved upon the central mystery of Chappaquiddick and the death of Mary Jo Kopechne. "Last year, Kennedy decided he could be invulnerable even to this. He was wrong. Voters have not forgiven that he got away with it in 1969 and thought he could get away with it again in 1980."

Bernie Flynn—the man who bent the rules to aid Kennedy at the inquest had also had a change of heart about the Senator. "When

Kennedy ran against Carter and he was screeching and yelling, I said to myself: 'Christ! This man doesn't deserve to be President.' I lost a lot of esteem for him."

Flynn had had no contact with the Senator since his security duty in 1976, and none whatever with Stephen Smith or Herbert Miller since their meeting at Logan airport a week before the inquest. Flynn had not found it necessary to cash in his job insurance policy. "If I was ambitious—and they were deciding on two different occasions to make U.S. Marshalls—I would have called up Stephen Smith to say, 'Now it's your turn to do me a favor,'" he said. "But it didn't cross my mind to see how far Kennedy would reciprocate." After 32 years in law enforcement, Flynn had had enough. He retired from the state police in 1980.

Stricken with cancer, George Killen had retired in 1975. Two months before his death in 1979, Killen was still lamenting Chappaquiddick as "the biggest mistake I ever made as a police officer." With the benefit of hindsight, Killen had dispensed with alternative theories and improbable scenarios to conclude Senator Kennedy had been drunk, in flight from "Huck" Look to avoid arrest and probably speeding at the time of the accident—his recklessness responsible for the death of Mary Jo Kopechne.

Chappaquiddick was equally fatal to Kennedy's presidential aspirations in 1980. The Senator made a spectacular appearance at the Democratic national convention on August 12 in a moment of defeat unprecedented for his family, to declare, "The dream shall never die." But his campaign had been a long struggle to overcome the stigma of Chappaquiddick. "The Senator told interviewer after interviewer that there was nothing new to say about the accident. Neither the public nor the press was persuaded," the *New York Times* said.

In his pursuit of the presidential nomination, Kennedy had run against Chappaquiddick. And Chappaquiddick had won.

So decisive a defeat was regarded merely as a "rehearsal" for 1984 by some of Kennedy's supporters. Conventional political wisdom held that Kennedy would not again have to face the specter of the accident. "A personal issue that's a problem in one campaign doesn't come back in the next," ran the argument.

By July 1982, polls were reporting Kennedy the leading candidate for the presidential nomination in 1984. Seeking Senate re-election in Massachusetts against a millionaire business man, Ray Shamie, hardly necessitated the expenditure of $2.5 million—three times what Kennedy had spent in 1976. Kennedy hoped to use the 1982 election as a "laboratory" to test ways to defuse the Chappaquiddick issue that had disabled his 1980 presidential campaign, "So this is partly a test run for the 1984 presidential sweepstakes," the *Wall Street Journal* predicted, "and to salvage some of the fabled political pride of the Kennedys."

But door-to-door polling revealed the "character issue" a bigger factor than in 1976. Kennedy launched a television advertising campaign created by a California media consultant which concentrated on his "compassionate side."

He needed just such image-burnishing: A 40-page comic book sent to two million Massachusetts households by Citizens Organized to Replace Kennedy portrayed him as a chubby black sheep, and zeroed in on his history of cheating at Harvard, Virginia traffic violations and Chappaquiddick. Kennedy's press secretary denounced the publication as, "The lowest level of propaganda. I find it appalling and hateful."

"The funny thing about it was, it's all true," Gargan said. Working on the campaign as usual, Gargan was taken to task "for sitting on your ass all winter doing nothing," by Ted Kennedy. Having joined Alcoholics Anonymous, involved in a courageous struggle to put his life back together, Gargan exploded. "I've given you 30 years of my life and what do I have to show for it? I'm a fool in the eyes of my own children because of Chappaquiddick. And that's *your* problem, not mine." One day, Gargan wanted the "real story" of the accident to be told.

Gargan stormed out of the campaign and resisted all overtures to return. A fixture for years as advance man, Gargan's absence was too conspicuous not be accounted for. Kennedy's office explained the Senator's "gradual *drift* from close friends such as cousin Joe Gargan with whom he has clashed on the sensitive issue of abortion."

———

Despite the huge expenditure of campaign money, Kennedy ran less well than in 1976. The outlook for a presidential candidacy was not as promising as his advisers hoped. Exit polls of the 1.2 million who voted for him indicated over half wouldn't support him for president. If Kennedy believed "some kind of a magical TV spot" could neutralize Chappaquiddick and the kind of sustained barrage about it he would face in another presidential campaign he was mistaken. Polls conducted in New Hampshire, exposed to the "character ads" on Boston television, indicated they had failed to reduce the hostility felt by a large number of voters. The idea that Chappaquiddick would fade over time had not proven to be true. Kennedy was in the strongest position of any candidate to gain the 1984 nomination, "But given the negative feelings about him, he would be pursuing a smaller pool of voters." He could win, "But it would be another long season of personal harangues and lurid press for him." One adviser suggested outgrowing Chappaquiddick by 1988 and the years beyond, when voters might treat a man in his late 50s "more kindly for the indiscretions of his 30s."

Citing family responsibilities and his decision to divorce his wife, Kennedy announced he wouldn't be a candidate or accept a draft for the nomination in 1984. He didn't rule out a future presidential campaign. "I don't think it's any mystery that I would like to be President," he said. Kennedy denied he had withdrawn because of public doubts about his character stemming mostly from Chappaquiddick. But an aide confirmed the Senator had feared "the impact on his children of another round of accusations and inquires about his role in the death of Mary Jo Kopechne."

For the first time in twenty-four years, a Kennedy was not a figure to be reckoned with at a Democratic national convention. Disappointed not to have been chosen as keynote speaker, Kennedy made a "gasbag of a speech," and appeared "incapable of seriousness" on the rostrum, laughing out loud at the traditional words of nomination.

Events would prove Kennedy lucky to have withdrawn from presidential contention early. In August 1983, Robert Kennedy, Jr., was arrested for possession of a gram of heroin. Revelations of drug use by a younger generation of Kennedys culminated in April 1984 in the death of David Kennedy from an overdose of cocaine, prescription pain killers and tranquilizers at a hotel in Palm Beach.

Senator Kennedy telephoned authorities to request the body of his nephew be removed so the investigation could be conducted in a less public setting. But this was Florida, not Massachusetts. Efforts to suppress information about the case didn't work. A court suit filed by a trio of newspapers sprung impounded records that revealed Caroline Kennedy to have visited the hotel 90 minutes before the body was discovered. Traces of drugs found in the room's toilet suggested efforts had been made to dispose of incriminating evidence—a "pure assumption," Herbert Miller said. Miller, the "shadow" counsellor of Chappaquiddick, was identified as a "Washington lawyer who represented the Kennedy family." A Miller-prepared statement over Caroline Kennedy's name denying she had entered the hotel room was released through Senator Kennedy's Washington office.

Kennedy kept a low profile until after the elections.

In December 1984, Kennedy made a highly publicized trip to Ethiopia to investigate famine conditions; then to South Africa on a fact-finding mission to study the racial problems of apartheid.

Accused of interfering in South Africa's internal affairs and exploiting a campaign-style barnstorming tour to launch his candidacy for the presidency in 1988, the *Financial Times* put Kennedy on its cover with the headline: "He's Teaching Us Morals?" An editorial inside, recalled the accident at Chappaquiddick in which a young woman had died in his car.

Kennedy was "seriously considering" running for President, an aide confirmed. "He's going to make a decision some time in the second half of 1985." Kennedy had made it clear, "I want very much to be President. I know I can make a difference."

By July 1985, Kennedy was leading all presidential preference polls. He "still must overcome the 16-year shadow of Chappaquiddick," but it was thought he had turned his "negatives" around. The character issue would rise again, but the "saliency" of Chappaquiddick had diminished since 1979 in the view of advisers. The Senator had reached a point, "Where enough people will take a look at him on the basis of his record and values to elect him," the *New Republic* reported. Kennedy's staff had been instructed "to assume there will be a presidential campaign and prepare for it."

But a *Boston Globe* survey of Democratic state chairmen offered little encouragement to a Kennedy candidacy. One chairman observed, "The Chappaquiddick situation will just kill him as far as ever being elected president. You just hear it on the street. People still remember."

Any mention of a Kennedy candidacy was sufficient to evoke the issue. Despite his lead in the polls, a Kennedy candidacy would be suicidal. Kennedy could expect "some guy in a frogman outfit carrying a sign" at every political rally. Opponents needed only to point out, "They were too high-minded to raise the Chappaquiddick issue, central to the judgment of a man's character though it may be," to devastate his candidacy. For the first time, Kennedy would have to give up his Senate seat to seek the presidency. A loss would mean oblivion.

On December 19, 1985, Kennedy produced a video, and purchased time on two Boston television stations to announce his intention not to run for president in 1988. A grave Kennedy addressed the camera in a manner reminiscent of his Chappaquiddick speech to announce, "I know that this decision means that I may never be president. But the pursuit of the presidency is not my life. Public service is."

For sixteen years, the ghost of Chappaquiddick had hovered over his career, resisting all efforts to persuade the public that the real story had been told. Lodged in the nation's memory, the legacy of Chappaquiddick had concretized into a monument beneath which Kennedy was burying his presidential hopes. No historian, but a poet could inscribe the epitaph for the death of the Kennedy dream:

> Chappaquiddick, Chappaquiddick
> Your syllables echo the sea
> Your rhythm caught the vulnerable note—
> Shattered the walls of a dynasty.

E65L-325M-TR13-2-69-948878

MUST TYPE OR PRINT

COMMONWEALTH OF MASSACHUSETTS
POLICE REPORT
OF MOTOR VEHICLE ACCIDENT

SEND ONE COPY TO:
REGISTRAR OF MOTOR VEHICLES
100 NASHUA STREET
BOSTON, MASS. 02114

POLICE DEPT. SUBMITTING REPORT
EDGARTOWN

REGISTRY USE ONLY

2-7

8-10

11-15 Date of Accident	16	Day of the Week							17 Hour	
Mo.	Day	Yr.	S 1	M 2	T 3	W 4	T 5	F 6	S 7	A.M. ☒ X / P.M. ☐ Y	12-1
7	19	69									

18 Did you notice any indication that an operator was under medication or had been using drugs? (explain on reverse) — Check one — YES 1 ☐ / NO 2 ☒

To your knowledge has any operator had a history of epilepsy, heart disease, fainting spells? (explain on reverse) — YES 3 ☐ / NO 4 ☒

19 Was this Accident investigated by an Officer? If Yes, Check One Box Below
1 ☒ Registry   4 ☐ State Police
2 ☐ MDC   5 ☒ Local Police
3 ☐ Other

VEHICLE 1

Name of Operator: KENNEDY, Edward M.

20 Number of Vehicles Involved: 1

21-26 Date of Birth: MO. 2 DAY 22 YR. 32

27 Sex: 1 ☒ M 2 ☐ F

Street Address: 3 Charles St., Boston, Mass.   City/Town   State

28-29 License Number and State: 040221W Mass.

Owners Name and Address (if same, write "same"): Same, Room 2400, JFK Bldg. Government Center, Boston, Mass.

Registration Number & State: L78-207 Mass.

Describe Damage to Vehicle: Front windshield smashed, dent in roof and on hood

Approximate Cost to Repair $ Over $200

Parked Car YES ☐ NO ☒

VEHICLE 2

Name of Operator:

30-35 Date of Birth: MO. DAY YR.

36 Sex: 1 ☐ M 2 ☐ F

Street Address: City/Town   State

37-38 License Number and State:

Owners Name and Address (if same, write "same"):

Registration Number & State:

Describe Damage to Vehicle:

Approximate Cost to Repair $

Parked Car YES ☐ NO ☐

VEHICLE 3

Name of Operator:

21-26 Date of Birth: MO. DAY YR.

27 Sex: 1 ☐ M 2 ☐ F

Street Address: City/Town   State

28-29 License Number and State:

Owners Name and Address (if same, write "same"):

Registration Number & State:

Describe Damage to Vehicle:

Approximate Cost to Repair $

Parked Car YES ☐ NO ☐

OTHER

Describe Other Property Damage

COMMONWEALTH EXHIBIT
No. 1.
10/20/69 P.

Name of Property Owner   Address

Approximate Cost to Repair $

39 Number Injured.

INJURED 1

Name of Injured: KOPECHNE, Mary Jo   Street: 2912 Olive St. NW   City/Town: Washington, D.C.   State

40-1 Age: 28

42 Sex: 1 ☐ M 2 ☒ F

45 Severity — Mark First One That Applies:
Killed ☒ (1) | Visible signs of injury, as bleeding wound, or distorted member; or had to be carried from scene (1) | Other visible injury, as bruises, abrasions, swelling, limping, etc. (2) | No visible injury but complaints of pain or momentary unconsciousness (3) | No visible injury (4)

43 Check if wearing Seat Belt 1 ☐

44 Check if Wearing Helmet 1 ☐

46 Person Injured:
1 ☐ Operator } in vehicle
2 ☒ Passenger   No. 1
3 ☐ Passenger in train, bus, etc.
4 ☐ Operator } On Motorcycle
5 ☐ Passenger
6 ☐ Pedestrian
7 ☐ Bicyclist
8 ☐ Other

INJURED 2

Name of Injured: Street   City/Town   State

47-8 Age:

49 Sex: 1 ☐ M 2 ☐ F

52 Severity — Mark First One That Applies:
Killed ☐ | Visible signs of injury, as bleeding wound, or distorted member; or had to be carried from scene (1) | Other visible injury, as bruises, abrasions, swelling, limping, etc. (2) | No visible injury but complaints of pain or momentary unconsciousness (3) | No visible injury (4)

50 Check if wearing Seat Belt 1 ☐

51 Check if Wearing Helmet 1 ☐

53 Person Injured:
1 ☐ Operator } in vehicle
2 ☐ Passenger   No.
3 ☐ Passenger in train, bus, etc.
4 ☐ Operator } On Motorcycle
5 ☐ Passenger
6 ☐ Pedestrian
7 ☐ Bicyclist
8 ☐ Other

INJURED 3

Name of Injured: Street   City/Town   State

40-1 Age:

42 Sex: 1 ☐ M 2 ☐ F

45 Severity — Mark First One That Applies:
Killed ☐ | Visible signs of injury, as bleeding wound, or distorted member; or had to be carried from scene (1) | Other visible injury, as bruises, abrasions, swelling, limping, etc. (2) | No visible injury but complaints of pain or momentary unconsciousness (3) | No visible injury (4)

43 Check if wearing Seat Belt 1 ☐

44 Check if Wearing Helmet 1 ☐

46 Person Injured:
1 ☐ Operator } in vehicle
2 ☐ Passenger   No.
3 ☐ Passenger in train, bus, etc.
4 ☐ Operator } On Motorcycle
5 ☐ Passenger
6 ☐ Pedestrian
7 ☐ Bicyclist
8 ☐ Other

BE SURE TO COMPLETE AND SIGN REPORT ON REVERSE SIDE

Appendix 1 Edgartown police report of the accident by Chief Dominick J. Arena. *Courtesy Dominick Arena.*

NOTE: Mark all items which apply. The diagram and description of what happened (below) need not be completed if separate 8½ x 11 size sheet with same detailed information is attached. Please sign report in space provided below.

LOCATION

City or Town Where Accident Occurred	Nearest Mile Marker	Reserved for Registry
Edgartown		

Street Name or Route Number

Dike Road

☐ at intersection with ___ N. S. E. W. Of nearest intersection,
or ___ feet ☐☐☐☐ bridge, mile marker, railroad.

Which direction was each vehicle traveling?

Vehicle N. S. E. W. No. N. S. E. W. No. N. S. E. W.
No. 1 ☐☒☒☐ 2 ☐☐☐☐ 3 ☐☐☐☐

Other Landmarks: On bridge at Dike

64
1 ☐ On ramp from route
2 ☐ Off ramp from route
3 ☐ At rotary

55
1 ☐ Area built up
2 ☒ Area not built up

TYPE

56 Accident Involved Collision With:

1 ☐ Pedestrian   4 ☐ Railroad train   7 ☐ Overturned in road
2 ☐ Motor Vehicle in Traffic   5 ☐ Ran off roadway hit fixed object ___ feet from road   8 ☐ Ran off roadway — non-collision
3 ☐ Motor Vehicle Parked   6 ☐ Bicycle   9 ☐ Fixed object on shoulder, sidewalk or island
                                            A ☒ Other

57 If collision involved two or more vehicles mark one of the following:

1 ☐ Rear end   2 ☐ Angle   3 ☐ Head on

SITUATION

What were vehicles doing prior to accident? Mark appropriate box.

	Vehicle 58-60					Vehicle					Vehicle			
	1	2	3			1	2	3			1	2	3	
1				Making right turn	8				Skidding	F				Parked
2				Making left turn	9				Slowing or stopping	G				Stalled or disabled
3				Making U turn	A				Crossing median strip	H				Stalled or disabled with flasher on
4	X			Going straight ahead	B				Driverless moving vehicle	J				In process of parking
5				Passing on right	C				Backing	K				Entering or exiting from alley or driveway
6				Passing on left	D				Starting in traffic	L				Other
7				Stop sign	E				Starting from parked position					

Where was pedestrian located at time of accident? Mark appropriate box.

	x			x	
1		At intersection	7		Getting on/off vehicle
2		Within 300 feet of intersection	8		Working on vehicle
3		More than 300 feet from intersection	9		Working in street
4		Walking in street with traffic	A		Playing in street
5		Walking in street against traffic	B		Not in street
6		Standing in street	C		Other

CONDITIONS

62	Light Conditions	**63**		Traffic Controls			**64**	Weather Conditions	**65**	Road Conditions
	X		X			X		X		X
1	Daylight	1	Stop sign	6	Railroad crossing gate	1	X Clear	1	X Dry
2	Dawn or dusk	2	Yield sign	7	Railroad automatic signal	2	Foggy	2	Wet
3	Darkness — road lighted	3	Warning sign	8	Control device not working	3	Cloudy	3	Snowy
4	X Darkness — road unlighted	4	Signal light	9	X No control present	4	Rain	4	Icy
		5	Officer or flagman			5	Snow	5	Other
						6	Sleet		

COLLISION CONDITIONS

66

	X			X			X			X			X	
1		Entered median	4		Hit guard rail	7		Hit signpost	A		Embankment	D		Stone wall
2		Crossed median	5		Hit curbing	8		Hit utility or light pole	B		Ditch	E		Other post
3		Hit median barrier	6		Hit abutment	9		Hit tree	C		Rock ledge	F		Bridge rail

DIAGRAM

= REFER TO ATTACHED DIAGRAM =

INDICATE ON THIS DIAGRAM WHAT HAPPENED

Use one of these outlines to sketch the scene of your accident, writing in street or highway names or numbers.

1. Number each vehicle and show direction of travel by arrow:
2. Use solid line to show path before accident; dotted line after accident.
3. Show pedestrian by:
4. Show railroad by:
5. Show distance and direction to landmarks; identify landmarks by name or number.
6. Indicate north by arrow, as:

INDICATE NORTH BY ARROW

VIOLATIONS

Operator (mark one or more)				Operator				Operator				Operator			
	1	2	3	67-75	1	2	3		1	2	3		1	2	3	
1				Operating Under Influence	6				Improper Passing	B				Disregarded Traffic Light	G	X			Leaving Scene of Accident
2				Operating After Drinking	7				On Wrong Side of Road Not Overtaking	C				Disregarded Warning or Stop Signs	H				Other Moving Violations (explain below)
3				Exceeding Lawful Speed	8				Failed to Give Proper Signal	D				Disregarded Other Traffic Control	J				Operating to Endanger
4				Failed to Grant Right of Way to Other Vehicle	9				Improper Turning Movement	E				Improper Start from Parked Position	K				Failed to Stop for a School Bus
5				Failed to Grant Right of Way to Pedestrian	A				Operating Unregistered Uninsured Vehicle	F				Improper Parked Position	L				No Violation

Describe What Happened: (Refer to Vehicles by Number)

Citation Number if issued   1032015

Car #1 being operated East on Dike Road at unknown rate of speed - oper. stated he had taken wrong turn (refer to attached statement) and was operating on an unfamiliar road - this roadway is a dirt road approx. 2 car widths wide - Oper descended a bit on roadway and came to a narrow (10'6" wide) bridge which went off to the left from the roadway at about

Signature ___ Dominick J. Arena Chief, Edgartown PD ___ Date 7-21-69
Name and Rank   Department

a 25-30 degree angle. Car 1 was unable to stop upon entering the bridge and hit the small
runn ing rail (approx. 4"high x 10" wide) which ran along sides of the bridge. The car went
off the bridge and turned over landing in the water. There were no lights in the area of the
bridge, no guardx rails on the sides, no warning signals approaching the bridge. This bridge
is usually used for foot traffic. The operator stated that he was able to get out of the car
and then made return trips into the water in an attempt to rescue the girl passenger but was
unsuccessful. The operator stated that he had been in a state of shock and exhaustion after
the accident and when he fully realized what had happend came to the police station to report
same. At the station the invest. officer received the following statement from the operator:
"On July 18, at approx. 11:15 PM on Chappaquidick Island, Martha's Vineyard, I was driving
my car on Main St. on my way back to get the ferry to Edgartown. I was unfamiliar with the
road and turned right on Dike Road instead of bearing hard left on Main St. After proceeding
for approx. 1/2 mile on Dike Road I descended a hill and came upon a narrow bridge. The car
went off the side of the bridge. There was one passenger with me, one Miss Mary Jo Kopechne
a former secretary of my brother Robert Kennedy. The car turned over and sank into the water
and landd with the roof resting on the bottom. I attempted to open the door and window of the
car but have no recollection of how I got out of the car. I came to the surface and then
repeatedly dove down to the car in an attempt to see if the passenger was still in the car.
I was unsuccesful in the attempt. I was exhausted and in a state of shock. I recall walking
back to where my friends were eating. There was a car parked in front of the cottage and I
climbed in the back seat. I then asked for someone to bring me back to Edgartown. I remember
walking around for a period of time and then going back to my hotel room. When I fully realized
what had happened this morning I immediately went to the police." /
~~IroxthexxiddidityxoxthexoxxxiexxxrxinxxryxofxdyxthxxSxxxxxRxxxxExdgxrtxxxxxxxxxxxxxxxxxhxxxdxx~~
~~xxxxxxxxxxxxxxxxxd~~ Chief Arena first received word of the accident at approx. 8:20 AM when
a call from a Mrs. Sylvia Malm was made to the Edgartown Police Station concerning xxx dxxxxx a
report received by her at her home from 2 boys who had been fishing on the Dike Road Brdige
that they had spotted a car in the water upside down. The invest. officer arrived at the scene
and upon observing the car for the first time found it almost completely submerged, part of
the left rear tire was above water - the invest officer entered the water and swam to the car
but because of the strong tide each time he went under he was unable to dtermine whether or
not anyone was in the car. Assistance was then requested from the Edgartown Fire Dept. scuba
squad and one John Farrar came to the scene and was able to enter the car and with the assistance of the invest. officer remove the body from the car gThe victim was a young lady, dressed
in white blouse, black slacks, and sandals; she was dead when removed. Dr. Donald Mills, MD,
of Edgartown, an associate Medical Examiner was notified and came to the scene and pronouncd
the victim (Miss Mary Jo Kopechne, 28, of 2912 Olive St., Washington, D.C.) dead of accidental
drowning. Her body had been found in the rear of the car. Her body was ordered removed to
the Martha's Vineyard Funeral Home. Also at the scene of the invest. were Registry Inspectors
George Kennedy and Robert Molla. The car was found to be registered to Sen. Edward Kennedy,
JFK Bldg., Boston. and a radio alert was put out to locate the Senator as at the time of the
accident the girl's identify had not yet been established. In the course of this Chief Arena
called his office regarding this alert and at this time was notified that the Sen. was at the
police office. Chief talked with him and Sen. advised that he would like to see the Chief at
Police Station - Chief went there and at this time the Sen. advised that he had been the operator of the vehicle,,and gave the above statement in regards to the accident. This was at about
9-10 A.M. and the accident was believed to have happend sometime between 12Mid and 1 A.M.
The whxxgabouts of the senxtor in the meantime was covered only in the above statement. It was
felt that because of the evidence at the scene, condition of the roadway and accident scene that
there was no negligence on the part of the operator in the accident. However due to the span
of time involved between the time of the accident and the report of same by the operator a
citation was issued to the operator citing violation of Chap. 90-24, leaving the scene. The
complaint application was made on Monday, July 21, 1969 at xx 10:00 AM and at this time the
complaining officer was advised that the defendant had requested a hearing before the complaint
would issue and the hearing was schedule for July 28, 1969 in the early afternoon.

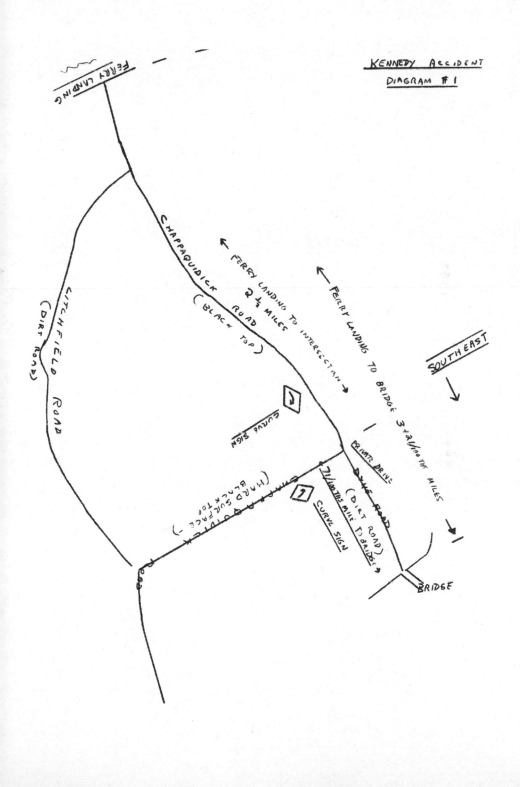

KENNEDY ACCIDENT
DIAGRAM #1

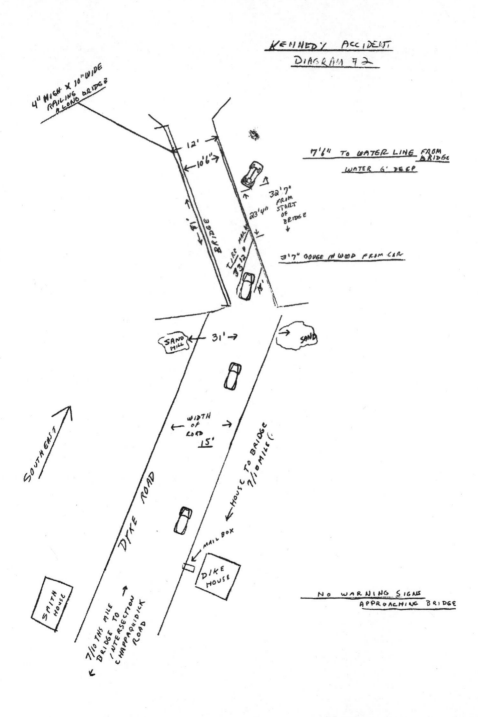

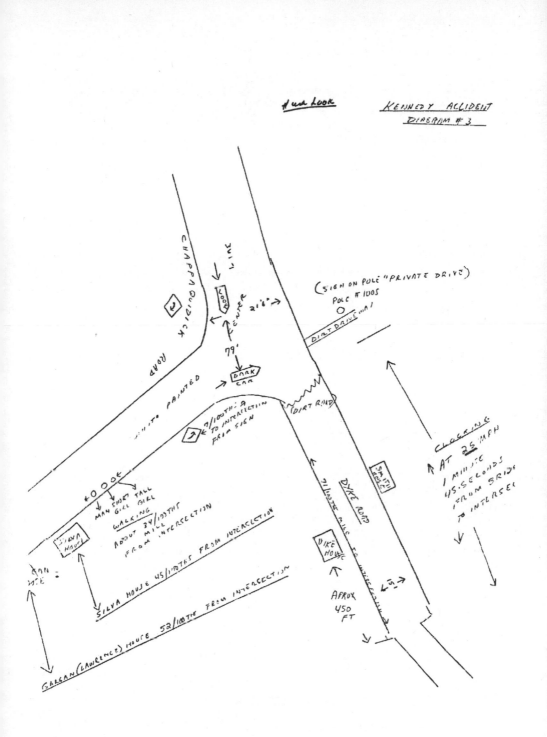

4 we LOOK

KENNEDY ACCIDENT
DIAGRAM #3

E65L-325M-TR13-2-69-948878

MUST TYPE OR PRINT

COMMONWEALTH OF MASSACHUSETTS
POLICE REPORT
OF MOTOR VEHICLE ACCIDENT

SEND ONE COPY TO:
REGISTRAR OF MOTOR VEHICLES
100 NASHUA STREET
BOSTON, MASS. 02114

POLICE DEPT. SUBMITTING REPORT

Oak Bluffs Registry

made out by George K.

300140

REGISTRY USE ONLY

2-7

8-10

11-15 Date of Accident	16	Day of the Week		17 Hour

18 Did you notice any indication that an operator was under medication or had been using drugs? (explain on reverse) — Check one — YES ☐ 1 NO ☒ 2

To your knowledge has any operator had a history of epilepsy, heart disease, fainting spells? (explain on reverse) — YES ☐ 3 NO ☒ 4

19 Was this Accident investigated by an Officer? If Yes, Check One Box Below
1 ☒ Registry 4 ☐ State Police
2 ☐ MDC
3 ☐ Other 5 ☒ Local Police

Mo. Day Yr. **7 - 18-69** S M T W T F S 1 2 3 4 5 6 7 A.M. ☐ X P.M. ☒ Y **11:20 PM**

VEHICLE 1

Name of Operator
Edward M. Kennedy

Street Address City/Town State
3 Charles River Street **Boston** **Mass.**

Owners Name and Address (if same, write "same")
same

Describe Damage to Vehicle:
Total

20 Number of Vehicles Involved. **1**

21-26 Date of Birth MO. **2** DAY **22** YR. **32**

27 Sex 1 ☒ M 2 ☐ F

28-29 License Number and State
040221W **Mass.**

Registration Number & State
L78207 **Mass.**

Approximate Cost to Repair $ **Total**

Parked Car YES ☐ NO ☒

VEHICLE 2

Name of Operator

Street Address City/Town State

Owners Name and Address (if same, write "same")

Describe Damage to Vehicle:

30-35 Date of Birth MO. DAY YR.

36 Sex 1 ☐ M 2 ☐ F

37-38 License Number and State

Registration Number & State

Approximate Cost to Repair $

Parked Car YES ☐ NO ☐

VEHICLE 3

Name of Operator

Street Address City/Town State

Owners Name and Address (if same, write "same")

Describe Damage to Vehicle:

21-26 Date of Birth MO. DAY YR.

27 Sex 1 ☐ M 2 ☐ F

28-29 License Number and State

Registration Number & State

Approximate Cost to Repair $

Parked Car YES ☐ NO ☐

OTHER

Describe Other Property Damage

Name of Property Owner Address

Approximate Cost to Repair $

39 Number Injured.

INJURED 1

Name of Injured Street City/Town State
Mary Jo Kopechne **2912 Olive Street, N.W.** **Washington** **D.C.**

40-1 Age **28**

42 Sex 1 ☐ M 2 ☒ F

45 Severity — Mark First One That Applies Killed ☒ | Visible signs of injury, as bleeding wound, or distorted member; or had to be carried from scene ☐ 1 | Other visible injury, as bruises, abrasions, swelling, limping, etc. ☐ 2 | No visible injury but complaints of pain or momentary unconsciousness ☐ 3 | ☐ 4

43 Check if wearing Seat Belt 1 ☐
44 Check if Wearing Helmet 1 ☐

46 Person Injured
1 ☐ Operator } in vehicle
2 ☒ Passenger } No.
3 ☐ Passenger in train, bus, etc.
4 ☐ Operator } On Motorcycle
5 ☐ Passenger
6 ☐ Pedestrian
7 ☐ Bicyclist
8 ☐ Other

INJURED 2

Name of Injured Street City/Town State

47-8 Age 49 Sex 1 ☐ M 2 ☐ F

52 Severity — Mark First One That Applies Killed ☐ | Visible signs of injury, as bleeding wound, or distorted member; or had to be carried from scene ☐ 1 | Other visible injury, as bruises, abrasions, swelling, limping, etc. ☐ 2 | No visible injury but complaints of pain or momentary unconsciousness ☐ 3 | ☐ 4

50 Check if wearing Seat Belt 1 ☐
51 Check if Wearing Helmet 1 ☐

53 Person Injured
1 ☐ Operator } in vehicle
2 ☐ Passenger } No.
3 ☐ Passenger in train, bus, etc.
4 ☐ Operator } On Motorcycle
5 ☐ Passenger
6 ☐ Pedestrian
7 ☐ Bicyclist
8 ☐ Other

INJURED 3

Name of Injured Street City/Town State

40-1 Age 42 Sex 1 ☐ M 2 ☐ F

45 Severity — Mark First One That Applies Killed ☐ | Visible signs of injury, as bleeding wound, or distorted member; or had to be carried from scene ☐ 1 | Other visible injury, as bruises, abrasions, swelling, limping, etc. ☐ 2 | No visible injury but complaints of pain or momentary unconsciousness ☐ 3 | ☐ 4

43 Check if wearing Seat Belt 1 ☐
44 Check if Wearing Helmet 1 ☐

46 Person Injured
1 ☐ Operator } in vehicle
2 ☐ Passenger } No.
3 ☐ Passenger in train, bus, etc.
4 ☐ Operator } On Motorcycle
5 ☐ Passenger
6 ☐ Pedestrian
7 ☐ Bicyclist
8 ☐ Other

BE SURE TO COMPLETE AND SIGN REPORT ON REVERSE SIDE

Appendix 2 Registry Inspector George Kennedy's preliminary report of the accident. *Courtesy Paula Golden, Massachusetts Registry of Motor Vehicles.*

NOTE: Mark all items which apply. The diagram and description of what happened (below) need not be completed if separate 8½ x 11 size sheet with same detailed information is attached. Please sign report in space provided below.

LOCATION

City or Town Where Accident Occurred **Edgartown** Chappaquiddick Island,	Nearest Mile Marker **NONE**	Reserved for Registry

Street Name or Route Number **Dike Road**

☐ at Intersection with_____
or
_____ feet N. S. E. W. ☐☐☐☐ Of nearest intersection, bridge, mile marker, railroad.

Which direction was each vehicle traveling?

Vehicle No. 1 N. S. E. W. ☐☐☒☐   No. 2 N. S. E. W. ☐☐☐☐   No. 3 N. S. E. W. ☐☐☐☐

Other Landmarks: **ON BRIDGE**

54		55
1 ☐ On ramp from route		1 ☐ Area built up
2 ☐ Off ramp from route		2 ☒ Area not built up
3 ☐ At rotary		

TYPE

56 Accident Involved Collision With:

1 ☐ Pedestrian   4 ☐ Railroad train   7 ☐ Overturned in road
2 ☐ Motor Vehicle in Traffic   5 ☐ Ran off roadway hit fixed object____feet from road   8 ☒ Ran off roadway — into non-collision river
3 ☐ Motor Vehicle Parked   6 ☐ Bicycle   9 ☐ Fixed object on shoulder, sidewalk or island
A ☐ Other

57 If collision involved two or more vehicles mark one of the following

1 ☐ Rear end   2 ☐ Angle   3 ☐ Head on

SITUATION

What were vehicles doing prior to accident? Mark appropriate box.

Vehicle 58-60	1 2 3		Vehicle 1 2 3		Vehicle 1 2 3	
1		Making right turn	B	Skidding	F	Parked
2		Making left turn	9	Slowing or stopping	G	Stalled or disabled
3		Making U turn	A	Crossing median strip	H	Stalled or disabled with flasher on
4	X	Going straight ahead	B	Driverless moving vehicle	J	In process of parking
5		Passing on right	C	Backing	K	Entering or exiting from alley or driveway
6		Passing on left	D	Starting in traffic	L	Other
7		Stop sign	E	Starting from parked position		

Where was pedestrian located at time of accident? Mark appropriate box.

	X	61		X	
1		At intersection	7		Getting on/off vehicle
2		Within 300 feet of intersection	8		Working on vehicle
3		More than 300 feet from intersection	9		Working in street
4		Walking in street with traffic	A		Playing in street
5		Walking in street against traffic	B		Not in street
6		Standing in street	C		Other

CONDITIONS

62	X	Light Conditions	63		X	Traffic Controls			X	
1		Daylight	1		Stop sign	6	Railroad crossing gate
2		Dawn or dusk	2		Yield sign	7	Railroad automatic signal
3		Darkness — road lighted	3		Warning sign	8	Control device not working
4	X	Darkness — road unlighted	4		Signal light	9	X No control present
			5		Officer or flagman		

64	X	Weather Conditions	65	X	Road Conditions
1	X	Clear	1	X	Dry
2		Foggy	2		Wet
3		Cloudy	3		Snowy
4		Rain	4		Icy
5		Snow	5		Other
6		Sleet			dirt road

COLLISION CONDITIONS

66	X			X			X			X	
1		Entered median	4		Hit guard rail	7		Hit signpost	A		Embankment	D		Stone wall
2		Crossed median	5		Hit curbing	8		Hit utility or light pole	B		Ditch	E		Other post
3		Hit median barrier	6		Hit abutment	9		Hit tree	C		Rock ledge	F	X	Bridge rail

DIAGRAM

INDICATE ON THIS DIAGRAM WHAT HAPPENED

Use one of these outlines to sketch the scene of your accident, writing in street or highway names or numbers.

1. Number each vehicle and show direction of travel by arrow:
2. Use solid line to show path before accident; dotted line after accident.
3. Show pedestrian by:
4. Show railroad by:
5. Show distance and direction to landmarks; identify landmarks by name or number.
6. Indicate north by arrow, as:

INDICATE NORTH BY ARROW

VIOLATIONS

Operator (mark one or more) 67-75	1 2 3		Operator	Operator	Operator
1		Operating Under Influ			
2		Operating After Drink			
3		Exceeding Lawful Spe			
4		Failed to Grant Right to Other Vehicle			
5		Failed to Grant Righ to Pedestrian			

Describe What Happened. (Refer to Vehicles by Number)

Citation Number if issued 1032015 Veh #1 driven by Edward M Kennedy was traveling on a dirt road known as Dike Rd. Being unfamiliar with the road and in the dark he had to cross a small wooden bridge with out any warning signs or guard rails. His right front wheel rolled over a 4 by 10 rub strip on the right of the bridge causing the vehicle to over turn into a pond upside down. He escaped thru one of the windows that was open or broken. The passanger was recovered the following AM died of accidential drowning. *G W Kennedy SD RMV*

E23-1000M-TR13-2-69-948878

MUST TYPE OR PRINT

COMMONWEALTH OF MASSACHUSETTS
OPERATOR'S REPORT
OF MOTOR VEHICLE ACCIDENT

REGISTRY USE ONLY

SEND ONE COPY TO:
REGISTRAR OF MOTOR VEHICLES
100 NASHUA STREET
BOSTON, MASS. 02114

ONE COPY TO:
POLICE DEPARTMENT in whose juris-
diction the accident occurred.

2-7

8-10

19
Was this Accident investigated by an Officer?
If Yes, Check One Box Below
1 ☐ Registry   4 ☐ State Police
2 ☐ MDC
3 ☐ Other   5 ☒ Local Police

11-15 Date of Accident	16 Day of the Week								17 Hour	18 Have you completed a Mass. driver Education course		
Mo. Day Yr.	S 1	M 2	T 3	W 4	T 5	F 6	S 7	A.M. ☐ X P.M. ☒ Y	11:15		YES ☐ X	NO ☒ Y
7 18 69						☒						

VEHICLE 1

Name of Operator Making Report
Edward M. Kennedy

20 Number of Vehicles Involved. 1

21-26 Date of Birth
MO. 2 DAY 22 YR. 32

27 Sex
1 ☒ M   2 ☐ F

Street Address · City/Town · State
3 Charles River Square, Boston, Mass.

28-29 License Number and State
040-221W Mass.

Owners Name and Address (if same, write "same")
SAME

Registration Number & State
L 78 207

Describe Damage to Vehicle:
Unknown - Submerged in water

Approximate Cost to Repair $ Unknown

Parked Car
YES ☐   NO ☐

VEHICLE 2

Name of Operator

30-35 Date of Birth
MO. DAY YR.

36 Sex
1 ☐ M   2 ☐ F

Street Address · City/Town · State

37-38 License Number and State

Owners Name and Address (if same, write "same")

Registration Number & State

Describe Damage to Vehicle:

Approximate Cost to Repair $

Parked Car
YES ☐   NO ☐

VEHICLE 3

Name of Operator

21-26 Date of Birth
MO. DAY YR.

27 Sex
1 ☐ M   2 ☐ F

Street Address · City/Town · State

28-29 License Number and State

Owners Name and Address (if same, write "same")

Registration Number & State

Describe Damage to Vehicle:

Approximate Cost to Repair $

Parked Car
YES ☐   NO ☐

OTHER

Describe Other Property Damage

Name of Property Owner · Address

Approximate Cost to Repair $

39 Number Injured.

INJURED 1

Name of Injured · Street · City/Town · State
Mary Jo Kopechne · 2912 Olive Street · Washington, D.C.

40-1 Age 28

42 Sex
1 ☐ M.   2 ☒ F.

43 Check if wearing Seat Belt 1 ☐

44 Check if Wearing Helmet 1 ☐

45 Severity
Mark First One That Applies   Killed 1 ☒

Visible signs of injury, as bleeding wound, or distorted member; or had to be carried from scene 1

Other visible injury, as bruises, abrasions, swelling, limping, etc. 2 ☐

No visible injury but complaints of pain or momentary unconsciousness 3 ☐

No visible injury 4 ☐

46 Person Injured
1 ☐ Operator } in vehicle
2 ☒ Passenger } No. 1
3 ☐ Passenger in train, bus, etc.
4 ☐ Operator } On Motorcycle
5 ☐ Passenger
6 ☐ Pedestrian
7 ☐ Bicyclist
8 ☐ Other

INJURED 2

Name of Injured · Street · City/Town · State
Edward M. Kennedy · 3 Charles River Square · Boston · Mass.

47-8 Age 37

49 Sex
1 ☒ M.   2 ☐ F.

50 Check if wearing Seat Belt 1 ☐

51 Check if Wearing Helmet 1 ☐

52 Severity
Mark First One That Applies   Killed 1 ☐

Visible signs of injury, as bleeding wound, or distorted member; or had to be carried from scene 1 ☐

Other visible injury, as bruises, abrasions, swelling, limping, etc. 2 ☐

No visible injury but complaints of pain or momentary unconsciousness 3 ☒

No visible injury 4 ☐

53 Person Injured
1 ☒ Operator } in vehicle
2 ☐ Passenger } No.
3 ☐ Passenger in train, bus, etc.
4 ☐ Operator } On Motorcycle
5 ☐ Passenger
6 ☐ Pedestrian
7 ☐ Bicyclist
8 ☐ Other

INJURED 3

Name of Injured · Street · City/Town · State

40-1 Age

42 Sex
1 ☐ M.   2 ☐ F.

43 Check if wearing Seat Belt 1 ☐

44 Check if Wearing Helmet 1 ☐

45 Severity
Mark First One That Applies   Killed 1 ☐

Visible signs of injury, as bleeding wound, or distorted member; or had to be carried from scene 1 ☐

Other visible injury, as bruises, abrasions, swelling, limping, etc. 2 ☐

No visible injury but complaints of pain or momentary unconsciousness 3 ☐

No visible injury 4 ☐

46 Person Injured
1 ☐ Operator } in vehicle
2 ☐ Passenger } No.
3 ☐ Passenger in train, bus, etc.
4 ☐ Operator } On Motorcycle
5 ☐ Passenger
6 ☐ Pedestrian
7 ☐ Bicyclist
8 ☐ Other

BE SURE TO COMPLETE AND SIGN REPORT ON REVERSE SIDE

Appendix 3 Operator's report of the accident submitted by Senator Kennedy. *Courtesy Paul Golden, Massachusetts Registry of Motor Vehicles.*

NOTE: Mark all items which apply. The diagram and description of what happened (below) need not be completed if separate 8½ x 11 size sheet with same detailed information is attached. Please sign report in space provided below.

LOCATION

City or Town Where Accident Occurred: Martha's Chappaquiddick, Vineyard, Mass.	Nearest Mile Marker	Reserved for Registry

Street Name or Route Number

Dyke Road Bridge

☐ at intersection with _____
or
☐ _____ feet   ☐☐☐☐   N. S. E. W. Of nearest intersection, bridge, mile marker, railroad.

Which direction was each vehicle traveling?

Vehicle No. 1 ☐☐☒☐ N. S. E. W.   No. 2 ☐☐☐☐ N. S. E. W.   No. 3 ☐☐☐☐ N. S. E. W.

Other Landmarks:

54
1 ☐ On ramp from route
2 ☐ Off ramp from route
3 ☐ At rotary

55
1 ☐ Area built up
☐ Area not built up

TYPE

56 Accident Involved Collision With:

1 ☐ Pedestrian
2 ☐ Motor Vehicle in Traffic
3 ☐ Motor Vehicle Parked
4 ☐ Railroad train
5 ☐ Ran off roadway hit fixed object _____ feet from road
6 ☐ Bicycle
7 ☐ Overturned in road
8 ☒ Ran off roadway — non-collision
9 ☐ Fixed object on shoulder, sidewalk or island
A ☐ Other

57 If collision involved two or more vehicles mark one of the following:

1 ☐ Rear end   2 ☐ Angle   3 ☐ Head on

SITUATION

What were vehicles doing prior to accident? Mark appropriate box.

Vehicle 58-60	1 2 3		Vehicle	1 2 3		Vehicle	1 2 3
1		Making right turn	8		Skidding	F	Parked
2	☒	Making left turn	9	-	Slowing or stopping	G	Stalled or disabled
3		Making U turn	A		Crossing median strip	H	Stalled or disabled with flasher on
4		Going straight ahead	B		Driverless moving vehicle	J	In process of parking
5		Passing on right	C		Backing	K	Entering or exiting from alley or driveway
6		Passing on left	D		Starting in traffic	L	Other
7		Stop sign	E		Starting from parked position		

Where was pedestrian located at time of accident? Mark appropriate box.

61

	X			X
1	At intersection	7	Getting on/off vehicle
2	Within 300 feet of intersection	8	Working on vehicle
3	More than 300 feet from intersection	9	Working in street
4	Walking in street with traffic	A	Playing in street
5	Walking in street against traffic	B	Not in street
6	Standing in street	C	Other

CONDITIONS

62 Light Conditions	X		**63** Traffic Controls	X				**64** Weather Conditions	X		**65** Road Conditions	X
1 Daylight		1 Stop sign		6 Railroad crossing gate		1 Clear	☒	1 Dry	☒
2 Dawn or dusk		2 Yield sign		7 Railroad automatic signal		2 Foggy		2 Wet	
3 Darkness — road lighted		3 Warning sign		8 Control device not working		3 Cloudy		3 Snowy	
4 Darkness — road unlighted	☒	4 Signal light		9 No control present	☒	4 Rain		4 Icy	
		5 Officer or flagman				5 Snow		5 Other	
						6 Sleet			

COLLISION CONDITIONS

66

	X			X			X			X			X
1 Entered median		4 Hit guard rail		7 Hit signpost		A Embankment		D Stone wall
2 Crossed median		5 Hit curbing		8 Hit utility or light pole		B Ditch		E Other post
3 Hit median barrier		6 Hit abutment		9 Hit tree		C Rock ledge		F Bridge rail

DIAGRAM

INDICATE ON THIS DIAGRAM WHAT HAPPENED

Use one of these outlines to sketch the scene of your accident, writing in street or highway names or numbers.

1. Number each vehicle and show direction of travel by arrow: →①←②→
2. Use solid line to show path before accident →①←②; dotted line after accident -----②
3. Show pedestrian by: ●——○
4. Show railroad by: ++++++++
5. Show distance and direction to landmarks; identify landmarks by name or number.
6. Indicate north by arrow, as: ⊘

INDICATE NORTH BY ARROW

Describe What Happened: (Refer to Vehicles by Number)

On July 18, 1969 at approximately 11:15 PM on Chappaquiddick, Martha's Vineyard, Mass. I was driving my car on Main Street., On my way to get the ferry back to Edgartown. I turned right onto Dyke Road instead of bearing hard left on Main Street. After proceeding for approximately 1/2 mile on Dyke Road I descended a hill and came upon a narrow bridge. The car went off the side of the bridge. The car turned over and sunk into the water and landed with the roof resting on the bottom.

My speed immediately prior to the accident was approximately about 20 m.p.h.

Signature of operator making report _____Edward M Kennedy_____   Date **July 23, 1969**

Date	Conn Time	Elap Time	Calling CO	Calling Loc	Term CO	Term No	Term Loc	Term Listing
7-18	10:08A	1:20	627	Edgartown	524	3878	Arlington Va.	Sen. Edw. M. Kennedy
7-18	12:13P	3:28	627	Edgartown	225	4545	Washington	U. S. Capitol
7-18	6:39P	3:32	627	Edgartown	775	7177	Hyannis	Joseph Kennedy
7-18	7:42P	:57	627	Edgartown	775	7177	Hyannis	Joseph Kennedy
7-19	10:57A	23:54	693	Vineyard Hav.	775	2145	Hyannis	Jacqueline Kennedy
7-19	2:36P	:21	627	Edgartown	532	0018	Falls Church	David Burke 6326 Street No
7-19	2:37P	:55	627	Edgartown	225	4418	Washington	U. S. Capitol
7-19	2:46P	:55	627	Edgartown	234	5929	So. Bend Ind	Jos F. Hurstel 817 Miner
7-19	2:49P	3:40	627	Edgartown	775	5231	Hyannis	Edw. M. Kennedy
7-19	3:44P	2:06	693	Vineyard Hav	225	4418	washington	U. S. Capitol
7-19	3:49P	:59	693	Vineyard Hav	337	8792	Washington	Miss Mary Carroll 2912 Olive NW
7-19	4:46P	8:42	693	Vineyard Hav	634	2881	New York	Frank Schuman 168 Beach 128th Queens
7-19	5:26P	10:12	627	Edgartown	775	5231	Hyannis	Edw. M. Kennedy
7-19	5:39P	5:03	693	Vineyard Hav	234	5929	So Bend Ind	Jos F Hurstel
7-19	6:01P	5:23	693	Vineyard Hav	775	5231	Hyannis	Edw. M. Kennedy
7-19	6:56P	:46	627	Edgartown	228	9813	Nantucket	W. A. Rock Macy Lane

Appendix 4 List of 17 phone calls made during July 18-19, 1969, submitted as Exhibit #4 at the inquest, shows no calls made during the more than nine-hour delay in reporting the accident. *Courtesy Phillip A. Rollins.*

"On July 18, 1969, at approximately 11:15 p.m. in Chappaquiddick, Martha's Vineyard, Massachusetts, I was driving my car on Main Street on my way to get the ferry back to Edgartown. I was unfamiliar with the road and turned right onto Dyke Road, instead of bearing hard left on Main Street. After proceeding for approximately one-half mile on Dyke Road I descended a hill and came upon a narrow bridge (arrow on map). The car went off the side of the bridge. There was one passenger with me, one Miss Mary (here the police chief paused, indicated that Kennedy was not sure of the spelling of the dead girl's last name, and offered a rough phonetic approximation), a former secretary of my brother Sen. Robert Kennedy. The car turned over and sank into the water and landed with the roof resting on the bottom. I attempted to open the door and the window of the car but have no recollection of how I got out of the car. I came to the surface and then repeatedly dove down to the car in an attempt to see if the passenger was still in the car. I was unsuccessful in the attempt. I was exhausted and in a state of shock. I recall walking back to where my friends were eating. There was a car parked in front of the cottage and I climbed into the back seat. I then asked for someone to bring me back to Edgartown. I remember walking around for a period of time and then going back to my hotel room. When I fully realized what had happened this morning, I immediately contacted the police."

Appendix 5 Statement of accident submitted to Chief Arena by Senator Kennedy. Inquest *Exhibit #2—Courtesy Philip A. Rollins.*

HEARING on FATAL ACCIDENT

OPERATOR _____ KENNEDY _____ DATE OF BIRTH 2-22-32.

    License Number, if any ___0402211___ **IN CAMERA**~~NUMBER~~ _____
    Date of Expiration
    Date of Issue

ATTORNEY ROBERT G. CLARK, JR. 231 Main St., Brockton, Mass.

WITNESSES ___None.___ _____ _____

Summary of Testimony and Evidence

    The Report shows that there were no warning devices, lights,
Reflectors, or signs in this area to warn a motorist that any such
dangerous condition as the bridge existed. It would appear that
Kennedy did not see the bridge in time and put on his brakes,
losing steering ability, and slid off the right side of the bridge.
I believe there was operation too fast for existing conditions in
this accident.

FINDINGS ___I do not find that the accident occurred without serious___
       fault.

ACTION _____

Supervising Inspector
Supervising Hearings Officer _[signature]_ DATE
                              HEARING
OFFICE ___HYANNIS.___ _____ HELD __MAY 18, 1970.__

P-Sug 4

Appendix 6 Report of Registry Hearing which found Senator Kennedy to have been speeding and at serious fault in the accident. *Courtesy Paula Golden, Massachusetts Registry of Motor Vehicles.*

The Commonwealth of Massachusetts

Registry of Motor Vehicles

100 Nashua Street, Boston 02114

May 27, 1970

IN CAMERA

Edward M. Kennedy
3 Charles River Square
Boston, Massachusetts

Dear Sir:

     Upon an investigation and after a hearing, I am unable to find that the fatal accident, in which a motor vehicle operated by you was involved, occurred without serious fault on your part.

     Under the law, the Registrar is compelled to revoke the license or suspend the right to operate, if not already revoked or suspended.

     Section 28 of Chapter 90 of the General Laws as amended reads as follows: "Any person aggrieved by a ruling or decision of the registrar may, within ten days thereafter, appeal from such ruling or decision to the board of appeal on motor vehicle liability policies and bonds created by section eight A of Chapter twenty-six, which board may, after a hearing, order such ruling or decision to be affirmed, modified or annulled; but no such appeal shall operate to stay any ruling or decision of the registrar."

Very truly yours,

Richard E. McLaughlin

Registrar

MNP-Sus 13 REV

CT6651
DMS

Appendix 7 Registrar Richard McLaughlin notified Senator Kennedy of the result of a hearing which found him at serious fault in the accident. Kennedy's license was revoked for an additional six months. *Courtesy Paula Golden, Massachusetts Registry of Motor Vehicles.*

Notes

10   "You probably can help keep traffic . . . else in it." Arena quoted by Look. Inquest, p.505.

10   "I saw a car last night . . . isn't the same one." Look. Inquest, p.505.

Chapter 2

13   "Do you know about the accident?" Antone Bettencourt to Dick Hewitt. Hewitt Police Statement, 7-22-69, p.3.

13   "Well, he's standing right over there . . ." Hewitt Police statement, p.3.

13   "Senator, do you know there's a girl . . . to the bridge?" Bettencourt to Arena. Arena interview 2-16-83.

13   "No, I'm going on over to town." Ted Kennedy. *Ibid.*

14   "We realized by this time . . . there for news." Steve Ewing. *New Bedford Standard Times,* 7-27-69.

14   "Senator, are you aware . . ." Hewitt Police Statement, p.3.

14   "Yes, we just heard about it." Hewitt Police Statement, p.3.

14   "This time Kennedy looked worried." Steve Ewing, *New Bedford Standard Times,* 7-27-69.

14   "That's why the picture isn't very good . . . sideways." Harvey Ewing. Interview 10-3-82.

14   "I figured if someone in his party . . ." Harvey Ewing. Interview 9-15-83.

15   "All I know is a car went into the drink . . . the car" Harvey Ewing. Interview 9-15-83.

15   "Don't be surprised . . . over there." Mrs. Thomas Teller. *The Bridge at Chappaquiddick* by Jack Olsen, Boston: Little, Brown & Co., 1970, pp.134–135.

15   "He's right here, Chief . . ." Carmen Salvador to Arena. Inquest, pp.579.

15   Arena-Ted Kennedy Dialogue. Arena. Inquest, p.579. Exhumation Hearings, p.7. Interview 3-15-83.

16   "a well-developed . . . young woman." Dr. Donald Mills. Exhumation Hearing, p.80.

17   "The characteristic foam . . ." Mills. Exhumation Hearing, p.87.

17   "I couldn't have removed her clothes . . ." Mills. Exhumation Hearing, p.82.

17   "I more or less kept my eyes open . . ." Eugene Frieh. Exhumation Hearing, p.116.

17   "That probably came from her stomach . . ." Frieh. Olsen, p.145.

17   "No, I'm pressing her chest . . ." Mills. Olsen, p.145.

17   "An obvious and clear . . . submerged automobile." Mills. Exhumation Hearing, p.86.

17   "certain non-medical factors . . ." Mills. Exhumation Hearing, p.90.

17   "If there's any Kennedy mixup . . ." Mills. Exhumation Hearing, p.90.

18   "There's been an accident . . . like to know." Richard Ferry to James Smith. Smith interview 2-14-83.

18   "as the one politician in Massachusetts . . ." James Smith. Interview 2-20-82.

19   "Cape Codders have wondered . . . mighty close." *Cape Cod News,* 8-26-65.

19   "How can we find out . . ." Warren O'Donnell to James Smith. Smith interview 2-14-83.

19   "very friendly, congenial . . . so provincial over there." James Smith. Interview 8-9-83.

19   "calling a shot a shot." *Ibid.*

Chapter 3

21   Carmen Salvador-Ted Kennedy dialogue. Olsen, p.138–139.

22   "He seemed to think . . . joy ride." Carmen Salvador. *Boston Herald Traveler,* 7-22-69.

22   Arena-Ted Kennedy dialogue. Arena interview 2-14-83 and Inquest, p.580.

22   "Nothing in my prior career . . . I was stunned." Arena's personal notes, p.1.

22   "Our roles could have been reversed . . ." Arena's personal notes, p.1.

22   "Do you happen to know . . . next of kin?" Arena. Interview 2-14-69.

22   "It isn't 'Cricket' Keough . . . her parents." Ted Kennedy to Arena. Arena interview 2-14-83.

23   "What would you like for me to do . . . for it." Ted Kennedy to Arena. Inquest, p.580.

23   "certainly worked a calming effect . . . traffic case." Arena's personal notes.

23   "The first thing we have to do . . . what happened." Arena. Inquest, p.580.

23 "Would it be all right if I wrote it out?" Ted Kennedy to Arena. Inquest, p.580.

23 "so the Senator could have some . . . got out and cleared OK." Arena's personal notes.

24 "Tell them I have the case of . . . asking for one." Mills. Exhumation Hearing, pp.99, 104.

24 "We almost never do autopsies . . . I'm no detective." Mills. Exhumation Hearing, p.106.

Chapter 4

25 "a good investigator . . . not too bright." Arena. Interview 2-14-83.

25 "You can call off . . . nobody else in the car." Arena. Interview 3-15-83 and Farrar, Inquest p.550.

26 "According to the skid marks . . . into the water." George Kennedy. Registry of Motor Vehicles Report of Investigator and Examiner, 7-25-69.

26 "No skid marks on the bridge . . . I could see." Arena. Interview 2-14-69.

26 "That's the same car . . . last night." Look. Police Statement to Arena and Exhumation Hearing, p.62.

26 "Do you know who was driving . . ." Arena. Look inquest testimony, p.506.

26 "Only what I told Bob . . . back seat." Look. Inquest, p.506.

26 "Holy Jesus! . . . see a thing." Look. Olsen, p.150.

26 "a vehicle with similar description . . . operating vehicle." Report of Investigator and Examiner, 7-25-69.

26 "For that reason . . . trapped inside." Farrar. *New Bedford Standard Times*, 8-1-69.

27 "I was far from being an expert . . . smashed in." Arena's personal notes, p.2.

28 "I'd only just found out . . . my doorstep." Arena. Interview 3-29-63.

28 "Reston was reverting . . . at this point." Harvey Ewing. Interview 9-15-83.

28 "We want to see if . . . gets away." James Reston to Harvey Ewing. Ewing interview 9-15-83.

28 "I found it hard to believe . . . sure I got it right." Arena's personal notes, p.2.

29 Arena-Carroll dialogue. Arena interview 2-28-83.

29 "Do you mind if I have this typed?" Arena. Inquest, p.584.

30 Kennedy Statement to Edgartown Police, 7-19-69.

30 "Ted Kennedy's in there . . . need you later." Arena. Interview 2-28-83.

31 "OK . . . a hold of Burke Marshall." Kennedy to Arena. Arena inquest testimony, p.585.

31 "part of the record . . . to Burke Marshall." Markham. Arena inquest testimony, p.588.

31 "The Senator will . . . his attorney." Paul Markham to Arena. Arena interview 2-28-83.

31 "I figured Kennedy . . . in my particular case." Arena. Interview 2-28-83.

31 Arena-Kennedy dialogue regarding driver's license. Arena interview 2-28-83.

31 Kennedy was "sure" it had been. Arena to *Brockton Enterprise*, 1-8-69.

31 "A lot of guys . . . change pants," Arena. *New Bedford Standard Times*, 1-22-70.

32 "actually engaged . . . walks into a police station . . ." Arena. *New Bedford Standard Times*, 1-22-70.

33 "Jesus, Walter . . . a bad accident." Tommy Teller. Olsen, p.154.

33 Steele-Markham dialogue about reporting the accident. Olsen, p.157–158.

34 "Sometimes I leave . . . it there." Ted Kennedy. Report of Investigator and Examiner, 7-25-69, p.3.

34 "I would like to know about something." George Kennedy. Inquest, p.481.

34 "I have nothing more to say . . . no comment." Ted Kennedy. George Kennedy inquest testimony, p.481.

35 Arena-Carroll dialogue: "Can you fly the Senator . . ." Arena interview 3-15-83.

35 "He looked like the wrath of God." Bob Hyde. *New Bedford Standard Times*, 7-20-69.

35   "Oh, my God, what has happened . . ." Ted Kennedy. George Kennedy inquest testimony, p.487.
35   "in a semi-state of shock . . ." John Celantano. *Boston Globe*, 7-20-69.

Chapter 5
37   "That kind of lulled . . . got to know her." Arena. Interview 3-23-83.
38   "Basically, I wanted . . . in the car." *Ibid.*
38   "who looked reputable . . ." Arena. *The Boston Globe*, 7-23-69.
38   "Maybe I gave it away . . . in it." Arena. Interview 3-23-83.
38   "She seemed very down in the dumps . . . accident?" Arena. Interview 3-23-83.
38   "I thought maybe . . . tell me something?" Arena. Interview 3-23-83.
38   "didn't add up at all . . ." Walter Steele. Olsen, p.167.
39   Arena-Steele dialogue regarding release of statement. Arena interview 2-14-83.
39   "We're in this case . . . he's *gone!*" Edmund Dinis to Arena. Arena interview 2-14-83.
39   "I don't know what's going . . . into the case." Arena. Interview 2-14-83.
40   "This is just a motor vehicles . . . your case." George Killen to Arena. Arena interview 10-23-83.
40   "Killen was right . . . he'd go apeshit." Arena. Interview 10-23-83.
40   "On Cape Cod . . . with my life." Edmund Dinis. *Cape Cod Standard Times*, 7-29-68.
40   "It seemed every time . . . I got a body.'" George Killen. *In His Garden* by Leo Damore. New York: Arbor House, 1981, p.29.
41   Killen-Flynn dialogue. Flynn interview 4-19-83.
41   "perfectly satisfied with Lieutenant Killen's decision." Mills. *Medical World News*, 8-22-69, p.12.
41   "I figured there should . . . indemnity claims." Eugene Frieh. *Philadelphia Sunday Bulletin*, 7-27-69.

42   "a very slight bit of moisture . . . much more moisture." Frieh. Exhumation Hearing, p.118.
43   "to keep ourselves refreshed . . . on our hands." Frieh. Exhumation Hearing, p.114.

Chapter 6
45   "That's up to the medical . . . was wrong." Arena. Interview 2-14-83.
45   "You've got a tiger . . . handle it." Killen to Arena. Arena interview 2-14-83.
46   Francis Broadhurst-Christopher Look, Sr. dialogue. Broadhurst interviews 12-27-82 and 7-26-83.
46   "I'm not saying a goddamned word!" Look to Broadhurst. Broadhurst interview 7-26-83.
46   "What do you know about all this . . ." Richard McCarron. Interview 7-29-83.
46   "More than I want to know . . ." Look to McCarron. McCarron interview 7-29-83.
46   "You ought to go down . . . young Farrar." Look to Broadhurst. Interview 12-27-82.
46   "She was in . . . would have been." Farrar. *Boston Herald Traveler*, 7-20-69.
46   "It seems likely . . . air to breathe." Farrar to Broadhurst. Interview 7-26-83.
47   "If an air bubble . . . the girl could have been saved." Farrar. *National Enquirer*, 10-12-69.
47   "This won't see the light . . . covered up." Woman to Broadhurst. Interview 12-27-82.
47   Bulletin: *Cape Cod Standard Times*, 7-19-69, p.1.
48   FBI Teletype. 7-19-69.

Chapter 7
49   "He was probably relieved . . . to handle it." Bernie Flynn. Interview 10-19-83.
49   "Personally, I thought it was . . . and let him run it." *Ibid.*
50   "Because he'd covered himself . . . report the thing." *Ibid.*
50   "Arena was in way over his head . . . doing anything." *Ibid.*

50 "Maybe we should . . . do an autopsy." Walter Steele. Olsen, p.169.

50 "OK, we've covered all bases . . . we think best." Steele to Arena. Arena interview 2-14-83.

51 "If everything had been clicking . . . clear everything up." Arena. Interview 6-6-83.

51 "They want the statement . . . release it." Arena. *Ibid.*

52 "Chief, we haven't been able . . . bit longer." Paul Markham to Arena. Arena interview 3-23-83.

52 "I'm sorry, I had to . . . investigation, that's all." Arena. Interview 3-23-83.

52 "And I think I'm a pretty good swimmer." Arena. *The Boston Globe,* 7-29-69.

52 "Don't do anymore talking." Walter Steele to Arena. Arena interview 3-23-83.

52 "I'd watched him closely . . . the accident?" Harvey Ewing. Interview 9-15-83.

53 "You could count on at least . . . on the beach." Harvey Ewing. Interview 10-3-83.

53 "Basically, it was Ted Kennedy . . . left up in the air." Harvey Ewing. Interview 9-15-83.

53 "They wanted anything I could give them . . . something else." Harvey Ewing. Interview 9-15-83.

54 "was still in a state of shock . . . discuss the accident." Associated Press. In *New Hampshire Sunday News* (Manchester, N.H.), 7-20-69.

Chapter 8

55 "All my relatives over there . . . enemy territory." James Smith. Interview 6-23-83.

55 "I haven't been called." Kenneth O'Donnell to James Smith. Smith interview 2-14-83.

56 "It's a fatal . . . driving charge." James Smith. Interview 2-14-83.

56 "Before Frank Keating came to town . . . care of it." Smith. Interview 2-10-83.

56 "a Democrat . . . young man." Letter to Senator Edward M. Kennedy dated 9-22-66.

56 "He always acted like a teacher . . . kid brother." James Smith. Interview 2-10-83.

56 "That's why Dinis . . . ran a good shop." James Smith. Interview 2-14-83.

57 "I know all about it . . . been called." Edmund Dinis to James Smith. Smith interview 2-10-83.

57 "We've got your buddy . . . the book at him!" Dinis to James Smith. Smith interview 2-10-83.

57 "It's just a motor vehicles accident . . ." Dinis to James Smith. Smith interview 2-10-83.

57 "You've got to listen to those two guys . . . right now!" David Burke to Joe Gargan. Gargan interview 6-2-83.

58 "The Boss went off . . . got killed." David Burke. *The Education of Edward Kennedy* by Burton Hersh, New York: Dell Publishing Co., Inc. 1980, p.519.

58 "Anything wrong . . . really." Hersh, p.519.

58 "He was very upset . . . with answers." Dick Drayne. Hersh, p.519.

58 "Waiting for the roof . . . already public." Drayne. Hersh, p.519.

59 "He just told me what happened . . . what happened." Gwen Kopechne. *New York Times,* 7-20-69.

59 "so upset . . . . what was happening to him." Burke Marshall. Hersh, p.521.

60 "The reason I thought he shouldn't . . . a medical problem." Burke Marshall. Hersh pp.521, 522.

60 There was a lapse in his memory . . . until 7:00 A.M. the next morning. Affidavit of Robert D. Watt. Inquest Relating to the Death of Mary Jo Kopechne, p.2.

61 "upon objective evidence . . . sustained by the patient." Dr. Robert Watt. Affidavit, pp.3–4.

61 "But I wouldn't say he . . . a sedative." Watt. *Medical World News,* 8-22-69, p.11.

61 "a mild concussion . . . shaken up." Watt. *The Boston Globe,* 7-21-69.

61   "blow on the head . . . all right."
     Watt. *New Bedford Standard
     Times,* 7-21-69.

Chapter 9

63   "simply on what Kennedy told him."
     Boston Globe, 10-29-74, p.18.

63   "It seems to be stretching . . . to fit
     the diagnosis." *Ibid.*

65   "to help in any way that makes sense
     . . ." Dun Gifford. Exhumation
     Hearing, p.207.

65   "You have no authority . . . Kielty
     funeral home." Eugene Frieh.
     Inquest, p.522.

65   "Drowning . . . made the finding."
     Frieh to Dun Gifford. Gifford
     Exhumation Hearing testimony,
     p.209.

65   "didn't want to cause any problem . .
     ." Frieh to John Farrar. Farrar
     quoted in *The Grapevine,* 2-13-80.

65   "run down and catch Dr. Mills . . .
     death certificate." Frieh. Inquest,
     pp.522–523.

66   "The reporters are here . . . to sell
     them." Dr. Robert Nevin. *Boston
     Record-American,* 8-16-69.

66   "I'm going down to see . . . going
     on." Mrs. Donald Mills. *Medical
     World News,* 8-22-69, p.13.

66   "What should I do Chief?" Mills to
     Arena. Arena interview 10-23-83.

66   "If the district attorney . . . for
     support or something." Arena.
     Interview 10-23-83.

66   "I still felt . . . autopsy to be done."
     Frieh. *Philadelphia Sunday Bulletin,*
     7-27-69.

67   "I've come up here . . . things
     along." Dun Gifford. *Medical World
     News,* 8-22-69, p.13.

67   "The required forms . . . anyway."
     Arena to Gifford. Gifford
     Exhumation Hearing testimony,
     p.211.

67   "I wouldn't go out on a limb . . .
     with him." Arena. Interview 10-23-
     83.

67   "I was still expecting to hear from
     these guys." Arena. Interview
     10-23-83.

67   "We were just honestly . . . take care
     of him." Arena. Interview 2-16-83.

67   "We talked about manslaughter . . .
     wilful conduct." Arena. Interview
     10-23-83.

68   "I really should have known better .
     . . a lot of doubts." Walter Steele.
     Cape Cod Standard Times, 7-14-79.

68   "A state trooper friend . . . probably
     true." Arena. Interview 2-16-83.

68   "The defense lawyer . . . that little
     technicality." Arena. Interview
     10-23-83.

69   "without stopping . . . more than
     two years." Chapter 90, Section 38,
     General Laws of the Commonwealth
     of Massachusetts, pp.313–314.

69   "We don't . . . back to you." George
     Kennedy to Arena. Arena interview
     2-16-83.

70   "a D.O.B. 2-22-32 Edward M.
     Kennedy." Report of Investigator
     and Examiner, 7-25-69, p.3.

70   "I'd always thought of him as
     Senator Ted Kennedy . . . what
     Kennedy it was." Mellino to Ralph
     Gordon. Unpublished news story,
     p.3.

71   "We get 800 to 1,000 . . . who he
     is." Richard McLaughlin. Interview
     8-10-82.

71   "So it doesn't get screwed up."
     Richard McLaughlin. Interview
     8-10-82.

Chapter 10

73   "pushed to the point of irrationality
     . . ." Mills. *Medical World News,*
     8-22-69.

73   "I'm being swamped . . . tell these
     people." *Ibid.*

73   "Tell them the girl died . . . the
     receiver." George Killen to Mills.
     Medical World News, 8-22-69,
     p.13.

74   Killen-Frank Keating dialogue.
     Keating interview 7-30-83.

75   "Don't you think you should . . .
     disclosure sure?" Reporter. Hersh,
     p.515.

75   "I don't think we're going . . . have
     to see." David Burke. Hersh, p.515.

75   "She talked about faith . . . at the
     funeral." Joseph Kopechne.
     Pittsburgh Press, 7-23-69.

75 "Nothing was explained . . . what happened." Joseph Kopechne to Ken Botwright. *Boston Globe,* 7-20-69.

76 "We didn't even know she was with Kennedy . . . last to know." Joseph Kopechne. *Ibid.*

76 "We assumed the girl . . . was killed." Joseph Kopechne. *Boston Globe,* 7-20-69.

76 "Politics was her life . . . anything like that." Joseph Kopechne. *Boston Globe,* 7-20-69.

76 "It was a good career . . . wanted to do." Gwen Kopechne. *New York Times,* 7-20-69.

76 "She left on Thursday . . . on Bobby's staff." Matt Reese. (UPI) *Cape Cod Standard Times,* 7-20-69.

77 "We were talking on the telephone . . . like to sunbathe." Gwen Kopechne. *The Grapevine* interview with Gerald Smith, 2-20-80.

77 "Ted came by to thank the girls . . . accident happened." Richard Drayne. *Boston Herald Traveler,* 7-20-69.

78 "That's one thing I objected to . . . on the spot." Arena. Interview 10-23-83.

78 "I know nothing of any party . . . a rumor." Arena. *New Bedford Standard Times,* 7-23-69.

78 "Nobody has proven to me . . . rented the house." Arena. *Boston Herald Traveler,* 7-23-69.

78 "I just kept answering . . . on the news." Arena. Interview 10-23-83.

78 "I was still living in a dream . . . from them." Arena. Interview 10-23-83.

78 "Boy, this is really a big one . . ." Arena. *Chicago Daily News,* 7-24-69, p.5.

79 "Reporters helped me realize . . . been different." Arena. Interview 2-14-83.

79 "This is the only aspect of the case . . . to press charges." Arena. *Ibid.*

79 That Senator Kennedy never attempted to brake the car . . . although the bridge angled to the left. *New York Times,* 7-21-69.

79 "No criminal negligence . . . reckless driving." Arena. *Boston Herald Traveler,* 7-20-69.

79 "as cooperative as . . . could be." Arena. *New Bedford Standard Times,* 7-20-69.

79 "But once again, I don't know . . . after the accident." Arena. *New Bedford Standard Times,* 7-30-69.

79 "At this time . . . strictly accidental." Arena. *New Bedford Standard Times,* 7-20-69.

80 "the most dismaying case . . ." Arena. *Boston Herald Traveler,* 7-22-69.

Chapter 11

82 "Gargan is used by Kennedy . . . saw to his education." *Time,* 8-1-69 and 9-5-69.

82 "The kind of things . . . to be so." Joe Gargan. Interview 6-22-83.

82 "Joey'll fix it." Gargan. Interview 2-13-83 (with James Smith).

82 "the intention was I stay . . . my summer vacation." Gargan. Interview 6-22-83.

83 "*My* father was . . . not Joe Kennedy." *Ibid.*

84 "My father looked down . . . in World War I." Gargan. *Ibid.*

84 "It was *my* father . . . Army-Notre Dame game." *Ibid.*

84 "It was the death of Joe, Jr . . . . opposed the war." *Ibid.*

84 "To me, Harvard was . . . went to Harvard." *Ibid.*

85 "I think that went back . . . in the old days." *Ibid.*

87 "There were a lot of elbows . . . to work together." *Boston Herald Traveler,* 5-4-68.

87 "It's inaccurate to say . . . wasn't drunk at all." Hersh, *The Education of Edward Kennedy,* p.427.

87 "I know I'm going to get my ass . . . don't want to." Ted Kennedy. *Time,* 8-1-69, p.14.

87 "After Bob died there was . . . like all of us were." Joe Gargan. Interview 2-15-83.

88 "She was very hurt . . . deeply wounded." Gargan. Interview 2-15-83.

88 "So, we combined to give . . . house in Nantucket." *Ibid.*

88 "Then we all went . . . a backyard cookout." *Ibid.*

88   "We all had a great time." Gargan to James Smith. Interview 2-9-83.

Chapter 12

91   "Like my three brothers . . . distinguished their lives." Ted Kennedy. *Time,* 8-1-68, p.11B.

91   "Yes, he picked up the . . . being President." Joe Gargan. *New Bedford Standard Times,* 7-28-69.

91   "He recognized that he had always . . . in any respect." Dun Gifford. *The Kennedys: An American Drama* by Peter Collier and David Horowitz, New York: Summit Books, p.366.

92   "He'd always been the spoiled . . . expected much." Collier and Horowitz, p.368.

92   "They were constantly measuring Ted . . . a tough act to follow." Gargan. Interview 2-17-83.

92   "already lustrous Presidential prospects . . ." *Time,* 1-10-69.

92   "the luxurious presumption . . . almost by inheritance . . ." *Newsweek,* 1-13-69.

92   "the most glamorous public . . . in the U.S." *New York Times Magazine,* 2-23-69.

92   "He wouldn't be a Kennedy if his goal were not the White House." Warren Rogers. *Look,* May 1969.

92   "like running the Boston Marathon . . ." Joe Mohbat. (AP) *New Bedford Standard Times,* 6-8-69.

92   "tougher, more decisive, less ebullient . . ." *Ibid.*

92   "a general discouragement . . ." Hersh, p.486.

92   "He has been a different . . . . a drunkard." *Time,* 7-28-69.

93   "The bad thing is the . . . hairy avoidances." Brock Brower. *Esquire* Magazine, February 1976, p.70.

93   "No one on board . . . the Senator himself." *Ibid.*

93   "A big, boiling broth . . . clearly showing." Brock Brower. *Life* Magazine, 8-1-69, p.22.

93   "They're going to shoot . . . they shot Bobby . . ." Hersh, p.484.

93   "Some thought his drinking . . . to relieve." Brower. *Life,* 8-1-69, p.22.

93   "We were going to have to say . . . side of Ted Kennedy." Brower. *Esquire,* February, 1976, p.7.

94   "The President of the poor people . . . . United States." *New Bedford Standard Times,* 4-5-69.

94   "The thing about being a Kennedy . . . raised all that excitement." Ted Kennedy to Joe Mohbat. (AP) *New Bedford Standard Times,* 6-8-69.

94   "Maybe over the summer . . . have some idea." Ted Kennedy. *Ibid.*

95   "Gee, that would be a lot of fun . . . do it." Ted Kennedy. Gargan interview 5-20-83.

95   "Because we liked to stay over . . . out by Saturday night." Gargan. Interview 5-20-83.

95   "way out in the sticks . . . far from the beach." Steve Gentle. Gargan interview 2-9-83 (with James Smith).

95   "We could stay . . . rented the place." Gargan. Interview 5-20-83.

95   "Jack was fit to be tied . . . where he lived." Gargan. Interview 2-17-83.

96   "The invitation was sort of hush-hush." Stan Moore. Interview 8-23-83.

97   "It was a lousy, uneventful . . . worked very hard." Gargan to James Smith. Interview 2-9-83.

97   . . . three drinks each . . . both were drinking rum and coke. Stan Moore. Interviews 8-23-83 and 7-18-82.

97   "Ted Kennedy never allowed . . . and fool around." Gargan. Interview 6-22-83.

98   "I thought more girls . . . supposed to be there, too." Gargan. Interview 5-20-83.

98   "I was interested in the food . . . all the preparations." Gargan Interview 6-22-83.

98   "A lot of things were a source . . . thing going at all." *Ibid.*

98   "Everyone sang old Irish songs . . ." Susan Tannenbaum. *Newsday,* 7-24-69.

99   "He laughed . . . of his crewmen." Esther Newberg. *Pittsburgh Press,* 7-24-69.

99   "The party was not that exciting . . . death with it." Gargan. Interview 5-20-83.

99   "I would have been drinking . . . had his pain." Gargan. Interview 6-22-69.

99   "We started getting the heave . . . I want everybody out." Gargan to James Smith 2-9-83; and James Smith and author 3-7-83.

99   Jesus Jack, you're stiff . . . going to get home?" Ted Kennedy. Gargan interview 6-22-69.

99   "Take a . . . cab." John Crimmins. *Ibid.*

99   "They talked that way . . . not driving you." Gargan. *Ibid.*

99   "'That's what we're doing . . . leaving right now.'" Ted Kennedy. Gargan interview 2-17-83.

99   "I was in the kitchen area . . . the living room with Mary Jo." Gargan. Interview 5-20-69.

99   I didn't question him . . . when he felt like it." Gargan. Interview 6-22-83.

100   "Maybe time went by faster . . . if he was going to the ferry." *Ibid.*

100   "But I hadn't driven over . . . people are still talking." *Ibid.*

100   "How it drifted past 12 o'clock . . . the time go by." Gargan. Interview 5-20-83.

100   "Some people at the party . . . except for Ray LaRosa." Gargan. Interview 6-22-69.

100   "Jack wanted everybody out . . . get 'em to hell out.'" Gargan to James Smith 2-9-83.

101   "They might have thought . . . gone with Ted Kennedy." Gargan. Interview 6-22-69.

Chapter 13

103   "The Senator . . . to see you." Gargan. Inquest, p.225.

103   "You better get Paul, too." Ted Kennedy. Gargan. Inquest, p.222.

103   "What do you want?" Paul Markham. Inquest, p.298.

103   "There's been a terrible accident . . . Mary Jo is in it." Ted Kennedy. Gargan inquest testimony, p.222.

103   "He didn't bark out . . . as quickly as possible." Gargan. Interview 6-22-83.

104   "The car is . . . on the right." Ted Kennedy. *Ibid.*

104   "Holy God!" Markham. Inquest, p.299.

104   "an automobile that . . . top sticking out." Gargan. Interview 5-20-83.

104   "As soon as I saw that . . . She's gone." Gargan. Interview 5-20-83.

104   "My timing was based . . . back to the bridge." *Ibid.*

104   "There had been one solution . . . you've got a shot." Gargan. Interview 2-17-83.

104   "Because if we are going . . . or something else." Gargan. Interview 2-15-83.

104   "All I was interested in . . . about anything else." Gargan. Interview 5-20-83.

105   "I felt there was . . . of saving Mary Jo." Gargan. Inquest, p.236.

105   "I was trying to feel . . . to get underwater." Gargan. Interview 5-20-83.

105   "Paul had all he could do . . . functioning perfectly well." Gargan. Interview 6-22-83.

105   "That wasn't going to work." *Ibid.*

105   "groping around to see if I could touch anything . . . it was completely submerged." Gargan. Interview 5-20-83.

105   "Because in turning . . . pushing myself out fiercely." Gargan. Interview 2-15-83.

106   "Can you see her? Is she in there?" Ted Kennedy. Gargan interview with James Smith and author 8-25-83.

106   Hands clasped . . . knees drawn up. Gargan. Interview 4-28-83 (with James Smith).

106   "Oh, my God . . . going to do?" Ted Kennedy. Gargan interview 2-13-83 with James Smith and author.

106   "I can't do it . . . I just can't get into the car." Gargan. Markham inquest testimony, p.305.

106   "The water was bad . . . I almost drowned." Gargan to James Smith 2-9-83.

106   "I just can't . . . this happened." Ted Kennedy. Gargan inquest testimony, p.237.

106   "Well, what . . . happened?" Gargan. *Ibid.*, p.237–238.

107   "Before I knew it . . . on the bridge."
Ted Kennedy. Markham inquest
testimony, p.306.

107   "I thought for sure . . . top of the
water." Ted Kennedy. Gargan
inquest testimony, p.238.

107   "I don't believe this . . . it could
happen." Ted Kennedy. Markham
inquest testimony, pp.305, 307.

107   "Well, it . . . happened." Markham,
Inquest, p.307.

107   "What am I . . . can I do?" Kennedy.
Ibid.

107   "There's nothing . . . can do."
Markham. *Ibid.*

107   "I had one thing in mind . . . be
reported immediately." Gargan.
Interview 6-22-83.

111   "I hope he drowns, the son of a
bitch." Gargan to James Smith 2-17-
83 and 3-22-83. Smith interview
3-3-83.

111   "The Senator's departure . . . was
cut short." Gargan. Interview 6-22-
83.

111   "He was going to report . . . back to
the cottage." Gargan. Interview
6-22-83.

111   "I wasn't satisfied . . . doing by
himself." Gargan. Interview 5-20-
83.

111   "I think one of us . . . I'll swim
across." *Ibid.*

111   "His leg was . . . have made it."
Gargan. Interview 6-22-83.

111   "To make sure the Senator . . . was
going to do." Gargan. *Ibid.*

112   "The Senator said he was . . . 'take
care of meant." Gargan. Interview
5-20-83.

112   "I felt I should go back . . . calm at
this time." Gargan. Inquest, p.244.

112   "The night was hot . . . was that
deadness." Gargan. Interview 6-22-
83.

112   "Jack, it's late . . . over in the
morning." Gargan. Interview 2-15-
83.

112   "lying around . . . trying to sleep."
Gargan. Interview 2-17-83.

112   "They were not . . . at this point."
Paul Markham. Inquest, p.313.

112   "kind of slumped back." *Ibid.*

112   "Watch out . . . on my legs." Esther
Newberg. Markham inquest
testimony, p.313.

112   "I'm sorry . . . believe what
happened." *Ibid.*, 313-314.

113   "Oh, don't even ask . . . looking for
boats." Gargan. Mary Ellen Lyons
inquest testimony, p.655.

113   "They said they had . . . to the other
side." *Ibid.*, p.653.

113   "Because of his back . . . dove in
after him." *Ibid.*, p.654.

113   "He told me she was . . . the last
ferry." *Ibid.*, p.656.

113   "He said not to worry . . . taken the
ferry." Rosemary Keough. Inquest,
p.734.

113   "I did not want to discuss . . . the
party and wait." Gargan. Interview
2-17-83.

113   "to be the first . . . to the cottage."
Gargan. Interview 2-15-83.

114   "I'm dealing with a guy . . . whatever
that is." Gargan. Interview 2-17-83.

114   "on the confidence that I ascribed . .
. able to function." Gargan.
Interview 5-20-83.

114   "I knew a confident, tough . . . dove
into the water." Gargan. Interview
2-17-83.

114   "In fact, I was . . . that he would."
Gargan. Interview 4-28-83.

114   "We hoped Ted was going . . . foggy
on that point." Paul Markham to
Edward Harrington. Harrington
interview 1-11-84 (with James
Smith).

115   "There were a lot of people . . . slept
very well." Gargan. Interview 2-15-
83.

115   "I didn't want to talk . . . get away
from them." Gargan. Interview
1-25-84.

Chapter 14

117   "Nobody had any money . . . let us
leave." Stan Moore. Interview 8-23-
83.

117   "By the way, could I borrow . . .
wallet upstairs." Ted Kennedy.
Olsen, *The Bridge at
Chappaquiddick*, p.119.

118   "He just said something . . . his wife,
Jean." Helga Wagner. *New York
Times*, 3-12-80.

118 "Ted's outside . . . you get up." Ross Richards. Marilyn Richards Gilbert interview 9-13-83.

118 "Ross, it isn't eight o'clock yet!" *Ibid.*

118 "Mostly, it was Stan Moore . . . when Joey Gargan arrived." *Ibid.*

118 "Joey looked awful . . . sticking out." *Ibid.*

118 "very definite about . . . Get in there!" Gargan. Interview 6-22-83.

119 "I was soaking wet . . . was going on." Gargan. Interview 5-20-83.

119 "That nothing had . . . was no commotion." Paul Markham. Inquest, p.321.

119 "What happened?" Markham. *Ibid.*

119 "I didn't report it." Markham. *Ibid.*

119 "When we got over there . . . hadn't reported it." Gargan to James Smith 2-9-83.

119 "What the fuck . . . the fucking accident." Gargan. *Ibid.*

120 "This thing is worse now . . . to do something." Gargan. Markham inquest testimony, p.323.

120 "We're reporting the accident right now!" Gargan. Interview 2-9-83.

120 "I'm going to say that Mary Jo was driving." Ted Kennedy. Gargan to James Smith and author 8-25-83.

120 "There's no way . . . placed at the scene." *Ibid.*

120 "Hey, you! Get out of here!" Gargan. Interview 6-22-83.

121 "I thought that in his eyes . . . something wrong." Charles Tretter. Inquest, p.254.

121 "I thought he was angry . . . conversation or what." *Ibid.*, p.192.

121 "Jesus! We've got to . . . let's go." Gargan to James Smith and author 8-25-83.

121 "He was still stuck . . . driving the car." Paul Markham. Edward Harrington to James Smith 1-11-84.

121 "I was very anxious . . . report the accident." Gargan. Interview 2-15-83.

121 "They were obviously in a big rush . . . without a greeting." Marilyn Richards Gilbert. Interview 9-13-83.

121 "To alert him to take care of . . . going to go out." Gargan. Interview 2-15-83.

122 "You've got to do . . . as fast as you can." Gargan. Interview 1-25-84.

122 "knew that something . . . what's happened?" Nance Lyons. Inquest, p.713.

122 "There's been an accident . . . can't find Mary Jo." Gargan. *Ibid.*

122 "I didn't know what had happened . . . which was brief." Gargan. Interview 2-15-83.

122 "Get all the stuff . . . cleaned up immediately." Gargan. Interview 5-20-83.

123 "Her pocketbook happened . . . my own things." Nance Lyons. Inquest, p.721.

123 Gargan-Nance Lyons dialogue. Gargan interview 5-20-83.

123 "Goddamn it, Joe you were smart . . . a total disaster." Gargan. Interview 5-20-83.

123 "Why can't we have . . . driving the car?" Nance Lyons. *Ibid.*

123 "We can't, that's all . . . was driving." Gargan. *Ibid.*

123 "This thing was . . . highly investigated." Gargan. Interview 2-17-83.

123 "But nobody specifically . . . in the car." Gargan. *Ibid.*

124 "We girls kept hoping . . . wandering around dazed." Esther Newberg. *Pittsburgh Press*, 7-24-69, p.1.

124 "One of the girls . . . happened to Mary Jo." Charles Tretter. Inquest, p.194.

124 "The Senator had driven off . . . and nobody did." Inquest, p.718.

124 "I think you ought to go . . . what to do." Charles Tretter. Gargan interview 6-22-83.

124 "I wanted to . . . I wasn't sure." Gargan. Interview 5-20-83.

124 "I asked if Mary Jo had been in the car . . . said, 'Yes'." Nance Lyons. Inquest, p.718.

125 "I want you to know . . . to save her." Joe Gargan. Esther Newberg inquest testimony, p.420.

125 "He said the Senator had called . . . Get me to Edgartown." Charles Tretter. Inquest, p.197.

125 "a tremendous emotional . . . nothing but crying." *Ibid.*, p.197.

125 "They were . . . very angry." Gargan. Interview 5-20-83.

125 "Because now I had the additional . . . I don't know." Gargan. *Ibid.*

125 "The only thing relevant . . . of any of that." Gargan. Interview 6-22-83.

125 "First, I was thinking of this as a civil case . . . to have a hearing." Gargan. Interview 5-20-83.

126 "Now that I saw the magnitude . . . now become a case." Gargan. Interview 2-17-83.

126 "I think what you ought to do . . . this whole thing." Gargan. *Ibid.*

126 "a very uncomfortable hour . . ." Charles Tretter. Inquest, p.199.

126 "Put them in the car . . . out of here." Gargan. Interview 5-20-83.

126 "sort of perused it . . . at that time." Gargan. Interview 2-15-83.

127 "Will you do us that favor . . . all screwed up." Gargan. Interview 6-22-83.

127 "He didn't take my advice." Gargan. Interview 13-28-83.

127 "We weren't asked . . . all very strange." Marilyn Richards Gilbert. Interview 9-13-83.

127 "It wasn't a scandalous party . . . to look like one." Gargan to James Smith and author 8-25-83.

128 "begun an affair during the weekend . . ." *New York Post*, 1-17-80.

128 "The whole problem about reporting . . . walk on water." Gargan. Interview 5-20-83.

129 "There were people involved . . . the accident happened." Gargan. Interview 2-17-83.

129 "talked about the accident . . . in his statement." Gargan. Interview 2-15-83.

130 "Maybe I should have realized . . . and so did Paul." Gargan. Interview 2-17-83.

130 "Up to that point . . . he was going to do." Gargan. *Ibid.*

130 "He didn't appear to be . . . he was or not." Gargan. Interview 6-22-83.

130 "The assumption was he was going . . . to take a swim." Gargan. *Ibid.*

130 "They both had comfortable hotel rooms . . . there for that purpose." Gargan. Interview 5-20-83.

130 "Look, I don't want you people . . . about the accident." Ted Kennedy. Markham inquest testimony, p.327.

Chapter 15

133 "When I looked in the trays . . . cards there." Herbert Burr. Interview 3-31-83.

134 "firmly convinced" . . . Arena. *Boston Herald Traveler* 7-21-69.

134 "But in the matter . . . leaving the scene." Arena. *The Boston Globe*, 7-21-69.

134 "If he sat . . . violation of the law." Arena. *Providence Journal*, 7-21-69.

134 "There was no other physical . . . is strictly accidental." Arena. *Boston Herald Traveler*, 7-21-69.

134 none of whom could be expected to contradict his account. *New York Times*, 7-21-69.

134 "I'm firmly convinced . . . tell the truth." Arena. *Boston Herald Traveler*, 7-21-69.

135 "I think the Senator was more . . . their attorney first." Arena. *Ibid.*

135 "I wouldn't say . . . some additional information." Arena. *New York Times*, 7-21-69.

135 "It wasn't in Kennedy's handwriting . . . threw it away." Arena. *New Bedford Standard Times*, 1-5-70.

135 "I felt it would be good . . . the hell it went." Arena. Interview 3-23-83.

135 "Chief, you better talk to Huck' Look." Arena. Interview 2-14-83.

136 "The question of time . . . in Kennedy's report." Arena. Interview 2-14-83.

136 "He is positive . . . he's not sure." Look. Statement of Chief Arena, 7-20-69.

136 "The thing that bothered . . . Kennedy's time." Arena. Interview 10-23-83.

136 "It's my day off . . . to my family." Arena. *Boston Globe*, 7-21-69.

136 "This was more a spectator thing . . . get the case." Bernie Flynn. Interview 6-15-83.

137 "George told me the colonel . . . call Bernie in." Frank Keating. Interview 7-30-83.

138 "Knowing the road . . . to be a shadow of some kind." Look. Exhumation Hearing, p.59.

138 "I observed in my rear-view . . . lost or something." Look. *Ibid.*

138 And I did sort of a photostatic . . . and the end." Look. p.60. *Ibid.*

138 "like a conga line . . . over there to our house." Look. Interview 10-4-83.

139 "I figured it was a man . . . getting lost." Look. *Ibid.*

139 "There's no way you could go . . . sore thumb." Bernie Flynn. Interview 7-28-83.

139 "I would have been there . . . within 15 minutes." Foster Silver to Hal Bruno. *Newsweek,* 8-11-69, p.21.

140 "They were real cute about that . . ." Sydney Lawrence. *Chicago Daily News,* 7-28-69.

140 "There was a lot of singing . . . damned loud, though." Foster Silva. Statement to Edgartown Police, 7-23-69.

140 "By one o'clock I was . . . called the police." Foster Silva. *New Bedford Standard Times,* 7-21-69.

140 "One of those loud, noisy . . . of hell-raising." *Manchester Union-Leader,* 7-22-69.

140 "You could still hear . . . at 2:30 A.M." Dodie Silva. *New York Post,* 7-23-69, p.5.

141 "a middle-aged man . . . towards the ferry." Dodie Silva. *Ibid.*

141 "The reason I stayed . . . was like glass." Jared Grant. Inquest, p.564–565.

142 "I was dead certain . . . I don't know." Grant. *Philadelphia Bulletin,* 7-21-69, p.7.

142 "We come out for any . . . accident or injury." Grant. *Time,* 8-8-69, p.15.

142 "If someone wanted . . . you ring the bell." Dick Hewitt. *Boston Herald Traveler,* 7-22-83.

142 "You tell me . . . with $20 bills?" Hewitt. *Washington Post,* 7-27-69, p.A10.

142 "I figure, we got a drunk driver . . . reveal himself." Bernie Flynn. Interview 4-19-83.

143 "Teddy Kennedy was running . . . find his direction." Bernie Flynn. Interview 7-28-83.

Chapter 16

146 "I just wanted to help . . ." Gifford. Exhumation Hearing, p.213.

146 "Mr. Kopechne had already . . . arrangements." Gifford. *New York Post,* 7-22-69, p.5.

146 "Because this is where her roots are . . ." Francis Kopen. *Boston Herald-Traveler,* 7-22-69.

146 "He said he wished . . . of Mary Jo." Joseph Kopechne. *New York Post,* 7-22-69, p.5.

146 "We are playing it by ear." Dr. Robert Watt. *Boston Herald-Traveler,* 7-21-69.

146 "There was no prosecutable charge . . . that's a different question." Joe Gargan. Interview 5-20-83.

152 "I'd pass them by . . . who I was." Gargan. Interview 2-15-83.

152 "After all, Senators are human . . ." Mike Mansfield. *Boston Globe,* 7-21-69.

152 "It's just one of those things . . . in any way." Mansfield. *Boston Herald Traveler,* 7-20-69.

152 "He's been going around . . . after the accident." Mansfield. *Boston Globe,* 7-22-69.

153 "at least 20 people" . . . Dick Drayne. *New York Times,* 7-21-69, p.2.

153 "Mary Jo was a sweet . . . wonderful person." Ethel Kennedy. *Boston Globe,* 7-21-69.

153 "Typing was the operative word . . . Mary Jo Kopechne hadn't." Nancy Cummings. Interview 7-26-83.

154 "Our coverage was justified . . . in history." Ian Menzies. *Newsweek,* 8-4-69, p.56.

154 "What's going on over in Edgartown?" Alvan Nickerson. Interview, 5-23-83.

154 "I'd love to tell . . . won't let me." James Reston to Alvan Nickerson. *Ibid.*

155 "They've just landed on the moon." *New York Times*, 7-21-69, p.28.
155 "one of great personal pride . . ." *Boston Globe*, 7-21-69.
155 "Instead, he was being forced . . . doctor's care." *Boston Globe*, Ibid.
155 "It's strictly . . . at Martha's Vineyard." *Boston Globe*, 7-21-69.
155 But at the last minute . . . to withhold comment. *Boston Globe*, 7-21-69.
155 "He was in a state of mind . . . right then." Dun Gifford. Hersh, p.524.

Chapter 17
157 "If you're in Edgartown . . . see us." Joe Gargan to James Smith. Smith interview 3-20-82.
157 "The invitation was given . . . been in battle." James Smith. Interview 3-20-82.
158 Memorandum From: Paul Kirk, 4-30-68.
160 "politically savvy, not mere secretaries." *Boston Globe*, 7-24-69.
160 "a Vietnam veteran . . . looking into." Memorandum—Pennsylvania Volunteers—Per Mary Jo Kopechne 202-659-9540.
160 As major a figure . . . not Humphrey. Memorandum TCS 4-26-68.
161 "I called this in to . . . any at all." Note appended to Memo TCS 4-26-68 signed MJK.
161 "drinking has a capacity . . . death of another person." Edmund Dinis. *New Bedford Standard Times*, 5-27-62.
161 "That poor woman . . . tell the truth?" Mrs. Dinis to James Smith. Smith interview 2-20-82.
162 "It was common knowledge . . . his mental health." Smith. Interview 5-22-82.
162 "Don't forget the guy . . . through so much." Smith. Interview 6-3-83.
162 "I feel sorry for him . . . Let's save him." Edmund Dinis to James Smith. Smith interview 6-3-82.
162 "It's a local matter . . . vehicles case." Dinis to Smith. Smith interview 6-3-82.
163 "You get a hold of Ted Kennedy . . . stay out of it." Dinis to Smith. Smith interviews 6-3-82 and 2-14-83.

163 "From me through you to Ted . . . Ted wants me to." Dinis to Smith. *Ibid*.

Chapter 18
165 James Smith-member of staff dialogue. Smith interview 2-14-83.
165 "It was a real bangdown . . . in my life." Smith. *Ibid*.
165 "In my heart . . . make sure I did." Smith. *Ibid*.
166 "Dinis just wants Teddy Kennedy to know . . . that's all." Smith. Interview 6-3-82.
166 Kenneth O'Donnell-James Smith dialogue. Smith interview 6-3-82.
166 "Ben's for the family." Ted Kennedy, Olsen, p.23.
167 Ben Smith-James Smith dialogue. James Smith interview 2-14-83.
167 "The nuts-and-bolts . . . get through." James Smith. Interview 6-3-82.
167 "John was such a straight arrow . . . help Teddy Kennedy, too." James Smith. Interview 10-14-83.
167 "I'm in a position . . . this thing." James Smith. Interview 10-14-83.
168 "Kenneth's not in it . . . to save him." James Smith. *Ibid*.
168 "They had some kind of a brain trust . . . called me." Smith. Interview 6-3-82.
168 "Why go to trial . . . plead *nolo*?" Smith. *Ibid*.
168 "How do you plead *nolo*?" Burke Marshall to James Smith. *Ibid*.
168 "Maybe it was just a quick . . . a guilty finding." James Smith. Interview 6-3-82.
168 "You can't very well . . . of the case." Smith. *Ibid*.
169 "They didn't trust Dinis . . . around him." Smith. *Ibid*.
169 "The case was being handled . . . ignore him." Smith. Interview 2-14-83.
169 "Inviting all those people . . . than he was." Smith. *Ibid*.
170 "Ed Hanify is the kind of lawyer . . . to argue it." Richard McCarron. Interview 7-29-83.
170 "Our kids played . . ." McCarron. Interview 10-3-83.

170   "At least now . . . somebody that was there." Arena. Interview 2-16-83.

171   "I asked him if he could . . . attended the party." Arena. Interview 10-23-83.

171   "Here I was, chief of a 5-man department . . . where to go." Arena. Interview 2-16-83.

171   "When you were a member of the alumni . . . things for you." Arena. Interview 10-23-83.

171   "My impression was . . . look into it." Arena. *Ibid.*

171   "helped push him to folly" Brock Brower. *Life Magazine.* Cited in *New Bedford Standard Times,* 7-28-69.

171   "Why didn't he call me . . . he call?" Arena to Brock Brower. *Esquire Magazine,* February, 1976, p.71.

Chapter 19

173   "I was leaning more . . . was Senator Kennedy's." Arena. Interview 10-12-83.

173   "Operator lost control . . . in the accident." Preliminary Report to the Chief Inspector, Registry of Motor Vehicles, July 21, 1969. George W. Kennedy, Investigator.

174   "I'm no pathologist." Dr. Mills. *Boston Herald Traveler,* 7-26-69.

174   "Keep it to yourself . . . what happens." Dinis to Dr. Mills. Exhumation Hearing, p.101.

174   "a very moderate . . . a highball afterwards." *Boston Herald Traveler,* 7-22-69.

174   "It was an open-and-shut . . . No nothing." Mills. *New York Times,* 7-22-69.

175   "worthy of Cecil B. DeMille." *Vineyard Gazette,* 7-22-69.

175   "Some people feel . . . if I don't.'" Arena. *Boston Herald Traveler,* 7-22-69.

175   "With any man of stature . . . any other police case." Arena. *Ibid.*

175   "I may very well be tampering . . . his defense." Arena. *Manchester (N.H.) Union-Leader,* 7-22-69.

176   "There's been a lot of hearsay . . . was there." Arena. *Boston Globe,* 7-22-69.

176   "a married man was driving . . . into the pond." *Manchester* (N. H.) *Union-Leader,* 7-21-69, p.1.

176   "to see if the girl's life . . . resign immediately?" *Ibid.,* p.6.

177   "completely discredited anything Look said" Walter Steele. *Ibid.*

177   "just seeking a little publicity . . ." Walter Steele. *Ibid.*

177   "I know what I saw . . . short to lie." "Huck" Look. *New Bedford Standard Times,* 8-17-69.

177   "Once Kennedy applied . . . up to that point." Arena. Interview 10-12-83.

178   "Tremendous pressure has built up . . . capable police officer." Edmund Dinis. *The Boston Globe,* 7-22-69.

178   "Some members of the press . . . this unfortunate incident." Dinis. *Ibid.*

178   "It's not our case . . . from the district court." George Killen. Interview 8-15-79.

178   "George was telling Arena . . . to protect the office." Bernie Flynn. Interview 10-19-83.

179   "I think he had something . . . he's no detective." Flynn. Interview 10-19-83.

179   "Positively not . . . all the attention." Flynn. Interview 7-28-83.

179   "George was on the phone . . . hands off." Flynn. Interview 10-19-83.

179   Dinis-Smith dialogue. Smith interview 6-3-82.

179   "Let *him* explain it . . . out of the case." George Killen to James Smith. Smith interview 6-3-82.

179   "What are they doing over there . . ." Smith. Interview 2-20-82.

180   "What did they think he could do . . . before it snowballs." Smith. *Ibid.*

180   "If he's attacked . . . always reacts." Smith. Interview 2-20-82.

180   "Everybody's thinking . . . to the ferry." Smith. Interview 6-27-83.

181   "Don't forget the geographical . . . simple mistake to make." Smith. Interviews 1-31-83 and 11-6-82.

181   "Advisers saw what the dangers . . . of the consequences." Hersh, p.507.

181   "I didn't want to set up . . . grief of the family." Ted Kennedy. Hersh, p.524.

182   "The marked straightening . . .
lateral projection" . . . X-Ray
Report, E. W Benjamin, M.D.,
Radiologist, 7-22-69.

182   "of indeterminable length . . . exact
time relationships." Report of Dr.
Milton F. Brougham, 7-22-69,
Exhibit B, p.1.

183   "It is safe to be dubious . . . properly
administered and interpreted."
Medical source to *The Boston
Globe*, 10-29-74.

183   "He's still under a doctor's care . . .
be considered." Richard Drayne.
Boston Herald-Traveler, 7-22-69.

183   "As of this moment . . . news
conference." Drayne. *Ibid.*

183   "a lot of different discussions . . .
about the funeral." Joe Gargan.
Interview.

Chapter 20
185   "and I described . . . knew who I
was." Gargan. Interview 2-15-83.

185   "I didn't have a discussion . . .
anything else." Gargan. *Ibid.*

186   "He'd come . . . were unconscious."
Kennedy aide. *New York Post*, 7-22-
69, p.5.

186   "Dun Gifford was very kind . . . was
a Kennedy man . . . ." Joseph
Kopechne. *The Grapevine*, 2-13-80.

187   "within the next few days." David
Harrison. *New York Post*, 7-22-69,
p.5.

187   "It was difficult . . . had a bad time."
Parish secretary. (UPI) *Manchester
Union-Leader*, 7-23-69.

187   "They wanted to see the Kennedys .
. . the Revolutionary War." Joseph
Kopechne. *The Pittsburgh Press*,
7-23-89.

188   "I'd seen so many people . . . myself
that way." Gwen Kopechne. *Ibid.*

188   "There he is!" *New York Times*,
7-23-69.

188   "Okay, you spectators . . . move
back!" Mayor Walter Burns. *Boston
Globe*, 7-23-69.

188   "Let's get to the car." Ted Kennedy.
New York Post, 7-22-69, p.5.

189   "We had a great time at lunch . . .
really something." Joseph Kopechne.
Pittsburgh Press, 7-23-69.

189   "I thought I was talking . . . all
about the area." Joseph Kopechne.
Ibid.

189   "working automatically to greet . . .
remember any of it." Gwen
Kopechne. *The Grapevine*, 2-13-80,
p.17.

189   "She was in an absolute daze."
Joseph Kopechne. *The Grapevine*,
2-13-80.

190   "We all talked at Wilkes-Barre . . .
be buried." Esther Newberg. *Boston
Sunday Advertiser*, 8-17-69.

190   "He asked me how I was . . . about
his wife." Esther Newberg. Inquest,
p.423.

190   "first indications . . . dripping wet . .
." *New York Times*, 7-23-69.

190   "where his friends had been holding
. . . is incredible!" *Ibid.*

190   "not to make any statement . . .
might never make one." *New
Bedford Standard Times*, 7-23-69.

Chapter 21
191   "This is the day of the funeral . . . at
the appropriate time." Ted Kennedy.
Boston Herald Traveler, 7-23-69.

191   "There has been some question . . .
political career." Liz Trotta. *Ibid.*

191   "I've just come from . . . comment to
make." Ted Kennedy. *Ibid.*

192   His remarks at the airport . . . to
pacify the press. Sources close to
Kennedy. *New Bedford Standard
Times*, 7-23-69.

192   "the mysterious *eminence grise* . . .
invincibility." Collier and Horowitz,
p.437.

192   "the capacity to move . . . quick
deadliness." Hersh, p.525.

192   "Half the press of the world . . .
gotten the attention." Stephen
Smith. Hersh, p.526.

192   "Our prime concern . . . charge of
manslaughter." Stephen Smith.
Hersh, p.526.

193   "Well, Bob . . . with this one."
Unnamed source. *New York Times*,
7-27-69, p.48.

193   "Steve's attitude was . . . to the
lawyers." Gargan. Interview 6-22-
83.

194   "I never heard from Killen . . . came
near me." Gargan. *Ibid.*

Chapter 22

195 "Unless we closed the police station." Walter Steele. *New Bedford Standard Times,* 7-27-69.

195 "Everyone was flying in . . . a zoo very quickly." Harvey Ewing. Interview 9-15-83.

196 "a story about getting the story . . . there was a tragic accident." *Vineyard Gazette,* 7-25-69.

196 "I left Boston to get away . . . investigating this case." Arena. *Chicago Daily News,* 7-24-69, p.5.

196 "The confusion . . . were working." *Boston Globe,* 7-23-69.

196 "One of the objects . . . heavy drinking . . ." Walter Steele. *Ibid.*

197 "These have all been . . . in such a manner." Walter Steele. *Ibid.*

197 "The investigation is . . . will be investigated." *Ibid.*

197 "I don't have, and probably . . . of a criminal sense," Walter Steele. *Boston Herald Traveler* 7-23-69.

197 "That hadn't been discussed . . ." Arena. Interview 2-16-83.

197 "We need someone . . . that manner." Arena. *Boston Globe,* 7-23-83.

197 "He walked steadily . . . he was drinking." Arena. *Chicago Daily News,* 7-24-69, p.5.

197 "It would have been a violation . . . up to that point." Arena. *Cape Cod Standard Times,* 7-23-69.

197 "There's no proof . . . of the vehicle." Arena. *Chicago Daily News,* 7-24-69, p.5.

197 "I've got to repeat again . . . involved in this accident." Arena. *Boston Globe,* 7-23-69.

198 "Aw, c'mon . . . What's the matter with you guys?" Arena. Interview 10-23-83.

198 "There is not . . . operation of the automobile." Walter Steele. *Boston Herald Traveler,* 7-23-69.

198 "We have certain evidence . . . where he was." Walter Steele. *Boston Globe,* 7-24-69.

198 "I think it's unfair . . . to his whereabouts." Walter Steele. *Ibid.*

198 "Yes, but for how long?" Arena. *Boston Globe,* 7-23-69.

199 "But we felt . . . the charge we did." Arena. *New Bedford Standard Times,* 7-30-69.

199 "But the Senator said . . . heard from him yet." Arena. *Ibid.*

199 "I just didn't think . . . might be thrown out." Arena. *Boston Herald Traveler,* 7-23-69.

199 "influenced to mishandle the case." Reporter. *Chicago Daily News,* 7-24-69, p.5.

200 "I've tried . . . to co-operate." Arena. *Ibid.*

200 "About the only thing . . . lose some weight." Arena. *Boston Herald Traveler,* 7-23-69.

200 "What bothers me . . . give to John Smith." Arena. *Albany Times-Union,* 7-23-69, p.20A.

200 "People can say . . . includes U.S. Senators." Arena. *Boston Globe,* 7-23-69.

200 "We played it straight . . . what had happened." Walter Steele to Hal Bruno. *Newsweek,* 8-11-69.

201 "The state was prepared . . . made voluntarily." *New York Times,* 7-24-69.

201 "There was no way . . . didn't want to." Arena. Interview 3-15-83.

201 "We can get Jack Crimmins . . ." McCarron to Arena. Arena interview 10-3-83.

201 "To get Arena off the hook . . . that much help." Dick McCarron. Interview 7-29-83.

Chapter 23

203 "When the Senator's closest associates . . . bafflingly obscure . . ." *Newsweek,* 7-28-69, p.33.

204 "The word has actually . . . talk to anybody." Campaign aide. *Boston Globe,* 7-24-69.

204 "I am a professional . . . to as such." Esther Newberg. *Boston Globe,* 10-30-74.

204 "It was a steak party . . . drinks apiece." Newberg. *Newsday,* 7-23-69.

204 "But everyone moved inside . . . a fun party." Newberg. *Ibid.*

205 "No one was sitting around . . . called to check, but there wasn't."

Newberg. *New York Times,* 7-24-69.

205   Her "Mickey Mouse" watch . . . wasn't working properly. *The Worcester* (Mass.) *Evening Gazette,* 7-23-69, p.2.

205   "On the way . . . had not been found." Newberg. *Pittsburgh Press,* 7-24-69.

205   "What else would you do?" Newberg. *The Worcester* (Mass.) *Evening Gazette,* 7-23-69, p.2.

206   "Ted Kennedy's office was five doors . . . to get information." Newberg. *Ibid.*

206   "Nobody's trying to hide anything." Newberg. *Boston Globe,* 7-24-69.

206   "First, Mary Jo is dead . . . tried to save her." Newberg. *Boston Herald Traveler,* 7-24-69.

206   "There was some vodka . . . a flippant-type person." Susan Tannenbaum. *Newsday,* 7-24-69.

206   "During the weekend . . . further to say." Tannenbaum. *Boston Herald Traveler,* 7-24-69.

207   "You can't begin to understand . . . over the papers." Tannenbaum. *Time,* 9-5-69.

207   "How would you feel . . . of married men." Tannenbaum. *Ibid.*

Chapter 24
209   "I thought, Hey, what's this . . . Kennedy accident case?'" Arena. Interview 2-16-83.

209   "We just wanted . . . without press coverage." Arena. Interview 3-15-83.

210   "Clark had always been a police-court . . . common-sense guy." Frank Keating. Interview 7-30-83.

211   "If I have anything . . . make that speech." Edward Hanify. McCarron interview 7-29-83.

211   "The lawyers wanted no statement . . . the Senator's career." McCarron. *Ibid.*

211   "Didn't cover it at all . . . was my interpretation." McCarron. Interview 10-3-83.

212   "Let's suggest . . . it wasn't considered." McCarron. *Ibid.*

212   "The law at that time . . . personal injury." McCarron. Interview 7-29-83.

212   "I'm not going to find you guilty . . . I'll sentence you." McCarron. *Ibid.*

213   "so rattled and unsure . . . unrealiable schoolboy." Hersh, p.490.

213   "As a time of great . . . difficult and complex." Ted Kennedy. Hersh, p.524.

213   "Kennedy was "obviously panicky still . . . that sort required." Hersh, p.523.

Chapter 25
215   "The nerve of these horse's asses . . . have some class." Walter Steele. Olsen, p.210.

216   "There is not a scintilla of evidence . . . leaving the scene." Walter Steele. *Worcester Evening Gazette* 7-23-69, p.1.

216   "Except for finishing touches." Walter Steele. *Boston Globe,* 7-24-69.

216   "To quell all the inferences . . . by natural conditions." Arena. *Boston Globe,* 7-23-69.

216   "There is not one iota . . . was involved." Arena. *Ibid.*

216   "We don't and probably will not . . . how that can change." Arena. *New York Times,* 7-24-69.

216   "We're satisfied that the accident . . . for the complaint." Arena. *Boston Globe,* 7-24-69.

217   Arena-Katz exchange at press briefing. Leonard Katz, *New York Post,* 7-24-69.

217   "It is not true . . . investigation is over." George Killen. *Worcester Evening Gazette,* 7-23-69, p.1.

217   "I see no need of . . . state police bureau." Killen. *Boston Globe,* 7-24-69.

217   "This isn't Argentina." Killen. Interview 7-16-79.

218   "This office will not . . . More facts will be presented." Edmund Dinis. *New Bedford Standard Times,* 7-23-69.

218   "between 11:15 P.M. and 11:45 P.M. . . . going fairly fast." Statement of Sylvia Malm to Edgartown Police.

218 "Nobody ever heard . . . hear anything." Arena. Interview 2-28-83.

218 "But I believe Mrs. Stewart did . . . that morning." Statement of Russell Peachey to Officer George Searle, 7-23-69.

219 "You are probably nearer . . . be a witness." Arena to Harvey Ewing. Ewing interview 10-3-83.

219 "Did you know the Registry . . . because of negligence?" Reporter to Arena. Arena interviews 2-16-83 and 4-15-83.

219 " 'Red' Kennedy was . . . from a reporter." Arena. Interview 2-16-83.

219 If the hearing resulted . . . at least six months. Statement of Registrar Richard McLaughlin on Kennedy Case. Press Release. 7-23-69.

219 "You must not again . . . been reinstated." Notice of Suspension of License to Edward M. Kennedy. File #CT6651. Registry of Motor Vehicles, 7-23-69.

220 "a matter of interpretation . . . to my woes." Arena. *Chicago Daily News,* 7-24-69, p.1.

220 "people were pulling the rug . . . on the spot." Arena. Interview 2-16-83.

220 "I got the feeling . . . avoiding me." Arena. Interview 6-6-83.

220 "a nice, easy-going guy . . . to snoop around." Arena. Interview 3-23-83.

222 FBI Report—Boston Office. Transmission 7-23-69.

222 "This is the case . . . I have." Arena. *Worcester Evening Gazette,* 7-23-69, p.1.

222 "This is my baby . . . *my* baby." Arena. *New Bedford Standard Times,* 7-24-69.

222 "taking tranquilizers because of this thing." Arena. *New York Times,* 7-24-69.

Chapter 26

223 "There are technical defenses . . ." Robert Clark. Olsen, p.210.

223 "by other considerations . . . criminal case." Clark. *Ibid.*

223 "I don't want evidence . . . against me." McCarron. Interview 7-29-83.

223 "The judge won't . . . neither do I." Walter Steele. Olsen, p.211.

224 "We've got enough to hook him . . ." Steele. *Ibid.*

224 "You'll get a fair shake . . . strictly by the book." Walter Steele. Arena interview 2-28-83.

225 "And here comes the same car . . . the right turn." Thomas Whitten to *The National Enquirer,* 9-2-69, p.19.

225 "reckless driving . . . Mass. registration." Commonwealth of Virginia, County of Albermarle Summons.

225 "That boy had . . . traffic ordinances." Thomas Whitten. *The National Enquirer,* 9-2-69, p.19.

226 "They were upset . . . with Huck' Look's." McCarron. Interview 7-29-83.

227 "Any person who wantonly . . . such a result." Chapter 265, Section 13. Massachusetts General Laws.

227 "Grave danger to others must have been apparent . . . act or omission." *Commonwealth v. Barnett Welansky,* 316 Mass. 383.

228 "unusually receptive . . ." *Ted Kennedy: Profile of a Survivor* by William Honan, New York: Manor Books, 1972, p.171.

228 "Felt pretty funny about it . . . asked us to write." Speechwriter. *Ibid.*

229 "a graduate . . . living Nebraskan." *New York Times,* 7-20-69.

229 "full of brooding . . . to the legacy." Hersh, p.526.

229 "I responded to the call . . ." Theodore Sorensen. *New York Times,* 8-22-69.

229 "The presence of a girl . . . the police immediately." *The Kennedy Legacy* by Theodore Sorensen, New York: Macmillan, 1969, p.302.

229 "To suspend my own moral judgments . . . misstatements of facts." Sorensen. *New York Times,* 8-22-69.

229 "about certain things . . . make certain about." Gargan. Interview 2-15-83.

229 "He can't let this thing . . . got some answers." *New York Times. Ibid.*

229 "still suffering from . . . the car." Ibid.

230   "Worse, there are good reasons . . . this tragic affair." *The Washington Post*, 7-24-69.

230   "To end speculation . . . the death of Mary Jo Kopechne." *Boston Record-American*, 7-24-69.

Chapter 27

231   "We don't know if the girl . . . from drowning." Robert Nevin. *Boston Globe*, 7-25-69.

231   "I wouldn't have let . . . change the picture." Nevin. *Medical World News*, 8-22-69, p.1.

231   "But the point is . . . could be answered." Nevin. *Boston Herald Traveler*, 7-25-69, p.1.

231   "The order could . . . district attorney." Nevin. *Ibid*.

232   "In my 11 years . . . vehicles accident." Edmund Dinis. *Boston Herald Traveler*, 7-25-69.

232   "And then for some reason . . . people will start talking." Dinis. *Chicago Daily News*, 7-25-69.

232   "You're saying that since . . . Joe Blow he wouldn't." Armand Fernandes. *Medical World News*, 8-22-69, p.13.

232   "would not be available . . . on this matter." *New Bedford Standard Times*, 7-24-69.

233   "I got hung with it . . . tried for months." James Smith. Interview 2-14-83.

233   "Where's all this Kennedy expertise . . . this thing ride." Edmund Dinis to James Smith. Smith interview 2-14-83.

233   "So much as the political time-bomb . . . the worse it got." James Smith. Interview 2-14-83.

233   The whole reaction of the parties . . . intentional or not. James Smith to Warren O'Donnell. Smith interview 3-17-83.

233   "Because of what was going on . . . working at all." James Smith. Interview 3-17-83.

234   "He can't duck the case forever." James Smith. Interview 2-14-83.

235   "I don't think an autopsy . . . do you?" Edmund Dinis to Dr. Mills. Exhumation Hearing, p.102.

235   "I really agree . . . guns on that." Mills. Exhumation Hearing, p.102.

235   "I don't want another Lee Harvey Oswald . . . Arena handle it." Dinis. *New Bedford Standard Times*, 8-7-69.

235   "In this particular case . . . the passage of time." Dr. John McHugh. Inquest, p.270.

236   "there shall be no presumption." McHugh. Interview 9-7-83.

236   "Chief, you're talking too much." Robert Quinn to Arena. (UPI) *Boston Globe*, 7-25-69.

236   "Pretrial publicity . . . it's unconstitutional." Bernie Flynn. *Cape Cod Standard Times*, 7-24-69.

236   "The two press conferences . . . it was a microphone." Bernie Flynn. Interview 7-28-83.

237   "Every time you turned . . . case away." George Killen. Interview 8-15-79.

237   "Better not blow your case." Albert Hinckley to Arena. Arena interview 2-14-83.

237   "I don't think I was told . . . were friendly calls." Arena. *Boston Herald Traveler*, 7-25-69.

237   "There will be no . . . Walter Steele." Robert Bruguiere. *Ibid*.

237   "But it is beyond belief . . . not even been asked." *The Nation*, 8-11-69, Vol. 209, No. 4, p.100.

238   "By talking a lot . . . knowing so little." Sherill, p.73.

238   "He is not only the best chief . . . his own career." Robert Carroll. *Boston Herald Traveler*, 7-25-69, p.11.

Chapter 28

239   "liked to hang around cops . . . and investigator." Arena. Interview 3-23-83.

239   "Jack was one of those . . . kept coming up." Arena. Interview 2-16-83.

240   "I thought . . . the night before." Arena. Interview 3-23-83.

240   "Here's a guy . . . at the party." Arena. Interview 2-16-83.

240   Arena-Crimmins dialogue. Arena interview 2-16-83.

241   Statement to Edgartown Police— John Crimmins. Catamaran Motel,

Falmouth, Mass., Thursday, 7-24-69.

241 "The statement certainly . . . corroborating Ted Kennedy." Arena. Interview 2-16-83.

242 "Reinforces the suspicions . . . for the tragic situation." *New York Times*, 7-31-69.

242 "All the surviving . . . fix with the judge." Barry Farrell. *Life Magazine*, 8-8-69.

242 "It's what lawyers . . . a more serious one." Richard McCarron. Interview 10-3-83.

243 "We didn't get . . . pitch or what." Arena. Interview 4-15-83.

243 "It was at this meeting . . . bomb at us." Arena. *Ibid*.

243 "How would you feel . . . for probation?" Robert Clark. Arena interview 4-15-83.

243 "First thing in the morning . . . what's happening." Robert Clark to Arena. Arena interview 4-15-83.

243 "Jesus! We forgot . . . the Judge!" Walter Steele. Olsen, p.227.

244 "Why should we . . . they ask for?" Judge James Boyle. Olsen, p.228.

244 "That's when we all pushed . . . he'll get upset." Arena. Interview 4-15-83.

244 Arena-Clark dialogue. Arena interview 2-16-83.

245 "A lot of time . . . was happening." Arena. *Ibid*.

245 Arena-McClure dialogue. Arena interview 2-16-83.

245 "I've got a brief . . . say no more." Robert Clark. *Boston Herald Traveler*, 7-25-69.

246 "I have no idea . . . decision on." Arena. (UPI) *Manchester Union-Leader*, 7-25-69.

246 "As of this moment . . . motor vehicles case." Arena. *Boston Herald Traveler*, 7-25-69.

246 "If a not guilty . . . for a continuance." Arena. *Ibid*.

246 "I'm ready . . . the witnesses ready." Walter Steele. (UPI) *Manchester Union-Leader*, 7-25-69.

246 "That's right . . . So sue me!" Walter Steele. *Pittsburgh Press*, 7-25-69, p.1.

246 "That's true . . . Take him out." Walter Steele. *Ibid*.

247 "If a lawyer had a serious case . . . against their client." Joe Donegan. Interview 2-29-84.

247 "Not as a legal advisor . . . going to court." Joe Gargan. Interview 4-28-83.

247 "So it wasn't difficult . . . make arrangements." Gargan. *Ibid*.

247 "I never discussed . . . for that matter." Gargan. *Ibid*.

247 "like some mystery ship . . ." Dick McCarron. Interview 7-29-83.

Chapter 29

249 "I never had a case . . . my client to jail." Robert Clark. *Boston Globe*, 10-31-74.

249 "Don't worry about it . . . made up his mind." Ted Kennedy to Dick McCarron. McCarron interview 10-3-83.

250 "He looked like . . . with the car." Harvey Ewing. Interview 9-15-83.

250 Transcript of *Commonwealth v. Edward M. Kennedy, New Bedford Standard-Times*, 7-27-69.

251 "that Ted Kennedy had tried . . . by delaying his report." *New York Times*, 7-27-69.

253 "The longest minute . . . his decision." Robert Clark. *Boston Globe*, 10-31-74.

Chapter 30

255 "You go out . . . it's all over." Walter Steele to Arena. Arena interview 2-16-83.

255 "Nobody else . . . cameras again." Arena. *Ibid*.

255 "We have prosecuted . . . case is closed." Arena. *Cape Cod Standard Times*, 7-25-69.

255 "I thought of letting out . . . the end of it." Arena. Interview 2-16-83.

256 "He said he'd called . . . for trespassing." Arena. Interview 2-16-83.

256 "This case is closed." Walter Steele. *Boston Herald-Traveler*, 7-26-69.

256 "I let them know . . . a plea were entered." Walter Steele. *Ibid*.

256 "People think once . . . always be doubts." Walter Steele. *Cape Cod Times*, 7-14-79.

256 "It was his decision . . . plead guilty." Dick McCarron. *Chicago Daily News*, 7-26-69.

257 "You had to enter . . . could suspend." McCarron. Interview 3-16-84.

257 "The statute called for . . . then suspend." Frank Keating. Interview 7-30-83.

257 "I see no reason . . . any different." Helen Tyra. *New Bedford Standard Times*, 7-29-69.

257 "a private matter . . . individual basis." Tyra. *Ibid*.

257 "But Senator Kennedy . . . travel at will." Tyra. *New York Daily News*, 7-27-69.

258 "I'm waiting for him . . . the public yet." Gwen Kopechne. (UPI) *Manchester Union-Leader*, 7-26-69.

258 "I know there are a lot of sick people . . . clear my daughter." Gwen Kopechne. *Ibid*.

258 "Although this call . . . without further advice." Dr. Donald Mills. *New Bedford Standard Times*, 7-21-69.

258 "Which I was . . . as soon as I did." Mills. *Ibid*.

259 "I believe the district attorney's . . . against speculation." Mills. *Boston Herald Traveler*, 7-26-69.

259 "I would have told . . . name was cleared." Mills. *Boston Globe*, 7-25-69.

259 "And the knowledge we had . . . once and for all." Mills. *Boston Herald Traveler*, 7-26-69.

259 "Reporters had a story . . . willing to do." Mills. *Medical World News*, 8-22-69, p.13.

259 "To send somebody . . . to help me." Mills. *Ibid*.

259 "didn't know the law . . ." Armand Fernandes. Cited by Mills. *Ibid*.

259 "that he fervently . . . the 'no autopsy'" Mills. *Ibid*.

260 "When I learned it was . . . was surprised." Joseph Mellino to Ralph Gordon. Gordon interview 6-19-83.

260 "Because I had a file card . . . funny as hell." Mellino. *Ibid*.

260 "But a while later . . . Saturday night." Mellino. *Ibid*.

260 "The expiration of a license . . . a motor vehicle." Richard McLaughlin to Ralph Gordon. Unpublished news story.

260 The Senator's license "had been taken care of." Hank Jonah to James Smith. Smith interview 2-10-83.

260 "Jack Kennedy often drove . . . license renewed." Joe Gargan. Interview 2-17-83.

261 "Senator Kennedy's license never expired." Richard McLaughlin to Ralph Gordon. Unpublished news story.

261 "In fact, he made it . . . any Registry office." McLaughlin. *Ibid*.

261 "He was always . . . his license." McLaughlin. *Ibid*.

261 "We never went . . . the Registry." Gargan. Interview.

261 "I see no . . . about it ever." Paul Markham. *New York Times*, 7-21-69, p.48.

262 "Can't you get . . . damaging this is?" Joseph Donahue, Jr. to Joe Gargan. Gargan interview 7-15-83.

262 "We indicated our feelings . . . thoughts and emotions." Gargan. Interview 6-23-82 (with James Smith).

Chapter 31

263 "I was pretty disillusioned over the press." Francis Broadhurst. Interview 12-27-82.

264 "You're going to Hyannis Port." Don Moore. Interview 6-16-83.

264 "You see those overhanging . . . for damages!" Irate neighbor. *Ibid*.

265 "He started to scream . . . in my face." Dr. Donald Mills. *Boston Record-American*, 8-16-69.

266–270 Senator Edward M. Kennedy television address. Inquest Exhibit #3. 15220.

271 "They were trying to say . . . outside of marriage." Richard Goodwin. Hersh, p.523.

272 "There was nothing heroic . . . of cowardice." *Time*, 8-29-69, p.19.

272 "She was having . . . sailing weekend." Joe Gargan. Interview 5-20-83.

272   "We got 100 calls . . . get through."
      Richard Drayne. (AP) Hartford
      Courant, 7-26-69.

272   "was overwhelmingly favorable . . .
      telegrams come in." Drayne. (UPI)
      Pittsburgh Press, 7-26-69, p.1.

272   "We're going to . . . than that."
      Drayne. *Boston Herald Traveler,*
      7-27-69.

273   "Senator Kennedy . . . and support."
      Mike Mansfield. (AP) *Hartford
      Courant,* 7-26-69.

273   "Senator Kennedy has been . . .
      slander and innuendo." Mansfield.
      New York Times, 7-25-69.

273   "Knowing Senator Kennedy as . . .
      between them." Edward Boland.
      New Bedford Standard Times,
      7-26-69, p.1.

273   "too significant . . . it concluded."
      Boland. *Brockton Enterprise,* 7-26-
      69.

273   "Senator Kennedy has the strength .
      . . this latest tragedy." Boland. *New
      Bedford Standard Times,* 7-26-69,
      p.2.

273   "I say that . . . need him badly."
      Thomas O'Neil. *New Bedford
      Standard Times,* 7-26-69.

273   "I have seen . . . by you people."
      O'Neil. *Ibid.*

274   "Unanimously anti-Kennedy . . ."
      New York Times, 7-26-69, p.10.

274   "I am satisfied . . . in the Senate."
      Gwen Kopechne. *New York Times,*
      7-25-69.

274   "I was satisfied . . . the unanswered
      questions." Gwen Kopechne.
      Sherrill, p.9.

274   "Whatever guilt was there . . . hurry
      up and *stop!*" James Smith.
      Interview 6-3-82.

274   "an assistant district attorney . . .
      Kennedy family." *Cape Cod
      Standard Times,* 7-26-69.

274   "I think he was . . . satisfactory to
      me." James Smith. *Ibid.*

275   "It was just foolish . . . nothing at
      all." George Killen. Interview 7-6-
      79.

275   "All this time . . . George's
      arguments." Bernie Flynn. Interview
      10-19-83.

275   "Watching that speech . . . ought to
      be shot." Flynn. *Ibid.*

275   "About 20 seconds . . . to do
      something." Armand Fernandes.
      Interview 6-2-83.

Chapter 32

277   "because Regatta weekends . . .
      other guests." Peachey. *Boston
      Globe,* 7-27-69.

277   Peachey-Kennedy dialogue. *Boston
      Sunday Advertiser,* 8-17-69.

278   "The courtyard was lit . . . the only
      one around at that time." Peachey.
      Brockton Enterprise, 7-27-83.

278   "He could have . . . to lose in high
      office." Peachey. *Philadelphia
      Evening Bulletin,* 7-28-69.

279   "I thought . . . with something
      new!" Arena. Interview 3-23-83.

279   "Because I thought . . . was a
      variation." Arena. Interview 2-16-
      83.

279   "Why the hell . . . as that place
      was." Arena. Interview 2-16-83.

279   "It was a moving . . . a man for
      that." Arena. *New York Sunday
      News,* 7-27-69, p.C3.

280   "It wouldn't have . . . the matter any
      further." Arena. *Boston Globe,*
      7-27-69.

280   "I'm not saying . . . don't believe it."
      Richard Hewitt. *New Bedford
      Standard Times,* 7-26-69.

280   "There's no question . . . a lot of
      baloney." Hewitt. *Philadelphia
      Evening Bulletin,* 7-28-69.

280   "But I wouldn't vote . . . for nine
      hours?" Hewitt to Mary McGrory.
      Boston Globe, 1-6-70.

280   "A man of Kennedy's swimming . . .
      his physical condition." John Farrar.
      New York News, 7-27-69.

280   "He didn't answer any questions . .
      ." John Farrar. *Philadelphia
      Bulletin,* 7-28-69.

280   "There was a great possibility . . .
      Mary Jo's life." Farrar. *New
      Bedford Standard Times,* 7-27-69.

281   "There would have been an airlock .
      . . a delay of 15 minutes." Farrar.
      Philadelphia Bulletin, 7-28-69.

281   "John had all this stuff . . . I didn't
      think so." Arena. Interview 2-16-
      83.

281   Having escaped from the car to
      swim to shore, the driver was

charged with negligent homicide. *Oregonian* (Portland, Oregon), 7-24-69.

281   "This is near . . . don't you?" Letter to Chief Arena dated 7-26-69.

282   "Chief Arena is getting . . . the thing to do." Carmen Salvador. *Philadelphia Evening Bulletin*, 7-28-69.

282   "Despite his bad back . . . do it." Arena. *Sunday New York Daily News*, 7-27-69.

282   "About a dog we used to see . . . Ted Kennedy could do it." Arena. Interview 3-23-69.

282   "a revelation that stunned . . . why it was not." Hal Bruno. *Newsweek*, 8-11-69, p.22.

282   "a moral . . . legal obligation." Arena. *New York Daily News*, 7-27-69.

282   "There's no violation . . . of any statute." Arena. *Philadelphia Sunday Bulletin* 7-27-69.

282   "A prompt call to the police . . . from drunken driving." *Time*, 8-1-69.

283   "That their efforts . . . off the hook." *Newsweek*, 8-11-69, p.22.

283   "In full possession of the facts . . . politically astute?" *The Nation*, 8-11-69, p.100.

283   "irritated and angry . . . no understanding of that." Gargan. Interview 5-20-83.

283   "because we had grown up together . . . the press loves." Gargan. Interview 2-17-83.

284   The Senator never did actually say . . . he was going to do." Gargan. *Ibid.*

284   "Nothing under the law . . . report the accident." Gargan. Interview 5-20-83.

284   "Everybody is saying . . . son of a bitch." Gargan. *Ibid.*

284   "There's no evidence . . . wanted them to do." Philip Sisk. *Cape Cod Standard Times*, 7-27-69.

285   "If a man is a . . . were trampled on." Sisk. *Ibid.*

285   "I think he assumed a lot more . . . leaving the scene." Sisk. *Ibid.*

285   "No one could get a fair trial . . . and God help you." Edmund Dinis. *New Bedford Standard Times*, 7-27-69.

285   "When the medical examiner . . . driver of the car." Dinis. *Ibid.*

285   "It's awfully easy . . . seek advice." Walter Steele. *Ibid.*

286   "Dinis was notified . . . I'll come down.'" Walter Steele. *New Bedford Standard Times*, 7-24-69.

286   "Dinis had at least 24 hours . . . to do neither." Steele. *Ibid.*

286   "An autopsy in this matter . . . Commonwealth's case." Steele, *New Bedford Standard Times*, 7-27-69.

286   "A lot of local people . . . putting them on." Arena. Interview 10-23-83.

286   "His headlights would have revealed . . . think you're kidding?" Letter to *New York Times* dated 7-26-69 from Dr. Edward Self. *New York Times*, 8-2-69.

287   "It seems like we've handled . . . are for him." *New York Times*, 7-26-69, p.10.

287   "a man who failed . . . moment of crisis." *Baltimore Sun*, 7-26-69.

287   "Further investigation . . . might be necessary." *The Hartford Courant*, 7-26-69.

287   "Just say she's pregnant . . . in February." Ted Kennedy. *New York Times*, 7-27-69.

288   The Senator made that clear . . . going to elaborate." Dick Drayne. *Boston Herald Traveler* 7-28-69.

288   "the ugly and destructive gossip . . . about the accident." *Times to Remember* by Rose Fitzgerald Kennedy, New York: Bantam, 1975, p.533 (paperback edition).

288   "Teddy has been so magnificent . . . the burden." Rose Kennedy. *Time*, 8-8-69, p.15.

288   "And how badly I felt . . . were with them." *Times to Remember*, p.534.

288   "I've always brought my children . . . ups and downs." Rose Kennedy. (UPI) *New Bedford Standard Times*, 9-6-69.

288   "God does not send . . . rise above all this." Rose Kennedy. *Time*, 8-8-69, p.15.

Chapter 33
289   "We're with you, Ted!" *New York Times*, 7-28-69.

289 "No test has been . . . to all men."
Monsignor William Thompson.
Cape Cod Standard Times, 7-28-69.

289 "Today we used it . . . Senator
Kennedy." Thompson. *Ibid.*

290 "This is church ground . . . of it."
New York Times, 7-28-69.

290 "disgusted, dismayed and shocked .
. . the emotions. *Cape Cod Standard
Times*, 7-28-69.

290 "emotion-charge . . . failure of
responsibility." *New York Times*,
7-27-69.

290 "had possibly sacrificed . . . name
out of it." *Ibid.*

290 "The speech . . . candor and style."
David Halberstam. Cited in Olsen,
p.249.

290 "who have no way . . . cast of
characters" James Reston. *New
York Times*, 7-27-69.

290 "Anything short of a formal . . . to
believe him." *Providence Journal*,
7-26-69.

291 "We've had calls . . . communicated
it to us." Eric Cochner. *Washington
Post*, 7-27-69.

291 "We are interested in his functions .
. . level of performance." Richard
McLaughlin. *Chicago Tribune*,
7-29-69.

291 "All such reports . . . a fatal
accident." McLaughlin. *Ibid.*

291 "a politician . . . State House." *New
Bedford Standard Times*, 7-3-71.

292 "We must make the consequence of
drunken driving . . . they drink."
McLaughlin. *New Bedford
Standard Times*, 3-11-70.

292 "It effectively deprives . . . how you
do it." Richard McLaughlin.
Interview 8-10-82.

293 "He has no immediate plans."
Richard Drayne. *New York Times*,
7-28-69.

293 "I know black from white." "Huck"
Look. *Time*, 8-8-69. p.15.

293 No one had come forward . . .
"probably unlikely." *New York
Times*, 8-2-69.

293 "Because at the time Look said . . .
Look was wrong." Joe Gargan.
Interview 5-20-83.

293 "But it was also highly criticized . . .
not have happened." Gargan.
Interview 2-15-83.

294 "more guilty . . . than Kennedy."
New Bedford Standard Times,
7-26-69, p.1.

294 "Take this and read it . . . in his
moccasins." Betty Gargan. Gargan
interview 2-17-83.

294 "She wanted to go on a talk show . .
. girls they were." Gargan. *Ibid.*

295 "I wouldn't have tried . . . is the
same." Gargan. Interview 6-22-83.

295 Telegram from Congressional
Delegation. *New Bedford Standard
Times*, 7-29-69.

295 "If there was less . . . it take place."
David Bartley. *Ibid.*

296 "It's a tough spot for me." Edmund
Dinis. *New Bedford Standard
Times*, 7-30-69.

Chapter 34

297 "as I was with our legal rights . . ."
Leslie Leland. *New Bedford
Standard Times*, 8-1-67.

297 "I wanted to clarify . . . for an
investigation." Leland. *New
Bedford Times*, 10-7-69.

297 "It's up to . . . a judge." Leland.
Vineyard Gazette, 8-1-69.

298 "Because of . . . repercussions."
Leland. *New Bedford Standard
Times*, 10-7-69.

298 "at one of the many meetings . . .
this matter . . . until the speech."
Armand Fernandes. Interview 6-2-
83.

298 "The effort to conceal the party . . .
about getting one." Fernandes. *Ibid.*

299 "We talked about this entire
situation . . . a Hobson's Choice." F.
Lee Bailey. Interview 5-2-84-

299 "The magistrate shall . . . his
arrest." Chapter 38, Section 12.
Massachusetts General Laws.

300 "Because the press . . . to do
something." Dinis to Killen. Killen
Interview 8-16-79.

300 "To hell with the press . . . was
cooperate." George Killen. *Ibid.*

300 "We don't prosecute . . . we know
about." Killen. *Ibid.*

300   "George had so much pride . . . manslaughter case." Frank Keating. Interview 7-30-83.

301   "There was Ted Kennedy . . . that whole approach." Keating. *Ibid.*

301   "a pure political animal . . . of the thing." Keating. *Ibid.*

301   "I won't have anything . . . I'll leave." Joseph Harrington to James Smith. Interview 3-20-82.

301   "Eddie knew better . . . not to do it." Peter Gay. Interview 8-20-84.

302   "My personal reaction . . . the Portuguese connection." James Smith. Interview 3-17-83.

302   I only . . . a lawyer." Fernandes. Interview 11-17-82.

302   "too contrived . . . the press." Evans and Novak Political Report, 7-30-69, #56, p.1.

302   "No fair assessment . . . his resignation." *Cape Cod Standard Times*, 7-29-69.

302   "It could hurt his image . . . on this basis." Josiah Spaulding. *Boston Globe*, 7-27-69.

302   "Senator Kennedy's situation . . . his ability to lead." Spaulding. *New York Times*, 7-29-69.

303   "Because he was a Kennedy . . . mysterious circumstances." *Boston Herald Traveler*. 7-30-69.

303   "I think the nation . . . in Teddy Kennedy." Emmanuel Celler to WCBS. Quoted in *New York Times*, 8-4-69.

303   "I never thought he'd run . . . he won't run." Mike Mansfield. *New York Times*, 7-29-69.

303   "The controversy . . . to common measurement." Edmund Muskie to Jack Bell, (AP) *Boston Globe*, 7-27-69.

303   "In the face of demands . . . in the political community." Evans and Novak Political Report, 7-30-69. p.2.

304   "He risked a hostile . . . in the balance." Evans and Novak. *Ibid.*

304   "But a personage engaged . . . of stagecraft." Sydney J. Harris. *Chicago Daily News*, 7-26-69.

304   To help him decide . . . isn't known." Dick Drayne. *Cape Cod Standard Times*, 7-30-69.

305   "There was never any essential . . . the statement." Source. *New York Times*, 7-27-69.

305   I've just got to gut this thing through." Ted Kennedy. Warren Rogers, *Look*, 8-10-71.

Chapter 35

307   "I have no reason . . . communicated it to anyone." Dick Drayne. *Washington Post*, 7-27-69.

308   Statement by Edward M. Kennedy Returning to the Senate. *New York Times*, 7-31-69.

308   I don't interpret . . . unambiguous to me." Dick Drayne. *Ibid.*

308   "A carefully-worked out . . . resolved in any sense." *New York Times*, 7-31-69.

309   "Mr. Kopechne and I can form . . . to believe this!" Gwen Kopechne. *New York Post*, 8-16-69.

309   "with the physical . . . its notoriety." *Vineyard Gazette*, 7-29-69.

309   "All of them are bothered . . . of the accident." *Vineyard Gazette*, 8-1-69, p.5.

309   "Miss Kopechne was dead . . . authorities do it." Statement by District Attorney Edmund Dinis of the Southern District, 8-2-69. Press Release, p.1.

309   "But as the days went by . . . courage into account." Dinis statement, p.2.

310   "A human being was dead . . . to demand an inquest." Dinis statement, p.5.

310   "That's right . . . if re-elected." Ted Kennedy. *New York Times*, 8-1-69.

310   "Come in here, Ted . . . you belong." Mike Mansfield. *Newsweek*, 8-11-69, p.19.

310   "The statement that I made . . . my full term." Ted Kennedy. *Boston Globe*, 8-1-69.

310   "I tried to the very best . . . any further comment." *Ibid.*

311   "Because it is crucial . . . is easily arrived at." *Washington Post*, 8-1-69.

311   "You're back at work . . . now and any time in the future." Letter to Ted Kennedy from James Smith, 7-31-69.

311   "And asked him to relay messages . . . I hope they helped." *Ibid.*
311   "Ed Dinis proved to be . . . when I see you." *Ibid.*
311   "To conduct an inquest . . . about July 18, 1969." Letter to Justice Joseph Tauro from Edmund Dinis, 7-31-69.

Chapter 36
313   "It is very bad judgment . . . notifying the court." Joseph Tauro. *New Bedford Standard Times*, 8-1-69.
313   "All relevant statutes . . . over such proceedings." Letter to Edmund Dinis from Joseph Tauro, 8-1-69.
313   "the confusion . . . unprecedented action." Letter to Edmund Dinis from Joseph Tauro, 8-6-69.
314   "To express my preference . . . like that better." Edmund Dinis. *Providence Journal*, 8-4-69.
314   "Inquests are practically . . . action is advisable." Kenneth Nash. *Boston Record American*, 9-4-69.
314   "I'll challenge Mr. Dinis . . . but he can't." Kenneth Nash. *New Bedford Standard Times*, 3-12-67.
314   "We have had . . . pleaded guilty." Walter Steele. *New Bedford Standard Times*, 8-1-69.
315   "After all . . . district attorney." Arena. *New Bedford Standard Times*, 8-1-69.
315   "Although the questioning . . . rumors about the case." Arena. *New York Daily News*, 8-7-69.
315   "Maybe we were just trying . . . party people at all." Arena. Interview 10-12-83.
315   "There's no rapport . . . two offices." Arena. *Cape Cod Standard Times*, 8-8-69.
316   "Dinis didn't want . . . Killen told him to." Bernie Flynn. Interview 4-7-83.
316   "One thing about Dinis . . . himself to any degree." Frank Keating. Interview 7-30-83.
316   "It wasn't the kind of case . . . the time to prepare." Keating. *Ibid.*
317   "Eddie turned sour . . . he usually does." James Smith. Interview 11-6-82.

317   "Dinis was being kind . . . his kindness." Smith. Interview 2-14-83.
317   "If he'd done that . . . been all over." Smith. *Ibid.*
317   "to state clearly . . . of Mary Jo Kopechne." Statement by District Attorney Edmund Dinis, 8-2-69.
317   "following some of the most . . . investigative agencies." *In His Garden* by Leo Damore, New York: Arbor House, 1981, p.237.
318   "but rather on the *lack* . . . finally to rest." Dinis statement, p.3.
318   "three young women" . . . *New York Times*, 8-2-69.
318   "He doesn't feel . . . for an inquest." Dick Drayne. *New Bedford Standard Times*, 8-4-69.
318   "It's still rather unclear . . . in any way." Ted Kennedy. *New Bedford Standard Times*, 8-1-69.
318   "After I accepted the responsibility . . . further kinds of legal action." Ted Kennedy. *Boston Globe*, 10-28-74, p.23.
318   "The common sense . . . the Senator's explanation on TV." James Reston. *New York Times*, 8-15-69.
318   "Should be welcomed . . . surrounded the tragedy." WCBS Editorial, 8-6-69. Broadcast at 8:20 and 11:20 P.M.
319   "at once self-pitying . . . remain to be asked." WCBS. *Ibid.*
319   "smacked of an attempt to . . . get publicity." WHDH-TV Reporter. *New Bedford Standard Times*, 8-2-69.
319   "No, I wouldn't . . . back to the Senate." Ted Kennedy. *Ibid.*
319   "to turn a tragedy into . . . political windfall." Kennedy source. *New Bedford Standard Times*, 8-2-69.
319   "Politically, this is not good . . . with any advantage?" Edmund Dinis to Greg Wierzynski, *Time*, 10-31-69.
319   "one of the most controversial . . . of Beacon Hill." *The Crime of Dorothy Sheridan* by Leo Damore. New York: Arbor House, 1978, p.81.

320 "But a requirement . . . food on the table." Armand Fernandes. Interview 11-17-82.

321 "He can decide . . . business to him." David Farrell. *Boston Herald Traveler,* 10-28-63.

321 "handsome, likeable . . . straight-talking . . ." *New Bedford Standard Times,* 10-3-70.

322 "I think for the most part . . . couldn't care less." Edmund Dinis. *Providence Journal,* 8-4-69.

322 "I am controversial . . . thought was right." Dinis. *New York Times,* 8-9-69.

322 "But to see that justice is done." Dinis. *New Bedford Standard Times,* 6-16-58.

Chapter 37

323 "I wasn't confident . . . case was getting." Joe Gargan. Interview 2-17-83.

324 "An imprecise process . . . don't know, never." Stephen Smith. Hersh, p.526.

324 "Steve Smith sort of came . . . for their interests." *Boston Globe,* 10-29-74, p.18.

324 "Because of what . . . or get into." *Ibid.*

324 "expressing some concern . . . I paid their attorneys." Ted Kennedy. *Boston Globe,* 10-28-74, p.23.

324 "One of the first . . . reporters or police." *Boston Globe,* 10-29-74.

325 "Until such time . . . now pending." Letter to Joseph Greelish from Robert G. Clark, Jr., 9-11-69.

325 "We have . . . that we legally can." Undated Memo. Registry of Motor Vehicles.

325 "As Senator Kennedy himself . . . he should have." Ted Sorensen. NBC Nightly News. *New Bedford Standard Times,* 8-1-69.

325 "To the best of my knowledge . . . of facts." Sorensen. *New York Times,* 8-22-69.

326 "And I don't think . . . in 1972." Sorensen. *Ibid.*

326 "There's no doubt it . . . don't know yet." Sorensen. *Boston Record-American,* 8-23-69.

326 "in light of these two . . . Robert Kennedy." Sorensen. *The Kennedy Legacy,* p.15.

327 "The eagerness to put off . . . and speechwriters." Sherrill, *The Last Kennedy,* p.32.

327 "A tragedy . . . a crucial moment." Mankiewicz. Cited in *Time,* 8-8-69, p.16.

327 "a moodiness and disorientation . . . core of integrity." James McGregor Burns. *New York Times,* 4-10-72.

327 "whose print-out . . . ten years old." James Smith. Interview 3-20-82.

327 "premature political burial . . ." *Before the Fall* by William Safire, New York: Belmon Tower Books, 1975, p.154.

327 "I don't know anything about it." Richard Nixon. *New York Times,* 7-21-69.

328 "It is doubtful . . . its former appeal." *The Nation,* 8-11-69.

328 "Much of the doubt . . . of the accident." *Time,* 8-8-69, p.17.

328 "And the public will continue . . . decisions under pressure." *Cape Cod Standard-Times,* 7-24-69.

328 "Kennedy refused to clear . . . a full disclosure." Robert Sherrill, *The Last Kennedy,* p.11.

329 "They wanted the names . . . on their own." Arena. Interview 6-6-83.

329 "as cold as . . . or colder." George Killen. Interview 8-15-79.

329 "George was kicking . . . done an autopsy." Bernie Flynn. Interview 4-19-83.

329 "He didn't look to me . . . in the morning." Russell Peachy to Charles Roberts. *Newsweek,* 9-8-69, p.22.

Chapter 38

331 "that dopey son of a bitch." George Killen. Leo Damore, *In His Garden,* p.77.

332 "Ross wasn't a member of . . . not Washington." Marilyn Richards Gilbert. Interview 9-13-83.

332 "I happened to win the race . . . 15 minutes." Ross Richards. Inquest, p.259.

332 "I remember the bell . . . join us later." Richards. Inquest, p.261.

332 "But as to what . . . I don't know." Ross Richards to Stan Moore. Moore interview 7-18-82.

332 "Are you thinking . . . for the first time." John Dunn. *Boston Globe*, 10-20-74.

332 "It sure looked that way." Ross Richards. *Ibid.*

332 "Ross was making faces . . . had gone on." Stan Moore. Interview 7-18-82.

333 "We weren't going to be . . . looking for." Moore. *Ibid.*

333 "The police asked me if . . . to me." Moore to John Kerr. *Cape Cod Standard-Times*, 1-11-70.

333 "Things like . . . Chappaquiddick at all." Moore. Interview 7-18-82.

333 "I was asked that . . . no comment." Moore. *Cape Cod Standard-Times*, 1-11-70.

333 "I didn't think it was . . . wasn't laced or anything." Moore. Interview 8-23-83.

333 "that kind of party . . . has no conscience.'" Moore. Interview 7-18-82.

334 "So he pulled over . . . heard about the accident." Bernie Flynn. Interview 4-19-83.

334 "On the fact that a man . . . you'd be frightened." Flynn. *Ibid.*

334 "Kennedy's talking to these people . . . back to the cottage." Flynn. *Ibid.*

335 "Not because of any telephone . . . didn't get out?' " Flynn. *Ibid.*

335 "Not unless somebody said . . . pretty damn good." Flynn. *Ibid.*

335 "Everybody thought it was . . . seeing the car." Flynn. Interview 6-15-83.

335 "If anything happened . . . now he's ready to run." Flynn. Interview 7-28-82.

335 "Ted Kennedy . . . gotten out alive." Flynn. *Ibid.*

335 "That was deliberate . . . doesn't *know* what happened." George Killen to Frank Keating. Keating interviews 7-30-83 and 7-18-83.

336 "Why wasn't it less harmless . . . himself in the water?" Keating. Interview 7-18-83.

336 "To hell with it . . . in the first place." Killen. Keating interview 7-30-83.

336 "Everybody was represented . . . to the attorney." Bernie Flynn. Interview 7-28-83.

336 "The letters we sent . . . refused to talk to police." Armand Fernandes. Interview 6-2-83.

336 "Quinn nearly fell . . . He was terrified." Edmund Dinis to James Smith. Smith interview 6-3-82.

337 "I have no more information . . . legal research." Robert Quinn. *New Bedford Standard Times*, 8-12-69.

337 "Let us hope that in the deep . . . to the people." Quinn. *Boston Herald Traveler*, 7-27-69.

337 "to submit evidence . . . Mary Jo Kopechne." Letter to Edmund Dinis from Judge James A. Boyle of the District Court of Edgartown, 8-5-69.

337 "All I'm trying to do . . . Senator Kennedy yet." Edmund Dinis. *New Bedford Standard Times*, 8-7-69.

337 "In order to have a pathologist . . . of the case." Dinis. *Ibid.*

338 "what practices and procedures . . ." Letter to Blythe Evans, Jr. from Edmund Dinis, 8-1-69.

338 "It's a court order . . . not a petition." Blythe Evans. *New Bedford Standard Times*, 8-7-69.

339 "If there was . . . had been committed." Evans. *Ibid.*

339 "I wouldn't do that . . . enough trouble." Dinis. *Ibid.*

339 "Mr. Dinis never bothered . . . who we are." Gwen Kopechne. *New Bedford Standard Times*, 8-7-69.

339 "We were told . . . after we buried her." Gwen Kopechne to Bill Ryan. *Hartford Times*, 9-30-69.

339 "We have had no collusion . . . tell us anything." Gwen Kopechne. Sherrill, *The Last Kennedy*, p.9.

339 "He'd make a trip . . . were prepared for it." Gwen Kopechne. *The Grapevine*, 2-11-80.

339   "pieced together . . . falsify the facts." Jack Anderson. *Washington Post,* 8-13-69, p.C7.

340   "Too fast for safety . . . without skidding." Anderson. *New Bedford Standard Times,* 8-8-69.

340   "After it was too late . . . presidential dream." Anderson. *Washington Post,* 8-13-69.

340   "In this state, he conceived . . . for the Kennedys." Anderson. *New Bedford Standard Times,* 8-8-69.

340   "It is entirely possible . . . the girl's body." Anderson. *Ibid.*

340   "Then Gargan and Markham rustled up a boat . . . of the accident." Anderson. *Washington Post,* 8-13-69.

340   "They wanted another look . . . in Poucha Pond." Anderson. *Ibid.*

340   "a nightmare of emotional trauma . . . what he had done." Anderson. *Ibid.*

340   "There were no rowboats . . . in the water." Gargan. Interview 6-22-83.

341   "There's no basis in fact . . . entirely untrue." Gargan. *New Bedford Standard Times,* 8-8-69.

341   "I don't think anybody was trying . . . protecting the Senator." Gargan. Interview 6-22-83.

341   "Their files contained this same report . . . they didn't use it." Jack Anderson. Interview 3-15-84.

341   "one of the great political stories of all time." Anderson. *Ibid.*

341   "Jack was representing me . . . on the long range." Anderson. *Ibid.*

341   "Those things are possible . . . the best we can do." Anderson. *Ibid.*

Chapter 39

343   "Because I thought . . . we had seen." C. Remington Ballou. *New Bedford Standard Times,* 8-19-69.

343   "the forms of three persons . . ." Ballou. *Ibid.*

343   "At this point . . . all was quiet." Ballou. *Ibid.*

343   "If there was a boat . . . swam across." Dick Drayne. *New Bedford Standard Times,* 8-23-69.

344   "categorically untrue." Ted Kennedy. *Boston Globe,* 8-14-69.

344   "legal restraints . . . rumor-filled atmosphere." Kennedy. *Ibid.*

344   "I can live with myself . . . no basis in fact." Kennedy. *Ibid.*

344   "He is ill-at-ease . . . the accident." Evans and Novak, Political Report, 8-13-69, #57, p.1.

344   "ashen-faced . . . defection." The Revival of Ted Kennedy by Sylvia Wright. *Life* Magazine, 10-3-69, p.38.

344   "an almost manic gaiety . . ." Sylvia Wright. *Ibid.*

344   "gloom and defeatism . . ." Evans and Novak, 8-13-69.

344   "thoughtful messages . . . easier for me." Letter to James Smith from Senator Edward Kennedy dated 8-13-69.

346   "legitimate and accredited . . . other news media." Judge James A. Boyle, *New York Times,* 8-9-69.

347   "For weeks media people . . . an *open* inquest!" Harvey Ewing. Interview 9-15-83.

347   "To make an effort . . . Mary Jo Kopechne." Edmund Dinis. *Newsweek,* 8-18-69, p.27.

347   "in going through the motions . . ." *Newsweek, Ibid.*

347   "That's what he said today . . . every possibility." Arena. *Time,* 8-15-69, p.20.

347   "It's understandable . . . angle is quite acute." Dinis. *New Bedford Standard Times,* 8-28-69.

347   "Now that he was doing it . . . on Ted Kennedy." F. Lee Bailey. Interview 5-2-84.

348   "To try to . . . of the accident." Andy Tuney. Interview 3-12-84.

348   "I didn't think a trial lawyer jumping . . . not get involved." Bailey. Interview 5-2-84.

348   "the impartiality of the law . . . conducted with great care." *New Bedford Standard Times,* 9-2-69.

348   "The statute . . . the Court will decide." Dinis. *Ibid.*

349   "I hope there will be . . . for the girl's family." *Boston Herald Traveler,* 8-7-69.

349   "That the sudden death . . . other than the deceased." Dinis petition.

350 "Because I've favored . . . debated facts." Robert Nevin.

350 "Dr. Mills committed an error . . . unless pushed." Nevin. *Medical World News*, 8-22-69, p.10.

350 "a strange man . . . knowing the facts." Dr. Donald Mills. *Ibid.*

350 "It was crystal clear . . . this case completely." Mills. *Ibid.*

350 "If the district attorney's office . . . have been avoided." Mills. *Ibid.*

350 "I've always been led . . . a pretty furtive affair." Mills. *Ibid.*

350 "That medical examiner can't . . . and he didn't." Dinis. *New Bedford Standard Times*, 8-14-69.

350 "On Sunday after the accident . . . released the body." Dinis. *Ibid.*

351 "strange that this should come . . . mention an autopsy." Mills. *Ibid.*

351 "The answer to these . . . trial by newspaper." George Killen to Roger Murray. *Cape Cod Standard-Times*, 8-20-69.

351 "If he'd asked . . . have gotten one." Killen. Interview 8-15-79.

351 "I've got 16 other things . . . in other states." Judge Bernard Brominski. *Boston Globe*, 8-14-69, p.10.

351 "They are a lot more formal . . . in Massachusetts." Dinis. *New York Times*, 8-16-69.

351 "We did not overrule him . . . hysteria that prevailed." Dinis. *New Bedford Standard Times*, 8-5-69.

352 "It's rather exciting . . . a United States Senator." Brominski. *Boston Record-American*, 8-26-69, p.12.

352 "all over the place . . . of the courthouse." Edmund Dinis. Interview 12-10-81.

352 "She was adamant . . . if at all possible." Joseph Flanagan. *New York Times*, 8-16-69.

352 "We can't understand . . . is only hurting us." Gwen Kopechne. *New Bedford Standard Times*, 8-15-69.

352 "I don't want my little girl's . . . drip a month ago." Gwen Kopechne. *Medical World News*, 8-22-69, p.13.

353 "Reading all the different versions . . . gets you confused." Gwen Kopechne. *New York Times*, 8-17-69.

353 "I would love to sit down and listen . . . how it happened." *Ibid.*

353 "I guess those girls . . . give us some answers." Gwen Kopechne to Representative of Jack Anderson. *New Bedford Standard Times*, 9-26-69.

353 "There's no sense denying it . . . went into shock." Gwen Kopechne. *New York Times*, 8-17-69.

353 "It is this question . . . me every day." Gwen Kopechne. (UPI) *New Bedford Standard Times*, 8-17-69.

353 "To clear up the questions . . . Kennedy to testify." *Ibid.*

353 "She didn't know what . . . the record straight." Gargan. Interview 6-22-83.

355 "I looked at some of their records . . . from the personal stuff." Dick McCarron. Interview 10-3-83.

355 "But I doubt . . . a fabrication." Dick Drayne. *New Bedford Standard Times*, 8-15-69.

355 "If he'd called me . . . the police promptly." Ted Sorensen. *New Bedford Standard Times*, 8-21-69.

355 "some elements . . . exaggerating rumors . . ." Sorensen. *New York Times*, 8-25-69.

355 "We knew he wasn't there . . . let them handle it.'" James Smith. Interview 6-27-83.

356 "the closest adviser . . . in the White House." *New York Times Magazine*, 11-4-73.

356 "Your brother is moving boldly . . . to support Kenneth O'Donnell." Letter to Ted Kennedy from James Smith, 8-8-66.

356 "Why should I help . . . makes him so great?" Ted Kennedy to James Smith. Smith interview 7-20-83.

356 "went dry in the mouth" . . . Smith. *Ibid.*

356 "Kenneth had made major . . . Massachusetts for years." Smith. Interview 10-14-83.

356 "There wasn't a major decision . . . did not share in." Robert Kennedy Friendship Dinner 1-22-66.

357 "Kenneth made a strong effort . . . a future contender." Letter to Ted Kennedy from James Smith. 10-3-66.

357   "Teddy didn't believe you should use . . . a moral issue." Hersh. *Education of Edward Kennedy*, p.373.

357   "That's two out of two . . . in this business." Kenneth O'Donnell. *Boston Herald Traveler*, 6-9-68.

357   "Paul was calling Kennedy up . . . because Paul told him." Cleo O'Donnell. Interview 9-22-82.

358   "Kenny would have knocked . . . to save himself." Cleo O'Donnell. *Ibid.*

358   "Teddy Kennedy was the weak kitten . . . other people are around." O'Donnell. *Ibid.*

358   "Kenny was amazed . . . they never hit it off." *Ibid.*

358   "I think he should stay on . . . his brothers showed." Kenneth O'Donnell. (AP) *New York Times*, 7-26-69.

358   "How do you think Teddy Kennedy felt . . . such a bad guy.'" James Smith. Interview 7-20-83.

358   "Kenneth was a moral man . . . light years." Smith. Interview 6-23-83.

359   "Kenneth was drinking a little bit . . . he handle anything else?" *Ibid.*

Chapter 40

361   "I thought the meetings Ted Kennedy had . . . from my friends.'" Paul Redmond. Interview 7-23-83.

361   "When I became involved in the case . . . strictly P.R." Redmond. *Ibid.*

362   "I was representing three guys and . . . amusement at the party." Redmond. *Ibid.*

362   "Everybody was talking about the defense . . . in there blind." Redmond. *Ibid.*

362   "Never mind the facts of the case . . . to the late 1800s." Redmond. *Ibid.*

363   "If I get over there with no ground rules . . . but just sit there." Redmond. *Ibid.*

363   "the first order of business . . ." Redmond. Pre-inquest Hearing, p.34.

363   "There was some question about extraditing . . . grand jury subpoena." Armand Femandes. Interview 6-2-83.

364   "There was no overwhelming response." Fernandes. *New Bedford Standard Times*, 8-21-69.

364   "I will voluntarily agree . . . fully and cooperatively." Rosemary Keough. *The Philadelphia Sunday Bulletin*, 8-24-69, p.1.

364   "Those rumors are untrue . . . about her death." Keough. *Ibid.*

364   "A ridiculous untruth . . . there is to it." Keough. *Ibid.*

365   "I'll do everything . . . obtain the nomination." Keough. *Ibid.*, p.9.

365   "just more Kennedy PR." Paul Redmond. Interview 7-23-83.

365   "The investigation was being blocked . . . talk to police." Armand Fernandes. Interview 6-2-83.

365   "But these were often wild-goose chases." Fernandes. *Ibid.*

365   "When you drown like that in a car . . . edge of clothing." John McHugh. Interview 9-7-83.

366   "We knew that's how she was . . . the elasticized waistband." McHugh. *Ibid.*

366   "You'd get a positive . . . water for many hours." McHugh. *Ibid.*

366   "The trouble was, everyone . . . the car was immersed." McHugh. *Ibid.*

366   "caved in like a wave . . . from the front." McHugh. *Ibid.*

366   "The logical person to survive . . . window close by." McHugh. *Ibid.*

367   "Because nobody saw him . . . got to prove that.' " McHugh. *Ibid.*

367   "Steering wheels can be difficult . . . washing away the print." James Sharkey. Interview 9-16-82.

367   "There were a lot of phone . . . highly-publicized cases." George Killen. Interview 7-16-79.

367   "Nobody's at the control tower . . . you take off." Killen. *Ibid.*

368   "because I don't want . . . directly to me." Killen. *Ibid.*

368   "Everyone came up a blank." Gordon Clarkson. Interview 6-3-83.

368   "The place was a madhouse . . . to kill you." Clarkson. *Ibid.*

369   "What his duty is . . . district attorney knows." Armand Fernandes Interview 6-2-83.

369   "The office was under . . . wild and woolly." Fernandes. Interview 6-2-83.

370 "Having failed to act . . . now powerless." Joseph Flanagan. *New Bedford Standard Times*, 8-25-69.

370 "To reveal grounds for suspecting . . . or anyone else." Flanagan. *Ibid.*

370 "whether or not criminal intent was suspected." Fernandes. *New York Times*, 8-2-69.

370 "Holding an inquest . . . for the inquest." Fernandes. *New Bedford Standard Times*, 8-25-69.

370 "autopsy is part of the . . . never be closed." Edmund Dinis. *New Bedford Standard Times*, 8-22-69.

370 "There must be an inquest . . . proceed without it." Dinis. *Boston Record-American*, 8-23-69, p.12.

Chapter 41

371 "Boyle was surprised . . . for ground rules." Paul Redmond. Interview 7-23-83.

371 "discuss matters . . . entitled to be filed." Judge James A. Boyle. Pre-inquest Hearing. Into the Death of Mary Jo Kopechne. Edgartown District Court, 8-27-69 and 8-28-69, p.13.

372 "And so were all the other lawyers . . . anything he wanted." Paul Redmond. Interview 7-23-83.

372 "just not going to accept . . . the United States Constitution." Redmond. Pre-inquest Hearing, p.15.

372 "You've had more time . . . to an inquest." Judge James A. Boyle. *Ibid.*, p.17.

372 "That went to the very heart of the issue." Robert Clark. *Ibid.*, p.20.

372 "a stake in an accusatory proceeding . . . constitutionally guaranteed him." *Jenkins versus McKeithon*, June 1969.

372 "archaic under present-day circumstances . . ." Clark. *Ibid.*, p.9.

373 "The investigative . . . trial-like proceedings." Cited in Sherrill, p.130.

373 "It's an investigation . . . of anyone." Boyle. Inquest, p.3.

373 "So that the rights . . . fully protected." Clark. Pre-inquest Hearing, 8-27-69, p.2.

373 "The Lord alone knows . . . to be asked." Pre-inquest Hearing—Part 2, p.31.

373 "in the nature of . . . is wide open?" Redmond. Pre-inquest Hearing, p.25.

373 "whose unlawful act . . . contributed thereto . . ." Boyle. *Ibid.*, p.28.

374 "the information that I need . . . and report." Boyle. *Ibid.*, Part 2, p.32.

374 "Except that I will make . . . without subpoena." Boyle. *Ibid.*

374 "At your request . . . you designate." Robert Clark. *Ibid.*, p.32.

374 "Then we are not going . . . that of our client." Edward Hanify. *Ibid.*, p.33.

374 "You heard that . . . want any ifs.'" Boyle. Pre-inquest Hearing.

375 "Before an inquest . . . allowed at an inquest." Clark. *Ibid.*, p.42.

375 "I'm doing what . . . wanted argument." Boyle. *Ibid.*, p.43.

375 "People file motions . . . accepted and docketed!" Clark. *Ibid.*, p.44.

375 "Give it to me . . . some law on this!" Boyle. *Ibid.*, p.45.

375 "To what Court . . . your exception?" Boyle. *Ibid.*, p.9.

375 "What I was saying in veiled terms . . . other remedies'" Paul Redmond. Interview 7-23-83.

376 "he must have stayed . . . to produce." Dick McCarron. Interview 7-29-83.

376 "to raise the issue . . . been the driver." Edward Hanify. *Ibid.*, Part 2, p.16.

376 "a person who had . . . of the inquest." *Ibid.*

376 "Because it had not been . . . no other reason." Boyle. *Ibid.*, p.15.

376 "more publicity . . . the world." Hanify. *Ibid.*, p.16.

376 "being less than cooperative . . . Senator from Massachusetts . . ." Hanify. *Ibid.*, p.26.

377 "as a private citizen . . . in the inquest." Hanify. *Ibid.*, pp.26–27.

377 "Because the end result . . . further criminal action." Redmond. *Ibid.*, p.36.

377 "The witnesses want to come . . . your Honor." Redmond. *Ibid.*

377 "We have nothing to hide."
     Redmond. *Ibid.*, p.34.
377 "we want the basic . . . situation is
     entitled." Redmond. *Ibid.*, Part 2,
     p.37.
377 "That's for the . . . not for me."
     Boyle. *Ibid.*, p.15.
377 "I was actually relieved . . . Senator
     Kennedy be there." Edmund Dinis.
     Boston Herald Traveler, 8-28-69.
377 "There are constitutional grounds . .
     . to be considered." Dinis.
     Newsweek, 8-25-69.
378 "to trace the movements . . . the
     accident." Dinis. *Time*, 8-29-69,
     p.19.
378 "All questions raised . . .
     satisfactorily answered." Dinis.
     Newsweek, 8-25-69, p.23.
378 "If Dinis is thorough . . . matter
     entirely." Leslie Leland. *Ibid.*, p.24.
378 "You'll get a full report . . . from
     Judge Boyle." George Killen. James
     Smith interview 6-3-82.
379 "My educated guess . . . soon as
     possible." Walter Steele. *Cape Cod
     Standard-Times*, 9-2-69.
379 "sanctioned publicity . . . judicial
     proceedings." *Edward M. Kennedy
     v. James A. Boyle*. Petition for Writ
     of Certiorari.

Chapter 42
381 "hurt my feelings . . . things didn't
     hurt so much." Joan Kennedy.
     McCalls, August 1978.
381 "I believe everything . . . in a
     confused state." Joan Kennedy.
     Ladies Home Journal, June 1970.
382 "No, I'm sure they weren't . . . the
     next day's race." Joan Kennedy.
     Ibid.
382 "a reasonable explanation . . . more
     rumors." Ted Kennedy. *New
     Bedford Standard Times*, 8-13-69.
382 "so stupid as to attend . . . late
     brother's staff." Ted Kennedy. *Time*,
     8-29-69, p.19.
383 "the careless . . . court reporting."
     Justice Paul Reardon. (UPI) *New
     Bedford Standard Times*, 9-3-69.
383 "That was Tommy's revenge . . .
     covering this thing." Harvey Ewing.
     Interview 9-15-83.

384 "It did look . . . had come to town."
     Vineyard Gazette, 8-29-69.
384 "They have these . . . all the time."
     Claire Markham. *The Philadelphia
     Inquirer*, 5-24-70.
384 "I never saw them myself . . . to see
     him." Joe Gargan. Interview 2-15-
     83.
384 "Paul was definitely having . . .
     couldn't deal with it." Edward
     Harrington to James Smith.
     Interview 1-11-84.
385 "as a fire . . . to protect Ted
     Kennedy." James Smith. Interview
     6-3-82.
385 "People were walking around
     Boston . . . by the press." Paul
     Redmond. Interview 7-23-83.
386 "It's no secret . . . took my spot."
     Redmond. *Ibid.*
386 "They haven't seen you . . . to say
     hello." Redmond. *Ibid.*
386 "a nice reunion . . . Very friendly."
     Gargan. Interview 5-20-83.
387 "massive descriptions . . ." Edward
     Hanify. Transcript Proceedings—
     *Edward M. Kennedy v. James A.
     Boyle, Justice of District Court of
     Dukes County*, (Reardon, J.) 9-2-
     69.
387 "of a gathering crescendo . . . each
     passing hour." Hanify. *Ibid.*, p.31.
387 "massive publicity . . ." Hanify. *Ibid.*
387 "preliminary relief . . . restraining
     order." Hanify. *Ibid.*, p.34.
387 "grave constitutional questions . . ."
     Hanify. *Ibid.*, p.35.
387 "But at this point . . . come into
     existence." Joseph Hurley. *Ibid.*,
     p.37.
387 "through the medium of the press . .
     ." Hurley. *Ibid.*, p.43.
388 "to terminate statements . . . the
     seeds of prejudice." Justice Reardon.
     Ibid., p.46.
388 "To mind their conduct . . ."
     Reardon. *Ibid.*, p.46.
388 "Now is the correct . . . its inquest
     laws." Walter Steele. *Boston
     Record-American*, 9-4-69.
388 "We'll have a much easier . . . in the
     year." Arena. *Boston Herald-
     Traveler*, 9-3-69.
388 "We've only got one . . . close that
     off." Arena. *Boston Globe*, 9-3-69.

Chapter 43

389   "I signed that prayer of . . . the Justice's declaration." Ted Kennedy. *New Bedford Standard Times*, 9-4-69.

390   "He did not want it thought . . . painful questions." *New York Times*, 9-7-69.

390   "The press would sit . . . verbally assassinated." Paul Redmond. *New Bedford Standard Times*, 10-9-69.

390   "with everyone else . . . wasn't necessary." Joe Gargan. Interview 2-17-83.

390   "The reason I went along . . . for years to come." Gargan. *Ibid*.

390   "There'll be any shuffling." John Powers. *New Bedford Standard Times*, 9-12-69.

391   "The state's judicial . . . the Senator's behalf." *Boston Globe*, 9-4-69.

391   "to join with me . . . dangerous practice." Robert Quinn. *Boston Record-American*, 9-4-69.

392   "had a feeling . . ." Leslie Leland. *New Bedford Standard Times*, 9-4-69.

392   "They were all shitting . . . grand jury action." James Smith. Interview 3-17-83.

392   "What he called me for . . . could do." Smith. Interview 6-27-83.

392   "If he didn't pursue the case . . . attacked his own reputation." Smith. *Ibid*.

393   "The credibility . . . medical area." Robert Nevin. *New Bedford Standard Times*, 9-2-69.

393   "I haven't been contacted." Edmund Dinis. *Boston Globe*, 9-2-69.

393   "Let's have it . . ." Bernard Brominski. *New Bedford Standard Times*, 9-4-69.

393   "name names . . . for an autopsy." Joseph Flanagan. *Boston Record-American*, 9-4-69.

394   "We offered to go to Massachusetts . . . was it going to prove?" Joseph Kopechne. *The Grapevine*, 2-13-80.

394   "I know she wasn't pregnant . . . with something else." Gwen Kopechne. *The Grapevine*, 2-13-80, p.15.

394   "In a way the appeal . . . no point to it." Edmund Dinis to James Smith. Smith interview 6-3-82.

394   "Don't these assholes . . . what I'm doing." Dinis to Smith. Smith interview 3-17-83.

394   "when she was in my arms . . . unusual at all." Arena. *New Bedford Standard Times*, 9-19-69.

395   "But I wasn't looking . . . out of the water." John Farrar. *Ibid*.

395   "You are putting me on . . . to answer." Eugene Frieh. *Chicago Daily News*, 9-18-69.

395   "Only a slight . . . from the nostrils." McCarron to Eugene Frieh, 9-15-69. McCarron interview 7-29-83.

395   "I would say those . . . to be disappointed." Ted Kennedy. *New Bedford Standard Times*, 9-19-69.

395   "could have caused . . . of blood." Senator's attorneys. *Ibid*.

395   "I figured we'd get . . . everybody go home.'" George Killen to Frank Keating. Keating interview 7-18-83.

396   "The investigation was unlike . . . are going through my head." Bernie Flynn. Interview 4-19-83.

396   "When Jack and Bobby got killed . . . gang going after him." Flynn. Interview 4-7-83.

397   "But I knew him by reputation." Flynn. Interview 4-19-83.

397   "I heard you're working . . . things going?" Andy Tuney. Flynn interview 6-15-83.

397   "I was telling him about . . . a raw deal." Flynn. Interview 4-19-83.

397   "That goddamned TV speech . . . and keeps lying." Flynn. Interview 6-15-83.

397   "Jesus, I'd like to help . . . in a bind." Flynn. Interview 5-19-83.

397   "Bernie was very anxious . . . to help Ted Kennedy." Andy Tuney. Interview 3-12-84.

398   "Andy said he knew where . . . see that he gets it." F. Lee Bailey. Interview 5-2-84.

398   "But I rather think . . . prepare him for the inquest." Bailey. *Ibid*.

398   "urgent and important . . . in the papers all the time." Tuney. Interview 3-12-84.

398   "Well, you can't do . . . not here."
Stephen Smith to Andy Tuney. *Ibid.*

398   "It had to be somebody close . . .
Kennedy family so much." Tuney.
Ibid.

398   "relay it direct . . . gets the message."
Stephen Smith. Tuney, *Ibid.*

Chapter 44

399   "At the time I talked . . . just
barroom talk." Bernie Flynn.
Interview 4-7-83.

399   "Tuney saying that . . . who I was."
Flynn. Interview 6-15-83.

400   "gave it a lot of thought . . ." Flynn.
Interview 4-7-83.

400   "The first time I've . . . not
comfortable with." Flynn. *Ibid.*

400   "I was put right through . . . who I
was." Flynn. Interview 7-28-83.

400   "I told him my position . . . on the
phone." Flynn. Interview 4-19-83.

400   "Maybe he was afraid . . . with
Teddy Kennedy." Flynn. Interview
6-15-83.

400   "check this out with the Senator."
Stephen Smith to Bernie Flynn.
Flynn interview 4-19-83.

401   "The most delicate political . . . kept
in the family." Gargan. Interview
6-2-83.

402   "I'll give you this name . . . in
Washington." Stephen Smith to
Flynn. Flynn interview 4-19-83.

402   "picayune case . . . as to when."
Flynn. Interview 6-15-83.

402   "When you hit Washington . . .
everybody called him Jack." Stephen
Smith to Bernie Flynn. Flynn
interview 6-15-83.

402   "Stay there . . . carrying a briefcase."
Herbert Miller. Flynn interview
4-19-83.

402   "Blonde hair . . . light color." Flynn.
Interview 5-19-83.

403   "Because I'd made the trip . . . lunch
or something.'" Flynn. *Ibid.*

403   "A good looking guy . . . very self-
confident." Flynn. *Ibid.*

403   "I said to myself . . . I'm no dummy."
Flynn. Interview 4-19-83.

403   "There was no reason for him . . . I
was expecting." Flynn. Interview
5-19-83.

403   "That's when I knew . . . I'm going
to do." Flynn. Interview 4-19-83.

403   "It kind of made me uneasy . . . what
I said." Flynn. Interview 5-19-83.

403   "I'm doing this because . . . he had
presidential aspirations." Flynn.
Interview 4-19-83.

403   "I kind of selected . . . delivered
verbally." Flynn. Interview 6-15-83.

404   "The man is honest . . . Kennedy
said it was." Flynn. Interview
4-19-83.

404   "The whole context . . . at the
inquest." Flynn. *Ibid.*

404   "The reason Look knows . . . to the
cemetery." Flynn. Interview 7-28-
83.

404   "Teddy Kennedy was in the bag . . .
driving under." Flynn. *Ibid.*

404   "The new witnesses we had . . . he
wasn't upset." Flynn. Interview 4-7-
83.

404   "He's just following the trend . . . on
the tape." Flynn. Interview 5-19-83.

404   "Is that it . . . anything else?"
Herbert Miller to Bernie Flynn.
Flynn interview 4-7-83.

405   "All lit up . . . really enjoyed that."
Flynn. Interview 5-19-83.

405   "Stephen Smith didn't send me . . .
pay your way down.' " Flynn.
Interview 4-7-83.

405   "I never called down . . . the case
with him." Andy Tuney. Interview
3-12-84.

405   "gave something to somebody . . . I
assumed, Judge Clark." F. Lee
Bailey. Interview 5-2-84.

406   "By the time this happened . . . of
the investigation, Ted Kennedy."
Bailey. *Ibid.*

Chapter 45

407   "Investigators for Kennedy . . .
change what I saw." "Huck" Look.
Boston Globe, 10-29-74, p.19.

407   "Because it didn't work . . . what he
said he saw." Dick McCarron.
Interview 10-3-83.

408   "It was the same problem . . . what I
was doing." McCarron. *Ibid.*

408   "Above all, Kennedy has told . . .
report the accident . . ." (AP) *New
Bedford Standard Times,* 1-5-70.

408 "that Senator Kennedy had tried . . . Miss Kopechne's death." *New York Times,* 7-27-69.

409 "sufficient to stun . . . a human being." *New Bedford Standard Times,* 9-7-69.

409 "How they can recreate . . . consulting firm didn't." John Farrar. *The National Enquirer,* 10-12-69.

409 "But I stand on my belief." John Farrar. *New Bedford Standard Times,* 8-1-69.

409 "John was a little screwy . . . of the accident." Dick McCarron. Interview 7-29-83.

410 "less than 3 seconds . . . miles per hour." Physical Factors Involved in the July 18, 1969 Accident on Dyke Bridge, Chappaquiddick Island, Edgartown, Martha's Vineyard. Prepared for Robert G. Clark, Jr. Arthur D. Little, Inc. p.51.

410 "Almost as though . . . been turned out . . ." Physical Factors Report, p.53.

410 "Braking only will not prevent . . . over the rail." *Ibid.,* p.52.

410 "Maybe an engineer could . . . on the bridge." Arena. Interview 2-28-83.

411 "well below the minimum . . . engineering criteria." Affidavit of Eugene D. Jones, District Court of Dukes County, 1-2-70.

411 "We use the breathalyzer . . . isn't a toy." John Palmiera. *New Bedford Standard Times,* 1-14-70.

412 "one widely-accepted line of speculation . . . had been alone in the car." Joseph Lelyveld. *New York Times,* 9-7-69.

412 "eroding the health . . . attacked the body." Ted Kennedy. Cited in *Life,* 10-3-69, p.38.

412 "lukewarm at best . . . a palpable dud . . ." *Newsweek,* 9-29-69, p.38.

412 "Ted Kennedy had been audacious . . ." Sylvia Wright in *Life,* 10-3-69.

412 "And acceptance of the fact . . . about the accident." *Ibid.,* p.39.

412 "There was much more . . . advice and solutions." *Ibid.*

413 "less frightening to him . . . on a TV panel." *Ibid.*

413 "For the rest, it will . . . just have to wait." Ted Kennedy to Sylvia Wright, *Ibid.,* p.39.

413 "Everyone agreed it had been a mistake." Dick McCarron. Interview 10-3-83.

413 "Nothing much was going on . . . under those circumstances." McCarron. Interview 10-3-83.

413 "He stayed on; we all did." McCarron. *Ibid.*

414 "The decision was made . . . wouldn't help." *Newsweek,* 9-29-69, p.38.

414 "The matter has to be cleared . . . all the information." Birch Bayh. *Boston Record-American,* 10-1-69.

414 "Some polls say . . . to forgive and forget." Bayh. *Ibid.*

416 "the hand maiden . . . judicial administration." *In re Oliver,* 33 U.S. 257, 268 (1948), cited in Reply Brief, p.7.

416 "but guarding against miscarriage . . . public scrutiny." *Ibid.*

416 "sometimes deploring its sensationalism." *Craig v. Henley.* Reply Brief, p.8.

416 "By their action . . . great prominence." Respondent's Brief.

417 "Because of the extreme interest . . . going on inside." Joseph Hurley. Appeal Proceedings. Massachusetts Judicial Court. 10-8-69.

417 "And preserve the good name . . . the hearing." Hurley. *Ibid.*

417 "There may be criminal . . . know of none." Hurley. *Ibid.*

417 "It is doubtful . . . holding an inquest." *Amicus Curiae. Edward M. Kennedy v. James A. Boyle— Supreme Judicial Court.* Brief of Civil Liberties Union of Massachusetts. October sitting, 1969. p.8.

417 "Accordingly, he faces . . . a manslaughter proceeding." *Ibid.,* p.8.

417 "Senator Kennedy would be spared . . . publicity." *Ibid.*

Chapter 46

419 "all fire and brimstone." Theresa Morse. *The Grapevine,* 2-6-80.

419   "He said he wanted . . . going to be known." Morse. *Ibid.*, p.8.
419   "by not getting in the way . . . co-operated with Mr. Dinis." Morse. *Ibid.*
420   "Such an action . . . that responsibility." Dinis. *New Bedford Standard Times*, 10-21-69.
421   "His battle against . . . with their opposition." Kennedy aides. *New Bedford Standard Times*, 12-3-69.
421   "the Kopechnes are . . . is someone else?" *Boston Record-American*, 8-23-69.
421   "This is our responsibility." Joseph Kopechne. *New Bedford Standard Times*, 9-30-69.
421   "We haven't stopped . . . as we have to." Joseph Kopechne to Anthony Burton. *New York Daily News*, 10-1-69.
421   "Because with the roll of the car . . . is just unbelievable." John Farrar. *The Grapevine*, 2-6-80, p.8.
422   "no human being can swear . . . alive, easily an hour." Farrar to Vera Glaser and Malvina Stephenson, *Philadelphia Inquirer*, 5-24-70, p.1.
422   "To become as close . . . which I observed." Farrar. Inquest, p.534.
423   "prejudiced, biased and anti-Kennedy . . ." Herbert Abrams Statement. Exhumation Hearing, p.37.
423   Look/Flanagan Examination. Exhumation Hearings, p.72.
424   "There were lights on the car . . . plate lights." "Huck Look" Exhumation Hearing, p.68.
425   "approximately 25 to 30 miles . . . going down the road." *Ibid.*, p.73.
425   "as a Washington attorney . . . I was concerned." Armand Fernandes. Interview 3-10-84.
425   "She had the characteristic foam . . . of injuries . . ." Exhumation Hearing, p.87.
425   "Mills/Flanagan Examination. Exhumation Hearing, p.94.
426   "quite substantial . . . of medical certainty." Dr. Cyril Wecht. *Ibid.*, pp.222–223.
426   "Would this include manual strangulation?" Fernandes. *Ibid.*, p.145.

426   "To stay away . . . of questioning." Brominski. *Ibid.*, p.145.
426   "Because we were trying . . . question was used." Fernandes. Interview 3-11-84.
427   "did not exclude . . . death." George Katsas. Exhumation Hearing, p.153.
427   "So obviously you . . . on the slacks." Bernie Flynn. Interview 7-28-83.
428   "You may exhume the girl . . . whether she drowned." Dr. Werner Spitz, Exhumation Hearing, p.246.
428   drowning resembled other . . . causes of death. Spitz. *Ibid.*, p.249.
428   "Because of the circumstances . . . be exhumed?" Spitz. *Ibid.*, p.250.
428   "That is *not* . . . other than drowning." Edmund Dinis. *Ibid.*, p.250.
428   "She may have . . . of the body . . ." Spitz. *Ibid.*, p.251.
428   "She may have injuries . . . exhume her or you don't." *Ibid.*, p.253.
429   "The issue Kennedy's lawyers . . . under the law." Fernandes. Interview 6-2-83.
429   "In a drowning case . . . benzidine reactions." Dr. Henry Freimuth. Exhumation Hearing, p.260.
430   "We do not want . . . in it at all." Joseph Kopechne. *Ibid.*, p.201.
430   "That's always . . . as of tonight." Dinis. *Wilkes-Barre Record*, 10-21-69, p.1.
430   "When the investigation . . . or incomplete." Dinis. Exhumation Hearing, p.180.
430   "Unless I was informed . . . a reason to." Dinis. *Ibid.*, p.187.
430   "positively ordered . . . the Kennedy people." Dinis. *Ibid.*, p.186.
430   "You cannot come . . . by facts." Brominski. *Ibid.*, p.185.
431   "a self-serving declaration." Joseph Flanagan. *Ibid.*, p.195.
432   "I can't think of a single . . . if we lose." *Wilkes-Barre Record*, 10-22-69, p.1.

Chapter 47

433   "The activities of the news media . . . which may follow." Massachusetts Supreme Judicial Court decision.

Boston Record-American, 10-31-69.

434 "a gathering crescendo . . . the scene of the accident . . ." *Wall Street Journal,* 10-7-69, p.22.

434 "So the bumbling . . . prying eyes." *Ibid.*

434 "Sooner or later the full . . . opportunities to do so." *Cape Cod Standard Times,* 10-27-69.

435 "So I can get on . . . the Court recommends." Ted Kennedy. *New Bedford Standard Times,* 10-31-69.

435 "that the inquest . . . action against him." Sources close to Kennedy to *Boston Record-American,* 11-1-69.

436 "We were disappointed . . . not here." Gwen Kopechne. *New York Daily News,* 10-1-69.

436 "I just wish . . . whole situation." Gwen Kopechne. *New Bedford Standard Times,* 9-30-69.

436 "We who are in public . . . baseless slander." Ted Kennedy to *Newsweek,* 12-15-69.

437 "Great spells . . . slain brothers." *New Bedford Standard Times,* 12-3-69.

437 "eager to clear up . . . remaining questions." *Ibid.*

437 "But I think we 11 win big." Ted Kennedy. *Ibid.*

438 "None of these . . . with death by drowning." Brominski. *New Bedford Standard Times,* 11-7-69.

438 "would give loose rein . . . facts of record." Brominski. *Ibid.*

439 "The irony is . . . to the grave." Melvin Belli. *Medical World News,* 8-22-69, p.12.

439 "I can't tell you . . . she had drowned." Gwen Kopechne. *New Bedford Standard Times,* 12-12-69.

439 "somewhat vocal . . . girlish than usual." *Boston Globe,* 10-30-74, p.60.

439 "Mary Jo was a wonderful . . . was a maiden lady." Gwen Kopechne to Anthony Burton. *New York Daily News,* 10-1-69.

439 "Because we're the parents . . . been a mystery." Gwen Kopechne. *Boston Record-American,* 11-9-70.

440 "There's a lot of questions . . . I just want to know what happened."

Joseph Kopechne. *New York Post,* 1-8-70.

440 "Because I realize . . . as soon as possible." Ted Kennedy. *Boston Record-American,* 12-11-69.

440 "We wanted him to have . . . make the arrangements." Kennedy aide. *Philadelphia Inquirer,* 1-5-70.

440 "That's just the way he is . . . not our kind of Irish." James Smith. Interview 4-23-83.

Chapter 48

441 "But a large, American-style automobile." Investigator Report of Witness Nancy T. McDonald. Interview 12-18-69, J. E. Gautreau, p.3.

442 "The reason I called . . . know already." Bernie Flynn. Interview 7-28-83.

442 "There's nothing else . . . at the inquest?" Stephen Smith to Bernie Flynn. Flynn interview 7-28-83.

442 "He told me the flight . . . going to arrive." Flynn. Interview 4-19-83.

442 "A nice, athletic-looking . . . haircut he had." Flynn. *Ibid.*

443 "He put the briefcase . . . over there." Flynn. Interview 4-19-83.

443 "The first time . . . tape it again?'" Flynn. Interview 7-28-83.

443 "Is there anything . . . can tell us?" Stephen Smith to Bernie Flynn. Flynn interview 6-15-83.

443 "What I was trying . . . your equilibrium." Flynn. Interview 4-7-83.

443 "I'm thinking of Ted Kennedy . . . dropped on him." Flynn. Interview 4-19-83.

443 "My whole thought was . . . caught in another lie." Flynn. Interview 4-11-83.

443 "This time when he tells his lie . . . swallow it." Flynn. Interview 6-15-83.

443 "He could walk into . . . seemed to like that." Flynn. Interview 4-19-83.

443 "They're interjecting . . . in a while." Flynn. *Ibid.*

443 "This information I have . . . already told you." Flynn. Interview 6-15-83.

443 "Are you sure . . . anything else?" Stephen Smith to Flynn. *Ibid.*

443   "No, that's it . . . nothing to fear." Flynn. *Ibid.*

444   "Except I know we had . . . get caught?" Flynn. Interview 4-19-83.

444   "I wanted Ted Kennedy . . . he's protected." Flynn. Interview 7-28-83.

444   "That's the reason the meeting . . . out at the inquest." Flynn. Interview 4-11-83.

444   "John was sitting . . . 'you bastard!'" Flynn. Interview 4-19-83.

444   "Are you *sure* . . . anything else?" Stephen Smith. Flynn interview 6-15-83.

444   "I'll get in touch . . ." Flynn. *Ibid.*

444   "What can I do . . . *you* want?" Stephen Smith. Flynn interview 4-19-83.

444   "You tell Ted Kennedy . . . in Pittsfield someplace." Flynn. *Ibid.*

445   "That's no problem . . . telephone call." Stephen Smith. Flynn interview 7-28-83.

445   "While I'm talking . . . tape that was there." Flynn. *Ibid.*

445   "Do you think . . . said about it." Ted Kennedy. *Chicago Daily News,* 12-27-69.

445   "Like he would . . . once and for all." Kennedy aide. *Philadelphia Inquirer,* 1-5-70.

446   "that it was ultimately from a Kennedy source." Eliot Fremont-Smith. *New Bedford Standard Times,* 1-16-70.

447   "No intelligent politician . . . ended Kennedy's career." Jack Olsen, *The Bridge at Chappaquiddick,* p.271.

447   "fudge a few minutes . . . wrong turn . . ." *Ibid.*

447   "The obvious answer . . . was she, 28?" Olsen. Interview with Patrick McGrady.

447   "The publisher . . . were played down." Olsen, *Ibid.*

448   "Why throw yourself . . . to believe him." Arena. Interview 3-15-83.

448   "I say to myself . . . wasn't in the car?'" Arena. Interview 2-16-83.

Chapter 49

451   "looking forward to . . . the Senate." Ted Kennedy. *New York Daily News,* 1-6-70.

451   "like a criminal . . ." James Reston. *New York Times,* 1-7-70.

451   "Are you glad . . . under way?" *Philadelphia Evening Bulletin,* 1-5-70.

451   "Yes, I am . . ." Ted Kennedy. *Ibid.*

452   "a stacked deck . . ." Bernie Flynn. 4-19-83.

452   "The pride of . . . the United States." Jack Anderson. *Philadelphia Evening Bulletin,* 1-2-70.

452   "She couldn't stay . . . the courthouse." Dick Drayne. *Women's Wear Daily,* 1-6-70.

452   "It was kind of . . . trial like that." Peter Gay. Interview 8-20-84.

453   "Witnesses, after testimony . . . or her counsel." Judge James A. Boyle. Inquest Into the Death of Mary Jo Kopechne, Edgartown District Court, p.5.

453   "I don't want . . . with another client." *Ibid.,* p.9.

453   "As an implicit . . . what goes on." Edward Hanify. *Ibid.,* p.8.

454   "Anything he says . . . a humiliating end." *New York Times,* 9-7-69.

454   (Footnote) "There was no discussion . . . home number." Charles Parrott to Richard J. Connolly. *Boston Globe,* 3-23-80.

454   (Footnote) "Judge Boyle was only . . . after the accident." Armand Fernandes. Interview 6-2-83.

454   (Footnote) "Doesn't at the moment . . . me anything." Judge Boyle. Inquest, p.93.

454   "Then, I think . . . drinks after that." Ted Kennedy. Inquest, p.23.

454   "engaged in . . . recollections . . ." *Ibid.,* p.22.

455   "I was talking . . . at that time." *Ibid.,* p.26–27.

455   "Mr. Crimmins, as well . . . back to Edgartown." *Ibid.,* p.27.

455   "any personal relationship . . . members of our family." Ted Kennedy. Inquest, p.69.

455   "I believe it is Main Street." *Ibid.,* p.28.

455   "I did not stop . . . no other person." *Ibid.,* p.29.

455   "approximately twenty miles an hour." *Ibid.,* p.35.

456 "A fraction of a second . . . to go off." *Ibid.*, p.33.

456 "The next thing I recall . . . out of the car." *Ibid.*, p.38.

456 "reaching what I thought . . . up to the surface." *Ibid.*, p.39.

456 "no idea . . . of that car." *Ibid.*, p.41.

456 "From the point . . . saw the bridge." Judge Boyle. *Ibid.*, p.42.

456 "I would estimate . . . was on the bridge." Ted Kennedy. *Ibid.*, p.42.

456 "Your attention . . . by anything else?" Boyle. *Ibid.*, p.43.

456 "No, it wasn't . . ." Kennedy. *Ibid.*, p.43.

456 "I want to . . . alcoholic beverages." Boyle, *Ibid.*, p.43.

456 "to go back . . . at the Shiretown?" *Ibid.*, p.44.

456 "a third of a beer at that time." Kennedy. *Ibid.*, p.44.

457 "Were you . . . influence of alcohol?" Boyle. *Ibid.*, p.47.

457 "Absolutely *not* . . ." Kennedy. *Ibid.*, p.47.

457 "absolutely sober . . ." *Ibid.*, p.48.

457 "by the tide . . . and coughing." *Ibid.*, p.48.

457 "Until at the very . . . any longer." *Ibid.*, p.52

457 "You were fully aware . . . was transpiring?" Dinis. *Ibid.*, p.52.

457 "Well, I was fully . . . hopelessly exhausted." Kennedy. *Ibid.*, p.52.

457 "But there was no . . . in the car." Dinis. *Ibid.*, p.53.

457 "I was doing the very best . . . or the door." Kennedy. *Ibid.*, p.53.

458 "I knew that I just . . . spent on the grass." *Ibid.*, p.54.

458 "I started going down . . . the two sides." *Ibid.*, p.55.

458 "I never saw . . . approximately 15 minutes." *Ibid.*, p.56.

458 "As I came up . . . get me Joe.'" *Ibid.*, p.57.

458 "There's been a . . . Let's go." *Ibid.*, p.58.

458 "I believe . . . was 12:20 A.M." *Ibid.*, p.59.

458 "I made a mistake . . . determine the time." Ted Kennedy. *Boston Globe*, 10-28-74, p.22.

458 "But I could see . . . some suggestions." Kennedy. Inquest, p.60.

458 "You were fully aware . . . at that time?" Dinis. *Ibid.*, p.60.

458 "fully aware . . . rescue that girl." Kennedy. *Ibid.*, p.60.

459 "Was there any . . . for assistance?" Dinis. *Ibid.*, p.61.

459 "No, other than . . . Mr. Markham." Kennedy. *Ibid.*, p.61.

459 "But they *failed* . . . Miss Kopechne." Dinis. *Ibid.*, p.61.

459 "quite a tussle . . . did afterward." Armand Fernandes. Interview 6-2-83.

459 "I want to avoid . . . trial technique." Judge Boyle. *Ibid.*, p.32.

460 "Was there any . . . fire department?" Dinis. *Ibid.*, p.62.

460 "Well, I intended . . . into the car." Ted Kennedy. *Ibid.*, p.62.

460 "Did something transpire to prevent this?" Dinis. *Ibid.*, p.62.

460 "If the court . . . in the car . . ." Kennedy. *Ibid.*, pp.62–63.

460 "I believe it was . . . report this accident." *Ibid.*, p.63.

460 "A lot of different . . . my wife." *Ibid.*, p.63.

460 "Even though I knew . . . down that road." *Ibid.*, pp.63–64.

461 "And about this time . . . I dove into the water." *Ibid.*, p.64.

461 "the girls to alarm . . ." *Ibid.*, p.80.

461 "Because I felt strongly . . . any one of them." *Ibid.*, p.80.

461 "I felt an extraordinary . . . right before me again." *Ibid.*, p.65.

462 "almost having no further . . . to what happened." *Ibid.*, p.66.

462 "But what I was . . . devoted friend." *Ibid.*, p.67.

462 "around me, on top of me . . . back into the room." *Ibid.*, p.68.

462 "I never really went to bed . . . escaped from the car." *Ibid.*, p.70.

463 "Because I was still . . . her existence and her life." Ted Kennedy. *Boston Globe*, 10-28-74.

463 "They asked had I . . . her daughter was dead." Ted Kennedy. Inquest, p.71–72.

463 "make a private phone . . . I have." *Ibid.*, p.73.

463   "I didn't feel . . . know the number." *Ibid.*, p.76.

464   "Because it was my thought . . . that responsibility." Ted Kennedy, Inquest, p.73.

464   "But you didn't go . . . to the police . . ." Dinis. *Ibid.*, p.73.

464   "Excuse me, Mr. Dinis . . . luncheon recess." Judge Boyle. *Ibid.*, p.74.

464   (Footnote) Interview of Ted Kennedy. *Boston Globe*, 10-28-74, p.23.

464   (Footnote) "He was trying to find . . . for Stephen Smith." Helga Wagner. *New York Times*, 3-12-80.

464   "didn't seem confident . . . he was trying to say." Peter Gay. Interview 3-20-84.

465   "When I fully realized . . . what you did?" Edmund Dinis. Inquest, p.77.

465   "Mr. Kennedy already said . . . speak for itself?" Judge Boyle. *Ibid.*, p.77.

465   Well, I don't think . . . of cross-examination." Dinis. *Ibid.*, p.247.

465   "There is no cross-examination . . . repetition of testimony." Boyle. *Ibid.*, p.248.

465   "I know we don't . . . occasionally." Dinis. *Ibid.*, p.248.

465   "I appreciate it . . . to the Court." *Ibid.*, p.247.

465   "No further questions." *Ibid.*, p.81.

465   "In the event . . . for anything." Boyle. *Ibid.*, p.81.

466   "I would hope . . . time this week." Kennedy. *Ibid.*, p.81.

466   "On one point . . . the bench on." *Ibid.*, p.82.

466   "Why did you not . . . Mary Jo?" Boyle. *Ibid.*, p.82.

466   "It is because I was . . . about the accident." Kennedy. *Ibid.*, pp.83–84.

466   "Since the alcoholic intake . . . part of the proceedings." *Ibid.*, p.83.

466   "One other occasion . . . quarter of one." *Ibid.*, p.83.

467   "immensely relieved . . . self-confident Ted Kennedy." Jeremiah Murphy. *Boston Globe*, 1-6-70.

467   "I'm satisfied I responded . . . district attorney." Ted Kennedy. *New York Daily News*, 1-6-70.

467   "I expect to be vindicated . . . to answer questions." Statement Released to *Chicago Daily News* through an aide. *Philadelphia Inquirer*, 1-8-70.

467   "Now, you don't expect me . . . secrets, do you?" Ted Kennedy. *Boston Globe*, 1-6-70.

Chapter 50

469   "Because how much . . . for a transcript." Joseph Donegan. Interview 2-29-84.

469   "The only testimony . . . very meager, really." *Ibid.*

470   "a voice . . . Senator Kennedy's." Ray LaRosa. Inquest, p.102.

470   "A man asked . . . of that nature." *Ibid.*, p.117.

470   "And I held my hands . . . on its way." *Ibid.*

470   "Hell, it could clear . . . really can't say." Ray LaRosa. *Boston Globe*, 10-30-74, p.11.

471   "The lawyers coached us . . . what to expect." LaRosa. *Boston Globe*, 10-31-74, p.55.

471   "I had to go by . . . white Valiant." Charles Tretter. Inquest, p.187.

471   "And there was . . . no cars." *Ibid.*, p.157.

472   "As far as I'm concerned . . . Edward Kennedy." Rosemary Keough. *Boston Globe*, 10-30-74, p.11.

472   "In preparing Tretter's . . . save his marriage." Paul Redmond. Interview 7-34-83.

473   "whose main interest was Ted Kennedy." Esther Newberg. Sherrill, *The Last Kennedy*, p.126.

473   "Just to escort . . . with microphones." Paul Redmond. Inquest, p.174.

473   "the lawyer friends who . . . post-accident silence." *Newsweek*, 9-8-69.

473   "Since they were presumably lucid . . . after his accident." *Time*, 9-5-69, p.18.

473   "I was simply going to tell . . . what I heard." Joe Gargan. Interview 2-17-83.

473   "having to hold onto the stay . . . the spinnaker out." Gargan. Inquest, p.210.

474 "I took out of the refrigerator . . . pass them around." Gargan. *Ibid.*, pp.216–217.

474 "Eddie was laughing . . . cooking instructions." James Smith. Interview 2-10-83.

474 "a tall glass . . . at that time." Gargan. Inquest, p.219.

474 "I saw him . . . I don't know." *Ibid.*, p.218.

474 "Mr. Crimmins was . . . at 12 o'clock." *Ibid.*, p.220.

474 "I didn't think it was necessary . . . everybody to go home." Gargan. Interview 6-22-83.

475 "The car had gone . . . fast as I could . . ." Gargan. Inquest, p.22.

475 "I didn't think there was anything . . . very disturbed." *Ibid.*, p., 237.

475 "He told me he was going . . . off into the water." *Ibid.*, p.238.

475 "But I do recall . . . accident immediately." *Ibid.*, p.240.

475 "to let the family know . . . best lawyer I know." *Ibid.*, p.242.

475 "Don't upset the girls . . . the way across." *Ibid.*, p.243.

475 "The Senator can swim . . . both ways." *Ibid.*, p.245.

475 "The Senator was going . . . around 2:15 A.M." *Ibid.*, p.244.

476 "I never spoke . . . or anything else." *Ibid.*, p.253.

476 "Yes, that was discussed . . . acted upon." Gargan. Interview 1-25-84 (with James Smith).

476 "a rum and coke . . . had arrived." Paul Markham. Inquest, p.293.

476 "We were singularly unsuccessful . . . report the accident." *Ibid.*, p.306.

476 "very emotional . . . sure it happened." *Ibid.*, p.322.

477 "The reason that you . . . after the swim?" Armand Fernandes. Inquest, p.328.

477 "That is what he told us." Markham. *Ibid.*, p.328.

477 "who besides Kennedy . . . explaining to do." *Time*, 9-15-69, p.18.

477 "It was the kind of overkill . . . things that were unnecessary." Joe Gargan. Interview 5-20-83.

477 "He didn't need that kind of help . . . but we were not." *Ibid.*

Chapter 51

479 "Don't believe everything you read." Paul Markham. Peter Gay interview 8-20-84.

479 "I'm still on the case. I'm not leaving." Edmund Dinis. *New Bedford Standard Times*, 1-6-70.

479 "But I'm going to find out." Dinis. *Boston Record-American*, 1-7-70.

479 "Dinis is folding up . . . not coming back." Dick Drayne. *Boston Record-American*, 1-7-70.

479 "I've led a very controversial life . . . the best I can." Edmund Dinis. *Boston Globe*, 1-8-70.

480 "People were drinking . . . of beer." Paul Markham. Inquest, p.287.

480 "I would say they looked damp . . . not say that, I'm sure." Ross Richards. *Ibid.*, p.262.

480 "Because I'd been with Ted . . . not real anxious about testifying." Stan Moore. Interview 7-18-82.

481 "We were on Ted's doorstep . . . a fast brush-off." Stan Moore. Interview 7-18-82.

481 "Both Richards and Moore . , . Moore wasn't called." Armand Fernandes. Interview 6-2-83.

482 "No one specifically missed . . . left the party." Esther Newberg. *New York Times*, 7-23-69.

482 "an informal group . . . at any given time." *Ibid.*

482 "I have a rather large watch . . . looked at it." Esther Newberg. Inquest, p.389.

482 "I saw him walk out . . . directly behind him." *Ibid.*, p.392.

482 "If you can use me as an expert." *Ibid.*, p.621.

482 "If I tell you that . . . in any respect?" Judge Boyle. *Ibid.*, p.622.

482 "Five or six drinks . . . way she lived." Newberg. *Ibid.*, p.624.

482 "I am only telling you . . . practically irrefutable." Boyle. *Ibid.*, p.624.

482 "Then, I'm the wrong . . . was completely sober." Newberg. *Ibid.*, p.624.

482 "And you saw her . . . she left?" Boyle. *Ibid.*, p.624.

482 "*Exactly* the time she left." Newberg. *Ibid.*, p.624.

482 "Something to the effect . . . back at the motel." *Ibid.*, p.404.
482 "How did you believe . . . to the motel?" Boyle. *Ibid.*, p.415.
483 "She had driven . . . without any trouble." Newberg. *Ibid.*, p.416.
483 "She had driven . . . she is going . . ." Boyle, *Ibid.*, p.467.
483 "now, you make an assumption . . . to the motel?" *Ibid.*, p.408.
483 "Later I had the assumption . . . get some rest." Newberg. *Ibid.*, p.408.
483 "Without her saying . . . at the party?" Boyle. *Ibid.*, p.408.
483 "At that time . . . motor vehicles gone?" Boyle. *Ibid.*, p.409.
483 "Suddenly you are left . . . isn't the plan?" *Ibid.*, p.411.
483 "There was some . . . make the ferry." Newberg. *Ibid.*, p.395.
483 "After one o'clock . . . attempt to sleep.' " p.410.
483 "We had no reason . . . was going to happen." *Ibid.*, p.412.
483 "We all wondered where . . . volunteered any information." Newberg. *Ibid.*, p.414.
484 "Later, when Mr. Gargan . . . in that motel room." *Ibid.*, p.415.
484 "She seemed like a nice girl . . . dislike to her." Armand Fernandes. Interview 6-2-83.
484 "Did you at any time . . . any reporters?" Boyle. Inquest, p.616.
484 "The last time . . . extreme duress." Newberg. *Ibid.*, pp.616–617.
484 "I can see what you are reading . . . anyone after July." *Ibid.*, p.618.
484 "Not to discuss . . . with any of them." Judge Boyle. *Ibid.*, p.424.
485 "Where have you been . . . What is happening?" Mary Ellen Lyons. Inquest, pp.656–657.
485 "They stated that they . . . to the Katama Shores." Nance Lyons. Inquest, p.664.
485 "Didn't you say to them . . . the Senator swims?" Boyle. *Ibid.*, p.664.
485 "Did you have some . . . was most peculiar?" *Ibid.*, p.665.
485 "No, not really . . ." Mary Ellen Lyons. *Ibid.*, p.665.
485 "We were just saying . . . stuck in the sand." *Ibid.*, p.650.

485 "Just after . . . weren't there." *Ibid.*, p.647.
485 "I would say . . . 11:15 P.M." Nance Lyons. *Ibid.*, p.691.
485 "Simply because people . . . all evening." *Ibid.*, p.722.
485 "And said in a rather loud . . . like to see you.'" *Ibid.*, p.694.
486 "And Mary Jo had already left." Susan Tannenbaum. *Ibid.*, p.757.
486 "Were you surprised . . . to Edgartown?" Judge Boyle. *Ibid.*, p.761.
486 "Yes, I was surprised." Tannenbaum. *Ibid.*, p.761.
486 "Was there not some discussion . . . us stranded here?" Boyle. *Ibid.*, p.761.
486 "Not that I remember." Tannenbaum. *Ibid.*, p.762.
486 "You are not accustomed . . . are you?" Boyle. *Ibid.*, p.762.
486 "You may leave . . . right to your friends." *Ibid.*, p.762.
486 "Would you just do . . . asked you to do?" Susan Tannenbaum to Joe Gargan. Gargan interview 6-22-83.
487 "that I may have been either . . . to protect Ted Kennedy." Gargan. *Ibid.*
487 "If you mean the time of Chappaquiddick . . . do it now." *Ibid.*
487 "having a few drinks . . . lot of fun." Joseph Donegan. Interview 2-29-84.
487 "That's the only time . . . old style barrister." Paul Redmond. Interview 7-23-83.
487 "I used to say to him . . . was very effective." Donegan. Interview 2-29-84.
487 "Some of the newspaper people . . . curious about everybody." *Ibid.*
487 "a non-story . . . current Kennedy inquiry." James Reston. *New York Times*, 1-7-70.

Chapter 52
489 "The real story . . . in that period." Esther Newberg. *Boston Globe*, 10-30-74, p.10.
489 "Either black . . . or dark green." Christopher Look. Inquest, p.509.
490 "Then you are unable . . . the previous night?" Boyle. *Ibid.*, pp.510–511.

490 "Maybe no other . . . I don't know." *Ibid.,* pp.569–570.

490 "I will even postpone . . . investigation be made." *Ibid.,* p.568.

490 "I will get on it . . . right away." Armand Fernandes. *Ibid.,* p.568.

490 "It was like 3:30 P.M. . . . the Registry." Bernie Flynn. Interview 4-11-83.

490 "And we aren't going to . . . driving alone: 'Nonsense.'" Kennedy spokesman. *New Bedford Standard Times,* 1-22-70.

490 "It would be improper . . . been adjudicated." Richard McLaughlin. *New Bedford Standard Times,* 1-8-70.

491 "And I don't believe . . . to the license." *Ibid.*

491 "It's not news . . . in a barefaced lie." *National Enquirer,* 2-22-70.

491 "How he votes . . . with satisfaction." Governor Francis Sargent. *New Bedford Standard Times,* 1-9-70.

491 "an open acknowledgment . . . must do business." *New Bedford Standard Times,* 7-3-71.

491 "Police have first-hand . . . Registry's muddled files." *Ibid.*

492 "I don't know . . . too late or what." Bernie Flynn. Interview 4-11-83.

492 "The attempt disclosed . . . would be helpful." Judge James Boyle. Inquest Report, p.8.

492 "would seriously affect . . . of the witnesses." *Ibid.,* p.8.

492 "They weren't needed." *New Bedford Standard Times,* 1-9-70.

492 "Did they . . . license *immediately?*" Armand Fernandes. *Ibid.,* p.479.

493 "At another date." George Kennedy. *Ibid.,* p.479.

493 "Now you are going . . . may not exist." Boyle. *Ibid.,* p.475.

493 "He doesn't know." Fernandes. *Ibid.*

493 "Let's ignore that." Boyle. *Ibid.*

493 "with the problem of . . . an immersed automobile." Edward Hanify. *Ibid.,* p.602.

494 "Testimony was not sought . . . purely speculative." Boyle. Inquest Report, p.9.

494 "Because such failure . . . criminal conduct." *Ibid.*

494 "the victim's head . . . air in the car." Farrar. Inquest, p.533.

494 "You don't *know* what was done . . . what you saw." Fernandes. *Ibid.*

494 "She suffocated . . . didn't drown." Farrar. *The Grapevine,* 2-20-80.

495 "then find out . . . I didn't obtain." Boyle. Inquest, p.763.

496 "You've got to remember . . . was merely received." Armand Fernandes. Interview 6-2-83.

496 "We put on the record . . . were available." Edmund Dinis. *New York Post,* 1-8-70.

496 "When we started . . . a helluva lot more." Dinis. *Hartford Courant,* 1-9-70.

496 "Traditionally, the grand jury . . ." Dinis. *Boston Globe,* 1-8-70.

496 "I'm glad it's over . . . business of the Senate." Ted Kennedy. *Boston Record-American,* 1-9-70.

497 "that Kennedy and Kopechne did *not* intend . . . been intentional." Report. Inquest *re Mary Jo Kopechne.* Commonwealth of Massachusetts, Dukes County District Court. Docket No. 15220, 2-18-70, p.11.

497 "A speed of even twenty miles . . . and possibly reckless." *Ibid.,* pp.11–12.

497 "But for some reason . . . the bridge." *Ibid.,* p.12.

498 "There is probable cause . . . death of Mary Jo Kopechne." *Ibid.,* p.12.

498 "We, of course, read the report . . . to the Superior Court." Dick McCarron. Interview 7-29-83.

499 "The judge is preparing . . . it is closed." Edmund Dinis. *New Bedford Standard Times,* 2-27-70.

499 "Our system is a rule . . . of men." Dinis. Fernandes interview 6-2-83.

499 "He could have, in his discretion . . . difficult to draw." Fernandes. Interview 6-2-83.

500 "Dinis didn't want . . . to save him." James Smith. Interview 6-3-83.

Chapter 53

501   "Most of us felt . . . of that girl." Grand juror. Sherrill, *The Last Kennedy*, p.167.

501   "We talked about bringing in . . . at the cookout." *Philadelphia Daily News*, 7-16-73.

501   "a duty and a responsibility . . . and for all." Leslie Leland. *Philadelphia Inquirer*, 4-5-70.

501   "Should have been . . . long time ago." Leland. *Boston Record-American*, 3-28-70.

502   "Everyone feels that a great injustice . . . found out what happened." Leland. Reported in *Reader's Digest*, February, 1980, p.238.

502   "We want to see . . . what isn't there." Leland. *New York Daily News*, p.C3.

502   "Leland wanted to keep . . . in the district court." James Smith. Interview 6-3-82.

502   "We want to finalize this matter . . . has floated over the case." Leland. *Boston Record-American*, 3-28-70.

503   "A violation of common law . . . in their deliberations." Dick McCarron. Interview 7-29-83.

503   "The one person . . . a Kennedyphile." Frank Keating. Interview 7-30-83.

504   "The reason to impound . . . of the public." Peter Gay. Interview 8-20-84.

504   "a report could lead . . . further criminal process." Edward Hanify Supreme Judicial Court Hearing. *New Bedford Standard Times*, 10-9-69.

504   "premature publicity about . . . a potential defendant." Supreme Court Decision. *Boston Record-American*, 10-31-69.

505   "Well, you were at the inquest . . . what was said." Grand juror. Armand Fernandes interview 6-2-83.

505   "We don't really believe . . . just an unfortunate accident." Dinis to Theresa Morse. *The Grapevine*, 2-6-80.

505   "We definitely discussed . . . to make that charge." Fernandes. Interview 6-2-83.

506   "didn't know anything about the case." Dick McCarron. Interview 3-16-84.

506   "It was very discouraging . . . well go home." Grand juror. *Philadelphia Daily News*, 7-16-73.

506   "I don't mean for a day . . ." Judge Wilfred Paquet. *Boston Record-American*, 4-7-70.

506   "It was made quite clear . . . support my family." Leland. *Boston Record-American*, 4-18-70.

506   "at the end of this . . . Mary Jo Kopechne." Edmund Dinis. *Philadelphia Inquirer*, 4-8-70.

506   "The case is closed." Dinis. *Boston Globe*, 4-7-70.

506   "They were on a wild goose . . . produce anything." Dinis. *Boston Globe*, 10-31-74, p.55.

507   "There's no question . . . them the case." Edmund Dinis. Interview 12-10-81.

507   "The investigative portion . . . stoop to doing that." Armand Fernandes Interview 6-2-83.

507   "If our office had appealed . . . have been overruled." Fernandes. *Ibid*.

507   "He'll do you a favor . . . and be damned." Joe Gargan. Interview 5-20-83.

507   "To hell with you . . . talk to you." Wilford Paquet. *Boston Globe*, 10-31-74, p.55.

508   "to insure order . . . public examination." Petition of Edward M. Kennedy. Supreme Judicial Court. By Edward B. Hanify. p.3.

508   "The only finding . . . could make . . ." Editorial "A Transcript Beyond Belief," *New Bedford Standard Times*, 5-2-70.

509   "trying to digest what I've heard." Leslie Leland. *Ibid.*, p.4.

509   "Things might have been different . . . get our hands on them." Dan Thomasson, Scripps-Howard, 4-30-69.

509   "But I'll have to . . . read the report." Leland. *Vineyard Gazette*, 5-1-70, p.4.

509   "A bigger bunch of dumbbells . . . impotent by Mr. Dinis." Theresa Morse. *The Grapevine*, 2-6-80.

509 "There were contributory . . . a hazard." Arena. *New Bedford Standard Times*, 5-1-70.

509 "I don't care what Boyle said . . . it was all right by me." Arena. Interview 2-16-83.

509 "In mystery . . . by authorities." *Cape Cod Standard Times*, 5-3-70.

510 "The case may be closed . . . a shadow on his future." *Boston Record-American*, 5-2-70.

510 "The facts of this incident . . . utterances and speculations." Ted Kennedy. *Boston Herald Traveler*, 4-30-70.

510 "The inferences and . . . I reject them." *Ibid.*

510 "No criminal action . . . remains to be seen." Robert Quinn. *Cape Cod Standard Times*, 5-1-70.

Chapter 54

511 "That his own testimony . . . not accurate or truthful." *New York Post*, 6-15-70.

511 "Every time I say something . . . any way to end it." Ted Kennedy. Honan, *Ted Kennedy: Profile of a Survivor*, p.98.

512 "That was last summer . . . more to say." *Ibid.*, p.99.

512 "the most difficult . . . we've ever done." Gwen Kopechne. *McCalls*, August 1970 and *New Bedford Standard Times*, 8-20-70.

512 "We finally realized . . . and contradictions." *Ibid.*

512 "The district attorney was falling apart . . . follow through." Gwen Kopechne. *The Grapevine*, 2-6-80.

512 "There were so many questions . . . thought of asking." Gwen Kopechne. *The Grapevine*, 2-13-80.

512 "It all sounds alike . . . it was rehearsed." Gwen Kopechne. *Ibid.*

512 "I began to disbelieve . . . it was unbelievable." Joseph Kopechne. *The Grapevine*, 2-20-80.

512 "If Senator Kennedy was . . . his negligence." George Killen to Frank Keating. Keating interview 7-30-83.

513 "Boyle's report put the ball . . . cheated at the inquest." Bernie Flynn. Interview 4-7-83-

513 "The insurance company . . . the car legally." Dick McCarron. Interview 7-29-83.

514 "It would appear that Kennedy . . . for existing conditions." Hearing on Fatal Accident. Summary of Testimony and Evidence. Report by Joseph P.Greelish, 5-15-70.

514 "Upon investigation and after . . . fault on your part." Letter to Edward M. Kennedy from Registrar Richard McLaughlin, 5-27-70.

514 "despite fairly heavy traffic." *Ted Kennedy: Triumphs and Tragedies*, by Lester David. New York: Award Books, 1975, p.332.

514 "The Senator never drove . . . was available." Joe Gargan. Interview 5-20-83.

515 "As long as I felt . . . on the issues." Ted Kennedy. *Cape Cod Standard Times*, 5-29-70.

515 "But Chappaquiddick . . . and by himself." James Reston. *New York Times*, 1-7-70.

515 "Even though . . . the tragic episode." *New Bedford Standard Times*, 10-20-70.

515 "The voters need reassurance . . . the way they see you." Ted Kennedy. *New York Times*, 8-27-70.

516 "At least one TV man . . . the anniversary." *Vineyard Gazette*, 7-17-70.

516 "My friend Mary Jo . . . with the wrong people." Rosemary Keough. *Boston Globe*, 10-30-74, p.11.

516 "accepted without protest." Joseph Flanagan. *Boston Globe*, 10-20-74.

516 "paid nothing . . . his own pocket." Flanagan. *Boston Globe*, 10-30-74.

516 "Obviously, a financial . . . it should be fair." Ted Kennedy. *Boston Globe*, 11-3-74.

516 "To put to rest . . . been torturing us." Gwen Kopechne. *Boston Record-American*, 8-20-70.

516 "leaves a bad taste . . . flow from it." Gwen Kopechne. *Ibid.*

517 "Among her boyfriends . . . named Senator Edward Kennedy." Gwen Kopechne. *McCall's*, August 1970.

517 "We also believe . . . along the way." *New Bedford Standard Times*, 8-20-70.

517   "Mr. Kopchne and I have . . . just an accident." *Ibid.*

518   "I look forward to being . . . within our society." Ted Kennedy. *Newsweek,* 11-16-70.

518   "too new in politics . . . in his attacks." Edmund Dinis. *New Bedford Standard Times,* 10-30-70.

518   "more a repudiation . . . for public office." *New Bedford Standard Times,* 11-4-70.

518   "But I would not hesitate . . . all over again." Dinis to WTEV-Channel 6, New Bedford. *New Bedford Standard Times,* 11-8-70.

518   "The girl died. And *I* got defeated." Dinis. Hersh, p.550.

519   "diligent and thorough search . . ." Registry of Motor Vehicles Inter-Office Memo. 6-29-83.

519   "our usual Massachusetts procedure . . . they respectively belong." Letter to District Attorney Philip A. Rollins, from Edward B. Hanify, 10-5-71.

519   "There was nothing . . . I knew about." George Killen. Interview 7-16-79.

519   "The return to the parents . . . at the inquest." Letter to Philip A. Rollins from Joseph F. Flanagan, 10-6-71.

520   "all exhibits introduced . . . or introduced." Inquest *in re: Death of Mary Jo Kopechne.* Order Re Exhibits by Justice Walter A. McLaughlin. 10-30-71.

520   "the specific articles . . . be destroyed." Letter to George Killen, Office of the District Attorney from Joseph Flanagan. 11-10-71.

521   "The clothing and sandals . . . insure total burning." Letter to Joseph Flanagan from George E. Killen, 11-17-71.

Chapter 55

523   "primarily a biological . . . are Chappaquiddick." William F. Buckley. *The National Review,* 10-7-69, p.1026.

523   "a sobriety of purpose . . . resolve." *Ibid.*

524   "faced up to the . . . after Chappaquiddick" *Look,* 8-10-71.

524   "In the minds of millions . . . debt to society." Warren Rogers. *Look,* 8-10-71.

524   "I don't discuss it . . . just not true." Ted Kennedy. *Ibid.*

524   "the commencement . . . of the United States." Honan. *Ted Kennedy: Profile of a Survivor.* p.19.

524   "In this context . . . will not die." James McGregor Burns. *New York Times,* 4-10-72.

524   "to come to grips . . . his soul." *Ibid.*

524   "A genuine draft . . . him electable." *Ibid.*

524   "It may be getting worse." *Harpers,* July 1972.

525   "He is thought of . . . run for President." Joseph Walsh. Memorandum to Jack Conway, 11-18-71, p.2.

525   "But now he is President . . . in Kennedy's case." *Ibid.*

526   "My political fortunes . . . to your book." Hersh, *The Education of Edward Kennedy,* p.14.

526   "wholly a fluke . . . and now." *Ibid.,* p.489.

526   "I really think I did . . . could have done." Ted Kennedy. *Ibid.,* p.532.

526   James Smith/Ted Kennedy conference. James Smith interviews 2-14-83 and 6-17-83.

527   "If that was the only way . . . sour memory of Chappaquiddick." *Newsweek,* 6-26-72.

527   "Nickel and dime stuff . . . anything really new." *All the President's Men* by Bernstein and Bob Woodward, Warner Popular Library, February 1975, p.275.

527   "The biggest political . . . the McCarthy hearings." Stewart Alsop. *Newsweek,* 10-2-73, p.98.

527   "the availability . . . Kennedy-Kopechne inquest." Letter to Clerk of Edgartown Superior Court, 12-3-71.

527   "the fine Kennedy hand." *The White House Transcripts.* Bantam Books, Inc., p.81.

528   "A responsible Congress . . . of impeachment." Ted Kennedy. *New York Times,* 9-16-73.

528 "the last person . . ." Barry Goldwater. *The Burlington Free Press,* 7-16-73.

528 "How the country would react . . . the man of Watergate." Tom Wicker. *New York Times,* 9-16-73."

528 "We have only pleasant feelings . . ." Joseph Kopechne. (AP) *New Bedford Standard Times,* 7-16-73.

528 "It's all over . . . do happen." *Ibid.*

528 "Not on account of . . . unpopular idea." Arena. Interview 2-16-83.

529 "There's a full response . . . be judged." Ted Kennedy. CBS "Face The Nation." Reported in *Burlington Free Press,* 3-4-74.

529 "Watergate had obscured . . . in a serious way." Sherrill."Chappaquiddick + Five." *New York Times,* 7-14-74.

529 "a multilayered, complex mystery . . . five years ago." *Ibid.*

529 "a case study . . . preference polls." Sherrill, *The Last Kennedy,* p.12.

530 "and have found nothing beyond the record." *Burlington Free Press,* 3-14-74.

530 Miller Memorandum. Cited in *Atlantic Monthly* by Seymour Hersh, August 1983, p.75.

531 "I think there may be . . . different situation." Ted Kennedy. *New Bedford Standard Times,* 11-1-74.

531 "Watergate was an attempt . . . a tragic accident." Ted Kennedy. *Boston Globe,* 10-28-74, p.23.

Chapter 56

533 "It may be said . . . Nixon's presidency." the *Palace Guard* by Dan Rather and Gary Paul Gates, Warner Paperback Library, July 1975, p.205.

533 "I can live with my testimony." Ted Kennedy. *Newsweek,* 10-7-74, p.35.

533 "His most obvious . . . indisputable facts." *McCall's,* November 1974.

534 Chappaquiddick would have neutralized. *Newsweek,* 6-2-75.

534 "no amount of sober . . . put to rest." *McCall's,* November 1974.

534 "We are not out . . . to be important." Tom Winship.*Time,* 11-11-74.

534 "I attempted . . . of my ability." Ted Kennedy. *Boston Globe,* 10-27-74.

534 "I was . . . state of mind." *Ibid.*

534 "nearly 100 discrepancies . . . inquest witnesses." *Boston Globe,* 10-29-74.

534 "Justice was not served . . . not pursued." *Boston Globe,* 10-31-74.

535 "ugly, untrue . . . articles of sensationalism." Ted Kennedy. *Boston Globe,* 11-3-74, p.31.

535 "Are harsh, complete . . . remind me." *Ibid.,* p.30.

535 "The problem is . . . have them answered." Ted Kennedy *Boston Globe,* 11-3-74.

535 "The real story . . . just don't exist." Ted Kennedy. *Newsweek,* 11-11-74.

535 "Sometimes I'd like to scream . . . hold it back." Gwen Kopechne. *Boston Globe,* 10-30-74, p.10.

535 "It would be . . . would speak up." Gwen Kopechne. *Ibid.*

535 "He was worried . . . and become upset." Gwen Kopechne. *The Grapevine,* 2-13-80.

535 "I was rather afraid . . . I had clean forgotten." Joseph Kopechne. *The Grapevine,* 2-20-80.

536 "It just becomes . . . or form." Christopher Look. (AP) *Sarasota Herald Tribune,* 2-22-76.

536 "He's so sure . . . have happened." Joseph Kopechne. *The Grapevine,* 2-6-80.

536 "It looks to me . . . at it objectively." Kopechne. *The Grapevine,* 2-6-80.

536 "The senator gave me . . . something to say." Gwen Kopechne. *The Grapevine,* 2-20-80.

536 "After all the . . . truth had not come out." John Farrar. *New York Daily News,* 7-19-74.

536 "I know she . . . didn't drown." Farrar. *New York Daily News,* 7-19-74.

536 "I felt that boy . . . real good." Gwen Kopechne. *The Grapevine,* 2-20-80.

536 "This is why . . . anybody advising him." *Ibid.*

537 "I'd like to know . . . got enough problems." *Ibid.*

537 "I'm the guy . . . about inquest evidence." Bernie Flynn. Interview 4-7-83.

537   "He was standing . . . who I was." Flynn. *Ibid.*

538   "Everyone makes mistakes . . . we won't interfere." Gwen Kopechne. *Newsweek,* 10-8-79.

538   "Because I will answer . . . in the past." Ted Kennedy. *Washington Post,* 11-11-79.

538   "seemed almost memorized . . . asked the question." *Ibid.*

539   "Many of the actions . . . irresponsible." Ted Kennedy. CBS-TV and *Newsweek,* 10-8-74.

539   "There hasn't been a new fact . . . and there cannot be." Ted Kennedy *New Bedford Standard Times,* 7-16-79.

539   "Because it doesn't exit." Ted Kennedy. *New Bedford Standard Times,* 7-16-79.

539   "No one has ever . . . charged him with." Arena. *The Concord Journal,* Minuteman Publications, Inc. 7-19-79.

539   "Expanding on it might . . . I still think the whole case deserves scrutiny." Arena. *Ibid.*

539   "cooperated fully and completely . . . What does Chief Arena want to be done?" Tom Southwick to *New York Post,* 7-21-79.

539   "I don't think . . ." Millicent Fenwick. *McCall's,* August 1979.

540   "Well, you mentioned . . . good one." Ronald Reagan. *Ibid.*

540   "He has become even more . . . for FDR." Arthur Schlesinger. *Ibid.*

540   "As I've said many times . . . except to support him." Ted Kennedy. *Boston Globe,* 6-8-79.

540   "We've had some crises . . . panicked in the crises." Jimmy Carter. *Time,* 10-8-79.

540   "I think the President . . . important to the country." Ted Kennedy. *Time,* 10-8-79.

541   "People may not believe me . . . is just all wrong." Ted Kennedy. *Time,* 11-5-79.

541   "They refused . . . still cloaked in mystery." *New York Times,* 3-17-80.

541   "a lawyer-client relationship . . . after the accident." *Ibid.*

541   "There is not going to be . . . to challenge my testimony." *Ibid.*

541   "There would be absolutely . . . of the United States." Ted Kennedy. NBC "Meet the Press." Reported in *Reader's Digest,* February 1980, p.24.

541   "The only major negative . . . your life forever." *Boston Globe,* 6-8-80, p.2.

541   "His family . . . if he was." *Boston Globe,* 6-8-80.

Chapter 57

543   "Do you think, Senator . . . of Chappaquiddick?" Roger Mudd. Quoted in *Reader's Digest,* February 1980, p.240.

543   Doubts about the propriety . . . six months . . . (UPI) *Cape Cod Standard Times,* 1-7-80.

544   "still felt queasy . . ." Betty Friedan. *Newsweek,* 12-10-79.

544   "The tide that night . . . Kennedy testified." Robert Morgan. *Vineyard Gazette,* 2-1-80.

545   "The clearly-documented facts . . . an abler judicial exercise." *Ibid.*

545   "a very serious misrepresentation . . ." Stephen Smith. *Washington Star,* 1-16-80.

546   "without written . . . Kennedy himself." *Reader's Digest,* February 1980, p.226.

546   "I knew that according . . . access to the report." Ronald Andrews. Letter to author from Ronald Andrews, 4-7-83.

546   "The invasion of personal privacy . . . for many, many years." Letter to author from Rico Matera, Legal Counsel, Registry of Motor Vehicles, 12-21-82.

546   "I never liked . . . stuff going on." Joseph Mellino. Interview 6-19-83.

546   "I have nothing to say about that." Herbert Burn. *Ibid.*

546   "I understand . . . about Chappaquiddick." Richard McLaughlin. Interview 6-19-83 with Ralph Gordon.

546   "that went straight . . . on the case." McLaughlin to Ralph Gordon. Unpublished newspaper story.

547 "You're insinuating something . . . in the radio room." *Ibid.*, p.4.

547 "not accepting . . . from you." Ralph Gordon. Interview 6-19-83.

547 "Beyond that, I didn't hear a thing . . . not to use it." Ralph Gordon. Interview 6-19-83.

547 "Negative feelings toward Kennedy . . . each month." *Washington Post*, 3-1-80.

547 "Last year . . . with it in 1980." *Rolling Stone*, 6-12-80.

548 "When Kennedy ran . . . of esteem for him." Bernie Flynn. Interview 4-7-83.

548 "If I was ambitious . . . Kennedy would reciprocate." Flynn. *Ibid.*

548 "The Senator told . . . press was persuaded." *New York Times*, 8-13-80, p.B1.

549 "A personal issue . . . back in the next." *The New Republic*, 11-2-85.

549 "So this is partly a test run . . . pride of the Kennedys." *Wall Street Journal*, 10-5-82.

549 "The lowest level . . . appalling and hateful." *Cape Cod Times*, 7-25-82.

549 "The funny thing about it was . . . all true." Gargan. To James Smith 6-25-82.

549 "I've given you 30 years . . . not mine." *Ibid.*

550 "gradual *drift* . . . issue of abortion." *Boston Globe*, 1-16-83.

550 "But given the negative . . . pool of voters." *Rolling Stone*, 1-20-83.

550 "personal harangues . . . for him." *Ibid.*

550 "more kindly . . . of his 30s." *New York Times*, 12-2-82.

550 "I don't think it's . . . to be President." Ted Kennedy. Anthony Lewis in *New York Times*, 12-2-82.

551 "the impact on his children . . . Mary Jo Kopechne." *New York Times*, 12-2-82.

551 "gasbag of a speech . . . incapable of seriousness." Ward Just. *New England Monthly*, October 1984.

551 "Washington lawyer . . . the Kennedy family." *New York Times*, 10-19-84.

552 "He's going to make . . . half of 1985." (UPI) *New Haven Register*, 2-10-85.

552 "I want . . . make a difference." Ted Kennedy. *Newsweek*, 4-8-85.

552 "still must overcome . . . shadow of Chappaquiddick." *USA Today*, 1-22-85.

552 "Where enough people . . . to elect him." *The New Republic*, 11-25-85, p.18.

552 "To assume there will be . . . prepare for it." *Ibid.*, p.18.

552 "The Chappaquiddick situation . . . still remember." *Boston Globe Magazine*, 11-24-85.

552 "some guy . . . carrying a sign." William Safire. *New York Times*, 12-12-85.

552 "They were too high-minded . . . though it may be." *Ibid.*

553 A loss . . . would mean oblivion. *Ibid.*

553 "I know that this . . . Public service is." Ted Kennedy. *Boston Herald*, 12-20-85.

553 "Chappaquiddick, Chappaquiddick . . . shattered the walls of a dynasty." *Say Over and Over* by Sylvia Spencer Ruggles. Used by permission of Theodore Ruggles.